HOUGHTON MIFFLIN HARCOURT

Literacy and Language Guide

Consultants
Irene C. Fountas
Shane Templeton

Grade 4

Printed in the U.S.A.

ISBN 978-0-547-86650-5

21 22 23 0877 21 20 19 18 17

4500676040 E F G

Houghton Mifflin Harcourt™

Literacy and Language Guide
Table of Contents

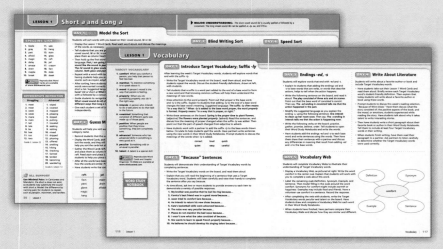

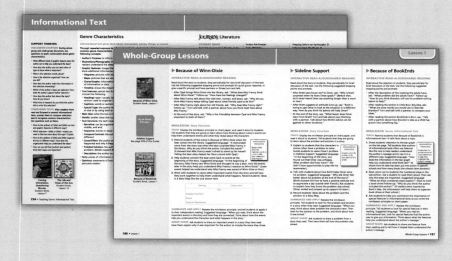

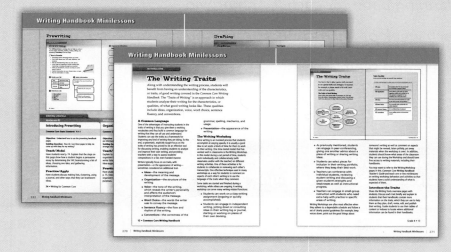

- Linguistic Transfer Support
- Qualitative Spelling Inventory
- Comprehensive Word List
- Leveled Readers Database
- Literature Discussion
- Bibliography

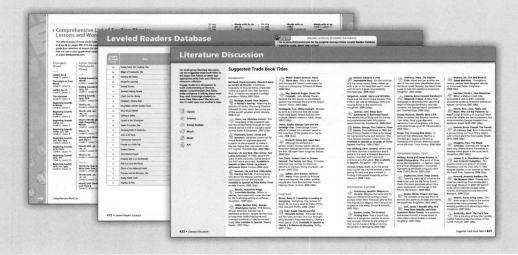

Literacy and Language Guide
Overview

In this Guide, you will find weekly lesson plans for Word Study, Reading, and Writing. A Planning page for each lesson provides a clear pathway through each week of instruction, connecting the parts of the plan cohesively and seamlessly.

INSTRUCTIONAL FOCUS
Each week's instructional focus at a glance—literature selections, comprehension skills, word work, and writing

READ ALOUD PASSAGES
Read Aloud Passages are reproduced in this Guide for ease of use

READING SELECTIONS
Reading selections for the week from the *Journeys* Student Book and Teacher's Edition

WORD STUDY
Spelling/Phonics and Oral Vocabulary Development lessons for the week

WRITING
Writing minilessons connect to *Journeys* instruction and provide students with additional handbook resources for writing practice during the week

GUIDED READING
Options for small-group teaching also appear in the complete Leveled Readers Database in the Resources section of this Guide

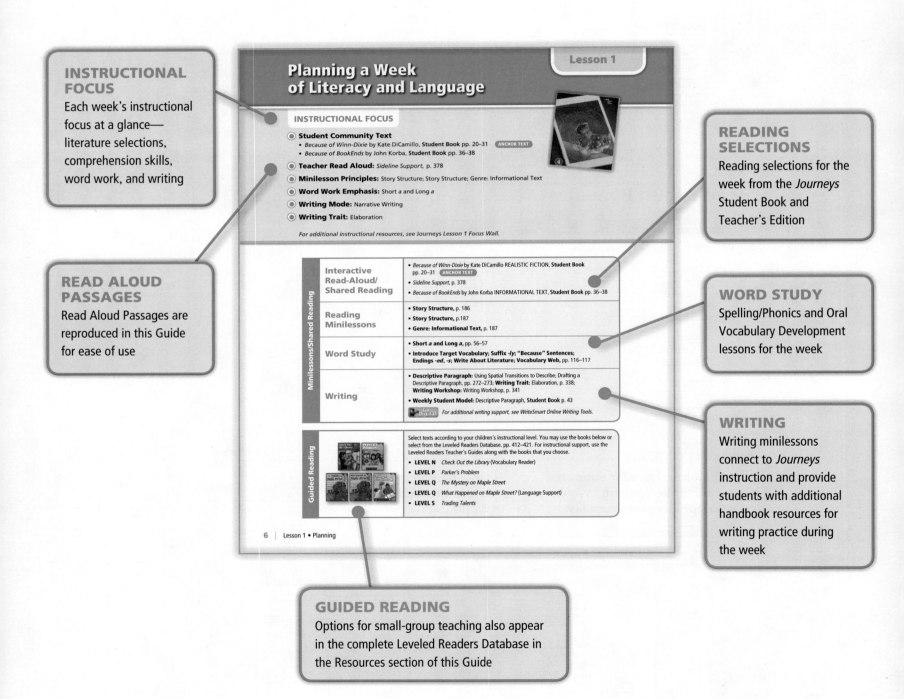

Table of Contents

Instructional Focus and Planning

Planning a Week of Literacy and Language

INSTRUCTIONAL FOCUS

- **Student Community Text**
  - *Because of Winn-Dixie* by Kate DiCamillo, **Student Book** pp. 20–31 ANCHOR TEXT
  - *Because of BookEnds* by John Korba, **Student Book** pp. 36–38
- **Teacher Read Aloud:** *Sideline Support,* p. 378
- **Minilesson Principles:** Story Structure; Story Structure; Genre: Informational Text
- **Word Work Emphasis:** Short *a* and Long *a*
- **Writing Mode:** Narrative Writing
- **Writing Trait:** Elaboration

For additional instructional resources, see Journeys *Lesson 1 Focus Wall.*

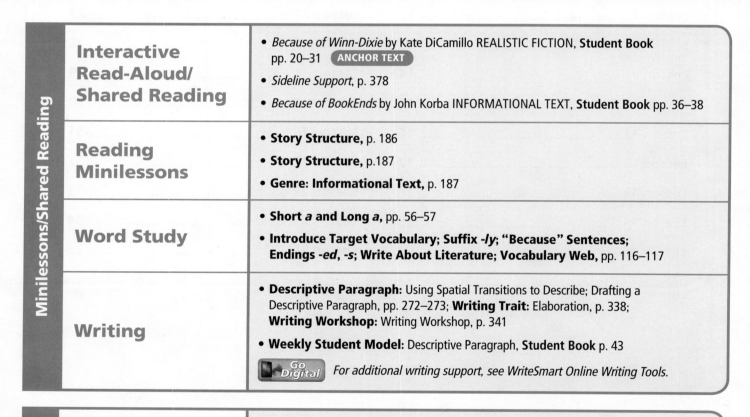

Minilessons/Shared Reading		
Interactive Read-Aloud/ Shared Reading	• *Because of Winn-Dixie* by Kate DiCamillo REALISTIC FICTION, **Student Book** pp. 20–31 ANCHOR TEXT • *Sideline Support,* p. 378 • *Because of BookEnds* by John Korba INFORMATIONAL TEXT, **Student Book** pp. 36–38	
Reading Minilessons	• **Story Structure,** p. 186 • **Story Structure,** p.187 • **Genre: Informational Text,** p. 187	
Word Study	• **Short *a* and Long *a*,** pp. 56–57 • **Introduce Target Vocabulary; Suffix *-ly*; "Because" Sentences; Endings *-ed*, *-s*; Write About Literature; Vocabulary Web,** pp. 116–117	
Writing	• **Descriptive Paragraph:** Using Spatial Transitions to Describe; Drafting a Descriptive Paragraph, pp. 272–273; **Writing Trait:** Elaboration, p. 338; **Writing Workshop:** Writing Workshop, p. 341 • **Weekly Student Model:** Descriptive Paragraph, **Student Book** p. 43 **Go Digital** *For additional writing support, see WriteSmart Online Writing Tools.*	

Guided Reading

Select texts according to your children's instructional level. You may use the books below or select from the Leveled Readers Database, pp. 412–421. For instructional support, use the Leveled Readers Teacher's Guides along with the books that you choose.

- **LEVEL N** *Check Out the Library* (Vocabulary Reader)
- **LEVEL P** *Parker's Problem*
- **LEVEL Q** *The Mystery on Maple Street*
- **LEVEL Q** *What Happened on Maple Street?* (Language Support)
- **LEVEL S** *Trading Talents*

Planning a Week of Literacy and Language

INSTRUCTIONAL FOCUS

◉ **Student Community Text**
- *My Brother Martin: A Sister Remembers Growing Up with the Rev. Dr. Martin Luther King Jr.* by Christine King Farris, **Student Book** pp. 48–61 ANCHOR TEXT
- *Langston Hughes: A Poet and a Dreamer* Poems by Langston Hughes, **Student Book** pp. 66–68

◉ **Teacher Read Aloud:** *The Troublemaker Who Healed a Nation,* p. 378

◉ **Minilesson Principles:** Genre: Biography; Author's Purpose; Genre: Poetry

◉ **Word Work Emphasis:** Short *e* and Long *e*

◉ **Writing Mode:** Narrative Writing

◉ **Writing Trait:** Purpose

For additional instructional resources, see Journeys *Lesson 2 Focus Wall.*

Minilessons/Shared Reading	**Interactive Read-Aloud/ Shared Reading**	• *My Brother Martin: A Sister Remembers Growing Up with the Rev. Dr. Martin Luther King Jr.* by Christine King Farris BIOGRAPHY, **Student Book** pp. 48–61 ANCHOR TEXT • *The Troublemaker Who Healed a Nation,* p. 378 • *Langston Hughes: A Poet and a Dreamer* by Langston Hughes POETRY, **Student Book** pp. 66–68
	Reading Minilessons	• **Genre: Biography,** p. 188 • **Author's Purpose,** p. 189 • **Genre: Poetry,** p. 189
	Word Study	• **Short *e* and Long *e*,** pp. 58–59 • **Introduce Target Vocabulary; Prefix *in-*; Word Associations; Prefix *re-*; Glossary Snapshots; Antonyms,** pp. 118–119
	Writing	• **Story:** Using Time-Order Words, Drafting a Story, pp. 274–275; **Writing Trait:** Purpose, p. 338; **Writing Forms:** Fictional Narrative, p. 360 • **Weekly Student Model:** Story, **Student Book** p. 73 **Go Digital** *For additional writing support, see WriteSmart Online Writing Tools.*

Guided Reading	 Select texts according to your children's instructional level. You may use the books below or select from the Leveled Readers Database, pp. 412–421. For instructional support, use the Leveled Readers Teacher's Guides along with the books that you choose. • **LEVEL O** *Sharing a Dream* • **LEVEL Q** *Separate Worlds* (Vocabulary Reader) • **LEVEL S** *Thurgood Marshall* (Language Support) • **LEVEL S** *A Voice for Equality* • **LEVEL U** *A Leader for All*

Planning a Week of Literacy and Language

INSTRUCTIONAL FOCUS

◉ **Student Community Text**
   - *My Librarian Is a Camel* by Margriet Ruurs, **Student Book** pp. 78–91   ANCHOR TEXT
   - *From Idea to Book* by Kim Becker, **Student Book** pp. 96–100

◉ **Teacher Read Aloud:** *Bridging the Gap*, p. 379

◉ **Minilesson Principles:** Cause and Effect; Cause and Effect; Genre: Informational Text

◉ **Word Work Emphasis:** Short *i* and Long *i*

◉ **Writing Mode:** Narrative Writing

◉ **Writing Trait:** Conventions

For additional instructional resources, see Journeys Lesson 3 Focus Wall.

Minilessons/Shared Reading	**Interactive Read-Aloud/ Shared Reading**	• *My Librarian Is a Camel* by Margriet Ruurs INFORMATIONAL TEXT, **Student Book** pp. 78–91 ANCHOR TEXT • *Bridging the Gap*, p. 379 • *From Idea to Book* by Kim Becker INFORMATIONAL TEXT, **Student Book** pp. 96–100
	Reading Minilessons	• **Cause and Effect,** p. 190 • **Cause and Effect,** p. 191 • **Genre: Informational Text,** p. 191
	Word Study	• **Short *i* and Long *i*,** pp. 60–61 • **Introduce Target Vocabulary; Prefix *im*-; Riddles; Suffix *-ly*; Write a Response; Four-Square Map,** pp. 120–121
	Writing	• **Dialogue:** Using Dialogue to Show Characters' Feelings; Drafting Dialogue, pp. 276–277; **Writing Trait:** Conventions, p. 340; **Evaluation:** Writing to a Prompt, p. 346 • **Weekly Student Model:** Dialogue, **Student Book** p. 105 Go Digital *For additional writing support, see WriteSmart Online Writing Tools.*

Guided Reading		Select texts according to your children's instructional level. You may use the books below or select from the Leveled Readers Database, pp. 412–421. For instructional support, use the Leveled Readers Teacher's Guides along with the books that you choose. • **LEVEL O** *Kids Can Save the Planet* • **LEVEL P** *Planes, Trains, and Snowmobiles* (Vocabulary Reader) • **LEVEL R** *Helping with Houses* (Language Support) • **LEVEL R** *Habitat for Humanity* • **LEVEL T** *Volunteer!*

Planning a Week of Literacy and Language

For additional instructional resources, see Journeys *Lesson 4 Focus Wall*.

INSTRUCTIONAL FOCUS

- **Student Community Text**
  - *The Power of W.O.W.!* by Crystal Hubbard, **Student Book** pp. 110–121 ANCHOR TEXT
  - *The Kid's Guide to Money* by Steve Otfinoski, **Student Book** pp. 126–128

- **Teacher Read Aloud:** *Bookmobile Rescue*, p. 379

- **Minilesson Principles:** Theme; Genre: Realistic Fiction; Genre: Informational Text

- **Word Work Emphasis:** Short *o* and Long *o*

- **Writing Mode:** Narrative Writing

- **Writing Trait:** Organization

Minilessons/Shared Reading		
Interactive Read-Aloud/ Shared Reading		• *The Power of W.O.W.!* by Crystal Hubbard PLAY, **Student Book** pp. 110–121 ANCHOR TEXT • *Bookmobile Rescue*, p. 379 • *The Kid's Guide to Money* by Steve Otfinoski INFORMATIONAL TEXT, **Student Book** pp. 126–128
Reading Minilessons		• **Theme,** p. 192 • **Genre: Realistic Fiction,** p. 193 • **Genre: Informational Text,** p. 193
Word Study		• **Short *o* and Long *o*,** pp. 62–63 • **Introduce Target Vocabulary; Prefix *mis*-; Rate Experiences; Root *spec/spect*; Word Pairs; Word Associations,** pp. 122–123
Writing		• **Fictional Narrative:** Using a Story Map, Developing the Characters, Setting, and Plot, pp. 278–279; **The Writing Process:** Prewriting, p. 332; **Writing Trait:** Organization, p. 337 • **Weekly Student Model:** Story Map, **Student Book** p. 133 ![Go Digital] *For additional writing support, see WriteSmart Online Writing Tools.*

Guided Reading

Select texts according to your children's instructional level. You may use the books below or select from the Leveled Readers Database, pp. 412–421. For instructional support, use the Leveled Readers Teacher's Guides along with the books that you choose.

- **LEVEL N**   *Nina Wows KWOW*
- **LEVEL O**   *Community Teamwork* (Vocabulary Reader)
- **LEVEL O**   *Friends on a Field Trip* (Language Support)
- **LEVEL P**   *A Friendly Field Trip*
- **LEVEL S**   *A.L.L. to the Rescue*

Planning a Week of Literacy and Language

INSTRUCTIONAL FOCUS

- **Student Community Text**
  - *Stormalong* by Mary Pope Osborne, **Student Book** pp. 138–153   ANCHOR TEXT
  - *Hoderi the Fisherman* retold by Kate McGovern, **Student Book** pp. 158–160
- **Teacher Read Aloud:** *Mighty Joe Magarac*, p. 380
- **Minilesson Principles:** Understanding Characters; Understanding Characters; Genre: Play
- **Word Work Emphasis:** Homophones
- **Writing Mode:** Narrative Writing
- **Writing Trait:** Conventions

For additional instructional resources, see Journeys Lesson 5 Focus Wall.

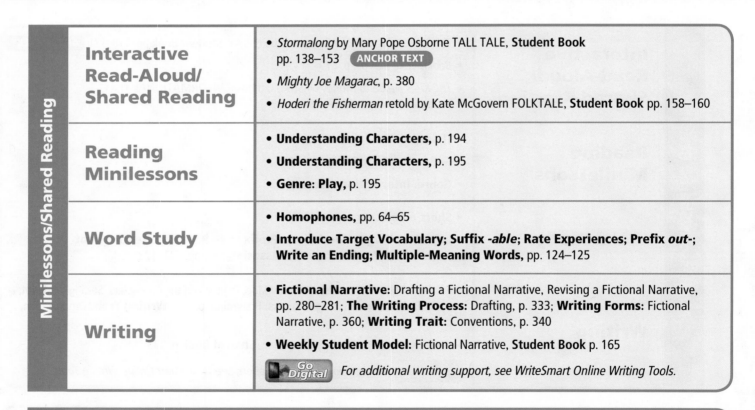

Minilessons/Shared Reading		
Interactive Read-Aloud/ Shared Reading	• *Stormalong* by Mary Pope Osborne TALL TALE, **Student Book** pp. 138–153 ANCHOR TEXT • *Mighty Joe Magarac*, p. 380 • *Hoderi the Fisherman* retold by Kate McGovern FOLKTALE, **Student Book** pp. 158–160	
Reading Minilessons	• **Understanding Characters,** p. 194 • **Understanding Characters,** p. 195 • **Genre: Play,** p. 195	
Word Study	• **Homophones,** pp. 64–65 • **Introduce Target Vocabulary; Suffix *-able*; Rate Experiences; Prefix *out-*; Write an Ending; Multiple-Meaning Words,** pp. 124–125	
Writing	• **Fictional Narrative:** Drafting a Fictional Narrative, Revising a Fictional Narrative, pp. 280–281; **The Writing Process:** Drafting, p. 333; **Writing Forms:** Fictional Narrative, p. 360; **Writing Trait:** Conventions, p. 340 • **Weekly Student Model:** Fictional Narrative, **Student Book** p. 165 **Go Digital** *For additional writing support, see WriteSmart Online Writing Tools.*	

Guided Reading

Select texts according to your children's instructional level. You may use the books below or select from the Leveled Readers Database, pp. 412–421. For instructional support, use the Leveled Readers Teacher's Guides along with the books that you choose.

- **LEVEL P**   *Mississippi Marvis Barnes*
- **LEVEL P**   *The Golden Age of Sail* (Vocabulary Reader)
- **LEVEL P**   *The Amazing Balina* (Language Support)
- **LEVEL Q**   *Balina*
- **LEVEL R**   *Whisper*

Planning a Week of Literacy and Language

INSTRUCTIONAL FOCUS

- **Student Community Text**
  - *Invasion from Mars* by Howard Koch, **Student Book** pp. 174–185   ANCHOR TEXT
  - *The History of Radio* by Vivian Fernandez, **Student Book** pp. 190–192

- **Teacher Read Aloud:** *The Tunguska Event,* p. 380

- **Minilesson Principles:** Story Structure; Story Structure; Genre: Informational Text

- **Word Work Emphasis:** Vowel Sounds /ŭ/, /yo͞o/, and /o͞o/

- **Writing Mode:** Informative Writing

- **Writing Trait:** Organization

For additional instructional resources, see Journeys Lesson 6 Focus Wall.

Minilessons/Shared Reading	**Interactive Read-Aloud/ Shared Reading**	• *Invasion from Mars* by Howard Koch PLAY, **Student Book** pp. 174–185 ANCHOR TEXT • *The Tunguska Event,* p. 380 • *The History of Radio* by Vivian Fernandez INFORMATIONAL TEXT, **Student Book** pp. 190–192
	Reading Minilessons	• **Story Structure,** p. 196 • **Story Structure,** p. 197 • **Genre: Informational Text,** p. 197
	Word Study	• **Vowel Sounds /ŭ/, /yo͞o/, and /o͞o/,** pp. 66–67 • **Introduce Target Vocabulary; Prefix *extra-*; Word Associations; Prefixes *re-*, *in-*; Act Out the Words; Guess My Category,** pp. 126–127
	Writing	• **News Report:** Writing a Headline and Lead Sentence, Drafting a News Report, pp. 282–283; **Writing Trait:** Organization, p. 337 **Technology:** Using the Internet, p. 342 • **Weekly Student Model:** News Report, **Student Book** p. 197 **Go Digital** *For additional writing support, see WriteSmart Online Writing Tools.*

Guided Reading		Select texts according to your students' instructional level. You may use the books below or select from the Leveled Readers Database, pp. 412–421. For instructional support, use the Leveled Readers Teacher's Guides along with the books that you choose. • **LEVEL N** *The Zeebo Encounter* • **LEVEL R** *The Golden Age of Radio* (Vocabulary Reader) • **LEVEL S** *The Amazing Game* (Language Support) • **LEVEL T** *Time Tag* • **LEVEL U** *Be Afraid*

Planning a Week of Literacy and Language

INSTRUCTIONAL FOCUS

- **Student Community Text**
  - *Coming Distractions* by Frank W. Baker, **Student Book** pp. 202–213 ANCHOR TEXT
  - *How Do They Do That?* by Allan Giles, **Student Book** pp. 218–220

- **Teacher Read Aloud:** *Steven Spielberg: A Filmmaker's Journey*, p. 381

- **Minilesson Principles:** Fact and Opinion; Fact and Opinion; Genre: Informational Text

- **Word Work Emphasis:** Vowel Sounds /o͞o/ and /o͝o/

- **Writing Mode:** Informative Writing

- **Writing Trait:** Evidence

For additional instructional resources, see Journeys Lesson 7 Focus Wall.

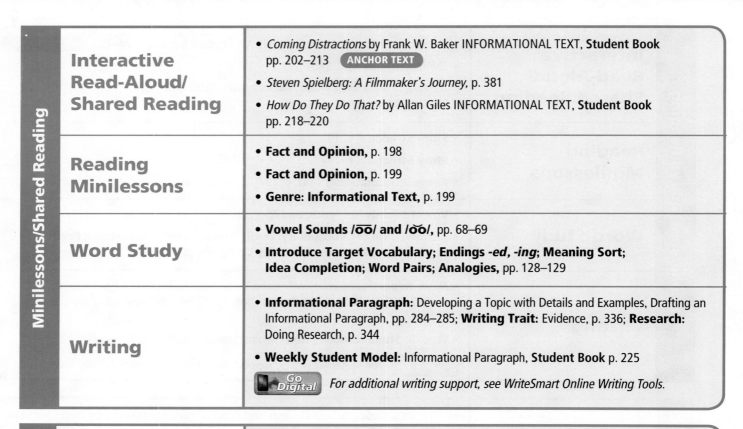

Minilessons/Shared Reading		
Interactive Read-Aloud/ Shared Reading	• *Coming Distractions* by Frank W. Baker INFORMATIONAL TEXT, **Student Book** pp. 202–213 ANCHOR TEXT • *Steven Spielberg: A Filmmaker's Journey*, p. 381 • *How Do They Do That?* by Allan Giles INFORMATIONAL TEXT, **Student Book** pp. 218–220	
Reading Minilessons	• **Fact and Opinion,** p. 198 • **Fact and Opinion,** p. 199 • **Genre: Informational Text,** p. 199	
Word Study	• **Vowel Sounds /o͞o/ and /o͝o/,** pp. 68–69 • **Introduce Target Vocabulary; Endings *-ed, -ing*; Meaning Sort; Idea Completion; Word Pairs; Analogies,** pp. 128–129	
Writing	• **Informational Paragraph:** Developing a Topic with Details and Examples, Drafting an Informational Paragraph, pp. 284–285; **Writing Trait:** Evidence, p. 336; **Research:** Doing Research, p. 344 • **Weekly Student Model:** Informational Paragraph, **Student Book** p. 225 Go Digital *For additional writing support, see WriteSmart Online Writing Tools.*	

Guided Reading

Select texts according to your students' instructional level. You may use the books below or select from the Leveled Readers Database, pp. 412–421. For instructional support, use the Leveled Readers Teacher's Guides along with the books that you choose.

- **LEVEL P** *Now Showing in Your Living Room*
- **LEVEL P** *Behind the Scenes* (Vocabulary Reader)
- **LEVEL T** *Making Movies* (Language Support)
- **LEVEL T** *The Magic of Movies*
- **LEVEL V** *Critics in Hollywood*

Planning a Week of Literacy and Language

◉ **Student Community Text**
  - *Me and Uncle Romie* by Claire Hartfield, **Student Book** pp. 230–243 ANCHOR TEXT
  - *Sidewalk Artists* by Sam Rabe, **Student Book** pp. 248–250

◉ **Teacher Read Aloud:** *Jazzy Jasmine*, p. 381

◉ **Minilesson Principles:** Understanding Characters; Understanding Characters; Directions

◉ **Word Work Emphasis:** Vowel Sounds /ou/ and /ô/

◉ **Writing Mode:** Informative Writing

◉ **Writing Trait:** Purpose

For additional instructional resources, see Journeys *Lesson 8 Focus Wall.*

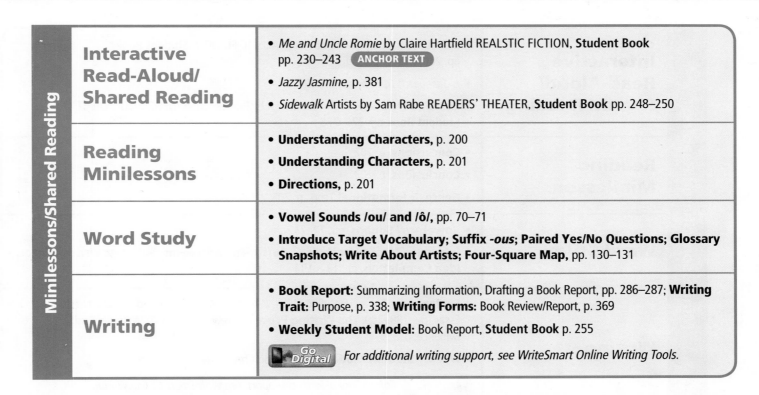

Minilessons/Shared Reading		
Interactive Read-Aloud/ Shared Reading	• *Me and Uncle Romie* by Claire Hartfield REALSTIC FICTION, **Student Book** pp. 230–243 ANCHOR TEXT • *Jazzy Jasmine*, p. 381 • *Sidewalk* Artists by Sam Rabe READERS' THEATER, **Student Book** pp. 248–250	
Reading Minilessons	• **Understanding Characters,** p. 200 • **Understanding Characters,** p. 201 • **Directions,** p. 201	
Word Study	• **Vowel Sounds /ou/ and /ô/,** pp. 70–71 • **Introduce Target Vocabulary; Suffix *-ous*; Paired Yes/No Questions; Glossary Snapshots; Write About Artists; Four-Square Map,** pp. 130–131	
Writing	• **Book Report:** Summarizing Information, Drafting a Book Report, pp. 286–287; **Writing Trait:** Purpose, p. 338; **Writing Forms:** Book Review/Report, p. 369 • **Weekly Student Model:** Book Report, **Student Book** p. 255 Go Digital *For additional writing support, see WriteSmart Online Writing Tools.*	

Guided Reading

Select texts according to your students' instructional level. You may use the books below or select from the Leveled Readers Database, pp. 412–421. For instructional support, use the Leveled Readers Teacher's Guides along with the books that you choose.

- **LEVEL M** *Recipe for Learning*
- **LEVEL R** *Romare Bearden* (Vocabulary Reader)
- **LEVEL S** *A Gift for Grandpa* (Language Support)
- **LEVEL S** *Gramp's Favorite Gift*
- **LEVEL S** *Stuck at Camp*

Planning a Week of Literacy and Language

INSTRUCTIONAL FOCUS

◎ **Student Community Text**
- *Dear Mr. Winston* by Ken Roberts, **Student Book** pp. 260–271 ANCHOR TEXT
- *Field Guide to Snakes of the Southwest* by Patrick Sutter, **Student Book** pp. 276–278

◎ **Teacher Read Aloud:** *Is Sasquatch Out There?*, p. 382

◎ **Minilesson Principles:** Conclusions; Conclusions; Genre: Informational Text

◎ **Word Work Emphasis:** Vowel + /r/ Sounds

◎ **Writing Mode:** Informative Writing

◎ **Writing Trait:** Evidence

For additional instructional resources, see Journeys Lesson 9 Focus Wall.

Minilessons/Shared Reading		
Interactive Read-Aloud/ Shared Reading	• *Dear Mr. Winston* by Ken Roberts REALISTIC FICTION, **Student Book** pp. 260–271 ANCHOR TEXT • *Is Sasquatch Out There?*, p. 382 • *Field Guide to Snakes of the Southwest* by Patrick Sutter INFORMATIONAL TEXT, **Student Book** pp. 276–278	
Reading Minilessons	• **Conclusions,** p. 202 • **Conclusions,** p. 203 • **Genre: Informational Text,** p. 203	
Word Study	• **Vowel + /r/ Sounds,** pp. 72–73 • **Introduce Target Vocabulary; Suffix -*ize*; Antonyms; Suffix -*y*; Write a Letter; Idea Completion,** pp. 132–133	
Writing	• **Explanatory Essay:** Deciding *What, Why*, and *How*, Organizing an Explanatory Essay, pp. 288–289; **The Writing Process:** Prewriting, p. 332; **Writing Trait:** Evidence, p. 336 • **Weekly Student Model:** Organization Chart, **Student Book** p. 283 Go Digital *For additional writing support, see WriteSmart Online Writing Tools.*	

Guided Reading

Select texts according to your students' instructional level. You may use the books below or select from the Leveled Readers Database, pp. 412–421. For instructional support, use the Leveled Readers Teacher's Guides along with the books that you choose.

- **LEVEL M** *Painting the Ocean*
- **LEVEL O** *Reptiles As Pets* (Vocabulary Reader)
- **LEVEL R** *Sisters Play Soccer* (Language Support)
- **LEVEL R** *Soccer Sisters*
- **LEVEL S** *Think Before You Speak*

Planning a Week of Literacy and Language

- **Student Community Text**
  - *José! Born to Dance* by Susanna Reich, **Student Book** pp. 288–299   ANCHOR TEXT
  - *Dance to the Beat* Poems by Leslie D.Perkins, Carl Sandburg, and Nikki Giovanni, **Student Book** pp. 304–306

- **Teacher Read Aloud:** *Mexican Dove*, p. 382

- **Minilesson Principles:** Genre: Biography; Author's Purpose; Genre: Poetry

- **Word Work Emphasis:** More Vowel + /r/ Sounds

- **Writing Mode:** Informative Writing

- **Writing Trait:** Elaboration

For additional instructional resources, see Journeys *Lesson 10 Focus Wall.*

Minilessons/Shared Reading	**Interactive Read-Aloud/ Shared Reading**	• *José! Born to Dance* by Susanna Reich BIOGRAPHY, **Student Book** pp. 288–299 ANCHOR TEXT • *Mexican Dove*, p. 382 • *Dance to the Beat* by Leslie D.Perkins, Carl Sandburg, and Nikki Giovanni POETRY, **Student Book** pp. 304–306
	Reading Minilessons	• **Genre: Biography,** p. 204 • **Author's Purpose,** p. 205 • **Genre: Poetry,** p. 205
	Word Study	• **More Vowel + /r/ Sounds,** pp. 74–75 • **Introduce Target Vocabulary; Suffix *-ful*; Shades of Meaning; Prefix *dis-*; "Because" Sentences; Meaning Sort,** pp. 134–135
	Writing	• **Explanatory Essay:** Drafting an Explanatory Essay, Revising for Exact Words, pp. 290–291; **The Writing Process:** Drafting, p. 333; **Writing Trait:** Elaboration, p. 338; **Evaluation:** Checklists and Rubrics, p. 347 • **Weekly Student Model:** Explanatory Essay, **Student Book** p. 311 **Go Digital** *For additional writing support, see WriteSmart Online Writing Tools.*

Guided Reading 	Select texts according to your students' instructional level. You may use the books below or select from the Leveled Readers Database, pp. 412–421. For instructional support, use the Leveled Readers Teacher's Guides along with the books that you choose. • **LEVEL O** *Isadora Duncan* • **LEVEL P** *Artists in Training* (Vocabulary Reader) • **LEVEL S** *The Life of Jackson Pollock* (Language Support) • **LEVEL S** *Jackson Pollock in Action* • **LEVEL W** *Luciano Pavarotti*

Planning a Week of Literacy and Language

INSTRUCTIONAL FOCUS

- **Student Community Text**
  - *Hurricanes: Earth's Mightiest Storms* by Patricia Lauber, **Student Book** pp. 320–329 `ANCHOR TEXT`
  - *Recovering from Katrina* by Alice Young, **Student Book** pp. 334–338

- **Teacher Read Aloud:** *The Big Storm,* p. 383

- **Minilesson Principles:** Text and Graphic Features; Genre: Realistic Fiction; Genre: Informational Text

- **Word Work Emphasis:** Compound Words

- **Writing Mode:** Opinion Writing

- **Writing Trait:** Purpose

For additional instructional resources, see Journeys Lesson 11 Focus Wall.

Minilessons/Shared Reading

Interactive Read-Aloud/ Shared Reading	• *Hurricanes: Earth's Mightiest Storms* by Patricia Lauber INFORMATIONAL TEXT, **Student Book** pp. 320–329 `ANCHOR TEXT` • *The Big Storm,* p. 383 • *Recovering from Katrina* by Alice Young NEWSPAPER ARTICLE, **Student Book** pp. 334–338
Reading Minilessons	• **Text and Graphic Features,** p. 206 • **Genre: Realistic Fiction,** p. 207 • **Genre: Informational Text,** p. 207
Word Study	• **Compound Words,** pp. 76–77 • **Introduce Target Vocabulary; Endings *-ed, -ing*; Root Chain; Prefix *en-*; Write Dialogue; Riddles,** pp. 136–137
Writing	• **Persuasive Paragraph:** Writing an Opinion Statement, Drafting a Persuasive Paragraph, pp. 292–293; **Writing Trait:** Purpose, p. 338; **Writing Workshop:** Writing Workshop, p. 341 • **Weekly Student Model:** Persuasive Paragraph, **Student Book** p. 343 **Go Digital** *For additional writing support, see WriteSmart Online Writing Tools.*

Guided Reading

Select texts according to your students' instructional level. You may use the books below or select from the Leveled Readers Database, pp. 412–421. For instructional support, use the Leveled Readers Teacher's Guides along with the books that you choose.

- **LEVEL P** *Volcanoes*
- **LEVEL Q** *Tornadoes* (Vocabulary Reader)
- **LEVEL R** *The Big, Dangerous Wave* (Language Support)
- **LEVEL S** *Tsunami*
- **LEVEL T** *Nature Destroys, Nature Renews*

Planning a Week of Literacy and Language

INSTRUCTIONAL FOCUS

- **Student Community Text**
  - *The Earth Dragon Awakes* by Laurence Yep, **Student Book** pp. 348–359   ANCHOR TEXT
  - *Twisters* by Laura Dameron, **Student Book** pp. 364–366

- **Teacher Read Aloud:** *Safe from Harm*, p. 383

- **Minilesson Principles:** Sequence of Events; Sequence of Events; Genre: Informational Text

- **Word Work Emphasis:** Words with *-ed* or *-ing*

- **Writing Mode:** Opinion Writing

- **Writing Trait:** Organization

For additional instructional resources, see Journeys Lesson 12 Focus Wall.

Minilessons/Shared Reading		
Interactive Read-Aloud/ Shared Reading	• *The Earth Dragon Awakes* by Laurence Yep HISTORICAL FICTION, **Student Book** pp. 348–359 ANCHOR TEXT • *Safe from Harm*, p. 383 • *Twisters* by Laura Dameron INFORMATIONAL TEXT, **Student Book** pp. 364–366	
Reading Minilessons	• **Sequence of Events,** p. 208 • **Sequence of Events,** p. 209 • **Genre: Informational Text,** p. 209	
Word Study	• **Words with *-ed* or *-ing*,** pp. 78–79 • **Introduce Target Vocabulary; Suffix *-age*; Guess My Category; Word Origins; Word and Picture Matching; Root Web,** pp. 138–139	
Writing	• **Problem-Solution Composition:** Using Words that Persuade, Drafting a Problem-Solution Composition, pp. 294–295; **Writing Trait:** Organization, p. 337; **Evaluation:** Checklists and Rubrics, p. 347; **Writing Forms:** Problem/Solution, p. 350 • **Weekly Student Model:** Problem-Solution Composition, **Student Book** p. 371 Go Digital *For additional writing support, see WriteSmart Online Writing Tools.*	

Guided Reading

Select texts according to your students' instructional level. You may use the books below or select from the Leveled Readers Database, pp. 412–421. For instructional support, use the Leveled Readers Teacher's Guides along with the books that you choose.

- **LEVEL N**   *Sailing to Safety*
- **LEVEL O**   *Keeping Safe in an Earthquake* (Vocabulary Reader)
- **LEVEL R**   *A New Name for Lois* (Language Support)
- **LEVEL S**   *Little Hare and the Thundering Earth*
- **LEVEL T**   *Two Against the Mississippi*

Planning a Week of Literacy and Language

INSTRUCTIONAL FOCUS

⦿ **Student Community Text**
- *Antarctic Journal: Four Months at the Bottom of the World* by Jennifer Owings Dewey, **Student Book** pp. 376–387   **ANCHOR TEXT**
- *Cold, Cold Science* by Dewey Badeaux, **Student Book** pp. 392–400

⦿ **Teacher Read Aloud:** *On My Way to Meet the Khan: Excerpts from Marco Polo's Adventures,* p. 384

⦿ **Minilesson Principles:** Sequence of Events; Sequence of Events; Genre: Informational Text

⦿ **Word Work Emphasis:** More Words with -*ed* or -*ing*

⦿ **Writing Mode:** Opinion Writing

⦿ **Writing Trait:** Evidence

For additional instructional resources, see Journeys *Lesson 13 Focus Wall.*

Minilessons/Shared Reading		
Interactive Read-Aloud/ Shared Reading	• *Antarctic Journal: Four Months at the Bottom of the World* by Jennifer Owings Dewey NARRATIVE NONFICTION, **Student Book** pp. 376–387 **ANCHOR TEXT** • *On My Way to Meet the Khan: Excerpts from Marco Polo's Adventures,* p. 384 • *Cold, Cold Science* by Dewey Badeaux INFORMATIONAL TEXT, **Student Book** pp. 392–400	
Reading Minilessons	• **Sequence of Events,** p. 210 • **Sequence of Events,** p. 211 • **Genre: Informational Text,** p. 211	
Word Study	• **More Words with -*ed* or -*ing*,** pp. 80–81 • **Introduce Target Vocabulary; Suffix -*ness*; Twenty Questions; Write a Journal Entry; Eponyms; Root Chain,** pp. 140–141	
Writing	• **Persuasive Letter:** Using Business Letter Format, Drafting a Persuasive Letter, pp. 296–297; **Writing Trait:** Evidence, p. 336; **Technology:** Writing for the Web, p. 343 • **Weekly Student Model:** Persuasive Letter, **Student Book** p. 405 **Go Digital** *For additional writing support, see WriteSmart Online Writing Tools.*	

Guided Reading

Select texts according to your students' instructional level. You may use the books below or select from the Leveled Readers Database, pp. 412–421. For instructional support, use the Leveled Readers Teacher's Guides along with the books that you choose.

- **LEVEL O**   *Amazing Birds of Antarctica*
- **LEVEL O**   *Really, Really Cold!* (Vocabulary Reader)
- **LEVEL R**   *A Visit to Antarctica* (Language Support)
- **LEVEL R**   *An Icy Adventure*
- **LEVEL V**   *Heroes of the Antarctic*

Planning a Week of Literacy and Language

INSTRUCTIONAL FOCUS

◉ **Student Community Text**
- *The Life And Times of the Ant* by Charles Micucci, **Student Book** pp. 410–423 `ANCHOR TEXT`
- *The Dove and the Ant* retold by Anne O'Brien, **Student Book** pp. 428–430

◉ **Teacher Read Aloud:** *Wicked Wind,* p. 384

◉ **Minilesson Principles:** Text and Graphic Features; Genre: Informational Text; Genre: Fable

◉ **Word Work Emphasis:** Final Long *e*

◉ **Writing Mode:** Opinion Writing

◉ **Writing Trait:** Purpose

For additional instructional resources, see Journeys Lesson 14 Focus Wall.

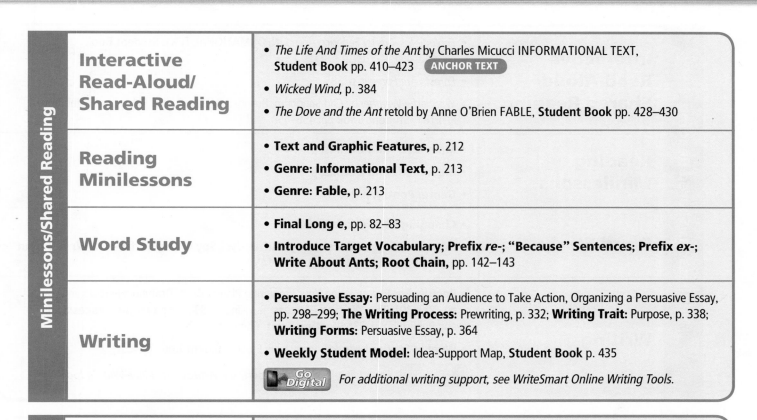

Minilessons/Shared Reading		
	Interactive Read-Aloud/ Shared Reading	• *The Life And Times of the Ant* by Charles Micucci INFORMATIONAL TEXT, **Student Book** pp. 410–423 `ANCHOR TEXT` • *Wicked Wind,* p. 384 • *The Dove and the Ant* retold by Anne O'Brien FABLE, **Student Book** pp. 428–430
	Reading Minilessons	• **Text and Graphic Features,** p. 212 • **Genre: Informational Text,** p. 213 • **Genre: Fable,** p. 213
	Word Study	• **Final Long *e*,** pp. 82–83 • **Introduce Target Vocabulary; Prefix *re*-; "Because" Sentences; Prefix *ex*-; Write About Ants; Root Chain,** pp. 142–143
	Writing	• **Persuasive Essay:** Persuading an Audience to Take Action, Organizing a Persuasive Essay, pp. 298–299; **The Writing Process:** Prewriting, p. 332; **Writing Trait:** Purpose, p. 338; **Writing Forms:** Persuasive Essay, p. 364 • **Weekly Student Model:** Idea-Support Map, **Student Book** p. 435 **Go Digital** *For additional writing support, see WriteSmart Online Writing Tools.*

Guided Reading		
		Select texts according to your students' instructional level. You may use the books below or select from the Leveled Readers Database, pp. 412–421. For instructional support, use the Leveled Readers Teacher's Guides along with the books that you choose. • **LEVEL O** *Ants of All Kinds* (Vocabulary Reader) • **LEVEL P** *The Lives of Social Insects* • **LEVEL S** *Arthropods Rule!* • **LEVEL S** *Arthropods Everywhere!* (Language Support) • **LEVEL T** *Love Those Bugs!*

Planning a Week of Literacy and Language

INSTRUCTIONAL FOCUS

- **Student Community Text**
  - *Ecology for Kids* by Federico Arana, **Student Book** pp. 440–451   `ANCHOR TEXT`
  - *Wonderful Weather* Poems by Carl Sandburg, Buson, Rob Hale, Aileen Fisher, and Calef Brown, **Student Book** pp. 456–458

- **Teacher Read Aloud:** *Forests Are Forever*, p. 385

- **Minilesson Principles:** Main Ideas and Details; Main Ideas and Details; Genre: Poetry

- **Word Work Emphasis:** Changing Final *y* to *i*

- **Writing Mode:** Opinion Writing

- **Writing Trait:** Conventions

For additional instructional resources, see Journeys Lesson 15 Focus Wall.

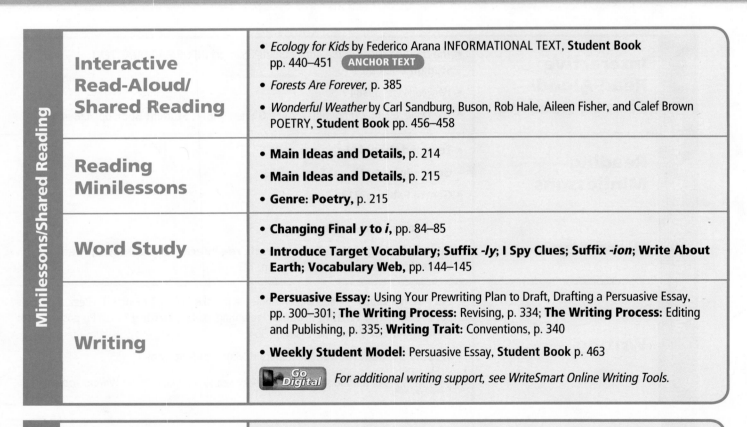

Minilessons/Shared Reading		
Interactive Read-Aloud/ Shared Reading	• *Ecology for Kids* by Federico Arana INFORMATIONAL TEXT, **Student Book** pp. 440–451 `ANCHOR TEXT` • *Forests Are Forever*, p. 385 • *Wonderful Weather* by Carl Sandburg, Buson, Rob Hale, Aileen Fisher, and Calef Brown POETRY, **Student Book** pp. 456–458	
Reading Minilessons	• **Main Ideas and Details,** p. 214 • **Main Ideas and Details,** p. 215 • **Genre: Poetry,** p. 215	
Word Study	• **Changing Final *y* to *i*,** pp. 84–85 • **Introduce Target Vocabulary; Suffix *-ly*; I Spy Clues; Suffix *-ion*; Write About Earth; Vocabulary Web,** pp. 144–145	
Writing	• **Persuasive Essay:** Using Your Prewriting Plan to Draft, Drafting a Persuasive Essay, pp. 300–301; **The Writing Process:** Revising, p. 334; **The Writing Process:** Editing and Publishing, p. 335; **Writing Trait:** Conventions, p. 340 • **Weekly Student Model:** Persuasive Essay, **Student Book** p. 463 **Go Digital** *For additional writing support, see WriteSmart Online Writing Tools.*	

Guided Reading	
	Select texts according to your students' instructional level. You may use the books below or select from the Leveled Readers Database, pp. 412–421. For instructional support, use the Leveled Readers Teacher's Guides along with the books that you choose. • **LEVEL N** *Squash in the Schoolyard* (Vocabulary Reader) • **LEVEL O** *The Seal Who Wanted to Live* • **LEVEL O** *The Princess and the Manatee* • **LEVEL P** *A Father's Garden* (Language Support) • **LEVEL Q** *Dad's Garden*

Planning a Week of Literacy and Language

INSTRUCTIONAL FOCUS

- **Student Community Text**
  - *Riding Freedom* by Pam Muñoz Ryan, **Student Book** pp. 472–483 **ANCHOR TEXT**
  - *Spindletop,* **Student Book** pp. 488–490
- **Teacher Read Aloud:** *Getting the Story,* p. 385
- **Minilesson Principles:** Genre: Historical Fiction; Genre: Biography; Compare and Contrast
- **Word Work Emphasis:** Words with /k/, /ng/, and /kw/
- **Writing Mode:** Narrative Writing
- **Writing Trait:** Development

For additional instructional resources, see Journeys Lesson 16 Focus Wall.

Minilessons/Shared Reading		
Interactive Read-Aloud/ Shared Reading	• *Riding Freedom* by Pam Muñoz Ryan HISTORICAL FICTION, **Student Book** pp. 472–483 **ANCHOR TEXT** • *Getting the Story,* p. 385 • *Spindletop* INFORMATIONAL TEXT, **Student Book** pp. 488–490	
Reading Minilessons	• **Genre: Historical Fiction,** p. 216 • **Genre: Biography,** p. 217 • **Compare and Contrast,** p. 217	
Word Study	• **Words with /k/, /ng/, and /kw/,** pp. 86–87 • **Introduce Target Vocabulary; Prefix *un-*; Meaning Sort; Similes; Word Pairs; Rate Experiences,** pp. 146–147	
Writing	• **Descriptive Paragraph:** Using Vivid Words, Drafting a Descriptive Paragraph, pp. 302–303; **Writing Trait:** Development, p. 339; **Writing Workshop:** Writing Workshop, p. 341 • **Weekly Student Model:** Descriptive Paragraph, **Student Book** p. 495 **Go Digital** *For additional writing support, see WriteSmart Online Writing Tools.*	

Guided Reading

Select texts according to your students' instructional level. You may use the books below or select from the Leveled Readers Database, pp. 412–421. For instructional support, use the Leveled Readers Teacher's Guides along with the books that you choose.

- **LEVEL N**   *Elizabeth's Stormy Ride*
- **LEVEL Q**   *Stagecoach Travel* (Vocabulary Reader)
- **LEVEL S**   *A Dangerous Trip* (Language Support)
- **LEVEL S**   *Perilous Passage*
- **LEVEL S**   *Come to Nicodemus*

Planning a Week of Literacy and Language

INSTRUCTIONAL FOCUS

- **Student Community Text**
  - *The Right Dog for the Job* by Dorothy Hinshaw Patent, **Student Book** pp. 500–511 **ANCHOR TEXT**
  - *Knowing Noses: Search-and-Rescue Dogs* by Ellen Gold, **Student Book** pp. 516–518

- **Teacher Read Aloud:** *Let Me Be Brave*, p. 386

- **Minilesson Principles:** Sequence of Events; Sequence of Events; Genre: Informational Text

- **Word Work Emphasis:** Words with Final /j/ and /s/

- **Writing Mode:** Narrative Writing

- **Writing Trait:** Purpose

For additional instructional resources, see Journeys *Lesson 17 Focus Wall.*

Minilessons/Shared Reading		
Interactive Read-Aloud/ Shared Reading	• *The Right Dog for the Job* by Dorothy Hinshaw Patent NARRATIVE NONFICTION, **Student Book** pp. 500–511 **ANCHOR TEXT** • *Let Me Be Brave*, p. 386 • *Knowing Noses: Search-and-Rescue Dogs* by Ellen Gold INFORMATIONAL TEXT, **Student Book** pp. 516–518	
Reading Minilessons	• **Sequence of Events**, p. 218 • **Sequence of Events**, p. 219 • **Genre: Informational Text**, p. 219	
Word Study	• **Words with Final /j/ and /s/,** pp. 88–89 • **Introduce Target Vocabulary; Prefix *dis*-; Idea Completion; Homophones; Riddles; Vocabulary Web,** pp. 148–149	
Writing	• **Friendly Letter:** Matching Words with Audience, Drafting a Friendly Letter, pp. 304–305; **Writing Trait:** Purpose, p. 338; **Writing Forms:** Personal Narrative, p. 370 • **Weekly Student Model:** Friendly Letter, **Student Book** p. 523 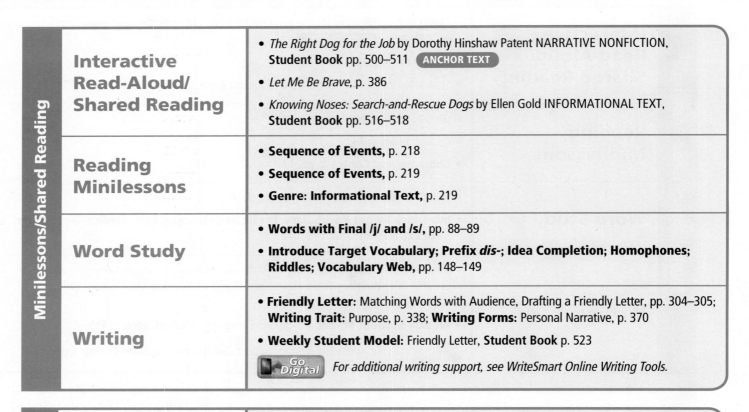 **Go Digital** *For additional writing support, see WriteSmart Online Writing Tools.*	

Guided Reading

Select texts according to your students' instructional level. You may use the books below or select from the Leveled Readers Database, pp. 412–421. For instructional support, use the Leveled Readers Teacher's Guides along with the books that you choose.

- **LEVEL N** *Animals Helping People* (Vocabulary Reader)
- **LEVEL N** *Animal Doctors*
- **LEVEL R** *Taking Care of Animals* (Language Support)
- **LEVEL R** *A Rural Veterinarian*
- **LEVEL T** *Helping Wild Animals*

Planning a Week of Literacy and Language

INSTRUCTIONAL FOCUS

- **Student Community Text**
  - *Hercules' Quest* by Martina Melendez, **Student Book** pp. 528–537 **ANCHOR TEXT**
  - *Zomo's Friends* by Tamara Andrews, **Student Book** pp. 542–550
- **Teacher Read Aloud:** *Theseus and the Minotaur*, p. 386
- **Minilesson Principles:** Story Structure; Story Structure; Genre: Folktale
- **Word Work Emphasis:** Prefixes *re-, un-, dis-*
- **Writing Mode:** Narrative Writing
- **Writing Trait:** Elaboration

For additional instructional resources, see Journeys Lesson 18 Focus Wall.

Minilessons/Shared Reading		
Interactive Read-Aloud/ Shared Reading	• *Hercules' Quest* by Martina Melendez MYTH, **Student Book** pp. 528–537 **ANCHOR TEXT** • *Theseus and the Minotaur*, p. 386 • *Zomo's Friends* by Tamara Andrews FOLKTALE, **Student Book** pp. 542–550	
Reading Minilessons	• **Story Structure,** p. 220 • **Story Structure,** p. 221 • **Genre: Folktale,** p. 221	
Word Study	• **Prefixes *re-, un-, dis-*,** pp. 90–91 • **Introduce Target Vocabulary; Suffix *-ful*; Word Associations; Base Word Build; Glossary Snapshots; Synonyms and Antonyms,** pp. 150–151	
Writing	• **Story:** Using Imagery, Drafting a Story, pp. 306–307; **Writing Forms:** Fictional Narrative, p. 360; **Writing Trait:** Elaboration, p. 338 • **Weekly Student Model:** Story, **Student Book** p. 555 **Go Digital** *For additional writing support, see WriteSmart Online Writing Tools.*	

Guided Reading

Select texts according to your students' instructional level. You may use the books below or select from the Leveled Readers Database, pp. 412–421. For instructional support, use the Leveled Readers Teacher's Guides along with the books that you choose.

- **LEVEL N**   *King Midas and the Golden Touch*
- **LEVEL R**   *The Story of Perseus* (Language Support)
- **LEVEL S**   *Long Ago in Greece* (Vocabulary Reader)
- **LEVEL T**   *The Adventures of Perseus*
- **LEVEL V**   *The Story of Icarus*

Planning a Week of Literacy and Language

INSTRUCTIONAL FOCUS

- **Student Community Text**
  - *Harvesting Hope: The Story of Cesar Chavez* by Kathleen Krull, **Student Book** pp. 560–571 ANCHOR TEXT
  - *The Edible Schoolyard* by Ned L. Legol, **Student Book** pp. 576–578

- **Teacher Read Aloud:** *The Father of India*, p. 387

- **Minilesson Principles:** Genre: Biography; Conclusions and Generalizations; Genre: Informational Text

- **Word Work Emphasis:** Suffixes *-ful, -less, -ness, -ment*

- **Writing Mode:** Narrative Writing

- **Writing Trait:** Organization

For additional instructional resources, see Journeys Lesson 19 Focus Wall.

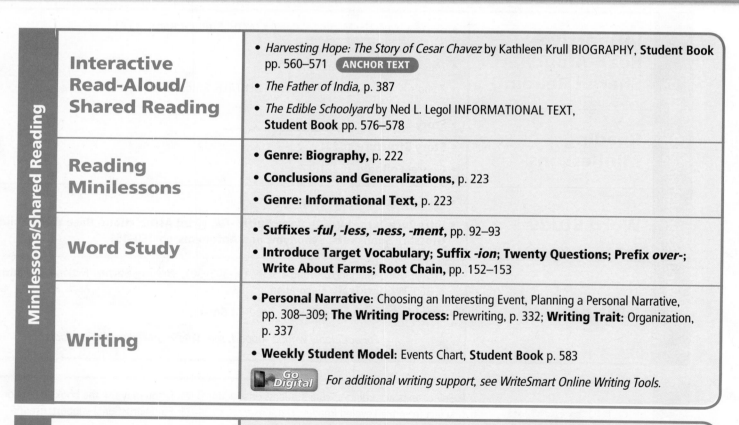

Minilessons/Shared Reading		
Interactive Read-Aloud/ Shared Reading	• *Harvesting Hope: The Story of Cesar Chavez* by Kathleen Krull BIOGRAPHY, **Student Book** pp. 560–571 ANCHOR TEXT • *The Father of India*, p. 387 • *The Edible Schoolyard* by Ned L. Legol INFORMATIONAL TEXT, **Student Book** pp. 576–578	
Reading Minilessons	• **Genre: Biography,** p. 222 • **Conclusions and Generalizations,** p. 223 • **Genre: Informational Text,** p. 223	
Word Study	• **Suffixes *-ful, -less, -ness, -ment*,** pp. 92–93 • **Introduce Target Vocabulary; Suffix *-ion*; Twenty Questions; Prefix *over-*; Write About Farms; Root Chain,** pp. 152–153	
Writing	• **Personal Narrative:** Choosing an Interesting Event, Planning a Personal Narrative, pp. 308–309; **The Writing Process:** Prewriting, p. 332; **Writing Trait:** Organization, p. 337 • **Weekly Student Model:** Events Chart, **Student Book** p. 583 Go Digital *For additional writing support, see WriteSmart Online Writing Tools.*	

Guided Reading

Select texts according to your students' instructional level. You may use the books below or select from the Leveled Readers Database, pp. 412–421. For instructional support, use the Leveled Readers Teacher's Guides along with the books that you choose.

- **LEVEL P** *Songs for the People*
- **LEVEL R** *A President for the People* (Language Support)
- **LEVEL R** *The People's President*
- **LEVEL S** *Tough Times* (Language Support)
- **LEVEL U** *The Story of Dorothea Lange*

Planning a Week of Literacy and Language

INSTRUCTIONAL FOCUS

- **Student Community Text**
  - *Sacagawea* by Lise Erdrich, **Student Book** pp. 588–603 **ANCHOR TEXT**
  - *Native American Nature Poetry* Poems by Teton Sioux, Crow, and Nootka, **Student Book** pp. 608–610
- **Teacher Read Aloud:** *Race Against Death*, p. 387
- **Minilesson Principles:** Main Ideas and Details; Genre: Narrative Nonfiction; Genre: Poetry
- **Word Work Emphasis:** Words with VCCV Pattern
- **Writing Mode:** Narrative Writing
- **Writing Trait:** Conventions

For additional instructional resources, see Journeys Lesson 20 Focus Wall.

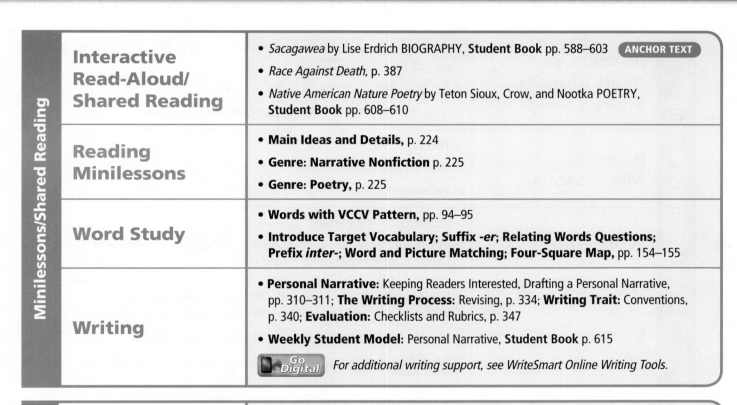

	Minilessons/Shared Reading	
Interactive Read-Aloud/ Shared Reading	• *Sacagawea* by Lise Erdrich BIOGRAPHY, **Student Book** pp. 588–603 **ANCHOR TEXT** • *Race Against Death*, p. 387 • *Native American Nature Poetry* by Teton Sioux, Crow, and Nootka POETRY, **Student Book** pp. 608–610	
Reading Minilessons	• **Main Ideas and Details,** p. 224 • **Genre: Narrative Nonfiction** p. 225 • **Genre: Poetry,** p. 225	
Word Study	• **Words with VCCV Pattern,** pp. 94–95 • **Introduce Target Vocabulary; Suffix *-er*; Relating Words Questions; Prefix *inter-*; Word and Picture Matching; Four-Square Map,** pp. 154–155	
Writing	• **Personal Narrative:** Keeping Readers Interested, Drafting a Personal Narrative, pp. 310–311; **The Writing Process:** Revising, p. 334; **Writing Trait:** Conventions, p. 340; **Evaluation:** Checklists and Rubrics, p. 347 • **Weekly Student Model:** Personal Narrative, **Student Book** p. 615 **Go Digital** *For additional writing support, see WriteSmart Online Writing Tools.*	

Guided Reading

Select texts according to your students' instructional level. You may use the books below or select from the Leveled Readers Database, pp. 412–421. For instructional support, use the Leveled Readers Teacher's Guides along with the books that you choose.

- **LEVEL O** *John Wesley Powell*
- **LEVEL Q** *Lewis and Clark's Packing List* (Language Support)
- **LEVEL R** *Laura Ingalls Wilder* (Vocabulary Reader)
- **LEVEL R** *Writer from the Prairie*
- **LEVEL U** *Chief Washakie*

Planning a Week of Literacy and Language

INSTRUCTIONAL FOCUS

- **Student Community Text**
  - *The World According to Humphrey* by Betty G. Birney, **Student Book** pp. 624–637 **ANCHOR TEXT**
  - *Make the Switch,* **Student Book** pp. 642–644

- **Teacher Read Aloud:** *Fun and Games on the Range,* p. 388

- **Minilesson Principles:** Theme; Genre: Informational Text; Persuasion

- **Word Work Emphasis:** Words with VCV Pattern

- **Writing Mode:** Informative Writing

- **Writing Trait:** Evidence

For additional instructional resources, see Journeys Lesson 21 Focus Wall.

Minilessons/Shared Reading	**Interactive Read-Aloud/ Shared Reading**	• *The World According to Humphrey* by Betty G. Birney FANTASY, **Student Book** pp. 624–637 **ANCHOR TEXT** • *Fun and Games on the Range,* p. 388 • *Make the Switch* ADVERTISEMENT, **Student Book** pp. 642–644
	Reading Minilessons	• **Theme,** p. 226 • **Genre: Informational Text,** p. 227 • **Persuasion,** p. 227
	Word Study	• **Words with VCV Pattern,** pp. 96–97 • **Introduce Target Vocabulary; Suffix -al; "Because" Sentences; Suffix -ate; I Spy Clues; Homophones,** pp. 156–157
	Writing	• **Summary:** Using Your Own Words, Drafting a Summary, pp. 312–313; **Writing Trait:** Evidence, p. 336; **Writing Forms:** Summary, p. 348 • **Weekly Student Model:** Summary, **Student Book** p. 649 **Go Digital** *For additional writing support, see WriteSmart Online Writing Tools.*

Guided Reading	Select texts according to your students' instructional level. You may use the books below or select from the Leveled Readers Database, pp. 412–421. For instructional support, use the Leveled Readers Teacher's Guides along with the books that you choose. • **LEVEL M** *The Magic of Teamwork* • **LEVEL Q** *Summer with Uncle Vince* (Language Support) • **LEVEL Q** *The Beltons' Imagination* • **LEVEL R** *The Truth About Rodents* (Vocabulary Reader) • **LEVEL S** *A Dragon's View*

Planning a Week of Literacy and Language

INSTRUCTIONAL FOCUS

- **Student Community Text**
  - *I Could Do That! Esther Morris Gets Women the Vote* by Linda Arms White, **Student Book** pp. 654–665 **ANCHOR TEXT**
  - *The Role of the Constitution* by Carl DeSoto, **Student Book** pp. 670–674

- **Teacher Read Aloud:** *Jane's Big Ideas*, p. 388

- **Minilesson Principles:** Cause and Effect; Cause and Effect; Genre: Informational Text

- **Word Work Emphasis:** VCCV and VCV Patterns

- **Writing Mode:** Informative Writing

- **Writing Trait:** Elaboration

For additional instructional resources, see Journeys *Lesson 22 Focus Wall.*

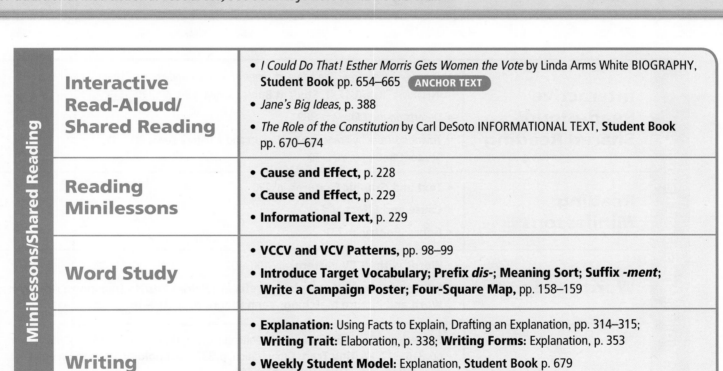

Minilessons/Shared Reading		
Interactive Read-Aloud/ Shared Reading	• *I Could Do That! Esther Morris Gets Women the Vote* by Linda Arms White BIOGRAPHY, **Student Book** pp. 654–665 **ANCHOR TEXT** • *Jane's Big Ideas*, p. 388 • *The Role of the Constitution* by Carl DeSoto INFORMATIONAL TEXT, **Student Book** pp. 670–674	
Reading Minilessons	• **Cause and Effect,** p. 228 • **Cause and Effect,** p. 229 • **Informational Text,** p. 229	
Word Study	• **VCCV and VCV Patterns,** pp. 98–99 • **Introduce Target Vocabulary; Prefix *dis-*; Meaning Sort; Suffix *-ment*; Write a Campaign Poster; Four-Square Map,** pp. 158–159	
Writing	• **Explanation:** Using Facts to Explain, Drafting an Explanation, pp. 314–315; **Writing Trait:** Elaboration, p. 338; **Writing Forms:** Explanation, p. 353 • **Weekly Student Model:** Explanation, **Student Book** p. 679 **Go Digital** *For additional writing support, see WriteSmart Online Writing Tools.*	

Guided Reading

Select texts according to your students' instructional level. You may use the books below or select from the Leveled Readers Database, pp. 412–421. For instructional support, use the Leveled Readers Teacher's Guides along with the books that you choose.

- **LEVEL P**   *The First Woman Doctor*
- **LEVEL S**   *Mill Girls* (Vocabulary Reader)
- **LEVEL S**   *Shirley Chisholm* (Language Support)
- **LEVEL S**   *A Champion of Change*
- **LEVEL U**   *The Writer Who Changed America*

Planning a Week of Literacy and Language

INSTRUCTIONAL FOCUS

◉ **Student Community Text**
- *The Ever-Living Tree: The Life and Times of a Coast Redwood* by Linda Vieira, **Student Book** pp. 684–699 `ANCHOR TEXT`
- *Towering Trees* Poems by Francisco X. Alarcón and J. Patrick Lewis, **Student Book** pp. 704–706

◉ **Teacher Read Aloud:** *Deserts on the Move?,* p. 389

◉ **Minilesson Principles:** Text and Graphic Features; Cause and Effect; Genre: Poetry

◉ **Word Work Emphasis:** Words with VCCV Pattern

◉ **Writing Mode:** Informative Writing

◉ **Writing Trait:** Organization

For additional instructional resources, see Journeys *Lesson 23 Focus Wall.*

Minilessons/Shared Reading		
Interactive Read-Aloud/ Shared Reading	• *The Ever-Living Tree: The Life and Times of a Coast Redwood* by Linda Vieira INFORMATIONAL TEXT, **Student Book** pp. 684–699 `ANCHOR TEXT` • *Deserts on the Move?,* p. 389 • *Towering Trees* by Francisco X. Alarcón and J. Patrick Lewis POETRY, **Student Book** pp. 704–706	
Reading Minilessons	• **Text and Graphic Features,** p. 230 • **Cause and Effect,** p. 231 • **Genre: Poetry,** p. 231	
Word Study	• **Words with VCCV Pattern,** pp. 100–101 • **Introduce Target Vocabulary; Prefix** *in-*; **Paired Yes/No Questions; Acronyms; Word and Picture Matching; Venn Diagram,** pp. 160–161	
Writing	• **Procedural Composition:** Using Sequential Order, Drafting a Procedural Composition, pp. 316–317; **Writing Trait:** Organization, p. 337; **Technology:** Using the Internet, p. 342; **Research:** Doing Research, p. 344 • **Weekly Student Model** Procedural Composition, **Student Book** p. 711 **Go Digital** *For additional writing support, see WriteSmart Online Writing Tools.*	

Guided Reading	
	Select texts according to your students' instructional level. You may use the books below or select from the Leveled Readers Database, pp. 412–421. For instructional support, use the Leveled Readers Teacher's Guides along with the books that you choose. • **LEVEL O** *Plants of the Redwood Forest* • **LEVEL P** *Forever Green* (Vocabulary Reader) • **LEVEL S** *Animals of the Redwood Forest* (Language Support) • **LEVEL S** *Life Among the Redwoods* • **LEVEL S** *Gentle Redwood Giants*

Planning a Week of Literacy and Language

INSTRUCTIONAL FOCUS

- **Student Community Text**
  - *Owen and Mzee: The True Story of a Remarkable Friendship* by Isabella Hatkoff, Craig Hatkoff, and Dr. Paula Kahumbu, **Student Book** pp. 716–727 **ANCHOR TEXT**
  - *Sea Sanctuary* by Rob Hale, **Student Book** pp. 732–734

- **Teacher Read Aloud:** *New Friends in the Newsroom,* p. 389

- **Minilesson Principles:** Compare and Contrast; Genre: Realistic Fiction; Summarize

- **Word Work Emphasis:** Words with VCCCV Pattern

- **Writing Mode:** Informative Writing

- **Writing Trait:** Purpose

For additional instructional resources, see Journeys Lesson 24 Focus Wall.

Minilessons/Shared Reading

Interactive Read-Aloud/ Shared Reading	• *Owen and Mzee: The True Story of a Remarkable Friendship* by Isabella Hatkoff, Craig Hatkoff, and Dr. Paula Kahumbu NARRATIVE NONFICTION, **Student Book** pp. 716–727 **ANCHOR TEXT** • *New Friends in the Newsroom,* p. 389 • *Sea Sanctuary* by Rob Hale INFORMATIONAL TEXT, **Student Book** pp. 732–734
Reading Minilessons	• **Compare and Contrast,** p. 232 • **Genre: Realistic Fiction,** p. 233 • **Summarize,** p. 233
Word Study	• **Words with VCCCV Pattern,** pp. 102–103 • **Introduce Target Vocabulary; Prefix *ex*-; Synonyms; Multiple-Meaning Words; Word Pairs; Shades of Meaning,** pp. 162–163
Writing	• **Research Report:** Seeking an Answer to a Question, Using an Outline to Organize, pp. 318–319; **The Writing Process:** Prewriting, p. 332; **Writing Trait:** Purpose, p. 338; **Writing Forms:** Notetaking Strategies, p. 372 • **Weekly Student Model:** Outline, **Student Book** p. 739 **Go Digital** *For additional writing support, see WriteSmart Online Writing Tools.*

Guided Reading

Select texts according to your students' instructional level. You may use the books below or select from the Leveled Readers Database, pp. 412–421. For instructional support, use the Leveled Readers Teacher's Guides along with the books that you choose.

- **LEVEL P** *Flying into History*
- **LEVEL P** *Dangerous Waves* (Vocabulary Reader)
- **LEVEL S** *Helen Keller's Special Friend* (Language Support)
- **LEVEL S** *Helen Keller's Lifelong Friend*
- **LEVEL S** *Champions on Ice*

Planning a Week of Literacy and Language

INSTRUCTIONAL FOCUS

◉ **Student Community Text**
- *The Fun They Had* by Isaac Asimov, **Student Book** pp. 744–753
- *Toys! Amazing Stories Behind Some Great Inventions* by Don Wulffson, **Student Book** pp. 758–762 `ANCHOR TEXT`

◉ **Teacher Read Aloud:** *The Future of Flight*, p. 390

◉ **Minilesson Principles:** Author's Purpose; Genre: Informational Text; Summarize

◉ **Word Work Emphasis:** Words with VV Pattern

◉ **Writing Mode:** Informative Writing

◉ **Writing Trait:** Elaboration

For additional instructional resources, see Journeys Lesson 25 Focus Wall.

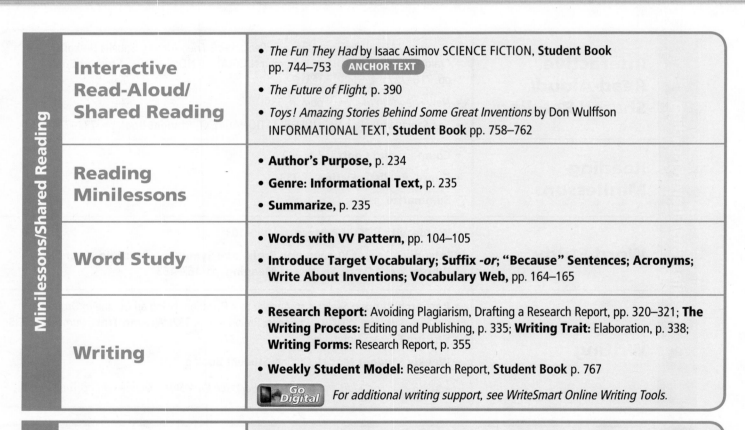

Minilessons/Shared Reading		
Interactive Read-Aloud/ Shared Reading	• *The Fun They Had* by Isaac Asimov SCIENCE FICTION, **Student Book** pp. 744–753 `ANCHOR TEXT` • *The Future of Flight*, p. 390 • *Toys! Amazing Stories Behind Some Great Inventions* by Don Wulffson INFORMATIONAL TEXT, **Student Book** pp. 758–762	
Reading Minilessons	• **Author's Purpose,** p. 234 • **Genre: Informational Text,** p. 235 • **Summarize,** p. 235	
Word Study	• **Words with VV Pattern,** pp. 104–105 • **Introduce Target Vocabulary; Suffix -or; "Because" Sentences; Acronyms; Write About Inventions; Vocabulary Web,** pp. 164–165	
Writing	• **Research Report:** Avoiding Plagiarism, Drafting a Research Report, pp. 320–321; **The Writing Process:** Editing and Publishing, p. 335; **Writing Trait:** Elaboration, p. 338; **Writing Forms:** Research Report, p. 355 • **Weekly Student Model:** Research Report, **Student Book** p. 767 **Go Digital** *For additional writing support, see WriteSmart Online Writing Tools.*	

Guided Reading

Select texts according to your students' instructional level. You may use the books below or select from the Leveled Readers Database, pp. 412–421. For instructional support, use the Leveled Readers Teacher's Guides along with the books that you choose.

- **LEVEL M**   *The Linney Twins Get Cooking*
- **LEVEL P**   *Remarkable Robots* (Vocabulary Reader)
- **LEVEL S**   *Dex is a Hero* (Language Support)
- **LEVEL S**   *A Hero Weighs In*
- **LEVEL T**   *Math Today and Tomorrow*

Planning a Week of Literacy and Language

INSTRUCTIONAL FOCUS

- **Student Community Text**
  - *The Girl Who Loved Spiders* by Karen Halvorsen Schreck, **Student Magazine** pp. 4–11 `ANCHOR TEXT`
  - *Web Wise* by Margaret Hall, **Student Magazine** pp. 12–13
  - *The Spider* by Jack Prelutsky, *Spider Ropes* by James Berry, **Student Magazine** pp. 14–15

- **Minilesson Principles:** Story Structure; Genre: Informational Text; Genre: Poetry

- **Word Work Emphasis:** Final Schwa + /r/ Sound

- **Writing Mode:** Opinion Writing

- **Writing Trait:** Evidence

For additional instructional resources, see Journeys Lesson 26 Focus Wall.

Minilessons/Shared Reading		
Interactive Read-Aloud/ Shared Reading	• *The Girl Who Loved Spiders* by Karen Halvorsen Schreck REALISTIC FICTION, **Student Magazine** pp. 4–11 `ANCHOR TEXT` • *Web Wise* by Margaret Hall INFORMATIONAL TEXT, **Student Magazine** pp. 12–13 • *The Spider* by Jack Prelutsky, *Spider Ropes* by James Berry POETRY **Student Magazine** pp. 14–15	
Reading Minilessons	• **Story Structure,** p. 236 • **Genre: Informational Text,** p. 237 • **Genre: Poetry,** p. 237	
Word Study	• **Final Schwa + /r/ Sound,** pp. 106–107 • **Review Target Vocabulary; Suffix *-able*; Synonyms; Root *mem*; Clipped Words; Riddles,** pp. 166–167	
Writing	• **Response to Fiction:** Using Examples from the Text, Drafting a Response to Fiction, pp. 322–323; **Writing Trait:** Evidence, p. 336; **Writing Forms:** Book Review/Report, p. 369 **Go Digital** *For additional writing support, see WriteSmart Online Writing Tools.*	

Guided Reading	
	Select texts according to your students' instructional level. You may use the novels below or select from the Leveled Readers Database, pp. 412–421. For instructional support, use the Leveled Readers Teacher's Guides along with the books that you choose. • **LEVEL P** *Justin and the Best Biscuits in the World* by Mildred Pitts Walter REALISTIC FICTION, pp. 1–27 • **LEVEL P** *Phineas L. MacGuire . . . Gets Slimed!* by Frances O'Roark Dowell REALISTIC FICTION, pp. 1–38 • **LEVEL V** *Sea Turtles: Ocean Nomads* by Mary M. Cerullo INFORMATIONAL TEXT, pp. 5–10

Planning a Week of Literacy and Language

INSTRUCTIONAL FOCUS

◉ **Student Community Text**
- *Amphibian Alert!* by Elliott Meiner, **Student Magazine** pp. 22–27 ANCHOR TEXT
- *The Frog in the Milk Pail* retold by M. C. Hall, **Student Magazine** pp. 20–21
- *Toad by the Road* by Joanne Ryder, *The Poison-Dart Frogs* by Douglas Florian, **Student Magazine** pp. 28–29

◉ **Minilesson Principles:** Main Ideas and Details; Genre: Fable; Genre: Poetry

◉ **Word Work Emphasis:** Final Schwa + /l/ Sound

◉ **Writing Mode:** Opinion Writing

◉ **Writing Trait:** Elaboration

For additional instructional resources, see Journeys *Lesson 27 Focus Wall.*

Minilessons/Shared Reading		
	Interactive Read-Aloud/ Shared Reading	• *Amphibian Alert!* by Elliott Meiner INFORMATIONAL TEXT, **Student Magazine** pp. 22–27 ANCHOR TEXT • *The Frog in the Milk Pail* retold by M. C. Hall FABLE, **Student Magazine** pp. 20–21 • *Toad* by the Road by Joanne Ryder, *The Poison-Dart Frogs* by Douglas Florian POETRY **Student Magazine** pp. 28–29
	Reading Minilessons	• **Main Ideas and Details,** p. 238 • **Genre: Fable,** p. 239 • **Genre: Poetry,** p. 239
	Word Study	• **Final Schwa + /l/ Sound,** pp. 108–109 • **Review Target Vocabulary; Suffix *-age*; Idea Completion; Similes and Metaphors; Glossary Snapshots; Four-Square Map,** pp. 168–169
	Writing	• **Journal Entry:** Expressing Thoughts and Feelings, Drafting a Journal Entry, pp. 324–325; **Writing Trait:** Elaboration, p. 338; **Technology:** Writing for the Web, p. 343; **Writing Forms:** Journal, p. 373 Go Digital *For additional writing support, see WriteSmart Online Writing Tools.*

Guided Reading	
	Select texts according to your students' instructional level. You may use the novels below or select from the Leveled Readers Database, pp. 412–421. For instructional support, use the Leveled Readers Teacher's Guides along with the books that you choose. • **LEVEL P** *Justin and the Best Biscuits in the World* by Mildred Pitts Walter REALISTIC FICTION, pp. 28–48 • **LEVEL P** *Phineas L. MacGuire . . . Gets Slimed!* by Frances O'Roark Dowell REALISTIC FICTION, pp. 39–75 • **LEVEL V** *Sea Turtles: Ocean Nomads* by Mary M. Cerullo INFORMATIONAL TEXT, pp. 11–18

Planning a Week of Literacy and Language

INSTRUCTIONAL FOCUS

Student Community Text
- *Museums: Worlds of Wonder* by Jody Cosson, **Student Magazine** pp. 34–39 ANCHOR TEXT
- *Making the Most from Trash* by H. G. Ellis, **Student Magazine** pp. 40–41
- *Dinosaur Bone* by Alice Schertle, *Museum Farewell* by Rebecca Kai Dotlich, **Student Magazine** pp. 42–43

Minilesson Principles: Fact and Opinion; Fact and Opinion; Genre: Poetry

Word Work Emphasis: Three-Syllable Words

Writing Mode: Opinion Writing

Writing Trait: Organization

For additional instructional resources, see Journeys *Lesson 28 Focus Wall.*

Minilessons/Shared Reading	**Interactive Read-Aloud/ Shared Reading**	• *Museums: Worlds of Wonder* by Jody Cosson INFORMATIONAL TEXT, **Student Magazine** pp. 34–39 ANCHOR TEXT • *Making the Most from Trash* by H. G. Ellis PHOTO ESSAY, **Student Magazine** pp. 40–41 • *Dinosaur Bone* by Alice Schertle, *Museum Farewell* by Rebecca Kai Dotlich POETRY **Student Magazine** pp. 42–43
	Reading Minilessons	• **Fact and Opinion,** p. 240 • **Fact and Opinion,** p. 241 • **Genre: Poetry,** p. 241
	Word Study	• **Three-Syllable Words,** pp. 110–111 • **Review Target Vocabulary; Suffix *-ize*; Riddles; Prefix *con-*; Write About Problem-Solving; Synonyms and Antonyms,** pp. 170–171
	Writing	• **Public Service Announcement:** Using Language to Affect Audience, Drafting a Public Service Announcement, pp. 326–327; **Writing Trait:** Organization, p. 337 Go Digital *For additional writing support, see WriteSmart Online Writing Tools.*

Guided Reading 	Select texts according to your students' instructional level. You may use the novels below or select from the Leveled Readers Database, pp. 412–421. For instructional support, use the Leveled Readers Teacher's Guides along with the books that you choose. • **LEVEL P** *Justin and the Best Biscuits in the World* by Mildred Pitts Walter REALISTIC FICTION, pp. 49–77 • **LEVEL P** *Phineas L. MacGuire . . . Gets Slimed!* by Frances O'Roark Dowell REALISTIC FICTION, pp. 76–109 • **LEVEL V** *Sea Turtles: Ocean Nomads* by Mary M. Cerullo INFORMATIONAL TEXT, pp. 19–25

Planning a Week of Literacy and Language

INSTRUCTIONAL FOCUS

○ **Student Community Text**
- *Save Timber Woods!* by Lillian Dietrich, **Student Magazine** pp. 48–55 `ANCHOR TEXT`
- *Following Muir: A Persuasive Essay* by Delia Greve, **Student Magazine** pp. 56–57
- *The Comb of Trees* by Claudia Lewis, *Enjoy the Earth* from Yoruba, Africa, **Student Magazine** pp. 58–59

○ **Minilesson Principles:** Understanding Characters; Persuasion; Genre: Poetry

○ **Word Work Emphasis:** Words with Silent Consonants

○ **Writing Mode:** Opinion Writing

○ **Writing Trait:** Organization

For additional instructional resources, see Journeys Lesson 29 Focus Wall.

Minilessons/Shared Reading	**Interactive Read-Aloud/ Shared Reading**	• *Save Timber Woods!* by Lillian Dietrich READERS' THEATER, **Student Magazine** pp. 48–55 `ANCHOR TEXT` • *Following Muir: A Persuasive Essay* by Delia Greve PERSUASIVE ESSAY, **Student Magazine** pp. 56–57 • *The Comb of Trees* by Claudia Lewis, *Enjoy the Earth* from Yoruba, Africa POETRY **Student Magazine** pp. 58–59
	Reading Minilessons	• **Understanding Characters,** p. 242 • **Persuasion,** p. 243 • **Genre: Poetry,** p. 243
	Word Study	• **Words with Silent Consonants,** pp. 112–113 • **Review Target Vocabulary; Suffix *-ful*; Word Associations; Suffix *-ity*; Write About Conservation; Four-Square Map,** pp. 172–173
	Writing	• **Opinion Essay:** Determining Audience and Purpose, Supporting an Opinion with Reasons, pp. 328–329; **The Writing Process:** Prewriting, p. 332; **Writing Trait:** Organization, p. 337; **Writing Forms:** Opinion Essay, p. 363 **Go Digital** *For additional writing support, see WriteSmart Online Writing Tools.*

Guided Reading 	Select texts according to your students' instructional level. You may use the novels below or select from the Leveled Readers Database, pp. 412–421. For instructional support, use the Leveled Readers Teacher's Guides along with the books that you choose. • **LEVEL P** *Justin and the Best Biscuits in the World* by Mildred Pitts Walter REALISTIC FICTION, pp. 78–94 • **LEVEL P** *Phineas L. MacGuire . . . Gets Slimed!* by Frances O'Roark Dowell REALISTIC FICTION, pp. 110–150 • **LEVEL V** *Sea Turtles: Ocean Nomads* by Mary M. Cerullo INFORMATIONAL TEXT, pp. 26–30

Planning a Week of Literacy and Language

INSTRUCTIONAL FOCUS

- **Student Community Text**
  - *Mystery at Reed's Pond* by Zoe Zolbrod, **Student Magazine** pp. 64–71 `ANCHOR TEXT`
  - *A Big Python Problem* by Trillio DeBernardi, **Student Magazine** pp. 72–73
  - *Naming the Turtle* by Patricia Hubbell, *Greater Flamingo* by Tony Johnston, **Student Magazine** pp. 74–75

- **Minilesson Principles:** Conclusions; Genre: Informational Text; Genre: Poetry

- **Word Work Emphasis:** Unusual Spellings

- **Writing Mode:** Opinion Writing

- **Writing Trait:** Conventions

For additional instructional resources, see Journeys *Lesson 30 Focus Wall.*

Minilessons/Shared Reading	**Interactive Read-Aloud/ Shared Reading**	• *Mystery at Reed's Pond* by Zoe Zolbrod MYSTERY, **Student Magazine** pp. 64–71 `ANCHOR TEXT` • *A Big Python Problem* by Trillio DeBernardi INFORMATIONAL TEXT, **Student Magazine** pp. 72–73 • *Naming the Turtle* by Patricia Hubbell, *Greater Flamingo* by Tony Johnston POETRY **Student Magazine** pp. 74–75
	Reading Minilessons	• **Conclusions,** p. 244 • **Genre: Informational Text,** p. 245 • **Genre: Poetry,** p. 245
	Word Study	• **Unusual Spellings,** pp. 114–115 • **Review Target Vocabulary; Prefix *pro-*; Rate Experiences; Suffix *-er*; Word Pairs; Vocabulary Web,** pp. 174–175
	Writing	• **Opinion Essay:** Writing an Effective Closing, Drafting an Opinion Essay, pp. 330–331; **Writing Process:** Editing and Publishing, p. 335; **Writing Trait:** Conventions, p. 340 **Go Digital** *For additional writing support, see* WriteSmart Online Writing Tools.

Guided Reading 	Select texts according to your students' instructional level. You may use the novels below or select from the Leveled Readers Database, pp. 412–421. For instructional support, use the Leveled Readers Teacher's Guides along with the books that you choose. • **LEVEL P** *Justin and the Best Biscuits in the World* by Mildred Pitts Walter REALISTIC FICTION, pp. 95–177 • **LEVEL P** *Phineas L. MacGuire . . . Gets Slimed!* by Frances O'Roark Dowell REALISTIC FICTION, pp. 151–197 • **LEVEL V** *Sea Turtles: Ocean Nomads* by Mary M. Cerullo INFORMATIONAL TEXT, pp. 31–38

Teacher's Notes

Word Study

Table of Contents

Spelling/Phonics

(continued)

Word Study

Table of Contents

Vocabulary

Why Is Word Study Important?

Word study is a developmentally based approach to phonics, spelling, and vocabulary instruction. Because of the critical role that word knowledge plays in reading and in writing, it is essential that our instruction be matched to students' developmental levels. The word study approach is grounded in research that has identified how learners develop an understanding of the structure of written words and how this structure reflects the alphabetic, pattern, and meaning layers of the language (Templeton, 2011).

Effective word study develops students' underlying *orthographic knowledge*— the understanding of how letters and letter patterns represent sound and meaning in language. As the diagram shown below illustrates, over time students move from an understanding of (1) alphabetic/sound relationships to (2) pattern/sound relationships to (3) *morphology*, or meaning, relationships. Orthographic knowledge forms the foundation of students' development in fluency, reading comprehension, and writing.

By understanding how we can best assess what our students know about word structure, we can then target our instruction most effectively at those aspects of word study that each of our students needs and is ready to learn (Bear, Invernizzi, Templeton, & Johnston, 2012).

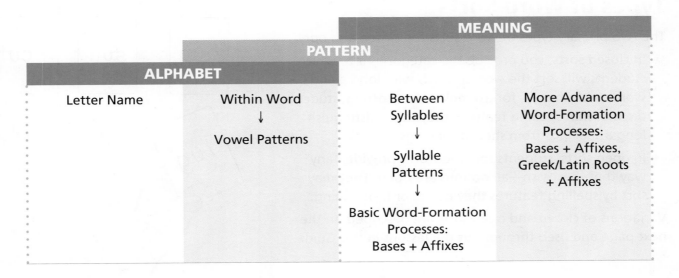

▸ Engaging and Effective Word Study

For word study to be effective, we need to make sure that our students are experiencing, examining, and talking about words from a variety of perspectives—taking them apart and putting them together (Ehri, 2005; Templeton & Bear, 2011). Through this type of analysis and synthesis, students will best internalize the features of words and apply this understanding efficiently in their reading and writing.

The most effective framework in which students may productively explore words and their patterns is through the process of comparing, contrasting, and analyzing in interactive word sort activities. Word sorts actively engage and motivate students, and the discussions allow students to share insights and discover generalizations about words. Word sorting combines student-exploratory and teacher-directed learning.

In *Journeys* and in this Guide, you are provided with words that will support students' discoveries and generalizations about the spelling of words at the alphabet, pattern, and meaning layers. First, you will guide students' explorations with appropriate modeling and questioning. As students follow up in their seatwork, they internalize these questions and develop ways to think critically about words.

Because word sorts are hands-on, they are motivating to students. Students work with *known* words because they cannot search for and discover patterns if they cannot identify some or most of the words they are examining. This involvement is in sharp contrast to many phonics and spelling approaches in which the "rule" is stated at the beginning of the lesson. Sorting words leads students towards generating the rule themselves. This framework supports the kind of processing that is the foundation of efficient, fluent reading and spelling.

Types of Word Sorts

The two primary types of word sorts are *closed* and *open*.

- In **closed sorts**, you provide the categories into which students will sort the words: words with long *a* and words with short *a*, for example. After sorting, students discuss what spelling features they think distinguish long *a* spellings from short *a* spellings.

- In **open sorts**, students sort the words provided any way that they wish—all options are open. They may sort by spelling features they notice or by meaning.

Variations of closed and open sorts are described on the next page and used throughout the lessons in this Guide.

Word Sort Variations

Repeated Sorting   It is important that students have multiple opportunities to sort and write the words for the week. Repeated sorting may be done after the initial group sort on Day 1. You may also send words home to be sorted with family members.

Blind Sorts   A blind sort focuses on strengthening the bond between sound and spelling. In blind sorts, students do not see the words to be sorted; they sort them based on the targeted sound/feature that the words represent. Words are shuffled and read aloud by you or a buddy without showing them to the writer. A key word is used to represent each of the sort categories. Students write the word that is called out under the appropriate key word.

Word Hunts   This activity helps students establish the connection between spelling words and reading words. After exploring the targeted features/patterns through sorting, students look back through familiar reading selections, hunting for words that are examples of these features/patterns. They record their discoveries in their Word Study Notebooks (see below).

Picture Sorts   Children in the early phases of spelling development sort both words and pictures. Pictures are particularly effective when children are focusing on sound because they must attend to particular sound patterns or phonemes within the pronounced word. Then they are able to focus more precisely on the sounds as they are represented either alphabetically or by spelling pattern.

Draw and Label, Cut-and-Paste   As children are learning the names and sounds of particular letters, they will draw pictures of things that begin with or contain these sounds. They label the pictures with the appropriate letter or try to spell as much of the label as they are able. Later, when words are sorted, they may be pasted into categories.

Guess My Category   This activity involves students in trying to guess categories after words have been sorted by you or by other students. The categories may be based on spelling patterns or on concepts. Students grow more creative in their categorization and guessing as they are exposed to more words and their features.

Speed Sorts   As students sort the words later in the week, they enjoy timing their sorts to see how rapidly they are able to complete the sort while maintaining accuracy. Many students keep track of their progress in their Word Study Notebooks.

Meaning/Concept Sorts   Pictures and words may be sorted according to meaning categories. When known words are grouped in different ways, new conceptual relationships are established. For example, younger children may sort a group of pictures according to things that may be found *indoors* and those that may be found *outdoors*; older students may sort a group of words according to concepts such as *mammal*, *amphibian*, or *bird*.

Word Study Notebooks

The Word Study Notebook is the home for word sorts, writing sorts, word hunts, interesting new words encountered in reading, and important new vocabulary. For younger children, the notebook may be a few pages of construction paper stapled or tied together. For older students, a loose-leaf binder works especially well because as more words and patterns are explored it is easy to add pages. Students may record and work with new spelling and vocabulary words—doing concept sorts, creating graphic organizers, or drafting sentences for the vocabulary.

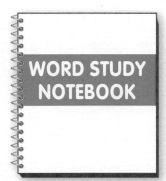

▶ Spelling/Phonics

The spelling/phonics lessons in this Guide may be used apart from or to complement the lessons in *Journeys*, providing additional exposure to and exploration of targeted word features. The five-day format of each lesson begins with an introduction and walk-through of the features and patterns in the spelling words. On subsequent days, the spelling words are compared and contrasted through the variety of sorts and activities described on page 41.

Throughout each lesson, there are several opportunities for students to share and discuss what they are observing and thinking with partners and with the group. The fifth day of each lesson is an assessment. Dictation sentences that include the spelling words are provided in Grades 1–6.

It is important that students interact with the spelling words every day. At all levels, you will introduce important phonics and spelling features at the beginning of the lesson. Depending on the students' developmental level, you may meet with some students on subsequent days. Every day, however, activities are provided that may be completed by the students at their seats, either in small groups or independently.

Components of a Typical Grade 4 Spelling/Phonics Lesson

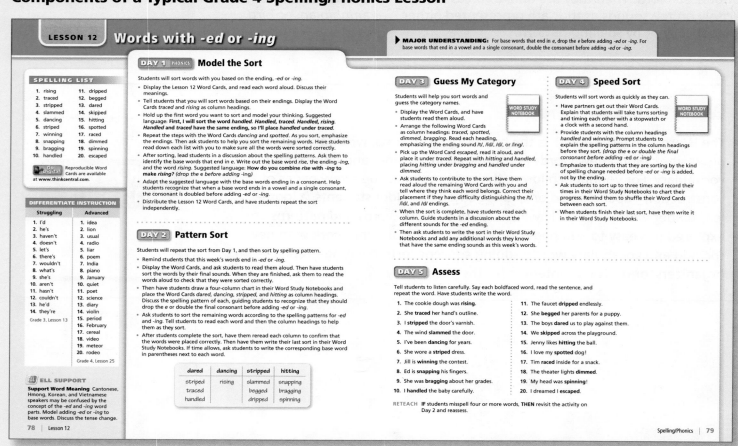

Characteristics of Most Grade 4 Spellers

- Most students will be in the syllables and affixes phase of spelling development. They will examine short and long vowel patterns in two-syllable words, and they will continue to explore less-frequent vowel spellings in words such as *sauce* (often spelled SAWCE) and *aloud* (ALOWD). For most students, *r*-controlled vowel patterns are still a challenge. Common misspellings are CHOOR, CHOORE (*chore*) and ERNE (*earn*).

- The basic understanding that students in this phase will develop is "what to do" at the juncture or place where syllables come together. This understanding is reinforced when students examine words to which the inflectional ending *-ed* or *-ing* has been added. Common errors are SKIPING (*skipping*), WASTEING (*wasting*), and DARRED (*dared*). Additional syllables and affixes conventions to be explored are V/CV (*human*/HUMMAN), VC/CV (*collect*/COLECT), and VC/V (*planet*/PLANNET).

- As students continue to learn about common syllable patterns, they will make errors at the juncture of syllables and in unstressed syllables: BACCON (*bacon*), BOTOM (*bottom*), ROCKIT (*rocket*), DAFEND (*defend*), PALICE (*palace*), RILATE (*relate*).

- Silent consonants constitute a common error pattern for students at this level: CLIME (*climb*), ANSER (*answer*), LISSEN (*listen*), OFFEN/OFEN (*often*). Historically, most of these sounds were pronounced.

Name _____

Lesson 12
SPELLING/PHONICS

rising	dripped
traced	begged
stripped	dared
slammed	skipped
dancing	hitting
striped	spotted
winning	raced
snapping	dimmed
bragging	spinning
handled	escaped

Word Study
© Houghton Mifflin Harcourt Publishing Company

Go Digital

Word Study Spelling/Phonics Lessons

- **Day 1:** Students sort by sound and then discuss pattern, realizing that sound determines the spelling at the juncture of the base words and the inflectional endings.

- **Day 2:** Students sort Word Cards by spelling pattern independently. Then they record their sort in their Word Study Notebooks.

- **Day 3:** Students recognize different sounds for the same spelling through an engaging category guessing game.

- **Day 4:** Students develop fluency in recognizing and categorizing by spelling pattern.

- **Day 5:** Assesses students' understanding.

Reproducible Word Cards

- Available at **www.thinkcentral.com**
- The lesson's Word Cards are used in a variety of ways throughout the week.

▶ Spelling/Phonics Development

What the Research Says

Word study instruction must match the needs of each student. A student's **instructional level** is a powerful determinant of what may be learned. Simply put, we must teach within each child's zone of understanding. The word features that are examined at each grade in *Journeys* should match the developmental level of most students. Students for whom the word study curriculum is not the appropriate developmental "fit," however, will have appropriate patterns and words provided.

The lower chart below presents the developmental nature of orthographic knowledge as students learn the relationships between letters in the printed word and the types of information the letters represent. The spellings reflect the types of orthographic information to which developing learners pay attention, from alphabetic through a deeper understanding of the structure of single-syllable words, two-syllable and multisyllabic words, and morphological relationships.

A developmental perspective on phonics and spelling instruction reveals that knowledge does not occur simply through repetition and memorization. For most students throughout the primary, intermediate, and middle grades, memory for words and patterns is supported by an awareness of underlying interrelationships among sound, spelling, meaning, and morphology.

Levels of Literacy Development

Emergent Literacy	Beginning Literacy	Transitional Literacy	Intermediate Literacy	Skilled/ Advanced Literacy
Pre-K to middle of Grade 1	Kindergarten to middle of Grade 2	Grade 1 to middle of Grade 4	Grade 3 through Grade 8	Grade 5 through Grade 12

Levels of Spelling Development

Emergent Phase	Letter Name-Alphabetic Phase	Within Word Pattern Phase	Syllables and Affixes Phase	Derivational Relations Phase
B—bed *CUS*—see you soon	*DT*—dot *BAD*—bed *SEP*—ship *LUP*—lump *JRIV*—drive	*TRANE*—train *FLOWT*—float *CATOL*—cattle *THOUT*—throat	*HABBIT*—habit *CAPCHURE*—capture *MIDDEL*—middle	*APPEARENCE*—appearance *OPPISITION*—opposition *DEPRAVATION*—deprivation *FEASABLE*—feasible *APARITION*—apparition *CLORINE*—chlorine

Phases of Spelling Development

Emergent Most preschoolers and kindergartners, as well as some first graders at the beginning of the school year, are emergent spellers. Emergent spelling may range from random marks to recognizable letters that correspond in some way to sound. Notably, children at the emergent phase are not yet phonemically aware—that is, they are not able consciously to attend to consonant and vowel sounds within syllables.

Letter Name-Alphabetic Becoming letter name-alphabetic spellers depends upon learning the *alphabetic principle*—the understanding that letters represent sounds in a systematic way and that words can be segmented into phonemes from left to right. Early on, children use the names of the letters to represent sounds. Beginning and ending sounds in syllables are represented, and medial vowels come in a bit later: BD spells *bed*; *we* may be spelled YE because the name of letter *y* contains the /w/ sound.

Typically, short vowel sounds may be spelled with the letter whose name is *closest* to the sound the child wants to spell: *bed* is spelled BAD because the name of the letter *a* is pronounced with a mouth position that is very similar to the mouth position that is used to pronounce the short *e* sound—more similar than any other vowel sound. As children learn about the conventional spellings for short vowel sounds, they learn about consonant digraphs and also blends, or how to separate the sound that each letter represents.

Within Word Pattern Within word pattern spellers are able to spell correctly most single-syllable short-vowel words, consonant blends, consonant digraphs, and the sounds that *m* and *n* represent when they occur before consonants, as in *bump* and *stand*. They are able to think in more than one dimension about word structure—how letters may be grouped into patterns that correspond predictably to sound—and they examine words by sound and pattern simultaneously. Because of this, within word pattern spellers come to understand that how sounds are spelled often depends on the following: where the sounds occur within words (long *a* at the end of words is spelled *ay*; in the middle, usually *a*-consonant-*e* or *ai*); other sounds that are around them (if a long vowel comes before a /j/ sound, /j/ is spelled *ge*; otherwise, /j/ is spelled *dge*); letters provide clues about the pronunciation of other letters within the word (the final *e* in *slide*).

During the within word pattern phase, students will first explore the common long vowel patterns (long *o* can be spelled *o*-consonant-*e* as in *broke*, *oa* as in *boat*, and *ow* as in *grow*), then less common patterns (VCC pattern in *told* and *host*), and later more challenging patterns (*au* in *taught*, *ough* in *through* and *though*).

Students begin to explore the role of *meaning* in the spelling system when they examine *homophones* such as *sail/sale* and *pail/pale*. The different spellings for the same sound are often explained by the fact that they occur in homophones, and we support children as they keep the word's meaning in mind while examining its spelling.

Syllables and Affixes Students' understanding about spelling patterns in single-syllable words is the foundation that supports their growth into the syllables and affixes phase. This understanding helps them to explore two-syllable words and the syllable patterns that determine what goes on at the juncture of syllables and morphemes. The juncture conventions all depend on an awareness of the relationship between sound and spelling. Morphological analysis—the exploration of word-formation processes involved in combining prefixes, suffixes, base words, and roots—may be facilitated by exploring how these units are represented in spelling.

The syllables and affixes phase is typically achieved in the intermediate grades. The first major convention to be explored at this phase is the addition of inflectional endings to base words. The vowel pattern in the base word determines what happens at the juncture of the base word and the ending: *make + ing = making* (drop *e*); *hit + ing = hitting* (double the final consonant to keep the short vowel sound in the base word); *wait + ing = waiting* (vowel pair in the base word, so no change when adding the ending).

Students' understanding of the relationship between short and long vowel sounds/patterns in base words and how they determine spelling when inflectional endings are added provides a solid foundation for their exploration of syllable patterns—what happens *within* words at the juncture of syllables. The vowel-consonant-consonant-vowel (VC/CV) pattern in *hitting* occurs in *hammer*. In both cases, the doubled consonant keeps the vowel in the first syllable short. The vowel-consonant-vowel (V/CV) pattern in *making* occurs in *diner*. In both cases, the single consonant signals a long vowel in the first syllable.

Derivational Relations   Some students may move into the derivational relations phase in Grade 4 or 5, but most students in this phase are in middle school and above. It is important to note that students will be *reading* many of the words to be studied at this phase when they are still syllables and affixes spellers.

In this phase, students explore the full range in which words are *derived* from a common base or Greek/Latin root to form spelling-meaning families. Word study at this level has the potential to expand students' vocabularies exponentially because most words students will encounter in specific domains of study will be understood and learned by examining their morphological structure. Students' spelling errors at this level are fairly sophisticated: schwas in unaccented syllables within multisyllabic words (DEPRAVATION/*deprivation*, DOMINENT/*dominant*) and consonant doubling in assimilated or "absorbed" prefixes (APARITION/*apparition*). Assimilated prefixes reflect the convention of changing the last consonant in a prefix to the first consonant of the base word or root (*in + mediate = immediate*; *ad + point = appoint*).

Where Do the Spelling/Phonics Words Come From?

The resources we have drawn upon to guide the selection of words in *Journeys* and in this Guide include extensive word frequency counts of English (Zeno et al., 1996). This informs us about the most frequently occurring words at each grade level in oral language as well as in print. To determine which words are likely to be known by students at different grade levels, we have used Biemiller's (2005) adaptation of Dale et al.'s (1981) extensive study. We have also drawn upon the developmental research that, as described above, has determined the scope and sequence of word features (Henderson & Templeton, 1986; Templeton & Bear, 1992). Consolidating this information allows us to select words representing the features that need to be addressed at each developmental level.

At the beginning of each grade, several lessons address important patterns that were also addressed in the previous grade. The words that represent the patterns, however, are appropriate for the new grade level. This is done in order to revisit and consolidate knowledge that may not have been exercised over the preceding break. If you teach in a year-round or multi-track system, you may decide whether or which students need to work through these lessons.

▶ Vocabulary

The vocabulary lessons in this Guide build on and extend the lessons and activities in *Journeys*. Each lesson addresses the research-based criteria for effective instruction using a grade-appropriate approach:

- Develop **word consciousness**—the appreciation of and interest in words, their meanings, and how they are used.

- Through discussion, **activate background knowledge** to determine what students already know about the words and the concepts they represent. Usually there is a range of understandings among students, so getting them involved in discussion is very important.

- Use a **variety of activities** that involve students in using words and thinking about their meanings. These include **sorting/categorizing** words, thinking of **words that are related** morphologically and semantically, **discussing** the words with examples and non-examples, and using **graphic organizers**.

- Reinforce how the structure or **morphology** of the words—affixes, base words, and roots—provides clues to their meanings.

- Teach and model the development of independent word-learning strategies that integrate the use of **contextual and morphological clues**.

- When necessary, **explain the meaning and give examples** of how the words are used. Make a point of using the words often.

Components of a Typical Grade 4 Vocabulary Lesson

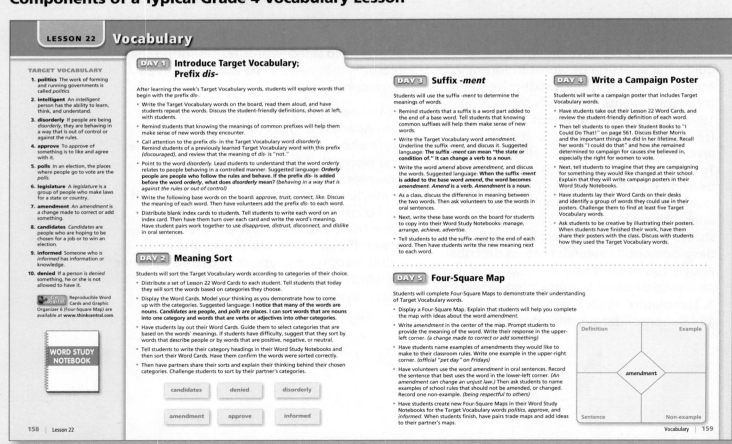

politics	legislature
intelligent	amendment
disorderly	candidates
approve	informed
polls	denied

Name _____

Lesson 22
VOCABULARY

Word Study
© Houghton Mifflin Harcourt Publishing Company

Go Digital

Word Study Vocabulary Lessons

- **Day 1:** Target Vocabulary words are discussed in the group, focusing on context and meaning. Morphology is addressed by targeting a prefix (*dis-*), and students learn how the meaning of a word may be determined by thinking about the meanings of its prefix and base word.

- **Day 2:** A meaning sort activity challenges students to generate categories of like words based on their understanding of the words' meanings.

- **Day 3:** Morphology is addressed by targeting a frequently occurring suffix (-*ment*).

- **Day 4:** Students apply understanding of Target Vocabulary words to writing. The topic connects to the week's Student Book selection.

- **Day 5:** Students generate graphic organizers to demonstrate understanding of words.

Reproducible Word Cards and Graphic Organizer Blackline Masters

- Available at **www.thinkcentral.com**

▸ Vocabulary Development

What the Research Says

We know that vocabulary knowledge is the single most powerful predictor of reading comprehension and academic learning. In Kindergarten and Grade 1, developing *oral* vocabulary is critical and absolutely necessary as a foundation for later vocabulary growth and learning.

For younger children who are not yet reading widely, there is a substantial, convincing body of research that supports the role of teacher read-alouds in developing language and vocabulary (Santoro, Chard, Howard, & Baker, 2008; Pilkulski & Templeton, 2010). However, significant vocabulary growth will occur only when you spend time with *explicit* attention to vocabulary in the contexts of both narrative and informational texts.

In Grades 2–6, we need to address the two major areas of vocabulary development: general academic vocabulary and content-area, or domain-specific, vocabulary (*Common Core State Standards*, 2010).

- **General academic vocabulary** includes those words that do not often occur in everyday spoken language—for example *transmit*, *paradox*, and *product*—but which students may encounter frequently in their reading across all content areas. These words also occur in more formal spoken language, such as a lecture format. Students may often have the underlying concept that such a word represents, but they lack the label that stands for that concept.

- **Content-area or domain-specific vocabulary** refers to words that occur primarily in specific content or subject matter areas such as science, history and social science, mathematics, and the arts. In contrast to general academic vocabulary, much content-specific academic vocabulary—for example *equilateral*, *condensation*, and *feudalism*—represents new concepts, and can therefore be more challenging to learn.

Journeys and this Guide offer a research-based, rich, and robust approach to vocabulary instruction using the important words that students need to learn. The lessons also teach them *about* words—for example, how prefixes, suffixes, base words, and roots combine to result in the meaning of words. When learners understand how this process works, they possess one of the most powerful understandings for vocabulary growth.

Where Does the Target Vocabulary Come From?

As with the selection of words for the spelling/phonics lessons, at Grades 2–6 we used Biemiller's (2005) adaptation of Dale et al.'s (1981) study to guide the selection of words for a particular grade level. We then used Zeno et al.'s frequency corpus (1996) as well as Hiebert's corpus (2005) to identify morphologically related words and cross-checked with Harris-Jacobsen (1982), Dale-Chall, and the Academic Word List.

This process ensured that words would be sufficiently challenging to be academic rather than conversational vocabulary, yet not so challenging that students will find them too difficult to learn and remember, even with good instruction and careful repetition. In Kindergarten and Grade 1, we used Zeno as well as cross-checking with traditional word frequency lists that still correlate highly with recent analyses.

Teacher's Notes

▶ Differentiated Instruction

Teachers differentiate for appropriate reading levels in their classrooms. It is important that children and older students be placed at their appropriate levels for word study as well. This will ensure that they have the experience with words and patterns that they are ready to explore.

Specific guidelines for determining your students' appropriate developmental levels for word study are provided on the next page and on pages 400–410 in the Resources section of this Guide. The Qualitative Spelling Inventory will help you determine your students' developmental spelling levels at the beginning of the school year. It may be administered again at the middle of the school year, and then toward the end of the year.

The relationship between word knowledge and reading level is very close. You will likely find that your below-level, on-level, and above-level students in word study are almost always your below-, on-, and above-level readers. This allows you to differentiate your instruction more effectively. For example, when meeting with your below-level reading group at the beginning of the week, you may introduce and sort the leveled spelling words after students have read an appropriately leveled selection.

For most students, the grade-level words and features that are presented in *Journeys* and in this Guide will be appropriate. For your students who are not on grade level, the Struggling and Advanced words and features offered in each lesson will address the needs of most. For those students who are significantly below- or above-level, use the word lists on pages 400–410 and access the appropriate lessons in another grade level of this Guide on **www.thinkcentral.com**.

Occasionally, it may be necessary to adjust the level for particular students, just as you adjust reading levels. The weekly assessments on Day 5 of each spelling/phonics lesson provide effective progress monitoring so that you will be able to know how students are progressing. This insight is also very helpful as you evaluate students' writing since that is where the depth of your students' learning is observed.

 **ELL SUPPORT**

In addition to the point-of-use notes located in the spelling/phonics lessons in this Guide, the information on the next page and on pages 392–396 of the Resources section will help you address the unique transfer support needs of your students who are English language learners (ELLs).

▶ Assessment to Inform Instruction

Assessing a student's spelling developmental phase is a powerful and precise method for planning instruction. By following the steps below and using the tools on the pages that follow, you can determine the phase of spelling development for each of your students and use the results to select appropriate lessons for students at varying phases.

① ASSESS

Administer the Qualitative Spelling Inventory (QSI) on the next page. Also collect a selection of each student's first-draft writing for comparison. The QSI results combined with examples from daily writing will offer a strong sampling for analysis. Emphasize to students that the assessment is not a test for a grade and it is okay if they don't know all the answers. Explain that their work will help you understand what they already know and what you need to help them learn.

② ANALYZE

Determine a spelling developmental phase for each student. Use the Qualitative Spelling Inventory Checklist (pages 397–399) to guide your decisions.

③ PLAN AND MONITOR

Organize small groups based on your diverse classroom needs. Monitor students' progress, and reorganize groups as needed throughout the year. For on-level students, use the lessons in your grade-level *Word Study Teacher's Guide*. Select lessons for Struggling and Advanced students:

- Suggested lessons for Differentiated Instruction are provided in each lesson in Grades 1–6.
- If your students' needs do not align with the suggested lessons, select an appropriate lesson using the word lists organized by spelling phase on pages 400–410.

Short *a* and Long *a*

SPELLING LIST

1. blade
2. gray
3. past
4. afraid
5. magic
6. delay
7. amaze
8. drain
9. maybe
10. break

11. sale
12. hang
13. stain
14. glass
15. raft
16. jail
17. crayon
18. fact
19. stale
20. steak

 Go Digital Reproducible Word Cards are available at **www.thinkcentral.com**.

DIFFERENTIATE INSTRUCTION

Struggling	Advanced
1. meet	1. wiped
2. meat	2. covered
3. week	3. mapped
4. weak	4. pleasing
5. mane	5. slipped
6. main	6. putting
7. tail	7. traveled
8. tale	8. seeking
9. be	9. visiting
10. bee	10. mixed
11. too	11. shipped
12. two	12. phoning
Grade 2, Lesson 22	13. offered
	14. smelling
	15. hiking
	16. checking
	17. fainted
	18. landed
	19. becoming
	20. wandering
	Grade 4, Lesson 13

ELL SUPPORT

Use Minimal Pairs In Cantonese and Mandarin, the short *a* does not exist, so students may substitute the sound with short *e*. Model the difference by naming pairs for students to repeat, such as *pan/pen*, *man/men*, and *tan/ten*.

DAY 1 PHONICS Model the Sort

Students will sort words with you based on their vowel sound, /ă/ or /ā/.

- Display the Lesson 1 Word Cards. Read each word aloud, and discuss the meanings of the words, as necessary.
- Tell students that you are going to sort the words into two categories based on the vowel sound, /ă/ or /ā/, in each word. Display the Word Cards *past* and *gray*, and place them as column headings.
- Then hold up the first word you will sort, and model your thinking. Suggested language: **First, I am going to sort the word *glass*. Does the vowel sound in *glass* sound like the sound in *past* or the sound in *gray*?** *Glass. Past, glass. Gray, glass.* **The /ă/ sound in *glass* sounds like the /ă/ sound in *past*, so I will place it in that column. Both *glass* and *past* have the short *a* sound.**
- Repeat with a word with long *a*. Then continue through the remaining Word Cards, having students help you sort the words. For words with more than one vowel sound, such as *crayon*, emphasize the sound for *a* as you read the word aloud.
- After sorting, have students read down each list with you to make sure all the words were sorted correctly. Help students recognize the spelling pattern in the short *a* list. Suggested language: **What vowel sound do all of the words in this list have?** *(/ă/ or short a)* **What do you notice about the spelling of /ă/?** *(It is spelled with a followed by a consonant.)*
- Guide students to recognize the spelling patterns for long *a*. Suggested language: **What vowel sound do all of the words in this list have?** *(/ā/ or long a)* **What are the different ways that long *a* is spelled?** *(ai, ay, ea, and CVCe)*
- Give each student a set of Lesson 1 Word Cards, and have them repeat the sort independently.

DAY 2 Guess My Category

Students will help you sort words based on their spelling pattern and guess the category name.

- Remind students that the words they are sorting this week have the /ă/ or /ā/ sound.
- Display the Word Cards, and have students read them aloud. Tell students that you will sort the words, and they will try to figure out the categories. Explain that students can help you sort the cards but should not reveal the categories until the sort is complete.
- Gather the Word Cards *raft, jail, maybe, steak,* and *sale*. Read the words aloud, and place them as column headings. Then read the word *fact* and place it under *raft*. Read *stain* and place it under *jail*. Continue sorting by spelling pattern, asking students to help you place the cards.
- After all the words have been sorted, have students analyze each column and describe how the words are similar. Prompt them to explain the spelling pattern in each column.
- Have students write the sort in their Word Study Notebooks.

raft	jail	maybe	steak	sale
fact	stain	crayon	break	amaze
past	drain	delay		blade
glass	afraid	gray		stale
magic				
hang				

DAY 3 Blind Writing Sort

Students will sort and write words that a partner says aloud.

WORD STUDY NOTEBOOK

- Have students divide a page in their Word Study Notebooks into two columns and write *fact* and *drain* as column headings.
- Group students into pairs, and have one pair demonstrate the activity for the class.
- Have one student read a Word Card aloud without showing the word. Have the second student write the word in the *fact* column if it has the short *a* sound or in the *drain* column if it has the long *a* sound.
- Then have the first student show the Word Card so the second student may confirm or correct the spelling. If the word was misspelled, have the second student cross out the word and write it correctly under the appropriate column heading.
- Have partners continue the activity until all the words have been written. The student writing the words should then read the words in each column aloud to confirm their placement.
- Have partners switch roles, shuffle the cards, and complete the activity again.

DAY 4 Speed Sort

Students will sort words as quickly as they can.

WORD STUDY NOTEBOOK

- Tell students that they will sort words by vowel sound with one partner and then sort by spelling pattern with a different partner.
- For the first sort, pair students and ask them to read their Word Cards aloud.
- Have one student sort the words into short *a* and long *a* categories as his or her partner keeps the time using a stopwatch or a clock with a second hand.
- Have students record their times in their Word Study Notebooks. Tell pairs to repeat the sort several times, alternating roles and trying to beat their last time with each new sort.
- Then have students change partners and complete another speed sort. This time student pairs will sort by spelling pattern.
- Provide students with the headings *past*, *stain*, *gray*, *break*, and *blade*. Ask partners to confirm that the words were sorted correctly.
- Have students write their last sort in their Word Study Notebooks.

DAY 5 Assess

Tell students to listen carefully. Say each boldfaced word, read the sentence, and repeat the word. Have students write the word.

1. Dad sharpened the saw **blade**.
2. The kitten is **gray** and white.
3. Dinosaurs lived in the **past**.
4. She was **afraid** of the big dog.
5. I did a **magic** trick for the kids.
6. The meeting will **delay** lunch.
7. His talent will **amaze** you.
8. My ring went down the **drain**.
9. **Maybe** we can go shopping.
10. The glass bottle may **break**.
11. I bought those shoes on **sale**.
12. Let's **hang** your picture here.
13. That shirt has a **stain** on it.
14. I would like a **glass** of juice.
15. We used a **raft** at the beach.
16. The outlaw went to **jail**.
17. Use a red **crayon** for the picture.
18. Is that a **fact** or your opinion?
19. The old bread was **stale**.
20. I like to eat **steak**.

RETEACH **IF** students misspell four or more words, **THEN** revisit the activity on Day 1 and reassess.

Short *e* and Long *e*

SPELLING LIST

1. west
2. steep
3. member
4. gleam
5. fresh
6. freedom
7. speed
8. steam
9. beast
10. believe
11. speck
12. kept
13. cheap
14. pretend
15. greed
16. shelf
17. least
18. eager
19. reason
20. chief

 Go Digital Reproducible Word Cards are available at **www.thinkcentral.com**.

DIFFERENTIATE INSTRUCTION

Struggling	Advanced
1. happy	1. turkey
2. pretty	2. lonely
3. baby	3. colony
4. very	4. steady
5. puppy	5. hungry
6. funny	6. valley
7. carry	7. hockey
8. lucky	8. starry
9. only	9. melody
10. sunny	10. movie
11. penny	11. duty
12. city	12. drowsy
	13. chimney
	14. plenty
	15. daily
	16. alley
	17. fifty
	18. empty
	19. injury
	20. prairie

Grade 2, Lesson 18.

Grade 4, Lesson 14.

ELL ELL SUPPORT

Linguistic Transfer Spanish speakers may have trouble with two letters representing one vowel sound. Model pronouncing each vowel pair, and have students repeat.

DAY 1 PHONICS **Model the Sort**

Students will sort words with you based on their vowel sound, /ĕ/ or /ē/.

- Display the Lesson 2 Word Cards, and read them aloud. Discuss the meanings of the words, as necessary.
- Tell students that you are going to sort the words into short *e* and long *e* categories. Display the Word Cards *west* and *steep*, and place them as column headings.
- Then show students the first word you will sort, and model your thinking. Suggested language: **First, I am going to sort the word *fresh*. Does *fresh* have the short *e* sound like *west* or the long *e* sound like *steep*? *Fresh*. *West*, *fresh*. *Steep*, *fresh*. The *e* sound in *fresh* is the same short *e* sound as in *west*, so I will place it in that column.**
- Model sorting a long *e* word. Then continue through the remaining Word Cards, asking students to help you sort the words. For words with more than one vowel sound, such as *pretend*, emphasize the *e* sound in the stressed syllable.
- When you have finished sorting, have students read down each list with you to make sure all the words have been sorted correctly. Help students discover the spelling pattern in the short *e* list. Suggested language: **What vowel sound do all of these words have in common?** *(/ĕ/ or short *e*)* **What do you notice about the spelling of /ĕ/?** *(It is spelled with *e* followed by a consonant.)*
- Then guide students to recognize the spelling patterns in the long *e* list. Suggested language: **What vowel sound do all of the words in this list have?** *(/ē/ or long *e*)* **What are the different ways that long *e* is spelled?** *(ee, ea, and ie)*
- Give each student a set of Lesson 2 Word Cards, and have them repeat the sort independently.

· ·

DAY 2 **Pattern Sort**

Students will sort words based on the spelling for /ĕ/ or /ē/.

- Remind students that this week's words have the short *e* or long *e* sound.
- Display the Word Cards, and have students read them aloud. Have students sort the words into short *e* and long *e* categories and then read their lists to make sure they sorted the words correctly.
- Then have students find the Word Cards *fresh, speed, beast,* and *chief* and place them as column headings. Have students sort the remaining Word Cards according to the spelling for short *e* or long *e*. Remind students to read each word aloud before placing it in a category.
- After completing the sort, have students read each column to confirm that they sorted the words correctly. Then have students write their sorts in their Word Study Notebooks.

fresh	speed	beast	chief
member	steep	reason	believe
speck	greed	gleam	
shelf	freedom	least	
pretend		eager	

DAY 3 Word Hunt

Students will sort words that they find in their reading.

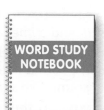

- Have students create a two-column chart in their Word Study Notebooks and write the headings *kept* and *least.*

- Tell students that they will sort words with the short *e* and long *e* vowel sounds that they find in their reading.

- Have students open their Student Books to page 49. Demonstrate how to search for words in "My Brother Martin" with the /ĕ/ or /ē/ sound. Help students understand the difference between skimming pages and reading the whole selection.

- Have students write the words they find under the appropriate heading. Have them check how they sorted the words by reading down each column aloud.

- Then have students compare their lists with a partner's and add other words they know that fit the categories.

(Possible responses: we, dear, peas, feet, best, piece, head, gleaming, behind, hedge, screams, bench)

DAY 4 Blind Writing Sort

Students will sort and write words that a partner says aloud.

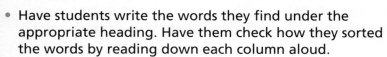

- Have students divide a page in their Word Study Notebooks into four columns and write *speck, greed, steam,* and *believe* as column headings.

- Ask students to work with a partner. Have one student read a Word Card aloud to his or her partner without showing the word. Have the other student write the word under the correct column heading according to the spelling pattern for short *e* or long *e.*

- After the word has been written, have the writer look at the Word Card to confirm or correct the spelling.

- Have partners continue the activity until all of the words have been written. Then have the students read the words in each column together and check the sort.

- Direct students to switch roles, shuffle the cards, and complete the activity again.

DAY 5 Assess

Tell students to listen carefully. Say each boldfaced word, read the sentence, and repeat the word. Have students write the word.

1. Jamie lives **west** of our school.
2. We climbed a very **steep** hill.
3. I am a **member** of a math club.
4. She had a **gleam** in her eyes.
5. Are those vegetables **fresh**?
6. Voting is a **freedom** we enjoy.
7. His bike raced at a high **speed**.
8. Does **steam** rise from boiling pots?
9. An ox is a strong **beast**.
10. I **believe** in what I'm doing.
11. The **speck** of paint splattered.
12. He **kept** money in the bank.
13. I can go if tickets are **cheap**.
14. Let's **pretend** we're on a boat.
15. Her **greed** made me angry.
16. Put the beans on the **shelf**.
17. He is at **least** ten minutes late.
18. I am **eager** to go camping.
19. I have a good **reason** for being late.
20. The fire **chief** gave directions.

RETEACH   IF students misspell four or more words, **THEN** revisit the activity on Day 2 and reassess.

Short *i* and Long *i*

SPELLING LIST

1. skill
2. crime
3. grind
4. tonight
5. brick
6. flight
7. live
8. chill
9. delight
10. build
11. ditch
12. decide
13. witness
14. wind
15. district
16. inch
17. sigh
18. fright
19. remind
20. split

 **Go Digital** Reproducible Word Cards are available at **www.thinkcentral.com**.

DIFFERENTIATE INSTRUCTION

Struggling	Advanced
1. lay	1. tiniest
2. real	2. hobbies
3. trail	3. copied
4. sweet	4. countries
5. today	5. pitied
6. dream	6. easier
7. seem	7. laziest
8. tea	8. families
9. treat	9. spied
10. afraid	10. happiest
11. leave	11. ladies
12. bait	12. friendlier
13. screen	13. studied
14. speed	14. busier
	15. breezier
	16. prettiest
	17. noisier
	18. healthier
	19. butterflies
	20. funniest
Grade 3, Lesson 3	Grade 4, Lesson 15

ELL SUPPORT

Use Minimal Pairs Students who speak Spanish may substitute a long *e* sound for short *i* (*leap* for *lip*). Help them differentiate by reading aloud minimal pairs, such as *tin/teen, fit/feet,* and *lid/lead.* Have students repeat the pairs.

DAY 1 PHONICS Model the Sort

Students will sort words with you based on their vowel sound, /ĭ/ or /ī/.

- Display the Lesson 3 Word Cards, and read each word aloud.
- Tell students that you are going to sort the words into short *i* and long *i* categories. Display the Word Cards *skill* and *crime*, and place them as column headings.
- Hold up the first word you will sort, and model your thinking. Suggested language: **Does the vowel sound in *live* sound like the sound in *skill* or *crime*? *Live, skill. Live, crime. Live* has the short *i* sound like *skill*, so let's place it in that column.**
- Then ask students to help you sort the remaining Word Cards. For words with more than one vowel sound, such as *witness,* emphasize the /ĭ/ or /ī/ sound. When you have sorted all the words, have students read each column aloud with you to make sure the words were sorted correctly.
- Help students recognize the spelling pattern for short *i*. Suggested language: **What vowel sound do all of these words have in common?** *(/ĭ/ or short* i*)* **What do you notice about the spelling of /ĭ/?** *(It is usually spelled* i *followed by a consonant.)*
- Point out the oddball *build*. Suggested language: **Look at this word, *build*. What letters stand for the /ĭ/ sound in *build*?** *(ui)*
- Then draw students' attention to the spelling patterns in the long *i* list. Suggested language: **What vowel sound do all of the words in this list have?** *(/ī/ or long* i*)* **What are the different ways that long *i* is spelled?** *(*i *followed by a consonant,* igh, *and CVCe)*
- Distribute the Lesson 3 Word Cards, and have students repeat the sort independently.

DAY 2 Repeat the Sort

Students will repeat the sort from Day 1 independently.

- Remind students that this week's words have the short *i* and long *i* sounds.
- Have students divide a page in their Word Study Notebooks into two columns and place the Word Cards *chill* and *sigh* as column headings.
- Tell students that they will sort the remaining Word Cards according to the vowel sound in each word. If a word has the /ĭ/ sound, they should place it under *chill*. If it has the /ī/ sound, they should place it under *sigh*. Remind students to read each card aloud before sorting it.
- After completing the sort, have students reread the words in each column to make sure they placed the words in the correct category. Then have students write the sort in their Word Study Notebooks.

chill	sigh
inch	remind
live	decide
brick	fright
build	tonight

> **MAJOR UNDERSTANDING:** The short vowel sound /ĭ/ is usually spelled *i* followed by a consonant. The long vowel sound /ī/ can be spelled *i* followed by a consonant, *igh*, and CVC*e*.

DAY 3 Guess My Category

Students will recognize the spelling patterns in words that you sort.

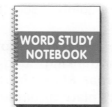
WORD STUDY NOTEBOOK

- Display the Word Cards and have students read them aloud. Tell students that you will sort the words, and they will try to figure out the categories.
- Gather the Word Cards *brick, grind, flight,* and *decide,* and place them as column headings.
- Choose a Word Card, read it aloud, and place it under the correct column heading according to its spelling pattern.
- After you have sorted several words, ask students to contribute to the sort by reading the Word Cards with you and telling where they think each word belongs.
- When you come to the oddball *build,* read the card aloud and attempt to match it to each column heading. Then set it aside.
- When the sort is complete, have students read each column aloud. Prompt students to explain how the words are sorted and to explain the spelling patterns. Have students describe why *build* is an oddball.
- Then have students shuffle the cards, repeat the sort independently, and write it in their Word Study Notebooks.

DAY 4 Buddy Sort

Students will repeat the sort from Day 3 with a partner.

WORD STUDY NOTEBOOK

- Tell students that they will sort their Word Cards with a partner based on the spelling pattern for /ĭ/ or /ī/.
- Have students divide a page in their Word Study Notebooks into five columns and label the columns *live, remind, fright, crime,* and *Oddballs.* Point out the spelling pattern for /ĭ/ or /ī/ in each word.
- Assign students to work together. Have one partner read each Word Card aloud and the other partner indicate the correct column.
- After all the words have been sorted, have partners read the words in each column aloud to make sure the words were sorted correctly. Then have students switch roles, shuffle the cards, and repeat the sort.
- Prompt students to discuss the spelling patterns and the oddball *build.* Then have them write their sorts in their Word Study Notebooks.
- Extend the activity by asking students to add any other words they know that have the same spelling patterns for /ĭ/ and /ī/ as the words in this lesson.

DAY 5 Assess

Tell students to listen carefully. Say each boldfaced word, read the sentence, and repeat the word. Have students write the word.

1. Passing is a **skill** in basketball.
2. The police solved the **crime**.
3. A butcher will **grind** the meat.
4. Judy is coming over **tonight**.
5. The **brick** wall was crumbling.
6. Our **flight** home was delayed.
7. He does not **live** in that house.
8. There's a **chill** in the air.
9. **Delight** showed on her face.
10. They plan to **build** a house.
11. Water ran through a **ditch**.
12. You **decide** where we will eat.
13. A **witness** spoke to the judge.
14. A strong **wind** damaged houses.
15. The school **district** closed.
16. I grew an **inch** taller this year!
17. Lee gave a **sigh** of relief.
18. His mask gave me a **fright**.
19. I'll **remind** you to pick me up.
20. The cook **split** the sandwich in half.

RETEACH IF students misspell four or more words, **THEN** revisit the activity on Day 3 and reassess.

SPELLING LIST

1. block
2. shown
3. oatmeal
4. wrote
5. fellow
6. scold
7. coast
8. odd
9. locate
10. slope
11. throat
12. host
13. online
14. shock
15. solve
16. known
17. remote
18. stock
19. boast
20. globe

 Reproducible Word Cards are available at **www.thinkcentral.com**.

DIFFERENTIATE INSTRUCTION

Struggling	Advanced
1. load	1. risky
2. open	2. track
3. told	3. topic
4. yellow	4. blank
5. soak	5. question
6. shadow	6. pocket
7. foam	7. monkey
8. follow	8. junk
9. glow	9. equal
10. sold	10. ache
11. window	11. public
12. coach	12. attack
13. almost	13. struck
14. throat	14. earthquake
Grade 3, Lesson 4	15. picnic
	16. banker
	17. electric
	18. blanket
	19. mistake
	20. stomach
	Grade 4, Lesson 16

 ELL SUPPORT

Linguistic Transfer Help Spanish speakers understand that the letter _o_ in English can stand for the /ŏ/ sound. (The letter _o_ in Spanish always stands for the long _o_ sound.)

DAY 1 PHONICS **Model the Sort**

Students will sort words with you based on their vowel sound, /ŏ/ or /ō/.

- Display the Lesson 4 Word Cards, and read each word aloud.
- Tell students that you are going to sort the words based on the vowel sound for _o_ in each word.
- Display the words _shown_ and _block_ as column headings. Hold up the first word you will sort, and model your thinking. Suggested language: **First, I'm going to sort the word _throat_. Shown, throat. Block, throat. The /ō/ sound in _throat_ sounds like the /ō/ sound in _shown_. Let's place _throat_ under _shown_.**
- Repeat with a word with short _o_ and continue through the list, having students help you sort the words. When words have more than one vowel sound, emphasize the sound for _o_ as you read the word aloud.
- Guide students to analyze what the words in each list have in common, starting with the short _o_ list. Suggested language: **What vowel sound do all the words in this list have?** (/ŏ/ or short o) **What do you notice about the spelling of /ŏ/?** (It is spelled with o followed by a consonant.)
- In the long _o_ list, guide students to recognize the different spellings for /ō/: _o_ followed by a consonant, _ow_, _oa_, and CVCe. Have students help you group the words with long _o_ by the spelling pattern for the sound /ō/.
- Give each student a set of Lesson 4 Word Cards, and have them repeat the sort independently.

DAY 2 **Pattern Sort**

Students will sort words based on the spelling for /ŏ/ or /ō/.

- Remind students that this week's words have the /ŏ/ and /ō/ sounds.
- Have students create a five-column chart in their Word Study Notebooks. Have them place the following Word Cards as column headings: _stock, host, known, coast, slope._
- Ask students to sort the remaining Word Cards according to the spelling for /ŏ/ or /ō/. Remind students to read each word aloud before placing it in a category.
- After all the words have been sorted, have students reread each list to confirm that the words have been sorted correctly. Then have them write their sorts in their Word Study Notebooks.

stock	host	known	coast	slope
odd	locate	shown	oatmeal	wrote
shock	scold	fellow	throat	remote
solve			boast	globe
online				
block				

DAY 3 ## Open Sort

Students will sort the words according to categories of their choice.

WORD STUDY NOTEBOOK

- Have students get out their Word Cards, read the words, and analyze the words for similarities and differences.

- Tell students that today they will select the categories for their sorts based on what they have noticed about the words.

- Tell students that their categories may be different from or the same as the categories they sorted by earlier in the week. Model analyzing the Word Cards and sorting them by the number of syllables in each word.

- If students have difficulty selecting categories, you may want to suggest sorting by parts of speech, or sorting by the location of the short *o* and long *o* sounds (beginning, middle, or end).

- Have students write column headings in their Word Study Notebooks and write each word in the correct column. Then have them confirm their choices and explain to a partner how they sorted the words.

DAY 4 ## Word Hunt

Students will sort words that they find in their reading.

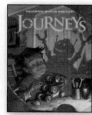

- Tell students that today they will sort words that they find in their reading with the sounds /ŏ/ and /ō/ by spelling pattern.

- Have students reproduce the Day 2 column headings in their Word Study Notebooks. Discuss the sound and spelling patterns.

- Ask students to open their Student Books to page 112. Have them skim each page in "The Power of W.O.W.!" to look for words that fit one of the five categories.

- Then have them write each word in the correct column and confirm the words were sorted correctly by reading down each column.

- Have students compare their lists with a partner's and add other words they know that fit the categories.

(Possible responses: own, golden, hold, nope, spotless, program, show, operate, mom, community, hose)

DAY 5 ## Assess

Tell students to listen carefully. Say each boldfaced word, read the sentence, and repeat the word. Have students write the word.

1. I know everyone on my **block**.
2. Sam has **shown** he is talented.
3. I like to eat hot **oatmeal**.
4. Lila **wrote** a note to her aunt.
5. Mr. Rivers is a friendly **fellow**.
6. I had to **scold** my brother.
7. We drove along the **coast**.
8. We learned about **odd** and even numbers in math class.
9. I need to **locate** the library.
10. I can sled on a snowy **slope**.
11. I had a cold and a sore **throat**.
12. Ben was the **host** of the party.
13. Tim used an **online** dictionary.
14. The movie's end was a **shock**.
15. We can **solve** the problem.
16. I've **known** Sasha for a year.
17. We hiked to a **remote** village.
18. The grocer has to **stock** the shelves in his store every day.
19. Tim likes to **boast** about his team.
20. I found the ocean on the **globe**.

RETEACH **IF** students misspell four or more words, **THEN** revisit the activity on Day 2 and reassess.

Homophones

SPELLING LIST

1. wait	11. sent
2. weight	12. cent
3. heard	13. scent
4. herd	14. feet
5. days	15. feat
6. daze	16. vain
7. heel	17. vane
8. heal	18. vein
9. peak	19. miner
10. peek	20. minor

 Reproducible Word Cards are available at **www.thinkcentral.com**.

DIFFERENTIATE INSTRUCTION

Struggling	Advanced
1. slight	1. glance
2. mild	2. judge
3. sight	3. damage
4. pie	4. package
5. mind	5. twice
6. tie	6. stage
7. pilot	7. carriage
8. might	8. since
9. lie	9. practice
10. tight	10. marriage
11. blind	11. baggage
12. fight	12. office
13. die	13. message
14. midnight	14. bridge
Grade 3, Lesson 5	15. chance
	16. notice
	17. ridge
	18. manage
	19. palace
	20. bandage
	Grade 4, Lesson 17

 **ELL SUPPORT**

Support Word Meaning
Homophones can be particularly challenging for ELLs. Support definitions with visuals and demonstrations to explain the differences in meaning.

DAY 1 PHONICS Model the Sort

Students will sort words with you based on the vowel sound in each word.

- Display the Lesson 5 Word Cards, and read each word aloud. Ask students what they notice about the words in this week's word list. *(They are words that sound alike but are spelled differently.)*
- Tell students that you will be sorting words based on the vowel sound in each word.
- Begin the sort by holding up the word *weight* and reading it aloud. Suggested language: **Weight** *has the long* a *sound. What other word has the long* a *sound and sounds like* weight**?** *(wait)* **Let's place** *wait* **under** *weight.*
- Adapt the suggested language for the homophones *heel* and *heal*, creating a column for long *e*. Repeat the process for *sent/cent/scent* (short *e*), *miner/minor* (long *i*), and *heard/herd* (/ûr/).
- Have volunteers show you where to place the remaining Word Cards. After all the words are sorted, have students read the columns aloud to confirm word placement. Guide students to identify the sounds by which the words are sorted. *(/ā/, /ē/, /ĕ/, /ī/, /ûr/)*
- Explain that words that sound the same are called homophones. Ask students to isolate the nine sets of homophones.
- Point to one homophone set and help students recognize the words' similarities and differences. Suggested language: **What is the same about these words?** *(They sound the same.)* **What is different about these words?** *(They are spelled differently, and they have different meanings.)*
- Guide students in analyzing each set of homophones to identify two or more spelling patterns for the same vowel sound. Then give each student a set of Lesson 5 Word Cards, and have them repeat the sort independently.

DAY 2 Repeat the Sort

Students will repeat the sort from Day 1 independently.

- Remind students that this week's words are homophones. Review that homophones are words that sound the same but have different spellings and meanings.
- Tell students to create a five-column chart in their Word Study Notebooks. Have them use the following column headings: *days, cent, feet, minor, herd.*
- Ask students to sort their Word Cards by vowel sounds. Explain that students should first match a set of homophones, and then they should place that set in the correct column according to the vowel sound.
- After sorting all the words, have students reread each column to confirm that they sorted the words correctly. Then have them write their sorts in their Word Study Notebooks.

days	cent	feet	minor	herd
daze	sent	feat	miner	heard
vein	scent	peak		
vane		peek		
vain				

DAY 3 Buddy Sort

Students will compare sorts with a partner, first by sound and then by homophone pair or set.

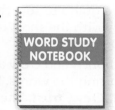

WORD STUDY NOTEBOOK

- Tell students that today they will sort their Word Cards independently into categories by vowel sound. Then they will sort each column into homophone pairs or sets.

- Direct students to choose their own column headings for the vowel sounds /ā/, /ē/, /ĕ/, /ī/, and /ûr/. Have students shuffle their Word Cards and sort the words into the sound categories.

- When students finish sorting, have them compare and confirm their sound sorts with a partner. Then have students independently sort each column into sets of homophones.

- Have students review their homophone sorts with a new partner. Then have them write the homophone sets in their Word Study Notebooks.

- Extend the activity by asking students to highlight or underline the different spelling patterns in each set of homophones.

DAY 4 Open Sort

Students will sort words according to categories of their choice.

WORD STUDY NOTEBOOK

- Have students take out their Word Cards, read the words aloud, and analyze the words for similarities and differences.

- Tell students that they will sort the words into categories of their choice. Explain that students' categories may be different from or the same as the categories they sorted by earlier in the week.

- If students have difficulty choosing categories, suggest that they sort by beginning or final consonant, short and long vowel sounds, or "things" and "actions."

- Give students time to sort the cards. When they complete their sorts, have students form small groups and explain their category choices and reasoning behind each word's placement.

- Have students write their sorts in their Word Study Notebooks.

- Extend the activity by challenging students to sort the Word Cards according to another student's categories.

DAY 5 Assess

Tell students to listen carefully. Say each boldfaced word, read the sentence, and repeat the word. Have students write the word.

1. I had to **wait** for the bus.
2. My cat is gaining **weight**.
3. Tom **heard** the doorbell ring.
4. A **herd** of cows ate the grass.
5. There are five **days** in a week.
6. I walked around in a **daze**.
7. That shoe hurts my **heel**.
8. My broken arm will **heal**.
9. He reached a mountain **peak**.
10. I took a **peek** at the baby.
11. She **sent** me an email.
12. The gum cost just one **cent**.
13. A skunk had a strong **scent**.
14. My **feet** ache from walking.
15. Winning the race was a great **feat**.
16. The handsome man was very **vain**.
17. The weather **vane** was on top of the barn.
18. I can see each **vein** in my arm.
19. The **miner** found gold in the mine.
20. It was just a **minor** error.

RETEACH **IF** students misspell four or more words, **THEN** revisit the activity on Day 2 and reassess.

Vowel Sounds /ŭ/, /yo͞o/, and /o͞o/

SPELLING LIST

1. bunch	11. clue
2. fruit	12. trunk
3. argue	13. amuse
4. crumb	14. suit
5. crew	15. rude
6. tune	16. trust
7. juice	17. dew
8. refuse	18. stuck
9. truth	19. rescue
10. young	20. brush

 Reproducible Word Cards are available at **www.thinkcentral.com**.

DIFFERENTIATE INSTRUCTION

Struggling	Advanced
1. three	1. colorful
2. scrap	2. weakness
3. street	3. movement
4. spring	4. endless
5. thrill	5. truthful
6. scream	6. illness
7. strange	7. cheerful
8. throw	8. useless
9. string	9. beautiful
10. scrape	10. restless
11. spray	11. clumsiness
12. threw	12. pavement
13. strong	13. peaceful
14. scratch	14. fondness
	15. neatness
Grade 3, Lesson 7	16. speechless
	17. statement
	18. wasteful
	19. penniless
	20. treatment
	Grade 4, Lesson 19

 ELL SUPPORT

Linguistic Transfer The /yo͞o/ sound may be challenging for Vietnamese and Hmong speakers. First, have students imitate words with the /o͞o/ sound. Then have them repeat /yo͞o/ words after you model them.

DAY 1 PHONICS Model the Sort

Students will sort words with you based on their vowel sounds, /ŭ/, /yo͞o/, and /o͞o/.

- Display the Lesson 6 Word Cards, and read each word aloud.
- Tell students that you are going to sort the words into two categories. One category will have words with the short *u* or /ŭ/ sound. The other will have words with the long /yo͞o/ or /o͞o/ sound.
- Display the Word Cards *bunch* and *crew* as column headings. Then model your thinking as you begin sorting the words. Suggested language: **First, I will sort the word *trust*. Bunch, trust. Crew, trust. The /ŭ/ sound in *trust* sounds the same as the /ŭ/ sound in *bunch*. I'll place *trust* under *bunch*.**
- Repeat with a word with /yo͞o/ or /o͞o/. Then ask students to help you sort the remaining Word Cards. When a word has more than one vowel sound, emphasize the /ŭ/, /yo͞o/, or /o͞o/ sound as you read it aloud.
- Guide students to identify what the words in each column have in common. Suggested language: **Let's look at the words in the *bunch* column. What vowel sound do all of the words have?** *(/ŭ/ or short* u*)* Explain that the /ŭ/ sound is usually spelled *u* followed by a consonant. Challenge students to identify the oddball in this column. *(*Young* is an oddball because its short* u *sound is spelled* ou.*)*
- Help students recognize the spelling patterns for the long vowel sounds /yo͞o/ and /o͞o/. After discussing the words' *ue, ew, ui,* and CVCe spellings, ask students if they noticed any oddballs in this column. *(*Truth* is the oddball because its long vowel sound is spelled* u *followed by a consonant.)*
- Give each student a set of Lesson 6 Word Cards. Have students repeat the sort independently.

DAY 2 Repeat the Sort

Students will repeat the sort from Day 1 independently.

- Remind students that this week's words have the /ŭ/, /yo͞o/, and /o͞o/ vowel sounds.
- Have students create a two-column chart in their Word Study Notebooks. Have them place the Word Cards *trunk* and *tune* as column headings.
- Tell students to sort the remaining Word Cards according to the /ŭ/, /yo͞o/, or /o͞o/ sound in each word. Remind students to read each word aloud before they sort.
- After students complete the sort, tell them to reread the words in each column to confirm that the words are in the correct columns. Then have students write their sorts in their Word Study Notebooks.

trunk	tune
crumb	dew
stuck	fruit
bunch	rude
young	clue

DAY 3   Guess My Category

Students will guess the category of words that you sort by spelling pattern.

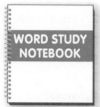

- Display the Word Cards, and have students read them aloud. Tell students that you will sort the words, and they will try to figure out the categories.
- Place the following five Word Cards as column headings: *stuck, rude, clue, fruit, dew.* Then create a sixth column and label it *Oddballs.*
- Select the word *tune,* read it aloud, and place it under *rude.* Next, sort *suit* under *fruit* and *rescue* under *argue.*
- Continue to sort the Word Cards by spelling pattern. Have students help you once they recognize the categories.
- When the sort is complete, have students read aloud the words in each column. Prompt students to explain the spelling patterns: /ŭ/ spelled *u* followed by a consonant; /yo͞o/ and /o͞o/ spelled *ue, ew, ui,* and CVC*e.*
- Ask students to explain why *young* and *truth* are oddballs. Then have students copy the sort into their Word Study Notebooks.

DAY 4   Buddy Sort

Students will sort by spelling pattern with a partner.

- Have students take out their Word Cards and read the words aloud with a partner. Tell students that they will work with a partner to sort words according to the spelling patterns for /ŭ/, /yo͞o/, and /o͞o/.
- Have students divide two pages in their Word Study Notebooks into six columns and write *crumb, amuse, rescue, juice, crew,* and *Oddballs* as column headings.
- Direct partners to take turns sorting the Word Cards according to the spelling patterns for /ŭ/, /yo͞o/, and /o͞o/. After one partner finishes, the other partner should shuffle the cards and sort the words.
- Remind students to read the words aloud before assigning them to a category and to watch out for oddballs.
- Instruct students to read each column to confirm that the words were sorted correctly. Then have students write their sorts in their Word Study Notebooks.
- Students may add other words they know that have the same spelling patterns.

DAY 5   Assess

Tell students to listen carefully. Say each boldfaced word, read the sentence, and repeat the word. Have students write the word.

1. He has a **bunch** of bananas.
2. Fresh **fruit** is healthy to eat.
3. Do not **argue** with friends.
4. One **crumb** of cake was left.
5. The **crew** washed the boat.
6. I heard the **tune** on the radio.
7. She drank some **juice**.
8. I **refuse** to go with you.
9. Was Gina telling the **truth**?
10. A **young** boy played outside.
11. That **clue** solved the puzzle.
12. She keeps clothes in a **trunk**.
13. A good book will **amuse** me.
14. I wore a **suit** to the concert.
15. Tanya is never **rude** to others.
16. I **trust** you to care for my dog.
17. Morning **dew** covers the grass.
18. The car is **stuck** in the mud.
19. I will **rescue** the cat in the tree.
20. Did you **brush** your hair?

RETEACH   **IF** students misspell four or more words, **THEN** revisit the activity on Day 3 and reassess.

Vowel Sounds /o͞o/ and /o͝o/

1. bloom
2. cookbook
3. tool
4. shampoo
5. put
6. wool
7. stool
8. proof
9. prove
10. group
11. brook
12. foolish
13. bush
14. crooked
15. booth
16. raccoon
17. hook
18. groom
19. roof
20. soup

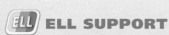 **Go Digital** Reproducible Word Cards are available at **www.thinkcentral.com**.

DIFFERENTIATE INSTRUCTION

Struggling	Advanced
1. itch	1. million
2. wreck	2. collect
3. knee	3. lumber
4. patch	4. pepper
5. wrap	5. plastic
6. knot	6. borrow
7. watch	7. support
8. knife	8. thirty
9. stretch	9. perfect
10. write	10. attend
11. knew	11. canyon
12. knock	12. traffic
13. match	13. fortune
14. wrong	14. danger
Grade 3, Lesson 8	15. soccer
	16. engine
	17. picture
	18. survive
	19. seldom
	20. effort
	Grade 4, Lesson 20

ELL SUPPORT

Linguistic Transfer To help students discriminate between the /o͞o/ and /o͝o/ sounds, say each word on the spelling list, exaggerating your mouth's shape for each vowel sound. Have students mimic and repeat.

DAY 1 PHONICS **Model the Sort**

Students will sort words with you based on their vowel sound, /o͞o/ or /o͝o/.

- Display the Lesson 7 Word Cards. Read each word aloud, and discuss the meanings of the words, as necessary.

- Tell students that you are going to sort the Word Cards into two categories based on the vowel sound in each word. Read aloud the words *bloom* and *put*, and place those cards as column headings.

- Then begin sorting the remaining words into the two sound categories. Suggested language: **The word is** *soup*. **Does the vowel sound in** *soup* **sound like the sound in** *bloom* **or the sound in** *put*? *Soooooup*. **The** /o͞o/ **sound in** *soup* **sounds like the** /o͞o/ **sound in** *bloom*, **so let's place it in that column.**

- Ask students to help you sort the remaining Word Cards. For words with more than one vowel sound, such as *shampoo*, emphasize the /o͞o/ or /o͝o/ sound. When you have finished sorting, have students read down each list with you to make sure all the words have been sorted correctly.

- Guide students to recognize the spelling patterns in the /o͞o/ list. Suggested language: **What vowel sound do all of the words in this list have?** (/o͞o/) **What are the different ways that** /o͞o/ **is spelled?** (oo, ou, *and* CVCe)

- Adapt the suggested language as you review the spelling patterns in the /o͝o/ list, leading students to recognize that /o͝o/ is usually spelled *oo* or *u*.

- Give each student a set of Lesson 7 Word Cards, and have them repeat the sort independently.

DAY 2 **Guess My Category**

Students will help you sort words based on their spelling patterns and guess the category name.

- Remind students that the words they are sorting this week have the /o͞o/ or /o͝o/ vowel sound.

- Display the Word Cards, and have students read them aloud. Tell students that you will sort the words, and they will try to figure out the categories. Remind students not to reveal the categories to the other students until the sort is complete.

- Gather the Word Cards *tool, soup, prove, hook,* and *bush*. Read the words aloud, and place them as column headings. Begin sorting the remaining Word Cards by spelling pattern, asking students to help you place the cards when they are able.

- After all the words have been sorted, have students read each column aloud and explain what the words have in common. Prompt them to describe the vowel sound and the spelling pattern in each column.

- Have students repeat the sort independently and then write the sort in their Word Study Notebooks.

tool	soup	prove	hook	bush
proof	group		wool	put
groom			crooked	
			cookbook	

DAY 3 Pattern Sort

Students will sort /o͞o/ and /o͝o/ words based on their spelling patterns.

- Remind students that this week's words contain the /o͞o/ and /o͝o/ sounds.
- Have students gather the Word Cards *booth*, *group*, *prove*, *wool*, and *put* and place them as column headings. Draw students' attention to the spelling pattern in each word.
- Ask students to sort the remaining Word Cards according to the spelling for /o͞o/ or /o͝o/. Remind students to read each word aloud before sorting it.
- After completing the sort, have students reread each column to make sure they sorted the words correctly.
- Have students compare their sort with another student's sort and discuss the spelling pattern in each column.
- Then have students write their sorts in their Word Study Notebooks.

DAY 4 Speed Sort

Students will sort words as quickly as they can.

- Tell students that they will sort words by vowel sound with one partner and then sort by spelling pattern with a different partner.
- For the first sort, pair students and ask them to read their Word Cards aloud. Then have one student sort the words into /o͞o/ and /o͝o/ categories as his or her partner keeps the time using a stopwatch or a clock with a second hand.
- Have students repeat the sort several times, shuffling the cards after each sort and alternating roles. Challenge students to beat their own best time.
- Then have students change partners and complete another speed sort. Have student pairs sort by spelling pattern. Provide them with the column headings *proof*, *soup*, *prove*, *brook*, and *bush*.
- Have partners check their sorts by reading the columns aloud. Then have them write their last sort in their Word Study Notebooks.

DAY 5 Assess

Tell students to listen carefully. Say each boldfaced word, read the sentence, and repeat the word. Have students write the word.

1. Tulips **bloom** in spring.
2. My **cookbook** has great recipes.
3. A **tool** will fix the wheel.
4. My **shampoo** smells like roses.
5. Where can you **put** the boxes?
6. My coat is made of **wool**.
7. Pull over a **stool** and sit down.
8. I showed my ticket as **proof**.
9. Can you **prove** your story?
10. The **group** works together.
11. The water in the **brook** is cold.
12. I felt **foolish** when I tripped.
13. My cat is hiding under a **bush**.
14. The path is **crooked**.
15. Line up for the voting **booth**.
16. A **raccoon** ate all of the trash.
17. A plant **hook** fell to the floor.
18. Sara left to **groom** her dog.
19. We replaced our leaky **roof**.
20. I would like a bowl of hot **soup**.

RETEACH **IF** students misspell four or more words, **THEN** revisit the activity on Day 3 and reassess.

Vowel Sounds /ou/ and /ô/

SPELLING LIST

1.	aloud	11.	howl
2.	bald	12.	false
3.	hawk	13.	dawn
4.	south	14.	allow
5.	faucet	15.	drown
6.	proud	16.	pause
7.	claw	17.	fault
8.	tower	18.	cause
9.	stalk	19.	amount
10.	couple	20.	cloudier

 Reproducible Word Cards are available at **www.thinkcentral.com**.

DIFFERENTIATE INSTRUCTION

Struggling	Advanced
1. clown	1. event
2. round	2. humor
3. bow	3. rapid
4. cloud	4. music
5. power	5. relief
6. crown	6. planet
7. thousand	7. detail
8. crowd	8. unite
9. sound	9. frozen
10. count	10. figure
11. powder	11. siren
12. blouse	12. polite
13. frown	13. hotel
14. pound	14. protest
Grade 3, Lesson 9	15. punish
	16. defend
	17. relay
	18. habit
	19. student
	20. moment
	Grade 4, Lesson 21

 ELL SUPPORT

Linguistic Transfer Haitian Creole speakers may need help matching the /ou/ sound with different spelling patterns. Brainstorm words that have the /ou/ sound, and list them by their spelling pattern.

DAY 1 PHONICS Model the Sort

Students will sort words with you based on their vowel sound, /ou/ or /ô/.

- Display the Lesson 8 Word Cards, and read each word aloud.
- Tell students that you are going to sort the words based on the vowel sounds /ou/ and /ô/. Display the Word Cards *south* and *hawk,* and place them as column headings.
- Model sorting a word based on its vowel sound. Suggested language: **Does the vowel sound in *bald* sound like the sound in *south* or *hawk*? *Bald, south. Bald, hawk. Bald* has the /ô/ sound like *hawk,* so let's place it in that column.**
- Continue through the remaining Word Cards, asking students to help you sort the words by sound. For words with more than one vowel sound, such as *cloudier,* emphasize the vowel sound in the stressed syllable.
- When you come to the oddball *couple,* emphasize the short *u* sound in the word, and make sure students recognize that it does not have the /ou/ or /ô/ sound. Place it in a category of its own.
- When you have finished sorting, have students read down each list with you to make sure all the words have been sorted correctly.
- Help students discover the spelling patterns in the /ou/ list. Suggested language: **What vowel sound do all of these words have in common?** *(/ou/)* **What are the spelling patterns for the sound /ou/?** *(ou or ow)*
- Then guide students to recognize the spelling patterns in the /ô/ list. Suggested language: **What vowel sound do all of the words in this list have in common?** *(/ô/)* **What are the different ways that /ô/ is spelled?** *(a followed by l, aw, and au)*
- Distribute the Lesson 8 Word Cards, and have students repeat the sort independently.

DAY 2 Pattern Sort

Students will sort words based on the spelling for /ou/ or /ô/.

- Remind students that most of this week's words have the /ou/ and /ô/ sounds. Ask students to read their Word Cards aloud and identify the word that does not have either sound. *(couple)*
- Have students create a six-column chart across two pages in their Word Study Notebooks. Have them use the following Word Cards as column headings: *proud, drown, bald, claw, pause.* Have students label the last column *Oddballs.*
- Ask students to read each word aloud to identify the /ou/ or /ô/ sound and then match the word to one of the spelling patterns. Remind them to watch out for the oddball, which may match a spelling pattern but not the sound.
- After sorting, have students reread each list to make sure they sorted the words correctly and then write their sorts in their Word Study Notebooks.

proud	drown	bald	claw	pause	Oddballs
amount	allow	false	hawk	fault	couple
aloud	tower	stalk	dawn	cause	
south	howl			faucet	
cloudier					

DAY 3 | Word Hunt

Students will sort words that they find in their reading.

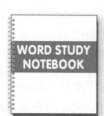

- Tell students that they will look for words in their reading that have the /ou/ and /ô/ sounds. Then they will sort those words by spelling pattern.

- Have students create a five-column chart in their Word Study Notebooks and label the columns *aloud, howl, false, dawn,* and *cause*. Discuss the sound and spelling pattern in each column heading.

- Ask students to open their Student Books to page 231 and look for /ou/ and /ô/ words in "Me and Uncle Romie."

- Students should identify the spelling pattern in each word and then write each word in the correct column in their Word Study Notebooks.

- After completing the sort, have students form small groups to compare their sorts. Students may add to their sorts using words that different group members found.

   (Possible responses: aunt, saw, down, found, call, out, crowds, houses, our, also, hall, loud, walking, around, how)

DAY 4 | Open Sort

Students will sort words according to categories of their choice.

- Have students take out their Word Cards, read the words aloud, and analyze the words for similarities and differences. Explain that students will sort the words using categories of their choice.

- Tell students to think about how they can sort the words in a way that is different from their sorts earlier in the week. If they have trouble identifying categories, suggest options such as parts of speech, number of syllables, or meaning-based categories.

- Give students time to sort their Word Cards. Then have them read each column to confirm that the words were sorted correctly.

- Have students record their completed sorts in their Word Study Notebooks.

- Have students explain their categories to a partner and then try sorting the Word Cards based on their partner's categories.

DAY 5 | Assess

Tell students to listen carefully. Say each boldfaced word, read the sentence, and repeat the word. Have students write the word.

1. The teacher read a story **aloud**.
2. A hat keeps a **bald** head warm.
3. The **hawk** circled the sky.
4. The town is just **south** of here.
5. I forgot to turn the **faucet** off!
6. Her mother was **proud** of her.
7. The crab had lost a **claw**.
8. A bird sat on top of the **tower**.
9. Tigers **stalk** their prey for days.
10. The **couple** were newlyweds.

11. The dog let out a sad **howl**.
12. She gave a **false** answer.
13. I like to wake up at **dawn**.
14. Mom won't **allow** me to go.
15. I **drown** my cereal in milk.
16. She took a long **pause** before speaking.
17. It was my **fault** we were late.
18. Lightning can **cause** fires.
19. He ate a huge **amount**.
20. Today is **cloudier** than yesterday.

RETEACH IF students misspell four or more words, **THEN** revisit the activity on Day 1 and reassess.

Vowel + /r/ Sounds

SPELLING LIST

1. spark
2. prepare
3. cheer
4. tear
5. scarf
6. scare
7. repair
8. earring
9. scarce
10. weird
11. sharp
12. rear
13. spare
14. gear
15. hairy
16. compare
17. alarm
18. harsh
19. upstairs
20. square

 Reproducible Word Cards are available at www.thinkcentral.com.

DIFFERENTIATE INSTRUCTION

Struggling	Advanced
1. talk	1. dentist
2. cross	2. final
3. awful	3. finish
4. law	4. narrow
5. cloth	5. shelter
6. cost	6. ahead
7. crawl	7. corner
8. chalk	8. hollow
9. also	9. divide
10. raw	10. famous
11. salt	11. recent
12. wall	12. silver
13. lawn	13. capture
14. always	14. cabin
	15. dinner
	16. minus
	17. minute
	18. value
	19. reward
	20. broken
Grade 3, Lesson 10	Grade 4, Lesson 22

 ELL SUPPORT

Linguistic Transfer Speakers of Hmong, Cantonese, and Korean may have difficulty with *r*-controlled vowels. Model the sounds /îr/, /är/, and /âr/. Have students practice pronouncing each sound.

DAY 1 PHONICS Model the Sort

Students will sort words with you based on the sound /îr/, /är/, or /âr/.

- Display the Lesson 9 Word Cards, and read each word aloud.

- Tell students that you are going to sort each word by its vowel sound. Display the Word Cards *cheer, spark*, and *scare* as column headings. Model your thinking as you sort. Suggested language: **The first word I want to sort is *rear*. Listen to the vowel sound as I say the word again: *reeeear. Rear, cheer. Rear, spark. Rear, scare.* The /îr/ sound in *rear* sounds like the same sound in *cheer*. I'll put *rear* under *cheer*.**

- Adapt the suggested language as you sort *scarf* with *spark* and *square* with *scare*. Have students help you sort the remaining Word Cards. After all the words have been sorted, ask students to read the words in each column.

- Discuss how the words under *cheer* are alike. Suggested language: **What do you notice about the spelling of /îr/?** (It is spelled *eer* or *ear*.) Guide students to recognize that one word is spelled differently. Then say: **The /îr/ sound is usually spelled *eer* or *ear*. *Weird* is an oddball because it has /îr/ spelled *ei*.** Students may also notice the homograph *tear*, which can have the /îr/ or /âr/ sound.

- Repeat with the *spark* and *scare* columns, leading students to understand that the /är/ sound in *spark* is usually spelled *ar*, and that the /âr/ sound in *scare* can be spelled *are* or *air*. Discuss the oddball *scarce*, which has the /âr/ sound but is spelled *ar*.

- Give each student a set of Lesson 9 Word Cards to repeat the sort independently.

DAY 2 Repeat the Sort

Students will repeat the Day 1 sort, sorting the words by the sound /îr/, /är/, or /âr/.

- Remind students that the words they are sorting this week have the sound /îr/, /är/, or /âr/.

- Have students create a three-column chart in their Word Study Notebooks. Have them use the following Word Cards as column headings: *gear, sharp, square*.

- Tell students that they will sort their remaining Word Cards according to the sound /îr/, /är/, or /âr/ in each word.

- Remind students to read each word aloud before they sort. Then have them compare the word's vowel + /r/ sound to the vowel + /r/ sound of each column heading.

- After students complete the sort, ask them to reread the words in each column to confirm that the words were placed in the correct columns. Then have them write their sorts in their Word Study Notebooks.

gear	sharp	square
weird	spark	prepare
cheer	harsh	upstairs
earring	alarm	hairy

DAY 3 Guess My Category

Students will guess the category of words that you sort by spelling pattern.

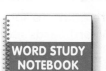

- Display the Word Cards, and have students read them aloud.
- Select the words *cheer, earring, sharp, compare,* and *upstairs*. Place each word as a column heading, and create another column heading labeled *Oddballs*.
- Choose the Word Card *gear*, read it, and place it under *earring*. Then repeat with *alarm* and *scarce*, placing *alarm* under *sharp* and *scarce* under *Oddballs*. Continue to sort by spelling pattern. Students may contribute to the sort once they have recognized the categories.
- Have students read the words aloud in each column. Guide them to explain the spelling patterns: /îr/ spelled *eer* and *ear*; /är/ spelled *ar*; /âr/ spelled *are* and *air*. Have students identify the spelling patterns in the two oddballs: /îr/ spelled *ei* in *weird*; /âr/ spelled *ar* in *scarce*.
- Then have students write the sort in their Word Study Notebooks and add any other words they know that fit the categories.

DAY 4 Blind Writing Sort

Students will sort and write words that a partner says aloud.

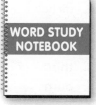

- Have students divide a page in their Word Study Notebooks into three columns. Tell them to write *tear, scarf,* and *spare* as column headings.
- Guide students to recognize the /îr/, /är/, and /âr/ sounds in the column headings. Tell students that they will sort words based on those sounds.
- Ask students to work with a partner. One partner reads each Word Card aloud without showing the word. The other partner writes each word in one of the columns.
- After each word has been written, the partner reading the Word Card places the card face up so the other partner can confirm that the word is spelled correctly. Students should correct any misspellings.
- Then have partners read aloud the words in each column and confirm whether the words were sorted correctly.
- After all the words have been sorted, have partners shuffle the Word Cards and switch roles.

DAY 5 Assess

Tell students to listen carefully. Say each boldfaced word, read the sentence, and repeat the word. Have students write the word.

1. A **spark** flew from the fire.
2. I'll **prepare** food for lunch.
3. I hear the **cheer** of the crowd.
4. A **tear** fell from her eye.
5. I gave my mom a new **scarf**.
6. The movie gave me a **scare**.
7. Dad can **repair** my TV.
8. Have you seen my lost **earring**?
9. Food for the deer was **scarce**.
10. The colorful painting was **weird**.

11. The shark's teeth look **sharp**.
12. I went to the **rear** of the bus.
13. Dad used the car's **spare** tire.
14. Mom shifted into first **gear**.
15. Our **hairy** dog needs a bath.
16. I can **compare** these stories.
17. I slept through my **alarm**.
18. The speaker used **harsh** words.
19. Look in the **upstairs** closet.
20. This monitor is **square**.

RETEACH **IF** students misspell four or more words, **THEN** revisit the activity on Day 3 and reassess.

More Vowel + /r/ Sounds

1. learn	11. worth
2. dirty	12. early
3. worn	13. return
4. sore	14. pure
5. thirst	15. world
6. burn	16. search
7. record	17. worse
8. cure	18. thirteen
9. board	19. sport
10. course	20. current

 Reproducible Word Cards are available at **www.thinkcentral.com**.

DIFFERENTIATE INSTRUCTION

Struggling	Advanced
1. joy	1. poster
2. spoil	2. secret
3. point	3. whether
4. toy	4. author
5. voice	5. rocket
6. joint	6. bushel
7. join	7. agree
8. boy	8. bucket
9. oil	9. ticket
10. soil	10. declare
11. coin	11. chicken
12. choice	12. clothing
13. noise	13. apron
14. boil	14. whiskers
Grade 3, Lesson 11	15. degree
	16. gather
	17. achieve
	18. rather
	19. bracket
	20. machine
	Grade 4, Lesson 23

 **ELL SUPPORT**

Linguistic Transfer Speakers of Mandarin and Cantonese may have difficulty pronouncing *r*-controlled vowels. Model pronouncing the sounds /ôr/, /ûr/, and /yŏŏr/. Have students repeat each sound after you.

DAY 1 PHONICS **Model the Sort**

Students will sort words with you based on the sound /ôr/, /ûr/, or /yŏŏr/.

- Display the Lesson 10 Word Cards, and read them aloud.
- Tell students that you are going to sort the words based on the vowel + /r/ sound in each word. Display the Word Cards *sport*, *dirty*, and *pure* as column headings.
- Hold up the word *learn* and read it along with each column heading. Suggested language: **The word is *learn*. Sport, learn. Dirty, learn. Pure, learn. The /ûr/ sound in *learn* sounds like the same sound in *dirty*, so I will put *learn* under *dirty*.**
- Ask students to help you sort the remaining Word Cards. For words with more than one syllable and vowel sound, such as *thirteen*, emphasize the vowel + /r/ sound when you read the word aloud.
- Starting with the /yŏŏr/ list, have students read down each column with you. Have them confirm that the words were sorted correctly and recognize the common sound in each list. Suggested language: **What sound do all the words in this list have?** *(/yŏŏr/)* **What do you notice about the spelling of /yŏŏr/?** *(It is spelled ure.)*
- Continue with the /ôr/ and /ûr/ columns, asking students to identify the common sounds in each column as well as how the sounds are spelled. Guide students to discover that /ôr/ is usually spelled *or* or *ore*, and /ûr/ can be spelled *ir*, *ur*, *ear*, and *or*. Point out the oddballs *board* and *course*, in which the /ôr/ sound is spelled *oar* and *our*.
- Distribute the Lesson 10 Word Cards, and have students repeat the sort independently.

· ·

DAY 2 **Pattern Sort**

Students will sort words by spelling patterns for vowel + /r/.

- Remind students that this week's words have the sound /ôr/, /ûr/, or /yŏŏr/.
- Display the Word Cards, and have students read them aloud. Have students sort the words by sound and then read their lists to make sure they sorted the words correctly.
- Have students create an eight-column chart across two pages in their Word Study Notebooks. Have them place the following Word Cards as column headings: *worn, sore, thirst, burn, learn, worth, pure*. Have students label the last column *Oddballs*.
- Ask students to sort the remaining Word Cards according to the sound and spelling pattern. Remind students to read each word aloud before placing it in a category.
- After sorting, have students reread each list to make sure they sorted the words correctly. Have them write their sorts in their Word Study Notebooks.

worn	sore	thirst	burn	learn	worth	pure	Oddballs
sport		thirteen	current	search	worse	cure	course
record		dirty	return	early	world		board

DAY 3 · Blind Writing Sort

Students will sort and write words that a partner says aloud.

- Have students create an eight-column chart across two pages in their Word Study Notebooks.

- Have students write the headings *or (sport), ore, ir, ur, ear, or (worth), ure,* and *Oddballs.* Explain that the first *or* column is for the /ôr/ sound in *sport,* and the second *or* column is for the /ûr/ sound in *worth.*

- Tell students that they will sort the words based on the spelling of the /ôr/, /ûr/, or /yŏŏr/ sound in each word.

- Pair students and have one student read a Word Card aloud without showing the card. Have the other student write the word under the correct column heading.

- After the student writes the word, the partner should reveal the Word Card so that the writer can confirm the word was spelled correctly or correct any misspellings.

- After all the words have been written correctly, have students read aloud the words in each column and confirm the words have been sorted correctly. Students should recognize the oddballs *board* and *course.*

- Then have partners shuffle the cards and switch roles.

DAY 4 · Word Hunt

Students will sort words that they find in their reading.

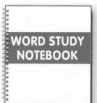

- Have students divide two pages in their Word Study Notebooks into seven columns and label the columns *sport, sore, dirty, return, early, world,* and *cure.*

- Tell students that they will sort words with the /ôr/, /ûr/, and /yŏŏr/ sounds that they find in their reading.

- Have students open their Student Books to page 289 and search for words in "José! Born to Dance" that have the /ôr/, /ûr/, and /yŏŏr/ sounds. Have them write the words in one of their seven spelling pattern categories.

- Tell students to compare their lists with a partner's list and to add other words they know that fit the categories.

  (Possible responses: born, surrounded, worked, skirts, border, heard, accordion, words, colorful, wore, soared, earth, swirled, forth)

DAY 5 · Assess

Tell students to listen carefully. Say each boldfaced word, read the sentence, and repeat the word. Have students write the word.

1. Jan will **learn** to speak Spanish.
2. The dishes in the sink are **dirty**.
3. Jack's old shirt was **worn**.
4. My inflamed throat is **sore**.
5. Water will satisfy my **thirst**.
6. Be careful not to **burn** yourself.
7. May I **record** this conversation?
8. Some diseases have no **cure**.
9. Use this **board** to build a ramp.
10. I am taking a history **course**.
11. That bike is not **worth** fixing.
12. It's too **early** to go shopping.
13. Please **return** the library book.
14. I use **pure** vanilla when I cook.
15. She travels around the **world**.
16. Let's **search** for the lost key.
17. My fever seems **worse** today.
18. Our country had **thirteen** original colonies.
19. The **sport** of football is fun.
20. Mary wears **current** fashions.

RETEACH **IF** students misspell four or more words, **THEN** revisit the activity on Day 2 and reassess.

Compound Words

SPELLING LIST

1. somebody
2. fireplace
3. nearby
4. toothbrush
5. homesick
6. make-believe
7. anything
8. all right
9. goodbye
10. forehead
11. classmate
12. flashlight
13. haircut
14. twenty-two
15. driveway
16. alarm clock
17. baby-sit
18. airport
19. forever
20. mailbox

 Reproducible Word Cards are available at www.thinkcentral.com.

DIFFERENTIATE INSTRUCTION

Struggling	Advanced
1. hole	1. hundred
2. whole	2. supply
3. its	3. single
4. it's	4. middle
5. hear	5. explain
6. here	6. surprise
7. won	7. pilgrim
8. one	8. sandwich
9. our	9. instead
10. hour	10. complete
11. their	11. monster
12. there	12. settle
13. fur	13. address
14. fir	14. farther
Grade 3, Lesson 12	15. sample
	16. although
	17. turtle
	18. athlete
	19. orchard
	20. kingdom
	Grade 4, Lesson 24

 **ELL SUPPORT**

Support Word Meaning Compound words are challenging for ELLs. Display pictures of each word within a compound word, and discuss its meaning. Then discuss the new meaning of the compound word.

DAY 1 PHONICS **Model the Sort**

Students will sort words with you based on the number of syllables in the words.

- Display the Lesson 11 Word Cards, and read each word aloud. Point out that all of this week's words are compound words, or words made up of two or more smaller words. Discuss the meanings of the words.
- Tell students you are going to sort the compound words by the number of syllables in each word. Display the Word Cards *nearby* and *somebody* as column headings.
- Then pick up the Word Card *alarm clock,* read it aloud, and begin to model the sort. Suggested language: **A-larm clock, near-by. A-larm clock, some-bod-y. I hear three syllables in** *alarm clock.* **I also hear three syllables in** *somebody.* **I'll place** *alarm clock* **under** *somebody.*
- Repeat the steps with the words *toothbrush* and *make-believe.* Then ask students to help you sort the remaining words. When the sort is complete, ask students to read the words down each column with you to confirm the words were sorted correctly.
- Draw students' attention to the column headings, starting with *nearby.* Guide students to recognize that *nearby* is made up of two smaller words, *near* and *by.* Then ask: **What smaller words make up the compound word** *somebody?* (some and body) Have students identify the smaller words in the remaining compound words.
- Guide students to recognize the different ways compound words are written. Tell students that some compound words are one word, some have a hyphen, and others are two separate words.
- Give each student a set of Lesson 11 Word Cards, and have them repeat the sort independently.

DAY 2 **Repeat the Sort**

Students will repeat the sort from Day 1, sorting according to the number of syllables in each word.

- Remind students that the words they are sorting this week are two- and three-syllable words.
- Have students divide a page in their Word Study Notebooks into two columns. Tell students to use the following Word Cards as column headings: *goodbye, anything.*
- Ask students to sort the remaining Word Cards according to the number of syllables in each word. Remind students to read aloud each word, emphasizing each syllable, before placing it in a category.
- After students have completed sorting the words into columns, have them read down each column to confirm that the words were sorted correctly.
- Then have them write their sorts in their Word Study Notebooks. Ask students to identify the smaller words in each compound word by underlining the first word and circling the second.

goodbye	anything
classmate	twenty-two
homesick	alarm clock
flashlight	forever
mailbox	

DAY 3 Open Sort

Students will sort words according to categories of their choice.

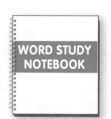

WORD STUDY NOTEBOOK

- Ask students to take out their Word Cards, read them aloud, and analyze the words for similarities and differences. Tell students they will sort the words using categories of their choice.

- Tell students to think about how they sorted words earlier in the week and to think of a way that is different from those sorts.

- If students are having difficulty choosing categories, suggest some options such as sorting by words that tell about people or objects, or sorting by single words, hyphenated words, and two separate words.

- Have students complete their sorts. When they are finished, ask them to read down each column to check that the words were sorted correctly.

- Have students write their sorts in their Word Study Notebooks.

- Then have partners work together to discuss their sorts and explain their category choices. Partners can challenge each other to sort the Word Cards based on each other's categories.

DAY 4 Word Hunt

Students will sort words that they find in their reading.

WORD STUDY NOTEBOOK

- Remind students that compound words can be written as one word, with a hyphen, or as two separate words.

- Tell students they will look for compound words in their reading and then sort the words according to their spelling pattern.

- Have students draw a three-column chart in their Word Study Notebooks and label the columns as follows: *forever, baby-sit, all right*. Discuss the spelling patterns.

- Have students turn to page 321 in their Student Books. Ask them to skim each page in "Hurricanes: Earth's Mightiest Storms" to look for compound words that fit one of the three categories.

- Students should write each compound word they find in the correct column in their Word Study Notebooks. When students are finished with their sorts, have them work with a partner to compare their findings.

(Possible responses: low-pressure, inside, within, counterclockwise, clockwise, air pressure, sunshine, sometimes, somewhere, water vapor, ice-cold, wind speed, outdoors, indoors, dateline, whirlwind)

DAY 5 Assess

Tell students to listen carefully. Say each boldfaced word, read the sentence, and repeat the word. Have students write the word.

1. Will **somebody** take the trash?
2. The cabin had a brick **fireplace**.
3. Our town has no mall **nearby**.
4. Ted has a blue **toothbrush**.
5. Eva got **homesick** at camp.
6. Tall tales are **make-believe**.
7. I'd give **anything** to sing.
8. Dad said it is **all right** to leave.
9. I said **goodbye** as I left.
10. Her hair fell on her **forehead**.
11. His **classmate** helped him with a project.
12. I used a **flashlight** in the cave.
13. I got a **haircut** on Saturday.
14. We have **twenty-two** guests.
15. Our **driveway** is steep.
16. He set his **alarm clock**.
17. I **baby-sit** for my sister.
18. I'll meet you at the **airport**.
19. She will love her dog **forever**.
20. I put the letters in the **mailbox**.

RETEACH IF students misspell four or more words, **THEN** revisit the activity on Day 2 and reassess.

Words with -ed or -ing

SPELLING LIST

1. rising	11. dripped
2. traced	12. begged
3. stripped	13. dared
4. slammed	14. skipped
5. dancing	15. hitting
6. striped	16. spotted
7. winning	17. raced
8. snapping	18. dimmed
9. bragging	19. spinning
10. handled	20. escaped

 Reproducible Word Cards are available at **www.thinkcentral.com**.

DIFFERENTIATE INSTRUCTION

Struggling	Advanced
1. I'd	1. idea
2. he's	2. lion
3. haven't	3. usual
4. doesn't	4. radio
5. let's	5. liar
6. there's	6. poem
7. wouldn't	7. India
8. what's	8. piano
9. she's	9. January
10. aren't	10. quiet
11. hasn't	11. poet
12. couldn't	12. science
13. he'd	13. diary
14. they're	14. violin
Grade 3, Lesson 13	15. period
	16. February
	17. cereal
	18. video
	19. meteor
	20. rodeo
	Grade 4, Lesson 25

 **ELL SUPPORT**

Support Word Meaning Cantonese, Hmong, Korean, and Vietnamese speakers may be confused by the concept of the -ed and -ing word parts. Model adding -ed or -ing to base words. Discuss the tense change.

DAY 1 PHONICS Model the Sort

Students will sort words with you based on the ending, -ed or -ing.

- Display the Lesson 12 Word Cards, and read each word aloud. Discuss their meanings.
- Tell students that you will sort words based on their endings. Display the Word Cards *traced* and *rising* as column headings.
- Hold up the first word you want to sort and model your thinking. Suggested language: **First, I will sort the word *handled*. Handled, traced. Handled, rising. Handled and *traced* have the same ending, so I'll place *handled* under *traced*.**
- Repeat the steps with the Word Cards *dancing* and *spotted*. As you sort, emphasize the endings. Then ask students to help you sort the remaining words. Have students read down each list with you to make sure all the words were sorted correctly.
- After sorting, lead students in a discussion about the spelling patterns. Ask them to identify the base words that end in *e*. Write out the base word *rise*, the ending -ing, and the word *rising*. Suggested language: **How do you combine *rise* with -ing to make *rising*?** (drop the e before adding -ing)
- Adapt the suggested language with the base words ending in a consonant. Help students recognize that when a base word ends in a vowel and a single consonant, the consonant is doubled before adding -ed or -ing.
- Distribute the Lesson 12 Word Cards, and have students repeat the sort independently.

DAY 2 Pattern Sort

Students will repeat the sort from Day 1, and then sort by spelling pattern.

- Remind students that this week's words end in -ed or -ing.
- Display the Word Cards, and ask students to read them aloud. Then have students sort the words by their final sounds. When they are finished, ask them to read the words aloud to check that they were sorted correctly.
- Then have students draw a four-column chart in their Word Study Notebooks and place the Word Cards *dared, dancing, stripped,* and *hitting* as column headings. Discuss the spelling pattern of each, guiding students to recognize that they should drop the *e* or double the final consonant before adding -ed or -ing.
- Ask students to sort the remaining words according to the spelling patterns for -ed and -ing. Tell students to read each word and then the column headings to help them as they sort.
- After students complete the sort, have them reread each column to confirm that the words were placed correctly. Then have them write their last sort in their Word Study Notebooks. If time allows, ask students to write the corresponding base word in parentheses next to each word.

dared	dancing	stripped	hitting
striped	rising	slammed	snapping
traced		begged	bragging
handled		dripped	spinning

Guess My Category

Students will help you sort words and guess the category names.

- Display the Word Cards, and have students read them aloud.

WORD STUDY NOTEBOOK

- Arrange the following Word Cards as column headings: *traced, spotted, dimmed, bragging*. Read each heading, emphasizing the ending sound /t/, /ĭd/, /d/, or /ĭng/.

- Pick up the Word Card *escaped*, read it aloud, and place it under *traced*. Repeat with *hitting* and *handled*, placing *hitting* under *bragging* and *handled* under *dimmed*.

- Ask students to contribute to the sort. Have them read aloud the remaining Word Cards with you and tell where they think each word belongs. Correct their placement if they have difficulty distinguishing the /t/, /ĭd/, and /d/ endings.

- When the sort is complete, have students read each column. Guide students in a discussion about the different sounds for the *-ed* ending.

- Then ask students to write the sort in their Word Study Notebooks and add any additional words they know that have the same ending sounds as this week's words.

DAY 4 **Speed Sort**

Students will sort words as quickly as they can.

- Have partners get out their Word Cards. Explain that students will take turns sorting and timing each other with a stopwatch or a clock with a second hand.

WORD STUDY NOTEBOOK

- Provide students with the column headings *handled* and *winning*. Prompt students to explain the spelling patterns in the column headings before they sort. *(drop the* e *or double the final consonant before adding* -ed *or* -ing*)*

- Emphasize to students that they are sorting by the kind of spelling change needed before *-ed* or *-ing* is added, not by the ending.

- Ask students to sort up to three times and record their times in their Word Study Notebooks to chart their progress. Remind them to shuffle their Word Cards between each sort.

- When students finish their last sort, have them write it in their Word Study Notebooks.

 Assess

Tell students to listen carefully. Say each boldfaced word, read the sentence, and repeat the word. Have students write the word.

1. The cookie dough was **rising.**
2. She **traced** her hand's outline.
3. I **stripped** the door's varnish.
4. The wind **slammed** the door.
5. I've been **dancing** for years.
6. She wore a **striped** dress.
7. Jill is **winning** the contest.
8. Ed is **snapping** his fingers.
9. She was **bragging** about her grades.
10. I **handled** the baby carefully.
11. The faucet **dripped** endlessly.
12. She **begged** her parents for a puppy.
13. The boys **dared** us to play against them.
14. We **skipped** across the playground.
15. Jenny likes **hitting** the ball.
16. I love my **spotted** dog!
17. Tim **raced** inside for a snack.
18. The theater lights **dimmed.**
19. My head was **spinning**!
20. I dreamed I **escaped.**

RETEACH **IF** students misspell four or more words, **THEN** revisit the activity on Day 2 and reassess.

SPELLING LIST

1. wiped	11. shipped
2. covered	12. phoning
3. mapped	13. offered
4. pleasing	14. smelling
5. slipped	15. hiking
6. putting	16. checking
7. traveled	17. fainted
8. seeking	18. landed
9. visiting	19. becoming
10. mixed	20. wandering

 Reproducible Word Cards are available at **www.thinkcentral.com**.

DIFFERENTIATE INSTRUCTION

Struggling	Advanced
1. horse	1. enter
2. mark	2. banner
3. storm	3. sugar
4. market	4. shower
5. acorn	5. motor
6. artist	6. collar
7. March	7. labor
8. north	8. finger
9. barking	9. mirror
10. stork	10. beggar
11. thorn	11. favor
12. forest	12. bother
13. chore	13. fever
14. restore	14. doctor
Grade 3, Lesson 14	15. temper
	16. actor
	17. polar
	18. sweater
	19. traitor
	20. whenever
	Grade 4, Lesson 26

ELL SUPPORT

Linguistic Transfer There are three English pronunciations for past tense verbs ending in -ed: /t/, /ĭd/, and /d/. Draw a three-column chart and have students categorize this week's words by their final sounds.

DAY 1 PHONICS **Model the Sort**

Students will sort words with you based on the ending, -ed or -ing.

- Display the Lesson 13 Word Cards, and read each word aloud. Discuss their meanings.
- Tell students that you will sort each word by its ending. Display the Word Cards *wiped* and *pleasing* as column headings.
- Hold up the first word you will sort and model your thinking. Suggested language: **Does *checking* have the same ending as *wiped* or *pleasing*? Checking, wiped. Checking, pleasing. Checking and pleasing have the same ending, so I'll place *checking* under *pleasing*.**
- Repeat the steps with the Word Card *mixed*. Then ask students to help you sort the remaining words. When the sort is complete, have students read the words in each column.
- Lead students in a discussion about the spelling patterns, beginning with the -ed list. Have students work with you to identify the base words ending in e. Guide students as they talk about what happens when -ed or -ing is added to a base word ending in e. (The e *is dropped.*)
- Call students' attention to the base words that end in a consonant. Help students understand what happens when -ed or -ing is added to words ending in a consonant. Have them observe how in some words the consonant is doubled and in other words there is no change before adding -ed or -ing.
- Then write out the base words *wipe, put,* and *mix,* and the endings -ed and -ing. Have students explain the spelling patterns when adding -ed or -ing to the base words.
- Give each student a set of Lesson 13 Word Cards, and have them repeat the sort independently.

DAY 2 **Guess My Category**

Students will guess the category of words that you sort by spelling pattern.

- Display the Word Cards, and have students read them aloud. Tell students that you will sort the words, and they will try to figure out the categories.
- Gather the Words Cards *phoning, shipped,* and *traveled,* and place them as column headings. Hold up each Word Card, read it aloud, and sort it into a category according to its spelling pattern.
- Continue to sort the Word Cards by spelling pattern. Have students help you once they recognize the sort categories: final e dropped, final consonant doubled, no spelling change. Tell them not to reveal what they think the sort categories are.
- After the sort is complete, have students read the columns aloud and discuss what the words in each column have in common. Prompt students to explain the spelling patterns.
- Then have students write the sort in their Word Study Notebooks. Ask students to write the corresponding base word in parentheses next to each word.

phoning	shipped	traveled
hiking	slipped	covered
wiped	mapped	offered
	putting	

DAY 3 Word Hunt

Students will sort words that they find in their reading.

- Tell students they will look for words in their reading that have the *-ed* and *-ing* endings and then sort them by word endings.

- Ask students to draw a two-column chart in their Word Study Notebooks and label the columns *covered* and *putting*.

- Have students open their Student Books to page 377 and skim each page in "Antarctic Journal" to find words with *-ed* and *-ing* endings.

- Remind students to read the column headings to help them sort by the endings of words they find. Have them write each word in the correct column in their Word Study Notebooks.

- When students complete the sort, have them form small groups to discuss and compare their findings. Students may add to their sorts using words that other group members found.

(Possible responses: protected, exploring, pounding, stranded, added, forbidding, needed, flagged, leaving, writing, sheltered)

DAY 4 Buddy Sort

Students will compare sorts with a partner, first by sound and then by spelling pattern.

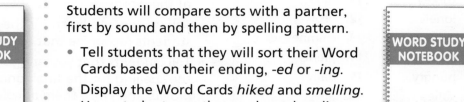

- Tell students that they will sort their Word Cards based on their ending, *-ed* or *-ing*.

- Display the Word Cards *hiked* and *smelling*. Have students use these column headings as they sort the remaining words by their endings.

- Remind students to read each word aloud as they sort. When students complete the sort, have them compare and confirm their sound sorts with a partner.

- Then have students add the Word Card *visiting* to their column headings. Tell them to shuffle and resort the Word Cards according to the spelling patterns for *-ed* and *-ing*: final e dropped, final consonant doubled, no spelling change.

- Have students compare and discuss their pattern sorts with a partner. Then have them write their sorts in their Word Study Notebooks.

DAY 5 Assess

Tell students to listen carefully. Say each boldfaced word, read the sentence, and repeat the word. Have students write the word.

1. She **wiped** sweat from her face.
2. Max **covered** his head with a hat.
3. We **mapped** out our trip.
4. The painting was **pleasing**.
5. I **slipped** on the step and fell.
6. Juan is **putting** away his book.
7. I have **traveled** to Canada.
8. He is **seeking** his lost bike.
9. My grandma is **visiting** us.
10. I **mixed** eggs with the flour.

11. Minja **shipped** the package.
12. Susan is **phoning** the guests.
13. Dad **offered** to give us a ride.
14. I like **smelling** the roses.
15. We went **hiking** in the woods.
16. Peg is **checking** her spelling.
17. Anna **fainted** from the heat.
18. The airplane **landed** safely.
19. Mom was **becoming** worried.
20. Luis went **wandering** through his new hometown.

RETEACH IF students misspell four or more words, **THEN** revisit the activity on Day 2 and reassess.

SPELLING LIST

1. turkey	11. duty
2. lonely	12. drowsy
3. colony	13. chimney
4. steady	14. plenty
5. hungry	15. daily
6. valley	16. alley
7. hockey	17. fifty
8. starry	18. empty
9. melody	19. injury
10. movie	20. prairie

 Reproducible Word Cards are available at **www.thinkcentral.com**.

DIFFERENTIATE INSTRUCTION

Struggling	Advanced
1. nurse	1. title
2. work	2. towel
3. shirt	3. battle
4. hurt	4. pedal
5. first	5. metal
6. word	6. simple
7. serve	7. eagle
8. curly	8. special
9. dirt	9. total
10. third	10. trouble
11. worry	11. nickel
12. turn	12. gentle
13. stir	13. barrel
14. firm	14. model
Grade 3, Lesson 15	15. tangle
	16. ankle
	17. marvel
	18. juggle
	19. squirrel
	20. riddle
	Grade 4, Lesson 27

 ELL SUPPORT

Linguistic Transfer Korean speakers may need help matching the final long e sound with different spelling patterns. Brainstorm words ending in the long e sound, and list them by their spelling pattern.

DAY 1 PHONICS — Model the Sort

Students will sort words with you based on the final long e sound, spelled -y, -ey, or -ie.

- Display the Lesson 14 Word Cards. Read each word aloud and discuss the meanings of the words, as necessary.
- Tell students to listen for the ending sound as you read some words aloud. Help students recognize that each word ends in the same sound. *(long e or /ē/)*
- Tell students that you are going to sort the words into three categories based on the spelling for the final long e sound. Display the Word Cards *lonely, turkey,* and *movie,* and place them as column headings.
- Hold up the first word you will sort. Read it aloud, and place it under each column heading to compare the final sounds and spellings. Model your thinking as you sort. Suggested language: **Hockey** has the final e sound spelled **-ey. Turkey** has the same final e sound spelled **-ey, so I'll place** *hockey* **under** *turkey***.**
- Continue through the list, having students sort with you. When the sort is complete, ask students to read the words aloud in each column.
- Guide students to identify what the words in each list have in common. Suggested language: **Let's look at the words in the** *lonely* **column. What final sound do all the words have?** *(/ē/ or long e)* **What do you notice about the spelling of /ē/?** *(It is spelled with* y.*)*
- Continue to discuss students' observations about the spelling patterns in the remaining lists, leading them to recognize that final long e can also be spelled -ey or -ie.
- Give each student a set of Lesson 14 Word Cards, and have them repeat the sort independently.

DAY 2 — Repeat the Sort

Students will repeat the sort from Day 1, sorting the Word Cards by the spelling patterns for the final long e sound.

- Remind students that this week's words have the final long e sound spelled -y, -ey, or -ie.
- Have students take out their Word Cards and create a three-column chart in their Word Study Notebooks. Tell them to place the Word Cards *valley, duty,* and *prairie* as column headings.
- Have students sort the remaining Word Cards according to the spelling patterns. Remind students to read each word aloud before placing the Word Card in a category.
- After students sort all the words, tell them to reread each list to confirm that the words were sorted correctly. Then have students write their sorts in their Word Study Notebooks.

valley	duty	prairie
hockey	plenty	movie
alley	daily	
turkey	steady	
	empty	

DAY 3 Open Sort

Students will sort words according to categories of their choice.

- Have students take out their Word Cards, read them aloud, and analyze the words for similarities and differences.

- Explain that students will sort words using categories that they choose. Tell students their categories may be different from or the same as the categories they sorted earlier in the week.

- If students have difficulty choosing categories, suggest options such as sorting by a beginning vowel or consonant, the first syllable's long or short vowel sound, or adjectives and nouns.

- You may want to model one of the suggested options for students who need more support.

- Have students sort their Word Cards. Then ask them to read down each column to confirm the words were sorted correctly.

- Have students write their completed sorts in their Word Study Notebooks. When they are finished, have partners work together to discuss their categories and explain why they sorted the words the way they did.

DAY 4 Word Hunt

Students will sort words that they find in their reading.

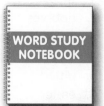

- Tell students that they will look for words in their reading that have the final long *e* sound spelled *-y, -ey,* or *-ie.*

- Have students draw a three-column chart in their Word Study Notebooks. Tell students to use the following column headings: *alley, hungry, movie.*

- Have students open their Student Books to page 411 and search for words in "The Life and Times of the Ant" that have the final long *e* sound. Students should identify the spelling pattern in each word and then write the word in one of the three spelling categories.

- Have students check how they sorted the words by reading the words aloud and comparing each word to the sound and spelling pattern of each column heading.

(Possible responses: only, gradually, dynasty, nursery, Shapley, twenty, factory, gluey, fifty, carry, hobby, frequently, many)

DAY 5 Assess

Tell students to listen carefully. Say each boldfaced word, read the sentence, and repeat the word. Have students write the word.

1. My favorite food is **turkey.**
2. I felt **lonely** when I moved.
3. I saw a **colony** of ants.
4. The runner has a **steady** pace.
5. I'm **hungry** for some pie.
6. I see the **valley** from our plane.
7. Players skate in **hockey.**
8. We looked up at the **starry** sky.
9. The song's **melody** is familiar.
10. I'd like to see a new **movie.**
11. It is my **duty** to help others.
12. The trip made me **drowsy.**
13. There is a nest in our **chimney.**
14. We prepared **plenty** of food.
15. I have a **daily** routine.
16. It was dark in the **alley.**
17. The goal is **fifty** yards away.
18. The **empty** house seemed sad.
19. The **injury** healed quickly.
20. Wildflowers grow on the **prairie.**

RETEACH **IF** students misspell four or more words, **THEN** revisit the activity on Day 2 and reassess.

Changing Final *y* to *i*

Model the Sort

Students will sort words with you based on the ending, *-ed, -er, -est,* or *-ies.*

- Display the Lesson 15 Word Cards, and read each word aloud. Discuss the meanings of the words and use them in a sentence, as necessary.

- Tell students that you are going to sort the words based on their ending sounds. Place the Word Cards *copied, easier, tiniest,* and *ladies* as column headings and read them aloud, emphasizing the ending sounds.

- Begin the sort by picking up the Word Card *prettiest.* Read it aloud and compare it to each column heading. Suggested language: **The word *prettiest* has the same ending sound as the word *tiniest,* so I'll place *prettiest* under *tiniest.***

- Repeat the steps with *studied, friendlier,* and *hobbies.* Once the categories are established, have volunteers help you sort the remaining words.

- When all the words have been sorted, have students read each column aloud with you to make sure the words were sorted correctly.

- Help students recognize the spelling patterns in each column, starting with the *copied* column. Suggested language: **What is the base word in the word *copied*?** *(copy)* **How do you combine *copy* with *-ed* to make *copied*?** *(change the* y *to* i *before adding* -ed*)*

- Then draw students' attention to the spelling patterns in the other columns. Adapt the suggested language, leading students to recognize that they should change the *y* to *i* before adding *-er* or *-est,* and they should drop the *y* before adding *-ies.*

- Distribute the Lesson 15 Word Cards, and have students repeat the sort independently.

Repeat the Sort

Students will repeat the sort from Day 1, sorting by words that end in *-ed, -er, -est,* or *-ies.*

- Remind students that the words they are sorting this week end in different sounds. Review with students the endings *-ed, -er, -est,* and *-ies.*

- Have students divide a page in their Word Study Notebooks into four columns and place the Word Cards *pitied, busier, funniest,* and *butterflies* as column headings.

- Tell students that they will sort the remaining Word Cards according to the ending sound in each word. Remind students to read each word aloud before they sort. Have them compare the ending sound in each word to the ending sound in each column heading.

- After students complete the sort, ask them to reread the words in each column to confirm that the words were placed in the correct category.

- Then have students write their sorts in their Word Study Notebooks. Ask them to write the corresponding base word in parentheses next to each word.

pitied	busier	funniest	butterflies
spied	friendlier	happiest	ladies
studied	healthier	prettiest	countries
	noisier	laziest	families
			hobbies

SPELLING LIST

1. tiniest	11. ladies
2. hobbies	12. friendlier
3. copied	13. studied
4. countries	14. busier
5. pitied	15. breezier
6. easier	16. prettiest
7. laziest	17. noisier
8. families	18. healthier
9. spied	19. butterflies
10. happiest	20. funniest

 Reproducible Word Cards are available at www.thinkcentral.com.

DIFFERENTIATE INSTRUCTION

Struggling	Advanced
1. air	1. library
2. wear	2. another
3. chair	3. hospital
4. stairs	4. example
5. bare	5. deliver
6. bear	6. history
7. hair	7. however
8. care	8. several
9. pear	9. vacation
10. pair	10. important
11. share	11. victory
12. near	12. imagine
13. ear	13. camera
14. beard	14. potato
Grade 3, Lesson 16	15. remember
	16. together
	17. memory
	18. favorite
	19. continue
	20. president
	Grade 4, Lesson 28

ELL SUPPORT

Linguistic Transfer To help ELLs understand changing final *y* to *i,* display the Word Cards *friendlier* and *funniest.* Identify the base words. Then model adding *-er* and *-est.* Repeat with other words from this week.

DAY 3 Buddy Sort

Students will sort by sound and compare their sorts with a partner.

- Tell students that they will sort their Word Cards based on the ending sounds in the words. Review the endings *-ed*, *-er*, *-est*, and *-ies* in this week's words.

- Display the Word Cards *studied*, *healthier*, *prettiest*, and *families*. Have students use these column headings as they sort the remaining words by their ending sounds.

- When students complete the sort, have them compare and discuss their sorts with a partner. Then have students write their sorts in their Word Study Notebooks.

- When students are finished writing, call attention to each column heading and the spelling pattern in each category. Prompt students to explain how the base words changed.

- Extend the activity by asking students to add any other words they know that have the same final sounds and spelling patterns as the words in this lesson.

DAY 4 Speed Sort

Students will sort words as quickly as they can.

- Tell students that they will sort words by their final sounds using the headings *spied*, *noisier*, *laziest*, and *countries*.

- Pair students and ask them to read their Word Cards aloud. Explain that one student will sort by ending sound while his or her partner keeps the time using a stopwatch or a clock with a second hand.

- Have students repeat the sort up to three times, shuffling the cards after each sort and taking turns timing each other.

- Challenge students to beat their own best time, while maintaining accuracy. Tell students to record their times in their Word Study Notebooks.

- When partners finish, have them read and confirm their sorts. Then have them write their sorts in their Word Study Notebooks.

- Extend the activity by having students try to sort their Word Cards faster than you. Model saying the words quietly as you sort the Word Cards one by one.

DAY 5 Assess

Tell students to listen carefully. Say each boldfaced word, read the sentence, and repeat the word. Have students write the word.

1. That doll has the **tiniest** feet.
2. Kyle has many **hobbies**.
3. I **copied** the letter neatly.
4. Ed visited three **countries**.
5. We **pitied** the team that lost.
6. Riding is **easier** than walking.
7. He was the **laziest** fellow!
8. The **families** held a block party.
9. He **spied** a rare type of bird.
10. Sara is **happiest** at home.
11. The **ladies** shopped for hats.
12. Dogs are **friendlier** than cats.
13. Abe **studied** late into the night.
14. This week was **busier** than last.
15. It is **breezier** on the porch.
16. She is the **prettiest** cat of all.
17. The car sounds **noisier** in the tunnel.
18. The right diet will make you **healthier**.
19. Let's catch **butterflies**!
20. She was the **funniest** comic.

RETEACH **IF** students misspell four or more words, **THEN** revisit the activity on Day 2 and reassess.

Words with /k/, /ng/, and /kw/

 Go Digital Reproducible Word Cards are available at www.thinkcentral.com.

DIFFERENTIATE INSTRUCTION

Struggling	Advanced
1. age	1. half
2. space	2. comb
3. change	3. mortgage
4. jawbone	4. honor
5. jacket	5. fasten
6. giant	6. kneel
7. pencil	7. wreath
8. circle	8. calm
9. once	9. answer
10. large	10. handsome
11. dance	11. wrinkle
12. jeans	12. listen
13. bounce	13. fetch
14. huge	14. yolk
Grade 3, Lesson 17	15. climb
	16. honest
	17. knuckle
	18. plumber
	19. limb
	20. folktale
	Grade 4, Lesson 29

ELL **ELL SUPPORT**

Linguistic Transfer Vietnamese speakers may not hear both the /k/ and the /w/ sounds. Model saying words with /kw/. Have students mimic your pronunciation.

DAY 1 PHONICS Model the Sort

Students will sort words with you based on the sound, /k/, /ng/, or /kw/.

- Display the Lesson 16 Word Cards, and read each word aloud.
- Tell students that you are going to sort the words into three categories based on the sound, /k/, /ng/ or /kw/, in each word. Display the Word Cards *track, junk,* and *question* as column headings.
- Hold up the Word Card *monkey,* read the word aloud, and model your thinking as you sort. Suggested language: **When I say *monkey,* I hear the /ng/ sound. I also hear the /ng/ sound in *junk,* but not in *track* or *question.* Since both *monkey* and *junk* have the /ng/ sound, I'll place *monkey* under *junk.***
- Repeat with the Word Cards *electric* and *equal.* Then continue with the remaining words, having students help you sort once the categories have been established. After sorting, have students check the placement of each word by reading down the columns aloud.
- Help students recognize the spelling patterns in the *track* column. Suggested language: **What sound do all of these words have in common?** *(/k/)* **What do you notice about the spelling of /k/?** *(It is spelled with* ck, k, *or* c.*)*
- Point out the oddballs *stomach* and *ache.* Suggested language: **Look at the words *stomach* and *ache.* What letters stand for the /k/ sound in *stomach* and *ache?*** *(ch)*
- Then adapt the suggested language as you guide students to discover the spelling patterns in the remaining columns. Students should recognize that the /ng/ sound is often spelled *nk* and the /kw/ sound is often spelled *qu.*
- Give each student a set of Lesson 16 Word Cards, and have them repeat the sort independently.

DAY 2 Pattern Sort

Students will repeat the sort from Day 1, and then sort by spelling pattern.

- Remind students that this week's words have the sound /k/, /ng/, or /kw/.
- Display the Word Cards, and have students read them aloud. Have students sort the words into /k/, /ng/, and /kw/ categories. When students are finished, have them read their lists to make sure they sorted the words correctly.
- Have students create a six-column chart across two pages in their Word Study Notebooks. Tell them to use the Word Cards *pocket, mistake, picnic, banker,* and *equal* as column headings.
- Discuss the target sound (/k/, /ng/, or /kw/) and spelling in each and tell students to underline the letters as shown below. Have them label the last column *Oddballs.*
- Ask students to sort the remaining words by their sound and spelling pattern. Remind students to read each word and then the column headings before placing it in a category.
- When the sort is complete, have students reread each list to make sure they sorted the words correctly. Have them write their sorts in their Word Study Notebooks.

po<u>ck</u>et	mista<u>k</u>e	pi<u>c</u>nic	ba<u>nk</u>er	e<u>qu</u>al	Oddballs
track	risky	public	blank	question	ache
attack		electric	monkey		
struck		topic			

DAY 3 Guess My Category

Students will guess how you have sorted words into categories.

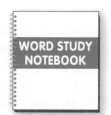
WORD STUDY NOTEBOOK

- Display the Word Cards, and have students read them aloud with you. Tell students that you will sort the words, and they will try to figure out the categories.

- Place the following Word Cards as column headings to represent words with the sound /k/, /ng/, or /kw/: *topic, blank, earthquake.* Pick up the Word Card *equal,* read it aloud, and place it under *earthquake.*

- Continue with *attack* and *junk,* placing *attack* under *topic* and *junk* under *blank.* Sort the remaining Word Cards without sharing the category types with students.

- When the sort is complete, have students read aloud the words in each column. Prompt students to explain how they think you sorted the words. *(by the sounds /k/, /ng/, and /kw/)*

- Then have students copy the column headings and write the sort in their Word Study Notebooks. Challenge students to write additional words they know that have the same sounds.

DAY 4 Buddy Sort

Students will sort by sound and spelling pattern and compare sorts with a partner.

WORD STUDY NOTEBOOK

- Have students take out their Word Cards and read them aloud. Review with students that they have sorted this week's words by the sounds /k/, /ng/, and /kw/.

- Display the Word Cards *public, blanket,* and *question,* and tell students to use these column headings as they sort the remaining words based on the sound /k/, /ng/, or /kw/.

- After students complete the sound sort, have them shuffle the Word Cards and sort the words again. This time have students sort the words by spelling pattern. Add these column headings to the ones from the sound sort: *risky, struck, Oddballs.*

- When students are finished sorting, have them read to confirm their sorts and then write their pattern sorts in their Word Study Notebooks.

- Then have students work with a partner to compare their sorts. Prompt students to discuss the spelling patterns and the oddballs *stomach* and *ache.*

DAY 5 Assess

Tell students to listen carefully. Say each boldfaced word, read the sentence, and repeat the word. Have students write the word.

1. It is **risky** to hike alone.
2. Alexa runs on the **track** team.
3. The speaker knew her **topic** well.
4. She filled in the **blank** spaces.
5. I asked a **question** about math.
6. My **pocket** is full of coins.
7. The **monkey** is very loud.
8. Please recycle the **junk** mail.
9. Rosa Parks wanted **equal** rights.
10. I **ache** when I have the flu.
11. Juan loves **public** speaking.
12. Lions **attack** to save a cub.
13. Sara **struck** the ball hard.
14. The **earthquake** did no harm.
15. Did ants spoil the **picnic**?
16. A **banker** can make loans.
17. Plug in the **electric** stove.
18. My wool **blanket** is so warm.
19. I made a **mistake** on the test.
20. My **stomach** is empty.

RETEACH IF students misspell four or more words, **THEN** revisit the activity on Day 2 and reassess.

Words with Final /j/ and /s/

1. glance
2. judge
3. damage
4. package
5. twice
6. stage
7. carriage
8. since
9. practice
10. marriage
11. baggage
12. office
13. message
14. bridge
15. chance
16. notice
17. ridge
18. manage
19. palace
20. bandage

 Reproducible Word Cards are available at **www.thinkcentral.com**.

DIFFERENTIATE INSTRUCTION

Struggling	Advanced
1. shark	1. meant
2. check	2. routine
3. queen	3. style
4. circus	4. flood
5. flake	5. month
6. crack	6. pleasant
7. second	7. guess
8. squeeze	8. women
9. quart	9. either
10. squeak	10. against
11. quick	11. disguise
12. coldest	12. sweat
13. Africa	13. magazine
14. Mexico	14. guard
Grade 3, Lesson 18	15. receive
	16. wonder
	17. league
	18. type
	19. ceiling
	20. money
	Grade 4, Lesson 30

ELL **ELL SUPPORT**

Linguistic Transfer Speakers of Spanish, Tagalog, and Korean may have trouble pronouncing the /j/ sound in English. Model saying words that begin or end with the /j/ sound. Have students repeat each word.

DAY 1 PHONICS Model the Sort

Students will sort words with you based on their final sound, /j/ or /s/.

- Display the Lesson 17 Word Cards, and read each word aloud. Discuss the meanings of the words, as necessary.
- Tell students that you are going to sort based on the ending sounds of the words. Display the Word Cards *damage* and *glance* as column headings.
- Show students the Word Card *twice*, read it aloud with each column heading, and model your thinking. Suggested language: **Does the final sound in *twice* have the /j/ sound like *damage* or the /s/ sound like *glance*? Damage, twice. Glance, twice. The /s/ sound in *twice* is the same sound as in *glance*, so I'll put *twice* under *glance*.**
- Model sorting a word that ends in /j/ like *stage*. Then continue through the remaining words, asking students to read each word with you. Have students help you place the words in the correct column. Continue until all the words are sorted and then ask students to read down each column with you to confirm that the words were sorted correctly.
- Guide students to recognize the spellings in the /j/ list. Suggested language: **What final sound do all of these words have in common?** *(/j/)* **What letters stand for /j/?** *(ge)* Then help students recognize the spellings in the /s/ list. Ask: **What final sound do all of the words in this list have?** *(/s/)* **What letters stand for /s/?** *(ce)*
- Distribute the Lesson 17 Word Cards, and have students repeat the sort independently.

DAY 2 Repeat the Sort

Students will repeat the sort from Day 1, sorting the words by their final sounds.

- Remind students that this week's words end in the sound /j/ or /s/.
- Have students create a two-column chart in their Word Study Notebooks. Have them find the Word Cards *judge* and *chance* and place them as column headings.
- Tell students to sort the remaining Word Cards by the sound they hear at the end of each word. Remind students to read the words aloud and to compare each word to the column headings before placing the Word Cards in the categories.
- After all the words have been sorted, have students reread each list to confirm the words have been sorted correctly. Then have students write their sorts in their Word Study Notebooks.

judge	chance
carriage	office
package	palace
bridge	notice
stage	

DAY 3 Speed Sort

Students will sort words as quickly as they can.

- Have students take out their Word Cards and read the words aloud with a partner.
- Tell students to create a two-column chart in their Word Study Notebooks and to place the Word Cards *message* and *palace* as column headings.
- Have partners use a stopwatch or a clock with a second hand as they take turns timing and sorting the words. Students should record their times in their Word Study Notebooks.
- Ask students to repeat the sort up to three times, working to improve their time with each sort. Have students shuffle the Word Cards between sorts.
- Have partners check their sorts by reading the columns aloud. Then have them write their last sort in their Word Study Notebooks.

DAY 4 Word Hunt

Students will sort words that they find in their reading.

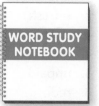

- Have students open their Word Study Notebooks to a clean page. Tell them to divide the page into two columns and write *stage* and *since* as column headings.
- Tell students that today they will look in their reading for words with the ending sound /j/ spelled -*ge* and the ending sound /s/ spelled -*ce*, and then they will sort those words according to their spelling patterns.

- Ask students to open their Student Books to page 501. Tell them to skim the selection "The Right Dog for the Job" for words that fit into one of the categories.
- Tell students to write each word in the correct column in their Word Study Notebooks. Then have students compare their lists with a partner's. Students may add to their sorts using words found by their partner.

(Possible responses: confidence, change, service, arranges, age, practice)

DAY 5 Assess

Tell students to listen carefully. Say each boldfaced word, read the sentence, and repeat the word. Have students write the word.

1. She gave the picture a **glance**.
2. Who will **judge** the show?
3. An early frost will **damage** the crops.
4. I got a **package** in the mail.
5. You are **twice** as old as I am.
6. Frogs are tadpoles in an early **stage** in life.
7. A baby **carriage** is expensive.
8. The sun has been up **since** six.
9. I **practice** singing every day.
10. We wished the couple a happy **marriage**.
11. Check your **baggage** here.
12. The doctor's **office** is closed.
13. The **message** was in a bottle.
14. The **bridge** was built in 1910.
15. This is your last **chance**.
16. Did you **notice** my haircut?
17. The sun rose over the **ridge**.
18. I can **manage** the children.
19. The king lives in a grand **palace**.
20. The nurse put a **bandage** on the wound.

RETEACH IF students misspell four or more words, **THEN** revisit the activity on Day 1 and reassess.

Prefixes re-, un-, dis-

SPELLING LIST

1. unused	11. untrue
2. refresh	12. unload
3. dislike	13. recall
4. replace	14. displease
5. unpaid	15. uneven
6. redo	16. rebuild
7. disorder	17. restart
8. unplanned	18. uncover
9. distrust	19. untidy
10. rewind	20. discolor

 Reproducible Word Cards are available at **www.thinkcentral.com**.

DIFFERENTIATE INSTRUCTION

Struggling	Advanced
1. unfold	1. breath
2. rejoin	2. wobble
3. untie	3. blister
4. reheat	4. crush
5. unfair	5. direct
6. unclear	6. promise
7. repaid	7. grasp
8. rewrite	8. numb
9. unhurt	9. hymn
10. recheck	10. shovel
11. unlucky	11. gravity
12. unwrap	12. frantic
13. reuse	13. swift
14. unsure	14. feather
Grade 3, Lesson 24	15. comic
	16. bundle
	17. solid
	18. weather
	19. energy
	20. stingy
	Grade 5, Lesson 1

ELL SUPPORT

Access Prior Knowledge Help Spanish speakers transfer their knowledge of Spanish prefixes. Using *correct* and *correcto*, demonstrate how adding the prefix *in-* to base words is the same in English and Spanish.

DAY 1 PHONICS Model the Sort

Students will sort words with you based on the prefixes *re-*, *un-*, and *dis-*.

- Display the Lesson 18 Word Cards, and read each word aloud. Discuss the meanings of the words and use them in sentences, as necessary.

- Tell students that you are going to sort the words based on the prefixes *re-*, *un-*, and *dis-*. Explain that prefixes are word parts that are added to the beginning of a base word. Then display the Word Cards *redo*, *untrue*, and *dislike* as column headings.

- Display the Word Card *unload* and model your thinking as you sort. Suggested language: **The word is *unload*. *Unload*, *redo*. *Unload*, *untrue*. *Unload*, *dislike*. I hear the prefix *un-* in the word *unload* and I hear the same prefix in the word *untrue*, so I'll place *unload* under *untrue*.**

- Ask students to work with you to sort the remaining words. Then have students read the words down each column to confirm that they have the same prefix.

- Discuss the common prefix in each column, beginning with *re-*. Suggested language: **What prefix do all the words have in common?** (the prefix *re-*)

- Help students identify the base words. Then discuss how adding a prefix to a base word changes the meaning of the word. Hold up the Word Card *redo*. Then say: **The prefix *re-* means "again." If you *redo* something, then you do it again.**

- Continue with the *un-* and *dis-* categories, discussing the base words and the new meanings after prefixes are added. Hold up the Word Cards *unused* and *displease*. Suggested language: **The prefixes *un-* and *dis-* mean "not." If something goes *unused*, then it is not used. If someone is *displeased*, then he or she is not pleased, or happy.**

- Distribute the Lesson 18 Word Cards, and have each student repeat the sort.

DAY 2 Repeat the Sort

Students will repeat the sort from Day 1, sorting words based on the prefixes *re-*, *un-*, and *dis-*.

- Remind students that this week's words have the prefix *re-*, *un-*, or *dis-* and that when a prefix is added to the beginning of a base word it changes its meaning.

- Ask students to get out their Word Cards and then create a three-column chart in their Word Study Notebooks. Tell them to use these column headings: *restart*, *unpaid*, *discolor*.

- Have students sort the remaining Word Cards according to their prefix. Remind students to read each word aloud before placing it in a category.

- When students finish sorting all the words into columns, have them reread each list to confirm that the words have been sorted correctly. Then have students write their sorts in their Word Study Notebooks. Tell them to write the corresponding base word in parentheses next to each word.

restart	unpaid	discolor
rewind	unplanned	disorder
replace	uneven	displease
refresh	untrue	dislike
rebuild		

MAJOR UNDERSTANDING: A prefix is a word part that is added to the beginning of a base word. Prefixes change the meaning of the base words.

DAY 3 Blind Writing Sort

Students will sort and write words that you say aloud.

- Have students create a three-column chart with the headings *rebuild, untidy,* and *disorder* in their Word Study Notebooks.

- Call attention to the prefix in each word and review what happens to the meaning of a base word when a prefix is added.

- Tell students that today they will sort the words based on the prefix they hear at the beginning of each word.

- Explain to students that you will read a Word Card aloud without showing the word to them. Tell students that they will write the word in one of the three columns. After students have written the word, reveal the Word Card so students can correct any misspellings.

- After all the words have been written, have students read aloud each column to confirm that they sorted the words correctly.

DAY 4 Speed Sort

Students will sort words as quickly as they can.

- Tell students that they will sort their Word Cards according to each word's prefix. Remind students that they have already sorted this week's words by the prefixes *re-, un-,* and *dis-*.

- Explain that partners will take turns sorting and timing each other. Tell students to sort the words by their prefix, using the following Word Cards as column headings: *replace, unused, displease.*

- Have partners use a stopwatch or a clock with a second hand to time each other. Explain that students can sort their cards up to three times as they work to improve their sorting time.

- Remind students to record their times in their Word Study Notebooks and to shuffle the Word Cards between each sort.

- When partners finish, have them read the words in the columns together and check their sorts. Then have them write their last sort in their Word Study Notebooks. Direct students to underline the prefixes and circle the base words.

DAY 5 Assess

Tell students to listen carefully. Say each boldfaced word, read the sentence, and repeat the word. Have students write the word.

1. We have an **unused** room.
2. I take a bath to **refresh** myself.
3. We **dislike** spicy food.
4. I will **replace** the plate.
5. The loan will help him settle his **unpaid** bills.
6. I had to **redo** my report.
7. The room was in **disorder** after the party.
8. We took an **unplanned** trip.
9. Why do you **distrust** me?
10. Please **rewind** the tape.
11. The story was **untrue**.
12. The movers will **unload** this.
13. Do you **recall** her name?
14. Your actions **displease** me.
15. The car bounced on the **uneven** road.
16. They will **rebuild** their house.
17. Please **restart** the movie.
18. He will **uncover** the scheme.
19. You have an **untidy** room.
20. Bleach will **discolor** your clothes.

RETEACH **IF** students misspell four or more words, **THEN** revisit the activity on Day 1 and reassess.

Suffixes -ful, -less, -ness, -ment

Go Digital

SPELLING LIST

1. colorful
2. weakness
3. movement
4. endless
5. truthful
6. illness
7. cheerful
8. useless
9. beautiful
10. restless
11. clumsiness
12. pavement
13. peaceful
14. fondness
15. neatness
16. speechless
17. statement
18. wasteful
19. penniless
20. treatment

Reproducible Word Cards are available at www.thinkcentral.com.

DIFFERENTIATE INSTRUCTION

Struggling	Advanced
1. singer	1. awake
2. loudly	2. feast
3. joyful	3. stray
4. teacher	4. greet
5. fighter	5. praise
6. closely	6. disease
7. powerful	7. repeat
8. farmer	8. display
9. quickly	9. braces
10. careful	10. thief
11. friendly	11. ashamed
12. speaker	12. sleeve
13. wonderful	13. waist
14. truly	14. beneath
Grade 3, Lesson 23	15. sheepish
	16. release
	17. remain
	18. sway
	19. training
	20. niece
	Grade 5, Lesson 2

ELL SUPPORT

Linguistic Transfer Cantonese or Hmong ELLs may be unfamiliar with suffixes. List five base words and the suffixes -ful, -less, -ness, and -ment. Add the suffixes to the words, and discuss the change in meanings.

DAY 1 PHONICS Model the Sort

Students will sort words with you based on the suffixes -ful, -less, -ness, and -ment.

- Display the Lesson 19 Word Cards, and read each word aloud. Tell students that today you are going to sort the words based on the suffix, or the word part at the end of each word.
- Find the Word Cards colorful, endless, weakness, and pavement, and display them as column headings. Ask students to identify the suffix in each word. Suggested language: **What suffix do you see at the end of colorful?** (-ful) Lead students in recognizing the other suffixes, -less, -ness, and -ment.
- Model sorting a few words. Suggested language: *Peaceful.* **What is the suffix in peaceful?** (-ful) **Which column heading has the suffix -ful?** (colorful) **Let's put peaceful under colorful.** Have volunteers show you where to place the remaining Word Cards. After all the words are sorted, have students read the columns aloud to confirm word placement.
- Point out the oddballs beautiful, clumsiness, and penniless, and have students identify the base words. Make sure students recognize that the spelling of these base words changes when suffixes are added. Suggested language: **When you add the suffix -ful to the base word beauty what happens to the base word?** (The y in beauty *changes to* i.)
- Guide students to recognize that adding suffixes changes the meanings of the base words. Hold up the Word Card restless. Then say: **The suffix -less means "without." If you are restless, then you are without rest.** Repeat with the other columns, identifying the suffix -ful as meaning "full of," -ness as meaning "the state or condition of," and -ment as meaning "the act of."
- Then give each student a set of Lesson 19 Word Cards, and have them repeat the sort independently.

DAY 2 Repeat the Sort

Students will repeat the sort from Day 1 independently.

- Remind students that this week's words have the suffixes -ful, -less, -ness, and -ment. Review that a suffix is added to the end of a base word and changes the word's meaning.
- Tell students to create a four-column chart in their Word Study Notebooks. Have them place the following Word Cards as column headings: cheerful, speechless, neatness, movement.
- Ask students to sort their Word Cards by suffix. After sorting all the words, have students reread each column to confirm that they sorted the words correctly.
- Have students copy their sorts into their Word Study Notebooks, writing the corresponding base word in parentheses next to each word. Then have students identify and circle the oddballs. Prompt students to explain why beautiful, clumsiness, and penniless are oddballs.

cheerful	speechless	neatness	movement
wasteful	useless	clumsiness	treatment
beautiful	penniless	illness	
truthful		fondness	

DAY 3 | Buddy Sort

Students will sort by parts of speech with a partner.

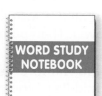
WORD STUDY NOTEBOOK

- Tell students that they will sort their Word Cards into two categories: adjectives and nouns.
- Review that a noun is a person, place, or thing and that an adjective is a word that describes a noun or pronoun.
- Direct partners to choose a Word Card and discuss whether the word is an adjective or a noun. If students need support, suggest that they try using the word in a sentence.
- When students finish sorting, have partners compare and confirm their sorts with another pair of students. Have students discuss any discrepancies until they are sure the words are sorted correctly.
- Ask students what they notice about the words in the two categories. Guide students to recognize that words that end with the suffixes -ment and -ness are nouns, and words that end with -ful and -less are adjectives.
- Have students write their sorts in their Word Study Notebooks.

DAY 4 | Blind Writing Sort

Students will sort and write words that you say aloud.

WORD STUDY NOTEBOOK

- Have students create a four-column chart in their Word Study Notebooks with the headings -ment, -ness, -ful, and -less. Review the meaning of each suffix.
- Tell students that you will read each spelling word aloud, and they will write the word in the correct column based on its suffix.
- Read each Word Card, and pause to give students time to write the word in one of the four columns. When students have written the word, show the Word Card and direct students to correct the spelling, if needed.
- After students have written all the words, have students read aloud each column and confirm the words were sorted correctly.
- Challenge students to use a dictionary, thesaurus, or other reference material to find and write more words that match the categories in their Word Study Notebooks.

DAY 5 | Assess

Tell students to listen carefully. Say each boldfaced word, read the sentence, and repeat the word. Have students write the word.

1. The girl wore a **colorful** hat.
2. I have a **weakness** for candy.
3. The class is reading about the civil rights **movement**.
4. The drive seemed **endless**.
5. That is not a **truthful** answer.
6. The long **illness** left me weak.
7. Play us a **cheerful** song.
8. Skis are **useless** in a desert.
9. The flowers are **beautiful**.
10. The baby is **restless** today.
11. My fall was due to my own **clumsiness**.
12. The **pavement** is cracking.
13. It was **peaceful** last night.
14. He has a **fondness** for dogs.
15. **Neatness** is not one of my virtues.
16. The vote left me **speechless**.
17. The mayor made a **statement**.
18. Using all that paper is **wasteful**.
19. The beggar was **penniless**.
20. What is the best **treatment** for the flu?

RETEACH **IF** students misspell four or more words, **THEN** revisit the activity on Day 2 and reassess.

Words with VCCV Pattern

SPELLING LIST

1.	million	11.	canyon
2.	collect	12.	traffic
3.	lumber	13.	fortune
4.	pepper	14.	danger
5.	plastic	15.	soccer
6.	borrow	16.	engine
7.	support	17.	picture
8.	thirty	18.	survive
9.	perfect	19.	seldom
10.	attend	20.	effort

 Go Digital Reproducible Word Cards are available at **www.thinkcentral.com**.

DIFFERENTIATE INSTRUCTION

Struggling	Advanced
1. mood	1. sign
2. wooden	2. groan
3. drew	3. reply
4. smooth	4. thrown
5. blue	5. strike
6. balloon	6. mighty
7. true	7. stroll
8. crooked	8. compose
9. chew	9. dough
10. tooth	10. height
11. hooves	11. excite
12. cool	12. apply
13. food	13. slight
14. pooch	14. define
Grade 3, Lesson 19	15. odor
	16. spider
	17. control
	18. silent
	19. brighten
	20. approach
	Grade 5, Lesson 3

ELL SUPPORT

Linguistic Transfer Double letters are rare in Spanish (except *ll* and *rr*), so Spanish speakers may have difficulty spelling words such as *pepper* and *traffic*. Brainstorm and list words that have double consonants.

DAY 1 PHONICS Model the Sort

Students will sort words with you based on each word's VCCV pattern.

- Display the Lesson 20 Word Cards, and read each word aloud.
- Guide students to see that all the words have the following pattern: vowel, consonant, consonant, vowel. Then point out that all of the words have two syllables.
- Explain to students that you will sort the words based on whether the two consonant sounds in the middle of the word sound the same or different. Display the Word Cards *pepper* and *plastic* as column headings. Read them aloud, emphasizing the middle consonants.
- Hold up the Word Card *borrow*. Suggested language: *Borrow*. **I hear two syllables in** *borrow*. **Bor-row. Both syllables have the same middle consonant sound, /r/.** *Pepper*. *Pepper* **also has two syllables.** *Pep-per*. **Both syllables in** *pepper* **have the same middle consonant sound, /p/. Let's place** *borrow* **under** *pepper*.
- Sort the Word Card *canyon* under *plastic*. Then ask students to help you finish the sort. When you come to the oddball *million*, make sure students are aware that one of the middle consonants is silent.
- After all the words have been sorted, have students read each column with you. Ask them whether the vowel sounds in the first syllables are long or short. *(short)* Guide students to notice that all the words break into syllables between the two middle consonants. Draw lines at the syllable breaks of a few words as an example. Then point out that syllables with short vowel sounds usually end with a consonant.
- Distribute the Lesson 20 Word Cards, and have students repeat the sort independently.

DAY 2 Pattern Sort

Students will repeat the sort from Day 1, and then sort by spelling pattern.

- Remind students that this week's words have the VCCV pattern. Review that words with the VCCV pattern are divided into syllables between the two middle consonants. Discuss how the middle consonants can be the same or different.
- Tell students to use their Word Cards to repeat the sort from Day 1, sorting the words based on whether the middle consonant sounds are the same or different. Remind students to read each word aloud before placing it in a category.
- Have students shuffle the Word Cards and focus on the spelling of the middle consonant sounds. Tell students to use *support* and *seldom* as column headings. If a word's middle consonant letters are the same, they should place the word under *support*. If they are different, they should place the word under *seldom*.
- Have students read each column aloud to check whether the words are sorted correctly. Then have students copy the column headings and write their sorts in a two-column chart in their Word Study Notebooks. Prompt students to divide each word into syllables by drawing a slash between the two middle consonants.

support	seldom
attend	perfect
traffic	danger
collect	engine
	lumber

> **MAJOR UNDERSTANDING:** Words with the VCCV pattern should be divided into syllables between the two middle consonants. Middle consonants can be the same or different.

DAY 3 Word Hunt

Students will sort words that they find in their reading.

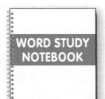

- Have students create a two-column chart in their Word Study Notebooks. Tell them to write the column headings *collect* and *thirty*.

- Explain that students will hunt for words with the VCCV pattern and then sort the words according to whether the middle consonants are the same or different.

- Tell students to turn to "Sacagawea" on page 589 of their Student Books. Give students time to skim the selection.

- Have students write the words they find in their Word Study Notebooks. Have them compare their words with a partner and confirm their understanding by reading the words aloud and checking the sound and spelling patterns.

- Extend the activity by having students identify the two middle consonants that make up each word's VCCV pattern. Have them draw a slash between the consonants.

  (Possible responses: mountain, rudder, matters, forty, blubber, wanted, offered, rescued, canyon, current, discuss, cactus)

DAY 4 Speed Sort

Students will try to sort words faster than you.

WORD STUDY NOTEBOOK

- Have students take out their Word Cards and read them aloud.

- Tell students that today they will sort words by the middle consonants they hear in each word. Remind students that they have already sorted this week's words by their middle consonant sounds.

- Explain to students that instead of taking turns sorting words with a partner they will try to sort their Word Cards faster than you.

- Display the column headings *effort* and *fortune*. Model saying the words quietly as you sort them one by one.

- Complete the sort two more times so that students have a chance to improve their speed. Have students shuffle their Word Cards between sorts and confirm word placement with a partner.

- Have students write their last sort in their Word Study Notebooks. Then ask students to underline the VCCV pattern in each word. Have them divide the words into syllables by drawing a slash between the two middle consonants.

DAY 5 Assess

Tell students to listen carefully. Say each boldfaced word, read the sentence, and repeat the word. Have students write the word.

1. A **million** people came to the parade.
2. I will **collect** the reports.
3. He bought **lumber** to build a shed.
4. I like **pepper** on my eggs.
5. The radio has a **plastic** case.
6. May I **borrow** five dollars?
7. Columns **support** the roof.
8. This month has **thirty** days.
9. The girl made a **perfect** dive.
10. I plan to **attend** the party.
11. A **canyon** is a deep valley.
12. Our car is in heavy **traffic**.
13. His family **fortune** was gone.
14. There is **danger** in skating on thin ice.
15. My sister likes to play **soccer**.
16. The **engine** makes the car move.
17. I took a **picture** of a lion.
18. Plants need water to **survive**.
19. Maria is **seldom** ill.
20. Climbing a mountain takes great **effort**.

RETEACH **IF** students misspell four or more words, **THEN** revisit the activity on Day 2 and reassess.

Words with VCV Pattern

SPELLING LIST

1. event	11. siren
2. humor	12. polite
3. rapid	13. hotel
4. music	14. protest
5. relief	15. punish
6. planet	16. defend
7. detail	17. relay
8. unite	18. habit
9. frozen	19. student
10. figure	20. moment

 Reproducible Word Cards are available at **www.thinkcentral.com**.

DIFFERENTIATE INSTRUCTION

Struggling	Advanced
1. birthday	1. glue
2. anyone	2. flute
3. sometimes	3. youth
4. everything	4. accuse
5. homework	5. bruise
6. afternoon	6. stew
7. airplane	7. choose
8. grandmother	8. loose
9. something	9. lose
10. without	10. view
11. himself	11. confuse
12. faraway	12. cruise
13. sunburned	13. jewel
14. daylight	14. execute
Grade 3, Lesson 20	15. route
	16. cartoon
	17. avenue
	18. include
	19. assume
	20. souvenir
	Grade 5, Lesson 4

 ELL SUPPORT

Linguistic Transfer Korean syllable-stress patterns differ from those in English. Korean speakers may need help learning the rhythm of English speech. Practice pronouncing the syllables of words in the spelling list.

DAY 1 PHONICS ## Model the Sort

Students will sort words with you based on the long or short vowel sound in the first syllable.

- Display the Lesson 21 Word Cards, and read each word aloud. Point out that all the words have two syllables.

- Tell students that you will sort each word by the long or short vowel sound in the first syllable. Display the Word Cards *rapid* and *event* as column headings, and read them aloud. Point out the /ă/ sound in *rapid* and the /ē/ sound in *event*. Then begin the sort with the word *frozen*. Suggested language: ***Frozen. Frooozen. I hear /ō/, a long vowel sound. Event has a long vowel sound, too. I'll place frozen under event.***

- Repeat with each Word Card, emphasizing the vowel sound in the first syllable of each word. Have students work with you to complete the sort and then read aloud each column's words.

- Tell students that all the words have the following pattern: vowel, consonant, vowel. Underline the letters that make up the VCV pattern in *rapid* and *event*.

- Have students help you divide the two words into syllables. Guide them to understand that when the first syllable ends with a short vowel sound, the first syllable is closed and the spelling of the first syllable will most likely end in a single consonant. When the first syllable ends with a long vowel sound, the first syllable is open and the spelling of the first syllable will usually end in a vowel.

- Ask volunteers to help you divide the remaining words by either the VC/V or the V/CV pattern, and prompt them to recognize how saying words and spelling them syllable by syllable can be helpful. Say: **Look at the words under rapid that all have a short vowel sound in the first syllable. What is the same about the spelling of the first syllable in each word?** *(They all end in a consonant.)* Repeat for the column of words with a long vowel sound in the first syllable.

- Distribute the Lesson 21 Word Cards. Have students repeat the sort independently.

DAY 2 ## Pattern Sort

Students will repeat the sort from Day 1 and then sort by spelling pattern.

- Remind students that this week's words have the VCV pattern. Review that words with the VCV pattern can be divided into syllables before or after the consonant, depending on the short or long vowel sound in the first syllable.

- Tell students to use their Word Cards to repeat the sort from Day 1, sorting the words based on the long or short vowel sound in the first syllable.

- Have students shuffle the Word Cards and focus on identifying the VC/V and V/CV syllable patterns. Have students place the Word Cards *planet* and *siren* as column headings. Students should place words with a short vowel in the first syllable under *planet*. Words with a long vowel in the first syllable should be placed under *siren*.

- When the sort is complete, have students read all the words to confirm the sort. Then ask them to make a two-column chart in their Word Study Notebooks and write the words. Tell students to divide each word into syllables by drawing a slash before or after the consonant at the syllable break.

planet	siren
rapid	humor
punish	student
habit	unite

> ▶ **MAJOR UNDERSTANDING:** Words with the VCV pattern can be divided into syllables before or after the consonant. A short vowel sound in the first syllable means divide after the consonant. A long vowel sound means divide before the consonant.

DAY 3 Blind Writing Sort

Students will sort and write words that a partner says aloud.

* Have students create a two-column chart with the headings *Short Vowel* and *Long Vowel* in their Word Study Notebooks.

* Remind students that the words in this week's sort can be divided into syllables before or after the middle consonant depending on if the vowel sound in the first syllable is short or long.

* Tell students they will sort the words based on the short or long vowel sound in the first syllable of each word.

* Pair students, and have one student read a Word Card without showing the word to his or her partner. Have the other student write the word in the correct column.

* After the student writes the word, the partner should place the card face up so the writer can confirm the word's correct spelling and placement. Have the student correct any misspellings at this time.

* After all the words are written, have students read the words to confirm the sort. Then ask them to shuffle the cards and switch roles.

DAY 4 Word Hunt

Students will sort words that they find in their reading.

* Have students draw a two-column chart in their Word Study Notebooks. Tell them to label the columns *punish* and *defend*.

* Explain to students that they will find and sort words with the VC/V and V/CV syllable patterns.

* Remind students to read the words they find with the column headings to compare the vowel sounds in the first syllables.

* Have students open their Student Books to page 625 and hunt for words in "The World According to Humphrey" that have the VCV pattern. Have them write the words under the correct column heading.

* Tell students to check how they sorted the words by reading down each column aloud.

(Possible responses: Friday, taking, cozy, baby, tigers, exit, minutes, power)

DAY 5 Assess

Tell students to listen carefully. Say each boldfaced word, read the sentence, and repeat the word. Have students write the word.

1. This is a happy **event**.
2. I have a good sense of **humor**.
3. My brother takes a **rapid** walk every morning.
4. I like to play **music**.
5. It was a **relief** to find our dog.
6. Mars is a small **planet**.
7. You forgot one small **detail**.
8. Let us **unite** in this cause.
9. The stream is **frozen**.
10. The mayor is a public **figure**.
11. The police car has a **siren**.
12. It is **polite** to say "thank you."
13. We stayed in a **hotel** on our vacation.
14. I **protest** doing this chore.
15. The law will **punish** criminals.
16. We chose to **defend** the fort.
17. Their team won the **relay**.
18. Cleaning my room became a **habit**.
19. He was a well-behaved **student**.
20. I could not sit still for one **moment**.

RETEACH **IF** students misspell four or more words, **THEN** revisit the activity on Day 2 and reassess.

VCCV and VCV Patterns

SPELLING LIST

1. dentist
2. final
3. finish
4. narrow
5. shelter
6. ahead
7. corner
8. hollow
9. divide
10. famous
11. recent
12. silver
13. capture
14. cabin
15. dinner
16. minus
17. minute
18. value
19. reward
20. broken

 Reproducible Word Cards are available at **www.thinkcentral.com**.

DIFFERENTIATE INSTRUCTION

Struggling	Advanced
1. coming	1. ounce
2. swimming	2. sprawl
3. dropping	3. launch
4. tapping	4. loyal
5. taping	5. avoid
6. invited	6. basketball
7. saving	7. moist
8. stared	8. haunt
9. planned	9. scowl
10. changing	10. naughty
11. joking	11. destroy
12. loved	12. saucer
13. gripped	13. pounce
14. tasted	14. poison
Grade 3, Lesson 21	15. August
	16. auction
	17. royal
	18. coward
	19. awkward
	20. encounter
	Grade 5, Lesson 5

 ELL SUPPORT

Linguistic Transfer With the exception of *ll* and *rr*, double letters are uncommon in Spanish. Model saying the spelling words with double consonants, and have ELLs pronounce the words after you.

DAY 1 PHONICS Model the Sort

Students will sort words with you based on each word's VCCV or VCV pattern.

- Display the Lesson 22 Word Cards, and read each word aloud. Discuss the words' meanings.

- Then display the Word Cards *narrow* and *final* as column headings. Point out that all the spelling words have two syllables. Help students recognize that this week's words have either the vowel, consonant, consonant, vowel pattern or the vowel, consonant, vowel pattern.

- Explain that you will sort the words based on whether a word has two consonant sounds in the middle of the word (VCCV) or vowel-consonant-vowel (VCV) sounds in the middle of a word.

- Begin the sort by holding up the Word Card *cabin*. Read the word aloud, emphasizing the vowel-consonant-vowel sounds. Suggested language: **Cabin. I hear a vowel-consonant-vowel pattern in the word *cabin*: cab-in. The word *final* has a vowel-consonant-vowel pattern, too: *final*.** Place *cabin* under *final*. Point out the VCV pattern in both words.

- Continue modeling as you sort *shelter* under *narrow*. Guide students to notice the VCCV pattern. Then ask students to help you sort the remaining Word Cards. After all the cards have been sorted, have students read each column with you.

- Then ask students to help you divide the words into syllables. Help them recognize that some words are divided into syllables between the two middle consonants (VCCV), and other words are divided into syllables before or after the consonant (VCV). Discuss how the short or long vowel sound in the first syllable of a VCV word determines where the word is divided. *(VC/V: short vowel; V/CV: long vowel)*

- Give each student a set of Lesson 22 Word Cards, and have them repeat the sort independently.

DAY 2 Guess My Category

Students will guess the category of words that you sort by spelling pattern.

- Display the Word Cards, and have students read them aloud.

- Sort the words based on these syllable patterns: double consonants (VC/CV), different consonants (VC/CV), a short vowel sound in the first syllable (VC/V), and a long vowel sound in the first syllable (V/CV).

- Tell students that you will begin the sort and that they are to guess how you are sorting. Display the Word Cards *hollow, dentist, cabin,* and *minus* as column headings. Choose the Word Card *reward,* read it aloud, and place it under *minus*.

- Continue sorting all the words without revealing the category types. When the sort is complete, have students read the words in each column. Have them share what the words in each column have in common. *(The words were sorted by VCCV and VCV patterns.)*

- Review what is the same about the words in each column. Then have students write the sort in their Word Study Notebooks.

hollow	dentist	cabin	minus
dinner	corner	minute	reward
narrow	silver	finish	famous
	shelter	value	

DAY 3 Pattern Sort

Students will repeat the sort from Day 1 and then sort by syllable pattern.

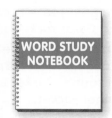

- Remind students that this week's words are two-syllable words that have the VCCV or VCV pattern. Display the Word Cards, and ask students to read them aloud.

- Have students sort the Word Cards by the two consonant sounds (VCCV) or the vowel-consonant-vowel sounds (VCV) they hear in the middle of each word. When they are finished, have students read the words for correct placement.

- Then have students draw a four-column chart in their Word Study Notebooks and arrange the following Word Cards as column headings: *dinner, silver, value, reward.* Ask students to sort the remaining words by their VCCV or VCV syllable patterns.

- Tell students to read each word and then the column heading to help them as they sort.

- Have students reread each column to confirm the sort. Then have them write their last sorts in their Word Study Notebooks.

DAY 4 Buddy Sort

Students will sort the words by sound and then review their sorts with a partner.

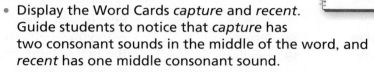

- Tell students that they will sort their Word Cards based on whether they have the VCCV pattern or the VCV pattern.

- Display the Word Cards *capture* and *recent.* Guide students to notice that *capture* has two consonant sounds in the middle of the word, and *recent* has one middle consonant sound.

- Have students use *capture* and *recent* as column headings as they sort the remaining words by their middle sounds. After the sort is complete, have partners work together to compare and confirm their sorts.

- Prompt students to discuss how to divide words into syllables when the word has double consonants (VC/CV) or different middle consonants (VC/CV). Then discuss how to divide words into syllables when the word has a short vowel sound in the first syllable (VC/V) or a long vowel sound in the first syllable (V/CV).

- Have students write their sorts in their Word Study Notebooks.

DAY 5 Assess

Tell students to listen carefully. Say each boldfaced word, read the sentence, and repeat the word. Have students write the word.

1. The **dentist** said I had no cavities.
2. I just read the **final** chapter.
3. It took me a week to **finish**.
4. The deer jumped across the **narrow** stream.
5. Trees provide **shelter**.
6. Please walk **ahead** of me.
7. There is a store on the **corner**.
8. A log or pipe is **hollow**.
9. **Divide** the pie into sections.
10. I met a **famous** writer.
11. This chair is a **recent** purchase.
12. Her necklace is made of **silver**.
13. The police will **capture** the criminal.
14. Abe Lincoln lived in a **cabin**.
15. What is for **dinner**?
16. Four **minus** one is three.
17. A **minute** is sixty seconds.
18. They **value** your friendship.
19. I **reward** my dog for good behavior.
20. Jessica's watch is **broken**.

RETEACH IF students misspell four or more words, **THEN** revisit the activity on Day 2 and reassess.

Words with VCCV Pattern

SPELLING LIST

1. poster	11. chicken
2. secret	12. clothing
3. whether	13. apron
4. author	14. whiskers
5. rocket	15. degree
6. bushel	16. gather
7. agree	17. achieve
8. bucket	18. rather
9. ticket	19. bracket
10. declare	20. machine

 Reproducible Word Cards are available at **www.thinkcentral.com**.

DIFFERENTIATE INSTRUCTION

Struggling	Advanced
1. person	1. glory
2. helmet	2. aware
3. until	3. carton
4. carpet	4. adore
5. Monday	5. aboard
6. enjoy	6. dairy
7. forget	7. ordeal
8. problem	8. pardon
9. Sunday	9. warn
10. garden	10. vary
11. order	11. barely
12. mistake	12. torch
13. umpire	13. barge
14. herself	14. soar
Grade 3, Lesson 26	15. beware
	16. absorb
	17. armor
	18. stairway
	19. perform
	20. former
	Grade 5, Lesson 6

 ELL SUPPORT

Linguistic Transfer Cantonese, Hmong, and Korean speakers may have difficulty with vowel sounds. Provide extra support as ELLs read words with the VCCV pattern.

DAY 1 PHONICS **Model the Sort**

Students will sort words with you based on the vowel sound in the first syllable.

- Display the Lesson 23 Word Cards, and read each word aloud.
- Tell students that you are going to sort each word by its vowel sound in the first syllable. Display the Word Cards *rocket* and *agree* as column headings.
- Point out the /ŏ/ sound in *rocket* and the /ə/ sound in *agree*. Then begin to model the sort. Suggested language: **Bracket. Braaacket. In the first syllable, I hear the /ă/ sound, a short vowel sound.** *Rocket* **also has a short vowel sound in the first syllable.** Place *bracket* under *rocket*.
- Repeat with the Word Card *declare*, placing it under *agree*. Have students work with you to sort the remaining Word Cards. Words with the short vowel sound in the first syllable should be added to the *rocket* column. Words with the long vowel sound or the /ə/ sound in the first syllable should be added to the *agree* column. When the sort is complete, have students read each column's words.
- Guide students to recognize that all the words have the following pattern: vowel, consonant, consonant, vowel. Call attention to the words that have two consonants that form a cluster *(whiskers)* and the words that have two consonants that stand for one sound *(author)*.
- Lead students in dividing the words into syllables. Help students notice that the words with a short vowel sound in the first syllable are divided after the two middle consonants. Then point out that the words with a long vowel sound or /ə/ sound in the first syllable are divided before the two consonants.
- Point out the oddballs *poster* and *clothing*. Lead students to understand these words have a long vowel sound in the first syllable but are divided after the two middle consonants.
- Distribute the Lesson 23 Word Cards, and have students repeat the sort independently.

DAY 2 **Repeat the Sort**

Students will repeat the sort from Day 1.

- Review that this week's words are two-syllable words that have the VCCV pattern.
- Display the Word Cards, and have students read them aloud. Tell students to place the Word Cards *bushel* and *declare* as column headings.
- Explain to students that they should sort the words by the vowel sound in the first syllable of each word. If they hear a short vowel sound, they should sort the word under *bushel*. If they hear a long vowel sound or the /ə/ sound in the first syllable, they should sort the word under *declare*.
- Have students reread the words in each column to confirm the words are sorted correctly. Then have them write their sorts in their Word Study Notebooks and draw a slash to divide each word into syllables.
- Tell students to circle the oddballs, which have a long vowel sound in the first syllable but are divided after the consonants. *(poster, clothing)*

bushel	declare
chicken	apron
whether	secret
gather	machine

DAY 3 Buddy Sort

Students will work with a partner to sort the words by vowel sound.

- Have partners work together to complete today's sort. Tell them to take out their Word Cards and read them aloud.

- Explain that they will sort their Word Cards based on the vowel sound they hear in the first syllable of each word.

- Display the Word Cards *ticket* and *apron*. Point out the VCCV pattern in each word and the vowel sound in the first syllable.

- Have students use the column headings as they sort the remaining words by the vowel sound in the first syllable.

- When partners finish sorting the words, have them read aloud the words in each column to confirm the sort.

- Then have students write their sorts in their Word Study Notebooks.

DAY 4 Open Sort

Students will sort words according to categories they choose.

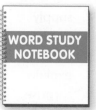

- Have students take out their Word Cards, read the words aloud, and analyze the words for similarities and differences.

- Tell students that they will sort the words based on what they notice about the words.

- Explain that students' categories may be different from or the same as the categories they sorted by earlier in the week.

- If students have trouble choosing categories, suggest options such as sorting by beginning or final consonant, parts of speech, or "animal" and "people" words.

- After students have sorted the words, have them write their sorts in their Word Study Notebooks.

- Then organize small groups. Ask group members to explain their categories and thinking behind how they sorted the words.

- Challenge students to sort the Word Cards according to another student's categories.

DAY 5 Assess

Tell students to listen carefully. Say each boldfaced word, read the sentence, and repeat the word. Have students write the word.

1. That is a great movie **poster**.
2. Can you keep a **secret**?
3. Tell me **whether** you can go.
4. I met a famous **author**.
5. A **rocket** provides power for a spacecraft.
6. A **bushel** is a unit of measurement.
7. Do you **agree** with my opinion?
8. Please fill up the **bucket**.
9. Dad paid for my **ticket**.
10. Who will **declare** the winner?
11. The **chicken** ate the grain.
12. This store sells men's **clothing**.
13. I wear an **apron** when I cook.
14. My cat has **whiskers**.
15. The temperature went up one **degree**.
16. People **gather** in the park.
17. I was able to **achieve** my goal.
18. He would **rather** sleep than go out.
19. More than one **bracket** holds up that shelf.
20. A lawn mower is a **machine**.

RETEACH   **IF** students misspell four or more words, **THEN** revisit the activity on Day 1 and reassess.

Words with VCCCV Pattern

SPELLING LIST

1. hundred	11. monster
2. supply	12. settle
3. single	13. address
4. middle	14. farther
5. explain	15. sample
6. surprise	16. although
7. pilgrim	17. turtle
8. sandwich	18. athlete
9. instead	19. orchard
10. complete	20. kingdom

 Reproducible Word Cards are available at **www.thinkcentral.com**.

DIFFERENTIATE INSTRUCTION

Struggling	Advanced
1. jelly	1. earth
2. bottom	2. peer
3. pillow	3. twirl
4. happen	4. burnt
5. butter	5. smear
6. lesson	6. further
7. cherry	7. appear
8. sudden	8. worthwhile
9. arrow	9. nerve
10. dollar	10. pier
11. hello	11. squirm
12. rabbit	12. weary
13. letter	13. alert
14. button	14. murmur
Grade 3, Lesson 27	15. thirsty
	16. reverse
	17. worship
	18. career
	19. research
	20. volunteer
	Grade 5, Lesson 7

ELL SUPPORT

Linguistic Transfer Consonant clusters do not exist in Cantonese syllables. Model how to pronounce consonant clusters in words with the VCCCV pattern, and have students repeat after you.

DAY 1 PHONICS   Model the Sort

Students will sort words with you based on the short vowel sound in the first syllable of each word.

- Display the Lesson 24 Word Cards, and read each word aloud. Discuss the meanings.
- Point out that each word has two syllables. Tell students you will sort the words based on the short vowel sound in the first syllable of each word.
- Display these Word Cards as column headings: *sandwich, explain, single, monster, hundred*. Read each word aloud and then model your thinking, beginning with *settle*. Suggested language: ***Settle*. Listen to the vowel sound in the first syllable: *set-tle*, /ĕ/. The first syllable in *explain* has the same short vowel sound, /ĕ/. I'll place *settle* under *explain*.**
- Continue modeling the sort, placing the Word Card *address* under *sandwich*. Have students help you sort the remaining Word Cards and then read them aloud.
- Help students recognize that all the words have the VCCCV pattern. Then guide them to notice that the VCCCV words have two consonants that stand for one sound or form a cluster and the first syllable usually has a short vowel sound.
- Have students work with you to divide the words into syllables. Ask volunteers to underline the two consonants that stand for one sound or form a cluster in each VCCCV word. Then divide the word into syllables before or after those consonants.
- Help students discover that most of the words are divided between the first two consonants (VC/CCV) and that the oddballs *sandwich, athlete,* and *kingdom* are different because they follow the VCC/CV pattern.
- Distribute the Lesson 24 Word Cards, and have students repeat the sort independently.

DAY 2   Pattern Sort

Students will repeat the sort from Day 1 and then sort by syllable pattern.

- Remind students that this week's words have the VCCCV pattern.
- Display the Word Cards, and have students read them aloud. Explain to students that they will sort the words based on the short vowel sound in the first syllable: /ă/, /ĕ/, /ĭ/, /ŏ/, or /ŭ/.
- When students finish, ask them to shuffle the Word Cards and prepare for a new sort. Have students create a two-column chart in their Word Study Notebooks and place the Word Cards *instead* and *kingdom* as column headings.
- Tell students that they will sort the remaining Word Cards according to how each word's VCCCV pattern is divided into syllables, VC/CCV or VCC/CV. Model reading the Word Card *complete* and sorting it under *instead*. Remind students to read each word aloud before sorting it.
- Have students reread the words in each column to confirm their placement. Then have them write their sorts in their Word Study Notebooks and draw a slash to divide each word into syllables.

instead	kingdom
complete	athlete
supply	sandwich
orchard	
address	

DAY 3 — Word Hunt

Students will sort words that they find in their reading.

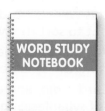

- Tell students to make a two-column chart in their Word Study Notebooks. Provide the following column headings: *turtle, athlete.*

- Review this week's words and the VC/CCV and VCC/CV syllable patterns. Model sorting a few words to support students' understanding.

- Explain that students will look for words with the VCCCV pattern. They will then sort each word based on its VC/CCV or VCC/CV syllable pattern.

- Have students turn to "Owen and Mzee" on page 717 of their Student Books and skim for words with the VCCCV pattern. Have students write each word in the correct column of their Word Study Notebooks.

- Then have students work with a partner to compare their words and confirm their understanding.

  (Possible responses: gentle, explained, unclear, countless, tickles)

DAY 4 — Guess My Category

Students will guess the category of words that you sort alphabetically.

- Display the Word Cards, and have students read them aloud.

- Sort the words into alphabetical order, but do not reveal how you are sorting.

- Tell students that you will sort the words and that they are to guess how you are sorting.

- Begin the sort by displaying these column headings: *address, middle, sample.* Choose the Word Card *although*, read it aloud, and place it under *address.*

- Continue sorting the remaining words, sorting each Word Card by its beginning vowel or consonant.

- When the sort is complete, have students read the words in each column.

- Then have them tell how they think you categorized the words. *(alphabetically)* If students have difficulty, ask them to look at the first letter of each word.

- Have students write the sort in their Word Study Notebooks.

DAY 5 — Assess

Tell students to listen carefully. Say each boldfaced word, read the sentence, and repeat the word. Have students write the word.

1. One **hundred** cents equals one dollar.
2. The rain will **supply** water.
3. The vase had a **single** flower.
4. We sat in the **middle** row.
5. Please **explain** your idea.
6. The party was a **surprise**.
7. The **pilgrim** traveled far.
8. I ate a turkey **sandwich**.
9. The chef used oil **instead** of butter.
10. Is this a **complete** set of tools?
11. The **monster** in the movie scared us.
12. We must **settle** this argument.
13. Write your name and **address**.
14. I walked **farther** than you did.
15. Try a **sample** of the ice cream.
16. **Although** I am tired, I will go.
17. A **turtle** is a reptile.
18. My sister is a great **athlete**.
19. We grow apples in the **orchard**.
20. The king ruled his **kingdom** wisely.

RETEACH   IF students misspell four or more words, **THEN** revisit the activity on Day 1 and reassess.

Words with VV Pattern

1. idea	11. poet
2. lion	12. science
3. usual	13. diary
4. radio	14. violin
5. liar	15. period
6. poem	16. February
7. India	17. cereal
8. piano	18. video
9. January	19. meteor
10. quiet	20. rodeo

 Go Digital Reproducible Word Cards are available at **www.thinkcentral.com**.

DIFFERENTIATE INSTRUCTION

Struggling	Advanced
1. painless	1. steel
2. sickness	2. steal
3. sadness	3. aloud
4. helpless	4. allowed
5. thankless	5. ring
6. kindness	6. wring
7. hopeless	7. lesson
8. darkness	8. lessen
9. fearless	9. who's
10. thickness	10. whose
11. careless	11. manor
12. goodness	12. manner
13. spotless	13. pedal
14. softness	14. peddle
	15. berry
	16. bury
	17. hanger
	18. hangar
	19. overdo
	20. overdue
Grade 3, Lesson 25	Grade 5, Lesson 8

ELL SUPPORT

Linguistic Transfer The VV pattern can be challenging for Mandarin speakers, who often have difficulty distinguishing English vowel sounds. Review vowel sounds individually before working with the words.

DAY 1 PHONICS Model the Sort

Students will sort words with you based on the number of syllables in each word.

- Display the Lesson 25 Word Cards, and read each word aloud. Discuss the meanings.
- Tell students that all of this week's words contain the vowel-vowel pattern. Then tell students that you want to sort the words by their number of syllables.
- Display the Word Cards *lion, idea,* and *January* as column headings. Read each heading aloud, emphasizing the syllables in each word.
- Then pick up the Word Card *radio,* and explain that you are going to sort it according to its number of syllables. Suggested language: **Ra-di-o. I hear three syllables in radio. Which column heading has three syllables?** *Li-on, i-de-a, Jan-u-ar-y. Idea has three syllables, so I'll put radio under idea.*
- Repeat the steps with the Word Card *poem.* Once the categories are established, have students read each word with you and help you sort it into the correct column. Continue until all the remaining words have been sorted. Have students read the words to check that they were sorted correctly.
- Lead students to reflect on this sort by explaining what the words in each column have in common. (Lion *column: two-syllable words;* idea *column: three-syllable words;* January *column: four-syllable words*)
- Guide students to divide the words into syllables. Help them notice that each word is divided into syllables between the vowels in its VV pattern and that the vowels in the VV pattern appear together, but they stand for different sounds.
- Give each student a set of Lesson 25 Word Cards. Have them repeat the sort independently.

DAY 2 Repeat the Sort

Students will repeat the sort from Day 1.

- Remind students that this week's words have the VV pattern.
- Display the Word Cards, and have students read them aloud. Tell students they will sort this week's words according to the number of syllables in each word.
- Have students create a three-column chart in their Word Study Notebooks and arrange the following Word Cards as column headings: *poet, rodeo, February.* Model reading the Word Card *violin* and sorting it under *rodeo.*
- Then ask students to sort the remaining Word Cards independently. Remind students to read each word and then the column headings before they sort.
- Have students reread the words in each column to confirm the words were sorted correctly. Then have them write their sorts in their Word Study Notebooks and draw a slash to divide each word into syllables.
- Have them circle the syllable breaks that are between two vowels.

poet	rodeo	February
science	violin	January
poem	India	
quiet	diary	
liar	cereal	

DAY 3 Speed Sort

Students will sort words as quickly as they can.

- Tell students that they will sort their Word Cards as fast as they can by the number of syllables in each word.
- Have student pairs read the Word Cards aloud. Then have one student sort the words by two-, three-, or four-syllable words.
- The second student will use a stopwatch or clock with a second hand to time the first student.
- Have students repeat the sort several times, shuffling the cards between each sort and switching roles.
- Have students record their times to chart their progress. Challenge them to improve their time with each sort.
- After partners complete the sort several times, have them read the words in each column aloud to confirm that the words were placed correctly.
- Then have them write their last sort in their Word Study Notebooks.

DAY 4 Word Hunt

Students will sort words that they find in their reading.

- Have students draw a three-column chart in their Word Study Notebooks. Provide these column headings: *quiet, violin, January*.
- Review this week's VV pattern. Remind students that the words are divided into syllables between the vowels.
- Tell students they will use their Student Books to find more words with the VV pattern and then sort those words according to their number of syllables.
- Ask students to open their Student Books to page 745. Tell students to skim "The Fun They Had" for words with the VV pattern. Remind them that the two vowels next to each other should stand for different sounds and be part of different syllables.
- Students should write each word they find in the correct column of their Word Study Notebooks and then divide each word into syllables.
- After completing the sort, have students form small groups to compare their sorts.

  (Possible responses: superior, dials, geography, actually, going)

DAY 5 Assess

Tell students to listen carefully. Say each boldfaced word, read the sentence, and repeat the word. Have students write the word.

1. Swimming is my **idea** of fun.
2. We saw a **lion** at the zoo.
3. We get the **usual** snow here in December.
4. I listen to music on the **radio**.
5. You cannot trust a **liar**.
6. My favorite **poem** is "The Wind."
7. **India** is a large country in Asia.
8. Juan can play **piano**.
9. **January** is the first month.
10. Be **quiet** in the library.
11. The **poet** signed my book.
12. Nora wants to study **science**.
13. Anne Frank wrote a **diary**.
14. A **violin** is played with a bow.
15. Our class is studying the **period** of World War II.
16. **February** can be cold here.
17. Roy eats **cereal** for breakfast.
18. I own that movie on **video**.
19. A shooting star is a **meteor**.
20. Bull riding is an event at a **rodeo**.

RETEACH **IF** students misspell four or more words, **THEN** revisit the activity on Day 2 and reassess.

SPELLING LIST

1.	enter	11.	favor
2.	banner	12.	bother
3.	sugar	13.	fever
4.	shower	14.	doctor
5.	motor	15.	temper
6.	collar	16.	actor
7.	labor	17.	polar
8.	finger	18.	sweater
9.	mirror	19.	traitor
10.	beggar	20.	whenever

 Reproducible Word Cards are available at **www.thinkcentral.com**.

DIFFERENTIATE INSTRUCTION

Struggling	Advanced
1. cities	1. wildlife
2. cried	2. uproar
3. puppies	3. home run
4. hurried	4. headache
5. stories	5. top-secret
6. flies	6. teammate
7. parties	7. wheelchair
8. tried	8. light bulb
9. pennies	9. well-known
10. fried	10. throughout
11. carried	11. life preserver
12. babies	12. barefoot
13. spied	13. part-time
14. ponies	14. warehouse
Grade 3, Lesson 22	15. overboard
	16. post office
	17. outspoken
	18. up-to-date
	19. awestruck
	20. newscast
	Grade 5, Lesson 9

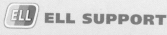 **ELL SUPPORT**

Access Prior Knowledge Many of this week's spelling words have Spanish cognates. The following words have the same spelling and meaning in English and Spanish: *doctor, actor, polar, motor.*

DAY 1 PHONICS Model the Sort

Students will sort words with you based on the spelling of the final /ər/ sound.

- Display the Lesson 26 Word Cards, and read each word aloud. Discuss each word's meaning and use it in a sentence, as necessary.
- Guide students to notice that all of this week's words have the same ending sound, /ər/, in an unstressed syllable. Tell students that the unstressed syllable is the syllable that is pronounced with less emphasis. Give an example, such as FA-vor.
- Then display these Word Cards and arrange them as column headings: *sugar, fever, doctor.* Read each word aloud, and explain that each word has the same ending sound, /ər/, but the sound is spelled differently.
- Display the Word Card *shower,* read it aloud, and model your thinking as you sort according to its spelling pattern. Suggested language: *Shower* has the same /ər/ ending sound as *sugar, fever,* and *doctor.*
- Hold the Word Card under each heading to compare the spellings. Then say: **Let's look to see which of these words matches the spelling of the ending sound. The ending sound of *shower* has the same spelling as the ending sound of *fever*. Let's place *shower* under *fever*.**
- Modify the suggested language as you sort *beggar* and *actor*. Once students recognize the spelling patterns, have them work with you to sort the remaining Word Cards. When the sort is complete, have them read down each column to confirm the sort.
- Guide students to analyze the categories. Ask what the words in each column have in common. *(They all have the /ər/ sound spelled* ar, er, *or* or.)
- Distribute the Lesson 26 Word Cards. Have students repeat the sort independently.

DAY 2 Repeat the Sort

Students will repeat the sort from Day 1 independently.

- Remind students that this week's words have the final /ər/ sound spelled *ar, er,* or *or.*
- Have students draw a three-column chart in their Word Study Notebooks and arrange the following Word Cards as column headings: *collar, bother, favor.*
- Tell students to sort the remaining Word Cards according to the spelling of each word's final /ər/ sound. Remind students to read each word aloud before they sort.
- After students complete the sort, tell them to reread the words in each column to confirm that the words are in the correct columns. Then have students write their sorts in their Word Study Notebooks.

collar	bother	favor
polar	shower	labor
sugar	banner	motor
beggar	enter	traitor
	temper	doctor

DAY 3 Buddy Sort

Student pairs will sort the words according to categories they choose.

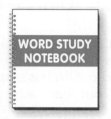

WORD STUDY NOTEBOOK

- Have partners work together for today's sort. Remind them that this week's words have the final /ər/ sound spelled *ar, er,* or *or.* Guide them to analyze the words' similarities and differences.

- Tell partners they will create their own sorting categories based on what they notice. Discuss how students' categories may be different from or the same as the categories they sorted by earlier in the week.

- Have students write column headings in their Word Study Notebooks and then sort the Word Cards into the correct category.

- When student pairs complete their sorts, ask them to read the words to confirm placement and then write their sorts in their Word Study Notebooks.

- Extend the activity by having partners brainstorm and write other words that fit the categories.

DAY 4 Speed Sort

Students will sort words as quickly as they can.

WORD STUDY NOTEBOOK

- Have students work with a partner as they sort this week's Word Cards. Tell students to look at their Word Cards as you review the different spellings for the final /ər/ sound.

- Ask students to draw a three-column chart in their Word Study Notebooks with the Word Cards *polar, enter,* and *motor* as column headings.

- Tell students that they will sort the remaining words by spelling pattern as quickly as they can while a partner times them. Challenge students to beat their best time.

- Have partners use a stopwatch or clock with a second hand as they take turns sorting the Word Cards and timing each other.

- Tell students to keep a record of their sorting times in their Word Study Notebooks so they can chart their progress. Explain that students can repeat the sort up to three times.

- Have partners check their sorts by reading the words in each column aloud. Then tell students to write their sorts in their Word Study Notebooks.

DAY 5 Assess

Tell students to listen carefully. Say each boldfaced word, read the sentence, and repeat the word. Have students write the word.

1. Should we **enter** the room?
2. A **banner** welcomed them.
3. Candy has lots of **sugar** in it.
4. I took a **shower**.
5. Dad started the boat's **motor**.
6. I put the pin on my **collar**.
7. The garden required **labor**.
8. I hurt my **finger**.
9. A **mirror** reflects your image.
10. The **beggar** wore old clothes.

11. Toby asked me for a **favor**.
12. Ants might **bother** us at a picnic.
13. I stayed home with a **fever**.
14. The **doctor** set my broken foot.
15. Carl has an even **temper**.
16. The **actor** took a bow.
17. Few people live in **polar** climates.
18. I like to wear a **sweater**.
19. The soldier was a **traitor**.
20. I skate **whenever** I go to the park.

RETEACH   **IF** students misspell four or more words, **THEN** revisit the activity on Day 2 and reassess.

Final Schwa + /l/ Sound

SPELLING LIST

1. title	11. nickel
2. towel	12. gentle
3. battle	13. barrel
4. pedal	14. model
5. metal	15. tangle
6. simple	16. ankle
7. eagle	17. marvel
8. special	18. juggle
9. total	19. squirrel
10. trouble	20. riddle

 Reproducible Word Cards are available at **www.thinkcentral.com**.

DIFFERENTIATE INSTRUCTION

Struggling	Advanced
1. taught	1. cellar
2. thought	2. flavor
3. rough	3. cougar
4. laugh	4. chapter
5. bought	5. mayor
6. cough	6. anger
7. ought	7. senator
8. caught	8. passenger
9. fought	9. major
10. daughter	10. popular
11. tough	11. tractor
12. through	12. thunder
13. enough	13. pillar
14. brought	14. border
Grade 3, Lesson 28	15. calendar
	16. quarter
	17. lunar
	18. proper
	19. elevator
	20. bitter
	Grade 5, Lesson 10

 ELL SUPPORT

Linguistic Transfer Speakers of South Asian languages, such as Hindi and Urdu, may pronounce the final e in words that end with le. As you listen to ELLs say le words, remind them that this e is silent.

DAY 1 PHONICS Model the Sort

Students will sort words with you based on the spelling of the final /əl/ sound.

- Display the Lesson 27 Word Cards, and read each word aloud. Discuss the meanings, and guide students to notice that all of this week's words end with the same sound, /əl/.

- Then display the Word Cards *nickel, total,* and *battle,* emphasizing the /əl/ sound in each word's unstressed syllable. Remind students that the unstressed syllable is the syllable that is pronounced with less emphasis. Point out that each word has the same ending sound, /əl/, but that each ending is spelled differently.

- Begin the sort by picking up the Word Card *riddle.* Model your thinking as you sort. Suggested language: **Riddle** *has the same /əl/ ending sound as* **nickel, total,** *and* **battle.** Place the Word Card under each heading to compare the spellings. Then say: **The ending sound of** *riddle* **has the same** *le* **spelling as the ending sound of** *battle.* **I'll put** *riddle* **under** *battle.*

- Adapt the suggested language as you repeat the steps with *model* and *metal.* Then ask students to help you sort the remaining words. When the sort is complete, have students read down each column with you.

- Ask students to analyze the categories. Have them tell what the words in each column have in common. *(The words in each column have the /əl/ sound spelled* el, al, *or* le.*)* Discuss students' responses.

- Give each student a set of Lesson 27 Word Cards, and have them repeat the sort independently.

DAY 2 Repeat the Sort

Students will repeat the sort from Day 1 independently.

- Remind students that this week's words have the final /əl/ sound spelled *el, al,* or *le.*
- Have students draw a three-column chart in their Word Study Notebooks. Tell them to place the following Word Cards as column headings: *marvel, pedal, eagle.*
- Then have students sort the remaining Word Cards according to the spelling of each word's final /əl/ sound. Remind students to read each word aloud and then the column heading before sorting a word.
- After students finish sorting all the words, have them reread the words in each column to confirm placement. Then have students write their sorts in their Word Study Notebooks.

marvel	pedal	eagle
nickel	total	tangle
towel	metal	ankle
barrel	special	simple
squirrel		juggle

DAY 3 Speed Sort

Students will sort words as quickly as they can.

WORD STUDY NOTEBOOK

- Have student pairs take out their Word Cards. Review that this week's words have the final /əl/ sound and that the sound can be spelled *el*, *al*, or *le*.
- Ask students to draw a three-column chart in their Word Study Notebooks and place the Word Cards *squirrel*, *special*, and *tangle* as column headings. Have students identify the spelling for final /əl/ in each word.
- Tell students that they are going to sort the remaining Word Cards by the *el*, *al*, or *le* spelling pattern as quickly as they can while a partner times them.
- Have partners use a stopwatch or clock with a second hand as they take turns sorting the Word Cards and timing each other. Remind students to record their times in their Word Study Notebooks. Have students repeat the sort up to three times.
- Have partners confirm their sorts by reading the words down each column. Then tell students to write their last sort in their Word Study Notebooks.

DAY 4 Blind Writing Sort

Students will sort and write words as you say them aloud.

WORD STUDY NOTEBOOK

- Have students create a three-column chart in their Word Study Notebooks and write the following spelling words as column headings: *barrel, metal, ankle.*
- Have partners compare how they spelled the words and correct any mistakes. Then review the final /əl/ sound and the *el*, *al*, or *le* spelling pattern in each word.
- Tell students that you will read a Word Card aloud without showing it to them. They will write the word under the column heading that has the same spelling pattern for the final /əl/ sound.
- After students have written the word, display the Word Card so that students can check the spelling and placement of the word.
- When all the words have been written, have students read aloud the words in each column to confirm understanding. As time allows, challenge students to brainstorm and write other words they know that fit the categories.

DAY 5 Assess

Tell students to listen carefully. Say each boldfaced word, read the sentence, and repeat the word. Have students write the word.

1. The book has a good **title**.
2. Use a **towel** to wipe it up.
3. The troops went to **battle**.
4. I had to **pedal** my bike fast.
5. My bracelet is made of **metal**.
6. Addition is **simple** math.
7. An **eagle** soared above us.
8. Cake is a **special** treat.
9. A **total** of ten people arrived.
10. Breaking rules causes **trouble**.
11. Five cents are in a **nickel**.
12. The calm dog was **gentle**.
13. The **barrel** was full of water.
14. I saw a **model** of the new school.
15. Wind can **tangle** your hair.
16. I fell and broke my **ankle**.
17. I **marvel** at the sunset.
18. I saw a clown **juggle** apples.
19. The **squirrel** gathered acorns.
20. Can you answer this **riddle?**

RETEACH **IF** students misspell four or more words, **THEN** revisit the activity on Day 2 and reassess.

Three-Syllable Words

1. library
2. another
3. hospital
4. example
5. deliver
6. history
7. however
8. several
9. vacation
10. important
11. victory
12. imagine
13. camera
14. potato
15. remember
16. together
17. memory
18. favorite
19. continue
20. president

Go Digital Reproducible Word Cards are available at **www.thinkcentral.com**.

DIFFERENTIATE INSTRUCTION

Struggling	Advanced
1. apple	1. bargain
2. river	2. journey
3. little	3. pattern
4. October	4. arrive
5. ladder	5. object
6. summer	6. suppose
7. purple	7. shoulder
8. later	8. permit
9. November	9. sorrow
10. giggle	10. tunnel
11. uncle	11. subject
12. winter	12. custom
13. center	13. suggest
14. double	14. perhaps
Grade 3, Lesson 29	15. lawyer
	16. timber
	17. common
	18. publish
	19. burden
	20. scissors
	Grade 5, Lesson 11

ELL ELL SUPPORT

Support Word Meaning Many of this week's spelling words lend themselves to visual depictions. Use pictures and photos to explain each word's meaning. Then have students draw their own pictures to confirm their understanding.

DAY 1 PHONICS Model the Sort

Students will sort words with you based on whether the first or second syllable is stressed.

- Display the Lesson 28 Word Cards. Read the words aloud and discuss their meanings.
- Tell students that all of this week's words have three syllables. Explain that you will sort each word according to whether its first or second syllable is stressed. Explain that a stressed syllable is pronounced with the most emphasis.
- Display the Word Cards *hospital* and *deliver,* and place them as column headings. Emphasize the division between each word's three syllables. Then underline the stressed first syllable in *hos-pi-tal* and the stressed second syllable in *de-li-ver.*
- Then display the first word you will sort, and model your thinking. Suggested language: **I am going to sort the word *victory*. *Vic-to-ry, hos-pi-tal, de-li-ver.* The first syllable is stressed in *victory* and *hospital*. Let's place *victory* under *hospital*.**
- Have students help you read and sort the remaining words. After all the words have been sorted, have students read down each column to confirm each word's correct placement. As students read a word, underline its stressed syllable.
- Guide students in analyzing how the words in each column are alike. *(The words in the* hospital *column have a stressed first syllable. The words in the* deliver *column have a stressed second syllable.)*
- Explain that when a three-syllable word has a stressed first syllable, it is important to pay close attention to the spelling of the unstressed syllables. Help students identify familiar spelling patterns in the words' unstressed syllables.
- Distribute the Lesson 28 Word Cards. Have students repeat the sort independently.

DAY 2 Repeat the Sort

Students will repeat the sort from Day 1 independently.

- Remind students that all of this week's words are three-syllable words.
- Write the column headings *history* and *vacation*. Read each heading aloud, emphasizing the syllables of each word. Explain that each word's stressed syllable is underlined.
- Have students divide a page in their Word Study Notebooks into two columns and copy the column headings you provided. Tell students to sort the remaining Word Cards according to whether each word's first or second syllable is stressed.
- If a word's first syllable is stressed, students should sort it into the same column as *history*. If the second syllable is stressed, they should sort the word under *vacation*. Remind students to read each card and column heading aloud before sorting.
- After students have finished sorting, have them reread the words in each column to make sure they placed the words in the correct category. Then have students write their sorts in their Word Study Notebooks.

hi̲story	vaca̲tion
library	potato
president	example
several	important

DAY 3 Concept Sort

Students will sort words according to whether the words are related to history.

- Have student pairs get out their Word Cards and read the words together. Have them discuss the meaning of each word.

- Monitor the discussions to ensure that students understand each word's meaning. Then explain that students will sort the words based on whether they are related to history.

- Have students create a two-column chart in their Word Study Notebooks with the headings *History* and *Other.* Tell partners to begin sorting the Word Cards. If a word does not relate to history, have them place it in the *Other* column.

- Emphasize to students that there are no right or wrong answers to how the words should be sorted, but they should be able to explain their thinking and decisions.

- Have each student write the completed sort in his or her Word Study Notebook. Ask students to share which words they placed in each category.

DAY 4 Open Sort

Students will sort words independently according to categories of their choice and compare sorts with a partner's.

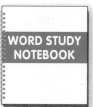

- Have students get out this week's Word Cards. Tell them to read the words and think about their similarities and differences.

- Explain that today students will sort words into categories that they select. Allow time for students to think about this week's words and how to organize their sort. Then have them write their chosen column headings in their Word Study Notebooks.

- Have students sort the Word Cards independently. After all the words have been sorted, have students read the words in each column aloud to make sure they were sorted correctly. Then have students write their sorts.

- Have partners compare their completed sorts and tell whether they sorted the words based on meaning or word features. Have them discuss the reasoning behind each word's placement.

- If time allows, challenge students to sort according to their partner's categories.

DAY 5 Assess

Tell students to listen carefully. Say each boldfaced word, read the sentence, and repeat the word. Have students write the word.

1. Our **library** has many books.
2. I could eat **another** taco.
3. Mom is a nurse at a **hospital**.
4. Here is an **example**.
5. Will Paul **deliver** the pizza?
6. That map is part of our **history**.
7. I thought I won; **however**, you did.
8. I took lessons for **several** years.
9. Our **vacation** was fun.
10. It's **important** to read.
11. My team celebrated our **victory**.
12. Can you **imagine** the future?
13. I took pictures with my **camera**.
14. Sam ate a baked **potato**.
15. I don't **remember** her name.
16. They went **together**.
17. I have no **memory** of that.
18. Blue is my **favorite** color.
19. We'll **continue** our talk later.
20. He is **president** of the group.

RETEACH **IF** students misspell four or more words, **THEN** revisit the activity on Day 2 and reassess.

Words with Silent Consonants

SPELLING LIST

1.	half	11.	wrinkle
2.	comb	12.	listen
3.	mortgage	13.	fetch
4.	honor	14.	yolk
5.	fasten	15.	climb
6.	kneel	16.	honest
7.	wreath	17.	knuckle
8.	calm	18.	plumber
9.	answer	19.	limb
10.	handsome	20.	folktale

 Reproducible Word Cards are available at www.thinkcentral.com.

DIFFERENTIATE INSTRUCTION

Struggling	Advanced
1. below	1. human
2. about	2. exact
3. belong	3. award
4. around	4. behave
5. again	5. credit
6. alone	6. basic
7. because	7. vivid
8. above	8. evil
9. between	9. modern
10. alive	10. nation
11. behind	11. robot
12. begin	12. panic
13. along	13. select
14. before	14. cousin
Grade 3, Lesson 30	15. item
	16. police
	17. prefer
	18. menu
	19. novel
	20. deserve
	Grade 5, Lesson 12

ELL SUPPORT

Access Prior Knowledge Tell students that English is not the only language with silent letters. Silent letters can often be explained by a word's origin or history. Ask students to share words with silent letters from their native languages.

DAY 1 PHONICS Model the Sort

Students will sort words with you based on the silent consonant in each word.

- Display the Lesson 29 Word Cards. Read each word aloud, and discuss the meanings of the words, as necessary.
- Ask students what they notice about the words. *(They all have silent letters.)* Explain that you will sort the words by their silent consonants.
- Display the following Word Cards as column headings: *climb, knuckle, honest, wrinkle.* Read each word aloud, and lead students to recognize the silent consonant in each word. Suggested language: *Climb.* **I can hear almost every letter in** *climb.* **/k/-/l/-/ī/-/m/. Which letter is not pronounced?** *(the consonant b)* Repeat for the remaining column headings. *(silent k, h, and w)*
- Then display and read aloud the Word Card *honor,* and model sorting the word based on its silent letter. Suggested language: *Honor.* **What is the silent letter in** *honor?* *(the consonant h)* **Let's place** *honor* **under** *honest,* **since both words have the same silent consonant.**
- Sort a few more words to establish the categories. Place words with silent letters other than *b, k, h,* and *w* in a fifth category called *Oddballs.* Then ask students to help you sort the remaining Word Cards.
- After sorting, guide students to read aloud the words in each column and recognize the spelling patterns: /m/ spelled *mb,* /n/ spelled *kn,* /ô/ spelled *ho,* and /r/ spelled *wr.* When discussing the *Oddballs* category, explain that some silent consonants form predictable patterns, but the silent letters in this category will need to be memorized.
- Give each student a set of Lesson 29 Word Cards, and have them repeat the sort independently.

DAY 2 Repeat the Sort

Students will repeat the sort from Day 1 independently.

- Remind students that this week's words have silent consonants. Since silent consonants are not pronounced, their spelling must be remembered.
- Tell students to create a five-column chart in their Word Study Notebooks. Have them use the following Word Cards as column headings: *comb, kneel, honor, wreath.* Have students create another column heading called *Oddballs.*
- Ask students to identify the silent consonant in each column heading. *(b, k, h, w)* Then have students sort the remaining Word Cards according to the silent consonant in each word. Remind students to read each word aloud before they sort the Word Card.
- After students complete the sort, ask them to reread the words in each column to confirm their placement. Ask students to explain the spelling patterns they notice in the first four columns. *(/m/ spelled mb, /n/ spelled kn, /ô/ spelled ho, /r/ spelled wr)* Then ask students to identify the silent consonants in the *Oddballs* column.
- Have students write their sorts in their Word Study Notebooks and underline the silent letters.

comb	kneel	honor	wreath	Oddballs
plumber	knuckle	honest	wrinkle	half
limb				listen
climb				handsome
				answer

DAY 3 · Blind Writing Sort

Students will sort and write words that a partner says aloud.

WORD STUDY NOTEBOOK

- Have students divide a page in their Word Study Notebooks into five columns.
- Tell students to write the following headings: *limb, knuckle, honest, wrinkle, Oddballs.* Display the corresponding Word Cards so that students may check their spellings.
- Tell students that they will sort words based on the silent consonant in each word. Have students circle or highlight the silent consonant in each column heading.
- Pair students and have one student read a Word Card aloud without showing the word. Have the partner write the word under the correct column heading.
- Then have the first student reveal the Word Card so that the partner may confirm or correct the word's spelling.
- After all the words have been written correctly, have students read aloud the words in each column and confirm their sorts. Ask students to circle or highlight the silent letter in each word.
- Have partners shuffle the Word Cards and switch roles.

DAY 4 · Guess My Category

Students will guess the category of words that you sort by number of syllables.

WORD STUDY NOTEBOOK

- Tell students that you will sort the words, and they will try to figure out the categories. Remind students not to reveal the categories until the sort is finished.
- Place the following Word Cards as column headings and read them aloud: *half, answer.* Then begin sorting the Word Cards by the number of syllables in each word.
- Select the Word Card *knuckle,* read it aloud, and place it under *answer.* Next, sort *climb* under *half* and *mortgage* under *answer.* Ask students to help you sort the words once they recognize the categories.
- When the sort is complete, have students read aloud the words in each column.
- Ask students what the words in each column have in common. *(The words in the first column have one syllable. The words in the second column have two syllables.)*
- Have students write the sort in their Word Study Notebooks.
- Extend the activity by asking students to shuffle the cards and repeat the sort independently.

DAY 5 · Assess

Tell students to listen carefully. Say each boldfaced word, read the sentence, and repeat the word. Have students write the word.

1. Here is **half** of an apple.
2. I should **comb** my hair.
3. Dad pays the **mortgage.**
4. The town will **honor** its veterans.
5. Please **fasten** your coat.
6. I **kneel** to scrub the floor.
7. My mom made a **wreath.**
8. I felt **calm** before the recital.
9. Ask for the **answer.**
10. He looks **handsome.**
11. She ironed the **wrinkle** in her skirt.
12. Bo likes to **listen** to music.
13. My dog will **fetch** the ball.
14. Kim never eats the egg's **yolk.**
15. Let's **climb** the hill.
16. It is not always easy to be **honest.**
17. I scraped my **knuckle.**
18. The **plumber** is coming tomorrow.
19. The cat sat on the tree **limb.**
20. I read an old African **folktale.**

RETEACH **IF** students misspell four or more words, **THEN** revisit the activity on Day 2 and reassess.

Unusual Spellings

SPELLING LIST

1. meant	11. disguise
2. routine	12. sweat
3. style	13. magazine
4. flood	14. guard
5. month	15. receive
6. pleasant	16. wonder
7. guess	17. league
8. women	18. type
9. either	19. ceiling
10. against	20. money

 Reproducible Word Cards are available at **www.thinkcentral.com**.

DIFFERENTIATE INSTRUCTION

Struggling	Advanced
1. wait	1. conflict
2. weight	2. orphan
3. heard	3. instant
4. herd	4. complex
5. days	5. simply
6. daze	6. burglar
7. heel	7. laundry
8. heal	8. laughter
9. peak	9. employ
10. peek	10. anchor
11. sent	11. merchant
12. cent	12. improve
13. scent	13. arctic
14. feet	14. mischief
15. feat	15. childhood
16. vain	16. purchase
17. vane	17. dolphin
18. vein	18. partner
19. miner	19. complain
20. minor	20. tremble
Grade 4, Lesson 5	Grade 5, Lesson 13

ELL SUPPORT

Support Word Meaning Show or draw pictures of the nouns and act out the verbs and adjectives in this week's word list. Then provide time for students to create their own images and demonstrations.

DAY 1 PHONICS Model the Sort

Students will sort words with you based on the number of syllables in each word.

- Display the Lesson 30 Word Cards, and read each word aloud. Discuss the meanings of the words, as needed.
- Tell students that you are going to sort the words by the number of syllables you hear. Display the Word Cards *meant, routine,* and *magazine.* Read the words aloud, and then read them again, emphasizing the number of syllables.
- Begin sorting the remaining Word Cards by the number of syllables in each word, and model your thinking. Suggested language: *Disguise.* **How many syllables are in** *disguise? Dis-guise.* **I hear two syllables.** *Rou-tine. Routine* **also has two syllables, so I will place** *disguise* **under** *routine.*
- Adapt the suggested language to sort a few more words. Once the categories are established, ask students to determine the number of syllables in each word and help you sort the remaining Word Cards.
- After completing the sort, have students read the words in each column to confirm that the words were sorted correctly. Tell students that this week's words have unusual spelling patterns.
- Challenge students to identify the unusual spelling patterns shared by some of the words, such as /ĕ/ spelled *ea* (meant, pleasant, sweat), /g/ spelled *gu* (guess, guard, disguise, league), /ī/ spelled *y* (type, style), /ŭ/ spelled *o* or *oo* (month, wonder, money, flood), and /ēn/ spelled *ine* (routine, magazine).
- Explain that noticing these unusual spelling patterns will help students remember how to spell the words.
- Give each student a set of Lesson 30 Word Cards, and have them repeat the sort independently.

DAY 2 Repeat the Sort

Students will repeat the sort from Day 1.

- Remind students that the words they are sorting this week have unusual spelling patterns that must be remembered.
- Have students create a three-column chart in their Word Study Notebooks and use the following Word Cards as column headings: *guard, either, magazine.*
- Tell students that they will sort the remaining Word Cards according to the number of syllables in each word. Remind students to read each word aloud and count the number of syllables before sorting it into a category.
- After students complete the sort, have them reread the words in each column to confirm that they sorted the words correctly. Then have them write their sorts in their Word Study Notebooks.

guard	either	magazine
flood	receive	
type	women	
league	wonder	
	pleasant	

DAY 3 Speed Sort

Students will sort words as quickly as they can.

- Tell students that they will sort words by their number of syllables while a partner times them.
- Pair students and ask them to read their Word Cards aloud, paying attention to the number of syllables in each word.
- Then have one student sort the words into one-, two-, and three-syllable categories while the other student uses a stopwatch or a clock with a second hand to time the sort.
- After each sort is completed, have students read the words in each category to check their sort. Then have them shuffle the Word Cards and switch roles. Tell students to keep track of their times in their Word Study Notebooks and to try to beat their own best time.
- Have students write their last sort in their Word Study Notebooks.
- Ask partners to discuss the unusual spelling patterns they notice in this week's words.

DAY 4 Blind Writing Sort

Students will sort and write words that a partner says aloud.

- Have students divide a page in their Word Study Notebooks into three columns. Have them label the columns *1 Syllable*, *2 Syllables*, and *3 Syllables*.
- Tell students that they will sort the spelling words into categories based on the number of syllables in each word.
- Have one partner read a Word Card aloud and the other partner write the word in the correct column.
- Have the first partner show the Word Card so the writer can correct any spelling mistakes. Have the writer circle the corrected word.
- When all the words have been written, have partners read aloud the words in each category and check that the words were sorted correctly. Then have students shuffle the Word Cards and switch roles.
- Extend the activity by asking partners to revisit their circled words and discuss ways to remember the correct spelling.

DAY 5 Assess

Tell students to listen carefully. Say each boldfaced word, read the sentence, and repeat the word. Have students write the word.

1. I knew what the code **meant**.
2. Exercise is in my daily **routine**.
3. She is dressed in a new **style**.
4. The storm may **flood** the land.
5. My birthday **month** is May.
6. The salesperson was **pleasant**.
7. Can you **guess** the riddle?
8. Many **women** are mothers.
9. I like **either** blue or purple.
10. The bed is **against** the wall.
11. The mask is a **disguise**.
12. I started to **sweat** as I ran.
13. I read the **magazine** article.
14. My dog is a **guard** dog.
15. She will **receive** an award.
16. I **wonder** how big a star is.
17. I joined a bowling **league**.
18. Jake likes any **type** of sport.
19. We painted the **ceiling**.
20. How much **money** do I owe you?

RETEACH **IF** students misspell four or more words, **THEN** revisit the activity on Day 1 and reassess.

Vocabulary

TARGET VOCABULARY

1. **comfort** When you *comfort* a person, you help that person to feel less bad.

2. **mention** To *mention* something is to speak about it.

3. **mood** A person's *mood* is the way that person is feeling.

4. **properly** When you do something *properly*, you do it the right way.

5. **intends** A person who *intends* to do a task plans to do that task in the future.

6. **consisted** Something that *consisted* of different parts was made up of those parts.

7. **positive** When people are *positive* that they know something, they are completely sure.

8. **advanced** Someone who has *advanced* skills in something is very good at it.

9. **peculiar** Something odd or unusual is *peculiar*.

10. **talent** A *talent* is a special skill.

 Reproducible Word Cards and Graphic Organizer 15 (Web) are available at **www.thinkcentral.com**.

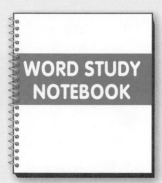

DAY 1 Introduce Target Vocabulary; Suffix -*ly*

After learning the week's Target Vocabulary words, students will explore words that end with the suffix -*ly*.

- Write the Target Vocabulary words on the board, read them aloud, and have students repeat the words. Discuss the student-friendly definitions, shown at left, with students.

- Tell students that a suffix is a word part added to the end of a base word to form a new word and that knowing common suffixes will help them understand the meanings of new words.

- Draw attention to the word *properly*. Point out that *proper* is the base word, and -*ly* is the suffix. Explain to students that adding -*ly* to the end of a base word changes the base word's meaning. Suggested language: **The suffix -*ly* often means "in a way that is."** When -*ly* is added to the base word *proper*, the word *properly* is formed. *Properly* means "in a way that is proper, or right."

- Write these sentences on the board: **Spring is the *proper* time to plant flowers.** (adjective) **The flowers were planted *properly*.** (adverb) Read the sentences, and discuss how the meaning of *proper* changed when the suffix -*ly* was added. Then point out that the part of speech changed from adjective to adverb.

- Have students work with a partner to add the suffix -*ly* to the base words shown below. Circulate to help students spell the words. Have partners write sentences using the new words in their Word Study Notebooks. Prompt students to discuss the meanings of the words when -*ly* is added.

correct	loud	quick
quiet	easy	careful

DAY 2 "Because" Sentences

Students will demonstrate their understanding of Target Vocabulary words by completing sentences.

- Write the Target Vocabulary words on the board, and read them aloud.

- Explain that you will read the beginning of a sentence that uses a Target Vocabulary word. Students will listen carefully and raise their hands to complete the sentence after you say *because*.

- As time allows, ask two or more students to provide answers to each item to demonstrate a variety of possible responses.

 1. **My brother was *positive* that he lost his ring because…**
 2. **Kamico's best friend was in a good *mood* because…**
 3. **Jason tried to *comfort* Sara because…**
 4. **He *intends* to return his new shoes because…**
 5. **Kate's basketball skills were *advanced* because…**
 6. **The noise was very *peculiar* because…**
 7. **Please do not *mention* the bad news because…**
 8. **I wasn't sure what the cake *consisted* of because…**
 9. **She wants to learn to speak French *properly* because…**
 10. **He believes he should develop his singing *talent* because…**

DAY 3 Endings *-ed, -s*

Students will explore words that end with *-ed* and *-s*.

- Explain to students that adding the endings *-ed* and *-s* to base words that are verbs, or words that describe actions, helps to tell when the action happens.

- Write the following sentence on the board, and read it aloud: **The play *consisted* of three acts and six scenes.** Point out that the base word of *consisted* is *consist.* Then say: **The *-ed* ending in *consisted* tells me that the action happened in the past.**

- Modify the suggested language as you explain the ending *-s*, using the following sentence: **She *intends* to clean up her room soon.** Then say: **The *-s* ending in *intends* tells me that the action is happening now.**

- Write the following verbs on the board: *practice, gather, promise, believe, order.* Tell students to open their Word Study Notebooks and write the words.

- Have students add the endings *-ed* and *-s* to each base word and write sentences using the words. Then have them share their sentences with a partner and discuss any differences in meaning that result from adding *-ed* and *-s* to the base words.

DAY 4 Write About Literature

Students will write about a favorite author or book and include Target Vocabulary words.

- Have students take out their Lesson 1 Word Cards and read them aloud. Briefly review each Target Vocabulary word's student-friendly definition. Then explain that today students will write about a favorite author or book using these words.

- Prompt students to discuss this week's reading selection, "Because of Winn-Dixie." Have them discuss what the story *consisted* of; the *positive* aspects of the book; and the *mood,* or emotions, students experienced while reading the story. Have students talk about why it takes *talent* to write interesting stories.

- Then have students write a short paragraph about their favorite book or author in their Word Study Notebooks. Tell them to include at least four Target Vocabulary words in their writing.

- When students finish writing, have them read their paragraph to a partner. Ask partners to listen carefully to determine whether the Target Vocabulary words were used correctly.

DAY 5 Vocabulary Web

Students will complete Vocabulary Webs to illustrate their understanding of Target Vocabulary words.

- Display a Vocabulary Web, as pictured at right. Write the word *comfort* in the center oval. Explain that students will work with you to complete a web about this word.

- Label the remaining ovals *Definition, Synonym, Example,* and *Sentence.* Then model filling in the ovals around the word *comfort.* Synonyms for *comfort* might include *warmth* or *happiness.* Examples may include *food* and *friends.* Have a volunteer use *comfort* in a sentence. Record the response.

- After completing the web with students, write the Target Vocabulary words *peculiar* and *talent* on the board. Have students draw and complete a Vocabulary Web for each word in their Word Study Notebooks.

- When students have finished, have partners compare their Vocabulary Webs and discuss how they are similar and different.

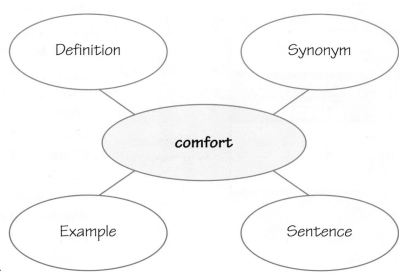

Vocabulary

TARGET VOCABULARY

1. **injustice** Something that is unfair is an *injustice.*

2. **numerous** If a person has *numerous* sheets of paper, he or she has many of them.

3. **segregation** A system called *segregation* kept African Americans and white Americans apart.

4. **nourishing** Something that is *nourishing* gives people what they need to grow and live.

5. **captured** If a person is caught while trying to get away, he or she has been *captured.*

6. **dream** A *dream* is something you want to happen very much.

7. **encounters** *Encounters* are meetings with people.

8. **preferred** If you *preferred* something, you liked it better than something else.

9. **recall** To *recall* something is to remember it.

10. **example** An *example* shows how to do something.

 Reproducible Word Cards and Graphic Organizer 12 (T-Map) are available at **www.thinkcentral.com**.

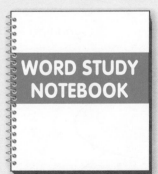

DAY 1 Introduce Target Vocabulary; Prefix *in-*

After learning the week's Target Vocabulary words, students will explore words that begin with the prefix *in-*.

- Write the Target Vocabulary words on the board, read them aloud, and have students repeat the words. Discuss the student-friendly definitions, shown at left, with students.

- Tell students that a prefix is a word part added to the beginning of a word that changes the word's meaning. Write the prefix *in-* on the board, and explain that it means "not."

- Write the word *justice* on the board, and explain the meaning. *(fairness)* Then add the prefix *in-* to the beginning of the word to make *injustice.* Suggested language: **The new word is *injustice.* The meaning changes from "something that is fair" to "something that is not fair."**

- Write these words on the board: *active, correct, complete, expensive, appropriate.* Have students copy the words into their Word Study Notebooks.

- Discuss each word's meaning. Then ask students to add the prefix *in-* before each word to change the word's meaning. Have them write the new words in their Word Study Notebooks.

- Have student pairs take turns reading the words and explaining how the meanings changed when the prefix *in-* was added. Have students write the new meaning next to each word.

- When students finish, have partners work together to record more words that begin with the prefix *in-* in their Word Study Notebooks.

DAY 2 Word Associations

Students will identify a Target Vocabulary word that they associate with related words and phrases.

- Distribute the Lesson 2 Word Cards, and have students display them on their desks.

- Explain that you will read several questions, and students should hold up the Word Cards that best answer the questions.

- As students hold up their Word Cards, share the answers provided and have students explain their reasoning.

  1. **Which word goes with *unfair, wrong*?** *(injustice, segregation)*
  2. **Which word goes with *show, sample*?** *(example)*
  3. **Which word goes with *caught, taken*?** *(captured)*
  4. **Which word goes with *many, abundant*?** *(numerous)*
  5. **Which word goes with *vision, goal*?** *(dream)*
  6. **Which word goes with *remember, memory*?** *(recall)*
  7. **Which word goes with *apart, groups*?** *(segregation)*
  8. **Which word goes with *meetings, visits*?** *(encounters)*
  9. **Which word goes with *healthy, growing*?** *(nourishing)*
  10. **Which word goes with *liked, favored*?** *(preferred)*

DAY 3 Prefix *re-*

Students will explore words that begin with the prefix *re-*.

- Remind students that a prefix is a word part added to the beginning of a word that changes the word's meaning. Remind students that knowing the meanings of common prefixes will help them determine the meanings of new words.

- Write *recall* on the board, and underline the prefix *re-*. Then explain the meaning of *re-*. Suggested language: **The prefix *re-* means "again." *Recall* means "to remember again."**

- Tell students that *re-* can be added to the beginning of many verbs. Write these word equations on the board:

$$re + dial = \underline{\hspace{2cm}}$$

$$re + count = \underline{\hspace{2cm}}$$

$$re + trace = \underline{\hspace{2cm}}$$

- Have volunteers combine the word parts and explain the meanings of the new words. Then have students copy the words and write the meanings in their Word Study Notebooks.

- Have students complete other word equations with *re-*, write the new meaning of each word, and share their words with a partner.

DAY 4 Glossary Snapshots

Students will create glossary entries for the Target Vocabulary words.

- Have students take out their Student Books and turn to the glossary in the back. Point out that all the words in a glossary appear in alphabetical order and each glossary entry is followed by a definition.

- Explain to students that they will create their own glossary entries for the Target Vocabulary words. Give each student ten index cards. Tell students they will use the index cards to create their glossary entries.

- Have students use one card for each entry. Have them write the word at the top of the card followed by its definition. Then have them turn the card over and provide an example sentence and a picture to support the meaning of the word.

- When students finish creating their glossary entries, tell them to put the word cards in alphabetical order.

- Have students share their glossary entries with a partner. Then have them compare their own glossary entries to those in the Student Book for the same Target Vocabulary words.

DAY 5 Antonyms

Students will use their knowledge of the Target Vocabulary words to determine their antonyms.

- Display a T-Map. Tell students that they will work with you to complete this map by listing Target Vocabulary words and their antonyms.

- Write the headings *Word* and *Antonym* at the top of the T-Map. Tell students that antonyms are words that have opposite meanings. Discuss a common antonym pair such as *young* and *old*.

- Write *recall* under the heading *Word*. Guide students to name an antonym for *recall*. Suggested language: **If I *recall* something, I remember it. If I *forget* something, I am unable to recall or remember it. *Recall* and *forget* are opposites. I will write *forget* under *Antonym*.**

- Have students copy the T-Map into their Word Study Notebooks. Tell them to write the column headings and the example you provided. Then tell students to write *numerous, captured,* and *nourishing* in the left column.

- Have students complete the T-Map by writing an antonym for each Target Vocabulary word in the right column, using a dictionary or thesaurus as necessary. Have student pairs discuss their completed T-Maps.

Word	Antonym
recall	forget
numerous	few
captured	freed
nourishing	unhealthy

TARGET VOCABULARY

1. **isolated** A place is *isolated* when it is separated or far from other places.

2. **virtual** Something that is *virtual* on a computer can be created, used, or read on a computer.

3. **access** When you have *access* to something, you have the ability or permission to use that thing.

4. **devour** People who *devour* books love to read and cannot easily stop reading a good book.

5. **impassable** Something that is *impassable* is impossible to get through or over because it is blocked.

6. **remote** A place that is *remote* is far from other places.

7. **obtain** *Obtain* means to get something as a result of work or planning.

8. **preserve** People who want to *preserve* their culture or past can keep it through clothing, language, music, and food.

9. **extremes** Two things that are at *extremes* are very different from or opposites of each other.

10. **avid** *Avid* means very interested in and eager about something.

 Reproducible Word Cards and Graphic Organizer 6 (Four-Square Map) are available at **www.thinkcentral.com**.

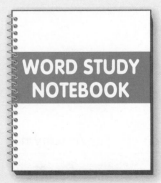

WORD STUDY NOTEBOOK

DAY 1 **Introduce Target Vocabulary; Prefix *im-***

After learning the week's Target Vocabulary words, students will explore words that begin with the prefix *im-*.

- Write the Target Vocabulary words on the board, read them aloud, and have students repeat the words. Discuss the student-friendly definitions, shown at left, with students.

- Remind students that a prefix is a word part added to the beginning of a word that changes the word's meaning. Then write the prefix *im-* on the board, and explain that it means "not" or "the opposite of."

- Rewrite the word *impassable* on the board. Underline the base word *pass*. Suggested language: **The base word *pass* is combined with the suffix *-able* to form the word *passable*,** meaning "able to be passed."

- Next, circle the prefix *im-*. Then ask: **When the prefix *im-* is added to the word *passable*, what might the new word, *impassable*, mean?** *(not able to be passed; not passable)*

- Next, write these words on the board for students to copy into their Word Study Notebooks: *polite, possible, personal*. Have students add the prefix *im-* to the beginning of each word. Then guide students to discuss the meaning of each new word after *im-* is added.

- Have students write a sentence for *impolite, impossible,* and *impersonal* in their Word Study Notebooks. Then invite volunteers to share their sentences with the class.

DAY 2 **Riddles**

Students will use their knowledge of word meanings to answer riddles about the Target Vocabulary words.

- Distribute copies of the Lesson 3 Word Cards.

- Tell students that you will read aloud a riddle that tells about a word. Tell them to listen carefully and choose the word that best answers the riddle.

- After you read a riddle, have students use their Word Cards to help them determine the answer and then record it in their Word Study Notebooks. Then review the answers together.

  1. **If you have this, come on in!** *(access)*
  2. **I really enjoy something. What kind of interest do I have?** *(avid)*
  3. **If you don't do this, things that are important to you might be lost.** *(preserve)*
  4. **I am all by myself. What am I?** *(isolated)*
  5. **I live far, far away. What am I?** *(remote)*
  6. **If you do this to books, you have a huge hunger for reading.** *(devour)*
  7. **You can see me on a computer, but you can't hold me. What am I?** *(virtual)*
  8. **There's no getting around this.** *(impassable)*
  9. **One is enormous. One is tiny. What are they?** *(extremes)*
  10. **If you want to do this, you'll likely have to work and plan.** *(obtain)*

DAY 3 Suffix -ly

Students will explore words that end with the suffix -ly.

- Remind students that a suffix is a word part added to the end of a base word to form a new word.

- Write the Target Vocabulary word *remote* on the board and review its meaning. Point out that *remote* is an adjective, a word used to describe a noun, as in this sentence: *They live in a remote village, high in the mountains.*

- Then add the suffix -ly to form *remotely.* Suggested language: **The suffix -ly can mean "in a way that is." When -ly is added to an adjective, it changes the adjective to an adverb.** Demonstrate using this sentence: *We communicate remotely using computers.*

- Then write the following Target Vocabulary words on the board: *extreme, virtual, avid.* Tell students to copy the words and add the suffix -ly to each word.

- Together, discuss how the meaning of each base word changes when the suffix -ly is added.

- Have students write a sentence using each new word. Then have volunteers share and discuss their work.

DAY 4 Write a Response

Students will write a response that includes Target Vocabulary words.

- Have students take out the Lesson 3 Word Cards and read them aloud. Briefly review each Target Vocabulary word's student-friendly definition. Then explain that today students will use these words in their writing.

- Guide students to think about this week's reading, "My Librarian Is a Camel." Discuss the creative ways in which books are shared.

- Tell students to imagine other ways books could be shared with others and provide the prompt for writing. Suggested language: **Write a response describing another way people in *remote* or *isolated* areas could gain *access* to books. Your ideas can be realistic or fanciful.**

- Have students shuffle their Word Cards and place them face down on their desks. Tell them to select four Word Cards randomly and use them to write their responses.

- Have students write their responses in their Word Study Notebooks. When students complete their writing, have them confirm with a partner that the vocabulary words were used correctly.

DAY 5 Four-Square Map

Students will complete Four-Square Maps to demonstrate their understanding of Target Vocabulary words.

- Display a Four-Square Map as shown at right. Students will work with you to complete the map for the Target Vocabulary word *devour.*

- Write *devour* in the center of the Four-Square Map. Have students explain what the word means. Write their response or the student-friendly definition in the upper-left corner. *(to consume something, like a book, quickly and eagerly)*

- Have students give examples of types of books students might devour. *(comic books, mysteries)* Write one of the examples in the upper-right corner. Then call on a volunteer to use the word *devour* in a sentence. Record the student's response in the lower-left corner. *(Shelley will devour any type of comic book.)*

- Then ask students to name some words or phrases that are the opposite of *devour,* such as *avoid, ignore, can't be bothered with.* Record one word or phrase as a non-example in the lower-right corner.

- When the class sample is complete, have students create Four-Square Maps for the Target Vocabulary words *preserve* and *isolated* in their Word Study Notebooks.

- Have students complete their Four-Square Maps independently. Then have them share and discuss their maps with a partner.

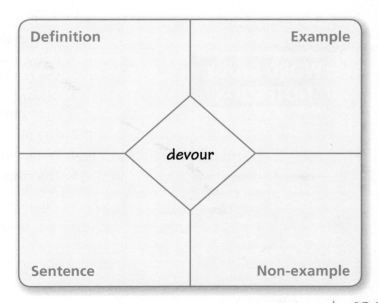

TARGET VOCABULARY

1. **assist** To *assist* someone is to help that person.

2. **burglaries** People who commit *burglaries* break into buildings and steal things.

3. **innocent** A person who is *innocent* has done nothing wrong.

4. **scheme** A *scheme* is a detailed plan to get something done.

5. **regretfully** If people say something *regretfully*, they say it in a way that shows they are sorry.

6. **misjudged** If a person has *misjudged* something, the person has formed an incorrect idea about it.

7. **suspect** A *suspect* is a person who people think might be guilty of a crime.

8. **favor** A *favor* is an act of kindness that someone does, even though he or she does not have to.

9. **speculated** If a person *speculated* about a situation, he or she made guesses about it.

10. **prior** An event that takes place *prior* to another event takes place before it.

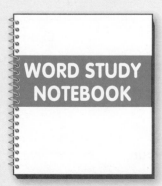 Reproducible Word Cards are available at **www.thinkcentral.com**.

WORD STUDY NOTEBOOK

DAY 1 Introduce Target Vocabulary; Prefix *mis-*

After learning the week's Target Vocabulary words, students will explore words that have the prefix *mis-*.

- Write the Target Vocabulary words on the board, read them aloud, and have students repeat the words. Discuss the student-friendly definitions, shown at left, with students.

- Review with students that a prefix is a word part that is added to the beginning of a base word to form a new word.

- Remind students that recognizing prefixes and knowing their meanings will help them understand new words. Rewrite *misjudged* and underline *mis-*. Suggested language: **The word part *mis-* is a prefix. *Judged* is the base word. The prefix *mis-* means "wrongly or badly." So, the word *misjudged* means "judged wrongly."**

- Write the following words on the board: *treat, read, understood, lead, spell, pronounce*. Have students add the prefix *mis-* to each base word and explain the meanings of the new words using their understanding of the prefix.

- Then have students write the following questions in their Word Study Notebooks: *What are some things that are easy to misplace? What are some ways that a toddler might misbehave?* Have students circle the word with the prefix *mis-* in each question. Then have them answer each question and share their answers with the class. Reinforce the meaning of *mis-* as students give their answers.

DAY 2 Rate Experiences

Students will use what they know about the Target Vocabulary words to rate experiences along a Word Line.

- Display a Word Line like the one shown below. Point out the words *Negative, Neutral,* and *Positive*. Explain the meanings of the words as needed.

- Tell students that you will read several sentences that use the Target Vocabulary words. Students should think about whether each experience you read about is positive, negative, or neutral.

- After you read aloud each sentence, have a student point to a place on the Word Line that shows how the sentence makes him or her feel and explain why.

- Ask other students whether they agree with the placement. Repeat for each word.
  1. Abby missed out on a friendship with Carlos because she *misjudged* him before she really got to know him.
  2. Oliver looked *regretfully* at his teammates after he missed a catch to win the championship game.
  3. She put on her hat *prior* to putting on her coat.
  4. Emma will *assist* her neighbor by doing a favor for him.
  5. The *suspect* says he was never at the scene of the crime.

Negative   Neutral   Positive

DAY 3 Root *spec/spect*

Students will use the root *spec/spect* to determine the meanings of new words.

- Tell students that a root is a word part that has meaning but cannot stand alone. Explain that knowing the meanings of common roots will help them understand the meanings of many words.

- Write the root *spec/spect* and the Target Vocabulary word *speculated* on the board. Underline the root *spec*, and explain its meaning. Suggested language: **The root *spec* or *spect* means "to see or observe."**

- Guide students to use the meaning of *spec* to understand that *speculated* means "to see ahead by guessing what might happen."

- Write these other words that have the root *spect* on the board: *inspect, spectacles, spectator, spectrum.*

- Ask student pairs to tell what they think each word means, based on the meaning of the root, and then confirm it in a dictionary.

- Have students write the words and their meanings in their Word Study Notebooks.

DAY 4 Word Pairs

Students will write sentences using Target Vocabulary words.

- Distribute copies of the Lesson 4 Word Cards.

- Have students place the Word Cards face down on their desks. Tell them to select two cards and turn them over.

- Ask students to write a sentence in their Word Study Notebooks that uses the words they have chosen. Then have them put the cards aside.

- Tell students that they may use different forms of the words as needed so their sentences make sense.

- Have students repeat until they have used all the Target Vocabulary words in sentences. Ask partners to confirm that the sentences use the words correctly.

> **burglaries**   **speculated**
>
> Police speculated that they would find who was responsible for the burglaries by viewing footage from the store's video camera.

DAY 5 Word Associations

Students will identify a Target Vocabulary word that they associate with related words and phrases.

- Have students lay out the Lesson 4 Word Cards on their desks.

- Tell students that you will read questions, and they should hold up the Word Card that best answers each question.

- As students hold up their Word Cards, discuss the different answers provided and have students explain their reasoning for answering as they did.

    1. Which word goes with *robberies, thefts?* (burglaries, suspect)

    2. Which word goes with *plan, idea?* (scheme)

    3. Which word goes with *wondered, guessed?* (speculated)

    4. Which word goes with *remorsefully, sorrowfully?* (regretfully)

    5. Which word goes with *first, before?* (prior)

    6. Which word goes with *help, lend a hand?* (assist, favor)

    7. Which word goes with *accused, assumed guilty?* (suspect)

    8. Which word goes with *misunderstood, misinformed?* (misjudged, innocent)

    9. Which word goes with *kindness, a friendly act?* (favor, assist)

    10. Which word goes with *not guilty, blameless?* (innocent, misjudged)

TARGET VOCABULARY

1. **seafaring** *Seafaring* means working or traveling at sea.

2. **tidal** Something that is *tidal* is affected by the tides, or the regular rise and fall of the sea level.

3. **foaming** A liquid that is *foaming* makes a layer of foam, or small bubbles.

4. **outcast** Someone who is not accepted by a group may feel like an *outcast*.

5. **yearning** A *yearning* is a strong desire for something.

6. **memorable** Something that is *memorable* is so special that it is worth remembering.

7. **betrayed** If you have *betrayed* someone, you have done something to disappoint or let that person down.

8. **condition** If a person is in poor *condition*, he or she may be sick or out of shape. If a building is in poor *condition*, it may need repairs.

9. **shortage** If there is not enough of something, there is a *shortage* of it.

10. **horrified** Someone who is *horrified* feels shock, terror, or fear because of something unpleasant.

 Reproducible Word Cards and Graphic Organizer 1 (Column Chart) are available at **www.thinkcentral.com**.

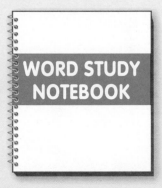
WORD STUDY NOTEBOOK

DAY 1 **Introduce Target Vocabulary; Suffix *-able***

After learning the week's Target Vocabulary words, students will explore words that have the suffix *-able*.

- Write the Target Vocabulary words on the board, read them aloud, and have students repeat the words. Discuss the student-friendly definitions, shown at left, with students.

- Rewrite the word *memorable*, and underline *-able*. Point out that *-able* is a suffix added to the base word *memory*.

- Remind students that a suffix is a word part that goes at the end of a base word to form a new word with a different meaning, using *memorable* as an example. Suggested language: **The suffix *-able* means "able to be" or "inclined to be." When *-able* is added to the base word *memory*, the word *memorable* is formed.** *Memorable* means "inclined, or likely, to be remembered."

- Explain to students that *-able* can be added to other words. Write the following words on the board: *achievable, believable, breakable, notable*. Have students identify the base word and meaning of each word ending with *-able*.

- Tell students to work with partners to add the suffix *-able* to the words *adore, flame, do, pleasure,* and *recycle*. Circulate to help students spell the new words. Have them write the words they form and their meanings in their Word Study Notebooks. Then have them share the meanings of the words with the class.

DAY 2 **Rate Experiences**

Students will use what they know about the Target Vocabulary words to rate experiences along a Word Line.

- Display a Word Line like the one below. Explain the meanings of *Negative, Neutral,* and *Positive* as needed.

- Tell students that you will read some sentences that use the Target Vocabulary words. Have students think about whether the person in each sentence has an experience that is negative, neutral, or positive.

- After reading each sentence, ask a volunteer to point to the place on the Word Line that he or she thinks describes the person's experience.

- Ask other students whether they agree with the placement on the line. Have them explain their reasoning. Repeat for each word.

  1. **Marley went on an exciting *seafaring* adventure.**
  2. **Devin watched the *tidal* currents of the ocean.**
  3. **Suzie felt *betrayed* when Max blurted out her secret.**
  4. **Javier worried that there would be a *shortage* of seats at the play.**
  5. **Mrs. Morgan was *horrified* when her wedding ring slipped down the drain.**

  Negative   Neutral   Positive

DAY 3 Prefix *out-*

Students will use the prefix *out-* to determine the meanings of new words.

- Review with students that adding a prefix to the beginning of a base word forms a new word. Help them recall that knowing the meanings of common prefixes will help them determine the meanings of many words.

- Write *outcast* on the board, and underline *out-*. Explain that the prefix *out-* means "away from," and the base word *cast* means "to send off."

- Then explain how to combine the meanings of the word parts. Suggested language: **The prefix *out-* and the base word *cast* form the word *outcast*. An *outcast* is someone who is sent away from a group or place.**

- Write *outdoors, outlaw,* and *outfield* on the board. Ask students to use their knowledge of the prefix *out-* to determine the meanings of the words.

- Have students write sentences in their Word Study Notebooks using the words on the board, as well as other words they can think of with the prefix *out-*. Tell students to share their sentences with a partner.

DAY 4 Write an Ending

Students will write an ending to a Student Book selection and include Target Vocabulary words.

- Have students take out the Lesson 5 Word Cards and read them aloud. Have volunteers explain the meaning of each word.

- Tell students that they will write a new ending to the folktale "Hoderi the Fisherman" from this week's reading. Have them brainstorm with a partner what might have happened to the Sea Princess when she disappeared into the sea.

- Students should use at least three of this week's Target Vocabulary words in their endings. Provide time for them to write in their Word Study Notebooks.

- When they finish, ask students to share their writing with a partner. Have partners identify whether the Target Vocabulary words were used correctly. They might also suggest places where additional Target Vocabulary words could have been used.

DAY 5 Multiple-Meaning Words

Students will complete a Column Chart to demonstrate their understanding of the multiple meanings of Target Vocabulary words.

- Explain to students that some words have more than one meaning. When students read, they can use context clues, or the words and sentences around a word, to determine how the word is being used. They can also use a dictionary to verify the word's meaning.

- Display a Column Chart with the headings *Word, Meaning 1,* and *Meaning 2.* List the words *condition, foaming,* and *yearning* in the *Word* column.

- In the *Meaning 1* column, have students help you write the meaning of *condition* based on the student-friendly definition provided on the previous page. Then model how to find a second meaning using a dictionary. Record the meaning in the chart.

- Have partners complete the Column Chart in their Word Study Notebooks. Extend the activity by having partners write sentences using both meanings of the words to confirm their understanding.

Word	Meaning 1	Meaning 2
condition	the state something or someone is in	something on which another thing depends
foaming	forming small bubbles	to be angry
yearning	feeling strong desire for something	to feel compassion

Vocabulary

1. **alarmed** To be *alarmed* is to be surprised, frightened, or amazed by something.

2. **reacted** *Reacted* means acted or responded to something.

3. **convey** To *convey* means to communicate something or make it known.

4. **daring** A person who is *daring* is fearless, brave, or adventurous.

5. **luminous** *Luminous* means giving off light.

6. **awe** *Awe* is a feeling of mixed fear, respect, and wonder about something.

7. **indescribable** Something that is *indescribable* cannot be described.

8. **extraordinary** *Extraordinary* means unusual, strange, or amazing.

9. **fade** To *fade* means to become less bright, loud, or visible.

10. **conferring** *Conferring* means meeting to discuss and compare information.

 Reproducible Word Cards and Graphic Organizer 1 (Column Chart) are available at **www.thinkcentral.com**.

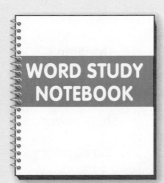

WORD STUDY NOTEBOOK

DAY 1 **Introduce Target Vocabulary; Prefix *extra-***

After learning the week's Target Vocabulary words, students will explore words that begin with the prefix *extra-*.

- Write the Target Vocabulary words on the board, read them aloud, and have students repeat the words. Discuss the student-friendly definitions, shown at left, with students.

- Rewrite the word *extraordinary*, and underline *extra-*. Explain that *extra-* is a prefix added to the word *ordinary*. Remind students that a prefix is a word part added to the beginning of a word to form a new word with a new meaning.

- Explain the meaning of the prefix *extra-* and how it changes the meaning of the word *ordinary*. Suggested language: **The prefix *extra-* can mean "outside" or "beyond." The base word *ordinary* means "common, not special." When the prefix *extra-* is added to *ordinary*, the new word, *extraordinary*, means "beyond ordinary; unusual or amazing."**

- Write these words on the board for students to copy into their Word Study Notebooks: *extrasensory, extraterrestrial, extravagant*.

- Work with students to explore how the prefix *extra-* shapes the meaning of each word. First, help students identify each base word: *sensory*, meaning "related to the senses"; *terrestrial*, meaning "related to land or the planet Earth"; the Latin root *vagari*, meaning "to wander." Then guide students to determine how the prefix *extra-* changes the meaning of each word.

- Have students write a sentence using each new word with *extra-* in their Word Study Notebooks. Then invite volunteers to share their sentences with the class.

- -

DAY 2 **Word Associations**

Students will identify a Target Vocabulary word that they associate with related words and phrases.

- Tell students to display the Lesson 6 Word Cards on their desks.

- Explain that you will read several questions, and that students should hold up the Word Card that best answers each question.

- As students hold up their Word Cards, share the answers provided and have students explain their reasoning.

  1. **Which word goes with *dim* and *grow quieter*?** *(fade)*
  2. **Which word goes with *beyond description* and *cannot explain*?** *(indescribable)*
  3. **Which word goes with *responded* and *acted*?** *(reacted)*
  4. **Which word goes with *glow* and *light*?** *(luminous)*
  5. **Which word goes with *unbelievable* and *amazing*?** *(extraordinary)*
  6. **Which word goes with *scared* and *surprised*?** *(alarmed)*
  7. **Which word goes with *discussing* and *sharing*?** *(conferring, convey)*
  8. **Which word goes with *fear* and *wonder*?** *(awe)*
  9. **Which word goes with *bold* and *courage*?** *(daring)*
  10. **Which word goes with *communicate* and *publicize*?** *(convey, conferring)*

DAY 3 Prefixes *re-, in-*

Students will explore words with the prefixes *re-* and *in-*.

- Review with students that a prefix is a word part added to the beginning of a base word to form a new word. Remind them that knowing the meanings of common prefixes will help them understand the meanings of many words.

- Write *reacted* on the board, and circle the prefix *re-*. Review that *re-* means "again" or "back." Model your thinking as you define *reacted*. Suggested language: ***Reacted* means "showed an action back in response to something else,"** as in *The spectators reacted noisily and angrily to the referee's decision.*

- Follow a similar procedure to define the word *indescribable*. Write *indescribable* on the board, and circle the prefix *in-*. Review that *in-* means "not." Identify the base word, *describe,* and the suffix *-able,* meaning "able to be." Then say: ***Indescribable* means "not able to be described,"** as in *The early pioneers often faced indescribable hardships.*

- Write the following words on the board, and have students copy them into their Word Study Notebooks: *restate, replace, reinvent, incapable, indestructible.* Together, discuss how the prefix *re-* or *in-* helps shape the meaning of each word.

DAY 4 Act Out the Words

Students will work with a partner to take turns acting out and guessing Target Vocabulary words.

- Display the Target Vocabulary words, and read each one aloud. Then briefly review the student-friendly definition for each word.

- Have students work with a partner to play a game similar to charades. Tell students that one partner will act out a Target Vocabulary word, and the other student will guess the word.

- Tell students to place a set of Word Cards face down on their desks. Have one partner choose a Word Card without revealing it to his or her partner, and then perform actions that will help the other student guess the correct Target Vocabulary word.

- Explain that if a word is difficult to act out using only gestures, such as *convey,* students can act as a character and use a short sentence that helps illustrate meaning, such as *I need to tell you something important!* Point out that the sentence should not include the Target Vocabulary word.

- When the correct word has been guessed, partners switch roles. They should continue until all of the Target Vocabulary words have been used.

DAY 5 Guess My Category

Students will guess the categories of Target Vocabulary words that you sort.

- Display a Column Chart. Explain that you will sort words into three columns and that students are to guess the categories, or how you are sorting the words.

- Display the Word Cards *awe, reacted,* and *luminous* as column headings to represent nouns, verbs, and adjectives. Choose the Word Card *conferring,* read it aloud, and place it under *reacted.* Continue sorting all the words without revealing the category types. (Noun: no additional words; Verb: *convey, fade;* Adjective: *alarmed, daring, indescribable, extraordinary*)

- When the sort is complete, have students read the words aloud in each column. Have them share what the words have in common. *(They were sorted by their parts of speech.)* Review that nouns name people, places, and things; verbs tell what people and things do; and adjectives describe people, places, and things.

- Wrap up the sort by writing *Noun, Verb,* and *Adjective* as the new column headings. Have students copy the chart into their Word Study Notebooks.

Noun	Verb	Adjective
awe	reacted	luminous
	conferring	alarmed
	convey	daring
	fade	indescribable
		extraordinary

Vocabulary

1. **entertaining** When something is *entertaining*, it is funny or enjoyable.

2. **promote** To *promote* something is to try to make it popular.

3. **focus** To *focus* on something is to pay attention to that thing.

4. **advertise** Companies *advertise* to inform the public about their products.

5. **jolts** *Jolts* are sudden bursts of energy or excitement.

6. **critics** People who judge artistic creations are *critics*.

7. **target** A *target* is a goal or aim.

8. **thrilling** Something that is *thrilling* is exciting.

9. **angles** *Angles* are the directions from which you see things.

10. **generated** If someone has *generated* something, that person has created or produced it.

 Reproducible Word Cards and Graphic Organizer 12 (T-Map) are available at **www.thinkcentral.com**.

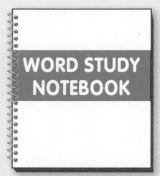

WORD STUDY NOTEBOOK

DAY 1 Introduce Target Vocabulary; Endings -ed, -ing

After learning the week's Target Vocabulary words, students will explore words that end with *-ed* and *-ing*.

- Write the Target Vocabulary words on the board, read them aloud, and have students repeat the words. Discuss the student-friendly definitions, shown at left.

- Explain that adding the ending *-ed* to base words that describe actions helps to tell when the action happens. Then say: **When you want to talk about something that happened in the past, add the ending -ed to a verb.**

- Rewrite the word *generated,* and underline *-ed*. Then say: **The -ed ending tells me the action happened in the past, as in I generated the project last night.**

- Explain that *-ed* can be added to the end of other verbs. Write the Target Vocabulary words *promote, focus,* and *advertise* on the board. Have students add *-ed* and explain how adding the ending *-ed* changes the meaning of the words.

- Focus students' attention on the word *generated*. Erase *-ed* and add *-ing* to make the word *generating*. Explain that the ending *-ing* can also be added to a verb to tell when the action happens. Suggested language: **The -ing ending tells me that the action is happening now, as in I am generating the project now.**

- Rewrite the Target Vocabulary words *promote, focus,* and *advertise* on the board. Have students add *-ing* to each word and explain how the meanings change.

- Have students write *promote, focus,* and *advertise* in their Word Study Notebooks and write sentences using each action word in the past and present tense.

DAY 2 Meaning Sort

Students will use their knowledge of the Target Vocabulary words to complete a T-Map.

- Distribute copies of the Lesson 7 Word Cards, and discuss the meanings of the words. Tell students that today they will help you sort the words into two categories: *words about making a movie, words about watching a movie.*

- Display a T-Map and write the headings *Making a Movie* and *Watching a Movie.* Have students copy the T-Map into their Word Study Notebooks. Have partners begin sorting the words. Explain that there are no right or wrong answers to how they sort the words, but they should be able to explain each word's placement.

- When the sort is complete, have partners share which words they placed in each category. Have them write their sorts in their Word Study Notebooks. Then have students circle any words that can fit into both categories.

Making a Movie	Watching a Movie
advertise	critics
target	entertaining
angles	thrilling
generated	jolts
promote	
focus	

DAY 3 Idea Completion

Students will demonstrate their understanding of Target Vocabulary words by completing sentence frames.

- Review the week's Target Vocabulary words with students.

- Then write the following sentence frames on the board. Students should use the Target Vocabulary word in parentheses to complete the sentences orally.

- Display the Word Card *critics* and model completing the first sentence frame. Then have students complete each sentence orally.

   1. The artwork was judged _____. *(critics)*
   2. Our science class _____. *(generated)*
   3. When I pay attention in class, _____. *(focus)*
   4. The students washing cars _____. *(target)*
   5. The scary movie sent _____. *(jolts)*
   6. The wooden roller coaster _____. *(thrilling)*
   7. The bake sale committee _____. *(advertise)*
   8. From high above I can see _____. *(angles)*
   9. Our school principal likes to _____. *(promote)*
   10. The actors in the play _____. *(entertaining)*

DAY 4 Word Pairs

Students will write sentences using Target Vocabulary words.

- Distribute copies of the Lesson 7 Word Cards, and review the words' meanings. Tell students that they will write sentences using two of the Target Vocabulary words.

- Display the Word Cards *critics* and *entertaining*. Write the example sentence below on the board, and underline *critics* and *entertaining*.

- Have students place their Word Cards face down on their desks. Explain that they will select two Word Cards, turn them over, and use the words to write a sentence in their Word Study Notebooks.

- Students may use different forms of the words as needed to ensure their sentences make sense. Have students continue until all Target Vocabulary words have been used. Have volunteers share their sentences.

| critics | entertaining |

The movie <u>critics</u> thought the new comedy was very <u>entertaining</u>.

DAY 5 Analogies

Students will use their knowledge of Target Vocabulary words to complete analogies.

- Tell students to display the Lesson 7 Word Cards on their desks. Explain that students will help solve analogies, or word puzzles, by analyzing how word pairs are related in the same way. Write the following analogy on the board and read it aloud: **Contests are to *judges* as *movies* are to _____.**

- Guide students to understand the relationship between *contests* and *judges*. Suggested language: **Judges are people who review contests. Who reviews movies?** *(critics)* Write *critics* in the blank. Explain that the word relationships in an analogy are often synonyms or antonyms.

- Tell students that you will read several analogies, and they should hold up the Word Card that best completes each analogy. Discuss each analogy, and have students explain their reasoning.

   1. *Frightening* **is to** *terrifying* **as** *exciting* **is to _____.** *(thrilling)*

   2. *Annoying* **is to** *amusing* **as** *boring* **is to _____.** *(entertaining)*

   3. *Tell* **is to** *recommend* **as** *inform* **is to _____.** *(advertise)*

   4. *Avoid* **is to** *notice* **as** *ignore* **is to _____.** *(focus)*

   5. *Destroyed* **is to** *ruined* **as** *created* **is to _____.** *(generated)*

Vocabulary

TARGET VOCABULARY

1. **glorious** Something that is *glorious* is wonderful.

2. **studio** A *studio* is a workshop for an artist.

3. **model** A *model* version of something is a sample or small version of it.

4. **concerned** To be *concerned* about something is to be worried.

5. **smeared** Something that is blurred or spread around is *smeared*.

6. **ruined** If something is *ruined*, it is destroyed.

7. **yanked** If something is *yanked*, it is pulled hard or jerked.

8. **streak** To *streak* is to move quickly.

9. **schedule** A *schedule* is a planned program of events.

10. **feast** A very large meal is a *feast*.

 Reproducible Word Cards and Graphic Organizer 6 (Four-Square Map) are available at **www.thinkcentral.com**.

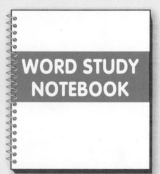

WORD STUDY NOTEBOOK

DAY 1 Introduce Target Vocabulary; Suffix *-ous*

After learning the week's Target Vocabulary words, students will explore words that have the suffix *-ous*.

- Write the Target Vocabulary words on the board, read them aloud, and have students repeat the words. Discuss the student-friendly definitions, shown at left, with students.

- Remind students that a suffix is a word part that goes after a base word to form a new word with a different meaning. Emphasize that knowing the meanings of common suffixes can help students determine the meanings of many words.

- Rewrite the word *glorious* on the board, and underline the suffix *-ous*. Explain that the addition of *-ous* changes the meaning of the base word *glory*. Suggested language: **The suffix *-ous* means "full of." It changes nouns into adjectives. When *-ous* is added to the noun *glory*, the adjective *glorious* is formed.** *Glorious* means "full of glory."

- Write the following words on the board: *advantage, courage, danger*. Ask students if the words are nouns, verbs, or adjectives. *(nouns)* Tell students to add the suffix *-ous* to each word. Then have them identify the new part of speech for each word. *(adjective)* Finally, have volunteers explain the meaning of each new word.

- Tell students to write the words *venomous, hazardous,* and *joyous* in their Word Study Notebooks. Have them underline each word's suffix and circle the base word. Then have students write a brief definition of each word. They should confirm their definitions with a partner.

DAY 2 Paired Yes/No Questions

Students will answer questions to show their knowledge of the Target Vocabulary words.

- Give each student an index card. Have students write *yes* on one side of the card and *no* on the other side.

- Explain that you will ask sets of two questions. After each question, students should hold up the *yes* or *no* side of their index cards to answer.

   1. **Does a doctor work in a *studio*?** *(no)* **Does a painter work in a *studio*?** *(yes)*

   2. **Would a paintbrush be *ruined* if you didn't wash it?** *(yes)* **Would a bar of soap be *ruined* if you didn't wash it?** *(no)*

   3. **Are you hungry after a *feast*?** *(no)* **Are you full after a *feast*?** *(yes)*

   4. **Do you look at a *schedule* to find out when a show is on?** *(yes)* **Do you look at a *schedule* to learn how to fix a television set?** *(no)*

   5. **Would your mom be *concerned* if you were doing poorly in class?** *(yes)* **Would your mom be *concerned* if you were doing well in class?** *(no)*

   6. **Can a *model* airplane be made of wind?** *(no)* **Can a *model* airplane be made of paper?** *(yes)*

   7. **If you *yanked* the end of a ball of yarn, would it unravel?** *(yes)* **If you *yanked* on a doorknob, would it unravel?** *(no)*

   8. **Might a sunset be described as *glorious*?** *(yes)* **Might an injury be described as *glorious*?** *(no)*

   9. **Does rain *streak* over a car?** *(yes)* **Does ice *streak* over a car?** *(no)*

   10. **Is fabric *smeared* on canvas?** *(no)* **Is paint *smeared* on canvas?** *(yes)*

DAY 3   Glossary Snapshots

Students will create glossary entries for the Target Vocabulary words.

- Distribute copies of the Lesson 8 Word Cards. Have students review the words and their meanings with a partner.

- Have students take out their Student Books and look at the glossary in the back. Review that the words are in alphabetical order, and each word is followed by a definition.

- Then give each student ten index cards. Have students write a Target Vocabulary word on each card. Explain that they will write glossary entries for each word.

- On the back of each card, students should include a definition, picture, and sentence using the word. They should then put the cards in alphabetical order.

- When students finish making their glossary entries, ask them to share their work with a partner.

- Partners should confirm that the words are correctly defined and that the pictures and sentences make sense.

DAY 4   Write About Artists

Students will write a paragraph that includes Target Vocabulary words.

- Provide students with the Lesson 8 Word Cards. Have volunteers read them aloud and explain their meanings.

- Tell students that they will write a descriptive paragraph about artists in their Word Study Notebooks. They can use what they already know, as well as what they learned from this week's reading of "Sidewalk Artists" in their Student Books.

- Explain that students should use at least four Target Vocabulary words in their paragraphs. Students might include information about what artists do, how and where they work, and what materials or tools they use.

- When students finish writing, have them read their paragraphs to a partner. Partners should confirm that the Target Vocabulary words are used correctly.

> **model**
>
> An artist might use clay to make a model train.

DAY 5   Four-Square Map

Students will complete Four-Square Maps to demonstrate their understanding of Target Vocabulary words.

- Display a Four-Square Map. Explain that students will help you complete the Four-Square Map for the word *studio.*

- Write *studio* in the center of the map. Have students explain the meaning of the word. Then write their response or the student-friendly definition in the upper-left corner. *(a place for artists to create things)*

- Have students share some examples of where they might find a studio. Record one response in the upper-right corner. *(in a school)*

- Then ask students to share some sentences using the word *studio.* Have students identify the sentence that best uses the word. Then write that sentence in the lower-left corner. *(I need to purchase new supplies for my art studio.)*

- Finally, ask students to come up with examples of places that are not studios. Write one non-example in the lower-right corner of the map. *(grocery store)*

- When the map is complete, have students create four more Four-Square Maps in their Word Study Notebooks. Tell students to use the words *model, yanked, streak,* and *feast.* Then have students share their completed maps with a partner.

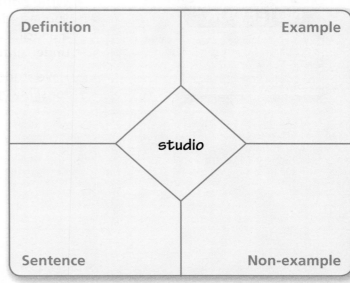

Vocabulary

1. **fault** When a person is responsible for a mistake, the mistake is his or her *fault*.

2. **borrow** To *borrow* is to take something for a while and then return it.

3. **reference** A *reference* is something that is used for information.

4. **fainted** If a person has *fainted*, he or she has lost consciousness from fear, hunger, or weakness.

5. **genuine** A person who is *genuine* is sincere and honest.

6. **local** Something that is *local* can be found nearby.

7. **apologize** To *apologize* is to say, "I'm sorry."

8. **proof** To show *proof* is to show that something is true.

9. **slimy** Something that is *slimy* is slippery and thick.

10. **insisted** If a person demanded something, he or she *insisted* on it.

 Reproducible Word Cards and Graphic Organizer 12 (T-Map) are available at **www.thinkcentral.com**.

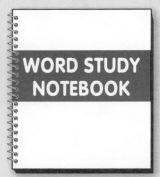

DAY 1 Introduce Target Vocabulary; Suffix *-ize*

After learning the week's Target Vocabulary words, students will explore words that have the suffix *-ize*.

- Write the Target Vocabulary words on the board, read them aloud, and have students repeat the words. Discuss the student-friendly definitions, shown at left, with students.

- Remind students that a suffix is a word part added to the end of a base word to form a word with a different meaning. Rewrite the word *apologize*. Guide students to identify the base word *apology*. Have a volunteer underline the suffix *-ize*.

- Discuss how the suffix *-ize* can change the meaning of a base word. Suggested language: **The suffix *-ize* can mean "to make or cause to be." It can change a noun into a verb.** Next, write these sentences on the board: **He wrote an *apology* to his neighbor.** (noun) **He had to *apologize* after breaking the window.** (verb) Read each sentence aloud, and help students define *apology* and *apologize*.

- Ask students to explain how *apology* changed in the second sentence. *(Meaning, spelling, and part of speech are different.)* Have students write the example sentences in their Word Study Notebooks. Have them underline the noun *apology* and circle the verb *apologize*.

- Read the base words below. Tell students to add the suffix *-ize* to the end of each word. Have them use their understanding of *-ize* to explain the meaning of each new word. Ask volunteers to write the new words on the board.

| **fossil** | **alphabet** | **motor** | **random** | **standard** |

DAY 2 Antonyms

Students will identify antonyms of Target Vocabulary words.

- Display a T-Map. Tell students that today they will complete this map by listing Target Vocabulary words and their antonyms.

- Write the headings *Word* and *Antonym*. Explain that antonyms are words that have opposite meanings. Discuss a common antonym pair such as *hot* and *cold*.

- Write *borrow* under *Word*. Guide students to identify an antonym for *borrow*. Suggested language: **If I ask to *borrow* your pencil, I need to use it. If I *lend* you a pencil, I am letting you use it. *Borrow* and *lend* are opposites. I will write *lend* under *Antonym*.**

- Have students copy the T-Map into their Word Study Notebooks and list antonyms for *slimy, genuine, insisted*, and *local*. Have pairs discuss their completed T-Maps.

Word	Antonym
borrow	lend
slimy	rough
genuine	fake
insisted	suggested
local	far away

DAY 3 Suffix -y

Students will use the suffix -y to determine the meanings of new words.

- Remind students that knowing the meanings of common suffixes will help them understand the meanings of many words.

- Write *slimy* on the board. Underline the suffix -y. Discuss the meaning of the base word *slime*, and explain that the suffix -y can mean "having." Then say: **The suffix -y and the base word *slime* form the word *slimy*. Something that is *slimy* has a slippery, sticky texture.**

- Write the following words on the board: *quirk, breeze, mist, crunch, curl*. Have students open their Word Study Notebooks and write the words on separate lines.

- Discuss the words' meanings. Then have students add the suffix -y to the end of each word. Tell students to drop the *e* at the end of *breeze* before adding -y.

- Have partners take turns reading a word and explaining how its meaning changes after adding -y. Have students write the new meaning next to each word.

DAY 4 Write a Letter

Students will write a letter that includes Target Vocabulary words.

- Distribute copies of the Lesson 9 Word Cards. Read each word aloud and review its student-friendly definition. Students will write a letter using some of these words.

- Ask students to think about this week's reading, "Dear Mr. Winston." Discuss with students why Cara had to write an apology letter to the librarian Mr. Winston. *(Cara brought a snake into the library. Mr. Winston got scared and fainted.)*

- Have students imagine that they are Cara, and they took a book from the library without checking it out. They must now write a short apology letter to Mr. Winston.

- Have students write the letter in their Word Study Notebooks using the Target Vocabulary words *fault, borrow, reference, proof,* and *insisted*.

- Have students read their letters to a partner. Partners should confirm that the Target Vocabulary words were used correctly. Have students correct any mistakes.

DAY 5 Idea Completion

Students will demonstrate their understanding of Target Vocabulary words by completing sentence frames.

- Write this week's Target Vocabulary words on the board. Assign pairs to read the words aloud and review their meanings.

- Explain to students that they will listen carefully as you read sentence frames. As you read each frame, display the Word Card that shows the Target Vocabulary word students will use to complete the sentence.

- Display the Word Card *fault*. Read the first sentence frame and model completing it aloud. Then have students complete each sentence orally.

   1. Luis made a mistake, but _____. *(fault)*
   2. Do you have an extra pen _____? *(borrow)*
   3. If you come across a word you don't know, use _____. *(reference)*
   4. When they told Sylvia that she won the lottery, _____. *(fainted)*
   5. If your friend is dishonest or fake, _____. *(genuine)*
   6. Places that are far away _____. *(local)*
   7. When the waiter realized that he brought us the wrong order, _____. *(apologize)*
   8. If you want others to believe your story, _____. *(proof)*
   9. That frog's skin _____. *(slimy)*
   10. The child didn't want to go to the dentist, but _____. *(insisted)*

Vocabulary

1. **debut** A performer's first public appearance is a *debut*.

2. **stubborn** Something that is *stubborn* is lasting and not easily changed.

3. **permission** If someone is given *permission*, she or he is allowed to do something.

4. **hauling** *Hauling* is pulling or carrying.

5. **mournful** Something that is *mournful* is sad and serious.

6. **towered** If something *towered* over something else, it stood above it.

7. **triumph** A *triumph* is a victory or success.

8. **discouraged** When someone feels hopeless or disappointed, he or she is *discouraged*.

9. **toured** If someone *toured* a place, they took a trip through that place.

10. **border** A *border* is a boundary or an edge.

 Reproducible Word Cards are available at **www.thinkcentral.com**.

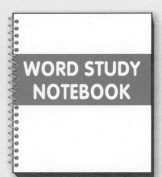

WORD STUDY NOTEBOOK

DAY 1 ## Introduce Target Vocabulary; Suffix *-ful*

After learning the week's Target Vocabulary words, students will explore words that have the suffix *-ful*.

• Write the Target Vocabulary words on the board, read them aloud, and have students repeat the words. Discuss the student-friendly definitions, shown at left, with students.

• Rewrite *mournful,* and underline *-ful*. Explain that *-ful* is a suffix added to the base word *mourn*. Remind students that a suffix is a word part that goes at the end of a base word to form a new word with a different meaning. Suggested language: **The suffix *-ful* means "full of." The base word *mourn* means "to be sad." *Mourn* plus the suffix *-ful* forms the word *mournful*. *Mournful* means "full of sadness."**

• Explain that *-ful* can be added to the end of other words. Write these word equations on the board:

$$color + ful = \underline{\hspace{2cm}}$$

$$grace + ful = \underline{\hspace{2cm}}$$

$$peace + ful = \underline{\hspace{2cm}}$$

$$power + ful = \underline{\hspace{2cm}}$$

• Have volunteers combine the word parts to write new words on the board. Discuss each word's meaning. Then have students copy the word equations into their Word Study Notebooks and write sentences for the new words. Students should revisit this page throughout the week to add more words that end with the suffix *-ful*.

DAY 2 ## Shades of Meaning

Students will use a Word Line to deepen their understanding of the Target Vocabulary word *mournful*.

• On the board, display a blank Word Line. Explain that today students will help you complete a Word Line with synonyms for *mournful*.

• Remind students that synonyms are words that have similar meanings. Review a common synonym pair such as *happy* and *glad*. Have volunteers identify other synonym pairs and discuss each word's meaning. Explain that some synonyms have slight differences in meaning that convey different degrees of feeling.

• Next, tell students that they will help you brainstorm synonyms for *mournful*. Have volunteers write several synonyms on the board. Then ask students to read aloud the synonym list.

• Have students draw a Word Line in their Word Study Notebooks. Tell them to write *mournful* in the center of the Word Line. Explain that students should place the synonyms that convey feelings that are not as strong as *mournful* to the left and stronger feelings to the right. Discuss students' choices, and have them explain each synonym's placement.

| sad | gloomy | mournful | depressed | miserable |

DAY 3 — Prefix *dis-*

Students will use the prefix *dis-* to determine the meanings of new words.

- Remind students that knowing the meanings of common prefixes will help them understand the meanings of many words. On the board, write the word *discouraged*. Underline the prefix *dis-*, and explain to students that *dis-* means "not."

- Discuss how the base word *courage* is about being strong and brave. Then guide students to explain the meaning of *discouraged*. Suggested language: **Courage means feeling strong, brave, and confident. If *dis-* is added before *couraged*, what does *discouraged* mean?** *(not feeling strong, brave, or confident)*

- Next, write the base words *honest*, *similar*, and *loyal*. Have students record the words in their Word Study Notebooks.

- Discuss the meaning of each word. Then have students add the prefix *dis-* to each word. Have pairs discuss how the meaning of each word changes after adding *dis-*.

- Have students write the new meaning next to each word.

DAY 4 — "Because" Sentences

Students will demonstrate their understanding of Target Vocabulary words by completing sentences.

- Display the Target Vocabulary words, and read them aloud.

- Explain that you will read the beginning of a sentence that uses a vocabulary word. Students must listen carefully and raise their hands to complete the sentence after you say *because*.

  1. The singer is excited about his *debut* because...
  2. Elena thinks her dad is *stubborn* because...
  3. The students need *permission* because...
  4. Tom is *hauling* his uncle's boat because...
  5. The family is *mournful* because...
  6. Her sister *towered* over her because...
  7. The team believed it would *triumph* because...
  8. His parents are *discouraged* because...
  9. Today they *toured* the island because...
  10. He carefully cut around the *border* because...

DAY 5 — Meaning Sort

Students will sort the Target Vocabulary words according to categories of their choice.

- Distribute a set of Lesson 10 Word Cards to each student. Before beginning the sort, explain that you will demonstrate how students can come up with their own categories when sorting.

- Model thinking about the words as you read the Word Cards aloud. Suggested language: **I notice some of these words give me a negative feeling. For example, the word *mournful* relates to sad events. I can sort words that are negative into one category and words that are positive or neutral into other categories.**

- Have students read the Word Cards aloud, analyze the words for similarities and differences, and select categories for their sorts based on what they notice about the word meanings. If students have difficulty selecting categories, suggest options such as sorting by parts of speech (nouns, verbs, adjectives).

- Have students write their chosen column headings in their Word Study Notebooks. Allow time for students to sort their Word Cards and write each word in the appropriate column. Remind students to reread their categories and confirm the placement of each word.

- Have student pairs share their sorts without revealing the category types. Have partners guess each other's categories. Then have partners discuss their sorts and explain their category choices.

mournful   triumph

stubborn   debut

discouraged   towered

1. **whirling** When something is *whirling,* it is spinning rapidly in a circle.

2. **rapidly** *Rapidly* means with great speed, quickly, or very fast.

3. **condense** To *condense* means to change from a gas (water moisture) to a liquid (water droplets).

4. **source** The *source* for something is what makes, causes, or begins it.

5. **rotating** *Rotating* means turning or going around in a circle.

6. **rage** Storms, winds, seas, or rivers that *rage* are ones that move in a strong or violent way.

7. **experience** When people or places *experience* something, they take part in or go through it.

8. **ancient** *Ancient* people are people who lived long ago, or a long time in the past.

9. **predict** To *predict* something is to say what you think will happen before it happens.

10. **registered** *Registered* means displayed or recorded on an instrument or machine.

 Reproducible Word Cards are available at **www.thinkcentral.com**.

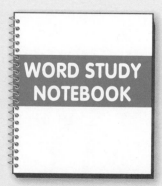

WORD STUDY NOTEBOOK

DAY 1 Introduce Target Vocabulary; Endings *-ed, -ing*

After learning the week's Target Vocabulary words, students will explore words with the endings *-ed* and *-ing.*

- Write the Target Vocabulary words on the board, read them aloud, and have students repeat the words. Discuss the student-friendly definitions, shown at left, with students.

- Review with students that an ending is a word part added to a base word. Then write the Target Vocabulary word *registered* on the board. Suggested language: **Register is a verb. The -ed ending in registered tells me that this action happened in the past.**

- Write the Target Vocabulary words *predict* and *condense* on the board. Guide students to add *-ed* to form the new words *predicted* and *condensed.* Have students tell how the *-ed* ending changes the meaning of each word.

- Remind students that the ending *-ing* shows that an action is happening now. Write the Target Vocabulary words *whirling* and *rotating* on the board. Point out the base word in each word. Then say: **The base words whirl and rotate are verbs. The -ing ending in whirling and rotating shows that these actions are taking place in the present.**

- Write the words *register* and *predict* on the board. Guide students to add *-ing* to each word to form new words that show that an action is taking place in the present.

- Have students write these words in their Word Study Notebooks: *gust, freeze, evaporate.* Tell students to add the endings *-ed* and *-ing* to each word. Then have partners work together to use each new word in a sentence, and record them in their Word Study Notebooks.

DAY 2 Root Chain

Students will observe and participate in the building of a Root Chain.

- Tell students that a root is a word part that has meaning but cannot stand alone. The same root may be a part of many different words. Write the Target Vocabulary word *predict* on the board, and underline the root *dict.*

- Have students name other words that contain the root *dict.* *(dictionary, dictate, verdict, dictator)* Write each word in a list, aligning and underlining *dict* as shown below.

- Guide students to use word parts to determine the meaning of *predict.* Explain that the prefix *pre-* can mean "earlier" or "before," and that the root *dict* means "say." Ask students what they think *predict* means. *(to say what will happen before it happens)*

- Have students use the root *dict* and the other word parts to explain the meanings of the remaining words in the Root Chain. Tell them to copy the Root Chain into their Word Study Notebooks, underline the root *dict* in each word, and write the word meanings next to the words. Allow students to use print or online dictionaries if needed.

pre<u>dict</u>
<u>dict</u>ionary
<u>dict</u>ate
ver<u>dict</u>
<u>dict</u>ator

DAY 3 Prefix *en-*

Students will use the prefix *en-* to determine the meanings of new words.

- Review with students that a prefix is a word part added to the beginning of a base word to form a new word. Remind students that knowing the meanings of common prefixes will help them understand the meanings of many words.

- Write the Target Vocabulary word *rage* on the board. Explain that *rage* can mean "to feel or show violent, uncontrollable anger."

- Then add the prefix *en-* to *rage*. Explain that *en-* means "to bring into or in." Suggested language: **When the prefix *en-* is added to *rage*, the new word, *enrage*, means "to make very angry."** *Losing its cub may enrage a mother bear.*

- Write *dear, tangle, close,* and *force* on the board. Have students record the words in their Word Study Notebooks. Discuss the meaning of each base word. Have students write the prefix *en-* in front of each word.

- Have student pairs take turns explaining how each word's meaning changed after they added the prefix *en-*. Have them confirm and then write the new meaning next to each word.

DAY 4 Write Dialogue

Students will write dialogue that uses the Target Vocabulary words.

- Distribute copies of the Lesson 11 Word Cards. Have students think about how they might use each Target Vocabulary word in dialogue, or everyday conversation. Prompt students to discuss their ideas with a partner.

- Have students choose three to five words. Ask students to write dialogue in their Word Study Notebooks that includes the Target Vocabulary words they chose.

- Remind students that dialogue should sound like real people talking to each other. Guide students to show expression through appropriate speaker tags.

- Ask volunteers to share a portion of their dialogue. Classmates should listen and discuss whether the Target Vocabulary words are used in a way that makes sense.

> **source**

> "What is the source of that awful clattering?" asked Mom. "Tomas set up a race track for his toy cars," said Marietta. "You should check it out!"

DAY 5 Riddles

Students will use their knowledge of word meanings to answer riddles about the Target Vocabulary words.

- Have students display the Lesson 11 Word Cards. Explain that as you read the riddles, students should hold up the Word Card that best answers each riddle.

- Discuss students' answers after each riddle.

1. **I turn round and round, sometimes fast and sometimes slow. What am I doing?** *(rotating, whirling)*
2. **When you want to get somewhere fast, you move this way.** *(rapidly)*
3. **Someone who is really, really mad might do this.** *(rage)*
4. **When water vapor becomes raindrops, it does this.** *(condense)*
5. **I'm spinning so fast that I'm dizzy! What am I doing?** *(whirling, rotating)*
6. **I'm so old that the olden days were new to me! What am I?** *(ancient)*
7. **You can be glad that your heartbeat did this on a monitor.** *(registered)*
8. **If you want to know why something happened, find me.** *(source)*
9. **When you go through something, you do this.** *(experience)*
10. **I'll bet you've already guessed who I am.** *(predict)*

whirling   rage

rapidly   experience

condense   ancient

source   predict

rotating   registered

Vocabulary

1. **trembles** *Trembles* means shakes.

2. **wreckage** *Wreckage* is what is left of something that has been ruined.

3. **slab** A broad, flat piece of something is a *slab*.

4. **possessions** *Possessions* are items that a person owns.

5. **tenement** A *tenement* is a low-quality apartment building.

6. **crushing** *Crushing* means smashing or squashing something.

7. **rubble** Broken or crumbled material from a destroyed building is *rubble*.

8. **debris** Pieces of broken things are *debris*.

9. **timbers** *Timbers* are large pieces of wood used for building.

10. **constructed** Something that is built is *constructed*.

 Reproducible Word Cards and Graphic Organizer 12 (T-Map) are available at **www.thinkcentral.com**.

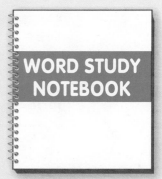

WORD STUDY NOTEBOOK

DAY 1 ## Introduce Target Vocabulary; Suffix *-age*

After learning the week's Target Vocabulary words, students will explore words that end with the suffix *-age*.

- Write the Target Vocabulary words on the board, read them aloud, and have students repeat the words. Discuss the student-friendly definitions, shown at left.

- Review that a suffix is a word part that has meaning and can be added to the end of a base word to form a new word. Remind students that knowing the meanings of common suffixes will help them make sense of new words.

- Rewrite *wreckage* and underline *-age*. Explain that *-age* is a suffix added to the base word *wreck*. Then say: **The suffix *-age* means "the result of." The base word *wreck* means "to ruin or destroy." *Wreck* plus the suffix *-age* forms *wreckage*. *Wreckage* means "the result of something that is ruined or destroyed."**

- Write the following base words on the board for students to copy into their Word Study Notebooks: *leak, shrink, block, break*. Have students add the suffix *-age* to each word and explain the new meanings after the suffix has been added.

- Then ask students the questions below, and prompt them to respond with one of the new words. Discuss students' answers. *(blockage, leakage, breakage, shrinkage)*

  1. **When a person stands in the middle of a doorway, what is the result?**

  2. **When water escapes through a hole in the roof, what is the result?**

  3. **When a vase falls to the floor, what is the result?**

  4. **When hot water causes a shirt to get smaller, what is the result?**

DAY 2 ## Guess My Category

Students will guess the categories of Target Vocabulary words that you sort.

- Display the Lesson 12 Word Cards. Briefly review the student-friendly definitions.

- Display a T-Map without headings. Explain that you will sort this week's words into each column and that students should guess how you are sorting them. Sort the words into two categories: *words about construction, words about destruction*.

- Place the Word Cards *timbers* and *rubble* in separate columns. Pick up the Word Card *constructed*, read it aloud, and place it under *timbers*. Continue sorting all the words without revealing the categories. Then have students read the words in each column and discuss what they have in common. *(The words on the left relate to building; the words on the right relate to destroying.)*

- Write the new headings *Construction* and *Destruction*, as shown below. Have students copy the T-Map into their Word Study Notebooks.

Construction	Destruction
timbers	rubble
constructed	wreckage
possessions	crushing
tenement	trembles
slab	debris

DAY 3 Word Origins

Students will explore the origins of the Target Vocabulary word *debris* and use this knowledge to discuss other word origins.

- Explain that students will learn the meanings and origins of common words. Suggested language: **Many words we use in the English language come from French words that were spoken long ago.**

- Write the Target Vocabulary word *debris* on the board. Discuss the definition, and use it in a sentence. Then say: **The word *debris* comes from the French word *debriser*, which means "to break into pieces or crush."**

- Have groups of three copy the following words and definitions into their Word Study Notebooks: (French origin words) *bon voyage, ballette, coller;* (Definitions) *a little dance; good journey; to glue.* Have students match each French origin word with its definition.

- Then write the modern version of each word on the board: *bon voyage, ballet, collage.* Discuss with students the common usage of these words. Then have them write a sentence for *bon voyage, ballet,* and *collage.*

DAY 4 Word and Picture Matching

Students will work with a partner to draw a picture for a Target Vocabulary word and guess the matching word.

- Distribute copies of the Lesson 12 Word Cards and ten index cards to student pairs. Explain that partners will take turns choosing a Target Vocabulary word, drawing a picture that represents the word, and then asking their partner to guess the matching word.

- Have partners place a set of Word Cards face down. Tell one student to select a word without revealing it. The student should draw a simple picture for the word on an index card. Then the partner will try to guess the correct vocabulary word.

- The student who guesses the word correctly should write the word on the back of the drawing and then use the word in a sentence. The student who draws the picture should confirm whether the Target Vocabulary word was used correctly.

- After students guess the words, write them, and use them in sentences, have partners switch roles and repeat the activity several times.

DAY 5 Root Web

Students will use the root *struct* to build new words and learn their meanings.

- Review that a root is a word part that has meaning but cannot stand alone. Explain that the same root may be a part of many different words.

- Write the root *struct.* Then write *constructed,* underline *struct,* and explain the root's meaning. Suggested language: **The root *struct* means "to build."**

- Review the definition of *constructed.* Explain how knowing the meaning of the root *struct* can help students understand the meaning of the word. Suggested language: **The prefix *con-* means "with or together" and the root *struct* means "to build," so the word *constructed* must mean "to build with or together."**

- Display a blank Root Web. Write *struct* in the center oval. Model adding the prefix *ob-* to the web and creating the word *obstruct.* Discuss the meaning of the new word. *(to block or make difficult)*

- Extend the web by writing the prefixes *in-, con-, de-* and the suffix *-ion,* as pictured. Explain the meanings of the prefixes and suffixes. Have students copy the web into their Word Study Notebooks.

- Have students complete the web, building new words by attaching each affix to the root *struct. (instruct, construction, destruction)* Then have small groups define and discuss the words. Have students write the meanings in their Word Study Notebooks.

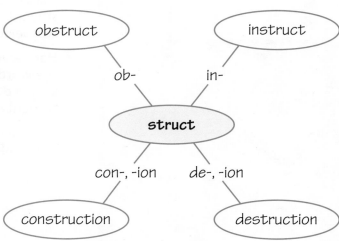

Vocabulary

1. **display** A *display* is something shown publicly.

2. **alert** To be *alert* is to be wide awake and paying attention.

3. **weariness** A person who is very tired experiences *weariness*.

4. **fractured** *Fractured* means cracked.

5. **standards** *Standards* are rules used for judging or measuring.

6. **vision** A *vision* is an idea of what something could be like in the future.

7. **huddle** When people or animals *huddle*, they crowd together.

8. **graceful** Something that moves smoothly and with ease is *graceful*.

9. **stranded** If a person is *stranded* in a place, he or she is unable to leave it.

10. **concluded** If a person has *concluded* something, he or she had made a decision or formed an opinion.

 Reproducible Word Cards are available at **www.thinkcentral.com**.

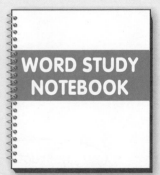

WORD STUDY NOTEBOOK

DAY 1 **Introduce Target Vocabulary; Suffix -*ness***

After learning the week's Target Vocabulary words, students will explore words that end with the suffix -*ness*.

- Write the Target Vocabulary words on the board, read them aloud, and have students repeat the words. Discuss the student-friendly definitions, shown at left, with students.

- Rewrite *weariness* and underline -*ness*. Explain that -*ness* is a suffix added to the base word *weary*. Remind students that a suffix is a word part that has meaning and can be added to the end of a base word. Then say: **The suffix -*ness* means "the state of." The base word *weary* means "tired." *Weary* plus the suffix -*ness* forms the word *weariness*. *Weariness* means "the state of being tired."**

- Point out the change in spelling in *weariness*: the *y* changed to an *i* before adding -*ness*. Explain that -*ness* can be added to the end of other words. Write the following word equations on the board:

$$\text{clever} + \text{ness} = \underline{\hspace{2cm}}$$

$$\text{famous} + \text{ness} = \underline{\hspace{2cm}}$$

$$\text{dark} + \text{ness} = \underline{\hspace{2cm}}$$

$$\text{alert} + \text{ness} = \underline{\hspace{2cm}}$$

- Have students add the word parts together to create new words. Have volunteers complete the word equations by writing the new words on the board. Discuss each word's meaning.

- Tell students to copy the word equations into their Word Study Notebooks. Then have them write sentences for *cleverness*, *famousness*, *darkness*, and *alertness*.

DAY 2 **Twenty Questions**

Students will ask a series of questions about the Target Vocabulary words and then guess the words.

- Distribute copies of the Lesson 13 Word Cards. Read each word aloud. Then briefly review the student-friendly definition for each word.

- Have students work with a partner to play the game Twenty Questions. Explain the rules of the game. One partner selects a Word Card without showing it to the other student. The other student will ask yes/no questions to try to determine which word was selected. When the student guesses correctly, the partner reveals the word.

- Have a volunteer select a Target Vocabulary word. Model asking questions about the word. Suggested language: **Is the word a verb? Is it an action that an animal would do? Does the word end with -*ed*?** Continue until you have guessed the student's word.

- Then have partners place a set of the Word Cards face down. Tell them to play the game, alternating roles until all the Word Cards have been used.

DAY 3 · Write a Journal Entry

Students will use Target Vocabulary words to write a journal entry about the Antarctic.

- Have students take out their Lesson 13 Word Cards and read them aloud. Briefly discuss the student-friendly definitions.

- Guide students to think about this week's reading, "Antarctic Journal." Discuss the author's experience in the Antarctic and how her journal entries recounted her adventures in vivid detail, such as the description of the crevasse in the glacier.

- Tell students to imagine that they have recently returned from a four-month adventure in the Antarctic. Ask them to write a short journal entry about their journey in their Word Study Notebooks.

- Write the Target Vocabulary words *concluded, graceful, weariness,* and *alert* on the board. Tell students to use these words as well as additional Target Vocabulary words of their choice in their writing.

- When students finish, have them share their journal entries with the class. Discuss how the Target Vocabulary words were used in their entries.

DAY 4 · Eponyms

Students will discover common eponyms through research.

- Have students open their Student Books to page 340, and lead them in a discussion about "The Coolest Marathon."

- Discuss why running in an Antarctic marathon might be a challenge. Point out the extreme weather conditions. Suggested language: **The Antarctic is the coldest place on Earth. The temperature generally does not reach above 32 degrees Fahrenheit, or 0 degrees Celsius.**

- Write the words *Fahrenheit* and *Celsius* on the board. Explain that these words are eponyms. Suggested language: **An eponym is a word that originates from the name of a real person, a fictional person, or a mythical character.**

- Tell students that Daniel Gabriel Fahrenheit was a real person who invented the temperature scale now named after him, as did Anders Celsius. Both temperature scales are used today.

- Then discuss the words *atlas* and *volcano*, and ask students to explore the origins of these eponyms.

- Have students write their findings in their Word Study Notebooks and share them with the class. (atlas: *named after a character in Greek mythology, Atlas;* volcano: *named after the Roman god of fire, Vulcan*)

DAY 5 · Root Chain

Students will observe and participate in the building of a Root Chain.

- Write the Target Vocabulary word *vision* on the board. Underline the root *vis.* Remind students that a root is a word part that has meaning but cannot stand alone. The same root may be a part of many different words.

- Guide students to use word parts to determine the meaning of *vision.* Suggested language: **The root *vis* means "to see," and the suffix *-ion* can mean "the act or process of."** Prompt students to think about the word parts and give a definition for *vision. (the act of seeing)*

- Ask students to name other words that contain the root *vis. (visual, visionary, visible, invisible, envision)* Write each word in a list, and align the root *vis* in each word as shown. Have volunteers underline the root *vis* in the words.

- Have students use the root *vis* and the other word parts to explain the meanings of the words in the Root Chain. Tell students to copy the Root Chain into their Word Study Notebooks and write the word meanings next to the words. Have students use print or online dictionaries, as needed.

vision
visual
visionary
visible
invisible
envision

TARGET VOCABULARY

1. **social** A *social* group is one in which people or animals live and work together.

2. **exchanges** In *exchanges,* things are given and received.

3. **excess** To have *excess* amounts is to have more than you need.

4. **reinforce** To *reinforce* something is to support it or make it stronger.

5. **storage** A place in which supplies are kept is called *storage.*

6. **transport** To move something from one place to another is to *transport* it.

7. **chamber** A room or enclosed area that has a special purpose may be called a *chamber.*

8. **scarce** If something is *scarce,* there is not enough of it.

9. **obstacles** *Obstacles* are things that get in the way.

10. **transfers** If a person *transfers* something, he or she moves it from one place to another.

 Reproducible Word Cards are available at **www.thinkcentral.com**.

WORD STUDY NOTEBOOK

DAY 1 **Introduce Target Vocabulary; Prefix *re-***

After learning the week's Target Vocabulary words, students will explore words that begin with the prefix *re-.*

- Write the Target Vocabulary words on the board, read them aloud, and have students repeat the words. Discuss the student-friendly definitions, shown at left, with students.

- Review with students that a prefix is a word part added to the beginning of a base word to form a new word with a different meaning. Then rewrite the word *reinforce,* and underline the prefix *re-.* Tell students that the prefix *re-* means "again or once more."

- Explain that knowing the meaning of *re-* can help students understand the meanings of other words with the prefix. Suggested language: **I recognize the word** *force* **in** *reinforce.* *Force* **means "strength or power." I know that** *re-* **means "again or once more," so** *reinforce* **must mean "to strengthen again or to make even stronger."**

- Write the words *fill, heat, place,* and *send* on the board, and have students copy the words into their Word Study Notebooks. Discuss the meaning of each base word.

- Have students add the prefix *re-* to each word and then write the new meaning next to each word in their Word Study Notebooks.

- Have students work with a partner to confirm the new words and their meanings. Then ask them to think of additional words they know with *re-* and add them to their lists.

DAY 2 **"Because" Sentences**

Students will demonstrate their understanding of Target Vocabulary words by completing sentences.

- Write the Target Vocabulary words, and read them aloud. Review the student-friendly definitions, as needed.

- Explain that you will read the beginning of a sentence that uses a Target Vocabulary word. Students will listen carefully and raise their hands to complete the sentence after you say *because.*

- As time allows, ask two or more students to provide answers to each item to demonstrate a variety of possible responses.

  1. **The judge met with the lawyers in her** *chamber* **because…**
  2. **I need to wipe up the** *excess* **glue because…**
  3. **You can tell that dogs are** *social* **animals because…**
  4. **The large truck will** *transport* **the supplies because…**
  5. **Race car drivers must look for road** *obstacles* **because…**
  6. **The postal worker carefully** *transfers* **the package because…**
  7. **Peaches were** *scarce* **this year because…**
  8. **She used the attic for** *storage* **because…**
  9. **Alfred** *exchanges* **a gift with his best friend every year because…**
  10. **The engineers must find a way to** *reinforce* **the dam because…**

DAY 3 Prefix *ex-*

Students will use the prefix *ex-* to determine the meanings of new words.

- Review with students that a prefix is a word part added to the beginning of a base word to form a new word. Remind students that knowing the meanings of common prefixes will help them understand the meanings of many words.

- Write *exchanges* on the board, and underline the prefix *ex-*. Discuss the word parts. Suggested language: **The prefix ex- means "out of."** *Exchanges* **means "the act of changing out, swapping, or sharing."**

- Then adapt the suggested language for the word *excess*, "outside of or beyond what is necessary or needed."

- Write *external, export,* and *exhale* on the board, and have students record the words in their Word Study Notebooks. Then tell students to circle the prefix *ex-* in each word.

- Have pairs write the meanings of *external, export,* and *exhale*. Allow students to use a dictionary, as needed. Then have partners write a sentence for each word.

DAY 4 Write About Ants

Students will use Target Vocabulary words to write about an ant's life from the ant's perspective.

- Distribute copies of the Lesson 14 Word Cards, and read them aloud. Review each Target Vocabulary word's student-friendly definition. Then explain that students will use many of these words in a writing activity.

- Guide students to discuss this week's reading, "The Life and Times of the Ant." Discuss the working lives of ants and their roles in the colony, such as foragers or tunnel diggers.

- Tell students to imagine that they are hard-working ants. Have them think creatively about what they would do from the ant's perspective.

- Then have students write about their experiences in their Word Study Notebooks using the Target Vocabulary words *social, storage, chamber, scarce, obstacles,* and *transfers*.

- When students complete their writing, have them read their selections to a partner. Have partners listen carefully to determine whether the Target Vocabulary words were used correctly.

DAY 5 Root Chain

Students will observe and participate in the building of a Root Chain.

- Review with students that a root is a word part that has meaning but cannot stand alone. The same root may be a part of many words, and the meanings of common roots can be clues to understanding the meanings of those words.

- Write the Target Vocabulary word *transport* on the board. Underline the root *trans*. Guide students to use word parts to determine the meaning of *transport*. Suggested language: **The root trans means "across," and the root port means "to carry."** Help students use the word parts to determine the meaning of *transport*. *(to carry across)*

- Write *transfers* on the board, and underline the root *trans*. Have students use what they know about the root to determine the meaning of the word. *(moves across from one place to another)* Review the student-friendly definition.

- Work with students to name other words that contain the root *trans*. *(transportation, transatlantic, transplant, transmit)* Write each word in a list, as pictured on the right. Align the root *trans* in each word as shown.

- Have students use the root *trans* and the other word parts to explain the meanings of the remaining words in the Root Chain. Tell students to copy the Root Chain into their Word Study Notebooks. Have students write each meaning next to the appropriate word. Allow students to consult print or online dictionaries, as needed.

transport
transfers
transportation
transatlantic
transplant
transmit

TARGET VOCABULARY

1. **organisms** *Organisms* are living things, such as plants or animals.

2. **directly** Something that happens *directly* happens right away, and with nothing or no one in between.

3. **affect** *Affect* means to cause a change in something.

4. **traces** *Traces* are signs, clues, or evidence that something was there.

5. **vast** Something that is *vast* is extremely large in amount, size, or area.

6. **habitats** *Habitats* are natural areas where certain kinds of plants and animals live and grow.

7. **variety** If you have a *variety* of something, you have several, or more than one, from which to choose.

8. **species** A *species* is a group of organisms that produces organisms of the same kind.

9. **banned** If something is *banned,* it is against the rules or against the law.

10. **radiation** *Radiation* is the invisible transfer of energy by waves through empty space.

 Reproducible Word Cards and Graphic Organizer 15 (Web) are available at **www.thinkcentral.com**.

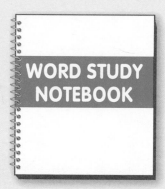

WORD STUDY NOTEBOOK

DAY 1 # Introduce Target Vocabulary; Suffix *-ly*

After learning the week's Target Vocabulary words, students will explore words that end with the suffix *-ly*.

- Write the Target Vocabulary words on the board, read them aloud, and have students repeat the words. Discuss the student-friendly definitions, shown at left, with students.

- Review with students that a suffix is a word part that has meaning and can be added to the end of a base word to form a new word with a different meaning. Remind students that knowing common suffixes will help them make sense of new words.

- Draw attention to the word *directly,* and underline the suffix *-ly*. Explain the meaning of the suffix *-ly*. Suggested language: **The suffix *-ly* means "in a certain way." It can change an adjective into an adverb.**

- Write these sentences on the board, and read them aloud: **My dad took the *direct* route to our house.** (adjective) **My dad drove *directly* to our house.** (adverb) Point out that the meaning of *direct* changed when the suffix *-ly* was added. Discuss the similarities and differences between the two words and their parts of speech.

- To extend the thinking to other examples, write the following base words on the board: *brave, polite, wise, swift, nervous.* Have students copy them into their Word Study Notebooks.

- Have students add the suffix *-ly* to each word to form a new word. Then organize students into small groups. Have them discuss the new meaning of each word and create sentence pairs using both the adjective and adverb forms of the words.

DAY 2 # I Spy Clues

Students will use clues to guess the correct Target Vocabulary word.

- Distribute copies of the Lesson 15 Word Cards. Briefly review this week's vocabulary.

- Explain that students will work in groups as they play a word game called I Spy. Tell students you will read a clue, and groups will hold up the Word Card that names what you are describing.

- Organize students into groups of three or four, and have them place a set of the Target Vocabulary Word Cards face up. Read the clues below.

  1. **I'm thinking of a word whose suffix means "in a certain way."** *(directly)*
  2. **I'm thinking of a word that is a category name for all animals of the same type.** *(species)*
  3. **I'm thinking of a verb that signals a change.** *(affect)*
  4. **I'm thinking of a word that means the same as *outlawed.*** *(banned)*
  5. **I'm thinking of a word that describes many different choices.** *(variety)*
  6. **I'm thinking of a word that means "all living things."** *(organisms)*
  7. **I'm thinking of a word that could be used to describe the Grand Canyon.** *(vast)*
  8. **I'm thinking of the name for animal homes in the wild.** *(habitats)*
  9. **I'm thinking of a word that describes clues a detective might find.** *(traces)*
  10. **I'm thinking of a word that describes invisible energy waves.** *(radiation)*

DAY 3   Suffix *-ion*

Students will explore words that end with the suffix *-ion*.

- Remind students that a suffix is a word part added to the end of a base word to form a new word with a different meaning.

- Write the Target Vocabulary word *radiation* on the board, and underline the suffix *-ion*. Tell students that *-ion* can mean "the result of an act or process."

- Explain that the suffix *-ion* is a word part that changes a verb to a noun. Write *radiate* above *radiation*. Discuss the two words. Suggested language: **Radiate is the base word. To *radiate* something results in *radiation*.**

- Write these sentences on the board and read them aloud: **The machine will *radiate* particles.** (verb) **The machine produces *radiation*.** (noun) Discuss the differences between the two words, including meaning and spelling changes.

- Write *donate*, *invent*, *celebrate*, and *connect* for students to copy into their Word Study Notebooks. Have students add *-ion* to each word. Then have partners discuss the change in meaning when the suffix is added.

DAY 4   Write About Earth

Students will write about the environment using Target Vocabulary words.

- Have students take out their Lesson 15 Word Cards and read them aloud. Briefly review each Target Vocabulary word's student-friendly definition.

- Guide students to discuss this week's reading, "Ecology for Kids." Discuss what an ecologist does and how this role can *affect* the environment we live in. Prompt students to talk about the *organisms* in an ecosystem and how the destruction of the environment results in the loss of animals' *habitats*.

- Have students imagine that they are ecologists taking a group of students on a tour through a forest. Explain that they will write the information they would tell the students about the environment in their Word Study Notebooks.

- Have students lay the Word Cards on their desks and choose three to five Target Vocabulary words to use in their writing. When they finish, ask them to read their finished piece to a partner to ensure the Target Vocabulary words were used correctly.

DAY 5   Vocabulary Web

Students will complete Vocabulary Webs to illustrate their understanding of Target Vocabulary words.

- Display a Vocabulary Web. Write the word *banned* in the center oval. Explain that students will deepen their understanding of the word *banned* as they help you complete a web about this word.

- Label the remaining ovals *Definition*, *Synonym*, *Example*, and *Sentence*. Ask students to state the meaning of *banned*. Write their response or the student-friendly definition in the upper-left oval. (*something that is against the rules or law*)

- Have students provide synonyms for *banned*. Record one of their responses in the upper-right oval. (*prohibited*) Then ask them to provide examples of things that are *banned*. Write one example in the lower-left oval. (*littering*)

- Ask volunteers to use *banned* in oral sentences. Have students determine the best use of the word, and record the sentence. (*Talking during a movie at a theater is banned.*)

- After the web is complete, write the Target Vocabulary words *vast* and *variety* on the board. Have students complete a web for each word in their Word Study Notebooks. Then have partners trade webs and add ideas to one another's webs. Prompt students to discuss their ideas about the words.

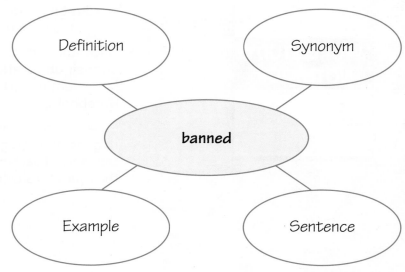

TARGET VOCABULARY

1. **escorted** To have *escorted* someone is to have gone with that person as a guide or protector.

2. **swelled** If something *swelled,* it grew larger than usual.

3. **relied** If you *relied* on someone, you depended on him or her to do something for you.

4. **reputation** The general public's opinions of a person form his or her *reputation.*

5. **worthy** When something is *worthy,* it is useful or valuable.

6. **churning** Something that is *churning* is stirred up and moving with great force.

7. **situation** A *situation* is what is happening at a specific time or place.

8. **deserve** If you *deserve* something, you have a right to it or have earned it.

9. **defended** If a person protected something from physical or verbal attack, he or she *defended* it.

10. **satisfied** A person who feels *satisfied* is happy with things that have happened or the work he or she has done.

 Reproducible Word Cards are available at **www.thinkcentral.com**.

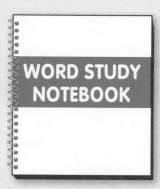

WORD STUDY NOTEBOOK

DAY 1 **Introduce Target Vocabulary; Prefix *un-***

After learning the week's Target Vocabulary words, students will explore words that have the prefix *un-.*

- Write the Target Vocabulary words on the board, read them aloud, and have students repeat the words. Discuss the student-friendly definitions, shown at left, with students.

- Rewrite the word *unworthy,* and underline *un-.* Explain that *un-* is a prefix added to the base word *worthy.* Have students recall that a prefix is a word part that is added to the beginning of a base word to form a new word with a different meaning.

- Tell students that *un-* means "not." Help them understand that knowing the meaning of *un-* can help them determine many word meanings. Suggested language: **If I am not sure what the word *unworthy* means, I can break the word into its word parts. I know that *un-* means "not," and *worthy* means "useful or valuable." *Unworthy* must mean "not useful or valuable."**

- Write the words *unafraid, uncommon, unequal, unacceptable, unkind, uncertain,* and *unusual* on the board. Tell students to break the words into their word parts to determine meaning. Guide students to understand that words with the prefix *un-* are antonyms of the base words.

- Have students use their knowledge of the prefix *un-* to figure out the meanings of the words *untalented, unhelpful,* and *unofficial.* Then have them write sentences using the words in their Word Study Notebooks.

. . . .

DAY 2 **Meaning Sort**

Students will sort the Target Vocabulary words according to concepts or features.

- Distribute copies of the Lesson 16 Word Cards. Review the meanings of the words with students.

- Tell students to look at their Word Cards and analyze the words for similarities and differences. Ask students to think about categories into which they could sort the words.

- Some students may need help selecting categories. Suggest that they sort by action words/non-action words or by words that have a positive/negative/neutral feeling associated with them.

- Once students decide on their categories, have them sort the Word Cards based on their observations. Ask students to reread their categories and confirm the placement of each word. Then have them record their sorts in their Word Study Notebooks.

- Have partners share their sorts without revealing the category types. Tell students to guess the categories their partner sorted by. Then have partners explain how they sorted each word. Challenge students to sort the Word Cards according to their partner's categories.

DAY 3 Similes

Students will listen to and describe the meanings of similes that use the Target Vocabulary words.

- Tell students that a simile uses the word *like* or *as* to compare two unlike things. Explain that you will read several similes that include Target Vocabulary words. Students should explain what each simile means.

- Write the following example on the board: **She *defended* her friend like a lioness protecting her cubs.**

- Model explaining the simile. Suggested language: **The girl's actions are being compared to those of a lioness. A lioness protects her cubs fiercely. The girl must have fiercely defended her friend.**

- Read the following similes, and have students describe the meanings.

  1. His ego *swelled* like a balloon.

  2. The *situation* became as hopeless as a ship lost at sea.

  3. The baby *relied* on her parents like a plant relies on sunlight.

DAY 4 Word Pairs

Students will write sentences using Target Vocabulary words.

- Tell students to place the Lesson 16 Word Cards face down on their desks. Have them choose two cards and turn them over.

- Have students write a sentence in their Word Study Notebooks using both words. Then have them set the cards aside.

- Have students keep drawing sets of Word Cards until all the Target Vocabulary words have been used.

- Explain that students can use different forms of the words as needed so that their sentences make sense.

- Then have students share their sentences in small groups. Group members should confirm that the sentences use the words correctly.

deserve	situation

The firefighters deserve an award for rescuing people from a dangerous situation.

DAY 5 Rate Experiences

Students will use what they know about the Target Vocabulary words to rate experiences along a Word Line.

- Display a Word Line like the one shown below. Write the labels *Negative, Neutral,* and *Positive*. Explain the meanings of the words as needed.

- Tell students that you will read some sentences that use the Target Vocabulary words. Students should think about whether the experiences in the sentences are negative, neutral, or positive.

- After you read each sentence, have partners discuss where they would place the experience. Have them point to that place on the Word Line and explain why.

  1. Her honesty makes her a *worthy* friend.
  2. Paul does not *deserve* that grade because he cheated.
  3. The watchdog *defended* the house from burglars.
  4. Nobody was *satisfied* with the school lunch today.
  5. The bride's father *escorted* her down the aisle.
  6. The kitten *relied* on its mother for milk.
  7. Maria found herself in an embarrassing *situation*.
  8. The false rumor damaged his *reputation*.
  9. Raj felt sick watching all the *churning* carnival rides.
  10. When I won the contest, my heart *swelled* with pride.

Negative   Neutral   Positive

TARGET VOCABULARY

1. **reward** To *reward* someone is to give that person something in return for doing something.

2. **graduate** To *graduate* from school is to complete it.

3. **symbol** A *symbol* is something that stands for something else.

4. **foster** A *foster* caretaker takes care of someone else's animal or child.

5. **disobey** To *disobey* is to not follow orders.

6. **confidence** When a person has a strong belief in his or her abilities, that person has *confidence*.

7. **patiently** If you do something *patiently*, you do it calmly and without complaining.

8. **confesses** When a person *confesses*, he or she admits that something is true or admits to having done something wrong.

9. **ceremony** A *ceremony* is an event that celebrates something special.

10. **performs** When a person *performs* a task, he or she does that task.

 Reproducible Word Cards and Graphic Organizer 15 (Web) are available at **www.thinkcentral.com**.

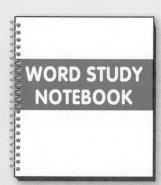

WORD STUDY NOTEBOOK

DAY 1 **Introduce Target Vocabulary; Prefix *dis-***

After learning the week's Target Vocabulary words, students will explore words that have the prefix *dis-*.

- Write the Target Vocabulary words on the board, read them aloud, and have students repeat the words. Discuss the student-friendly definitions, shown at left, with students.

- Ask students to recall what a prefix is. *(a word part that is added to the beginning of a base word to form a new word with a different meaning)* Remind them that learning the meanings of common prefixes can help them determine the meanings of many words.

- Rewrite *disobey* on the board, and underline *dis-*. Model using what you know about the word parts to figure out the meaning of the word. Suggested language: **The prefix *dis-* means "not." The base word *obey* means "to follow orders." *Disobey* must mean "to not follow orders."**

- Write the words *trust, agree, like*, and *believe* on the board. Have students add *dis-* to each word and determine the meanings of the new words. Help students understand that words with the prefix *dis-* are antonyms of the base words.

- Have students brainstorm other words they know that have the prefix *dis-* with a partner and write the words in their Word Study Notebooks. Have partners discuss the words' meanings.

- Tell students to use the words with *dis-* to write questions in their Word Study Notebooks. Then have them work with a partner to ask and answer each other's questions.

DAY 2 **Idea Completion**

Students will complete sentence frames using the Target Vocabulary words.

- Have students review the Target Vocabulary words and their meanings.

- Tell students that you will read several sentence frames. Students should complete each sentence with a partner using the Target Vocabulary word on the Word Card that you display, shown in parentheses below.

- Have partners write their sentence endings in their Word Study Notebooks. After completing the activity, ask volunteers to share their endings with the class.

   1. **I will feel accomplished when _____.** *(graduate)*
   2. **When I do well at something, I like to _____.** *(reward)*
   3. **The best part of the show is _____.** *(performs)*
   4. **The students will get in trouble if _____.** *(disobey)*
   5. **As Marco waits for his food, _____.** *(patiently)*
   6. **The animal shelter is looking for _____.** *(foster)*
   7. **When I see a picture on a recycling bin, I know _____.** *(symbol)*
   8. **Keisha's dance routine went well because _____.** *(confidence)*
   9. **Sam will only be found guilty if _____.** *(confesses)*
   10. **Last weekend, I attended _____.** *(ceremony)*

DAY 3 Homophones

Students will determine the meanings of homophones.

- Tell students that homophones are words that sound the same but have different spellings and meanings.

- Write the Target Vocabulary word *symbol* on the board. Have students recall its meaning. *(something that stands for something else)*

- Write *cymbal* on the board, and read it aloud. Explain that a cymbal is a type of instrument. Help students understand why *symbol* and *cymbal* are homophones.

- As a class, share sentences using the words *symbol* and *cymbal*. Write the sentences on the board.

- Give partners a pair of homophones on index cards, such as *bored/board* or *pain/pane*. Have partners discuss the differences in word meanings and then write sentences using the words.

- Ask partners to share their finished sentences with the class as they show the spellings of the homophones on the index cards. Prompt the class to identify and discuss the differences between the homophone pairs.

DAY 4 Riddles

Students will use their knowledge of word meanings to answer riddles about the Target Vocabulary words.

- Distribute copies of the Lesson 17 Word Cards.

- Explain that you will read riddles, and students will hold up the Word Card that they think best answers them.

   1. **You do this when your dog performs a trick.** *(reward)*
   2. **I am how people must wait in line.** *(patiently)*
   3. **This means not following the rules.** *(disobey)*
   4. **I am what a singer does on stage.** *(performs)*
   5. **You do this when you finish school.** *(graduate)*
   6. **Some caretakers are this.** *(foster)*
   7. **I could be a graduation.** *(ceremony)*
   8. **Your friend does this when she admits the truth.** *(confesses)*
   9. **You have this when you believe in yourself.** *(confidence)*
   10. **I stand for something else.** *(symbol)*

DAY 5 Vocabulary Web

Students will complete Vocabulary Webs to illustrate their understanding of Target Vocabulary words.

- Display a Vocabulary Web. Label the outside ovals *Definition, Sentence, Antonym,* and *Example*. Write the word *reward* in the center oval. Tell students that they will help you complete the web.

- Point to *reward,* and say it aloud. Have students repeat. Then ask students to state the meaning of *reward*. Write their response or the student-friendly definition in the upper-left oval. *(to give someone something in return for something he or she did)*

- Have volunteers use *reward* in a sentence. Remind students that *reward* should be used as a verb. Write the best use of the word in the upper-right oval. *(The teacher will reward us for good behavior.)*

- Ask students to name words that mean the opposite of *reward,* such as *punish, penalize,* or *harm*. Write one of their responses in the lower-left oval. Then have students provide examples of things people might do to reward someone. Pick one example to record in the lower-right oval. *(award a prize)*

- Next, write the Target Vocabulary words *confidence* and *patiently* on the board. Have students complete a web for each word in their Word Study Notebooks. Have them share their completed webs with a partner to confirm their understanding and use of the words.

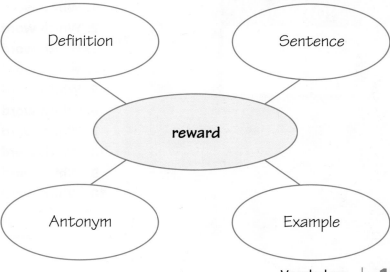

Vocabulary

1. **acquire** To *acquire* means to gain something through one's own efforts.

2. **unfortunate** *Unfortunate* means unlucky or having undeserved bad luck.

3. **coerce** To *coerce* other people means to try to force them to act in a certain way by using pressure or threats.

4. **boasted** *Boasted* means spoke with too much pride about something.

5. **beamed** *Beamed* means smiled widely.

6. **glared** *Glared* means gave a fixed and angry stare.

7. **ceased** *Ceased* means stopped or came to an end.

8. **declared** *Declared* means said something strongly.

9. **devised** *Devised* means planned in one's mind.

10. **resourceful** People who are *resourceful* can act using their imaginations in a difficult situation.

 Reproducible Word Cards and Graphic Organizer 1 (Column Chart) are available at **www.thinkcentral.com**.

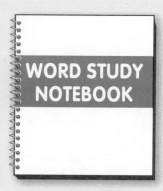

DAY 1 Introduce Target Vocabulary; Suffix *-ful*

After learning the week's Target Vocabulary words, students will explore words that have the suffix *-ful*.

- Write the Target Vocabulary words on the board, read them aloud, and have students repeat the words. Discuss the student-friendly definitions, shown at left, with students.

- Rewrite the word *resourceful* on the board. Underline the suffix *-ful,* and remind students that it means "full of."

- Explain how adding the suffix *-ful* changes the meaning of the word *resource.* Suggested language: **The word *resource* means "something that is a source of help or information." When the suffix *-ful* is added to *resource,* the new word, *resourceful,* describes someone who is full of resources, or ways to help.**

- Next, explain that *-ful* can be added to other words. Write the words *boast* and *thought* on the board. Guide students to define each word. Then have volunteers add *-ful* to each word. Discuss the meanings of *boastful* and *thoughtful.*

- Have students copy the words *grace, deceit,* and *plenty* into their Word Study Notebooks. Discuss the meaning of each word. Then have students add the suffix *-ful* to each base word. Use the fact that the *y* in *plenty* changes to *i* when *-ful* is added to remind students that spelling changes may occur in suffixed words.

- Ask volunteers to tell the meaning of the words *graceful, deceitful,* and *plentiful.* Have students write a sentence for each word. Then have volunteers share their sentences with the class.

DAY 2 Word Associations

Students will identify a Target Vocabulary word that they associate with related words and phrases.

- Distribute the Lesson 18 Word Cards, and have students display them on their desks.

- Explain that you will read several questions, and students should hold up the Word Card that best answers each question.

- As students hold up their Word Cards, share the answers provided. Have students explain their Word Card choices.

   1. **Which word goes with *ended* and *stopped*?** *(ceased)*
   2. **Which word goes with *pride* and *bragged*?** *(boasted)*
   3. **Which word goes with *creative* and *solution*?** *(resourceful)*
   4. **Which word goes with *pressure* and *threaten*?** *(coerce)*
   5. **Which word goes with *smiled* and *brightly*?** *(beamed)*
   6. **Which word goes with *stated* and *announced*?** *(declared)*
   7. **Which word goes with *planned* and *dreamed up*?** *(devised)*
   8. **Which word goes with *gain* and *get*?** *(acquire)*
   9. **Which word goes with *stare* and *scowl*?** *(glare)*
   10. **Which word goes with *unlucky* and *bad*?** *(unfortunate)*

DAY 3 **Base Word Build**

Students will explore adding word parts to a base word to create new words.

- Write the Target Vocabulary word *cease* on the board and review its meaning with students.

- Remind students that word parts can change word meanings. Suggested language: **Cease is a base word. We can add different word parts, like prefixes and suffixes, to *cease* to form new words with new meanings.**

- First, add the ending *-ed* to *cease* to form the Target Vocabulary word *ceased*. Ask students to tell what the ending *-ed* indicates, and what the word *ceased* means. *(happened in the past; stopped or came to an end)*

- Follow a similar process to add the suffixes *-less* and then *-ly* to *cease* to form *ceaseless* and *ceaselessly*. Guide students to tell what each new word means.

- Invite students to think of other word parts or words they can add to *cease* to form new words. *(ceasing, unceasing, ceasefire)* Discuss the meaning of each new word.

- Have students write sentences in their Word Study Notebooks for three of the words they can build with the base word *cease*.

DAY 4 **Glossary Snapshots**

Students will create glossary entries for the Target Vocabulary words.

- Ask students to take out their Student Books. Have them turn to the glossary in the back of the book. Remind students that all the words in a glossary appear in alphabetical order, and each glossary entry is followed by a definition.

- Give each student ten index cards, and explain that students will create a glossary entry on each card. Tell students that they will use one card for each Target Vocabulary word.

- Have students write the word at the top of the card followed by its definition. Then have students turn the card over. Have them write a sentence using the word and draw a picture to support the meaning of the word.

- When students finish creating their glossary entries, have them arrange the cards in alphabetical order.

- Have students share their glossary entries in small groups. Then have each student compare his or her glossary entries to those in the Student Book for the same Target Vocabulary words.

DAY 5 **Synonyms and Antonyms**

Students will complete a Column Chart with synonyms and antonyms to deepen their understanding of Target Vocabulary words.

- Display a Column Chart as shown at right. Tell students that they will work with you to complete this chart by listing Target Vocabulary words and their synonyms and antonyms.

- Write the headings *Word, Synonym,* and *Antonym* in the Column Chart. Review the meanings of *synonym* and *antonym*. Remind students that synonyms are words with similar meanings, and antonyms are opposites.

- Write the word *acquire* in the *Word* column. Ask students to explain what *acquire* means. Then guide students to name a synonym for *acquire*. Model your thinking. Suggested language: **A little league team wanted to *acquire* new uniforms. They planned to *get* them by selling refreshments at games. The word *get* is a synonym for *acquire*.**

- Have students identify an antonym for *acquire* and record it. Then tell students to copy the Column Chart into their Word Study Notebooks. Allow time for students to write the headings and examples you provided.

- Ask students to select three more Target Vocabulary words. Have them write each word in the first column and complete the chart independently. Students should use a dictionary or thesaurus as necessary. Have partners compare their completed Column Charts.

Word	Synonym	Antonym
acquire	get	lose
declared	stated	asked
unfortunate	unlucky	lucky
coerce	pressure	beg

TARGET VOCABULARY

1. **overcome** To *overcome* a difficulty is to solve it or conquer it.

2. **association** An *association* is a group of people officially organized for a certain purpose.

3. **capitol** A *capitol* is a building in which a government meets to create laws.

4. **drought** During a *drought*, there is little or no rain.

5. **dedicate** To *dedicate* something is to devote it to a special purpose.

6. **publicity** *Publicity* is information given out to get the public's attention.

7. **violence** *Violence* is the use of physical force to cause harm.

8. **conflicts** When people have *conflicts*, they have problems or disagreements with each other.

9. **horizon** The place at which the earth and sky meet is the *horizon*.

10. **brilliant** Something that is *brilliant* is very bright.

 Reproducible Word Cards are available at **www.thinkcentral.com.**

WORD STUDY NOTEBOOK

DAY 1 Introduce Target Vocabulary; Suffix *-ion*

After learning the week's Target Vocabulary words, students will explore words that have the suffix *-ion.*

• Write the Target Vocabulary words on the board, read them aloud, and have students repeat the words. Discuss the student-friendly definitions, shown at left, with students.

• Rewrite the word *association,* and underline *-ion*. Point out that *-ion* is a suffix. Help students recall that a suffix is a word part that goes at the end of a base word to form a new word with a different meaning.

• Discuss the word parts in *association*. Suggested language: **The word part *-ion* is a suffix. The suffix *-ion* can mean "the act or process of." *Associate* is the base word. *Associate* means "to join together or connect with." An *association* is a group of people who join together for a certain purpose. It is the act of associating.**

• Explain that *-ion* can be added to the end of other words. Write the following word equations on the board:

correct + ion = _____   elect + ion = _____

inspect + ion = _____   infect + ion = _____

• Have students add the word parts together to create new words. Ask volunteers to write the new words on the board. Discuss each word's meaning.

• Have students copy the completed word equations and their meanings into their Word Study Notebooks.

- -

DAY 2 Twenty Questions

Students will ask a series of questions about the Target Vocabulary words and then guess the words.

• Briefly review the Target Vocabulary words and their student-friendly definitions.

• Have students work in small groups of two teams. Provide each team with a set of Lesson 19 Word Cards. Ask the teams to shuffle their cards and stack them face down on their desks.

• Explain that one team will choose a Word Card without revealing the card or saying the word aloud. The other team will take turns asking yes/no questions to try to guess which Target Vocabulary word was selected.

• Model the activity with a volunteer. Have the student select a Target Vocabulary word. Then ask questions to try to guess the word. Tell the student to respond to each question by saying *yes* or *no*. Continue asking questions until you can guess the word.

• Tell teams that they will now play the game with the remaining Target Vocabulary words. Have each team take turns selecting a Word Card until all the words are guessed. When one team chooses a word that has already been used, have them place the card in a separate pile and select another word from the stack.

• When students are finished, have them explain which words were the most difficult to guess and which words were the easiest to guess.

| brilliant | capitol | drought |

DAY 3 Prefix *over-*

Students will use the prefix *over-* to determine the meanings of new words.

- Review with students that a prefix is a word part added to the beginning of a base word to form a new word. Remind students that knowing the meanings of common prefixes will help them recognize the meanings of many words.

- On the board, write the word *overheat*. Underline the prefix *over-*, and circle the base word *heat*. Explain to students that *over-* can mean "excessively." Suggested language: **The word *overheat* means "to heat up excessively."**

- Write the Target Vocabulary word *overcome* and underline *over-*. Tell students that in this case, *over-* means "completely." Discuss what it means to overcome a problem.

- Write *overexcite, overjoy, overconfident, overpower,* and *overhaul*. Have volunteers underline each word's prefix. Then discuss the words' meanings. Tell students to write the words and their meanings in their Word Study Notebooks.

- Have students distinguish between words in which *over-* means "excessively" *(overexcite, overconfident)* and words in which *over-* means "completely" *(overjoy, overpower, overhaul)*.

DAY 4 Write About Farms

Students will write about farms and include Target Vocabulary words in their writing.

- Write the Target Vocabulary words on the board. Read them aloud, and discuss each word's student-friendly definition.

- Tell students that they will write a short paragraph that describes farms. They can use what they know, as well as what they learned from the Student Book selections "Harvesting Hope" and "The Edible Schoolyard." Discuss the selections with students, as needed.

- Tell students to use at least four Target Vocabulary words in their writing. Explain that a good way to describe a farm is to compare it to something similar. Suggest that students compare farms to gardens.

- When students finish writing, have them read their paragraphs to a partner. Partners should confirm that the Target Vocabulary words were used correctly.

> **drought**
>
> A long drought can ruin the crops grown on a farm or in a garden.

DAY 5 Root Chain

Students will observe and participate in the building of a Root Chain.

- Tell students that a root is a word part that has meaning but cannot stand alone. Help students understand that the same root may be a part of many words.

- Write the Target Vocabulary word *publicity* on the board, and underline the root *pub*. Explain that *pub* means "people." Help students recognize that *publicity* is information that is given out to get people's attention.

- Ask students to name other words that contain the root *pub*. Write each word in a list, aligning and underlining *pub* as shown at right.

- Guide students to use word parts to determine the meaning of *publication*. Point out the root *pub*, and review the meaning of the suffix *-ion*. *(the act or process of)* Then discuss the meaning of *publication*. *(the act of publishing printed material to share with people)*

- Have students use the root *pub* and other word parts to explain the remaining words in the Root Chain. Have them copy the Root Chain into their Word Study Notebooks and write the word meanings next to the words. Provide students with dictionaries if needed.

publicity
publication
public
publish
publicly
publicize
nonpublic

1. **territory** An area of land is a *territory*.

2. **accompany** To go somewhere with someone is to *accompany* him or her.

3. **proposed** If something is *proposed*, it is suggested.

4. **interpreter** An *interpreter* translates words from one language to another.

5. **duty** A person's *duty* is his or her job or responsibility.

6. **supplies** *Supplies* are the important items that people need.

7. **route** A *route* is a road or path between two places.

8. **corps** A *corps* is a group that works together.

9. **clumsy** Something that is *clumsy* is awkward or done without skill.

10. **landmark** A *landmark* is a familiar or easily seen object that identifies a place.

 Reproducible Word Cards and Graphic Organizer 6 (Four-Square Map) are available at **www.thinkcentral.com**.

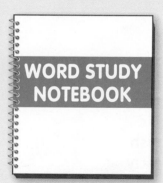

DAY 1 ## Introduce Target Vocabulary; Suffix *-er*

After learning the week's Target Vocabulary words, students will explore words that have the suffix *-er*.

• Write the Target Vocabulary words on the board, read them aloud, and have students repeat the words. Discuss the student-friendly definitions, shown at left, with students.

• Remind students that a suffix is a word part added to the end of a base word to form a new word with a different meaning. Emphasize that knowing the meanings of common suffixes can help students determine the meanings of many words.

• Introduce the suffix *-er*. Suggested language: **The suffix *-er* can mean "someone who." When *-er* is added to the end of a verb, the new word is a noun.**

• Rewrite the word *interpreter* on the board, and underline the suffix *-er*. Explain that the addition of *-er* changes the meaning and part of speech of the base word *interpret*. Suggested language: **When the suffix *-er* is added to the verb *interpret*, the noun *interpreter* is formed. An *interpreter* is someone who interprets, or translates words.**

• Write the following verbs on the board: *admire, report, cater, defend*. Then have volunteers come to the board and add the suffix *-er* to each word. Have students identify the new part of speech for each word. *(noun)* Ask students to explain the meaning of each new word.

• Tell students to copy the words *admirer, reporter, caterer,* and *defender* in their Word Study Notebooks. Have them underline each word's suffix and circle the base word. Then have them write a brief definition of each word. Have pairs share their definitions to confirm their understanding.

- -

DAY 2 ## Relating Words Questions

Students will identify related Target Vocabulary words in a question and use knowledge of their meanings to answer.

• Display the Lesson 20 Word Cards. Briefly review each word's student-friendly definition.

• Explain that you will read several questions to students, and they should listen for the Target Vocabulary words used in each sentence.

• Tell students to use their knowledge of the words to help them answer the questions. Prompt them to explain their reasoning.

• Allow two or more students to reply to each question to demonstrate a variety of possible responses.

1. **What is the most important *duty* of an *interpreter*?**

2. **Why would someone driving an emergency vehicle need to know the quickest *route* to deliver *supplies*?**

3. **Could it be dangerous to *accompany* someone who is *clumsy*? Why or why not?**

4. **What would be the best way to label a *landmark* on the map of a *territory*?**

5. **Why would it be important for a *corps* to work together to achieve the goals it *proposed*?**

DAY 3   Prefix *inter-*

Students will use the prefix *inter-* to determine the meanings of new words.

- Review with students that a prefix is a word part added to the beginning of a base word to form a new word. Remind students that knowing the meanings of common prefixes will help them understand the meanings of many words.

- Write *interpreter* on the board. Underline the prefix *inter-*, and explain to students that *inter-* means "between or among." Review the meaning of *interpreter*. *(someone who translates, or interprets, between languages)*

- Explain that *inter-* can be added to the beginning of other words. Write *international, intercom, interact, interject,* and *interstate* on the board.

- Have volunteers come to the board and underline the prefix *inter-* in each word. Tell students to write the words in their Word Study Notebooks. As a class, define each word and discuss how the prefix can help determine the meaning of the words.

- Extend the activity by having partners identify each word's part of speech. Then have them use each word in an oral sentence.

DAY 4   Word and Picture Matching

Students will work with a partner to draw a picture for a Target Vocabulary word and guess the matching word.

- Have partners take out this week's Word Cards and review the words' meanings.

- Explain that today students will take turns drawing pictures and guessing which Target Vocabulary words they represent. Model the activity by drawing a simple map. Outline an area of land, and guide students to guess the word *territory*.

- Distribute blank index cards to student pairs. Have one student in each pair select a Word Card and begin drawing. The partner will try to guess which Target Vocabulary word the picture represents.

- Explain that when the partner guesses the correct word, he or she will write the word on the back of the drawing and use the word in a sentence. Then have partners switch roles.

- Continue the activity until all Target Vocabulary words have been drawn and guessed correctly. Ask students which words were the most challenging to draw or guess. Have students explain their reasoning.

DAY 5   Four-Square Map

Students will complete Four-Square Maps to demonstrate their understanding of Target Vocabulary words.

- Display a Four-Square Map as shown at right. Explain that the class will work together to complete it with ideas about the Target Vocabulary word *supplies*.

- Write *supplies* in the center of the map. Ask students to explain what the word means. Write their response or the student-friendly definition in the upper-left corner. *(items people need)*

- Have a volunteer use *supplies* in a sentence. Write his or her answer in the lower-left corner. *(Don't forget to bring your supplies for the science project.)*

- Have students name some examples of *supplies*. Record one response in the upper-right corner. *(pencils)* Then guide students to name things that are not supplies, such as *pets* or a *home*. Record one non-example in the lower-right corner.

- When the class example is completed, have students create Four-Square Maps in their Word Study Notebooks for the Target Vocabulary words *accompany, route,* and *corps.*

- Have students compare and discuss their completed maps with a partner.

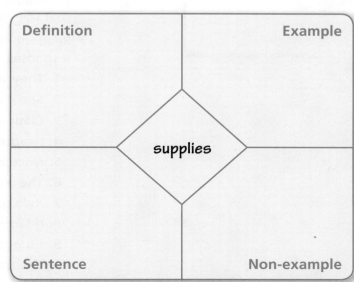

TARGET VOCABULARY

1. **appreciate** When you *appreciate* something, you know what is good about it.

2. **blaring** When something is *blaring*, it is making a loud, unpleasant noise.

3. **combination** A *combination* is a mixture.

4. **promptly** If you do something *promptly*, you do it right away.

5. **introduce** When you *introduce* people, you present them to each other for the first time.

6. **nocturnal** *Nocturnal* animals and people are active mostly at night.

7. **feats** *Feats* are difficult actions.

8. **effort** A person who makes an *effort* tries hard to do something.

9. **suggest** To *suggest* is to put forward an idea.

10. **racket** A *racket* is loud, bothersome noise.

 Reproducible Word Cards are available at **www.thinkcentral.com**.

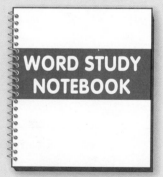

WORD STUDY NOTEBOOK

DAY 1 **Introduce Target Vocabulary; Suffix -al**

After learning the week's Target Vocabulary words, students will explore words that end with the suffix -al.

- Write the Target Vocabulary words on the board, read them aloud, and have students repeat the words. Discuss the student-friendly definitions, shown at left, with students.

- Remind students that a suffix is a word part added to the end of a base word to form a new word. Tell them that recognizing common suffixes will help them understand the meanings of new words.

- Rewrite *nocturnal,* underline the suffix -al, and discuss the word parts. Suggested language: **The suffix -al can change a noun to an adjective. The suffix -al means "having the characteristics of or relating to."** Circle *noct* and draw a square around *-urn*. Then say: **The root *noct* means "night," and the suffix -urn means "a place for." *Nocturn* must mean "a place for night." *Nocturn* plus the suffix -al forms the adjective *nocturnal*.**

- Discuss the meaning of *nocturnal. (having the characteristics of or relating to night)*

- Write the following words on the board: *monument, norm, music, tradition, universe.* Have students copy the words into their Word Study Notebooks and add the suffix -al to make adjectives. Point out that for words ending in e, they must drop the e before adding the suffix.

- Then have partners work together to write the meanings of *monumental, normal, musical, traditional,* and *universal.* Allow students to use a print or online dictionary, as needed.

· ·

DAY 2 **"Because" Sentences**

Students will demonstrate their understanding of Target Vocabulary words by completing sentences.

- Review the week's Target Vocabulary words with students. Then explain that you will read the beginning of a sentence that contains a vocabulary word. Tell students to write an ending for every sentence they hear in their Word Study Notebooks.

- Tell students that each sentence starter will end with the word *because.* Explain that the word *because* signals that they should begin writing their endings.

- Read the following sentence starters, and allow time for students to write their responses. Have volunteers share their sentence endings with the class.

  1. **They were asked to turn down the *blaring* noise because…**
  2. **She made an *effort* to visit her friend because…**
  3. **Claudia *promptly* turned onto the next street because…**
  4. **I *appreciate* my friends because…**
  5. ***Nocturnal* animals sleep during the day because…**
  6. **The jackhammer made a terrible *racket* because…**
  7. **Kyle does not like the *combination* of sweet and sour food because…**
  8. **If I *introduce* myself to someone, it is because…**
  9. **I *suggest* that you wear the blue shirt because…**
  10. **The trapeze artist performed *feats* that were extraordinary because…**

DAY 3 · Suffix *-ate*

Students will explore the meanings of words with the suffix *-ate*.

- Remind students that knowing the meanings of common suffixes can sometimes help them understand a word's meaning.

- Write the Target Vocabulary word *appreciate* on the board. Underline the suffix *-ate*, and discuss its meaning. Suggested language: **The suffix -ate can mean "to make or do or cause to be." The word *appreciate* means "to be thankful."**

- Use the word *appreciate* in the following oral sentence and ask students to identify its part of speech: **I appreciate a loyal friend. What part of speech is appreciate?** *(verb)*

- Write the following words on the board: *calculate, graduate, animate, eliminate*. Have students copy them into their Word Study Notebooks and circle the suffix *-ate* in each word.

- Have students work with a partner to determine the meaning of each word and its part of speech. Then have students write a sentence for each word.

- Ask volunteers to share their sentences with the class.

DAY 4 · I Spy Clues

Students will use clues to guess Target Vocabulary words.

- Distribute copies of the Lesson 21 Word Cards. Briefly review the Target Vocabulary words.

- Explain that today partners will use this week's vocabulary to play a word game called I Spy.

- Explain the purpose of the game. One partner will choose a word and provide clues that relate to the word's meaning or its word parts. The other student will try to guess the word.

- Have partners place the Word Cards face up on their desks so that they can both see the cards. Then tell students to begin each clue with "I'm thinking of a word that…"

- Model giving a clue for the word *nocturnal*, and have students guess the word. Suggested language: **I'm thinking of a word that has to do with nighttime activity. What is the word?** *(nocturnal)*

- Remind partners to take turns after guessing a word correctly, and have students play until all the words have been used.

DAY 5 · Homophones

Students will determine the meanings of homophones.

- Review with students that homophones are words that sound the same but have different spellings and meanings.

- Then write the Target Vocabulary word *feats* on the board. Ask students to provide the meaning of the word. *(difficult actions)* Then erase the ending *-s*. Review that *feat* is the base word, and the ending *-s* makes the noun plural.

- Next to the word *feat*, write the word *feet* and read it aloud. Prompt students to share the meaning of *feet*. *(what we stand on and move with)* Guide students to understand that *feat* and *feet* are homophones.

- Work with students to create sentences for the words *feat* and *feet*. Write the sentences on the board, and have students copy them into their Word Study Notebooks.

- Then organize students into small groups, and write the following homophone pairs on the board: *principle/principal, creak/creek, presence/presents*. Assign each group a homophone pair, and have them write sentences using the words.

- Have groups share their sentences with the class. Then take a class vote for the most creative sentences, and write them on the board.

TARGET VOCABULARY

1. **politics** The work of forming and running governments is called *politics*.

2. **intelligent** An *intelligent* person has the ability to learn, think, and understand.

3. **disorderly** If people are being *disorderly*, they are behaving in a way that is out of control or against the rules.

4. **approve** To *approve* of something is to like and agree with it.

5. **polls** In an election, the places where people go to vote are the *polls*.

6. **legislature** A *legislature* is a group of people who make laws for a state or country.

7. **amendment** An *amendment* is a change made to correct or add something.

8. **candidates** *Candidates* are people who are hoping to be chosen for a job or to win an election.

9. **informed** Someone who is *informed* has information or knowledge.

10. **denied** If a person is *denied* something, he or she is not allowed to have it.

 Reproducible Word Cards and Graphic Organizer 6 (Four-Square Map) are available at **www.thinkcentral.com**.

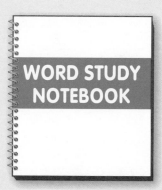

WORD STUDY NOTEBOOK

DAY 1 Introduce Target Vocabulary; Prefix *dis-*

After learning the week's Target Vocabulary words, students will explore words that begin with the prefix *dis-*.

- Write the Target Vocabulary words on the board, read them aloud, and have students repeat the words. Discuss the student-friendly definitions, shown at left, with students.

- Remind students that knowing the meanings of common prefixes will help them make sense of new words they encounter.

- Call attention to the prefix *dis-* in the Target Vocabulary word *disorderly*. Remind students of a previously learned Target Vocabulary word with this prefix (*discouraged*), and review that the meaning of *dis-* is "not."

- Point to the word *disorderly*. Lead students to understand that the word *orderly* relates to people behaving in a controlled manner. Suggested language: **Orderly people are people who follow the rules and behave. If the prefix *dis-* is added before the word *orderly*, what does *disorderly* mean?** *(behaving in a way that is against the rules or out of control)*

- Write the following base words on the board: *approve, trust, connect, like*. Discuss the meaning of each word. Then have volunteers add the prefix *dis-* to each word.

- Distribute blank index cards to students. Tell students to write each word on an index card. Then have them turn over each card and write the word's meaning. Have student pairs work together to use *disapprove, distrust, disconnect,* and *dislike* in oral sentences.

DAY 2 Meaning Sort

Students will sort the Target Vocabulary words according to categories of their choice.

- Distribute a set of Lesson 22 Word Cards to each student. Tell students that today they will sort the words based on categories they choose.

- Display the Word Cards. Model your thinking as you demonstrate how to come up with the categories. Suggested language: **I notice that many of the words are nouns.** *Candidates* **are people, and** *polls* **are places. I can sort words that are nouns into one category and words that are verbs or adjectives into other categories.**

- Have students lay out their Word Cards. Guide them to select categories that are based on the words' meanings. If students have difficulty, suggest that they sort by words that describe people or by words that are positive, negative, or neutral.

- Tell students to write their category headings in their Word Study Notebooks and then sort their Word Cards. Have them confirm the words were sorted correctly.

- Then have partners share their sorts and explain their thinking behind their chosen categories. Challenge students to sort by their partner's categories.

candidates	denied	disorderly
amendment	approve	informed

DAY 3 | Suffix -ment

Students will use the suffix -ment to determine the meanings of words.

- Remind students that a suffix is a word part added to the end of a base word. Tell students that knowing common suffixes will help them make sense of new words.

- Write the Target Vocabulary word *amendment*. Underline the suffix -ment, and discuss it. Suggested language: **The suffix -ment can mean "the state or condition of." It can change a verb to a noun.**

- Write the word *amend* above *amendment*, and discuss the words. Suggested language: **When the suffix -ment is added to the base word *amend*, the word becomes *amendment*. *Amend* is a verb. *Amendment* is a noun.**

- As a class, discuss the difference in meaning between the two words. Then ask volunteers to use the words in oral sentences.

- Next, write these base words on the board for students to copy into their Word Study Notebooks: *manage, arrange, achieve, advertise.*

- Tell students to add the suffix -ment to the end of each word. Then have students write the new meaning next to each word.

DAY 4 | Write a Campaign Poster

Students will write a campaign poster that includes Target Vocabulary words.

- Have students take out their Lesson 22 Word Cards, and review the student-friendly definition of each word.

- Then tell students to open their Student Books to "I Could Do That!" on page 561. Discuss Esther Morris and the important things she did in her lifetime. Recall her words "I could do that" and how she remained determined to campaign for causes she believed in, especially the right for women to vote.

- Next, tell students to imagine that they are campaigning for something they would like changed at their school. Explain that they will write campaign posters in their Word Study Notebooks.

- Have students lay their Word Cards on their desks and identify a group of words they could use in their posters. Challenge them to find at least five Target Vocabulary words.

- Ask students to be creative by illustrating their posters. When students have finished their work, have them share their posters with the class. Discuss with students how they used the Target Vocabulary words.

DAY 5 | Four-Square Map

Students will complete Four-Square Maps to demonstrate their understanding of Target Vocabulary words.

- Display a Four-Square Map. Explain that students will help you complete the map with ideas about the word *amendment*.

- Write *amendment* in the center of the map. Prompt students to provide the meaning of the word. Write their response in the upper-left corner. *(a change made to correct or add something)*

- Have students name examples of amendments they would like to make to their classroom rules. Write one example in the upper-right corner. *(official "pet day" on Fridays)*

- Have volunteers use the word *amendment* in oral sentences. Record the sentence that best uses the word in the lower-left corner. *(An amendment can change an unjust law.)* Then ask students to name examples of school rules that should not be amended, or changed. Record one non-example. *(being respectful to others)*

- Have students create new Four-Square Maps in their Word Study Notebooks for the Target Vocabulary words *politics, approve,* and *informed.* When students finish, have pairs trade maps and add ideas to their partner's maps.

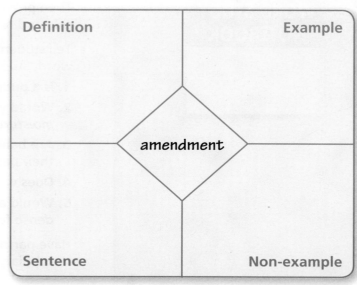

Vocabulary

1. **resources** *Resources* are an available supply of something that can be used when needed.

2. **dense** Something that is *dense* has its parts packed together closely.

3. **evaporate** When liquids *evaporate*, they become gases.

4. **shallow** If something is *shallow*, it is not deep.

5. **moisture** Tiny drops of water in the air or on a surface are *moisture*.

6. **civilized** A *civilized* society is advanced and has reasonable laws.

7. **continent** A *continent* is one of the main landmasses of Earth.

8. **opportunities** *Opportunities* are chances for a person to do something.

9. **customs** The common ways of behaving in a society are called *customs*.

10. **independent** If you are *independent* of something, you don't rely on that thing.

 Reproducible Word Cards and Graphic Organizer 14 (Venn Diagram) are available at **www.thinkcentral.com**.

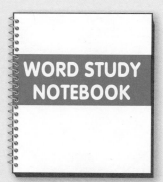

WORD STUDY NOTEBOOK

DAY 1 ## Introduce Target Vocabulary; Prefix *in-*

After learning the week's Target Vocabulary words, students will explore words that begin with the prefix *in-*.

- Write the Target Vocabulary words on the board, read them aloud, and have students repeat the words. Discuss the student-friendly definitions, shown at left, with students.

- Remind students that a prefix is a word part added to the beginning of a word that changes the word's meaning.

- Draw attention to the Target Vocabulary word *independent*, underline the prefix *in-*, and review the meaning of the prefix. Suggested language: **The prefix *in-* means "not."**

- Then write the word *dependent* on the board, and discuss its meaning with students. Lead students to understand that when a person is dependent, he or she needs the help or support of others. Then add the prefix *in-* to *dependent*. Suggested language: **The new word is *independent*. What is the meaning of this word?** *(not needing the help or support of others)*

- Explain that *in-* can be added to the beginning of other words. Write the following word equations on the board:

$$\text{in} + \text{definite} = \rule{2cm}{0.15mm} \qquad \text{in} + \text{capable} = \rule{2cm}{0.15mm}$$

$$\text{in} + \text{frequent} = \rule{2cm}{0.15mm} \qquad \text{in} + \text{sincere} = \rule{2cm}{0.15mm}$$

- Have students add the word parts together to create new words, and ask volunteers to write the new words on the board. Discuss each word's meaning.

- Ask students to copy the word parts and the new words into their Word Study Notebooks. Then have them write a sentence for each new word.

DAY 2 ## Paired Yes/No Questions

Students will answer questions to show their knowledge of Target Vocabulary words.

- Write the Target Vocabulary words on the board, and review the words' meanings with students.

- Then provide each student with a blank index card. Have students write *yes* on one side and *no* on the other side.

- Tell students that you will ask pairs of questions featuring a Target Vocabulary word. Students should hold up the *yes* or *no* side of the card to answer.

   1. Is a puddle *shallow*? *(yes)* Is an ocean *shallow*? *(no)*
   2. Would you find a lot of *moisture* in a desert? *(no)* Would you find a lot of *moisture* in a rain forest? *(yes)*
   3. Are babies *independent* from their parents? *(no)* Are adults *independent* from their parents? *(yes)*
   4. Does water *evaporate*? *(yes)* Do trees *evaporate*? *(no)*
   5. Would a forest fire create a *dense* forest? *(no)* Would trees and plants create a *dense* forest? *(yes)*

- Have partners continue to ask their own paired questions using the Target Vocabulary words *resources, civilized, continent, opportunities,* and *customs.*

DAY 3 Acronyms

Students will learn about space-related acronyms.

- Have students open their Student Books to "The Ever-Living Tree" on page 597. Call attention to the phrase *space station*.

- Introduce the concept of acronyms by writing *ISS* on the board next to *International Space Station*. Discuss the acronym. Suggested language: **An acronym is a word whose letters stand for a longer phrase or name. *ISS* is an acronym for the *International Space Station*, a famous research facility.**

- Underline the initial letter of each word in *International Space Station* to demonstrate how an acronym is formed. Then have students explore other space-related acronyms. Write the following on the board: *unidentified flying object, Kennedy Space Center, National Aeronautics and Space Administration*.

- Have volunteers underline the initial letter of each word, and ask the class to determine the acronyms that are formed. *(UFO, KSC, NASA)*

- Circle *and* in *National Aeronautics and Space Administration*. Explain that the initial letter in *and, the, for,* and *of* is usually not included in acronyms.

DAY 4 Word and Picture Matching

Students will work with a partner to draw a picture for a Target Vocabulary word and guess the matching word.

- Distribute to student pairs one set of the Lesson 23 Word Cards and ten blank index cards.

- Explain that partners will take turns choosing a Target Vocabulary word, drawing a picture that represents the word, and guessing which word the picture represents.

- Have partners place one set of Word Cards face down on their desk. Ask one student to select a Word Card without revealing it to the other student.

- The first student should draw a picture of the word he or she selected and then show it to the second student. The second student should try to guess the correct Target Vocabulary word.

- The student who guesses the word should write the correct word on the back of the drawing and then use the word in a sentence. The student who draws the picture should confirm whether the Target Vocabulary word was used correctly.

- Have students continue the game, taking turns until all words have been guessed.

DAY 5 Venn Diagram

Students will use their knowledge of the Target Vocabulary words to complete a Venn Diagram.

- Write the Target Vocabulary words. Review the words as they relate to the selection "The Ever-Living Tree" on page 585 in the Student Book. Then display a Venn Diagram. Explain that students will work with you to write the vocabulary words in the diagram. Label the circles.

- Tell students that they will use what they know about each vocabulary word to sort based on their relationship to land (*Continent*) or people (*Civilized*).

- Model sorting *customs*: **People have *customs*, such as taking your shoes off before entering a house. Which category best fits *customs*?** (Civilized; customs *deal with what people do*.)

- Guide students to write the remaining words in the diagram. Explain that some words fit in both categories. They should be placed in the overlapping circle in the middle of the diagram.

- As students give their answers, prompt them to share their thinking behind each word's placement.

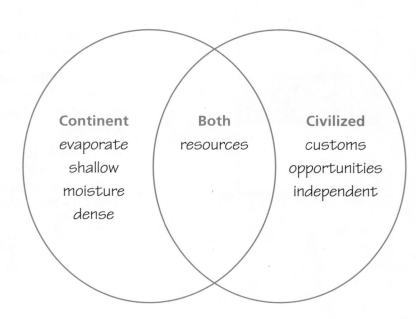

Continent: evaporate, shallow, moisture, dense

Both: resources

Civilized: customs, opportunities, independent

TARGET VOCABULARY

1. **bond** A *bond* between people is a feeling of close friendship.

2. **suffered** If someone felt pain or great sadness, he or she *suffered*.

3. **intruder** One who enters a place without permission is an *intruder*.

4. **companion** A *companion* is someone who spends time with you.

5. **enclosure** An area that is fenced off and used for a special purpose is an *enclosure*.

6. **inseparable** People or things that are *inseparable* are always together.

7. **charged** If an animal *charged* at someone, it moved quickly toward that person.

8. **chief** The *chief* part of something is the most important or largest part.

9. **exhausted** A person who is *exhausted* is tired and has no energy.

10. **affection** *Affection* is a feeling of fondness for someone or something.

 Reproducible Word Cards and Graphic Organizer 12 (T-Map) are available at **www.thinkcentral.com**.

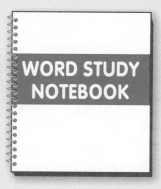

WORD STUDY NOTEBOOK

DAY 1 Introduce Target Vocabulary; Prefix *ex-*

After learning the week's Target Vocabulary words, students will explore words that begin with the prefix *ex-*.

- Write the Target Vocabulary words on the board, read them aloud, and have students repeat the words. Discuss the student-friendly definitions, shown at left, with students.

- Review with students that a prefix is a word part added to the beginning of a base word to form a new word.

- Remind students that they have learned the common prefix *ex-*. Write the word *exhale* on the board, and ask students to take in a deep breath and then let it out. Have students share what they did. *(let out air)* Underline *ex-* in *exhale,* and confirm that *ex-* means "out of."

- Then draw attention to the Target Vocabulary word *exhausted,* underline the prefix *ex-*, and discuss the word's meaning. Suggested language: **When people say they are *exhausted*, do they have energy or are they out of energy?** *(out of energy)*

- Write these words on the board and have students copy them into their Word Study Notebooks: *excavate, extend, exclaim.* Have students underline the prefix *ex-* in each word. As a class, discuss the meaning of each word.

- Then have students write the following questions in their Word Study Notebooks: *What kinds of things might a scientist want to excavate? When would you extend your hand to someone? What situation might make you exclaim, "Oh, no!"?*

- Have students circle the word with the prefix *ex-* in each question. Then ask students to answer each question and share their answers with the class.

- -

DAY 2 Synonyms

Students will use their knowledge of the Target Vocabulary words to determine their synonyms.

- Display a T-Map. Tell students that they will complete this map with Target Vocabulary words and their synonyms.

- Write the headings *Word* and *Synonym*. Remind students that synonyms are words that have the same or similar meanings, such as *strong* and *powerful*.

- Begin with the word *charged*. Guide students to identify a synonym for *charged*. Suggested language: **If an animal *rushed* towards someone, then that animal *charged* at that person. *Charged* and *rushed* are the same. I will write *rushed* under *Synonym*.**

- Tell students to copy the T-Map into their Word Study Notebooks and add the following vocabulary words in the left column: *intruder, companion, enclosure, inseparable, affection, suffered.* In the right column, have them write synonyms to complete the T-Map. Then have pairs discuss their completed T-Maps.

Word	Synonym
charged	rushed
intruder	invader
companion	friend

DAY 3 Multiple-Meaning Words

Students will explore words that have more than one meaning.

- Tell students that some words have more than one meaning.

- Explain that when students read a word and are unsure of the word's meaning, they can use context clues to help them determine its meaning. Tell students they can also use a dictionary to clarify a word's meaning.

- Write the Target Vocabulary words *bond, charged,* and *chief* on the board. Discuss the student-friendly definition for each word. Then explain that student pairs will work together to determine a different meaning for each word.

- Have students take out their Word Study Notebooks and copy the words. Then guide them to use a print or online dictionary to locate new meanings for *bond, charged,* and *chief.*

- For each word, have partners write two sentences: one sentence that uses the student-friendly definition and another sentence that uses a different meaning of the word. When students are finished, have them share their sentences with the class and discuss the words' multiple meanings.

DAY 4 Word Pairs

Students will write sentences using Target Vocabulary words.

- Distribute copies of the Lesson 24 Word Cards, and review the student-friendly definition for each word.

- Display the Word Cards *companion* and *affection,* and write the sample sentence below. Circle the Target Vocabulary words *companion* and *affection,* and tell students that they will write sentences that use two of the Target Vocabulary words.

- Then tell students to place their Word Cards face down. Explain that they will choose two Word Cards, turn them over, and use the words to write a sentence in their Word Study Notebooks.

- Tell students that they may use different forms of the words as needed to ensure their sentences make sense.

- Have students use all the Target Vocabulary words. Then ask volunteers to share their sentences.

companion	affection

The furry companion wagged its tail when it received affection.

DAY 5 Shades of Meaning

Students will rank synonyms on a Word Line by their shades of meaning.

- Remind students that synonyms are words that have the same or similar meanings. Prompt students to brainstorm synonyms for *exhausted,* and record them on the board. *(fatigued, overexerted, weakened, tuckered out, drained)*

- Help students understand that the synonyms suggested have slight differences in meaning, or they may have different feelings associated with them.

- Display and label a Word Line as shown below. Have students copy the Word Line into their Word Study Notebooks.

- Tell students to rank the synonyms along the Word Line according to whether they give the sense of "least tired," "most tired," or somewhere in the middle.

- Have partners compare their completed Word Lines. Lead them to discuss what they discovered about the Target Vocabulary word *exhausted* and its synonyms.

Least Tired   exhausted   Most Tired

TARGET VOCABULARY

1. **progress** If someone makes *progress*, he or she is improving.

2. **calculated** If someone *calculated* an answer, he or she worked with numbers to find an answer.

3. **dispute** If you *dispute* something, you say that it is not true.

4. **centuries** *Centuries* are periods of one hundred years.

5. **superior** Something *superior* is better than other things of its type.

6. **insert** To *insert* something is to put one object inside another.

7. **waste** To spend or throw away something thoughtlessly is a *waste*.

8. **inspector** A person who checks to make sure that things are working as they should is an *inspector*.

9. **mechanical** A machine with movable working parts is *mechanical*.

10. **average** Something that is *average* is typical or normal.

 Reproducible Word Cards and Graphic Organizer 15 (Web) are available at **www.thinkcentral.com**.

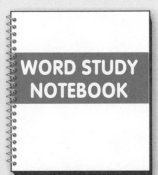

WORD STUDY NOTEBOOK

DAY 1 ## Introduce Target Vocabulary; Suffix *-or*

After learning the week's Target Vocabulary words, students will explore words that end with the suffix *-or*.

- Write the Target Vocabulary words on the board, read them aloud, and have students repeat the words. Discuss the student-friendly definitions, shown at left, with students.

- Remind students that knowing the meanings of common suffixes can sometimes help them understand a word's meaning.

- Write the word *inspect*, use it in a sentence, and ask students to identify its part of speech. Suggested language: **How is the word *inspect* used in the following sentence? He will *inspect* the car engine to make sure it runs properly.** *(verb)*

- Add the suffix *-or* to the end of *inspect* to make *inspector*. Underline the suffix, and discuss its meaning. Suggested language: **The suffix *-or* can mean "someone who." An *inspector* is someone who inspects, or checks, things to make sure they are working properly.** Point out that adding the suffix *-or* to *inspect* changes the word from a verb to a noun.

- Modify the suggested language as you repeat with the suffix *-er*. Use the word *teacher* as you review with students that *-er* can also mean "someone who."

- Write these words for students to copy into their Word Study Notebooks: *invent, sculpt, act, direct, collect*. Ask students to add the suffix *-or* to each word.

- Discuss the new meanings of the words. Then have student pairs create riddles, such as *I like to perform in movies. Who am I?* (actor) Have partners trade riddles with another student pair. Partners should use the new *-or* words to answer the riddles.

DAY 2 ## "Because" Sentences

Students will demonstrate their understanding of Target Vocabulary words by completing sentences.

- Distribute copies of the Lesson 25 Word Cards, and read them aloud. Briefly review the meanings of this week's vocabulary words with students.

- Explain that you will read the beginning of a sentence that contains a Target Vocabulary word. Students will use their knowledge of the word to write an ending in their Word Study Notebooks. When you say *because*, they should begin writing.

- Have volunteers share their sentence endings with the class.

  1. The school bus has a *mechanical* problem because…
  2. Vanessa correctly *calculated* how much food to buy because…
  3. He knew that the castle was at least two *centuries* old because…
  4. Please do not *waste* paper because…
  5. My little sister made *progress* riding her new bike because…
  6. The *inspector* examined the toy because…
  7. The city received higher than *average* rainfall because…
  8. Karl did not want to *dispute* what his best friend said because…
  9. I think my new skateboard is far *superior* to my old one because…
  10. My dad had to *insert* the DVD into another DVD player because…

DAY 3 Acronyms

Students will learn about technology-related acronyms.

- Have students open their Student Books to page 638. Discuss the technology-related words *telebooks* and *television* in the selection "The Fun They Had."

- Write *television* and discuss its acronym. Suggested language: **An acronym is a word whose letters stand for a longer phrase or name. What is the acronym for *television*?** (*TV*)

- Review with students that often the initial letter of each word in a phrase or name forms an acronym. Demonstrate by writing the phrase *compact disc* on the board. Underline the initial letters *c* and *d*, and then write the acronym *CD*.

- Discuss other technology-related acronyms. Write these phrases on the board and have students copy them into their Word Study Notebooks: *digital versatile disc, instant messaging,* and *personal computer.*

- Have partners determine the acronyms that are formed. (*DVD, IM, PC*) Then have students share their experiences with these technologies, and prompt them to use the acronyms in their discussions.

DAY 4 Write About Inventions

Students will write about future inventions using Target Vocabulary words.

- Have students take out their Lesson 25 Word Cards, read the words aloud, and review their definitions. Explain that students will use these words to write about an invention that will change classrooms in the future.

- Have students think about this week's reading selection "The Fun They Had." Recall Margie's mechanical teacher and how Margie did not enjoy her studies.

- Tell students to imagine they are inventors in the future. Explain that they have invented creative ways for students to have fun while learning. Tell students they will write about one of their amazing inventions.

- Have students lay out their Word Cards on their desks and separate a group of words they will use in their writing. Ask students to use at least four Target Vocabulary words.

- Tell students to complete their writing in their Word Study Notebooks. When students finish, have volunteers share their work with the class. Discuss whether the Target Vocabulary words were used correctly.

DAY 5 Vocabulary Web

Students will complete Vocabulary Webs to illustrate their understanding of Target Vocabulary words.

- Display a Vocabulary Web. Write the word *superior* in the center oval. Explain that students will help you complete a web for the word *superior*.

- Label the remaining ovals *Definition, Antonym, Example,* and *Sentence.* Ask students to provide the meaning of *superior*. Write their response or the student-friendly definition in the upper-left oval. (*something that is better than other things of its type*)

- Prompt students to provide antonyms for *superior*, such as *inferior* or *worse*. Record one of their responses in the upper-right oval. Then ask students to provide examples of technology-related gadgets they think are superior. Write one example in the lower-left oval. (*tablet computer, cell phone*)

- Have volunteers use *superior* in a sentence. Have students determine the best use of *superior* and then record the sentence in the lower-right oval. (*Video games in the future will be superior to the ones we have now.*)

- Next, write *progress* and *dispute*. Have students complete a Vocabulary Web for each word in their Word Study Notebooks. Then organize students into small groups to share and discuss their completed webs.

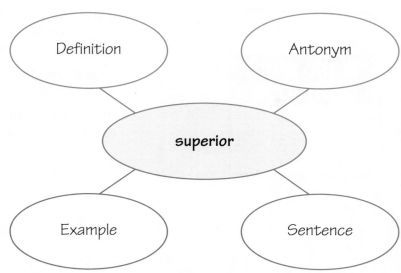

TARGET VOCABULARY

1. **peculiar** Something odd or unusual is *peculiar*.

2. **intends** A person who *intends* to do a task plans to do that task in the future.

3. **captured** If a person is caught while trying to get away, he or she has been *captured*.

4. **nourishing** Something that is *nourishing* gives people what they need to grow and live.

5. **isolated** A place is *isolated* when it is separated or far from other places.

6. **obtain** *Obtain* means to get something as a result of work or planning.

7. **assist** To *assist* someone is to help that person.

8. **favor** A *favor* is an act of kindness that someone does, even though he or she does not have to.

9. **condition** If a person is in poor *condition*, he or she may be sick or out of shape. If a building is in poor *condition*, it may need repairs.

10. **memorable** Something that is *memorable* is so special that it is worth remembering.

 Reproducible Word Cards and Graphic Organizer 12 (T-Map) are available at **www.thinkcentral.com**.

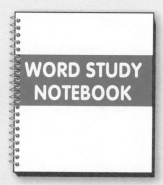

DAY 1 Review Target Vocabulary; Suffix *-able*

After reviewing Target Vocabulary words from previous lessons, students will explore words that have the suffix *-able*.

- Write the Target Vocabulary words on the board, read them aloud, and have students repeat the words. Discuss the student-friendly definitions, shown at left, with students.

- Rewrite the word *memorable,* and underline *-able*. Remind students that they have seen the suffix *-able* before. Explain that *-able* is a suffix added to the base word *memory*. Suggested language: **The suffix *-able* means "able to be" or "inclined to be."** When *-able* is added to the base word *memory,* the word *memorable* is formed. What does *memorable* mean?** (likely to be remembered)

- Write the following sentences on the board:

  The vacation was <u>enjoyable</u>.

  The bed is <u>comfortable</u>.

  We knew our opponent was <u>beatable</u>.

- Have students determine each underlined word's meaning by looking at the word parts. Then have students write other words with *-able* in their Word Study Notebooks. Tell students to write their own sentences using those words.

DAY 2 Synonyms

Students will use their knowledge of the Target Vocabulary words to determine their synonyms.

- Display a T-Map with the headings shown below. Tell students that today they will work with you to complete this map by listing Target Vocabulary words and their synonyms. Help students recall that synonyms are words that have the same or almost the same meaning.

- Write *isolated* under *Word*. Then model finding synonyms for *isolated*. Suggested language: **If a place is *isolated,* it is remote or far away from other people. *Remote* and *isolated* are synonyms because they have the same meaning.** Guide students to identify other synonyms for *isolated*. (apart, lonely)

- If students have difficulty, model using a thesaurus to find additional synonyms. Suggested language: **Sometimes I can't think of synonyms. When that happens, I use a thesaurus.** Write any additional words you find in the *Synonyms* column.

- Repeat the steps with *peculiar*. Then have students copy the T-Map and the examples provided in their Word Study Notebooks.

- Have them work in small groups to identify synonyms for *captured, nourishing, assist, intends, obtain, condition,* and *favor*. Have groups compare their T-Maps.

Word	Synonyms
isolated	remote, apart, lonely
peculiar	odd, unusual, strange, bizarre

DAY 3 Root *mem*

Students will use the root *mem* to determine the meanings of new words.

- Remind students that a root is a word part that has meaning but cannot stand alone as a word. Point out that knowing the meanings of common roots will help students determine the meanings of many words.

- Write the word *memorable* on the board. Underline *mem* and explain that it is the root of the word *memorable*. Suggested language: **The root *mem* means "mind." Knowing this helps me understand the word *memorable* because something that is memorable stays in your mind.**

- List the following words on the board: *remember, memoir, memento*. Discuss the meaning of each word, and guide students to understand how *mem* contributes to their meanings.

- Have students write the words in their Word Study Notebooks and underline the root *mem* in each word. Then have students write sentences using the words.

DAY 4 Clipped Words

Students will discuss and use animal-related clipped words.

- Remind students that a clipped word is a word that has been "clipped," or taken directly, from a longer word.

- Write the word *zoo* on the board as an example of a clipped word.

- Explain that *zoo* comes from the longer term *zoological garden*. Suggested language: ***Zoological garden* is very long to say, so people have "clipped" out the word *zoo*, which is much easier to say.**

- Explain that many animal-related words are clipped words. Discuss with students the clipped words that come from the following longer words: rhinoceros *(rhino)*, alligator *(gator)*, hippopotamus *(hippo)*, raccoon *(coon)*, veterinarian *(vet)*.

- Tell students to write sentences in their Word Study Notebooks using two of the animal-related clipped words. If they think of additional animal-related clipped words, they may write sentences using those words.

DAY 5 Riddles

Students will answer riddles about Target Vocabulary words to deepen their understanding of word meanings.

- Distribute copies of the Lesson 26 Word Cards.

- Explain that you will read riddles, and students should hold up the Word Card that answers each riddle. Discuss students' answers.

1. **You won't ever forget me because I'm this.** *(memorable)*

2. **A cat wearing sunglasses would be this.** *(peculiar)*

3. **If you can't lift a heavy box by yourself, you need someone to do this.** *(assist)*

4. **When a neighbor helps you mow your lawn, she is doing this.** *(favor)*

5. **When Gloria caught the lizard, she did this.** *(captured)*

6. **The boy who says he will clean his room tomorrow does this.** *(intends)*

7. **A log cabin deep in the woods would be this.** *(isolated)*

8. **This is what you do when you get something you want or need.** *(obtain)*

9. **Giving water is this to a plant.** *(nourishing)*

10. **When you buy a used bike, make sure this is good.** *(condition)*

TARGET VOCABULARY

1. **shortage** If there is not enough of something, there is a *shortage* of it.

2. **betrayed** If you have *betrayed* someone, you have done something to disappoint or let that person down.

3. **species** A *species* is a group of organisms that produces organisms of the same kind.

4. **continent** A *continent* is one of the main landmasses of Earth.

5. **scarce** If something is *scarce*, there is not enough of it.

6. **focus** To *focus* on something is to pay attention to that thing.

7. **convey** To *convey* means to communicate something or make it known.

8. **alert** To be *alert* is to be wide awake and paying attention.

9. **introduce** When you *introduce* people, you present them to each other for the first time.

10. **opportunities** *Opportunities* are chances for a person to do something.

 Reproducible Word Cards and Graphic Organizer 6 (Four-Square Map) are available at **www.thinkcentral.com**.

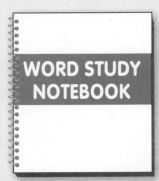

WORD STUDY NOTEBOOK

DAY 1 **Review Target Vocabulary; Suffix *-age***

After reviewing Target Vocabulary words from previous lessons, students will explore words that have the suffix *-age*.

- Write the Target Vocabulary words on the board, read them aloud, and have students repeat the words. Discuss the student-friendly definitions, shown at left, with students.

- Rewrite the word *shortage*, and underline *-age*. Remind students that they learned about the suffix *-age* in a previous lesson. Have them recall the suffix's meaning. *(the result of)*

- Review that a suffix is a word part that goes at the end of a base word to form a new word with a different meaning. Emphasize that if students learn to recognize common suffixes, they will be able to determine the meanings of many words.

- Explain the meaning of *shortage* using what you know about its suffix, *-age*. Suggested language: **The base word in *shortage* is *short*, which means "not having enough." When I combine the base word *short* with the suffix *-age*, I know that *shortage* must mean "the result of not having enough."**

- Write the words *coverage* and *outage* on the board. Then ask volunteers to circle the base word and underline the suffix in each word. As a class, discuss the meanings of the words.

- Have students write the following words in their Word Study Notebooks: *spoilage, sinkage, wastage*. Have partners use what they know about the suffix *-age* to determine the meanings of the words. Then have students write a brief definition next to each word.

DAY 2 **Idea Completion**

Students will complete sentence frames using the Target Vocabulary words.

- Distribute copies of the Lesson 27 Word Cards, and read them aloud. Have volunteers share the meaning of each word.

- Explain that you will read several sentence frames. Tell students to complete each sentence with a partner using the Target Vocabulary word on the Word Card you display, shown in parentheses below.

- Have partners write their sentence endings in their Word Study Notebooks. Have volunteers share their endings with the class.

    1. It was difficult to start a campfire because _____. *(scarce)*
    2. Graduating from college will _____. *(opportunities)*
    3. If I could travel anywhere, _____. *(continent)*
    4. When I take a test, _____. *(focus)*
    5. If two people are meeting for the first time, they _____. *(introduce)*
    6. When I wake up in the morning, _____. *(alert)*
    7. When I give a speech, I think about _____. *(convey)*
    8. I felt upset when _____. *(betrayed)*
    9. When I go to the zoo, I see _____. *(species)*
    10. Sometimes the supermarket _____. *(shortage)*

DAY 3 Similes and Metaphors

Students will listen to and describe the meanings of similes and metaphors.

- Write the following sentences on the board: **The frog jumps like a spring. The frog is a spring leaping across the pond.**

- Remind students that a simile uses the words *like* or *as* to compare two unlike things. Reread the first sentence, and provide an explanation of its meaning. Suggested language: **The first sentence is a simile. It uses the word *like* to compare the motion of a spring to how a frog jumps.**

- Then explain that a metaphor compares two unlike things without using *like* or *as*. Reread the second sentence. Then say: **This sentence is a metaphor. It says the frog *is* a spring, even though as readers we know the writer is just making an interesting comparison.**

- Then have students identify whether the following sentences are similes or metaphors: **The frog was as still as a statue.** *(simile)* **Its tongue was lightning.** *(metaphor)* **An army of flies gathered.** *(metaphor)* Guide students to explain the meaning of each simile or metaphor.

DAY 4 Glossary Snapshots

Students will create glossary entries for the Target Vocabulary words.

- Have students take out the Lesson 27 Word Cards and review the words and their meanings.

- Tell students that today they will write glossary entries for the Target Vocabulary words. Display the glossary in the back of the Student Book. Review that the words are in alphabetical order, and that each word is followed by a definition.

- Provide each student with ten index cards. Have students write a Target Vocabulary word on each card.

- On the back of each card, have students include a definition, picture, and sentence using the word. Then have students arrange the cards in alphabetical order.

- Give students time to share their glossary entries with a partner. Partners should confirm that the definitions make sense and that the words are used correctly in the sentences.

> **continent**
>
> A continent is one of the main landmasses of Earth.
> Asia is the largest continent.

DAY 5 Four-Square Map

Students will complete Four-Square Maps to demonstrate their understanding of Target Vocabulary words.

- Display a Four-Square Map. Explain that today students will work with you to complete a Four-Square Map for the word *species*.

- Write *species* in the center of the map. Ask students how they would define *species*. Write their response in the upper-left corner.

- Ask students to think of some examples of species, and write one example in the upper-right corner. *(blue whale, Komodo dragon)*

- Ask a volunteer to use *species* in a sentence. Write the sentence in the lower-left corner. *(Many species of animals live in the rain forest.)*

- Have students identify things that are not species, such as *book* or *kitten*. Record one of their responses in the lower-right corner.

- Tell students to make three more Four-Square Maps in their Word Study Notebooks for the words *continent*, *scarce*, and *alert*.

- Have students compare their completed maps in small groups. If they find information on a group member's map helpful, they should add it to their maps.

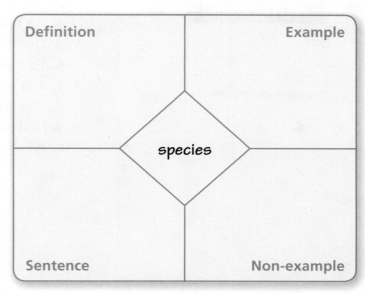

Vocabulary

1. **apologize** To *apologize* is to say, "I'm sorry."

2. **genuine** A person who is *genuine* is sincere and honest.

3. **triumph** A *triumph* is a victory or success.

4. **source** The *source* for something is what makes, causes, or begins it.

5. **registered** *Registered* means displayed or recorded on an instrument or machine.

6. **display** A *display* is something shown publicly.

7. **concluded** If a person has *concluded* something, he or she has made a decision or formed an opinion.

8. **obstacles** *Obstacles* are things that get in the way.

9. **affect** *Affect* means to cause a change in something.

10. **vast** Something that is *vast* is extremely large in amount, size, or area.

 Reproducible Word Cards and Graphic Organizer 1 (Column Chart) are available at **www.thinkcentral.com**.

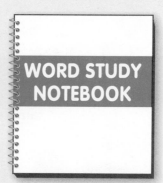

DAY 1 Review Target Vocabulary; Suffix *-ize*

After reviewing Target Vocabulary words from previous lessons, students will explore words that have the suffix *-ize*.

- Write the Target Vocabulary words on the board, read them aloud, and have students repeat the words. Discuss the student-friendly definitions, shown at left, with students.

- Write the word *apologize* on the board, and underline the suffix *-ize*. Review that a suffix is a word part that can be added to the end of a base word to form a new word with a different meaning. Remind students that they can use the meanings of common suffixes to help them determine the meanings of unfamiliar words.

- Discuss the word *apologize*. Suggested language: **The word *apologize* combines *apology* and the suffix *-ize*. An *apology* is something a person says or writes to another person to say they are sorry for doing something wrong. The suffix *-ize* means "to make or cause to be." These clues help me know that *apologize* must mean "to make an apology."** Review that adding the suffix *-ize* to a noun changes it to a verb.

- Write the following nouns on the board and have students copy them into their Word Study Notebooks: *central, category, emphasis*. Ask them to add the suffix *-ize* to each noun to form a verb. (*centralize, categorize, emphasize*) Have partners discuss and compare the meaning of each base word with the meaning of each new word.

DAY 2 Riddles

Students will use their knowledge of word meanings to answer riddles about the Target Vocabulary words.

- Distribute the Lesson 28 Word Cards. Explain that as you read the riddles, students should hold up the Word Card that answers each riddle.

- Discuss students' answers after each riddle.

  1. **These are things that stand in your way.** *(obstacles)*
  2. **This is something I did when I wanted to take a dance class.** *(registered)*
  3. **I am as big as the Grand Canyon.** *(vast)*
  4. **If a team wins a game, it is this.** *(triumph)*
  5. **This is what you do when you cause a change in something.** *(affect)*
  6. **You should do this if you step on someone's foot.** *(apologize)*
  7. **You might gaze at this in a store window.** *(display)*
  8. **This is where something comes from or where it begins.** *(source)*
  9. **I am honest and true. What am I?** *(genuine)*
  10. **When you reached a decision about something, you did this.** *(concluded)*

DAY 3 | Prefix *con-*

Students will use the prefix *con-* to determine the meanings of new words.

- Remind students that a prefix is a word part added to the beginning of a word that changes the word's meaning.

- Write the prefix *con-* on the board, and explain that it means "with" or "together."

- Write *concluded* on the board. Have a volunteer tell what the word means. Explain that when someone concludes something, they bring their ideas or opinions together to make a decision.

- Write more words that have the prefix *con-* on the board: *concert*, *connect*, *construct*, *contract*, *converse*. Guide students to determine what each word means, using the meaning of the prefix as a clue.

- Tell students to write sentences using the new words in their Word Study Notebooks. When students finish writing, have volunteers share their sentences.

DAY 4 | Write About Problem-Solving

Students will write a paragraph that includes Target Vocabulary words.

- Have students take out the Lesson 28 Word Cards and read them aloud. Have volunteers explain the meaning of each word. Tell students that they will use some of these words in a paragraph they will write.

- Ask students to think about problem-solving. Remind them that they read about ways to solve the problem of too much trash in the Student Magazine selection "Making the Most from Trash."

- Tell students to write a paragraph in their Word Study Notebooks that describes a problem and proposes a solution. Have them use the Target Vocabulary words *genuine*, *source*, *obstacles*, *affect*, and *vast* in their paragraphs.

- Have students share their finished writing with a partner. Partners should confirm whether the Target Vocabulary words were used correctly.

DAY 5 | Synonyms and Antonyms

Students will complete a Column Chart with synonyms and antonyms to deepen their understanding of Target Vocabulary words.

- Display a Column Chart as shown, and write the headings *Word*, *Synonym*, and *Antonym*.

- Tell students that they will work with you to complete this chart by listing Target Vocabulary words and their synonyms and antonyms. Remind students that synonyms are words that mean the same thing, and antonyms are words that mean the opposite.

- Write the word *triumph* in the first column. Ask students to explain what the word means. Then model thinking of a synonym and an antonym for *triumph*. Write the synonym and antonym in the appropriate columns.

- Have students copy the Column Chart into their Word Study Notebooks. Allow time for students to write the headings and examples you provided.

- Then ask students to select three more Target Vocabulary words. Have them write each word in the first column and complete the chart independently. Students should use a dictionary or thesaurus as necessary.

- Have partners compare and confirm their completed Column Charts.

Word	Synonym	Antonym
triumph	victory	failure
vast	immense	tiny
genuine	real	fake
obstacles	barriers	advantages

Vocabulary

TARGET VOCABULARY

1. **defended** If a person protected something from physical or verbal attack, he or she *defended* it.

2. **satisfied** A person who feels *satisfied* is happy with things that have happened or the work he or she has done.

3. **confidence** When a person has a strong belief in his or her abilities, that person has *confidence*.

4. **symbol** A *symbol* is something that stands for something else.

5. **boasted** *Boasted* means spoke with too much pride about something.

6. **resourceful** People who are *resourceful* can act using their imaginations in a difficult situation.

7. **brilliant** Something that is *brilliant* is very bright.

8. **publicity** *Publicity* is information given out to get the public's attention.

9. **territory** An area of land is a *territory*.

10. **proposed** If something is *proposed*, it is suggested.

 Reproducible Word Cards and Graphic Organizer 6 (Four-Square Map) are available at **www.thinkcentral.com**.

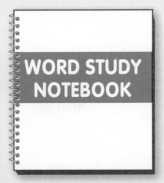

WORD STUDY NOTEBOOK

DAY 1 ## Review Target Vocabulary; Suffix *-ful*

After reviewing Target Vocabulary words from previous lessons, students will explore words that have the suffix *-ful*.

- Write the Target Vocabulary words on the board, read them aloud, and have students repeat the words. Discuss the student-friendly definitions, shown at left, with students.

- Write the word *resourceful* on the board, and underline the suffix *-ful*. Review that a suffix is a word part that can be added to the end of a base word. Explain that adding a suffix to a base word forms a new word with a different meaning. Remind students that they can use the meanings of common suffixes to help them determine the meanings of unfamiliar words.

- Discuss the word *resourceful*. Suggested language: **The word *resourceful* combines *resource* and the suffix *-ful*. A *resource* is something that helps you to do work or to solve a problem. The suffix *-ful* means "full of." These clues help me know that *resourceful* must mean "full of ways to do things or solve problems."**

- Explain to students that the suffix *-ful* can be added to the end of other words. Write the following word equations on the board:

  force + ful =   waste + ful =

  grace + ful =   success + ful =

- Tell students to copy these word equations into their Word Study Notebooks. Ask them to add the suffix to the base words to form new words. Have partners discuss and compare the meaning of each base word with the meaning of each new word.

DAY 2 ## Word Associations

Students will identify a Target Vocabulary word that they associate with related words and phrases.

- Distribute the Lesson 29 Word Cards, and have students lay them face up on their desks.

- Tell students that you will read questions, and they will hold up the Word Card that best answers each question.

- As students hold up their Word Cards, discuss the different answers provided and have students explain why they answered the way they did.

  1. **Which word goes with *suggested, recommended*?** *(proposed)*
  2. **Which word goes with *land, area*?** *(territory)*
  3. **Which word goes with *protected, safeguarded*?** *(defended)*
  4. **Which word goes with *pride, belief*?** *(confidence)*
  5. **Which word goes with *emblem, representation*?** *(symbol)*
  6. **Which word goes with *happy, content*?** *(satisfied)*
  7. **Which word goes with *advertisements, media*?** *(publicity)*
  8. **Which word goes with *bragged, showed off*?** *(boasted)*
  9. **Which word goes with *bright, dazzling*?** *(brilliant)*
  10. **Which word goes with *creative, imaginative*?** *(resourceful)*

DAY 3 | Suffix *-ity*

Students will explore words that have the suffix *-ity*.

- Write the word *publicity* on the board. Ask students to define the base word *public*. *(freely available to people)*

- Underline the suffix *-ity*, and tell students that it means "the state of being." Remind them that adding the suffix *-ity* to a base word changes the meaning of the word.

- Guide students to connect the base word *public* with the meaning of the suffix *-ity*. Suggested language: **Public plus the suffix -ity forms the word publicity. Publicity is "information used to get the attention of many people."**

- Write the words *popular*, *elastic*, and *captive*. Use each word in a sentence and discuss its meaning. Tell students to write the words in their Word Study Notebooks and add the suffix *-ity* to the words. Remind students to drop the final *e* before adding the suffix to the word *captive*.

- Have students write sentences in their Word Study Notebooks using the new words. When students are finished, ask volunteers to share their sentences.

DAY 4 | Write About Conservation

Students will write a paragraph that includes Target Vocabulary words.

- Have students take out the Lesson 29 Word Cards and briefly review their student-friendly definitions.

- Tell students to shuffle their Word Cards, place them face down on their desks, and choose six cards. Explain that they will use these words to write a paragraph.

- Ask students to think about the John Muir essay they read in the Student Magazine. Remind them that John Muir worked hard to protect wild places. Tell students that they will write a paragraph about why people should protect nature and what people can do to help conserve wild areas.

- Have students write a paragraph in their Word Study Notebooks about preserving wild places. Remind them to include their six Target Vocabulary words in their paragraphs.

- When students are finished writing, have partners read their paragraphs to each other. Ask partners to listen for whether the vocabulary words were used correctly.

DAY 5 | Four-Square Map

Students will complete Four-Square Maps to demonstrate their understanding of Target Vocabulary words.

- Display a Four-Square Map. Tell students that they will help you complete the map for the Target Vocabulary word *proposed*.

- Write *proposed* in the center of the map. Have students define the word. Write their response or the student-friendly definition in the upper-left corner. *(something that is suggested)*

- Ask volunteers to use *proposed* in a sentence. Then have students identify the sentence that best uses the word, and write that sentence in the upper-right corner. *(My father proposed that we spend the day at the science museum.)*

- Next, have students name things that are examples of *proposed*. Write one example in the lower-left corner. *(a suggestion to make peanut butter sandwiches for lunch on Friday)*

- Guide students to name things that are not examples of *proposed*. Write one of their suggestions in the lower-right corner. *(an order that must be followed)*

- Then write *confidence*, *symbol*, and *brilliant* on the board. Have students open their Word Study Notebooks and create three maps using the words. Have partners share their completed maps.

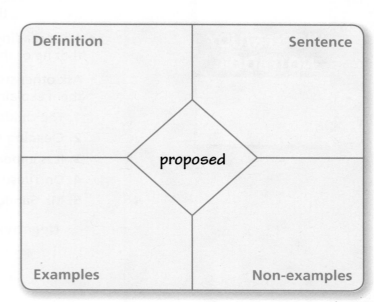

TARGET VOCABULARY

1. **appreciate** When you *appreciate* something, you know what is good about it.

2. **effort** A person who makes an *effort* tries hard to do something.

3. **denied** If a person is *denied* something, he or she is not allowed to have it.

4. **informed** Someone who is *informed* has information or knowledge.

5. **shallow** If something is *shallow*, it is not deep.

6. **resources** *Resources* are an available supply of something that can be used when needed.

7. **average** Something that is *average* is typical or normal.

8. **suffered** If someone felt pain or great sadness, he or she *suffered*.

9. **inspector** A person who checks to make sure that things are working as they should is an *inspector*.

10. **progress** If someone makes *progress*, he or she is improving.

 Reproducible Word Cards and Graphic Organizer 15 (Web) are available at **www.thinkcentral.com**.

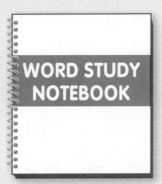

WORD STUDY NOTEBOOK

DAY 1 **Review Target Vocabulary; Prefix *pro-***

After reviewing Target Vocabulary words from previous lessons, students will explore words that begin with the prefix *pro-*.

- Write the Target Vocabulary words on the board, read them aloud, and have students repeat the words. Discuss the student-friendly definitions, shown at left, with students.

- Review with students that a prefix is a word part added to the beginning of a base word to make a new word. Adding a prefix to a base word changes the meaning.

- Write the word *progress*, underline the prefix *pro-*, and explain that the prefix gives a clue about the word's meaning. Suggested language: **The prefix *pro-* means "forward."** Have a volunteer explain what the word *progress* means. Then guide students to connect the student-friendly definition with the prefix. Suggested language: **If someone makes *progress*, he or she moves forward, or improves.**

- Write the following words on the board: *project, promote, proceed, procession.*

- Guide students to use their knowledge of the prefix *pro-* to figure out the meaning of each word. Suggested language: **If I *project* my voice, I am moving it outward, or forward, so that you can hear me.** Repeat with *promote (to move forward, to advance), proceed (to move forward toward a goal),* and *procession (the act of moving forward).*

- Tell students to copy the words into their Word Study Notebooks. Have students work with a partner to write definitions for the words. When students finish writing, have them use a dictionary to confirm their definitions.

DAY 2 **Rate Experiences**

Students will use what they know about the Target Vocabulary words to rate experiences along a Word Line.

- Display a Word Line like the one below. Explain the meanings of *Negative, Neutral,* and *Positive* as needed.

- Tell students that you will read some sentences that use the Target Vocabulary words. Have students think about whether the person in each sentence has an experience that is negative, neutral, or positive.

- After reading each sentence, ask a volunteer to point to the place on the Word Line that he or she thinks describes the person's experience.

- Ask other students whether they agree with the word's placement on the line. Have them explain their reasoning. Repeat for each word.

  1. **The children greatly *appreciate* the new playground.**
  2. **Cleaning the garage took so much *effort* that Ali had no more energy.**
  3. **It is important to have the right *resources* when fixing a house.**
  4. **On Tuesday, the temperature was *average* for this time of year.**
  5. **Mr. Sandusky *suffered* for days after he sprained his ankle.**

Negative   Neutral   Positive

DAY 3 Suffix -er

Students will explore words that have the suffix -er.

- Remind students that knowing the meanings of common suffixes will help them understand the meanings of new words.

- Write the words *inspector* and *baker* on the board. Underline the suffixes -*or* and -*er*. Remind students that both suffixes can mean "someone who."

- Have a volunteer tell what the base word *inspect* means. *(to check)* Explain that an *inspector* is someone who inspects, or checks, things to make sure they are working properly. Then call on another volunteer to explain the meaning of *baker*. *(someone who bakes)*

- Write the following words on the board: *designer, composer, bargainer, entertainer, traveler*. Explain that the words are made up of a base word and the suffix -*er*. Discuss the meaning of each word by identifying the base word and how the suffix -*er* changes the meaning.

- Have students write the words in their Word Study Notebooks. Then tell partners to take turns using each word in an oral sentence.

DAY 4 Word Pairs

Students will write sentences using Target Vocabulary words.

- Distribute copies of the Lesson 30 Word Cards. Review the definitions of the words, as necessary.

- Tell students that they will write sentences using two of the Target Vocabulary words. Model the activity with the Word Cards *effort* and *progress*. Display the cards, and write the example sentence below.

- Have students place their Word Cards face down. Direct students to choose two cards. Have them use the words to write a sentence in their Word Study Notebooks.

- Tell students that they may use different forms of the words so their sentences make sense. Have students repeat the process until they have used all the words.

- Ask volunteers to share their sentences.

| effort | progress |

If you make an effort, you will make progress.

DAY 5 Vocabulary Web

Students will complete Vocabulary Webs to illustrate their understanding of Target Vocabulary words.

- Display a Vocabulary Web as shown. Explain that students will help you complete the web for the word *appreciate*.

- Write the word *appreciate* in the center oval. Have students state the meaning of the word. Then write their response or the student-friendly definition in the upper-left oval. *(to know what is good about something)*

- Have students share some synonyms or words that have the same meaning as *appreciate*. Record one synonym in the upper-right oval. *(value, enjoy)* Then have volunteers give examples of *appreciate*. Write one example in the lower-left oval. *(thanking someone)*

- Ask students to share sentences using *appreciate*. Have students identify the sentence that best uses the word and then write that sentence in the lower-right oval. *(Tom stopped to appreciate the lovely day.)*

- Write the words *shallow, informed, denied,* and *progress*. Have students complete a Vocabulary Web for each word in their Word Study Notebooks. Have students share their completed webs as you discuss and reinforce the meaning and usage of each Target Vocabulary word.

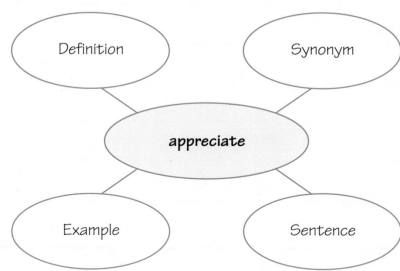

Teacher's Notes

Meet Irene Fountas

Journeys Leveled Readers offer a variety of engaging, interesting fiction and nonfiction text—very carefully leveled, so you can count on the supports and challenges in each text to be appropriate for children in their development.

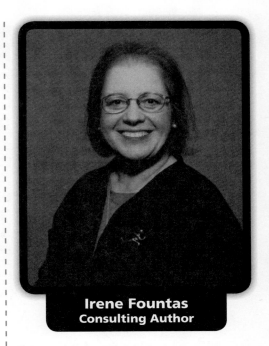

Irene Fountas
Consulting Author

The **Journeys** Reader's Workshop approach supports an emphasis on students reading and writing complex literature and informational text.

Weekly Plans for Whole Group and Small Group instruction enable teachers to:

- increase students' ability to read, think, and write critically about text.

- meet students at their instructional level and move them forward.

- allow for lesson flexibility to fit the strengths and needs of students.

Irene Fountas is a Professor in the School of Education of Lesley University in Cambridge, Massachusetts. Irene's research has focused on leveled texts, reader's and writer's workshop, assessment, classroom management, and professional development.

Table of Contents

Whole-Group Lessons

- Interactive Read-Aloud/Shared Reading
- Reading Minilessons

Introduction

What Are Effective Instructional Practices in Literacy?

Your goal in literacy teaching is to bring each student from where he is to as far as you can take him in a school year, with the clear goal of helping each student develop the competencies of proficiency at the level. Proficient readers and writers not only think deeply and critically about texts but also develop a love of reading. The roots of lifelong literacy begin with a rich foundation in the elementary school.

The lessons in this section provide a structure for organizing your literacy teaching, linking understandings across the language and literacy framework, and building a strong foundation of reading strategies and skills. On the pages that follow, you will find an overview of how to use this section along with your *Journeys* materials in three different instructional contexts: Whole-Group Teaching, Small-Group Teaching, and Independent Literacy Work.

WHOLE GROUP
Interactive Read-Aloud/Shared Reading
(heterogeneous)

WHOLE GROUP
Reading Minilesson
(heterogeneous)

SMALL GROUP
Guided Reading
(temporary homogeneous)

SMALL GROUP
Literature Discussion
(heterogeneous)

INDEPENDENT
Independent Reading,
Literacy Work

Whole-Group Teaching

Whole-Group Lessons are related lesson sequences you may want to use across a week. At the core of each lesson is a Journeys literature selection, chosen to highlight a certain aspect of reading that is important for students to learn and apply in various contexts.

Interactive Read-Aloud/Shared Reading sets the stage for the day's focus and provides a common foundation of experience for students at various levels of reading proficiency (Fountas and Pinnell, 2006).

As you read aloud to students, use the questions and prompts at planned stopping points in the text to encourage discussion of the reading through classroom collaboration.

Reading aloud to students in this context

- helps students appreciate literature.

- gives students a model of how to think about ideas in the text and from the thinking of their peers.

- models fluent, expressive, phrased reading.

- has students think actively about what they read.

- allows students to hear and share a variety of perspectives and interpretations through classroom collaboration.

- is the common text used in the Reading Minilesson.

The **Reading Minilesson** is focused instruction about a specific topic or skill, called the Minilesson Principle (Fountas and Pinnell, 2001). Using this principle, you help your students think like effective, independent readers. The literature selection from the Interactive Read-Aloud/Shared Reading context is used as the example to demonstrate the principle.

Whole-Group Lessons

▶ Because of Winn-Dixie

INTERACTIVE READ-ALOUD/SHARED READING

Read aloud the story to students. Stop periodically for very brief discussion of the text. Use the following suggested stopping points and prompts for quick group response, or give a specific prompt and have partners or threes turn and talk.

- After Opal brings Winn-Dixie into the library, ask: "What does Miss Franny think about Winn-Dixie?" Follow-up: "How have her feelings changed?"
- After Miss Franny tells about the wild men, women, and bears, ask: "Why do you think Miss Franny keeps telling Opal about what Florida used to be like?"
- After Miss Franny sighs about her old friends, ask: "Why does Miss Franny sigh?" Follow-up: "Turn and talk with a partner about how you think Opal feels about Miss Franny."
- At the end of the story, ask: "Why is the friendship between Opal and Miss Franny important to both of them?"

Because of Winn-Dixie
Student Book, Lesson 1

Read Aloud Passages

Sideline Support
See page 378 of this Guide

Because of BookEnds
Student Book, Lesson 1

MINILESSON Story Structure

TEACH Display the minilesson principle on chart paper, and read it aloud to students. Tell students that they are going to learn about how thinking about a story's events can help them understand events and what they reveal about the characters.

1. Remind students of the scene in *Because of Winn-Dixie* when the bear comes into the library. Suggested language: "A memorable scene from the story was when the bear surprised Miss Franny in the library. Why do you think the author included this scene?" *(It showed that Miss Franny wasn't afraid to stand up for herself. Telling the bear story helped her form a bond with Opal.)*

   > **MINILESSON PRINCIPLE**
   > Readers think about the important events in a story to help them understand what happens.

2. Help students connect the bear scene back to events at the beginning of the story. Suggested language: "In the beginning of the story, Miss Franny saw Winn-Dixie and thought he was a bear. How did events later in the story help you understand Miss Franny's reaction to Winn-Dixie?" *(Later events helped me understand why Miss Franny was scared of Winn-Dixie at first.)*

3. Work with students to name other important events from the story and tell how they work together to help them understand what happens. Record students' ideas in a Story Map like the one shown here.

Setting	Characters
Plot	
Problem (Conflict)	
Events	
Solution (Resolution)	

SUMMARIZE AND APPLY Restate the minilesson principle, and tell students to apply it to their independent reading. Suggested language: "When you read, think about the important events in the story and how they are connected. Think about how the events help you understand the characters and what happens in the story."

GROUP SHARE Ask students to share an important event in a story they have read. Have them explain why it was important for the author to include the scene they chose.

186 • Lesson 1

The **Group Share** has students apply the minilesson principle to the text. As students think deeply about the text, they are able to make the connection to the minilesson principle, deepening their comprehension.

TEACHER'S ROLE

- Engage students in thinking deeply about texts.
- Provide a learning environment in which students feel comfortable sharing their thinking with each other.
- Prepare explicit lessons that are tailored to students' needs.
- Provide a model of phrased, fluent reading in interactive read-aloud.

- Prompt students with comments and questions at planned stopping points to promote active thinking in interactive read-aloud/shared reading.
- Provide explicit teaching of critical literacy concepts in reading minilessons.
- Expose students to a wide variety of genres, authors, and topics.
- Monitor students' understanding to plan for future lessons.

STUDENT'S ROLE

- Listen actively.
- Share ideas and opinions with others.
- Make connections to other readings and to own experiences.
- Ask genuine questions and build on the ideas of others.
- Demonstrate understanding of critical literacy concepts.

Informational Text

Genre Characteristics

Informational text gives facts about real people, places, things, or events.

Through repeated exposure to informational texts, students should learn to notice common genre characteristics. Use friendly language to help them understand the following concepts:

- **Author's Purpose:** to inform; to persuade
- **Illustrations/Photographs:** show the information being described accurately and help readers understand the ideas in the text
- **Graphic Features:** images that help the reader understand information in the text or show additional information; may include the following:
  - **Diagrams:** pictures with labels that identify or explain specific parts
  - **Maps:** pictures that are used to show the physical layout of an area
  - **Charts/Graphs:** information arranged in a way that helps readers compare pieces of information or data
  - **Timeline:** shows the important events related to a topic over a period of time
- **Text Features:** special text that helps the reader understand what is important; may include the following:
  - **Headings:** type—usually larger, darker, or both—at the beginning of a new section; used to organize information into sections that make sense for the topic
  - **Captions:** words or sentences that explain an image
  - **Special Type:** the author may emphasize words and ideas by using a different color or size or by using bold or italic print
- **Main Idea:** what the text is mostly about
- **Details:** smaller ideas that support the main idea and tell more about the topic
- **Text Structure:** the text's overall structure
  - **Narrative:** can be organized and have the feeling of a story with a clear beginning, middle, and end
  - **Sequence:** events or steps in a process are told in order
  - **Compare/Contrast:** the author's main goal is to tell how things are alike and different
  - **Cause/Effect:** the author explains a topic by telling about something that happened and why it happened
  - **Problem/Solution:** the author explains a problem and offers a solution to the problem; details support the author's solution
  - **Description:** the author explains what something is and what it is like
- **Facts:** pieces of information that are true and can be proved
- **Opinions:** statements of how the author feels about a subject; may be used to try to persuade readers

SUPPORT THINKING

DISCUSSION STARTERS During whole-group and small-group discussion, use questions to spark conversation about genre characteristics.

- What different kinds of graphic features does the author use to help you understand the topic?
- How does the author use size and colors of type to show what is important?
- What is the selection mostly about?
- How is the selection organized? How can you tell?
- How does the author make the information in this selection interesting?
- Which of the author's ideas are opinions? How does the author support his/her opinions?
- How does the author feel about the topic? How do you know?
- What kind of research do you think the author did to write this selection?

COMPARING TEXTS After students have read and listened to several informational texts, prompt them to compare selections and to recognize common characteristics. Use questions such as these:

- How do the authors of [title] and [title] use text and graphic features in different ways?
- Which selection—[title] or [title]—makes you want to find out more about the topic? Explain.
- How do the authors of [title] and [title] organize the text in different ways? How does the organization help you understand the ideas?
- How can you tell that [author] and [author] think their topics are important?

Coming Distractions: Questioning Movies, Student Book, Lesson 7

The Life and Times of the Ant, Student Book, Lesson 14

254 • Teaching Genre: Informational Text

Genre instruction is a powerful tool for helping students develop the competencies of effective readers and writers. The questions and teaching points in this section can be used over and over across the year as students encounter different genres and increasingly difficult texts within a particular genre.

Discussion Starters are provided to spark discussion about genre characteristics.

Prompts for **Comparing Texts** guide students to compare the various texts they have read in a particular genre.

Small-Group Teaching

JOURNEYS **RESOURCES** FOR
SMALL-GROUP TEACHING
- Leveled Readers
- Leveled Readers Teacher's Guides

Small-group lessons are the individualized sessions in which you help students develop as readers based on their needs, challenges, and sometimes their preferences.

In **GUIDED READING** lessons, you use *Journeys* Leveled Readers to work with small groups of students who will benefit from teaching at a particular instructional level. You select the text and guide the readers by supporting their ability to use a variety of reading strategies (Fountas and Pinnell, 1996, 2001). Guided reading groups are flexible and should change as a result of your observations of your students' growth.

In this section, whole-group lessons provide the foundation for small-group instruction. Skills introduced in whole group can be developed and expanded according to students' needs in a smaller group with the appropriate level text. On the planning pages, Leveled Readers that connect to the whole-group experience are suggested, though you may need to select from the complete Leveled Readers Database (pp. 412–421) to match your students' instructional levels.

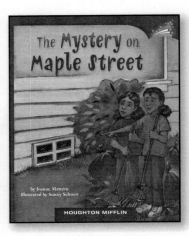
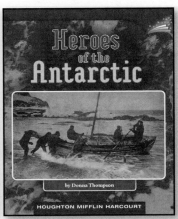

▲ JOURNEYS Leveled Readers

Select Leveled Readers according to the instructional levels of your students.

Guided Reading Level

Every Reader has been carefully analyzed and leveled by Irene Fountas, and the titles are presented in ascending order.

Reading Recovery Level

Each Reader has been assessed with a quantitative readability score, indicating its Lexile level.

Genre

The Leveled Readers have been written in a wide variety of genres, directly corresponding to those of the Anchor Texts with which they appear. Instruction for and additional information about each genre can be found in the Teaching Genre section of this Guide.

Leveled Readers Database

Guided Reading Level	Title	Grade Pack	DRA Level	Lexile Level	Genre	Word Count
M	Linney Twins Get Cooking, The	4 ●	28	610	Science Fiction	968
M	Magic of Teamwork, The	4 ●	28	530	Fantasy	873
M	Painting the Ocean	4 ●	28	400	Realistic Fiction	885
M	Recipe for Learning	4 ●	28	620	Realistic Fiction	879
N	Animal Doctors	4 ●	30	710	Narrative Nonfiction	801
N	Animals Helping People	4VR	34	940	Informational Text	1,016
N	Check Out the Library	4VR	30	820	Informational Text	839
N	Elizabeth's Stormy Ride	4 ●	34	310	Historical Fiction	815
N	King Midas and the Golden Touch	4 ●	30	550	Myth	759
N	Nina Wows KWOW	4 ●	30	NP	Play	791
N	Sailing to Safety	4 ●	34	560	Historical Fiction	1,005
N	Squash in the Schoolyard	4VR	34	700	Informational Text	620
N	Zeebo Encounter, The	4 ●	30	NP	Play	884
O	Amazing Birds of Antarctica	4 ●	34	650	Narrative Nonfiction	619
O	Ants of All Kinds	4VR	38	890	Informational Text	898
O	Community Teamwork	4VR	38	910	Informational Text	1,101
O	Friends on a Field Trip	4 ◆	38	NP	Play	1,266
O	Isadora Duncan	4 ●	38	780	Biography	915
O	John Wesley Powell	4 ●	38	830	Biography	888
O	Keeping Safe in an Earthquake	4VR	38	780	Informational Text	949
O	Kids Can Save the Planet	4 ●	34	690	Informational Text	703
O	Plants of the Redwood Forest	4 ●	38	730	Informational Text	913
O	Princess and the Manatee, The	4 ■	38	710	Fantasy	1,655
O	Really, Really Cold!	4VR	38	690	Informational Text	781
O	Reptiles As Pets	4VR	38	800	Informational Text	1,109

412 • Leveled Readers Database

🧑 TEACHER'S ROLE

GUIDED READING

- Form groups based on students' instructional levels.
- Establish routines and meeting times.
- Select and introduce the book.
- Monitor students' reading through the use of running records and specific questioning.
- Record observations.

LITERATURE DISCUSSION

- Form groups based on students' reading preferences.
- Demonstrate routines for effective discussion.
- Facilitate discussions, and redirect student talk as needed.
- Summarize students' ideas and engage them in self-evaluation of their contributions.

👥👥👥 STUDENT'S ROLE

GUIDED READING

- Apply skills learned during whole-group instruction.
- Share ideas.
- Make connections to other readings and to own experiences.
- Ask questions.
- Support thinking with evidence from the text.

LITERATURE DISCUSSION

- Choose a book.
- Prepare by reading and thinking about the text.
- Listen politely and respectfully to others.
- Share opinions and raise questions.

▼ JOURNEYS Leveled Readers Teacher's Guides

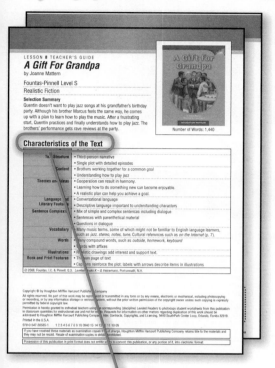

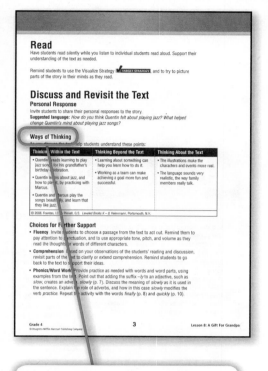

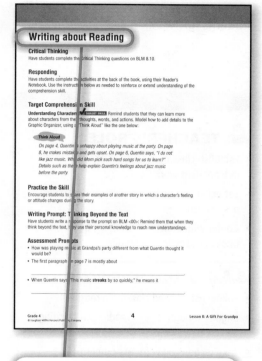

Characteristics of the Text

The qualitative features of each Reader include genre, text structure, content, book and print features, themes and ideas, language and literary features, and sentence complexity.

Ways of Thinking

The Leveled Readers Teacher's Guides outline how to lead students to read closely as they are prompted to think within, beyond, and about the text.

Writing About Reading

Students have multiple opportunities to demonstrate through writing their thinking within, beyond, and about the text they have just read.

In **LITERATURE DISCUSSION,** a small group of students of varying abilities and a common interest—a topic, a genre, or an author—selects one book to read. Each student comes prepared to discuss it.

In this collaborative group, you facilitate discussion of the book and encourage students to share their thinking and to build upon each other's ideas as they gain a deeper understanding of the text (Fountas and Pinnell, 2001).

Literature discussion groups will change as students select different books to read. Guide students to select books by encouraging them to page through a book or read a short segment in order to determine whether it is too easy or too difficult before they make a final selection.

The suggested trade book titles on pp. 422–425 are appropriate for Grade 4 students to engage in literature discussions and represent a wide variety of genres, authors, and topics.

Independent Literacy Work

Independent literacy work includes meaningful and productive activities for your students to do while you work with small groups.

INDEPENDENT READING The best way to develop reading skills is to read more. Independent reading is a time for students to explore their interests, select books that are "just right" for them, and read continuous text for an established period of time.

Support your students as they make book choices because too-hard books will only frustrate them. Teach them how to choose books that they can read with understanding and that don't present too many challenges. Having a large, accessible collection of books—whether in your classroom or in the library—is the best way to support readers.

Suggested Trade Book Titles
Select books from a variety of genres, topics, and themes for students to read independently or in Literature Discussion Groups.

TEACHER'S ROLE

- Establish classroom routines for independent work time.
- Set expectations for what students should accomplish.
- Confer with individual students to discuss books or sample oral reading.

STUDENT'S ROLE

- Follow established classroom routines.
- Engage thoughtfully in reading and writing tasks.
- Take responsibility for assignments, and demonstrate progress.

Literature Discussion

For small-group literature discussion, use the suggested trade book titles on the pages that follow, or select age-appropriate texts from your library or classroom collection.

Engage students in discussions to build understanding of the text, deepen comprehension, and foster their confidence in talking about what they read. Encourage students to share their ideas about the text and also to build upon one another's ideas.

- 📖 Classic
- 🔬 Science
- 🗺️ Social Studies
- 🎵 Music
- ➗ Math
- 🎨 Art

Suggested Trade Book Titles

BIOGRAPHY

Bertrand, Diane Gonzales. *Ricardo's Race/La carrera de Ricardo.* A bilingual biography of Ricardo Romo, a talented runner as a youth who later earned a Ph.D. in history and became a college president. Piñata, 2007 (32p).

 Burleigh, Robert. *Paul Cézanne: A Painter's Journey.* Rejecting the opinions of others, the young Cézanne followed his own vision, becoming one of the world's greatest artists. Abrams, 2006 (31p).

 Dunn, Joe. *Abraham Lincoln.* This biography of the president who saw the United States through its most divisive period is told in a graphic-novel format. Abdo & Daughters, 2007 (32p).

 FitzGerald, Dawn. *Vinnie and Abraham.* Abraham Lincoln sat for Vinnie Ream, an eighteen-year-old sculptor, as she prepared to create a life-size statue that now stands in the U.S. Capitol. Charlesbridge, 2000 (48p).

Guzmán, Lila and Rick. *Ellen Ochoa: First Latina Astronaut.* In 1993, aboard the space shuttle *Discovery,* Ochoa became the first Latina astronaut. **Available in Spanish as** *Ellen Ochoa: La primera astronauta latina.* Enslow, 2006 (32p).

 Guzmán, Lila and Rick. *Frida Kahlo: Painting Her Life.* This biography tells about the Mexican painter who is best-known for her self-portraits. **Available in Spanish as** *Frida Kahlo: Pintó su vida.* Enslow, 2006 (32p).

 Martin, Jacqueline Briggs. *Snowflake Bentley.* Wilson A. Bentley, fascinated with snow, devoted his life to photographing snowflakes. Houghton, 1998 (32p).

Miller, Barbara Kiely. *George Washington Carver.* This famous African American scientist was a dedicated professor, taught farmers how to keep their fields productive, and invented hundreds of uses for various crops. **Also available in Spanish.** Weekly Reader, 2007 (24p).

Parker, Robert Andrew. *Piano Starts Here.* This is the story of jazz virtuoso Art Tatum's enthusiasm for music as a young boy. Schwartz & Wade, 2008 (40p).

Ray, Deborah Kogan. *Down the Colorado.* John Wesley Powell became the first person to scientifically explore the Colorado River and the Grand Canyon. Farrar, 2007 (48p).

Streissguth, Tom. *Wilma Rudolph.* Stricken by polio as a child and told she would never walk again, Wilma Rudolph won multiple Olympic medals in track. Lerner, 2007 (120p).

Taylor, Gaylia. *George Crum and the Saratoga Chip.* Chef George Crum's efforts to please his customers result in the invention of the potato chip. Lee & Low, 2006 (32p).

Wyckoff, Edwin Brit. *Heart Man.* Although he worked as a janitor, Vivien Thomas was an African American medical technician who directed the first 100 open-heart surgeries. Enslow, 2008 (32p).

Yoo, Paula. *Sixteen Years in Sixteen Seconds: The Sammy Lee Story.* A Korean American boy realizes his dream to become an Olympic diving champion. Lee & Low, 2005 (32p).

Zalben, Jane Breskin. *Paths to Peace.* From Gandhi to Princess Diana and beyond, the author profiles people who have devoted their lives to helping others. Dutton, 2006 (48p).

FANTASY

Birney, Betty G. *Friendship According to Humphrey.* Humphrey, the hamster of Room 26, isn't sure what to make of the new class pet. Puffin, 2006 (150p).

Dahl, Roald. *Charlie and the Chocolate Factory.* Although there are five lucky winners of a tour through Willy Wonka's chocolate factory, Charlie is most special of all. **Available in Spanish as** *Charlie y la fábrica de chocolate.* Puffin, 2007 (176p).

Teacher's Notes

Whole-Group Lessons

Because of Winn-Dixie
Student Book, Lesson 1

Read Aloud Passages

Sideline Support
See page 378 of this Guide.

Because of BookEnds
Student Book, Lesson 1

▶ Because of Winn-Dixie

INTERACTIVE READ-ALOUD/SHARED READING

Read aloud the story to students. Stop periodically for very brief discussion of the text. Use the following suggested stopping points and prompts for quick group response, or give a specific prompt and have partners or threes turn and talk.

- After Opal brings Winn-Dixie into the library, ask: "What does Miss Franny think about Winn-Dixie?" Follow-up: "How have her feelings changed?"
- After Miss Franny tells about the wild men, women, and bears, ask: "Why do you think Miss Franny keeps telling Opal about what Florida used to be like?"
- After Miss Franny sighs about her old friends, ask: "Why does Miss Franny sigh?" Follow-up: "Turn and talk with a partner about how you think Opal feels about Miss Franny."
- At the end of the story, ask: "Why is the friendship between Opal and Miss Franny important to both of them?"

MINILESSON Story Structure

TEACH Display the minilesson principle on chart paper, and read it aloud to students. Tell students that they are going to learn about how thinking about a story's events can help them understand events and what they reveal about the characters.

1. Remind students of the scene in *Because of Winn-Dixie* when the bear comes into the library. Suggested language: "A memorable scene from the story was when the bear surprised Miss Franny in the library. Why do you think the author included this scene?" *(It showed that Miss Franny wasn't afraid to stand up for herself. Telling the bear story helped her form a bond with Opal.)*

> **MINILESSON PRINCIPLE**
>
> Readers think about the important events in a story to help them understand what happens.

2. Help students connect the bear scene back to events at the beginning of the story. Suggested language: "In the beginning of the story, Miss Franny saw Winn-Dixie and thought he was a bear. How did events later in the story help you understand Miss Franny's reaction to Winn-Dixie?" *(Later events helped me understand why Miss Franny was scared of Winn-Dixie at first.)*

3. Work with students to name other important events from the story and tell how they work together to help them understand what happens. Record students' ideas in a Story Map like the one shown here.

Setting	Characters
Plot	
Problem (Conflict)	
Events	
Solution (Resolution)	

SUMMARIZE AND APPLY Restate the minilesson principle, and tell students to apply it to their independent reading. Suggested language: "When you read, think about the important events in the story and how they are connected. Think about how the events help you understand the characters and what happens in the story."

GROUP SHARE Ask students to share an important event in a story they have read. Have them explain why it was important for the author to include the scene they chose.

▶ Sideline Support

INTERACTIVE READ-ALOUD/SHARED READING

Read aloud the story to students. Stop periodically for brief discussion of the text. Use the following suggested stopping points and prompts:

- After Brett says *Excuse me?* to Omar, ask: "Why is Brett surprised when he hears Omar speak?" (*Before then, he'd never heard Omar say anything longer than a word or two.*)
- After Brett suggests an *attitude tune-up*, say: "Brett is trying to get Omar to look at the situation in a different way. How do you think his advice will help Omar?"
- At the end of the story, say: "What lesson does Omar learn from Brett? Turn and talk about your thinking with a partner. Talk about how Brett's advice can be applied to other situations."

MINILESSON Story Structure

TEACH Display the minilesson principle on chart paper, and read it aloud to students. Tell students that they are going to learn about the problem and solution in a story.

1. Explain to students that the characters in stories often have a problem to solve. Guide students to name Omar's problem in *Sideline Support*. Suggested language: "In the beginning of the story, you found out that Omar was unhappy. What problem did Omar have?" (*He didn't have opportunities to play like his teammates.*)

> **MINILESSON PRINCIPLE**
>
> Readers notice the problem in the story and how it is solved.

2. Talk with students about how Brett helps Omar solve his problem. Suggested language: "Why did Omar feel better about his problem at the end of the story?" (*Brett showed him how to have a positive attitude and to appreciate a day outside with friends.*) Ask students to explain how they know the problem was solved. (*Omar smiled and jumped up to support his team.*)

3. Record students' ideas about the problem and the solution in a Story Map.

SUMMARIZE AND APPLY Restate the minilesson principle. Tell students to look for the problem and solution in a story when they read. Suggested language: "When you read, think about what problem the characters have. Then look for the solution to the problem, and think about how it was solved."

GROUP SHARE Ask students to share a problem from a story they read. Then have them tell how the problem was solved.

▶ Because of BookEnds

INTERACTIVE READ-ALOUD/SHARED READING

Read aloud the selection to students. Stop periodically for brief discussion of the text. Use the following suggested stopping points and prompts:

- After the description of the meeting the adults have, ask: "What problem did the adults have?" Follow-up: "How do you think Brandon will use his problem-solving talent to help?"
- After reading the section A Little Boy's Big Idea, ask: "What are some words you would use to describe Brandon? Turn and talk with a partner to compare your ideas."
- After reading the section BookEnds Is Born, say: "Talk with a partner about how Brandon's idea as a child has grown into something big."

MINILESSON Genre: Informational Text

TEACH Remind students that *Because of BookEnds* is informational text—it tells facts about a topic.

1. Direct students' attention to the bar graph on the last page. Tell students that authors of informational texts often use features like this one to help readers understand the author's message and to see it in a different way. Suggested language: "How does the information in the bar graph help you understand what Brett did?" (*It shows how his idea has been put into action in specific schools and how many books the schools have donated.*)

> **MINILESSON PRINCIPLE**
>
> Readers look for special features in informational text to help them understand the author's message.

2. Next, point out to students the numbered steps in the last section. Ask a student to read them aloud. Then ask why the steps are important. Suggested language: "What do these numbered steps explain?" (*how to hold a book drive*) Follow-up: "Why do you think the author included this section?" (*If readers were inspired by Brett's idea, the information will help them to organize book drives at their school.*)

3. Ask students to help you summarize the importance of special features in informational texts as you write the minilesson principle on chart paper.

SUMMARIZE AND APPLY Restate the minilesson principle. Tell students to look for special features in their reading. Suggested language: "When you read an informational text, look for special features that the author uses to give you information. Think about what the features help you understand about the author's message."

GROUP SHARE Ask students to share one feature from their reading and to tell how it helped them understand the author's message.

Whole-Group Lessons

My Brother Martin: A Sister Remembers Growing Up with the Rev. Dr. Martin Luther King Jr.
Student Book, Lesson 2

Read Aloud Passages

The Troublemaker Who Healed a Nation
See page 378 of this Guide.

Langston Hughes: A Poet and a Dreamer
Student Book, Lesson 2

▶ My Brother Martin

INTERACTIVE READ-ALOUD/SHARED READING

Read aloud the biography to students. Stop periodically for very brief discussion of the text. Use the following suggested stopping points and prompts for quick group response, or give a specific prompt and have partners or threes turn and talk.

- After reading the first page, ask: "Who is telling this story?" (*Martin's sister*) Follow-up: "How does this make the selection more interesting to read?"
- After reading about where Martin and his family lived in Atlanta, ask: "How would you describe where Martin and his family lived?" Follow-up: "What was it like for them to live there?"
- At the end of the selection, say: "The author gives information about Martin's parents. Turn and talk with a partner about how Martin's parents were a good example for Martin."

MINILESSON Genre: Biography

TEACH Explain to students that a biography is a kind of writing that tells facts about a real person's life. Then display the minilesson principle on chart paper, and read it aloud to students. Tell students that they are going to think about what the author of *My Brother Martin* wanted them to believe and understand about the subject, or the person the biography is about.

1. Point out to students that Martin's sister told about events in Martin's childhood. Suggested language: "Almost all of this biography told about some important things that happened to Martin as a child. What were some of these events?"

2. Discuss with students that by choosing these events, the author shared information that she felt was important to know about her brother. Suggested language: "We found out that early in Martin's life, some of his friends stopped playing with him. Because of that experience, he made a promise to make changes in the world. The author wanted us to know that Martin's experiences as a child inspired him throughout his life."

3. Work with students to name other things the author wanted readers to believe and understand about Martin. Guide them to recognize that Martin's parents were a positive influence and inspired Martin to dream. Records students' ideas in a T-Map that explains events and why they were important.

> **MINILESSON PRINCIPLE**
>
> Readers think about what the author of a biography wants them to believe and understand about the subject.

Event	Why Event Was Important

SUMMARIZE AND APPLY Restate the minilesson principle. Then tell students to apply it to their independent reading. Suggested language: "When you read a biography, think about what the author wants you to believe and understand about the subject."

GROUP SHARE Ask students to share information from a biography they read. Have them tell what the author wanted them to believe and understand about the subject.

▶ The Troublemaker Who Healed a Nation

INTERACTIVE READ-ALOUD/SHARED READING

Read aloud the biography to students. Stop periodically for brief discussion of the text. Use the following suggested stopping points and prompts:

- After reading the first paragraph, ask: "Why do you think a troublemaker would make an unlikely candidate for a Nobel Peace Prize?"
- After reading about Robben's Island, ask: "Why do you think the author tells you that Mandela refused special treatment in prison?"
- At the end of the selection, ask students to turn and tell a partner one reason why people respect Mandela.

MINILESSON Author's Purpose

TEACH Display the minilesson principle on chart paper, and read it aloud to students. Tell students that they are going to learn how to use the genre of a text to explain the author's purpose, or reason, for writing.

1. Remind students that the genre of *The Troublemaker Who Healed a Nation* is biography. Suggested language: "How do you know that this is a biography?" (*It gives facts about a real person named Nelson Mandela.*) Follow-up: "What did you learn about Mandela's life from this biography?"

> **MINILESSON PRINCIPLE**
>
> Readers think about the genre of a text to help them explain the author's purpose for writing.

2. Explain to students that authors write for different purposes. Suggested language: "Authors can write to entertain, to inform, or to persuade. Thinking about what kind of writing a book is and what the author wants you to gain from reading it can help you explain the author's purpose. What is the author's purpose for writing this biography?" (*to inform readers about Mandela's life*) Follow-up: "How do you know?" (*Biographies give information about someone's life, and this biography tells about Nelson Mandela.*)

SUMMARIZE AND APPLY Restate the minilesson principle. Tell students to apply it to their independent reading. Suggested language: "When you read, think about the genre of the book and how it helps you explain the author's purpose for writing."

GROUP SHARE Ask students to name the genre of a book they read. Then have them explain the author's purpose for writing it.

▶ Langston Hughes: A Poet and a Dreamer

INTERACTIVE READ-ALOUD/SHARED READING

Read aloud the selection to students. Stop periodically for brief discussion of the text. Use the following suggested stopping points and prompts:

- After reading the introduction, say: "What have you learned about Langston Hughes?"
- After reading the first poem, ask: "What do you think this poem is about?" (*It's about how having dreams can change the world.*) Follow-up: "How does this poem connect to what you learned about Langston Hughes's life?"
- After reading the last poem, ask students to turn and tell a partner which poem they liked best and why. Have students explain what the poem means to them.

MINILESSON Genre: Poetry

TEACH Display the minilesson principle on chart paper, and read it aloud to students. Explain that they are going to look back at *Langston Hughes* to learn to notice the words a poet uses to show how he feels about the topic.

1. Explain to students that words can make them feel a certain way. Ask students to volunteer words that make them feel excited, nervous, and sad. Then tell them that poets choose words carefully to help readers understand precisely how they feel about a topic.

> **MINILESSON PRINCIPLE**
>
> Readers notice how poets use words in unique ways to express feeling.

2. Reread the poem "Dreams" aloud to students. Then focus on the words in the first stanza. Suggested language: "Let's look at the first part of the poem. The poet says that life without dreams is like a bird that cannot fly. How do you think he feels about dreams?"

3. Next, discuss the second stanza. Point out the phrase *barren field,* and discuss the literal meaning with students. Then ask: "How would looking at a barren field make you feel?" Follow-up: "The poet says that without dreams, life is like a barren field. Why do you think he chose these words to show how he feels about dreams?"

SUMMARIZE AND APPLY Restate the minilesson principle. Tell students to apply it to their independent reading. Suggested language: "When you read a poem, look for the ways the poet uses words in unique ways to express their feelings."

GROUP SHARE Ask students to share a poem with others and to talk about how the poet used words to express feelings.

Whole-Group Lessons

My Librarian Is a Camel
Student Book, Lesson 3

Read Aloud Passages

Bridging the Gap
See page 379 of this Guide.

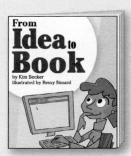

From Idea to Book
Student Book, Lesson 3

▶ My Librarian Is a Camel

INTERACTIVE READ-ALOUD/SHARED READING

Read aloud the book to students. Stop periodically for very brief discussion of the text. Use the following suggested stopping points and prompts below for quick group response, or give a specific prompt and have partners or threes turn and talk.

- After reading the section Canada, ask: "Why do you think it is important for people to have access to books?"
- After reading the section Kenya, ask: "Why are camels a good way to transport library books?"
- After reading the section Thailand, ask: "What do all these places have in common?"
- At the end of the book, ask: "Why do you think the author named this book, *My Librarian Is a Camel*? Turn and talk about your ideas with a partner."

MINILESSON Cause and Effect

TEACH Display the minilesson principle on chart paper, and read it aloud to students. Explain that a cause is an action or event that makes something else happen. An effect is what happens as a result of the cause. Tell students that they are going to learn how some events in *My Librarian Is a Camel* cause other events to happen.

1. Use an event from the book to help students understand cause-and-effect relationships. Suggested language: "A boat brings books to children who live on islands off the coast of Finland because there are no libraries on the islands. Having no libraries is the cause. The effect is that a boat brings books to children."

> **MINILESSON PRINCIPLE**
>
> Readers notice how some events cause other events to happen.

2. Focus on another event in the book, such as the book programs in Thailand. Suggested language: "Why are elephants used to transport library books to some parts of Thailand?" *(because elephants can carry heavy loads to mountain regions)*

3. Work with students to name other causes and effects in the book. Record their ideas in a T-Map like the one shown here.

Cause	Effect

SUMMARIZE AND APPLY Restate the minilesson principle. Then tell students to apply it to their independent reading. Suggested language: "When you read a book, think about the events that cause other events to happen."

GROUP SHARE Have students tell about a cause and effect relationship from their independent reading.

▶ Bridging the Gap

INTERACTIVE READ-ALOUD/SHARED READING

Read aloud the book to students. Stop periodically for brief discussion of the text. Use the following suggested stopping points and prompts:

- After reading the first page, ask: "What problem does the OLPC organization work to improve?"
- After reading the first paragraph on the second page, ask: "How are the OLPC laptops different from standard ones? Why are they different?"
- At the end, ask: "Why do you think having access to computers is important for children? Turn and talk about your ideas with a partner."

MINILESSON Cause and Effect

TEACH Display the minilesson principle on chart paper, and read it aloud to students. Tell students that they will learn how authors explain what causes something to happen.

1. Discuss the principle with students, using examples from *Bridging the Gap*. Focus on an event in the text such as children not having access to computers. Suggested language: "The author wrote that children do not have a chance to develop skills that could get them a good job as a result of not having access to computers. Not having access to computers causes children to not get good jobs.

> **MINILESSON PRINCIPLE**
>
> Readers notice when the author is explaining what causes something else to happen.

2. Point out another cause-and-effect relationship in the text, such as why the OLPC was formed. Suggested language: "OLPC has donated more than two million laptops to schools around the world. Why did they do this?" *(They want to help bridge the gap between people that have computers and people that don't.)* Point out that authors use words and phrases like *because, so,* and *as a result* to identify causes and effects.

3. Work with students to identify more examples of causes and effects. Record students' ideas in a T-Map.

SUMMARIZE AND APPLY Restate the minilesson principle. Then tell students to apply it to their independent reading. Suggested language: "When you read, think about how the author explains what causes something else to happen."

GROUP SHARE Ask students to name an event in a book they read. Have them explain what caused the event to happen.

▶ From Idea to Book

INTERACTIVE READ-ALOUD/SHARED READING

Read aloud the book to students. Stop periodically for brief discussion of the text. Use the following suggested stopping points and prompts:

- After reading the third paragraph on the second page, ask: "How is an editor's job similar to an author's job? How is it different?"
- After reading about printing presses, ask: "Why do you think many pages of a book are printed on one big sheet of paper at a time?"
- At the end, ask: "Which would you prefer to read, an eBook or a print book? Why? Turn and talk about your ideas with a partner."

MINILESSON Genre: Informational Text

TEACH Display the minilesson principle on chart paper, and read it aloud to students. Tell students that they will learn about ways that an author shows the steps in a procedure.

1. Discuss the principle with students, using *From Idea to Book*. Suggested language: "In this book, the author explained a procedure, or the steps in a process, for making a book in two ways. What were these ways? *(in the text and in a diagram)* Follow-up: "What other ways could you show steps in a procedure?" *(in a numbered list)*

> **MINILESSON PRINCIPLE**
>
> Readers notice how an author shows steps in a procedure in different ways.

2. Focus on how the text and diagram are related. Suggested language: "The author described the different steps and roles of people involved in making a book. The author also included a diagram to show the procedure. Why do you think the author included this diagram?" *(It makes it easier for readers to understand the procedure.)*

SUMMARIZE AND APPLY Restate the minilesson principle. Tell students to apply it to their independent reading. Suggested language: "When you read, notice how an author shows steps in a procedure. Think about how it helps you understand how to do something."

GROUP SHARE Ask students to share an example of a procedure from their reading. Have them tell what it helped them understand.

Whole-Group Lessons

The Power of W.O.W.!
Student Book, Lesson 4

Read Aloud Passages

Bookmobile Rescue
See page 379 of this Guide.

The Kid's Guide to Money
Student Book, Lesson 4

▶ The Power of W.O.W.!

INTERACTIVE READ-ALOUD/SHARED READING

Read aloud the play to students. Stop periodically for very brief discussion. Use the following suggested stopping points and prompts for quick group response, or give a specific prompt and have partners or threes turn and talk.

- After reading Act One, Scene One, ask: "What problem do the characters have?"
- After reading Act One, Scene Two, say: "It sounds like these friends are devising a plan to save W.O.W. Why do you think they ask for Jake's advice?"
- After Ileana gets Mr. Diaz to agree to have the car wash, ask: "How would you describe Ileana? Turn and talk with a partner about your thinking."
- At the end of the play, ask: "How do Ileana and the others solve the problem?"

MINILESSON Theme

TEACH Display the minilesson principle on chart paper, and read it aloud to students. Explain to students that authors may write a story to share a message or a lesson about life. Tell students that they are going to think about how they can look at the characters' actions to understand the lesson about life that the author is trying to teach. Explain that the message is called the story's theme.

1. Guide students as they discuss what Ileana and the others did in *The Power of W.O.W.!* Suggested language: "When Ileana discovered that the bookmobile was going to stop running, she met with others to talk about what they could do to save it. What plan did they make?"

> **MINILESSON PRINCIPLE**
>
> Readers think about how the characters' actions teach a lesson about life.

2. Discuss the theme of the play with students. Suggested language: "Think about how many people in the community helped to save the bookmobile. How was each one of their actions important?" *(Everyone who contributed something played an important role—the children who organized it, Mr. Diaz's donation of the water and parking lot, and the people who mailed in money.)* Follow-up: "What lesson did the characters' actions teach you?" *(People working together can accomplish more than one person can accomplish alone.)*

3. Have students recall another story they have read. Guide them to explain the lesson about life that they learned from the characters' actions.

SUMMARIZE AND APPLY Restate the minilesson principle. Then tell students to apply it to their independent reading. Suggested language: "When you read a story or play, think about how the characters' actions teach you a lesson about life."

GROUP SHARE Ask students to share some lessons they learned in stories and plays they read.

▶ Bookmobile Rescue

INTERACTIVE READ-ALOUD/SHARED READING

Read aloud the story to students. Stop periodically for brief discussion of the text. Use the following suggested stopping points and prompts:

- After Jessica and Alex talk, ask: "What problem does Alex have?" (*He needs to find a computer to write a report.*)
- After reading about Aunt Clara's idea, ask: "Why do you think that Aunt Clara's solution will work? Turn and talk with a partner about your thinking."
- At the end of the story, ask: "How do Jessica and Alex feel about Aunt Clara?" Follow-up: "What makes you think they feel that way?"

MINILESSON Genre: Realistic Fiction

TEACH Tell students that knowing what different kinds of stories are like will help them understand what happens and what to expect as they read. Tell students that realistic fiction is one kind of story. Display the minilesson principle on chart paper, and read it aloud. Then use *Bookmobile Rescue* to discuss the genre characteristics of realistic fiction.

1. Focus on one event in the story, such as the discussion that Jessica and Alex had. Help students understand that this event could really happen in today's world. Suggested language: "Jessica and Alex seem just like people that I know. Why do you think their discussion seemed like one that two friends could really have in today's world?" (*They talked like kids today. They had a problem that kept them from writing a report, which is a problem that I could have.*)

> **MINILESSON PRINCIPLE**
>
> Readers think about how the events in realistic fiction could really happen in today's world.

2. Guide students to identify other events in the story that could happen in today's world. Have them describe how the story's events make the story seem realistic.

SUMMARIZE AND APPLY Restate the minilesson principle. Tell students to apply it to their independent reading. Suggested language: "When you read a story, think about whether the events could really happen in today's world."

GROUP SHARE Ask students to tell whether the story they read was realistic fiction. Have them point out events that could or could not happen in today's world.

▶ The Kid's Guide to Money

INTERACTIVE READ-ALOUD/SHARED READING

Read aloud the book to students. Stop periodically for brief discussion of the text. Use the following suggested stopping points and prompts:

- After reading the first page, ask: "What is a budget?" Follow-up: "Why does the author think that making a budget is a good idea?"
- After reading the list of steps, ask: "Why do you think you should list things you need before listing the things you want?"
- At the end, ask: "Do you think you might want to try the author's idea of making a budget? Why or why not? Turn and talk about your ideas with a partner."

MINILESSON Genre: Informational Text

TEACH Display the minilesson principle on chart paper, and read it aloud to students. Tell students that authors use special features like charts to help readers understand information.

1. Discuss the principle with students, using the chart in *The Kid's Guide to Money*. Help students understand that a chart helps readers understand an author's ideas. Suggested language: "The author wrote about why it's important to create a budget. He included a chart showing a sample budget to help readers understand how to create one."

> **MINILESSON PRINCIPLE**
>
> Readers think about how charts can help them understand information.

2. Guide students in examining the chart. Help them understand that the titles on the chart tell them what information is included in each column, and that the labels identify all the parts. Read aloud the titles and labels and have students explain what the information on the chart means. Ask: "How did this student figure out that he has $6.50 left over?" (*He subtracted his weekly needs from his weekly income.*)

3. Continue to discuss the information on the chart, including how it helps readers compare information. Ask: "How does the amount the student lists for his total needs compare to his total wants?" (*The cost for his needs is a lot less than the cost for his wants.*)

SUMMARIZE AND APPLY Restate the minilesson principle. Tell students to apply it to their independent reading. Suggested language: "When you read, notice charts and how they help you understand information."

GROUP SHARE Ask students to share a chart from a book they read. Have them explain how the chart made it easy to understand information.

Whole-Group Lessons

Stormalong
Student Book, Lesson 5

Read Aloud Passages

Mighty Joe Magarac
See page 380 of this Guide.

Hoderi the Fisherman
Student Book, Lesson 5

▶ Stormalong

INTERACTIVE READ-ALOUD/SHARED READING

Read aloud the story to students. Stop periodically for very brief discussion of the text. Use the following suggested stopping points and prompts for quick group response, or give a specific prompt and have partners or threes turn and talk.

- After the villagers name the giant baby Stormy, ask: "How do you know this is not a realistic story?"
- After Stormy meets the captain in Boston Harbor, ask: "What problem does Stormy have?" Follow-up: "How does he plan to solve it?"
- After Stormy returns to Boston because he yearns for the sea, say: "The author describes Stormy's condition after he returns to Boston. Why are the sailors surprised when they see him?"
- At the end of the story, ask: "How do the other sailors feel about Stormy?" Follow-up: "How do they show that they like him?"

MINILESSON Understanding Characters

TEACH Display the minilesson principle on chart paper, and read it aloud to students. Tell students that they are going to learn how details in a story will help them imagine and understand the main character.

1. Discuss the main character of *Stormalong* with students. Suggested language: "This story was about a giant sailor named Stormy. The author shared details that helped you imagine and understand what Stormy was like. What details helped you imagine the way he looked and sounded?" (*He was 18 feet tall; he cried as loud as a foghorn; ten people patted his back.*)

2. Point out that the author also gave readers details about how Stormy felt and why he did certain things. Suggested language: "How did Stormy feel when he left Cape Cod? What details did the author tell you to help you understand?"

3. Page through the story with students to locate more details about Stormy that paint a picture of him in readers' minds. Work with students to record details about Stormy in a Column Chart like the one shown here.

> **MINILESSON PRINCIPLE**
>
> Readers look for details to help them imagine and understand the main character.

How a Character Looks and Sounds	How a Character Feels	What a Character Does

SUMMARIZE AND APPLY Restate the minilesson principle. Then tell students to apply it to their independent reading. Suggested language: "When you read a story, think about the details the author includes to help you imagine and understand the main character."

GROUP SHARE Ask students to name the main characters in a story they read. Have them share details that helped them imagine and understand the character.

▶ Mighty Joe Magarac

INTERACTIVE READ-ALOUD/SHARED READING

Read aloud the story to students. Stop periodically for brief discussion of the text. Use the following suggested stopping points and prompts:

- After reading that Joe was made of steel, ask: "How does the author help you imagine young Joe and where he lives?"
- After reading about how Joe built a new fleet, ask: "In what other ways could Joe have helped people? Turn and talk with a partner about your thinking."
- At the end of the story, ask: "How is Joe like a real man?" Follow-up: "How is Joe not like a real man?"

MINILESSON Understanding Characters

TEACH Display the minilesson principle on chart paper, and read it aloud to students. Explain to students that thinking about what characters are like can help them predict what characters will do in stories such as *Mighty Joe Magarac*.

1. Discuss Joe's characteristics with students. Suggested language: "In the story you learned what Joe looked like. You also learned about the kind of man he was. What are some words that describe what Joe was like?" (*strong, helpful, hardworking, unselfish, successful*)

> **MINILESSON PRINCIPLE**
>
> Readers think about what characters are like to predict what they will do next.

2. Point out to students that when Joe first reported for work, he worked longer and harder than anyone else. He also did things that no one else could do.

3. Connect this information to making predictions about what Joe will do. Suggested language: "At the beginning of the story, Joe could do no wrong. He completed and succeeded at every task he was given. Knowing this information about Joe, what did you expect to happen when you read about the shortage of ships in the 1940s?"

4. Guide students to explain other predictions they could make about Joe based on his characteristics at the beginning of the story and at the end.

SUMMARIZE AND APPLY Restate the minilesson principle. Tell students to apply it to their independent reading. Suggested language: "When you read a story, think about what the characters are like to help you predict what they might do."

GROUP SHARE Ask students to describe some characters in a story they read. Have them tell how knowing what these characters were like helped them to predict what they did in the story.

▶ Hoderi the Fisherman

INTERACTIVE READ-ALOUD/SHARED READING

Read aloud the play to students. Stop periodically for brief discussion of the text. Use the following suggested stopping points and prompts:

- After reading the first page, ask: "What information does the author include on the first page?" (*the play's title, the characters' names and how to say them, the play's setting—where and when it takes place*)
- After reading the second page, ask: "What kind of information does the narrator tell you in this play?" (*The narrator gives information that isn't included in the dialogue, such as what the characters do.*)
- At the end of the play, ask: "How might the play have ended if Katsumi listened to her father? Turn and talk with a partner about your thinking."

MINILESSON Genre: Play

TEACH Display the minilesson principle on chart paper, and read it aloud to students. Explain that stage directions are parts of a play that are not read aloud. They tell the actors what to do, and they explain how to set up the stage for a performance. Tell students that they are going to look at the stage directions in *Hoderi the Fisherman* to help them understand the setting and action.

1. Focus on one stage direction in Scene One, such as *[Hoderi dives into the water.]*. Suggested language: "This stage direction tells you what a character is doing. If you were watching a performance of the play, the actor playing Hoderi would dive into water."

> **MINILESSON PRINCIPLE**
>
> Readers notice stage directions in a play to understand the setting and action.

2. Point out to students that stage directions often explain how a line should be read and the emotion that the character should have. Have students point out stage directions in this play that explain emotion.

3. Draw students' attention to stage directions that describe setting and discuss them.

SUMMARIZE AND APPLY Restate the minilesson principle. Tell students to apply it to their independent reading. Suggested language: "When you read a play, use the stage directions to understand the action and setting."

GROUP SHARE Ask students to share a stage direction from a play they read. Have them tell how it helped them understand something about the play.

Whole-Group Lessons

Invasion from Mars
Student Book, Lesson 6

Read Aloud Passages

The Tunguska Event
See page 380 of this Guide.

The History of Radio
Student Book, Lesson 6

▶ Invasion from Mars

INTERACTIVE READ-ALOUD/SHARED READING

Read aloud the story to students. Stop periodically for very brief discussion of the text. Use the following suggested stopping points and prompts below for quick group response, or give a specific prompt and have partners or threes turn and talk.

- After reading the first two pages, ask: "How is a radio play different from a stage play?"
- After Phillips stops reporting to change positions, ask: "How does the author build suspense?"
- At the end, ask: "How do you think you would have felt if you had been listening to this radio report? Why? Turn and talk about your ideas with a partner."

MINILESSON Story Structure

TEACH Display the minilesson principle on chart paper, and read it aloud to students. Tell students that they are going to learn how thinking about the setting, characters, and events in a play can help them understand it better.

1. Discuss the principle with students, using details from *Invasion from Mars.* Suggested language: "We read a radio play that was broadcast many years ago. Where did the events in the play take place?" *(a field on a farm, at night)*

2. Focus on the character Phillips. Suggested language: "In a radio play, the audience cannot see the characters. How do you know what Phillips is like?" *(from the things he says and the way he says them)* Follow-up: "Who are the other characters in the play? What are they like?"

3. Then guide students to retell the important events. Record students' responses in a Story Map like the one shown here.

> **MINILESSON PRINCIPLE**
>
> Readers think about setting, characters, and important events in a play.

Setting	Characters
Plot	
Beginning	
Middle	
End	

SUMMARIZE AND APPLY Restate the minilesson principle. Then tell students to apply it to their independent reading. Suggested language: "When you read a play or story, think about the setting, characters, and important events."

GROUP SHARE Have students share the setting, characters, and important events in a story or play they read.

▶ The Tunguska Event

INTERACTIVE READ-ALOUD/SHARED READING

Read aloud the book to students. Stop periodically for brief discussion of the text. Use the following suggested stopping points and prompts:

- After reading the first page, ask: "What was so strange about the event in Tunguska?"
- After reading the second paragraph on the second page, ask: "What made it difficult for scientists to learn about what happened in Tunguska?"
- At the end, ask: "Do you agree with what scientists believed happened in Tunguska? Why or why not? Turn and talk about your ideas with a partner."

MINILESSON Story Structure

TEACH Display the minilesson principle on chart paper, and read it aloud to students. Tell students that they will learn to look for details that help them understand the setting and important events in an informational text.

1. Guide students to identify important details about the setting in *The Tunguska Event*. Suggested language: "The second paragraph tells that it happened on June 30, 1903, early in the morning. What other details about Tunguska did you learn from the story?" *(It is in Siberia, near the North Pole, a place where few people live.)*

> **MINILESSON PRINCIPLE**
>
> Readers notice details that tell them about setting and important events in an informational text.

2. Explain that students can also look for details that tell about important events. Suggested language: "Witnesses said that the sky suddenly lit up. What other details tell about what happened?" *(It got really hot and windy; there was a huge explosion; the light faded and people could see that trees had been flattened for miles and miles around.)*

3. Continue in the same way, focusing on important events, such as how scientists tried to determine what had happened at Tunguska. Suggested language: "What made it difficult for scientists to figure out what happened?" *(Many years had passed; some people did not want to talk about it.)* Record students' responses on a Story Map.

SUMMARIZE AND APPLY Restate the minilesson principle. Then tell students to apply it to their independent reading. Suggested language: "When you read, pay attention to details that tell you about the setting and important events."

GROUP SHARE Ask students to share details about the setting and important events in a book they read. Have them explain how the details helped them understand what they read.

▶ The History of Radio

INTERACTIVE READ-ALOUD/SHARED READING

Read aloud the book to students. Stop periodically for brief discussion of the text. Use the following suggested stopping points and prompts:

- After reading the first paragraph on the second page, ask: "How was listening to radio similar to watching television?"
- After reading the second page, ask: "What happened to make radio less popular? Why?"
- At the end, ask: "Do you think radio will continue? Why or why not? Turn and talk about your ideas with a partner."

MINILESSON Genre: Informational Text

TEACH Display the minilesson principle on chart paper, and read it aloud to students. Tell students that they will learn about the features of a historical text.

1. Discuss the principle, using examples from *The History of Radio*. Suggested language: "A historical text tells about a particular subject during a time in the past. Authors often use dates to present events in the order they happened. What are some dates the author presents in *The History of Radio*?" *(The first transmission of voices and music took place on December 24, 1906; many people had radios in their homes by the 1920s; President Roosevelt gave his first "fireside chat" on March 12, 1933.)*

> **MINILESSON PRINCIPLE**
>
> Readers notice the features of a historical text.

2. Tell students that a historical text often includes a timeline. Explain that a timeline helps them quickly see important dates and events. Suggested language: "This timeline shows important events in the history of radio. How do the events on the timeline relate to the information in the text?" *(They include information that is not in the text.)*

SUMMARIZE AND APPLY Restate the minilesson principle. Then tell students to apply it to their independent reading. Suggested language: "When you read a historical text, look for important dates and features like timelines that help you understand what happened during a time in history."

GROUP SHARE Ask students to share what they learned about a time in history from their reading. Have them tell how they learned about important dates and events.

Whole-Group Lessons

***Coming Distractions:
Questioning Movies***
Student Book, Lesson 7

Read Aloud
Passages

***Steven Spielberg:
A Filmmaker's Journey***
See page 381 of this Guide.

How Do They Do That?
Student Book, Lesson 7

▶ Coming Distractions: Questioning Movies

INTERACTIVE READ-ALOUD/SHARED READING

Read aloud the book to students. Stop periodically for very brief discussion of the text. Use the following suggested stopping points and prompts for quick group response, or give a specific prompt and have partners or threes turn and talk.

- After reading the section Painting a "Bad" Picture, ask: "What is the author saying about the choices that moviemakers make?" *(They sometimes leave things out of a movie to keep the movie interesting and so that viewers don't get bored.)*
- After reading the section How Does the Message Get My Attention?, ask: "How do movie studios advertise?" Follow-up: "Which technique do you think is best to get the attention of people your age? Turn and talk about your ideas with a partner."
- After reading the section Jolts Per Minute, say: "The author tells about some of the ingredients that make movies fun. Turn and talk with a partner about how some of these ingredients were used in your favorite movies."

MINILESSON Fact and Opinion

TEACH Display the minilesson principle on chart paper, and read it aloud to students. Explain that facts are statements that can be proved. Opinions are someone's thoughts, feelings, or beliefs about something. Tell students that it is important to notice the difference between facts and opinions as they read because they can agree or disagree with opinions.

1. Discuss the principle, using examples from *Coming Distractions: Questioning Movies.* Suggested language: "The author said that 'a leading man doesn't look as good driving a rusty old car.' Is this a fact or an opinion?" *(opinion)* "How do you know?" *(The idea can't be proved by checking in a reference book or another reliable source.)*

2. Reread the section Mixing Up a Movie with students. Guide them to name a fact or an opinion and tell how they know.

3. Explain to students that some words and phrases are clues that the author is stating an opinion. Write the following examples on chart paper: *should, best, I think, believe.*

4. Elicit from students additional examples of facts and opinions in the selection. Record students' ideas in a T-Map like the one shown here. Have volunteers tell whether they agree with the opinions and why.

> **MINILESSON
> PRINCIPLE**
>
> Readers notice the difference between facts and the author's thoughts, feelings, or beliefs.

Fact	Opinion

SUMMARIZE AND APPLY Restate the minilesson principle. Then tell students to apply it to their independent reading. Suggested language: "When you read, look for facts and what the author thinks, feels, or believes. Think about how you know the difference between facts and opinions."

GROUP SHARE Ask students to share a fact and an opinion they found in their reading. Tell them to explain how they knew it was a fact or an opinion.

▶ Steven Spielberg: A Filmmaker's Journey

INTERACTIVE READ-ALOUD/SHARED READING

Read aloud the book to students. Stop periodically for brief discussion of the text. Use the following suggested stopping points and prompts:

- After reading the first paragraph, ask: "Why does the author explain that some people discover their dream jobs early in life and some do not?"

- After reading the second paragraph, ask: "What was Steven Spielberg's life like when he was young?" Follow-up: "How do you think this affected the kinds of films he makes? Turn and talk about your thinking with a partner."

- At the end of the selection, ask: "Why do you think the author wrote this selection?"

MINILESSON Fact and Opinion

TEACH Display the minilesson principle on chart paper, and read it aloud to students. Tell students they are going to learn about how to recognize the difference between facts and opinions. Remind them that facts can be proved and opinions tell a person's thoughts, feelings, or beliefs about something.

1. Discuss the principle with students, using examples from *Steven Spielberg.* Suggested language: "The author says that Steven Spielberg is the most successful filmmaker of all time. Think about whether this statement can be proved. Is it a fact or an opinion?" *(fact)* "How do you know?" *(The author says that his movies have earned nearly 8 billion dollars.)*

> **MINILESSON PRINCIPLE**
>
> Readers recognize that facts can be proved and that opinions cannot be proved.

2. Read aloud a mixture of facts and opinions from the selection as you record them in a T-Map on chart paper. Ask students to explain whether they are facts or opinions.

3. Encourage students to explain how the facts can be proved and whether they agree with the opinions.

SUMMARIZE AND APPLY Restate the minilesson principle. Tell students to apply it to their independent reading. Suggested language: "When you read, think about the ideas in the selection and whether they are facts that can be proved or opinions."

GROUP SHARE Ask students to share a statement from a selection they read. Have them tell whether it is a fact or an opinion.

▶ How Do They Do That?

INTERACTIVE READ-ALOUD/SHARED READING

Read aloud the book to students. Stop periodically for brief discussion of the text. Use the following suggested stopping points and prompts:

- After reading the second page, ask: "Why do filmmakers use green or blue screens to create special effects?"

- After reading the second paragraph on the second page, ask: "How does the author help you understand CGI effects?"

- At the end, ask: "How have special effects affected the kind of movies that are made today? Turn and talk about your ideas with a partner."

MINILESSON Genre: Informational Text

TEACH Display the minilesson principle on chart paper, and read it aloud to students. Tell students that they will learn how photographs and captions help them better understand ideas in an informational text.

1. Discuss the principle with students, using examples from *How Do They Do That?* Explain that informational texts often include photographs. Have students examine the photograph of a T-rex model. Suggested language: "Photographs help readers visualize ideas in an informational text. How did this photograph help you understand how large the model of T-rex is?" *(It helped me compare its size to a real person.)* Follow-up: "What else did the photograph help you understand?" *(what the model looked like, how it was set up)*

> **MINILESSON PRINCIPLE**
>
> Readers think about how features like photographs and captions help them understand information.

2. Next, focus on the captions. Have students read the caption for the photograph of the motion capture scene. Ask: "What additional information does the caption tell you about the motion capture technique?" *(It explains what the red lights on the suit do.)*

3. Continue in the same way, having students tell how the photographs and captions helped them understand the ideas in the text.

SUMMARIZE AND APPLY Restate the minilesson principle. Then tell students to apply it to their independent reading. Suggested language: "When you read, notice photographs and captions and how they help you understand the ideas in the text."

GROUP SHARE Ask students to share a photograph and caption from a book they read. Have them tell how it helped them understand an idea in the text.

Whole-Group Lessons

Me and Uncle Romie
Student Book, Lesson 8

Read Aloud Passages

Jazzy Jasmine
See page 381 of this Guide.

Sidewalk Artists
Student Book, Lesson 8

▶ Me and Uncle Romie

INTERACTIVE READ-ALOUD/SHARED READING

Read aloud the story to students. Stop periodically for very brief discussion of the text. Use the following suggested stopping points and prompts for quick group response, or give a specific prompt and have partners or threes turn and talk.

- After James and Aunt Nanette climb the stairs to the apartment, ask: "Who is telling this story?" Follow-up: "Where does the story take place?"
- After Aunt Nanette tells James she has to go away, ask: "Why doesn't James want his Aunt Nanette to leave? Turn and talk about your thinking with a partner."
- After Aunt Nanette returns home, ask: "How do James's feelings about Uncle Romie change after he spends time with him?" *(He realizes Uncle Romie is a good man and that they have a lot in common.)*
- Focus on the picture at the end of the selection. Ask: "What does James do at the end of the story?" Follow-up: "How does he make his collage special for Uncle Romie?"

MINILESSON Understanding Characters

TEACH Display the minilesson principle on chart paper, and read it aloud to students. Explain that authors use different clues to help readers get to know characters and understand what they are like.

1. Discuss the principle, using examples from *Me and Uncle Romie*. Suggested language: "At the beginning of the story, the author started including clues to help you understand Uncle Romie. Aunt Nanette said he's preparing for a big art show and working hard. She also said he's a collage artist. One way to learn about characters is by reading what others characters say about them."

> **MINILESSON PRINCIPLE**
>
> Readers notice the ways in which the author helps them get to know the characters.

2. Ask students to think about Uncle Romie once he and James spent time together. Suggested language: "Another way to get to know characters is by what they say and do. What did you learn about Uncle Romie when he spent time with James?" *(He was caring because he made James's birthday special. He was also mischievous because he said he snuck pepper jelly when Grandma wasn't looking.)*

3. Elicit from students additional clues showing what characters in the story were like. Record students' ideas in a T-Map like the one shown here.

Clue	What We Learn About the Character

SUMMARIZE AND APPLY Restate the minilesson principle. Then tell students to apply it to their independent reading. Suggested language: "When you read, think about what the characters say and do. Notice what other characters say about them. These clues will help you get to know the characters."

GROUP SHARE Ask students to share what they learned about one character in a story they read. Have them explain clues that helped them know what that character was like.

▶ Jazzy Jasmine

INTERACTIVE READ-ALOUD/SHARED READING

Read aloud the story to students. Stop periodically for brief discussion of the text. Use the following suggested stopping points and prompts:

- After reading the first page, ask: "What kind of person is Jasmine?" Follow-up: "How do you know?"
- After Saji asks Jasmine if she has *listened* to Jack the Saxman, say: "Saji doesn't seem to be impressed with Jasmine's playing. What is she trying to tell Jasmine?" *(Playing the saxophone is more about how you sound than how you look.)*
- At the end of the selection, ask: "What does Jasmine learn in this story? Turn and talk about your thinking with a partner."

MINILESSON Understanding Characters

TEACH Display the minilesson principle on chart paper, and read it aloud to students. Tell students that they will learn how a character in *Jazzy Jasmine* is influenced by others.

1. Talk with students about Jasmine's reason for wanting a saxophone. Suggested language: "Jasmine wanted to look like Jack the Saxman when she played. Watching him play influenced Jasmine to want her own shiny instrument to play."

2. Then tell students that characters can change how other characters feel. Have students explain how Jasmine felt after playing for Saji. Suggested language: "Saji told Jasmine that Jack the Saxman moved around because he felt the music and not to look good. How did Jasmine feel right after talking to Saji?" *(She was upset because she didn't think she could ever sound like Jack the Saxman.)*

3. Remind students that Jasmine was happier by the end of the story. Work with them to explain what changed for Jasmine and who influenced her to change what she did and how she felt.

> **MINILESSON PRINCIPLE**
>
> Readers notice how characters influence one another to understand what they do and how they feel.

SUMMARIZE AND APPLY Restate the minilesson principle. Tell students to apply it to their independent reading. Suggested language: "When you read, notice how characters influence one another. Think about how it helps you understand what the characters do and how they feel."

GROUP SHARE Ask students to share an example from a story they read of how one character influenced another to do something or feel a certain way. Have them tell what they learned about those characters.

▶ Sidewalk Artists

INTERACTIVE READ-ALOUD/SHARED READING

Read aloud the play to students. Stop periodically for brief discussion of the text. Use the following suggested stopping points and prompts:

- After reading the first page, ask: "What do you think you will learn from this selection?" *(how to do wet-chalk drawing)* Follow-up: "How do you know?" *(The students are preparing for an art show, and Ms. Lee is about to review the steps.)*
- At the end of the selection, ask: "What have the students discovered?" *(a new technique for making chalk drawings)* Follow-up: "How do the students feel about their new artwork? How do you know?"

MINILESSON Directions

TEACH Display the minilesson principle on chart paper, and read it aloud to students. Tell students that they are going to learn about ways that authors show steps for how to do something.

1. Discuss the principle with students, using examples from *Sidewalk Artists*. Suggested language: "In the selection, the author used two different ways to give instructions for how to create a wet-chalk drawing. What are these ways?" *(through dialogue and through numbered steps)* Follow-up: "What other ways could you show steps in a process? Turn and talk about your ideas with a partner."

2. Focus on the numbered steps at the end. Suggested language: "The author used a numbered list to show the steps for making a wet-chalk drawing. Why is a numbered list easier to use when you are following steps in a process?"

> **MINILESSON PRINCIPLE**
>
> Readers notice how authors may show steps in a process in different ways.

SUMMARIZE AND APPLY Restate the minilesson principle. Explain to students that they should notice how authors show steps in a process as they read. Suggested language: "When you read, notice how the author shows steps in a process. Think about how it helps you understand how to do something."

GROUP SHARE Ask students to share an example of steps in a process from a selection they read. Have them explain how it helped them understand the process.

Whole-Group Lessons

Dear Mr. Winston
Student Book, Lesson 9

Is Sasquatch Out There?
See page 382 of this Guide.

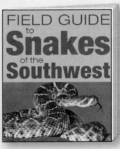

Field Guide to Snakes of the Southwest
Student Book, Lesson 9

▶ Dear Mr. Winston

INTERACTIVE READ-ALOUD/SHARED READING

Read aloud the story to students. Stop periodically for very brief discussion of the text. Use the following suggested stopping points and prompts for quick group response, or give a specific prompt and have partners or threes turn and talk.

- After reading the first page, ask: "How is this story different from most stories?" *(It is a letter.)* Follow-up: "Why do you think the author writes the story in the form of a letter?"
- After reading the second page, ask: "What do you think about the girl's apology so far? Turn and talk with a partner about whether you think it's sincere."
- After reading that Jake Lambert says the snake is perfectly harmless, ask: "What does the girl think of Mr. Winston's fear of snakes? What does the author say to make you think that?"
- At the end of the selection, ask: "What makes this story so funny? Turn and talk with a partner about your thinking."

MINILESSON Conclusions

TEACH Display the minilesson principle on chart paper, and read it aloud to students. Explain that authors gives clues in a story to help readers figure out things that are not stated. Tell students that when they figure out something that the author did not say, they have drawn a conclusion.

1. Discuss the principle, using examples from *Dear Mr. Winston*. Suggested language: "On the second page of the letter, the writer said that she wanted to remind Mr. Winston about something before he was taken away in an ambulance. What does it mean when an ambulance picks someone up?" Use students' responses to point out that the writer didn't say that Mr. Winston was hurt, but they figured it out because of what they already know about ambulances.

> **MINILESSON PRINCIPLE**
>
> Readers notice that they can use clues to figure out things the author does not tell them.

2. Guide students to draw conclusions about how Cara's parents felt about what she did in the library. Help students recognize clues that helped them figure out that they were very upset with Cara. *(They made her write an apology letter, they didn't allow her to watch her favorite show anymore, and they sent Mr. Winston flowers.)*

3. Next, explain to students that the author gave clues throughout the letter that showed how the writer really felt about Mr. Winston's reaction to the snake in the library. Guide students to identify clues that helped them understand how Cara felt.

4. Record students' ideas in a T-Map like the one shown here.

Cara's Feelings	Clues

SUMMARIZE AND APPLY Restate the minilesson principle. Then tell students to apply it to their independent reading. Suggested language: "When you read, notice clues that authors include to help you figure out things they don't tell you in their stories."

GROUP SHARE Ask students to explain something in a story they read that the author did not tell them, but they figured out using clues and what they already know. Then have students tell the clues that helped them figure it out.

▶ Is Sasquatch Out There?

INTERACTIVE READ-ALOUD/SHARED READING

Read aloud the selection to students. Stop periodically for brief discussion of the text. Use the following suggested stopping points and prompts:

- After reading the first paragraph, ask: "How do you think the author feels about legends?" Follow-up: "How can you tell?"
- After reading the second paragraph, say: "The author compares legends to a game called Telephone. Turn and talk with a partner about how this comparison helps you understand how legends change."
- At the end of the selection, ask: "What do you think the author believes about whether Sasquatch exists?"

MINILESSON Conclusions

TEACH Display the minilesson principle on chart paper, and read it aloud to students. Tell students they are going to think about whether the ideas an author gives are believable.

1. Tell students that sometimes authors share facts and different people's ideas about something, and they allow readers to draw their own conclusions about them. Explain that forming an opinion about whether something is believable is a type of conclusion.

> **MINILESSON PRINCIPLE**
>
> Readers think about whether the ideas an author gives are believable to form their own opinions.

2. Recall with students that there is a debate as to whether Sasquatch really exists. Focus on the part of the selection that discusses how some scientists, including Jane Goodall, have claimed that they believe Sasquatch may be real. Ask: "Knowing that some scientists believe it possible, do you believe that it is possible that Sasquatch exists? What is your opinion?" Have students turn and talk with a partner about their thinking.

3. Discuss the other evidence people have used to convince others that Sasquatch exists. Have students tell whether they think the evidence is believable and how it affects their own opinions.

SUMMARIZE AND APPLY Restate the minilesson principle. Tell students to apply it to their independent reading. Suggested language: "When you read, think about whether the ideas the author gives are believable to help you form your own opinions."

GROUP SHARE Ask students to share an idea from a book they have read. Have them tell whether they think the idea is believable and explain why.

▶ Field Guide to Snakes of the Southwest

INTERACTIVE READ-ALOUD/SHARED READING

Read aloud the selection to students. Stop periodically for brief discussion of the text. Use the following suggested stopping points and prompts:

- After reading the first page, ask: "What evidence does the author give to support the idea that snakes are amazing?" Follow-up: "Why do you agree or disagree?"
- After reading the three display boxes, ask: "What kinds of information does the author tell you about each snake?"
- At the end of the selection, ask: "How do you think the author feels about snakes? Turn and talk with a partner about your thinking."

MINILESSON Genre: Informational Text

TEACH Display the minilesson principle on chart paper, and read it aloud to students. Tell students that they are going to learn about how information can be organized into categories to explain a topic.

1. Discuss the principle with students, using examples from *Field Guide to Snakes of the Southwest*. Suggested language: "In the selection, the author grouped information about snakes of the southwest into three categories, or sections. He told all about one snake and then he told all about the next snake. How does this kind of organization help you understand the information?"

> **MINILESSON PRINCIPLE**
>
> Readers notice that authors may organize information in categories to explain a topic.

2. Focus on one of the boxes, such as the box for Western Diamond-Backed Rattlesnake, and explain that this is one category of information. Ask students to explain the information in this category.

3. Then move to the next category, and ask students to explain the information in it. Elicit from students that the same kinds of information are presented in each category.

SUMMARIZE AND APPLY Restate the minilesson principle. Tell students to apply it to their independent reading. Suggested language: "When you read, notice how the author organizes information in categories. Think about how this helps you understand the topic."

GROUP SHARE Ask students to share how information is organized in a selection they read. Have them explain how it helped them understand the topic.

Whole-Group Lessons

José! Born to Dance
Student Book, Lesson 10

Read Aloud Passages

Mexican Dove
See page 382 of this Guide.

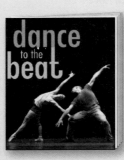

Dance to the Beat
Student Book, Lesson 10

▶ **José! Born to Dance**

INTERACTIVE READ-ALOUD/SHARED READING

Read aloud the selection to students. Stop periodically for very brief discussion of the text. Use the following suggested stopping points and prompts for quick group response, or give a specific prompt and have partners or threes turn and talk.

- After José's family leaves their home, ask: "Where did José live?" (*Mexico*) Follow-up: "What was it like in Mexico when José was young, and how did this affect his life?"
- After José gives up art, say: "The author uses the words *cemetery* and *jungle of stone* to describe how José felt about New York. How do these words make you feel about New York?"
- After reading about José's dancing, ask: "The author uses some words from earlier in the selection when describing José's dancing. Why do you think she does this?" (*to show how José used everything he learned in life in his dancing*)
- At the end of the selection, ask: "What does José's life teach you? Turn and talk about your thinking with a partner."

MINILESSON Genre: Biography

TEACH Display the minilesson principle on chart paper, and read it aloud to students. Remind students that biographies tell facts about a person's life. Explain that authors sometimes write biographies to show how a person overcomes hardships to succeed. Tell students that thinking about the hardships a person faced can help them understand what the person is like.

1. Discuss the principle, using examples from *José! Born to Dance.* Suggested language: "When José first went to school in the United States, he didn't know how to speak English. Why was this difficult for him?" (*He couldn't read or communicate, and others teased him.*) Follow-up: "How did José overcome this hardship?" (*He told himself that he would learn English better than any of his classmates, and within three years he was confident when he spoke English.*)
2. Work with students to discuss other hardships José overcame in Mexico, California, and New York. Have students tell how he overcame each of these hardships.
3. Record students' ideas in a T-Map like the one shown here.

> **MINILESSON PRINCIPLE**
>
> Readers notice how the subject of a biography overcomes hardships to succeed.

Hardship	How José Overcame It

SUMMARIZE AND APPLY Restate the minilesson principle. Then tell students to apply it to their independent reading. Suggested language: "When you read a biography, notice how the person you are reading about overcame hardships to succeed. Think about what it helps you learn about the person."

GROUP SHARE Ask students to share an example of a biography they read in which the person overcame a hardship to succeed.

▶ Mexican Dove

INTERACTIVE READ-ALOUD/SHARED READING

Read aloud the biography to students. Stop periodically for brief discussion of the text. Use the following suggested stopping points and prompts:

- After reading the first paragraph, ask: "Who is this biography about?" *(Frida Kahlo)* Follow-up: "How does the author make you want to know more about Frida?"
- After reading about Frida's paintings, say: "Frida used the same vibrant colors and symbols that the native Mexicans used. What does that tell you about how she feels about Mexico?"
- At the end of the biography, ask: "How does Frida overcome her hardships? Turn and talk with a partner about how painting helped her."

MINILESSON Author's Purpose

TEACH Display the minilesson principle on chart paper, and read it aloud to students. Tell students that thinking about how an author feels about a subject can help them understand why the author wrote about that subject.

1. Discuss the principle, using examples from *Mexican Dove*. Focus on the first paragraph of the selection. Guide students to understand the author's feelings for Frida Kahlo. Suggested language: "How does the author feel about Frida?" Follow-up: "What words or phrases did the author use to let you know?" *("fragile and small," "stubborn interest," "shout her story")*

> **MINILESSON PRINCIPLE**
>
> Readers think about authors' feelings about their subject to understand why they wrote about it.

2. Reread the last paragraph aloud. Work with students to describe the author's feelings and to identify words or phrases that help them know. Guide students to recognize that the author thinks Frida's life story is important to share because her experiences may inspire other people to overcome problems.

3. Point out to students that authors often write biographies about subjects that they admire. Have students turn and talk with a partner about why authors would want to write about a person they admire.

SUMMARIZE AND APPLY Restate the minilesson principle. Tell students to apply it to their independent reading. Suggested language: "When you read, notice how the author feels about the subject. Think about how these feelings help you understand why the author wrote about the subject."

GROUP SHARE Ask students to share a selection they read. Have them tell how the author of the selection felt about the subject. Then ask them to tell how they knew.

▶ Dance to the Beat

INTERACTIVE READ-ALOUD/SHARED READING

Read aloud the poems to students. Stop periodically for brief discussion of the text. Use the following suggested stopping points and prompts:

- After reading the introduction, ask: "Why does the author compare poems to music and dance?"
- After reading "The Song of the Night," ask: "How does this poem make you feel about dancing? Turn and talk about your thinking with a partner."
- After reading the poem about Gene Kelly, ask: "Why does the author include a short biography of Gene Kelly?" *(If you don't know who Gene Kelly is, it helps you understand why the poet wrote a poem for him to dance to.)*

MINILESSON Genre: Poetry

TEACH Display the minilesson principle on chart paper, and read it aloud to students. Tell students that they are going to learn about how poets use the sound of words to create rhythm.

1. Explain to students that in poems rhythm is the beat of how the words are read. Like the beat of a song, a poem's rhythm can be fast or slow.

> **MINILESSON PRINCIPLE**
>
> Readers notice how poets use the sound of words to create rhythm.

2. Discuss the principle with students, using examples from "The Song of the Night." First, reread the poem, emphasizing the rhythm as you read. Then discuss the rhythm with students. Suggested language: "The poet used the sound of words to create a beat. She repeated the word *dance* to emphasize the beat. She also included rhyming words to create rhythm."

3. Focus on the other poems. Have students tell how the repeating words and rhyming words helped to create a rhythm. Ask students to read selected lines aloud to show the rhythm.

SUMMARIZE AND APPLY Restate the minilesson principle. Tell students to apply it to their independent reading. Suggested language: "When you read a poem, notice how the sound of the words helps create rhythm."

GROUP SHARE Ask students to share a poem they read. Have them point out how the sound of the words creates rhythm.

Whole-Group Lessons

Hurricanes: Earth's Mightiest Storms
Student Book, Lesson 11

Read Aloud Passages

The Big Storm
See page 383 of this Guide.

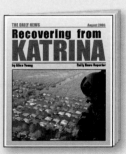

Recovering from Katrina
Student Book, Lesson 11

▶ Hurricanes: Earth's Mightiest Storms

INTERACTIVE READ-ALOUD/SHARED READING

Read aloud the book to students. Stop periodically for very brief discussion of the text. Use the following suggested stopping points and prompts below for quick group response, or give a specific prompt and have partners or threes turn and talk.

- After reading the section The Making of a Hurricane, ask: "Why does the author call hurricanes 'Earth's mightiest storms'?"
- After reading the section Some Weather Instruments, ask: "What do scientists use an anemometer for?" Follow-up: "What problems sometimes occur with them?"
- After reading the section World Names, ask: "What different parts of the world do names for storms come from?"
- At the end of the book, ask: "What new things did you learn about hurricanes? Turn and talk about your ideas with a partner."

MINILESSON Text and Graphic Features

TEACH Display the minilesson principle on chart paper, and read it aloud to students. Tell students that they are going to learn how using text and graphic features can help them understand more about a topic.

1. Discuss the principle with students, using examples from *Hurricanes: Earth's Mightiest Storms*. Suggested language: "In *Hurricanes: Earth's Mightiest Storms*, the author uses different features to help readers understand hurricanes. What are some of these features?" *(headings, captions, photographic images, diagram, charts)*

2. Focus on the diagram that shows how a hurricane begins. Suggested language: "This diagram shows how a hurricane forms. How does it help you understand this idea?" *(It helps you visualize what happens.)*

3. Next, focus on the chart that tells about different types of weather instruments. Ask: "What information does this chart give?"*(It shows what each instrument looks like and what it does.)* Follow-up: "How does putting the information in a chart help you better understand the subject?" *(The chart helps you focus on each instrument; you can easily compare the instruments.)*

4. Guide students to identify more examples of text and graphic features used in the book. Record their responses and ideas in a Column Chart like the one shown here.

> **MINILESSON PRINCIPLE**
>
> Readers notice special features that help them better understand an author's ideas.

Text or Graphic Feature	Page Number	Information

SUMMARIZE AND APPLY Restate the minilesson principle. Then tell students to apply it to their independent reading. Suggested language: "When you read, notice the special features the author includes to help you understand ideas in a text."

GROUP SHARE Have students share an example of a special feature in a book they read. Have them tell how that feature helped them understand an author's ideas.

▶ The Big Storm

INTERACTIVE READ-ALOUD/SHARED READING

Read aloud the story to students. Stop periodically for brief discussion of the text. Use the following suggested stopping points and prompts:

- After reading the first page, ask: "What is this story about?"
- After reading the first paragraph on the second page, ask: "What happened?" Follow-up: "How do you think the narrator feels?"
- At the end of the story, ask: "Have you ever been in a big storm? What was it like? Turn and talk about your ideas with a partner."

MINILESSON Genre: Realistic Fiction

TEACH Display the minilesson principle on chart paper, and read it aloud to students. Tell students that they will learn to notice how events in a story are like events that could happen in real life.

1. Explain to students that there are different kinds of stories. Tell them that some stories have events that could happen in real life. Explain that this kind of story is realistic fiction.

> **MINILESSON PRINCIPLE**
>
> Readers think about how events in realistic fiction could happen in real life.

2. Focus on one event in *The Big Storm,* such as how the rain started slowly but soon became a downpour. Help students understand that this is something that happens in real life. Suggested language: "The storm in the story reminds me of a storm we had. At first it didn't seem like a big storm, but after awhile the rain came down harder and harder."

3. Guide students to identify events in the story that could happen in real life. Have them describe how the story's events make the story seem realistic.

SUMMARIZE AND APPLY Restate the minilesson principle. Then tell students to apply it to their independent reading. Suggested language: "When you read a story, notice whether the events could happen in real life."

GROUP SHARE Ask students to tell whether the story they read was realistic fiction. Have them describe events that could or could not happen in real life.

▶ Recovering from Katrina

INTERACTIVE READ-ALOUD/SHARED READING

Read aloud the article to students. Stop periodically for brief discussion of the text. Use the following suggested stopping points and prompts:

- After reading the first page, ask: "Does this article tell about an event that just happened, or one that happened in the past? How do you know?"
- At the end of the second page, ask: "What effect did Hurricane Katrina have on New Orleans and other areas nearby?"
- At the end of the article, ask: "Why do you think it might take a long time for regions to rebuild and recover from Hurricane Katrina? Turn and talk about your ideas with a partner."

MINILESSON Genre: Informational Text

TEACH Display the minilesson principle on chart paper, and read it aloud to students. Tell students that they will learn about how an author explains events that happened in the past.

1. Discuss the principle with students, using examples from *Recovering from Katrina.* Suggested language: "In a newspaper article, reporters often tell about events in the order they happened. What events about Hurricane Katrina did the reporter describe?" *(the direction Katrina traveled once it made landfall; the damage it caused and left behind; what happened to people living in the area)*

> **MINILESSON PRINCIPLE**
>
> Readers notice how an author tells about an event that happened in the past.

2. Explain that sometimes an author includes comparisons. Suggested language: "Sometimes an author will compare one event with another. What event did the reporter compare Hurricane Katrina to?" *(Hurricane Andrew)* Follow-up: "What did this help you understand?" *(It helped me understand that Hurricane Katrina was more severe and damaging than Hurricane Andrew.)*

SUMMARIZE AND APPLY Restate the minilesson principle. Then tell students to apply it to their independent reading. Suggested language: "When you read a newspaper article, notice what the author does to help you understand an event that happened in the past."

GROUP SHARE Ask students to share a newspaper article they read. Have them tell how the author helped them understand events that happened in the past.

Whole-Group Lessons

The Earth Dragon Awakes
Student Book, Lesson 12

Read Aloud Passages

Safe from Harm
See page 383 of this Guide.

Twisters
Student Book, Lesson 12

▶ The Earth Dragon Awakes

INTERACTIVE READ-ALOUD/SHARED READING

Read aloud the story to students. Stop periodically for very brief discussion of the text. Use the following suggested stopping points and prompts for quick group response, or give a specific prompt and have partners or threes turn and talk.

- After reading the introduction, ask: "Why does the author put the text in the introduction in different type?" (*to show it's not part of the regular story*)
- After the ceiling drops on Chin and Ah Sing, say: "The author describes the earthquake in so much detail that you feel that you are experiencing it. Turn and talk with a partner about words the author uses to make you see, hear, and feel the earthquake."
- After reading about the city's collapsing buildings, direct attention to the illustration and ask: "How does the illustration give you a better sense of what was happening during the earthquake?"
- At the end of the story, say: "The author doesn't tell you if Chin is able to save his father. Turn and talk with a partner about how the ending makes you feel."

MINILESSON Sequence of Events

TEACH Display the minilesson principle on chart paper, and read it aloud to students. Tell students that they are going to learn about how dates and clue words can help them understand the sequence of events in a story.

1. Discuss the principle with students, using examples from *The Earth Dragon Awakes*. Focus on the introduction to show how the author used dates and other time words to help readers understand the sequence of events. Suggested language: "At the beginning of the story, the author told you what day and time it was to help you understand how much time passes as you keep reading."

> **MINILESSON PRINCIPLE**
>
> Readers look for dates and clue words to understand the sequence of events.

2. Page through the selection with students, pointing out the times and dates shown every few pages.

3. Work with students to find other examples of words the author used to show the sequence of events. Have them look for clue words such as *then* and *until*.

4. Draw on chart paper a Flow Chart like the one shown below. Guide students to identify the most important story events, and have them tell you in which order to write the events in the chart. Ask students to label the events with dates and clue words to show the order of events.

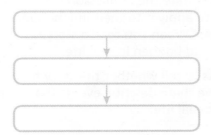

SUMMARIZE AND APPLY Restate the minilesson principle. Then tell students to apply it to their independent reading. Suggested language: "When you read a story, think about how the author uses dates, time, and clue words to help you understand the sequence of events."

GROUP SHARE Ask students to retell a short scene from a story they read, using clue words to explain the order of events.

▶ Safe from Harm

INTERACTIVE READ-ALOUD/SHARED READING

Read aloud the story to students. Stop periodically for brief discussion of the text. Use the following suggested stopping points and prompts:

- After reading about how a mudslide could crush Jia's house, say: "Turn and talk with a partner about how the author lets you know that Jia is worried."
- After reading about the wreckage from the mudslide, ask: "How does the author make you feel as he describes what Jia and her parents see when they return to her house?"
- At the end of the story, ask: "Why do you think that Jia is a good friend?"

MINILESSON Sequence of Events

TEACH Display the minilesson principle on chart paper, and read it aloud to students. Tell students that they are going to think about the sequence of events to understand how much time has passed in a story.

1. Discuss the principle with students, using examples from *Safe from Harm*. Remind students that authors have different ways of helping readers understand how much time has passed in a story. Focus on the words *The next week* as you discuss how much time has passed since Jia and her parents talked about the possibility of a mudslide. Suggested language: "The author used the words *The next week* to let readers know that time has passed since the conversation between Jia and her parents."

> **MINILESSON PRINCIPLE**
>
> Readers think about the sequence of events to understand how much time has passed.

2. Work with students to identify other words the author used to help readers know that time has passed, including *just two weeks later* and *for five long days*.

3. Display a Flow Chart on chart paper. Have students explain the order of events in the story as you write them on the chart. Discuss events that happened one right after another, as well as gaps in the story that are explained using clue words and phrases.

SUMMARIZE AND APPLY Restate the minilesson principle. Tell students to apply it to their independent reading. Suggested language: "When you read a story, think about the sequence of events and how the author lets you know that time has passed."

GROUP SHARE Have students tell about the sequence of events in a story they read. Ask them to tell how the author let them know that time had passed in the story.

▶ Twisters

INTERACTIVE READ-ALOUD/SHARED READING

Read aloud the book to students. Stop periodically for brief discussion of the text. Use the following suggested stopping points and prompts:

- After reading the first page, ask: "What is the author saying about tornadoes and Texas?"
- After reading the section Supercells and Funnel Clouds, ask: "How do meteorologists know a tornado might form?"
- At the end, ask: "Would you be more concerned to hear about a tornado watch or a tornado warning? Turn and talk with a partner about your thinking."

MINILESSON Genre: Informational Text

TEACH Display the minilesson principle on chart paper, and read it aloud to students. Remind students that authors of informational books use special features like diagrams to give information to readers.

1. Discuss the principle with students, using the section Supercells and Funnel Clouds in *Twisters*. Suggested language: "In this section, the author told you how tornadoes form. The information in the first paragraph was illustrated in the diagram at the bottom of the page."

> **MINILESSON PRINCIPLE**
>
> Readers understand how diagrams can help them understand information.

2. Help students understand that the title of a diagram tells them what kind of information it explains and that labels identify specific parts. Read aloud the labels and have students point to what they refer to.

3. Ask students to use the diagram and the caption to explain in their own words how a tornado forms.

SUMMARIZE AND APPLY Restate the minilesson principle. Tell students to apply it to their independent reading. Suggested language: "When you read, think about the diagrams that authors use to give information. Think about how they help you understand information in the text."

GROUP SHARE Ask students to explain a diagram from a book they read. Tell them to explain how the diagram helped them to understand the information in the book.

Whole-Group Lessons

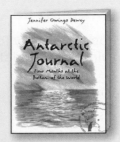

Antarctic Journal: Four Months at the Bottom of the World
Student Book, Lesson 13

Read Aloud Passages

On My Way to Meet the Khan: Excerpts from Marco Polo's Adventures
See page 384 of this Guide.

Cold, Cold Science
Student Book, Lesson 13

▶ Antarctic Journal

INTERACTIVE READ-ALOUD/SHARED READING

Read aloud the book to students. Stop periodically for very brief discussion of the text. Use the following suggested stopping points and prompts for quick group response, or give a specific prompt and have partners or threes turn and talk.

- After reading the introduction, say: "This selection is a journal. What is a journal?"
- After reading the entry from November 27th, ask: "How is a journal organized?" Follow-up: "How does this organization help you understand the information the author tells you?"
- After reading the entry on December 3rd, say: "The author includes a photograph of a penguin. Turn and talk with a partner about how the photograph helps you understand more about the author's experiences."
- At the end of the selection, have students turn and talk with a partner about the most interesting thing they learned about Antarctica.

MINILESSON Sequence of Events

TEACH Display the minilesson principle on chart paper, and read it aloud to students. Tell students that they are going to learn about how authors use dates and other clue words to show the sequence, or order of events. Explain that noticing the sequence of events will help them better understand what they read.

1. Discuss the principle with students, using examples from *Antarctic Journal*. Focus on the first two journal entries to show how the author used dates to help readers understand the sequence of events. Suggested language: "The author included headings with a date and a place to help you understand how much time had passed. How much time passed between the first two events?" *(six days)*

> **MINILESSON PRINCIPLE**
>
> Readers look for dates and clue words to understand the sequence of events.

2. Page through the story, having students point out the dates and places shown every few pages. Have them find other examples of words the author used to show the sequence of events. Have them look for clue words such as *before, after* and *earlier*.

3. Guide students to note the sequence of events that takes place on December 24th at Palmer Station. Work together to create a Flow Chart like the one shown here. Have students suggest signal words that help clarify the order.

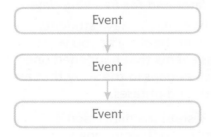

SUMMARIZE AND APPLY Restate the minilesson principle. Then tell students to apply it to their independent reading. Suggested language: "When you read, think about how the author uses dates and other clue words to help you understand the sequence of events."

GROUP SHARE Ask students to retell the sequence of events from a story they read. Have them use clue words to describe the order of events.

▶ On My Way to Meet the Khan

INTERACTIVE READ-ALOUD/SHARED READING

Read aloud the book to students. Stop periodically for brief discussion of the text. Use the following suggested stopping points and prompts:

- After reading the introduction, say: "Marco Polo lived a long time ago. How do you think he traveled to China?"
- After reading all the stories, say: "Turn and talk with a partner about which place in China you would like to have seen and explain why."
- At the end, ask: "How do you think people felt when they heard Marco Polo's tales about China?"

MINILESSON Sequence of Events

TEACH Display the minilesson principle on chart paper, and read it aloud to students. Remind students that signal words such as *first, before, next, then,* and *finally,* help readers notice the order in which things happen in a story.

1. Discuss the principle with students, using examples from *On My Way to Meet the Khan*. Focus on the first story of Marco Polo's travels. Ask: "What did he describe in this story?" *(traveling after leaving the Kingdom of Kirman)* Follow-up: "What word helped you understand the order of events?" *(after)*

> **MINILESSON PRINCIPLE**
>
> Readers notice signal words that tell about the sequence of events in a story.

2. Focus on the story at the top of the second page. Ask: "Which words helped you understand the order of Marco Polo's travels?" *(On the way to, on the fourth day)*

3. Continue in the same way, having students identify signal words that help them understand the sequence of events.

SUMMARIZE AND APPLY Restate the minilesson principle. Then tell students to apply it to their independent reading. Suggested language: "When you read, notice words that help you understand the order of events."

GROUP SHARE Ask students to share details about a sequence of events in a story they read. Have them use signal words to tell about the events.

▶ Cold, Cold Science

INTERACTIVE READ-ALOUD/SHARED READING

Read aloud the book to students. Stop periodically for brief discussion of the text. Use the following suggested stopping points and prompts:

- After reading the section Frozen Sculptures, ask: "Why do scientists study glaciers and ice shelves?"
- After reading the section Antarctica's Wildlife, ask: "Why is it important for scientists to study animal life?"
- At the end of the article, ask: "Which of the things that scientists study at Palmer Station would you like to work on? Turn and talk about your ideas with a partner."

MINILESSON Genre: Informational Text

TEACH Display the minilesson principle on chart paper, and read it aloud to students. Tell students that they will learn how authors use secondhand accounts in informational texts.

1. Discuss the principle with students, using *Cold, Cold Science*. Focus on the first paragraph. Suggested language: "A secondhand account is written by the author based on research from books or the Internet, or from information the author gathers from someone who has actually experienced events the author wants to write about. What is one secondhand source the author used?" *(He used the words of a scientist who had been there.)*

> **MINILESSON PRINCIPLE**
>
> Readers notice how an author uses secondhand accounts to share information.

2. Guide students to examine the rest of the article and think about what sources the author might have used to write the article. Together, create a chart to list examples of possible secondhand accounts or sources.

SUMMARIZE AND APPLY Restate the minilesson principle. Then tell students to apply it to their independent reading. Suggested language: "When you read an informational text, notice whether the author includes secondhand accounts to share information."

GROUP SHARE Ask students to share an example of a secondhand account from an article or informational text they read. Have them tell how they know it is a secondhand account.

Whole-Group Lessons

The Life and Times of the Ant
Student Book, Lesson 14

Read Aloud
Passages

Wicked Wind
See page 384 of this Guide.

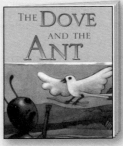

The Dove and the Ant
Student Book, Lesson 14

▶ The Life and Times of the Ant

INTERACTIVE READ-ALOUD/SHARED READING

Read aloud the selection to students. Stop periodically for very brief discussion of the text. Use the following suggested stopping points and prompts for quick group response, or give a specific prompt and have partners or threes turn and talk.

- After reading the section Masters of the Earth, ask: "How does the author describe ants?" Follow-up: "Why does the author call them *masters of the earth?*"
- After reading the section A Life of Work, ask: "How is the information in this section organized?" *(It is organized by types of ants and their jobs.)* Follow-up: "How does this organization help you understand the information?"
- After reading the section A Dangerous World, say: "The author tells about some of the dangers that ants face in a big world. Turn and talk with a partner about what you think ants see when they look out at the world."
- At the end of the selection, ask students to turn and tell a partner about the most interesting thing they learned about ants.

MINILESSON Text and Graphic Features

TEACH Display the minilesson principle on chart paper, and read it aloud to students. Tell students that they are going to learn how using text and graphic features can help them learn more about a topic as they read.

> **MINILESSON PRINCIPLE**
>
> Readers use text and graphic features to help them learn more about the topic.

1. Discuss the principle with students, using examples of text and graphic features from *The Life and Times of the Ant*. Suggested language: "In the selection, the author used different kinds of writing and graphic features to help you learn more information about ants. What were some of these features?" *(headings, diagrams, illustrations, charts, timeline)*

2. Focus on the diagram of the anteater. Suggested language: "The author used a diagram of an anteater to give you information about what anteaters do. What specific information did the diagram show?" *(It showed how each part of the anteater's body helps it hunt for ants.)*

3. Point out how the diagram's callouts highlight the different parts of the anteater's body. Ask partners to select one callout and discuss how it helps them understand anteaters.

4. Work with students to identify more examples of text and graphic features from the selection. Record students' ideas in a T-Map like the one shown here.

Text or Graphic Feature	Information It Gives Readers

SUMMARIZE AND APPLY Restate the minilesson principle. Explain to students that they should notice text and graphic features as they read. Suggested language: "When you read, think about the text and graphic features the author uses to give information. Think about how it helps you understand more about the topic."

GROUP SHARE Ask students to share what they noticed about one text or graphic feature in their reading. Tell them to explain what the feature is and the information it gives.

▶ Wicked Wind

INTERACTIVE READ-ALOUD/SHARED READING

Read aloud the selection to students. Stop periodically for brief discussion of the text. Use the following suggested stopping points and prompts:

- After reading the introduction, ask: "How does the author get your attention with this first paragraph?" *(by talking directly to the reader and telling exactly what you might see and hear as a tornado approaches)*
- After reading the section Tornado Forces, say: "The author tells how tornadoes affect survivors. Turn and talk with a partner about how you might help people who have survived a tornado."
- At the end of the selection, ask: "What do you think is the best advice the author gives to help people prepare for tornadoes?"

MINILESSON Genre: Informational Text

TEACH Display the minilesson principle on chart paper, and read it aloud to students. Tell students that they are going to learn about how the author's description helps them understand what something is like.

1. Explain to students that authors use precise words to help readers "see" and "hear" what is being described. Using *Wicked Wind*, discuss the author's description of the sound of a tornado. Suggested language: "In the first paragraph, the author described how a tornado sounds. What words did the author use to help you imagine how tornadoes sound?" *(a distant hum that gets louder and louder; a train that is about to crash through your door)*

> **MINILESSON PRINCIPLE**
>
> Readers think about the author's description of something to understand how it looks and sounds.

2. Have students identify other words in the selection that describe what a tornado is like. *(violent, spinning, huge, large, destroy, damage, scary)* Display students' ideas in a Web labeled *Tornado*.

SUMMARIZE AND APPLY Restate the minilesson principle. Tell students that when they read, they should think about the descriptions authors give. Suggested language: "When you read, think about how the author describes how things look and sound to help you understand what they are like."

GROUP SHARE Ask students to share a description they found in their reading that explains how something looks or sounds.

▶ The Dove and the Ant

INTERACTIVE READ-ALOUD/SHARED READING

Read aloud the story to students. Stop periodically for brief discussion of the text. Use the following suggested stopping points and prompts:

- After the Dove tells the Ant about the river, ask: "How does the author show what the Dove and the Ant are like?" Follow-up: "Which character would you rather have as a friend?"
- After the Ant gets back on shore, say: "The ant seems really grateful for the Dove's help. What does she mean when she says *Life is hard and such kindness is scarce?*"
- At the end of the story, have students turn and talk with a partner about how the Ant and the Dove are alike.

MINILESSON Genre: Fable

TEACH Display the minilesson principle on chart paper, and read it aloud to students. Then reread with students the introduction of *The Dove and the Ant*, emphasizing that it is fable.

1. Introduce students to the idea that fables are written to teach readers a lesson about life. Explain to students that knowing what to expect when they read a fable will help them understand what they read. Suggested language: "In the story, the Ant learned a lesson when the Dove saved her life. Sometimes readers apply a story's lesson to their own lives in different ways. What lesson did you take away from reading the fable?" *(We can make friends by doing kind things for others.)*

> **MINILESSON PRINCIPLE**
>
> Readers think about the lesson or moral in a fable.

2. Point out to students that the author used story details such as the characters' traits and what they did to explain the lesson. Guide students to identify story details that supported the author's message about being kind.

SUMMARIZE AND APPLY Restate the minilesson principle. Then ask students to apply it to their independent reading. Suggested language: "When you read fables, think about the lesson or moral of the story."

GROUP SHARE Ask students to share a lesson they learned from a story they read. Tell them to explain how details in the story were used to teach the lesson.

Whole-Group Lessons

Ecology for Kids
Student Book, Lesson 15

Read Aloud Passages

Forests Are Forever
See page 385 of this Guide.

Wonderful Weather
Student Book, Lesson 15

▶ Ecology for Kids

INTERACTIVE READ-ALOUD/SHARED READING

Read aloud the selection to students. Stop periodically for very brief discussion of the text. Use the following suggested stopping points and prompts for quick group response, or give a specific prompt and have partners or threes turn and talk.

- After reading the section Ecology, ask: "What do you predict you will learn from reading this selection?" Have students turn and talk with a partner about their predictions.
- After reading the section Destruction of the Forests, ask: "How does the author organize the information in the selection?" Follow-up: "How do the headings help you find information?"
- After reading the section An Ocean of Resources, ask: "What is similar about this section and the section about forests that we read before it?" *(They both tell about important resources and how we should use them.)*
- At the end of the selection, say: "The author ends the selection with ideas about how you can protect Earth. Turn and talk with a partner about why you think he includes this information."

MINILESSON Main Ideas and Details

TEACH Display the minilesson principle on chart paper, and read it aloud to students. Tell students that they are going to learn about how to use details in a selection to figure out what the main idea is. Explain that the main idea is what a text is mostly about.

1. Discuss the principle with students, using examples from *Ecology for Kids.* Suggested language: "In the section Ecosystem, the author gave you a lot of details about ecosystems and the things that live in them. These details all told about the main idea. The main idea of this section is that an ecosystem is a natural area where living and nonliving things live and interact with each other. This is what the section is mostly about."

> **MINILESSON PRINCIPLE**
>
> Readers use details in a text to figure out the main idea, or what a text is mostly about.

2. Work with students to name the main idea of the other sections of the selection. Have them identify details in the text that helped them identify the main idea.

3. Record students' responses in an Idea-Support Map like the one shown here.

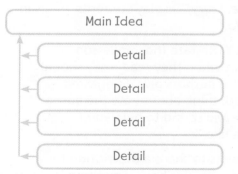

SUMMARIZE AND APPLY Restate the minilesson principle. Then tell students to apply it to their independent reading. Suggested language: "When you read, think about the details the author gives to help you figure out the main ideas."

GROUP SHARE Ask students to name a main idea from a book they read. Then have them name details that helped them figure out what the main idea was.

▶ Forests Are Forever

INTERACTIVE READ-ALOUD/SHARED READING

Read aloud the selection to students. Stop periodically for brief discussion of the text. Use the following suggested stopping points and prompts:

- After reading the first paragraph, ask: "How does the author's introduction make you curious about forests?"

- After reading about how people can affect a forest in good ways, ask: "What are some other ways that people can affect a forest in a good way? Turn and talk with a partner about your thinking."

- At the end of the selection, ask: "What is the most important thing you learned from the selection?"

MINILESSON Main Ideas and Details

TEACH Display the minilesson principle on chart paper, and read it aloud to students. Tell students that authors often state the main idea of a paragraph in the first or last sentence. Then explain that in some cases, authors do not state the main idea at all, but they expect readers to figure it out using details provided.

1. Focus on the second paragraph of *Forests Are Forever*, and reread it aloud to students. Guide them to understand that the main idea of this paragraph is stated in the first sentence: *Forests are home to many living things*. Have students name details in the paragraph that tell about this main idea.

> **MINILESSON PRINCIPLE**
>
> Readers notice that the author's main idea may be stated or unstated.

2. Next, focus on the last paragraph, and reread it aloud to students. Tell students that the main idea of this paragraph is not stated. Suggested language: "The author doesn't directly state the main idea of this paragraph. You have to think about the details in the paragraph and figure out the main idea. The main idea of this paragraph is: *The ozone layer needs to be saved in order to protect the planet*." Have students name details the author gives that tell about this main idea. Record their responses in an Idea-Support Map.

SUMMARIZE AND APPLY Restate the minilesson principle. Tell students to apply it to their independent reading. Suggested language: "When you read, think about what the main idea is. Think about whether the author states the main idea or expects you to figure it out."

GROUP SHARE Have students name a main idea from a book they read. Have them tell whether the main idea was stated or unstated.

▶ Wonderful Weather

INTERACTIVE READ-ALOUD/SHARED READING

Read aloud the poems to students. Stop periodically for brief discussion. Use the following suggested stopping points and prompts:

- After reading the poem "Fog," ask: "How does this poem make you feel?"

- After reading the poem "Weather," ask: "What is special about the words that the poet uses to tell about weather sounds?"

- After the last poem, say: "Each poem tells about weather in a different way. Which poem do you think is most memorable? Turn and talk about your thinking with a partner."

MINILESSON Genre: Poetry

TEACH Display the minilesson principle on chart paper, and read it aloud to students. Explain to students that they are going to learn how rhyming words give poems rhythm and form.

1. Read aloud "Weatherbee's Diner" to students, emphasizing the rhythm and rhyme. Guide them to understand how rhyming words such as *eat* and *street* and *rain* and *Maine* help to give the poem rhythm. Suggested language: "Poems often have rhyming words in them. When you read a poem, these rhyming words help to give the poems a musical feeling, or rhythm."

> **MINILESSON PRINCIPLE**
>
> Readers notice how rhyming words give a poem rhythm and form.

2. Have students identify the rhyming words in "Weather." Have them take turns reading the poem and emphasizing the rhyming words. Discuss how the rhyming words help to give the poem its rhythm and its shape or form.

3. Last, discuss the poem "Umbrella." Guide students to notice where the rhyming words fall. Ask: "Where do the rhyming words fall in this poem?" *(at the end of the second and fourth lines)* Point out that the pattern of rhyming words adds to a poem's rhythm and its form.

SUMMARIZE AND APPLY Restate the minilesson principle. Tell students to apply it to their independent reading. Suggested language: "When you read a poem, think about how the rhyming words give it rhythm and form."

GROUP SHARE Ask students to share a poem they have read. Tell them to name the rhyming words in it. Then have them read aloud a few lines from the poem to show its rhythm and form.

Whole-Group Lessons

Riding Freedom
Student Book, Lesson 16

Read Aloud Passages

Getting the Story
See page 385 of this Guide.

Spindletop
Student Book, Lesson 16

▶ Riding Freedom

INTERACTIVE READ-ALOUD/SHARED READING

Read aloud the story to students. Stop periodically for very brief discussion of the text. Use the following suggested stopping points and prompts for quick group response, or give a specific prompt and have partners or threes turn and talk.

- After Charlotte sets a goal to have ten good round-trip runs, ask: "What can you tell so far about the main character of this story?" *(She is determined; she sets a goal and works hard to achieve it.)*
- After James agrees to let Charlotte drive, ask: "What do you think will happen when James watches Charlotte drive the stagecoach?"
- After Charlotte checks the bridge, ask: "What is Charlotte's plan for crossing the bridge?"
- At the end of the story, say: "The passengers in the stage thought Charlotte was a boy. What do you think they would have done if they knew the truth? Turn and talk about your thinking with a partner."

MINILESSON Genre: Historical Fiction

TEACH Display the minilesson principle on chart paper, and read it aloud to students. Explain that in historical fiction, the setting is important to what happens in the story. The events happen in a time and a real place in the past. Tell students they will learn to notice details about the setting that help them recognize that a story is historical fiction.

1. Discuss the principle, using examples from *Riding Freedom*. Suggested language: "In the introduction, you found out that the story took place in the 1800s, when girls were not allowed to have paid jobs. This tells you that the story happened in the past."

2. Have a volunteer reread the introduction aloud, and ask students to listen for other details about the setting. Ask them to share what they discovered as you write the details in a Web like the one shown below.

> **MINILESSON PRINCIPLE**
>
> Readers notice that the setting in historical fiction is a time and a real place in the past.

Details About Setting

3. Focus students' attention on other details in the story that describe the setting. Ask: "What other details in the story helped you understand that the story happened in the past?" *(people used horses for transportation, a stagecoach delivered mail and brought passengers from place to place)* Continue adding to the Web as students explain their findings.

SUMMARIZE AND APPLY Restate the minilesson principle. Then tell students to apply it to their independent reading. Suggested language: "When you read, notice details about the setting that explain where and when the story takes place. Think about how the setting helps you understand what kind of story you are reading."

GROUP SHARE Ask students to share details about setting from their reading that helped them understand what kind of story they read.

▶ Getting the Story

INTERACTIVE READ-ALOUD/SHARED READING

Read aloud the biography to students. Stop periodically for brief discussion of the text. Use the following suggested stopping points and prompts:

- After reading the first page, ask: "What was it like when Nellie Bly lived?" *(Many women didn't work, and many people didn't accept the idea of it.)*
- After reading that Nellie Bly was an investigative reporter, say: "Why do you think the kinds of stories that Nellie Bly wrote were called investigative reporting? Turn and talk about your ideas with a partner."
- At the end of the selection, ask: "Throughout her life, how did Nellie Bly react when people told her she couldn't do something?"

MINILESSON Genre: Biography

TEACH Display the minilesson principle on chart paper, and read it aloud to students. Tell students that the subject of a biography—the real person that the writing is about—often accomplished something in life that other people may find interesting or even inspiring. Explain that thinking about what a subject tried to do and why it was important can help them understand more about the subject's life.

1. Discuss the principle, using examples from *Getting the Story*. Suggested language: "The author wrote that Nellie Bly quit her job because she wasn't satisfied with writing about fashion and flowers. She wanted to write about more important things. Why do you think this is important? Turn and talk about your thinking with a partner."

> **MINILESSON PRINCIPLE**
>
> Readers think about what a subject tried to do and why it was important.

2. Discuss Nellie Bly's accomplishments with students, and have them explain why the accomplishments were important. Ask: "Why were the things Nellie did important to others?" *(She proved that women could be good journalists. She wrote the kind of stories that caused change.)*

SUMMARIZE AND APPLY Restate the minilesson principle. Tell students to apply it to their independent reading. Suggested language: "When you read, think about what the subject tried to do and why it was important."

GROUP SHARE Ask students to share an example of a biography they read. Have them tell what the person tried to do and why it was important.

▶ Spindletop

INTERACTIVE READ-ALOUD/SHARED READING

Read aloud the selection to students. Stop periodically for brief discussion of the text. Use the following suggested stopping points and prompts:

- After reading the first page, ask: "Why do you believe Pattillo Higgins thought that Spindletop was an important area to explore?"
- After Lucas finds oil, ask: "What was so important about Lucas's discovery?" *(The oil field produced more barrels of oil than any other oil field in Texas.)*
- After reading the last page, ask: "What information does the e-mail add to the selection? Why do you think the author includes it?"

MINILESSON Compare and Contrast

TEACH Display the minilesson principle on chart paper, and read it aloud to students. Tell students that they are going to learn to think about similarities and differences in two different selections. Explain that thinking about how selections are alike and different will help them recognize when one book they read reminds them of another book they have read.

1. Remind students that in *Riding Freedom* and *Spindletop*, they read about several people who faced challenges. Have students recall that in both selections the characters had to convince others to believe in them. Point out that this is a similarity between the selections.

> **MINILESSON PRINCIPLE**
>
> Readers look for similarities and differences between two texts they read.

2. Ask students to explain how the challenges that the people faced in *Riding Freedom* and *Spindletop* were different. Ask: "What was different about the people in these selections?" Record students' responses in a Venn Diagram.

3. Have students volunteer other similarities and differences between the two selections as you add their ideas to the Venn Diagram. Tell students to think about genre, characters' traits, and text features.

SUMMARIZE AND APPLY Restate the minilesson principle, and tell students to apply it to their independent reading. Suggested language: "When you read, look for similarities and differences between what you are reading and something you've read before."

GROUP SHARE Ask students to share how two books they read are alike and different.

Whole-Group Lessons

The Right Dog for the Job: Ira's Path from Service Dog to Guide Dog
Student Book, Lesson 17

Read Aloud Passages

Let Me Be Brave
See page 386 of this Guide.

Knowing Noses
Student Book, Lesson 17

▶ The Right Dog for the Job

INTERACTIVE READ-ALOUD/SHARED READING

Read aloud the book to students. Stop periodically for very brief discussion of the text. Use the following suggested stopping points and prompts for quick group response, or give a specific prompt and have partners or threes turn and talk.

- After reading the first two pages, ask: "Why do you think the training of service dogs is so important?" Follow-up: "Why is something like picking up keys important for service dogs to learn?"
- After reading the section in which Ira completes his training to become a service dog, ask: "What qualities does a service dog need to have?" Follow-up: "Turn and talk with a partner about why you think these qualities are important."
- After reading about the graduation, ask: "How do you think Sandy feels at the graduation?" Follow-up: "How do you think Don feels?"
- After reading the selection, remind students that authors have a reason, or purpose, for writing. Ask: "Why do you think the author wrote this selection? Turn and talk about your thinking with a partner."

MINILESSON Sequence of Events

TEACH Display the minilesson principle on chart paper, and read it aloud to students. Tell students that noticing how the author organizes information and why can help them recognize what is most important about a selection.

1. Discuss the principle with students, using examples from *The Right Dog for the Job*. Focus on the first paragraph. Suggested language: "The author began by telling you about the place where Ira was born and what he was like. This is a clue that information is organized in the order things happened."

2. Remind students that time-order words and phrases are clues that information is organized by the sequence of events. Ask students to point out time-order words and phrases on the first two pages of the selection.

3. On chart paper, draw a Flow Chart, and explain to students that they will identify important events in the selection as you write them in the chart. Tell students to focus on the key parts of Ira's training.

4. Ask students to turn and talk with a partner about why the organization of this selection makes sense for the topic. Tell them to think about how the organization helps them understand the dogs' training.

> **MINILESSON PRINCIPLE**
>
> Readers notice how the author organizes information and why.

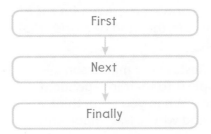

SUMMARIZE AND APPLY Restate the minilesson principle. Then tell students to apply it to their independent reading. Suggested language: "When you read, notice how the author organizes the text. Think about how it helps you understand the information."

GROUP SHARE Ask students to explain how the author organized the information in a book they read. Have them tell why they think the author organized it that way.

▶ Let Me Be Brave

INTERACTIVE READ-ALOUD/SHARED READING

Read aloud the biography to students. Stop periodically for brief discussion of the text. Use the following suggested stopping points and prompts:

- After reading that Liinah's father died, ask: "What difficult decision did Liinah have to make?" Follow-up: "Why do you think she made the decision that she did?"
- After reading about the Irish social workers who are at Liinah's race, ask: "Do you think the tragedy in Liinah's life will affect her race? Why or why not?"
- At the end of the selection, ask: "Why do you think the author wrote about Liinah? Turn and talk about your thinking with a partner."

MINILESSON Sequence of Events

TEACH Display the minilesson principle on chart paper, and read it aloud to students. Tell students they will learn how clue words can help them understand the sequence of events.

1. Discuss the principle with students, using examples from *Let Me Be Brave*. Read aloud the second paragraph again, and ask students to raise their hand when they hear a clue word that indicates sequence.

> **MINILESSON PRINCIPLE**
>
> Readers look for clue words to understand the sequence of events.

2. Tell students that dates and other clues about time can also help to explain the sequence of events. Point out the example *just two months before*.

3. Have students turn and talk with a partner to retell the events in Liinah Bukenya's life that led up to the 2003 Special Olympics. Tell them to use clue words to explain the sequence of events.

SUMMARIZE AND APPLY Restate the minilesson principle. Tell students to apply it to their independent reading. Suggested language: "When you read, look for clue words to understand the sequence of events."

GROUP SHARE Ask students to share a book they read. Have them explain how the author used clue words to help them understand the sequence of events.

▶ Knowing Noses

INTERACTIVE READ-ALOUD/SHARED READING

Read aloud the selection to students. Stop periodically for brief discussion of the text. Use the following suggested stopping points and prompts.

- After reading the section Noses to the Rescue!, ask: "Why are SAR dogs so useful?"
- After reading the section Qualities of a Good SAR Dog, ask: "What qualities does a SAR dog need to have?" Follow-up: "Turn and talk with a partner about which quality you think is most important."
- After reading the special feature, ask: "How is this section different from everything else in this selection?"

MINILESSON Genre: Informational Text

TEACH Display the minilesson principle on chart paper, and read it aloud to students. Explain to students that they are going to learn to use special features that will help them locate information in informational text.

1. Point out and read aloud the headings in *Knowing Noses*. Tell students that headings usually tell what a section is about, and they help to organize the author's ideas.

> **MINILESSON PRINCIPLE**
>
> Readers look for the features of informational text to locate information.

2. Write the selection's four headings on chart paper. Work with students to list the kinds of information in each section. Help them recognize that the heading relates to the information that follows it.

3. Explain to students that they can use headings to find information. Guide students to understand how headings help readers locate information. Suggested language: "Look at the headings. In which section would you look to find information about what kind of dog would be good for this job?" Repeat for the other sections.

SUMMARIZE AND APPLY Restate the minilesson principle. Tell students to apply it to their independent reading. Suggested language: "When you read informational text, read the headings. They can help you know where different kinds of information are located."

GROUP SHARE Ask students to share informational texts they read. Have them read several headings and briefly describe the kinds of information they read about after each one.

Whole-Group Lessons

Hercules' Quest
Student Book, Lesson 18

Read Aloud Passages

Theseus and the Minotaur
See page 386 of this Guide.

Zomo's Friends
Student Book, Lesson 18

▶ Hercules' Quest

INTERACTIVE READ-ALOUD/SHARED READING

Read aloud the myth to students. Stop periodically for very brief discussion of the text. Use the following suggested stopping points and prompts below for quick group response, or give a specific prompt and have partners or threes turn and talk.

- After reading the first page, ask: "What kind of a person is Hera?" Follow-up: "What does she do to make you think that?"
- After Hercules delivers the golden apples, ask: "How does Hercules handle each task? What does that tell you about him?"
- At the end of the myth ask: "How did Hercules change during the story? Turn and talk about your ideas with a partner."

MINILESSON Story Structure

TEACH Display the minilesson principle on chart paper, and read it aloud to students. Tell students that noticing the problem in a story and how it is solved will help them better understand the story.

1. Remind students that myths are stories that have been told for many years. Explain that in many myths a hero must face certain challenges to prove himself or herself in some way.

2. Guide students to understand the challenges Hercules faced in *Hercules' Quest*. Suggested language: "What did Zeus order Hercules to do?" *(serve King Eurystheus)* Follow-up: "Why must Hercules do this?" *(to show his father he is worthy of his strength)*

3. Focus on the first task that King Eurystheus gave Hercules. Suggested language: "What did King Eurystheus want Hercules to do? *(kill the Nemean lion)* Follow-up: "Why was this a problem?" *(because the lion was evil and strong and everyone thought it was impossible to kill him)* Have students tell how Hercules solved the problem.

4. Work with students to identify Hercules' other tasks, and how he was able to complete them. Record students' ideas in a Story Map like the one shown here.

> **MINILESSON PRINCIPLE**
>
> Readers notice the problem a character faces and how the character solves it.

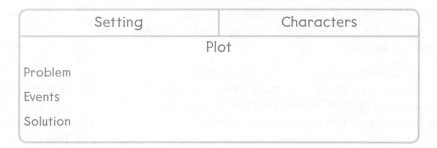

Setting	Characters
Plot	
Problem	
Events	
Solution	

SUMMARIZE AND APPLY Restate the minilesson principle. Then tell students to apply it to their independent reading. Suggested language: "When you read a myth, think about the problem a character has and how it is solved.

GROUP SHARE Have students share a problem from a story they read. Have them explain how the character solved the problem.

▶ Theseus and the Minotaur

INTERACTIVE READ-ALOUD/SHARED READING

Read aloud the myth to students. Stop periodically for brief discussion of the text. Use the following suggested stopping points and prompts:

- At the end of the second paragraph, ask: "Why did the people of Athens make a deal with King Minos?"
- At the end of the first page, ask: "Who volunteered to go to Crete?" Follow-up: "What do you think will happen? Turn and talk about your predictions with a partner."
- At the end, ask: "How did Theseus defeat the Minotaur?"

MINILESSON Story Structure

TEACH Display the minilesson principle on chart paper, and read it aloud to students. Remind students that thinking about story elements such as settings, characters, and important events will help them better understand a story.

1. Discuss the principle with students, using details from *Theseus and the Minotaur*. Suggested language: "Who is the main character?" *(Theseus)* Follow-up: "What did you learn about him?" *(He is the son of a king; he volunteered to go to Crete; he said he would kill the Minotaur.)*

> **MINILESSON PRINCIPLE**
>
> Readers think about important parts of a story, such as the characters, setting, and important events.

2. Next, focus on the setting. Suggested language: "An important setting is the labyrinth on Crete. What makes this place important?" *(It is where Theseus has to defeat the Minotaur.)* Follow-up: "In what other places does the myth take place?"

3. Finally, work with students to identify and discuss important events. Record students' responses on a Story Map.

SUMMARIZE AND APPLY Restate the minilesson principle. Then tell students to apply it to their independent reading. Suggested language: "When you read a myth, think about important story elements, like characters, settings, and important events."

GROUP SHARE Ask students to share details about an important event in a story they read. Have them explain why that event was important.

▶ Zomo's Friends

INTERACTIVE READ-ALOUD/SHARED READING

Read aloud the tale to students. Stop periodically for brief discussion of the text. Use the following suggested stopping points and prompts.

- After Zomo goes to see Sky God, ask: "Why does Zomo want to visit Sky God?"
- After Zomo leaves Crocodile, ask: "What does Zomo learn from his visit with Crocodile?"
- At the end of the folktale, ask: "Do you agree with Zomo that it is great to be clever, but having friends is even better? Turn and talk about your ideas with a partner."

MINILESSON Genre: Folktale

TEACH Display the minilesson principle on chart paper, and read it aloud to students. Tell students that they will learn about the sayings that come from folktales and the lessons they share.

1. Discuss the principle with students, using examples from *Zomo's Friends*. Suggested language: "Sayings called proverbs and adages are short statements that tell a basic truth. Proverbs and adages are often found in folktales. When Zomo first visited Sky God, what proverb did Sky God share?" *(The only way to have friends is to be one yourself.)* Follow-up: Why did he tell Zomo this? *(to help Zomo understand why he didn't have any friends)*

> **MINILESSON PRINCIPLE**
>
> Readers think about proverbs and adages that are found in folktales.

2. Continue in the same way, using other examples of proverbs and adages. Suggested language: "When Zomo returned to Sky God after meeting with Zebra, Sky God shared this proverb: 'A little rain each day will fill the rivers to overflowing.' What do you think Sky God means?" *(Zomo still needs to learn that to make and keep friends, he must continue being kind to others.)*

3. Guide students to identify other proverbs and adages, and discuss their meanings. Together, create a chart to show the lessons Zomo learns.

SUMMARIZE AND APPLY Restate the minilesson principle. Then tell students to apply it to their independent reading. Suggested language: "When you read a folktale, pay attention to proverbs and adages, and think about how characters learn about these basic truths."

GROUP SHARE Ask students to share a proverb or adage from a folktale they read. Have them explain how a character learned this truth.

Whole-Group Lessons

Harvesting Hope: The Story of Cesar Chavez
Student Book, Lesson 19

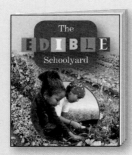

Read Aloud Passages

The Father of India
See page 387 of this Guide.

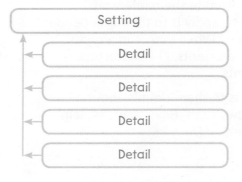

The Edible Schoolyard
Student Book, Lesson 19

▶ Harvesting Hope

INTERACTIVE READ-ALOUD/SHARED READING

Read aloud the biography to students. Stop periodically for very brief discussion of the text. Use the following suggested stopping points and prompts for quick group response, or give a specific prompt and have partners or threes turn and talk.

- After reading the introduction, say: "This selection is a biography. How is a biography different from a story?"
- After reading about the family earning thirty cents a day for their work, ask: "What was Cesar's life like when he began traveling from one farm to another for work?"
- After the first meeting Cesar has with other workers, say: "Why do you think Cesar feels strongly about the idea of nonviolence?"
- At the end of the selection, remind students that Cesar Chavez did not think violence could help solve problems. Then say: "Do you agree or disagree? Turn and talk about your thinking with a partner."

MINILESSON Genre: Biography

TEACH Display the minilesson principle on chart paper, and read it aloud to students. Tell students that people in different parts of the world and in different times face different problems. Remind students that in a biography, the setting is a real place. Then tell students that they are going to think about how the place where the subject of a biography lives can affect the person's life.

1. Discuss the principle with students, using examples from *Harvesting Hope*. Suggested language: "When Cesar was a boy, he lived on a ranch in Arizona. He learned what it was like to work on a farm."

2. Contrast Cesar's life in Arizona to his life as a migrant worker. Suggested language: "Cesar's life changed when he moved to California. Why were the conditions that he worked in such a shock?"

3. Guide students to understand how Cesar's life changed when he moved from Arizona to California. Point out that the place where he lived inspired him to fight for better working conditions. Have students give details about what California was like and how it affected Cesar. Record students' ideas in an Idea-Support Map like the one shown here.

> **MINILESSON PRINCIPLE**
>
> Readers think about the setting of a biography and how it affected the person's life.

```
          ┌─────────────────────┐
          │       Setting       │
          └─────────────────────┘
            ┌───────────────────┐
          ← │      Detail       │
            └───────────────────┘
            ┌───────────────────┐
          ← │      Detail       │
            └───────────────────┘
            ┌───────────────────┐
          ← │      Detail       │
            └───────────────────┘
            ┌───────────────────┐
          ← │      Detail       │
            └───────────────────┘
```

SUMMARIZE AND APPLY Restate the minilesson principle. Then tell students to apply it to their independent reading. Suggested language: "When you read a biography, think about the setting and how it affects the person's life."

GROUP SHARE Ask students to tell about a person from a biography they have read. Have them tell how the setting affected that person's life.

▶ The Father of India

Read aloud the biography to students. Stop periodically for brief discussion of the text. Use the following suggested stopping points and prompts:

- After reading the first paragraph, ask: "How does the author help you imagine what it used to be like to live in India?"
- After reading the first page, ask: "Why do you think the author tells you that Gandhi wore simple clothes and had a modest lifestyle? Turn and talk about your thinking with a partner."
- At the end of the book ask: "Why do you think Gandhi's strategies to create change influenced other people?"

MINILESSON Conclusions and Generalizations

TEACH Display the minilesson principle on chart paper, and read it aloud to students. Tell students that authors give clues in a book to help readers figure out things that they don't say. Explain that when readers use information from the text and their own ideas, they are drawing conclusions.

1. Discuss the principle with students, using details from *The Father of India*. Suggested language: "Think about how Gandhi looked, behaved, and acted. Did his qualities make him an appealing leader? What conclusion can you draw about why others listened to him?" *(Yes; Gandhi's personal qualities made others trust and want to follow him.)*

> **MINILESSON PRINCIPLE**
>
> Readers notice clues in the text to think about what the author does not tell them.

2. Next, guide students to use information from the text to make generalizations. Suggested language: "Gandhi believed that violence was not a good way to protest unfair laws. Think about putting this idea into action. Can nonviolence be an effective way to bring change?" *(Yes; Gandhi proved nonviolence can bring about change.)*

3. Continue in the same way, having students use details from the text and their own ideas to draw conclusions and make generalizations.

SUMMARIZE AND APPLY Restate the minilesson principle. Then tell students to apply it to their independent reading. Suggested language: "When you read, use information from the text and what you already know to help you draw conclusions or make generalizations."

GROUP SHARE Ask students to share something they figured out in a book they read. Have them explain how they formed their ideas.

▶ The Edible Schoolyard

Read aloud the book to students. Stop periodically for brief discussion of the text. Use the following suggested stopping points and prompts:

- After reading the introduction, ask: "What do you think happens in the Edible Schoolyard program?"
- After reading the section Time to Get Cooking, say: "Students who work in the garden learn about different foods, but they also learn to work together. Turn and talk with a partner about how the garden teaches them many important skills."
- At the end of the book ask: "Do you agree with the author that the Edible Schoolyard program is 'part garden, part kitchen, and part classroom?' Support your thinking with ideas in the text."

MINILESSON Genre: Informational Text

TEACH Display the minilesson principle on chart paper, and read it aloud to students. Remind them that informational texts like *The Edible Schoolyard* give information about a topic. Explain to students that authors often include pictures, graphs, and other visuals that relate to information in the text in order to help readers understand the topic and why it is important.

1. Direct students' attention to the graph on the last page. Tell students that when they see a graph, they should first think about what it shows. Suggested language: "What does the information in the graph help you understand?" *(what foods are healthy and how much people should eat each day)*

> **MINILESSON PRINCIPLE**
>
> Readers notice information shown in graphs and how it relates to the text.

2. Have students summarize what the Edible Schoolyard program is and why it is important. Then tell students to think about how the graph relates to the ideas in the main text. Ask: "How does the graph relate to the information in the text?" *(It shows that the foods the students are growing in the garden are healthy. The fruits and vegetables they grow are part of the diet recommended by the U.S. government.)*

SUMMARIZE AND APPLY Restate the minilesson principle. Tell students to apply it to their independent reading. Suggested language: "When you read, notice how information in a graph relates to the text. Think about how the graph helps you understand more about the topic."

GROUP SHARE Ask students to share an example of a graph from their reading. Have them tell how it relates to the text.

Whole-Group Lessons

Sacagawea
Student Book, Lesson 20

Read Aloud Passages

Race Against Death
See page 387 of this Guide.

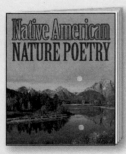

Native American Nature Poetry
Student Book, Lesson 20

▶ Sacagawea

INTERACTIVE READ-ALOUD/SHARED READING

Read aloud the biography to students. Stop periodically for very brief discussion of the text. Use the following suggested stopping points and prompts for quick group response, or give a specific prompt and have partners or threes turn and talk.

- After reading that Charbonneau and Sacagawea will join the Corps, ask: "How have the lives of the two different groups now joined? What experience will they share?"
- After Sacagawea rescues the captains' supplies, ask: "How do you think the captains felt about having Sacagawea on the journey?" Follow-up: "How did they show their appreciation?"
- After the explorers reach the Pacific Ocean, ask: "What do you think it was like for Sacagawea to go on this journey?" Have students use examples from the selection to support their answers.
- At the end of the selection, ask: "How can you tell that the captains respected Sacagawea by the end of the journey? Turn and talk with a partner about your thinking."

MINILESSON Main Ideas and Details

TEACH Display the minilesson principle on chart paper, and read it aloud to students. Tell students that they are going to learn about how to use details in a text to figure out the main idea.

1. Discuss the principle with students, using examples from *Sacagawea*. Suggested language: "The main idea of a story is what the story is mostly about. The author supports the main idea with important details. What are some important details in this story?" As students give their responses, write them in an Idea-Support Map like the one shown below.

2. Guide students to recognize what the important details have in common. Elicit from students that Sacagawea played an important role in an important expedition.

3. Work with students to write a main idea statement that describes what the selection is mostly about. Add the main idea statement to the Idea-Support Map.

> **MINILESSON PRINCIPLE**
>
> Readers look for important details in a text to figure out the main idea.

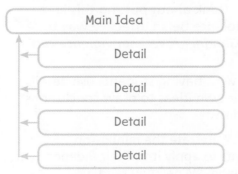

SUMMARIZE AND APPLY Restate the minilesson principle. Then tell students to apply it to their independent reading. Suggested language: "When you read, think about the important details the author gives to help you figure out the main idea."

GROUP SHARE Ask students to share a main idea from a book they read. Then have them name details that helped them figure it out.

▶ Race Against Death

INTERACTIVE READ-ALOUD/SHARED READING

Read aloud the selection to students. Stop periodically for brief discussion of the text. Use the following suggested stopping points and prompts:

- After reading the first paragraph, ask: "How do you know this is a true story?" *(The author includes dates and quotes.)*
- After reading the first page, ask: "Why do you think the author calls the relay a race against death? Turn and talk about your thinking with a partner."
- At the end of the selection, ask: "What words and phrases does the author use to help you understand the dangers the sled dog teams faced on their journey?"

MINILESSON Genre: Narrative Nonfiction

TEACH Display the minilesson principle on chart paper, and read it aloud to students. Explain that authors share information in different ways to make information interesting. Explain that narrative nonfiction has some of the characteristics of a story, but it is about real people, events, and places.

1. Discuss the principle with students, using examples from *Race Against Death*. Suggested language: "One characteristic of a story is that the author uses a technique called suspense. Suspense is when the author gets the reader excited about learning the outcome of the events."

> **MINILESSON PRINCIPLE**
>
> Readers think about how the author shares information to make it interesting.

2. Ask students to explain how the author of *Race Against Death* used suspense. Elicit from students that the author revealed the events to readers just as they happened. Readers had to wait to find out whether the medicine would arrive in time, just as the people who experienced the events.

3. Have students explain how the characteristics of narrative nonfiction are similar to and different from other informational texts. Have them turn and talk to a partner about whether they enjoy reading about real people, events, and places in the form of a story.

SUMMARIZE AND APPLY Restate the minilesson principle. Tell students to apply it to their independent reading. Suggested language: "When you read, think about techniques the author uses to make the information interesting."

GROUP SHARE Have students share an example from their reading that shows how the author made information interesting.

▶ Native American Nature Poetry

INTERACTIVE READ-ALOUD/SHARED READING

Read aloud the poems to students. Stop periodically for brief discussion of the text. Use the following suggested stopping points and prompts:

- After reading the first poem, ask: "How does this poem make you feel about the moon? Turn and talk about your thinking with a partner."
- After reading the information about cylinder recorders, ask: "Why does the author include this information?" *(to tell the reader that it was an important tool Native Americans used to preserve their stories)*
- After reading the last poem, say: "Poems can make you feel different things such as sad, hopeful, lazy, or scared. Which of these poems gives you the strongest feeling? Tell a partner how it makes you feel."

MINILESSON Genre: Poetry

TEACH Display the minilesson principle on chart paper, and read it aloud to students. Explain to students that they are going to learn how the words in poems can help them create images in their minds.

1. Remind students that poets choose words for a poem very carefully so that readers will understand the precise meaning that the poet wants to share.

> **MINILESSON PRINCIPLE**
>
> Readers notice how poets use words to create images in readers' minds.

2. Read aloud "The Wind" to students again. Then ask: "What words in this poem help you visualize the wind?" Follow-up: "What does the wind look like? What does it sound like? How does the wind feel?" Tell students to answer the questions based on the image they have in their mind after reading the poem.

3. Next, ask a volunteer to read aloud the Nootka poem. Then have students explain what they see in their mind when they listen to the poem.

4. Guide students to recognize that if they replaced one or more words in the poem, its imagery and meaning would change. Work with students to replace the words *beautiful* and *rainbow* to create a different image in readers' minds.

SUMMARIZE AND APPLY Restate the minilesson principle. Tell students to apply it to their independent reading. Suggested language: "When you read a poem, think about the words the poet uses to help you create images in your mind."

GROUP SHARE Ask students to share a poem they read. Have them point out words in the poem that helped them create images in their mind.

Whole-Group Lessons

The World According to Humphrey
Student Book, Lesson 21

Read Aloud Passages

Fun and Games on the Range
See page 388 of this Guide.

Make the Switch
Student Book, Lesson 21

▶ The World According to Humphrey

INTERACTIVE READ-ALOUD/SHARED READING

Read aloud the story to students. Stop periodically for very brief discussion of the text. Use the following suggested stopping points and prompts for quick group response, or give a specific prompt and have partners or threes turn and talk.

- After A. J. introduces Humphrey, ask: "Who is telling this story?" (*Humphrey the hamster*)
- After the Thomases talk about breakfast, ask: "Why does the author use all capital letters for the conversation the Thomases are having?" (*to let readers know that they are talking very loudly*) Follow-up: "What has Humphrey noticed about the Thomases?"
- After Humphrey pulls out the plug, ask: "How does Humphrey feel about TV?" Follow-up: "How do you think the family will respond to Humphrey's Big Idea?"
- At the end of the story, say: "A. J.'s parents have changed. How do they feel about TV now? Turn and talk with a partner about why you think they feel this way now."

MINILESSON Theme

TEACH Display the minilesson principle on chart paper, and read it aloud to students. Tell students that they are going to think about how the lesson that characters learn in a story can help them determine the theme, or what the author is really trying to say to readers.

1. Discuss the principle with students, using examples from *The World According to Humphrey*. Focus on how the Thomas family changes when the TV goes off. Suggested language: "After Humphrey pulls out the plug, the Thomas family learns that there are a lot of fun things to do besides watching TV. How would you describe the lesson they learned?"

> **MINILESSON PRINCIPLE**
>
> Readers think about the lesson in the story to understand the theme, or what the author is really trying to say.

2. Guide students to understand the theme of the story. Suggested language: "The theme of a story is what the author is really trying to say to readers. What is the author really trying to say to readers by sharing this lesson about watching TV?" (*that people shouldn't watch so much TV*) Have students turn and talk with a partner about whether they agree with the author.

3. Explain to students that readers can interpret the theme of a story in different ways. Ask volunteers to explain how they would describe the theme in a way that makes it personal to them.

SUMMARIZE AND APPLY Restate the minilesson principle. Then tell students to apply it to their independent reading. Suggested language: "When you read a story, think about the lesson the author teaches to understand the theme."

GROUP SHARE Ask students to tell about a lesson the characters learned in a story they read. Have them explain how the lesson helped them understand the story's theme.

▶ Fun and Games on the Range

INTERACTIVE READ-ALOUD/SHARED READING

Read aloud the selection to students. Stop periodically for brief discussion of the text. Use the following suggested stopping points and prompts:

- After reading about the sounds of life in 1850, say: "Compare your life at home with the lives of children in 1850. Turn and talk with a partner about how it is the same and how it is different."
- After reading about how pioneers had fun, ask: "Why do you think pioneers combined work and having fun?" Follow-up: "Which of these activities would you like to do?"
- At the end of the selection, ask: "How did the author of this selection organize information?"

MINILESSON Genre: Informational Text

TEACH Display the minilesson principle on chart paper, and read it aloud to students. Tell students that authors use interesting words and examples to get readers' attention.

1. Focus on the first paragraph of *Fun and Games on the Range*. Guide students to understand that the author grabs their attention with an interesting beginning. Suggested language: "The author describes a scene right at the beginning to get your attention and to make you feel like you are experiencing the sights and sounds. What interesting words does the author use?" (*TV is blaring, jangles your nerves, cuts through the racket*)

> **MINILESSON PRINCIPLE**
>
> Readers notice how the author uses words and interesting examples to get their attention.

2. Next, reread the paragraph about how pioneers relaxed. Point out to students that the author begins with a question to draw readers in to the paragraph and so that they will read on to answer it. Have students recall examples of relaxing activities that answer the question.

3. Ask students to think about the two techniques—using questions and making readers feel like they are part of the scene. Have them turn and talk with a partner about which technique they think is more effective in getting readers' attention.

SUMMARIZE AND APPLY Restate the minilesson principle. Tell students to apply it to their independent reading. Suggested language: "When you read, think about how the author uses words and interesting examples to get your attention."

GROUP SHARE Have students tell about words and interesting examples that got their attention when they read a story.

▶ Make the Switch

INTERACTIVE READ-ALOUD/SHARED READING

Read aloud the selection to students. Stop periodically for brief discussion of the text. Use the following suggested stopping points and prompts:

- After reading the introduction, ask: "What is the author saying about ads and how they try to influence you?" Follow-up: "What do you expect to see as you continue reading?"
- After reading the posters, ask: "How do the arrows and text help give you information?" (*They show some of the persuasive techniques used in ads.*)
- After reading the selection, say: "The author ends the selection by challenging you. Turn and talk with a partner. Explain what you think about the positive and negative effects of the posters."

MINILESSON Persuasion

TEACH Display the minilesson principle on chart paper, and read it aloud to students. Tell students that they are going to learn how authors use words and visuals to try to persuade them.

1. Guide students to understand the principle by focusing on the first poster in *Make the Switch*. Read the title aloud and ask: "How does the author want a reader to feel after reading the title?" Elicit from students that it makes sitting and watching the TV seem like a lazy thing to do.

> **MINILESSON PRINCIPLE**
>
> Readers notice how the author uses words and visuals to try to persuade them.

2. Focus on the visuals. Ask: "How does the boy look as he watches TV? How do you think he feels about the TV character? Turn and talk with a partner about how the author wants you to feel about watching TV."

3. Discuss the other poster with students. Have them point out how the words and visuals are used to persuade readers that the activities shown are a lot more fun to do than watching TV.

4. Have students share their ideas about which poster is more persuasive.

SUMMARIZE AND APPLY Restate the minilesson principle. Tell students to apply it to their independent reading. Suggested language: "When you read an ad or poster, think about how the author uses words and visuals to persuade you to think or act in a certain way."

GROUP SHARE Ask students to tell about an ad or poster they have read. Have them tell how the words and visuals try to persuade them to do something or think in a certain way.

Whole-Group Lessons

I Could Do That! Esther Morris Gets Women the Vote
Student Book, Lesson 22

Jane's Big Ideas
See page 388 of this Guide.

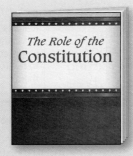

The Role of the Constitution
Student Book, Lesson 22

▶ I Could Do That!

INTERACTIVE READ-ALOUD/SHARED READING

Read aloud the biography to students. Stop periodically for very brief discussion of the text. Use the following suggested stopping points and prompts for quick group response, or give a specific prompt and have partners or threes turn and talk.

- After Esther opens a hat shop, ask: "What kind of person do you think Esther was?" Follow-up: "What makes you think that?"
- After Esther moves to Illinois, say: "What pattern are you starting to see about what happened when people told Esther that she could not do something?"
- After women win the right to vote in Wyoming, ask: "How did Esther persuade the candidates to introduce a bill to allow women to vote?" *(She got everyone to agree that people in Wyoming were not afraid to try new things.)*
- At the end of the selection, ask: "How do you think Esther felt when she cast her first vote in Wyoming? Turn and talk about your thinking with a partner."

MINILESSON Cause and Effect

TEACH Display the minilesson principle on chart paper, and read it aloud to students. Remind students that a cause makes something else happen and that an effect is the result of a cause. Then tell students that they are going to learn to notice how many events can lead to one effect.

1. Discuss the principle with students, using cause-and-effect relationships in *I Could Do That!* Draw an Inference Map on chart paper, and write the following sentence in the bottom box: *In 1870, women in Wyoming voted for the first time.* Label the box *Effect*.

> **MINILESSON PRINCIPLE**
> Readers notice how many events can lead to one effect.

2. Then challenge readers to ask the question, "Why did this happen?" Tell students that when they think about why something happened, they are thinking about the cause of an event.

3. As students share their ideas about the causes for the event, write their responses in the Inference Map. Guide students to recognize that there were several causes that led to the effect.

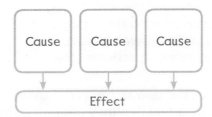

SUMMARIZE AND APPLY Restate the minilesson principle. Then tell students to apply it to their independent reading. Suggested language: "When you read, think about how many events can lead to one effect, or result."

GROUP SHARE Ask students to tell about causes and effects in a book they read. Have them explain several events that led to one effect.

▶ Jane's Big Ideas

INTERACTIVE READ-ALOUD/SHARED READING

Read aloud the biography to students. Stop periodically for brief discussion of the text. Use the following suggested stopping points and prompts:

- After reading the first paragraph, ask: "What do you think the author means by saying that Jane Addams had big ideas?"

- After reading about Jane's pamphlet, ask: "What was Jane's reason for writing this pamphlet? Turn and talk about your thinking with a partner."

- At the end of the selection, ask: "Why do you think the author calls Jane a *tough cookie*?" Have students use examples from the selection to support their answers.

MINILESSON Cause and Effect

TEACH Display the minilesson principle on chart paper, and read it aloud to students. Remind them that a cause makes something else happen. The effect is the result of a cause. Then tell students that a cause can be a person's ideas. What the person does as a result of the ideas is the effect.

1. Discuss the principle with students, using examples from *Jane's Big Ideas*. Suggested language: "Jane Addams felt strongly about what women should be able to do. What were her big ideas?" After students summarize Jane's feelings about women's right to vote, tell students that her big ideas became the cause for change.

> **MINILESSON PRINCIPLE**
>
> Readers notice how a person's big ideas can cause changes for many people.

2. Next, ask students to think about the effects of Jane's big ideas. Suggested language: "Let's think about the result of Jane's big ideas. How did her ideas change life for many people?" Elicit from students that Jane challenged people to think about why women's ideas would be valuable in politics, and she influenced many people to change their views. Students should recognize that the 19th amendment was passed partly as a result of Jane's ideas.

SUMMARIZE AND APPLY Restate the minilesson principle. Tell students to apply it to their independent reading. Suggested language: "When you read a story, think about how a person's ideas cause changes in other people's lives."

GROUP SHARE Ask students to describe a person they read about. Have them tell how the person's ideas caused changes in other people's lives.

▶ The Role of the Constitution

INTERACTIVE READ-ALOUD/SHARED READING

Read aloud the book to students. Stop periodically for brief discussion of the text. Use the following suggested stopping points and prompts:

- After reading the second paragraph on the second page, ask: "Why is our country called a democracy?" Follow-up: "What document explains this information?"

- After reading the section The Three Branches, ask: "What are the three branches of our government?" Follow-up: "What main areas does each branch include?"

- After reading the section Rights and Freedoms, ask: "Which rights and freedoms do you think are most important? Turn and talk about your ideas with a partner."

MINILESSON Genre: Informational Text

TEACH Display the minilesson principle on chart paper, and read it aloud to students. Tell students that they will learn about how the information in graphs relates to the ideas in the text.

1. Discuss the principle with students, using the graph in *The Role of the Constitution*. Explain why authors of informational texts sometimes include graphs. Suggested language: "A graph shows information about numbers or data in a visual way. Graphs help readers make comparisons. This type of graph is called a bar graph. What information does this graph help you understand?" (*It tells about voter turnout rates from 1960–2008.*)

> **MINILESSON PRINCIPLE**
>
> Readers think about how information in graphs relates to the text.

2. Have students think about how the information in the graph relates to the ideas in the main text. Suggested language: "How does the graph relate to the information in this section?" (*The text explained that voting is a citizen's duty. The graphs show how many people actually voted over a period of time.*)

SUMMARIZE AND APPLY Restate the minilesson principle. Tell students to apply it to their independent reading. Suggested language: "When you read, notice how information in a graph relates to the text. Think about how the graph helps you understand ideas in the text."

GROUP SHARE Ask students to share a graph from a book they read. Have them tell how it relates to the text.

The Ever-Living Tree: The Life and Times of a Coast Redwood
Student Book, Lesson 23

Read Aloud Passages

Deserts on the Move?
See page 389 of this Guide.

Towering Trees
Student Book, Lesson 23

▶ The Ever-Living Tree

INTERACTIVE READ-ALOUD/SHARED READING

Read aloud the selection to students. Stop periodically for very brief discussion of the text. Use the following suggested stopping points and prompts for quick group response, or give a specific prompt and have partners or threes turn and talk.

- After reading the first page, ask: "What kind of selection is this?" Follow-up: "What is the author telling you about?"
- After reading the second page, say: "The author did something interesting here by telling you about some events happening on the other side of the world. Why do you think she did this in a selection about a tree?"
- After reading about the Native Americans, ask: "Now that we've read several pages, what pattern do you see with how the author has organized information?"
- After reading about man walking on the moon, ask: "Why do you think the author included this information about space travel? Turn and talk about your ideas with a partner."
- At the end of the selection, ask: "Why do you think the author wrote this? How does it make you feel about the sequoia tree?"

MINILESSON Text and Graphic Features

TEACH Display the minilesson principle on chart paper, and read it aloud to students. Tell students that they are going to learn about why an author uses visuals such as diagrams, symbols, and timelines to help them understand the topic.

> **MINILESSON PRINCIPLE**
>
> Readers notice how visuals are related to a text and why the author used them.

1. Discuss the principle, using examples from the first two pages of *The Ever-Living Tree*. Suggested language: "Look at the timeline in the top left corner of the page. Now look at the symbols at the beginning of each paragraph. What do you notice?" *(The symbols are the same.)* Tell students that the timeline shows the year when the tree started to grow and important events that happened later. Guide students to page through the selection to see how the timeline grows as the tree grows and time passes in history.

2. Ask students to explain whether they think the author's choice to include a timeline and symbols helps them understand information about the sequoia.

3. Guide students to explain how other visuals in the selection support and relate to the main text. Draw their attention to the map, the diagram, and the illustrations.

4. Record students' responses in a T-Map like the one shown here. Have them explain how each visual connects to the ideas in the text.

Visual	What It Explains

SUMMARIZE AND APPLY Restate the minilesson principle. Then tell students to apply it to their independent reading. Suggested language: "When you read a selection, think about why the author used certain visuals to help you understand the topic."

GROUP SHARE Ask students to share what they learned from a visual in a book they read. Have them explain how the author used the visual, how it relates to the text, and how it helped them understand the topic.

▶ Deserts on the Move?

INTERACTIVE READ-ALOUD/SHARED READING

Read aloud the selection to students. Stop periodically for brief discussion of the text. Use the following suggested stopping points and prompts:

- After reading the section Creeping Sands, ask: "How does the author make the information about deserts interesting?" *(by explaining how the land and people's lives change at the same time as the deserts change)*

- At the end of the selection, ask: "What does the author mean by saying that humans create the problem and also help to solve it? Turn and talk about your thinking with a partner."

MINILESSON Cause and Effect

TEACH Display the minilesson principle on chart paper, and read it aloud to students. Remind students that some events cause other events to happen. The first event that happens is the cause. The effect is what happens as a result. Tell students that they will learn to notice the language an author uses to explain causes and effects.

1. Discuss the principle, using examples from *Deserts on the Move?* Reread paragraph four aloud to students. Then say: "One way that authors show causes and effects is by using clue words such as *because, if, so,* and *when.*" Reread the two sentences that begin with *If* to help students recognize the cause-and-effect relationships.

> **MINILESSON PRINCIPLE**
>
> Readers notice the language the author uses to explain causes and effects.

2. Write the causes and effects in a T-Map to illustrate the relationships.

3. Work with students to identify other causes and effects in the selection as you reread selected sentences. Have students indicate when the author used a clue word to help them understand causes and effects.

SUMMARIZE AND APPLY Restate the minilesson principle. Tell students to apply it to their independent reading. Suggested language: "When you read, think about the words the author uses to explain causes and effects."

GROUP SHARE Ask students to share a cause and an effect from a book they read. Have them give examples of words the author used to explain that cause and effect.

▶ Towering Trees

INTERACTIVE READ-ALOUD/SHARED READING

Read aloud the poems to students. Stop periodically for brief discussion of the text. Use the following suggested stopping points and prompts:

- After reading the introduction and "Ancestors of Tomorrow," ask: "How do the ideas in this poem relate to the topic of ancestors?" *(Ancestors are people who came before you. The poet compares people and their ancestors to trees and their branches and seeds.)* Follow-up: "What do you think about this comparison?"

- After reading about the Eon Tree, ask: "How does this poem tell a story? Turn and talk about your ideas with a partner."

- After reading the last poem, ask: "How does the poet help you picture the sequoia? What words and phrases does he use?"

MINILESSON Genre: Poetry

TEACH Display the minilesson principle on chart paper, and read it aloud to students. Explain to students that they are going to learn to recognize that poets can express ideas about a topic such as trees in different ways.

1. Discuss the principle, using examples from *Towering Trees.* Suggested language: "The three poems are about trees. Each poet expresses ideas about the trees in different ways. What do the trees in all the poems have in common?" *(They are all very old.)*

> **MINILESSON PRINCIPLE**
>
> Readers notice how poets can express ideas about the same topic in very different ways.

2. Next, point out the differences in the poems, including their structure and the feeling each poem gives the reader. Suggested language: "What is different about the ways the poems look?" Follow-up with questions that help students explain the mood and tone of the poems. Have students explain their answers to each question. Suggested language: "Which poem ends with a feeling of hope? Which poem makes the tree sound majestic? Which poem gives you a feeling of comfort?"

3. Have volunteers tell how they might approach writing a poem about a tree and how their poems would be different from the ones they read.

SUMMARIZE AND APPLY Restate the minilesson principle. Tell students to apply it to their independent reading. Suggested language: "When you read a poem, think about the unique way that the poet expresses ideas about a topic."

GROUP SHARE Ask students to share part of a poem they read. Have them point out words and techniques the poet used to make ideas about the topic unique.

Whole-Group Lessons • **231**

Whole-Group Lessons

Owen and Mzee: The True Story of a Remarkable Friendship
Student Book, Lesson 24

New Friends in the Newsroom
See page 389 of this Guide.

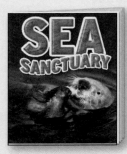

Sea Sanctuary
Student Book, Lesson 24

▶ **Owen and Mzee**

INTERACTIVE READ-ALOUD/SHARED READING

Read aloud the selection to students. Stop periodically for very brief discussion of the text. Use the following suggested stopping points and prompts for quick group response, or give a specific prompt and have partners or threes turn and talk.

- After reading the first page, ask: "Why was Haller Park a good place for Owen to go?"
- After the introduction to Mzee, ask: "What do you predict will happen with Mzee and Owen?"
- After reading that Owen would feed beside Mzee, ask: "Why do you think Owen felt safe with Mzee?"
- At the end of the selection, say: "The author gives a lot of reasons for why Owen and Mzee may have bonded. Which reasons do you think are correct? Turn and talk about your ideas with a partner."

MINILESSON Compare and Contrast

TEACH Display the minilesson principle on chart paper, and read it aloud to students. Remind students that comparing is telling how two things are alike and that contrasting is telling how two things are different. Tell students that comparing and contrasting ideas in a text can help them understand it better.

1. Discuss the principle with students, using examples from *Owen and Mzee*. Suggested language: "This selection tells about two unlikely friends. The reason their friendship is so surprising is because they are two very different animals. How are Owen and Mzee different?"

2. As students answer the question, write their responses on chart paper in a Venn Diagram.

3. Next, ask students to explain how the two animals are alike. Tell students to think about where they live, their friendship, and how they treat each other. Add students' responses to the Venn Diagram.

> **MINILESSON PRINCIPLE**
>
> Readers compare and contrast ideas to understand how things are alike and different.

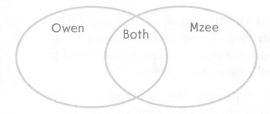

SUMMARIZE AND APPLY Restate the minilesson principle. Then tell students to apply it to their independent reading. Suggested language: "When you read, compare and contrast ideas to understand how things are alike and different."

GROUP SHARE Ask students to share two ideas from a book they have read. Have them explain how they are alike and different.

▶ New Friends in the Newsroom

INTERACTIVE READ-ALOUD/SHARED READING

Read aloud the story to students. Stop periodically for brief discussion of the text. Use the following suggested stopping points and prompts:

- After reading the first two paragraphs, ask: "Why will Anna have a hard time finding things from her old home in the place where she lives now?"

- At the end of the story, ask: "How did Sarah make Anna comfortable in the city?" Follow-up: "How do you think writing the article helped Anna? Turn and talk about your ideas with a partner."

MINILESSON Genre: Realistic Fiction

TEACH Display the minilesson principle on chart paper, and read it aloud to students. Tell students that the setting of a story can be as important as the characters. Explain that looking for the author's description of the setting will help them understand when and where the story takes place and also how it affects the characters.

1. Discuss the principle with students, using examples from *New Friends in the Newsroom*. Focus on the first paragraph. Suggested language: "The author says that Anna just started a new school and that she has to ride a bus for an hour because the city is so big. This tells you that the story takes place at a school in a city."

> **MINILESSON PRINCIPLE**
>
> Readers look for the author's description of the setting to understand when and where the story takes place.

2. Focus on other details in the story that describe when the story takes place. Ask: "Does this story take place now or long ago?" *(now)* "How does the author let you know this?" Have students give details from the story to support their answers. Then ask students to talk with a partner about why the setting of the story is important.

SUMMARIZE AND APPLY Restate the minilesson principle. Tell students to apply it to their independent reading. Suggested language: "When you read, look for the author's description of the setting to understand where and when the story takes place. Think about how the setting affects the characters."

GROUP SHARE Ask students to share an example of how the author described the setting in a story they read. Have them explain why the setting was important.

▶ Sea Sanctuary

INTERACTIVE READ-ALOUD/SHARED READING

Read aloud the selection to students. Stop periodically for brief discussion of the text. Use the following suggested stopping points and prompts:

- After reading the first page, ask: "Based on the information the author has told you, what is a sanctuary?" Follow-up: "What is unique about the sanctuary that the author describes?"

- After reading the section Seafood Chain, ask: "How has the author organized the information in this section?" *(cause and effect)*

- After reading the section Flower Garden Banks, ask: "How is this sanctuary the same as or different from the Monterey Bay National Marine Sanctuary?"

- At the end of the selection, ask: "Why do you think sea sanctuaries are important? Turn and talk about your thinking with a partner."

MINILESSON Summarize

TEACH Display the minilesson principle on chart paper, and read it aloud to students. Tell students that summarizing a text in their own words is a strategy they can use to be sure they understand what they read.

1. Discuss the principle with students by using the selection *Sea Sanctuary*. Suggested language: "When you summarize, you explain the main ideas and the most important details of a text in your own words. Look at the first two pages of the selection. What is the main idea of these pages?" *(The Monterey Bay National Marine Sanctuary is an ecosystem where animals live and find good sources of food.)* Write students' correct responses on chart paper.

> **MINILESSON PRINCIPLE**
>
> Readers summarize a text in their own words to be sure they understand it.

2. Repeat the process for the second page.

3. Work with students to combine the main idea statements into a two- or three-sentence summary. *(Sea sanctuaries are places where marine animals live and thrive because they are protected. In Monterey Bay and Flower Garden Banks Sanctuaries, each animal is part of a food chain.)* Point out to students that the summary is much shorter than the complete text, and it does not include minor details.

SUMMARIZE AND APPLY Restate the minilesson principle. Tell students to apply it to their independent reading. Suggested language: "When you read, summarize the ideas in your own words to be sure you understand them."

GROUP SHARE Ask students to summarize a book they read. Remind them to tell about the ideas in their own words.

Whole-Group Lessons

The Fun They Had
Student Book, Lesson 25

Read Aloud Passages

The Future of Flight
See page 390 of this Guide.

Toys! Amazing Stories Behind Some Great Inventions
Student Book, Lesson 25

▶ The Fun They Had

INTERACTIVE READ-ALOUD/SHARED READING

Read aloud the story to students. Stop periodically for very brief discussion of the text. Use the following suggested stopping points and prompts for quick group response, or give a specific prompt and have partners or threes turn and talk.

- After reading the first page, ask: "When does this story take place?" *(in the future)* Follow-up: "Besides the diary entry, how do you know that this is the future?"
- After the man fixes the mechanical teacher, ask: "How do you think the author wants you to feel about the mechanical teacher? Turn and talk with a partner about details that let you know."
- After Tommy walks away with the book, say: "Margie wants to read the old book some more. How do you think she feels about schools in the past?"
- At the end of the story, have students turn and talk with a partner about whether they would rather go to schools like we have today or schools in the future like the author describes. Have them use text evidence to explain their thinking.

MINILESSON Author's Purpose

TEACH Display the minilesson principle on chart paper, and read it aloud to students. Remind students that authors have different reasons for writing. Tell students that they are going to look for details that will help them figure out the author's reason for writing.

1. Discuss the principle with students, focusing on the author's use of humorous details in *The Fun They Had*. Suggested language: "The author included some funny details in the story he told about the future."

2. Work with students to identify humorous details in the story. Guide them to understand that the details were funny because of the characters' reactions to learning about what schools were like in the past. For example, they had never seen a book.

3. Write on the board the following purposes for writing: to inform, to entertain, to persuade. Ask students to explain the author's reason for writing *The Fun They Had*. Elicit from students that the humorous details indicate that the story was written to entertain readers.

> **MINILESSON PRINCIPLE**
>
> Readers look for details to figure out the author's reason for writing.

SUMMARIZE AND APPLY Restate the minilesson principle. Then tell students to apply it to their independent reading. Suggested language: "When you read, think about details that help you understand the author's reason for writing."

GROUP SHARE Ask students to tell about a story they read. Have them name details in the story that helped them figure out the author's reason for writing it.

▶ The Future of Flight

INTERACTIVE READ-ALOUD/SHARED READING

Read aloud the selection to students. Stop periodically for brief discussion of the text. Use the following suggested stopping points and prompts:

- After the first paragraph, ask: "How do you think the author feels about flight? Turn and talk with a partner about your thinking."
- After the first page, ask: "What problems do airplanes cause?"
- At the end of the selection, ask: "Why do you think the author wrote this selection? Turn and talk about your thinking with a partner."

MINILESSON Genre: Informational Text

TEACH Display the minilesson principle on chart paper, and read it aloud to students. Explain to students that authors use evidence to explain why they think a topic is important. Tell students that it is their job to think about what the author writes and decide whether they agree.

1. Discuss the principle with students, using examples from *The Future of Flight*. Have students identify reasons the author gives to show that the field of flight is important. (*It is inexpensive compared with earlier types of travel, it's quicker, and it gives people access to other cultures and opportunities.*)

> **MINILESSON PRINCIPLE**
>
> Readers think about why the author feels the subject is important and decide whether they agree.

2. Next, have students explain other evidence the author gives to support the idea that flight is an ideal way to travel.

3. Explain to students that they may agree or disagree with an author's ideas. Tell them that they should evaluate the evidence to form their own opinions. Have students turn and talk with a partner about whether they think the subject of flight is important for people to learn about. Have them use evidence to explain their thinking.

SUMMARIZE AND APPLY Restate the minilesson principle. Tell students to apply it to their independent reading. Suggested language: "When you read, think about why the author feels the subject is important. Look at the evidence the author gives and decide whether you agree."

GROUP SHARE Have students share a book they read and tell why the author felt the subject was important. Then have them tell whether they agree and why.

▶ Toys!

INTERACTIVE READ-ALOUD/SHARED READING

Read aloud the selection to students. Stop periodically for brief discussion of the text. Use the following suggested stopping points and prompts:

- After the first two paragraphs, ask: "How are windup toys similar to those in the past? How are they different?"
- After reading through the third page, ask: "How does the information in the diagram connect to the text?"
- At the end of the selection, ask: "How does the author feel about automatons and windup toys?" Follow-up: "How did the automaton inventors of the past contribute to new technology today?"

MINILESSON Summarize

TEACH Display the minilesson principle on chart paper, and read it aloud to students. Tell students that summarizing information can help them understand it.

1. Guide students to understand the principle by focusing on the first page of *Toys!* Suggested language: "When you summarize, you tell about the main ideas and the important details that support the main ideas. What is the main idea of this page, or what is it mostly about?" (*Windup toys in the past were more elaborate and were intended for adults, not children.*) Have students point out details that support this main idea.

> **MINILESSON PRINCIPLE**
>
> Readers summarize information in their own words to be sure they understand it.

2. Focus on the second through fifth pages of the selection. Suggested language: "What is the main idea of this section?" (*Inventors made increasingly elaborate and complex automatons that amazed people.*)

3. Repeat for the last page of the selection.

4. Work with students to combine all the main ideas into a two- or three-sentence summary of the selection. Remind students that they should use their own words in a summary.

SUMMARIZE AND APPLY Restate the minilesson principle. Tell students to apply it to their independent reading. Suggested language: "When you read, summarize the main ideas and details to be sure you understand the information."

GROUP SHARE Ask students to summarize part of a book they read. Remind them to include the main ideas and details in it.

Whole-Group Lessons

The Girl Who Loved Spiders
Student Magazine, Lesson 26

Web Wise
Student Magazine, Lesson 26

Poetry Place: "The Spider" and "Spider Ropes"
Student Magazine, Lesson 26

▶ The Girl Who Loved Spiders

INTERACTIVE READ-ALOUD/SHARED READING

Read aloud the story to students. Stop periodically for very brief discussion of the text. Use the following suggested stopping points and prompts for quick group response, or give a specific prompt and have partners or threes turn and talk.

- After reading the first page, ask: "Who is telling this story?" (*a boy*) Follow-up: "How does this make the selection more interesting to read?"

- After reading the second page, ask: "How do you think Luis feels about moving to Florida? What does he say that makes you think this?"

- After Ashanti stalks away, ask: "Why does Ashanti stalk away?" (*She is still angry with Luis for surprising her and frustrated that he doesn't like spiders.*) Follow-up: "Turn and talk with a partner about how you think Luis feels about Ashanti."

- After Ashanti shows Luis the poster of Anansi, ask: "Do you think Luis and Ashanti will become friends? Turn and talk with a partner about your thinking."

- At the end of the selection, ask: "How does the author use photographs and captions in the story?" (*to show you what real spiders look like and to give facts that help you learn about them*)

MINILESSON Story Structure

TEACH Display the minilesson principle on chart paper, and read it aloud to students. Tell students that they are going to learn about the problem and solution in a story.

1. Explain to students that the characters in stories often have a problem to solve. Guide students to identify Luis's problem in *The Girl Who Loved Spiders*. Suggested language: "At the beginning of the story, you learned that Luis hates spiders. Why was this a problem for Luis?" (*He moved to Florida and there are all kinds of spiders there.*)

> **MINILESSON PRINCIPLE**
>
> Readers notice the problem in a story and how it is solved.

2. Talk with students about how Ashanti helped Luis solve his problem. Ask: "How did Luis feel about spiders at the end of the story?" (*He was not afraid of them anymore.*) Follow-up: "How do you know?" (*He said they are kind of cool, and he wanted to know what kinds of spiders were in his yard.*)

3. Record students' ideas about the problem and solution in a Story Map like the one shown here.

Setting	Characters
Plot	
Problem (Conflict)	
Events	
Solution (Resolution)	

SUMMARIZE AND APPLY Restate the minilesson principle. Tell students to look for a problem and solution in their reading. Suggested language: "When you read, think about what problem the characters have. Then think about how the problem was solved."

GROUP SHARE Ask students to share a problem from a story they read. Then have them tell how the problem was solved.

▶ Web Wise

INTERACTIVE READ-ALOUD/SHARED READING

Read aloud the selection to students. Stop periodically for brief discussion of the text. Use the following suggested stopping points and prompts:

- After reading the introduction, ask: "What will you learn about in this selection?" (*spider webs*) Follow-up: "How does the author feel about spiders? How do you know?"
- After reading the section Web Shots, ask: "Why do you think scientists and photographers want to take pictures of spider webs? Turn and talk with a partner about your thinking."
- After reading the section Strange, but True!, ask: "Do you think spiders are intelligent? What did you learn from this selection that makes you think that way?"

MINILESSON Genre: Informational Text

TEACH Display the minilesson principle on chart paper, and read it aloud to students. Remind students that *Web Wise* is an informational text—it tells facts about a topic. Tell students that they are going to use features in the text to help them locate information.

1. Discuss the principle with students, using the introduction from *Web Wise* as an example. Point out the introduction. Suggested language: "At the beginning of the selection, the author wrote a short introduction. I read the introduction to find out what the selection is about."

> **MINILESSON PRINCIPLE**
>
> Readers use the features of informational text to locate information.

2. Next, point out the headings and read them aloud. Guide students to understand the purpose of headings. Suggested language: "The author used headings to organize the information. What section would you read to learn about how to photograph spider webs?" (*Web Shots*)

3. Finally, talk with students about how the author used photos in the selection. Ask: "Why did the author use photos in the selection?" (*to help readers better understand the information in each section*)

SUMMARIZE AND APPLY Restate the minilesson principle. Tell students to apply it to their independent reading. Suggested language: "When you read an informational text, look for special features that can help you locate different kinds of information."

GROUP SHARE Have students share an informational text from their reading. Have them name the features in the text and tell how those features helped them locate information.

▶ Poetry Place

INTERACTIVE READ-ALOUD/SHARED READING

Read aloud the poems to students. Stop periodically for brief discussion of them. Use the following suggested stopping points and prompts:

- After reading "The Spider," ask: "What is this poem about?" (*how a spider captures its prey*) Follow-up: "How does the poet make this information interesting?" (*The poet uses interesting adjectives to describe the spider and its web.*)
- After reading "Spider Ropes," ask: "What does this poem tell about?" (*It tells about a child who goes exploring in the woods.*) Follow-up: "Explain whether you think 'Spider Ropes' is a good name for this poem. Turn and talk with a partner about your thinking."

MINILESSON Genre: Poetry

TEACH Display the minilesson principle on chart paper, and read it aloud to students. Tell students they will learn to look for clues in poems that help them understand their meaning.

1. Guide students to understand the principle by focusing on "The Spider." Suggested language: "This poem doesn't say what the spider will do with the flies. What do you think the spider will do?" (*eat the flies*) Follow-up: "What clues does the poet give to make you think that?" (*The poet says the spider is sly and that she won't apologize for the flies getting stuck in the web.*)

> **MINILESSON PRINCIPLE**
>
> Readers look for clues to understand a poem's meaning.

2. Read "Spider Ropes" aloud. Then ask: "What does this poem tell about?" (*a walk in the woods*) Follow-up: "What clues does the poet give to help you understand its meaning?" (*The poet tells about things you can come across, such as leaves and spiders' webs, when exploring in the woods.*)

SUMMARIZE AND APPLY Restate the minilesson principle. Tell students to apply it to their independent reading. Suggested language: "When you read a poem, look for clues that help you understand its meaning."

GROUP SHARE Ask students to share a poem they read. Have them point out the clues in the poem that helped them understand its meaning.

Whole-Group Lessons

Amphibian Alert!
Student Magazine, Lesson 27

The Frog in the Milk Pail
Student Magazine, Lesson 27

**Poetry Place: "Toad by the Road"
and "The Poison-Dart Frogs"**
Student Magazine, Lesson 27

▶ Amphibian Alert!

INTERACTIVE READ-ALOUD/SHARED READING

Read aloud the selection to students. Stop periodically for very brief discussion of the text. Use the following suggested stopping points and prompts for quick group response, or give a specific prompt and have partners or threes turn and talk.

- After reading the first page, say: "What kind of information does the author give about amphibians?"
- After reading the first two pages, ask: "How do you think the author feels about amphibians?" Follow-up: "What does the author say to make you think that?"
- After reading the section Introduced Species and Fungus, say: "The author tells about some things that are a threat to the lives of amphibians. Turn and talk with a partner about which threat you think is the most serious and why."
- At the end of the selection, ask: "How does the author organize the information in the selection?" Follow-up: "How does this help you understand the information?"

MINILESSON Main Ideas and Details

TEACH Display the minilesson principle on chart paper, and read it aloud to students. Tell students that authors often state the main idea of a paragraph in the first or last sentence. Then explain that in some cases, authors do not state the main idea at all, but they expect readers to figure it out using details provided.

1. Discuss the principle with students, using examples from *Amphibian Alert!* Focus on the section Habitat Loss and Pollution. Tell students that the main idea of this section is not stated. Suggested language: "The author doesn't directly state the main idea of this section. You have to think about the details in the section and figure out the main idea. The main idea of this paragraph is *Loss of habitat and water pollution are two things that threaten the lives of amphibians.*" Have students name details the author gives that tell about this main idea.

> **MINILESSON PRINCIPLE**
>
> Readers notice that the main idea can be stated or unstated.

2. Next, focus on the section Plans to Help. Guide students to understand that the main idea of this section is stated in the first sentence: *Scientists and conservation groups from around the world are putting plans together to help save amphibians.* Have students name details in the section that tell about this main idea.

3. Work with students to state the main idea of other sections in the selection. Have them name details that tell about the main idea. Record their responses in an Idea-Support Map like the one shown here.

SUMMARIZE AND APPLY Restate the minilesson principle. Tell students to apply it to their independent reading. Suggested language: "When you read, think about whether the author states the main idea or expects you to figure it out."

GROUP SHARE Have students name a main idea from a book they read. Have them tell whether the main idea was stated or unstated.

▶ The Frog in the Milk Pail

INTERACTIVE READ-ALOUD/SHARED READING

Read aloud the fable to students. Stop periodically for brief discussion of the text. Use the following suggested stopping points and prompts:

- After reading the first page, say: "The frog is curious and determined. Give examples from the story that help you know this." (*The frog tastes new things he comes upon as he goes exploring. The frog does not let any difficulties that come his way discourage him.*)

- After reading the section The Science of Butter, ask: "Why do you think the author includes this information? Turn and talk about your thinking with a partner."

MINILESSON Genre: Fable

TEACH Display the minilesson principle on chart paper, and read it aloud to students. Tell students you are going to think about how a character's actions are used to explain a lesson or moral in a fable.

1. Remind students that fables are written to teach readers a lesson about life. Explain that thinking about what the characters do in a fable can help them understand the lesson. Suggested language: "In the fable *The Frog in the Milk Pail*, the frog kept hopping along and exploring no matter what happened to him. How did not giving up help the frog?" (*The frog was able to get out from being stuck in the milk pail.*)

> **MINILESSON PRINCIPLE**
>
> Readers notice how characters' actions are used to explain a lesson or moral.

2. Tell students that the author included other details to help explain the lesson. Guide them to identify details about the frog's actions that support the lesson that you should never give up.

SUMMARIZE AND APPLY Restate the minilesson principle. Tell students to apply it to their independent reading. Suggested language: "When you read a fable, think about how the characters' actions help to explain the lesson or moral of the story."

GROUP SHARE Have students share a lesson they learned in their reading. Tell them to explain how the characters' actions in the story helped explain the lesson.

▶ Poetry Place

INTERACTIVE READ-ALOUD/SHARED READING

Read aloud the poems to students. Stop periodically for brief discussion of the text. Use the following suggested stopping points and prompts:

- After reading "Toad by the Road," ask: "What does this poem tell you about what toads are like?" (*that toads like to be still and like to sing*) Follow-up: "How does the rhyme in the poem make it more interesting to read?"

- After reading "The Poison-Dart Frogs," ask: "What does the author mean by saying that the frogs are 'Masters of Fine Art'?" (*The author thinks the frogs' colors are as beautiful as fine art.*) Follow-up: "How does the author describe each frog?"

MINILESSON Genre: Poetry

TEACH Display the minilesson principle on chart paper, and read it aloud to students. Have students name the five senses as you write them on chart paper. Tell them they will learn to notice how poets use strong verbs and adjectives to appeal to the readers' senses.

1. Discuss the principle with students, using examples from "Toad by the Road." Suggested language: "Poets often use more exciting verbs to make their writing lively and interesting. Strong verbs such as *hustle* and *hurry* help you see and feel what is happening better than verbs like *go* or *pass by* would."

> **MINILESSON PRINCIPLE**
>
> Readers notice how poets use strong verbs and adjectives to appeal to the senses.

2. Point out other verbs and adjectives the author uses, such as *wiggle*, *flicker*, *glorious*, and *savor*. Have students tell how these words make the poem more interesting.

3. Then read "The Poison-Dart Frogs" aloud. Ask: "What do you see and feel when you read this poem?" Follow-up: "What words does the poet use to make you see and feel those things?"

SUMMARIZE AND APPLY Restate the minilesson principle. Tell students to apply it to their independent reading. Suggested language: "When you read a poem, notice the words the poet uses to appeal to your senses."

GROUP SHARE Ask students to share a poem they read. Have them point out strong verbs and adjectives that appeal to their senses.

Museums: Worlds of Wonder
Student Magazine, Lesson 28

Making the Most from Trash
Student Magazine, Lesson 28

**Poetry Place: "Dinosaur Bone" and
"Museum Farewell"**
Student Magazine, Lesson 28

▶ Museums: Worlds of Wonder

INTERACTIVE READ-ALOUD/SHARED READING

Read aloud the selection to students. Stop periodically for very brief discussion of the text. Use the following suggested stopping points and prompts for quick group response, or give a specific prompt and have partners or threes turn and talk.

- After reading the first page, ask: "What information does the map give you?"
- After reading about the National Air and Space Museum, ask: "How does the author organize the information in the selection?"
- After reading about the Field Museum, ask: "What information does the photograph give you?" Have students turn and talk with a partner about how the photograph helps them understand more about the text.
- At the end of the selection, ask: "Which museum would you like to visit? Turn and talk with a partner about your choice."

MINILESSON Fact and Opinion

TEACH Display the minilesson principle on chart paper, and read it aloud to students. Remind them that facts tell true information that can be proved. The author's thoughts, feelings, or beliefs are opinions. Explain that it is important to notice the difference between facts and the author's opinions as they read because they can agree or disagree with opinions.

> **MINILESSON PRINCIPLE**
>
> Readers notice the difference between facts and the author's thoughts, feelings, or beliefs.

1. Discuss the principle with students, using examples from *Museums: Worlds of Wonder*. Suggested language: "The author states that museums are wonderful places. This statement is not a fact. It tells how the author feels about museums. The author also states that there are different kinds of museums. That is a fact. It gives information that can be proved."

2. Reread the section City Museum of St. Louis, Missouri. Have students identify a fact or an opinion. Suggested language: "The author said that *there's an amazing playground* at the museum. Is this a fact or an opinion?" (*opinion*) Follow-up: "How do you know?" (*It tells how the author feels about the playground. The idea can't be proved.*)

3. Explain to students that some words and phrases are clues that the author is stating a thought, feeling, or belief. Write the following examples on chart paper: *should, best, I think, believe*.

4. Elicit from students additional examples of facts and opinions. Record students' responses in a T-Map. Have volunteers tell whether they agree with the author's opinions and why.

Facts	Thoughts, Feelings, Beliefs

SUMMARIZE AND APPLY Restate the minilesson principle. Then tell students to apply it to their independent reading. Suggested language: "When you read, look for facts and what the author thinks, feels, or believes. Think about how you know the difference between facts and opinions."

GROUP SHARE Have students tell about a book they read. Ask them to share a fact that the author states and one of the author's thoughts, feelings, or beliefs. Have them explain how they know it is a fact or the author's opinion.

▶ Making the Most from Trash

INTERACTIVE READ-ALOUD/SHARED READING

Read aloud the selection to students. Stop periodically for brief discussion of the text. Use the following suggested stopping points and prompts:

- After reading the introduction, ask: "How does the author feel about trash?" (*The author thinks the amount of trash people make is a problem.*)
- After reading the section Flakes to Fleece, ask: "How does the author organize information in this section?" (*in time order*)
- At the end of the selection, ask: "Why do you think the author wrote this selection? Turn and talk about your thinking with a partner."

MINILESSON Fact and Opinion

TEACH Display the minilesson principle on chart paper, and read it aloud to students. Tell students that authors often use facts to support their opinions. They give facts that explain how they formed that opinion.

1. Discuss the principle with students, using examples from *Making the Most from Trash*. Suggested language: "The author has the opinion that people can do something about the trash problem by reducing, reusing, and recycling. The author then gives facts about different ways this can be done."

> **MINILESSON PRINCIPLE**
>
> Readers notice how authors support opinions with facts.

2. Work with students to name the different facts that the author used to support the opinion that the trash problem can be solved. (*We can reduce the amount of things we use, reuse things instead of throwing them out, and recycle tires and different kinds of plastic.*)

3. Ask students to tell whether they agree with the author's opinion about trash. Suggested language: "Do you think the author included enough facts to support this opinion? Why or why not?"

SUMMARIZE AND APPLY Restate the minilesson principle. Tell students to apply it to their independent reading. Suggested language: "When you read, think about the author's opinion and the facts the author uses to support that opinion."

GROUP SHARE Ask students to name an opinion from a book they read. Have them tell facts the author provided to support that opinion.

▶ Poetry Place

INTERACTIVE READ-ALOUD/SHARED READING

Read aloud the poems to students. Stop periodically for brief discussion of the text. Use the following suggested stopping points and prompts:

- After reading "Dinosaur Bone," ask: "Where is the dinosaur bone?" (*in a museum*) Follow-up: "How does the illustration help you to know this?"
- After reading "Museum Farewell," ask: "What is this poem about?" (*closing time at a museum*) Follow-up: "How does the rhyme make the poem more interesting to read? Turn and talk with a partner about your thinking."

MINILESSON Genre: Poetry

TEACH Display the minilesson principle on chart paper, and read it aloud to students. Explain that poets choose words carefully to help readers feel a certain way.

1. Guide students to understand the principle by focusing on "Dinosaur Bone." Suggested language: "This poem told the thoughts someone had while looking at a dinosaur bone in a museum. Think about the words *secret* and *tell me* in the poem. What feeling do these words give you?" (*a feeling of mystery*)

> **MINILESSON PRINCIPLE**
>
> Readers think about the feeling the poem gives them.

2. Then focus on the questions in the poem. Ask: "The poet also used a lot of questions in the poem. How do the questions contribute to this feeling of mystery? Turn and talk about your thinking with a partner."

3. Next, reread "Museum Farewell." Ask: "How does this poem make you feel?" Guide students to recognize that words in the poem convey a feeling of peace and quiet.

SUMMARIZE AND APPLY Restate the minilesson principle. Tell students to apply it to their independent reading. Suggested language: "When you read a poem, think about the feeling the poem gives you."

GROUP SHARE Ask students to share a poem from their reading. Have them tell about the feeling the poem gives them.

Whole-Group Lessons

Save Timber Woods!
Student Magazine, Lesson 29

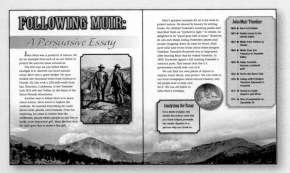

***Following Muir:** A Persuasive Essay*
Student Magazine, Lesson 29

**Poetry Place: "The Comb of Trees"
and "Enjoy the Earth"**
Student Magazine, Lesson 29

▶ Save Timber Woods!

INTERACTIVE READ-ALOUD/SHARED READING

Read aloud the play to students. Stop periodically for very brief discussion of the text. Use the following suggested stopping points and prompts for quick group response, or give a specific prompt and have partners or threes turn and talk.

- After previewing the play, ask: "How is a play different from a story?" (*A play is a story that can be performed for an audience.*) Follow-up: "Turn and talk with a partner about the features you find in a play."
- After the students find out that Timber Woods is going to be sold, ask: "Why don't the students want Timber Woods to be sold?" (*They will lose a place to camp and picnic; animals will lose their homes.*)
- After reading Scene II, ask: "What do the friends decide to do to persuade the town to buy Timber Woods?" (*They decide to go to the town council meeting and give reasons why the town should buy Timber Woods.*) Follow-up: "Do you think their idea will work? Turn and talk about your thinking with a partner."
- At the end of the play, ask: "Why do you think the author wrote this play?"

MINILESSON Understanding Characters

TEACH Display the minilesson principle on chart paper, and read it aloud to students. Explain to students that thinking about the things characters say and do can help them understand the reasons for their actions.

1. Discuss the principle with students, using Gina from *Save Timber Woods!* as an example. Suggested language: "Gina talks about the deer that are eating trees in her family's backyard. Saving backyards from the deer is the reason Gina wants to save Timber Woods."

2. Focus on another character in the play, such as Lucas. Suggested language: "Why does Lucas want to save Timber Woods?" (*Lucas wants to save animals' homes.*) Follow-up: "What does Lucas say and do to help you know that?"

3. Work with students to understand reasons for other characters' actions in the play. Record their ideas in a T-Map like the one shown here.

> **MINILESSON PRINCIPLE**
>
> Readers notice what characters say and do to understand the reasons for their actions.

Characters	Reasons

SUMMARIZE AND APPLY Restate the minilesson principle. Then tell students to apply it to their independent reading. Suggested language: "When you read, think about what the characters say and do. Think about how that helps you understand the reasons for their actions."

GROUP SHARE Ask students to tell about a character in a story they read. Have them give reasons for the character's actions.

▶ Following Muir

INTERACTIVE READ-ALOUD/SHARED READING

Read aloud the selection to students. Stop periodically for brief discussion of the text. Use the following suggested stopping points and prompts:

- After reading the first page, ask: "How did the walks John Muir took help him decide what to do with his life?"
- After reading about Yosemite, ask: "Why do you think the author tells you about Yosemite?"
- After reading the selection, ask: "Do you think protecting nature is important? Turn and talk about your thinking with a partner."

MINILESSON Persuasion

TEACH Display the minilesson principle on chart paper, and read it aloud to students. Explain to students that they are going to learn how authors use details in a selection to support their persuasive message.

1. Discuss the principle with students, using *Following Muir: A Persuasive Essay*. Tell students that the author wanted to persuade readers about the importance of preserving nature. Explain that the author shared this message by using John Muir as an example. Suggested language: "The author wanted to persuade readers that John Muir set a good example for how people can protect nature. The author gave details about the things John Muir did to learn about the importance of nature."

> **MINILESSON PRINCIPLE**
>
> Readers look for support in a text to understand the author's persuasive message.

2. Discuss the example of how John Muir explored the outdoors. Ask: "What did John Muir learn as he explored the wilderness?" (*He learned all about rocks, plants, and animals.*) Follow-up: "Why was this important?" (*It helped him understand the importance of the wilderness.*)

3. Work with students to identify other things John Muir did to learn about the importance of nature. Ask: "Why does the author believe that John Muir is a good example to follow for people who want to protect nature?" Follow-up: "What details did she include to make you think that way?"

SUMMARIZE AND APPLY Restate the minilesson principle. Tell students to apply it to their independent reading. Suggested language: "When you read, look for details that support the author's message."

GROUP SHARE Have students tell about the author's message in a book they read. Have them give examples of details the author used to support his or her message.

▶ Poetry Place

INTERACTIVE READ-ALOUD/SHARED READING

Read aloud the poems to students. Stop periodically for brief discussion of the text. Use the following suggested stopping points and prompts:

- After reading "The Comb of Trees," ask: "Why does the poet compare the trees to a comb?" (*to help the reader visualize what the trees look like*) Follow-up: "How does the poet feel about the trees? What does the poet say to let you know that?"
- After reading "Enjoy the Earth," ask: "What does the poet mean by the phrase enjoy the earth gently?" (*The poet means that it is okay to enjoy what the earth has to offer, but that we should also take care of it.*) Follow-up: "Do you agree with the poet's message? Turn and talk with a partner about your thinking."

MINILESSON Genre: Poetry

TEACH Display the minilesson principle on chart paper, and read it aloud to students. Tell students that they are going to learn about how poets use language to help the reader see, feel, and hear what they are describing.

1. Tell students that poets use language in special ways that help readers share an experience or feeling. Read aloud "The Comb of Trees." Then ask: "What language did the poet use to help you visualize the trees?"

> **MINILESSON PRINCIPLE**
>
> Readers notice language that helps them see, feel, and hear what the poet describes.

2. Talk about other words or phrases the poet used to help the reader see, hear, or feel what the trees are like.

3. Next, read aloud "Enjoy the Earth." Then ask: "How does this poem make you feel? Turn and talk about your thinking with a partner."

4. Guide students to recognize that if they replaced one or more words in the poem, its imagery and meaning would change. Work with students to replace the words *enjoy* and *gently* to create a different image in readers' minds.

SUMMARIZE AND APPLY Restate the minilesson principle. Tell students to apply it to their independent reading. Suggested language: "When you read a poem, notice the language that helps you see, feel, and hear what the poet describes."

GROUP SHARE Ask students to share a poem from their reading. Have them point out words that help them see, feel, and hear what the poet describes.

Whole-Group Lessons

Mystery at Reed's Pond
Student Magazine, Lesson 30

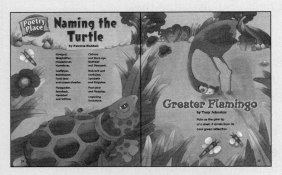

A Big Python Problem
Student Magazine, Lesson 30

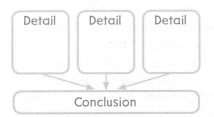

**Poetry Place: "Naming the Turtle"
and "Greater Flamingo"**
Student Magazine, Lesson 30

▶ Mystery at Reed's Pond

INTERACTIVE READ-ALOUD/SHARED READING

Read aloud the story to students. Stop periodically for very brief discussion of the text. Use the following suggested stopping points and prompts for quick group response, or give a specific prompt and have partners or threes turn and talk.

- After reading the first page, ask: "Where does the story take place?" (*at a pond*)
- After the children find the bag with lettuce, ask: "What problem do the children have?" (*They can't find Brownie and don't know what happened to the nest and eggs.*) Follow-up: "Turn and talk with a partner about what you think might have happened."
- After the children find information about turtles on the computer, ask: "What information do the photographs and captions give you?" (*They show you what real turtles look like and give more information about each turtle.*)
- At the end of the story, ask: "What did you learn from this story? Turn and talk with a partner about your thinking."

MINILESSON Conclusions

TEACH Display the minilesson principle on chart paper, and read it aloud to students. Explain that authors give details in a story to help readers figure out things they don't say. Remind students that when they figure out something that the author did not say, they have drawn a conclusion.

1. Discuss the principle with students, using an example from *Mystery at Reed's Pond*. Suggested language: "The children find a paper bag with lettuce in it. The author didn't say who left the bag and why there was lettuce in it, but you can figure it out. You know that people carry things in paper bags. You also know that pet turtles eat lettuce. This information helps you know that someone might have had a turtle in the bag."

> **MINILESSON PRINCIPLE**
>
> Readers notice that they can use details in a story to figure out things the author does not say.

2. Guide students to draw conclusions about how Adrian felt about turtles. Help students recognize details that helped them know that Adrian likes turtles. (*He was the first to spot Brownie. He was worried when they didn't find him and happy when they saw him again.*)
3. Work with students to draw other conclusions using details from the story. Have students tell which details helped them figure out things that the author didn't say.
4. Record students' responses on an Inference Map like the one shown here.

Detail	Detail	Detail

Conclusion

SUMMARIZE AND APPLY Restate the minilesson principle. Then tell students to apply it to their independent reading. Suggested language: "When you read, think about details in the story that can help you figure out things the author doesn't say."

GROUP SHARE Ask students to share a story from their reading. Have them tell about something they figured out that the author didn't say. Then have them name details in the story that helped them figure it out.

▶ A Big Python Problem

INTERACTIVE READ-ALOUD/SHARED READING

Read aloud the selection to students. Stop periodically for brief discussion of the text. Use the following suggested stopping points and prompts:

- After reading the section A Dangerous Predator, ask: "What information do the photo and caption give you about pythons?" (*They show what a python looks like and tell how much they can weigh.*)
- After reading the section Can the Problem Be Solved?, ask: "Do you think the author thinks that the python problem can be solved? Turn and talk with a partner about why you think so."
- At the end of the selection, ask: "Why do you think the author wrote this selection? Turn and talk about your thinking with a partner."

MINILESSON Genre: Informational Text

TEACH Display the minilesson principle on chart paper, and read it aloud to students. Tell students that authors often share problems and ways to solve them.

1. Explain to students that authors often write about a problem because they believe it is an important problem to solve. They want readers to agree that the problem is important.
2. Focus on the first section of *A Big Python Problem*. Guide students to understand what the problem is. Suggested language: "The author tells about pet pythons and how people are letting them loose in the Everglades. This is the problem the author is sharing."
3. Work with students to tell the information the author shares about how to solve this problem. Guide them to understand that park officials are using radio transmitters and dogs to help them find and catch the pythons.

> **MINILESSON PRINCIPLE**
>
> Readers notice when an author shares a problem and how to solve it.

SUMMARIZE AND APPLY Restate the minilesson principle. Tell students to apply it to their independent reading. Suggested language: "When you read a selection, think about the problems and solutions that the author shares."

GROUP SHARE Have students tell about a problem and solution the author shared in something they read.

▶ Poetry Place

INTERACTIVE READ-ALOUD/SHARED READING

Read aloud the poems to students. Stop periodically for brief discussion of the text. Use the following suggested stopping points and prompts:

- After reading "Naming the Turtle," ask: "What does this poem tell about?" (*names to give to different kinds of turtles*) Follow-up: "How does the poet make the poem interesting?"
- After reading "Greater Flamingo," ask: "What does the poet mean by the phrase *pale as the pink lip of a shell*?" (*The author is describing the color of the flamingo by comparing it to the part of a shell near its opening.*) Follow-up: "How does the poet describe the water?" (*cool and green*)

MINILESSON Genre: Poetry

TEACH Display the minilesson principle on chart paper, and read it aloud to students. Remind students that poems can make readers feel a certain way. Tell them they will think about how a poem makes them feel.

1. Explain to students that different words can make them feel different ways. Have them name words that make them feel excited, sad, or scared. Remind students that poets choose words carefully to create different feelings in readers.
2. Reread "Naming the Turtle." Suggested language: "This poem tells about different names for turtles. How does the poem make you feel?" Guide students to understand that the poem makes readers think about all the different characteristics of turtles.
3. Focus on "Greater Flamingo." Ask: "How does this poem make you feel? Turn and talk about your thinking with a partner." Guide students to understand that the image in the poem may give them a feeling of calm or serenity.

> **MINILESSON PRINCIPLE**
>
> Readers think about how a poem makes them feel.

SUMMARIZE AND APPLY Restate the minilesson principle. Tell students to apply it to their independent reading. Suggested language: "When you read a poem, think about how the poem makes you feel."

GROUP SHARE Ask students to share a poem they read. Have them tell how the poem made them feel.

Teacher's Notes

Teaching Genre

Table of Contents

Genre instruction and repeated exposure to a variety of genres are essential components of any high-quality literacy program. Access to the tools students need to understand information in different genres will make them better readers. When students understand the characteristics of a variety of genres, they will be able to:

- gain an appreciation for a wide range of texts
- develop a common vocabulary for talking about texts
- begin reading texts with a set of expectations related to genre
- make evidence-based predictions
- develop preferences as readers
- understand purposes for reading and writing
- recognize the choices an author makes when writing
- compare and contrast texts
- think deeply about what they read

The pages in this section provide a framework for discussing genre with your students in an age-appropriate way. You can use the lists on the following pages to organize for genre discussion.

- **Genre Characteristics:** teach and review the salient features
- **Discussion Starters:** begin and maintain productive discussions
- **Comparing Texts:** encourage students to make connections across texts
- **Literature:** select *Journeys* literature for discussion

Realistic Fiction

SUPPORT THINKING

DISCUSSION STARTERS During whole-group and small-group discussion, use questions to spark conversation about genre characteristics.

- Who is telling the story?
- Who are the main characters in the story?
- What is [character name] like? How can you tell?
- What problem does [character name] have?
- How does [character name]'s problem get solved by the end of the story?
- How does [character name] change from the beginning of the story to the end?
- What are the most important events in the story?
- How are the story's events like things that could happen in real life?
- How is the story's setting like a real place?
- What lesson do the characters learn? What lesson do you learn from reading the story?

COMPARING TEXTS After students have read and listened to several realistic fiction stories, prompt them to compare selections and to recognize common characteristics. Use questions such as these:

- What do the characters in [title] and [title] have in common?
- What could [character name] learn from [character name from another story]?
- How are the themes of [title] and [title] different?
- Which realistic fiction stories that you have read make you want to read more stories by the same author? What do you like most about them?

Because of Winn-Dixie,
Student Book, Lesson 1

Me and Uncle Romie,
Student Book, Lesson 8

Genre Characteristics

Realistic fiction is a made-up story that could really happen in today's world.

Through repeated exposure to realistic fiction, students should learn to notice common genre characteristics. Use friendly language to help them understand the following concepts:

- **Author's Purpose:** to entertain
- **Characters:** characters are like real people and may remind students of people they know; readers learn about characters through the author's descriptions and by thinking about what the characters think, say, and do
- **Setting:** where and when the story takes place; could be based on a real place
- **Plot:** events that could really happen; includes a problem or conflict that characters face, a series of events that occur as characters try to solve the problem, and a resolution
- **Dialogue:** the words that characters say reveal what they are like and what other characters are like
- **Point of View:** the narrator or speaker of the story; in first-person point of view, the narrator is part of the story; in third-person point of view, the narrator is an outside observer who tells the story
- **Theme:** the story's message, or what the author is trying to say to readers; theme can often be determined through what characters in the story learn

JOURNEYS Literature

STUDENT BOOK
Because of Winn-Dixie
Dear Mr. Winston
Me and Uncle Romie

STUDENT MAGAZINE
The Girl Who Loved Spiders

TEACHER'S EDITION READ-ALOUD
The Big Storm
Bookmobile Rescue
Jazzy Jasmine

New Friends in the Classroom
Safe from Harm
Sideline Support

LEVELED READERS
A Gift for Grandpa **S**
Gramp's Favorite Gift **S**
The Mystery on Maple Street **Q**
Painting the Ocean **M**
Parker's Problem **P**
Recipe for Learning **M**
Safe from Harm

Sisters Play Soccer **R**
Soccer Sisters **R**
Stuck at Camp **S**
Think Before You Speak **S**
Trading Talents **S**
What Happened on Maple Street? **Q**

Historical Fiction

Genre Characteristics

Historical fiction is a made-up story that could have happened in a real time and place in the past.

Through repeated exposure to historical fiction, students should learn to notice common genre characteristics. Use friendly language to help them understand the following concepts:

- **Author's Purpose:** to entertain
- **Characters:** characters are realistic, but they may look or talk like people from the past; readers learn about characters through the author's descriptions and by thinking about what the characters think, say, and do
- **Setting:** where and when the story takes place; setting is important to the story and shows something about a period or place in history
- **Plot:** what happens in the story—could contain an author's imagined details about real events; includes a problem that characters face, a series of events that occur as characters try to solve the problem, and a resolution
- **Dialogue:** the words that characters say may show how people of a certain time talked to one another—for example, formal, informal, or the use of slang
- **Point of View:** the narrator or speaker of the story; in first-person point of view, the narrator is part of the story; in third-person point of view, the narrator is an outside observer who tells the story
- **Theme:** the story's message, or what the author is trying to say to readers; theme may center around an important issue during the time in which the story takes place

JOURNEYS Literature

SUPPORT THINKING

DISCUSSION STARTERS During whole-group and small-group discussion, use questions to spark conversation about genre characteristics.

- Where and when does this story take place?
- What is important about the setting of this story?
- What is [character name] like?
- Which of [character name]'s traits help you know that he/she lived in the past?
- What happens in this story?
- What is the main problem in this story?
- How is the setting important to what happens?
- What is the author trying to tell you with this story?
- What kinds of issues were important to the people in this story?

COMPARING TEXTS After students have read and listened to several historical fiction stories, prompt them to compare selections and to recognize common characteristics. Use questions such as these:

- How are the settings in [title] and [title] different? In which time and place would you rather live?
- How are the characters in [title] and [title] different in the ways they talk, think, and act? How are they the same?
- Which historical fiction story that you've read makes you want to learn more about where and when the characters lived?

The Earth Dragon Awakes, Student Book, Lesson 12

Riding Freedom, Student Book, Lesson 16

Traditional Tale

SUPPORT THINKING

DISCUSSION STARTERS During whole-group and small-group discussion, use questions to spark conversation about genre characteristics.

- Who are the main characters in this story? Who are the minor characters?
- Which characters have qualities that represent good? How can you tell?
- How do the characters in the story change from the beginning to the end?
- What lesson does the author want you to learn by reading this story? How could you apply the lesson to your life?
- What does this story help you learn about the people or group that first told the story long ago?

COMPARING TEXTS After students have read and listened to several traditional tales, prompt them to compare selections and to recognize common characteristics. Use questions such as these:

- Which characters in [title] and [title] have something in common?
- Why do you think the lessons in stories like [title] and [title] have been shared for many years?
- Think about the ending of [title]. How is this ending similar to the ending of [title]? How is it different?

 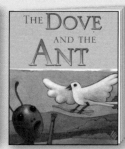

Stormalong,
Student Book,
Lesson 5

The Dove and the Ant,
Student Book,
Lesson 14

Genre Characteristics

Traditional tales are short, made-up stories that have been retold over and over for many years.

Through repeated exposure to traditional tales, students should learn to notice common genre characteristics. Use friendly language to help them understand the following concepts:

- **Author's Purpose:** to entertain; to teach a lesson
- **Characters:** characters could be like real people or they could have exaggerated traits or amazing abilities; talking animals and objects are common in traditional tales; characters are usually good or evil
- **Setting:** usually set long ago in a specific place (often where the story originated)
- **Plot:** what happens in the story; could have magical elements or events that are unrealistic; includes a problem that characters face, a series of events that occur as characters try to solve the problem, and a resolution
- **Theme:** the lesson that the author wants to teach readers; often tells about the beliefs of a group of people; may explain how something came to be
- **Variants:** different versions of the same story may be told in different cultures and places
- **Subgenres:** can be classified into subgenres such as fable, folktale, fairy tale, tall tale, trickster tale, myth—each having its own unique features

JOURNEYS Literature

STUDENT BOOK
The Dove and the Ant
Hercules' Quest
Hoderi the Fisherman
Stormalong
Zomo's Friends

STUDENT MAGAZINE
The Frog and the Milk Pail

TEACHER'S EDITION READ-ALOUD
Mighty Joe Magarac
Theseus and the Minotaur

LEVELED READERS
The Adventures of Perseus **T**
The Amazing Balina **P**
Balina **Q**

King Midas and the Gold
Touch **N**
Mississippi Marvis Barnes
The Story of Icarus **V**
The Story of Perseus **R**
Whisper **R**

Fantasy

Genre Characteristics

A fantasy is a made-up story that could not happen in real life.

Through repeated exposure to fantasy, students should learn to notice common genre characteristics. Use friendly language to help them understand the following concepts:

- **Author's Purpose:** to entertain
- **Characters:** characters often have human qualities but can do amazing or magical things; animals and objects may have human characteristics and may talk; the main character usually has a goal to accomplish
- **Setting:** often set in a different time, in a magical or imaginary world, or both
- **Plot:** what happens in the story could not happen in the real world, but the plot is believable in the world that the author has created; includes a problem, a series of events that occur as characters try to solve the problem, and a resolution; the problem may be a fight against evil characters who get in the way of a goal
- **Theme:** the lesson that the author wants to teach readers

JOURNEYS Literature

STUDENT BOOK

The World According to Humphrey

TEACHER'S EDITION READ-ALOUD

Tim Wishes Twice

LEVELED READERS

The Beltons' Imagination **Q**

A Dragon's View **S**

The Magic of Teamwork **M**

The Princess and the Manatee **O**

The Seal Who Wanted to Live **O**

Summer with Uncle Vince **Q**

SUPPORT THINKING

DISCUSSION STARTERS During whole-group and small-group discussion, use questions to spark conversation about genre characteristics.

- What is special about the setting of this story?
- Which events in this story could not really happen? How do you know?
- Which characters in this story could not be a part of a realistic fiction story? Explain.
- What is [character name] trying to do in this story? Who or what is getting in the way?
- Why is the setting of the story important to what happens?
- How is [character name]'s problem resolved by the end of the story?

COMPARING TEXTS After students have read and listened to several fantasy stories, prompt them to compare selections and to recognize common characteristics. Use questions such as these:

- Would you rather be a character in the story [title] or [title]? Explain.
- How are [fantasy title] and [realistic fiction title] alike? How are they different?
- Are the characters in [title] or [title] closer to being like people in the real world? Explain your thinking.

The World According to Humphrey, Student Book, Lesson 21

Science Fiction

SUPPORT THINKING

DISCUSSION STARTERS During whole-group and small-group discussion, use questions to spark conversation about genre characteristics.

- Where does the story take place?
- When does the story take place?
- How is the world the author has created different from today's world?
- What words and images does the author use to help you imagine the setting?
- What problem does the setting create for the characters?
- What part does science or technology have in helping the characters solve the problem?
- What do you learn about the characters by what they say and do?
- What is the author trying to tell you with this story?
- Which events in this story could happen in today's world? Which events could not happen in today's world?

COMPARING TEXTS After students have read and listened to several science fiction stories, prompt them to compare selections and to recognize common characteristics. Use questions such as these:

- How are the worlds created by the authors in [title] and [title] different?
- How are the problems in [title] and [title] different?
- How are the messages in [title] and [title] different? Why do you think the authors used a time in the future to teach these lessons?

The Fun They Had,
Student Book,
Lesson 25

Genre Characteristics

Science fiction is a made-up story that is based on scientific ideas or technology.

Through repeated exposure to science fiction, students should learn to notice common genre characteristics. Use friendly language to help them understand the following concepts:

- **Author's Purpose:** to entertain
- **Characters:** characters may be people, animals, or objects that have human problems but can do or experience things that are not realistic in today's world
- **Setting:** description of setting shows the author's ideas about what it would be like to live in the future or on another planet
- **Plot:** events are usually driven by what happens to characters as a result of the author's imagined world; includes a problem that characters face, a series of events that occur as characters try to solve the problem, and a resolution
- **Theme:** what the author is trying to say to readers

JOURNEYS Literature

STUDENT BOOK
The Fun They Had

LEVELED READERS
Dex Is a Hero **S**

A Hero Weighs In **S**
The Linney Twins Get Cooking **M**
Math Today and Tomorrow **T**

Play

Genre Characteristics

A play is a story that is meant to be performed for an audience.

Through repeated exposure to plays, students should learn to notice common genre characteristics. Use friendly language to help them understand the following concepts:

- **Author's Purpose:** to entertain
- **Characters:** portrayed by the actors in the play; may include a narrator who provides background information and fills in details about the characters, setting, or events
- **Stage Directions:** notes from the writer of the play that tell actors how to move or with what emotion certain lines should be read; give information about how to set up the stage for the play, including props to use and what the actors might wear; stage directions usually appear in parentheses and in italic type
- **Dialogue:** the conversations between characters that are read aloud by actors; a play is made up almost entirely of dialogue
- **Plot:** the action of the story, or what happens, as revealed through dialogue and stage directions; may be based on real events and people or made up by the writer
- **Setting:** can be any place, real or imaginary; usually described in stage directions
- **Acts:** large sections of a play between breaks; can be further divided into scenes
- **Scene:** a part of the play in which the setting does not change

JOURNEYS Literature

STUDENT BOOK
Hoderi the Fisherman
Invasion from Mars
The Power of W.O.W.!
Sidewalk Artists

STUDENT MAGAZINE
Save Timber Woods!

LEVELED READERS
A.L.L. to the Rescue **S**
The Amazing Game **S**
Be Afraid **U**
A Friendly Field Trip **P**
Friends on a Field Trip **O**
Nina Wows KWOW **N**
Time Tag **T**
The Zeebo Encounter **N**

SUPPORT THINKING

DISCUSSION STARTERS During whole-group and small-group discussion, use questions to spark conversation about genre characteristics.

- What information does the writer give at the beginning of the play?
- What is the narrator's role in this play?
- Who are the most important characters? Why do you think so?
- What information do you learn about the characters from the stage directions?
- How do the stage directions help you understand the setting?
- What is the most exciting part of the play? Explain.
- If you were to act in this play, which character would you want to play? How would you use the stage directions to help you with your role?

COMPARING TEXTS After students have read and listened to several plays, prompt them to compare selections and to recognize common characteristics. Use questions such as these:

- How do the writers of [title] and [title] help you understand what is happening in the play?
- How are the settings of [title] and [title] different?
- In which play—[title] or [title]—do you think the dialogue is more realistic? Explain.
- What would it be like to have [character] and [character from another play] in the same play?

Hoderi the Fisherman, Student Book, Lesson 5

The Power of W.O.W.! Student Book, Lesson 18

Informational Text

Genre Characteristics

SUPPORT THINKING

DISCUSSION STARTERS During whole-group and small-group discussion, use questions to spark conversation about genre characteristics.

- What different kinds of graphic features does the author use to help you understand the topic?
- How does the author use size and colors of type to show what is important?
- What is the selection mostly about?
- How is the selection organized? How can you tell?
- How does the author make the information in this selection interesting?
- Which of the author's ideas are opinions? How does the author support his/her opinions?
- How does the author feel about the topic? How do you know?
- What kind of research do you think the author did to write this selection?

COMPARING TEXTS After students have read and listened to several informational texts, prompt them to compare selections and to recognize common characteristics. Use questions such as these:

- How do the authors of [title] and [title] use text and graphic features in different ways?
- Which selection—[title] or [title]—makes you want to find out more about the topic? Explain.
- How do the authors of [title] and [title] organize the text in different ways? How does the organization help you understand the ideas?
- How can you tell that [author] and [author] think their topics are important?

Coming Distractions: Questioning Movies, Student Book, Lesson 7

The Life and Times of the Ant, Student Book, Lesson 14

Informational text gives facts about real people, places, things, or events.

Through repeated exposure to informational texts, students should learn to notice common genre characteristics. Use friendly language to help them understand the following concepts:

- **Author's Purpose:** to inform; to persuade
- **Illustrations/Photographs:** show the information being described accurately and help readers understand the ideas in the text
- **Graphic Features:** images that help the reader understand information in the text or show additional information; may include the following:
  - **Diagrams:** pictures with labels that identify or explain specific parts
  - **Maps:** pictures that are used to show the physical layout of an area
  - **Charts/Graphs:** information arranged in a way that helps readers compare pieces of information or data
  - **Timeline:** shows the important events related to a topic over a period of time
- **Text Features:** special text that helps the reader understand what is important; may include the following:
  - **Headings:** type—usually larger, darker, or both—at the beginning of a new section; used to organize information into sections that make sense for the topic
  - **Captions:** words or sentences that explain an image
  - **Special Type:** the author may emphasize words and ideas by using a different color or size or by using bold or italic print
- **Main Idea:** what the text is mostly about
- **Details:** smaller ideas that support the main idea and tell more about the topic
- **Text Structure:** the text's overall structure
  - **Narrative:** can be organized and have the feeling of a story with a clear beginning, middle, and end
  - **Sequence:** events or steps in a process are told in order
  - **Compare/Contrast:** the author's main goal is to tell how things are alike and different
  - **Cause/Effect:** the author explains a topic by telling about something that happened and why it happened
  - **Problem/Solution:** the author explains a problem and offers a solution to the problem; details support the author's solution
  - **Description:** the author explains what something is and what it is like
- **Facts:** pieces of information that are true and can be proved
- **Opinions:** statements of how the author feels about a subject; may be used to try to persuade readers

Journeys Literature

STUDENT BOOK

Antarctic Journal: Four Months at the Bottom of the World

Because of BookEnds

Cold, Cold Science

Coming Distractions: Questioning Movies

Ecology for Kids

The Edible Schoolyard

The Ever-Living Tree

Field Guide to Snakes of the Southwest

The History of Radio

How Do They Do That?

Hurricanes: Earth's Mightiest Storms

From Idea to Book

The Kid's Guide to Money

Knowing Noses: Search-and-Rescue Dogs

The Life and Times of the Ant

Make the Switch

My Librarian Is a Camel

Owen and Mzee

Recovering from Katrina

The Right Dog for the Job

The Role of the Constitution

Sea Sanctuary

Spindletop

Toys! Amazing Stories Behind Some Great Inventions

Twisters

STUDENT MAGAZINE

Amphibian Alert!

A Big Python Problem

John Muir: A Persuasive Essay

Making the Most from Trash

Museums: Worlds of Wonder

Web Wise

TEACHER'S EDITION READ-ALOUD

Bridging the Gap

Deserts on the Move?

Forests Are Forever

Frisky Whiskers

Fun and Games on the Range

The Future of Flight

Is Sasquatch Out There?

On My Way to Meet the Khan: Excerpts from Marco Polo's Adventures

Race Against Death

Safe from Harm

Steven Spielberg: A Filmmaker's Journey

The Tunguska Event

Wicked Wind

LEVELED READERS

Amazing Birds of Antarctica O

Animal Doctors N

Animals Helping People N

Animals of the Redwood Forest S

Ants of All Kinds O

Arthropods Everywhere! S

Arthropods Rule! S

Artists in Training P

Behind the Scenes P

The Big, Dangerous Wave R

Champions on Ice S

Check Out the Library N

Community Teamwork O

Critics in Hollywood V

Dangerous Waves P

Flying into History P

Forever Green P

Gentle Redwood Giants S

The Golden Age of Radio R

The Golden Age of Sail P

Habitat for Humanity R

Helen Keller's Lifelong Friend S

Helen Keller's Special Friend S

Helping Wild Animals T

Helping with Houses R

Heroes of the Antarctic V

An Icy Adventure R

Keeping Safe in an Earthquake O

Kids Can Save the Planet O

Lewis and Clark's Packing List Q

Life Among the Redwoods S

The Lives of Social Insects P

Long Ago in Greece S

Love Those Bugs! T

The Magic of Movies T

Making Movies T

Mill Girls S

Nature Destroys, Nature Renews T

Now Showing in Your Living Room P

Planes, Trains, and Snowmobiles P

Plants of the Redwood Forest O

Really, Really Cold! O

Remarkable Robots P

Reptiles As Pets O

Romare Bearden R

A Rural Veterinarian R

Separate Worlds Q

Squash in the Schoolyard N

Stagecoach Travel Q

Taking Care of Animals R

Tornadoes Q

Tough Times S

The Truth About Rodents R

Tsunami S

A Visit to Antarctica R

Volcanoes P

Volunteer! T

Biography

SUPPORT THINKING

DISCUSSION STARTERS During whole-group and small-group discussion, use questions to spark conversation about genre characteristics.

- Who is this biography about?
- What is the subject like?
- What are [subject name]'s strengths? What are [subject name]'s weaknesses?
- Where did [subject name] live?
- How did other people influence [subject name] and affect his/her life?
- What did other people think about [subject name]?
- What can you tell about [subject name] by what he/she says?
- Why is it important to know about [subject name]'s life?
- What does the author think about [subject]?

COMPARING TEXTS After students have read and listened to several biographies, prompt them to compare selections and to recognize common characteristics. Use questions such as these:

- What things about [subject name] and [subject name] are alike? What things are different?
- If you were to meet [subject name], what questions would you ask him/her? How would the questions be different from questions you might ask [different subject name]?
- Which author do you think had more difficult research to do about the subject? Why do you think so?

José! Born to Dance, Student Book, Lesson 10

Sacagawea, Student Book, Lesson 20

Genre Characteristics

A biography is the true story of a real person's life.

Through repeated exposure to biographies, students should learn to notice common genre characteristics. Use friendly language to help them understand the following concepts:

- **Author's Purpose:** to inform; to show why this person's life is important
- **Characters:** the real person the biography is about is the subject; a biography tells what the subject accomplished and why he or she is important; other characters in the biography are real people who influenced the life of the subject in some way
- **Setting:** thinking about the time and place in which the subject lived will help readers understand more about the person
- **Narrative Structure:** events are told in order as a story; events may span the person's entire life or may represent a specific time in the person's life
- **Facts and Opinions:** most parts of a biography are facts that are accurate and can be proved; the author's opinions may be included
- **Point of View:** usually third-person point of view—the narrator is an outside observer who tells the story

JOURNEYS Literature

STUDENT BOOK

Harvesting Hope: The Story of Cesar Chavez

I Could Do That! Esther Morris Gets Women the Vote

José! Born to Dance

My Brother Martin: A Sister Remembers Growing Up with the Rev. Dr. Martin Luther King Jr.

Sacagawea

TEACHER'S EDITION READ-ALOUD

The Father of India

Getting the Story

Jane's Big Ideas

Let Me Be Brave

Mexican Dove

The Troublemaker Who Healed a Nation

LEVELED READERS

A Champion of Change **S**

Chief Washakie **U**

The First Woman Doctor **P**

Isadora Duncan **O**

Jackson Pollock in Action **S**

John Wesley Powell **O**

Laura Ingalls Wilder **R**

A Leader for All **U**

The Life of Jackson Pollock **S**

Luciano Pavarotti **W**

The People's President **R**

A President for the People **R**

Sharing a Dream **O**

Shirley Chisholm **S**

Songs for the People **P**

The Story of Dorothea Lange **U**

Thurgood Marshall **S**

A Voice for Equality **S**

Writer from the Prairie **R**

The Writer Who Changed America **U**

Poetry

Genre Characteristics

Poetry is a piece of writing in which words and their sounds are used to show images and express feelings and ideas.

Through repeated exposure to poetry, students should learn to notice common genre characteristics. Use friendly language to help them understand the following concepts:

- **Author's Purpose:** to entertain or express
- **Form:** includes free verse, narrative, lyric, haiku
- **Stanzas:** the sections of a poem; a stanza may focus on one central idea or thought; lines in a stanza are arranged in a way that looks and sounds pleasing
- **Rhyme:** words that have the same ending sound may be used at the ends of lines to add interest to the poem and to make it fun to read
- **Rhythm:** the beat of how the words are read; may be fast or slow
- **Sensory Words:** words that describe how things look, feel, taste, smell, and sound
- **Figurative Language:** similes, metaphors, and personification; the comparison of things that might not ordinarily seem similar
- **Onomatopoeia:** the use of words that imitate the sounds they describe
- **Alliteration:** the repetition of the same initial consonant sounds
- **Punctuation:** tells a reader when to pause; can make a poem sound short and choppy or long and flowing; may not be present at all

JOURNEYS Literature

STUDENT BOOK	STUDENT MAGAZINE	
Dance to the Beat	The Comb of Trees	The Poison-Dart Frogs
Langston Hughes: A Poet and a Dreamer	Dinosaur Bone	The Spider
Native American Nature Poetry	Enjoy the Earth	Spider Ropes
Towering Trees	Greater Flamingo	Toad by the Road
Wonderful Weather	Museum Farewell	
	Naming the Turtle	

SUPPORT THINKING

DISCUSSION STARTERS During whole-group and small-group discussion, use questions to spark conversation about genre characteristics.

- What does this poem describe?
- Which words in the poem help you picture or experience what the poet describes?
- Which words in the poem describe sounds? Which words describe smells? Which words describe tastes?
- How does the poem make you feel?
- How would you describe the rhythm of the poem? What feeling does the rhythm give you when you read the poem?
- Which of the poem's images do you like best? Why?
- How does the title of the poem fit what the poem says?
- What kinds of decisions did the writer of this poem make as he/she wrote it?

COMPARING TEXTS After students have read and listened to several poems, prompt them to compare poems and to recognize common characteristics. Use questions such as these:

- How are the images in [title] and [title] different?
- How do the writers of [title] and [title] create poems with different feelings?
- How are the shapes or forms of [title] and [title] different?

Dance to the Beat,
Student Book,
Lesson 10

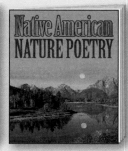

Native American Nature Poetry,
Student Book,
Lesson 20

Teacher's Notes

Writing Handbook Minilessons

Writing Handbook Minilessons

Writing Handbook Minilessons

How to Use This Book

The *Writing Handbook* was designed to complement the writing instruction in your reading program as well as meet all academic standards for writing. It consists of two components: a handbook for students that they can refer to as a resource as well as practice writing in throughout the year, and a Teacher's Guide that supports instruction by providing minilessons for every handbook topic.

Components

Two easy-to-use components make up the *Writing Handbook* program:

- For Grades 2–6, a 160-page partially consumable student handbook with 30 writing topics that correlate to your reading program's lessons.

  The first section of each grade-level handbook includes writing models along with interactive practice to scaffold or reinforce students' understanding of opinion, informational/explanatory, and narrative writing. As students practice writing, they build additional examples of forms to refer to throughout the year as well as develop a deeper understanding of each form's structure.

  The second section of the handbook is a resource tool that students can refer to whenever they write. Topics range from writing strategies to how to use technology to do research.

- For Grade 1, a 96-page partially consumable student handbook also includes 30 correlated handbook topics followed by a resource section on writing strategies, such as the writing process and writing traits.

- For Grades K–6, a Teacher's Guide with 60 minilessons for section 1 (two minilessons for each section 1 student handbook topic) plus one minilesson, as needed, for each remaining page of the resource handbook. The Kindergarten Teacher's Guide includes an abundance of copying masters.

Minilessons

Minilessons are short, focused lessons on specific topics. For each minilesson, you will demonstrate an aspect of writing before students try their own hand. In this Teacher's Guide, minilessons are provided for each topic in the handbook. In the first section are two minilessons for each topic. Each of these minilessons consists of the following parts:

- Topic title
- Tab with section name
- Minilesson number and title
- Objective and guiding question
- Easy-to-follow instruction in an *I Do*, *We Do*, and *You Do* format
- Modeled, collaborative, and independent writing
- Conference and evaluation information

6 • Writing Handbook

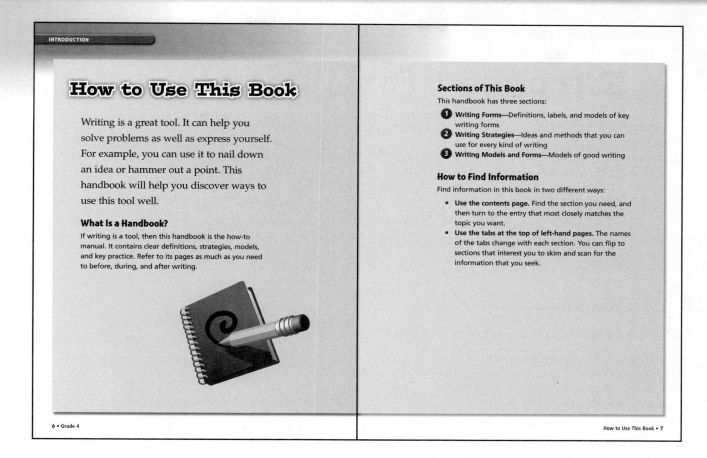

How to Use This Book

Writing is a great tool. It can help you solve problems as well as express yourself. For example, you can use it to nail down an idea or hammer out a point. This handbook will help you discover ways to use this tool well.

What Is a Handbook?

If writing is a tool, then this handbook is the how-to manual. It contains clear definitions, strategies, models, and key practice. Refer to its pages as much as you need to before, during, and after writing.

Sections of This Book

This handbook has three sections:

1. **Writing Forms**—Definitions, labels, and models of key writing forms
2. **Writing Strategies**—Ideas and methods that you can use for every kind of writing
3. **Writing Models and Forms**—Models of good writing

How to Find Information

Find information in this book in two different ways:

- **Use the contents page.** Find the section you need, and then turn to the entry that most closely matches the topic you want.
- **Use the tabs at the top of left-hand pages.** The names of the tabs change with each section. You can flip to sections that interest you to skim and scan for the information that you seek.

6 • Grade 4

How to Use This Book • 7

- Technology references
- Reduced facsimiles of student handbook pages
- Tips for corrective feedback
- A feature that further explores the lesson's writing trait

Each writing minilesson has been correlated to your reading program's writing lessons so that all minilessons and corresponding writing handbook pages within this section are used at least once during the school year. Additional minilessons are provided throughout the Teacher's Guide and correlate to each remaining page in the handbook. Use these minilessons, as needed, to clarify concepts for students and provide additional support.

Student-Page Walk-Through

Have students turn to and read pages 6 and 7 in their books. Explain to them that their handbook is a tool that they can use whenever they write. It can help them find information quickly about any writing question they have, and they can use it to help them during writing. Guide students to find

each of these parts in their handbooks:

- Table of contents
- Introductory pages, including overviews of the writing process and the writing traits
- Writing form pages, each with a section tab, title, definition, and helpful bulleted points, followed by a clear example of the writing model as well as a write-in activity page
- Additional reference pages on topics ranging from writing strategies to revising to using technology, as well as more examples of writing models they may need or want to refer to during the year for projects and other assignments
- An index. Remind students that the table of contents is in order of presentation while the index is ordered alphabetically.

Grade 4 • **7**

Purposes for Writing

The *Writing Handbook* spirals writing instruction up the grade levels to coincide with writing standards that spiral. Over the years, as students explore and practice writing, their sophistication in writing for different purposes and audiences will grow. Students across all grades will learn about and practice opinion/argument, informative/explanatory, and narrative writing.

Purpose and Form

Writers choose specific writing forms to communicate their intended meaning. To choose effectively, they target their purpose and audience before and while they write. Over the years, students will practice writing in different genres to build up a repertoire of writing forms from which to choose. This increasing practice as well as access to information about writing will help students feel more comfortable about writing and, hopefully, enjoy doing it.

In this handbook, the writing forms and models presented coincide primarily with the purposes expressed through the academic standards. These are to inform, to explain, to narrate, and to persuade. There are other purposes for writing as well, but these four are emphasized to best prepare students for college and career readiness.

TO INFORM The purpose for writing to inform is to share facts and other information. Informational texts such as reports make statements that are supported by facts and truthful evidence.

TO EXPLAIN The purpose for writing to explain is to tell *what, how,* and *why* about a topic. An example is to explain in writing how to do or make something.

TO NARRATE The purpose of writing to narrate is to tell a story. The story can be made up or truthful. Most forms of narrative writing

have a beginning, middle, and end. Examples are fictional stories and personal narratives.

TO PERSUADE Writing that has a purpose to persuade states an opinion or goal and supports it with reasons and supporting details in order to get the audience to agree, take action, or both. At Grade 6, the emphasis shifts to argument.

Over the years, as their writing grows more sophisticated, students may find that their purpose for writing is a hybrid of two or more purposes. An example would be literary nonfiction that includes elements of storytelling although it may be written primarily to inform and explain. Another example would be historical fiction that tells a story but relates events accurately in order to inform the reader as well.

Success in School and Life

Students and adults are often judged by how well they can communicate. Students are encouraged to learn to write effectively to be successful in their studies. In particular, by the upper grades, they need to master the basic essay format that includes

- An introductory paragraph that identifies the topic or statement of purpose.

- Supporting paragraphs that provide related details and examples.

8 • Writing Handbook

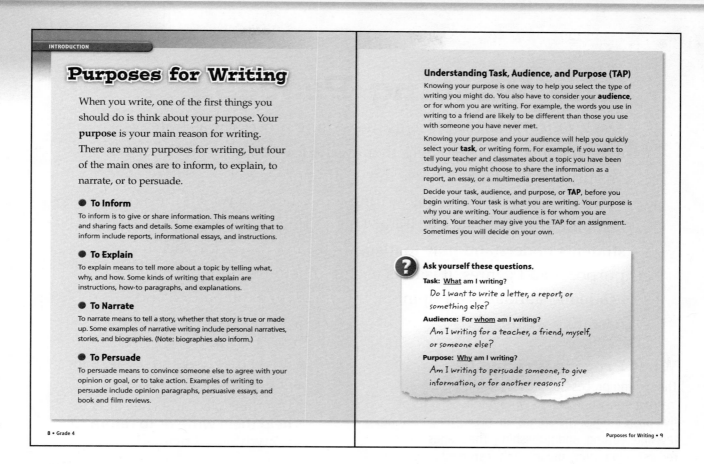

Purposes for Writing

When you write, one of the first things you should do is think about your purpose. Your **purpose** is your main reason for writing. There are many purposes for writing, but four of the main ones are to inform, to explain, to narrate, or to persuade.

● **To Inform**
To inform is to give or share information. This means writing and sharing facts and details. Some examples of writing that to inform include reports, informational essays, and instructions.

● **To Explain**
To explain means to tell more about a topic by telling what, why, and how. Some kinds of writing that explain are instructions, how-to paragraphs, and explanations.

● **To Narrate**
To narrate means to tell a story, whether that story is true or made up. Some examples of narrative writing include personal narratives, stories, and biographies. (Note: biographies also inform.)

● **To Persuade**
To persuade means to convince someone else to agree with your opinion or goal, or to take action. Examples of writing to persuade include opinion paragraphs, persuasive essays, and book and film reviews.

8 • Grade 4

Understanding Task, Audience, and Purpose (TAP)

Knowing your purpose is one way to help you select the type of writing you might do. You also have to consider your **audience**, or for whom you are writing. For example, the words you use in writing to a friend are likely to be different than those you use with someone you have never met.

Knowing your purpose and your audience will help you quickly select your **task**, or writing form. For example, if you want to tell your teacher and classmates about a topic you have been studying, you might choose to share the information as a report, an essay, or a multimedia presentation.

Decide your task, audience, and purpose, or **TAP**, before you begin writing. Your task is what you are writing. Your purpose is why you are writing. Your audience is for whom you are writing. Your teacher may give you the TAP for an assignment. Sometimes you will decide on your own.

Ask yourself these questions.
Task: <u>What</u> am I writing?
    Do I want to write a letter, a report, or something else?
Audience: For <u>whom</u> am I writing?
    Am I writing for a teacher, a friend, myself, or someone else?
Purpose: <u>Why</u> am I writing?
    Am I writing to persuade someone, to give information, or for another reasons?

Purposes for Writing • 9

● A closing paragraph that sums up and concludes.

Students will use this essay form to produce reports, literary analyses, theses, and critiques throughout their academic career. They will also be tested on their ability to write effective essays in standardized tests. In later life, as adults, they will need to be able to communicate clearly in writing to coworkers, bosses, and clients. This requires extensive and ongoing exposure to exemplary writing models and explicit instruction in a variety of areas, as well as opportunities to practice different forms of writing. In all cases, their purpose for writing must be clear. Evidence suggests that the more time student writers spend on writing, developing their writing skills, and deepening their writing experience, the better writers they become.

The Reading-Writing Connection

The ability to communicate their thinking about texts for a variety of purposes and audiences will serve students well in preparation for college and career readiness. When students write about what they read, reflecting on content, craft, or another aspect of a text, they provide evidence of their thinking. This helps teachers know how well students have understood a text. Additionally, the more students write in response to texts, the more they increase their ability to reflect and improve their critical writing ability. Also, students learn to cite evidence from texts in supporting their claims or supporting their main ideas. This ability becomes particularly useful in writing reports and opinion pieces.

Introduce the Purposes

Have students turn to page 8 and read the text. Explain that these are the key purposes for writing that will be explored in their handbooks. Give or elicit an example of a writing form that might be used for each purpose. Examples might include an informational paragraph or a research report *to inform,* directions or a how-to essay *to explain,* a story or personal narrative *to narrate,* and an opinion essay or letter to the editor *to persuade.* Then have students read the next page. Discuss how students should always consider their TAP—or task, audience, and purpose—to help them better target the message of their writing.

Grade 4 • **9**

The Writing Process

The *Writing Handbook* presents the writing process as a strategy that students can use to help them write for any task, audience, or purpose. Students can use the writing process independently or as part of writing workshops in which they respond to each other's writing. The writing process can help students understand how to plan, write, and revise for various purposes and genres. It is thus useful in helping students meet academic standards for opinion, informative/explanatory, and narrative writing.

What Process Writing Is

The writing process, or process writing, is an instructional approach to writing that consists of five basic stages. The stages are prewriting, drafting, revising, editing, and publishing. The stages are recursive in nature, meaning that students are encouraged to go back and forth between the stages as needed.

The characteristics of the stages of the writing process are as follows:

Prewriting

This is the stage where students begin to plan their writing. Students:

- Define a task and purpose.
- Identify an audience.
- Brainstorm ideas.
- Narrow and choose a topic.
- Plan and organize information.

Drafting

During drafting, students make their first attempt at fleshing out the prewriting idea and forming it into a written work. In other words, students put their ideas in writing. In this stage, students:

- Write a first draft.
- Do not yet worry about perfecting their writing.

- Know that they can revise, edit, and proofread later.
- Use their plan and checklists to help them write or to return to prewriting, as needed.

Revising

A draft is reread and decisions are made to rework and improve it. In this stage, students might:

- Read aloud their work to others to determine how it sounds and how it might be improved.
- Conference with other students or their teachers.
- Add information.
- Delete unnecessary information.
- Rearrange sentences and paragraphs.
- Combine sentences.

Editing

During editing, the draft is polished. In this stage, students reread and correct their writing for the following:

- Grammar
- Spelling
- Mechanics
- Usage

10 • Writing Handbook

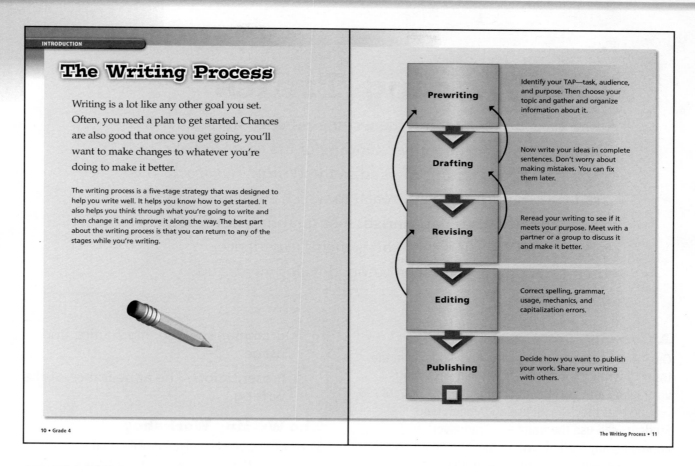

The Writing Process

Writing is a lot like any other goal you set. Often, you need a plan to get started. Chances are also good that once you get going, you'll want to make changes to whatever you're doing to make it better.

The writing process is a five-stage strategy that was designed to help you write well. It helps you know how to get started. It also helps you think through what you're going to write and then change it and improve it along the way. The best part about the writing process is that you can return to any of the stages while you're writing.

Prewriting — Identify your TAP—task, audience, and purpose. Then choose your topic and gather and organize information about it.

Drafting — Now write your ideas in complete sentences. Don't worry about making mistakes. You can fix them later.

Revising — Reread your writing to see if it meets your purpose. Meet with a partner or a group to discuss it and make it better.

Editing — Correct spelling, grammar, usage, mechanics, and capitalization errors.

Publishing — Decide how you want to publish your work. Share your writing with others.

10 • Grade 4

The Writing Process • 11

Publishing

Students share their writing with others. In this stage, students typically:

- Make a final, clean copy.
- Use their best handwriting, if writing by hand. If they are sharing their work electronically, they typically choose typefaces and other elements to make their writing readable and attractive.
- Combine their writing with art or graphics.
- Make multiple copies, read their writing aloud, post it electronically, or share and display it in some other way.

Introduce the Process

Have students read pages 10–11. Explain that the writing process is a strategy that they can use to help them write about any topic. Point out how the graphic on page 11 has arrows, indicating that students can go back and forth between the stages as needed. For students who have no previous orientation to the writing process, simplify your introduction by emphasizing at first only the three key stages of planning, drafting, and revising. Elicit how most tasks of any nature require planning, doing or making something, and then thinking about what might be done better and making those improvements. Compare how these same basic stages can be used each time students write.

Have students turn to the table of contents and locate the section in their handbooks devoted to the writing process (pages 74–81). Explain that they can use these handbook pages whenever they need help with specific stages or writing in general. Point out that each stage in the handbook has one or two pages devoted to it that tell more about the stage. As an example, have students turn to the Prewriting pages 74–75, and point out how they show the different organizational plans students can use for the different kinds of writing they will do. Encourage students to use their handbooks as a resource whenever they write.

Grade 4 • **11**

The Writing Traits

Along with understanding the writing process, students will benefit from having an understanding of the characteristics, or traits, of good writing covered in the *Writing Handbook*. The "Traits of Writing" is an approach in which students analyze their writing for the characteristics, or qualities, of what good writing looks like. These qualities include evidence, organization, purpose, elaboration, development, and conventions.

A Common Language

One of the advantages of instructing students in the traits of writing is that you give them a working vocabulary and thus build a common language for writing that they can all use and understand. Students can use the traits as a framework for improving any kind of writing they are doing. To this end, a systematic, explicitly taught focus on the traits of writing has proved to be an effective tool for discussing writing, enabling students to analyze and improve their own writing, and providing teachers with a way to assess students' compositions in a fair, even-handed manner.

Writers typically focus on six traits, with presentation—or the appearance of writing— sometimes considered an additional trait.

- **Evidence**—the details and examples that explain ideas and support opinions.
- **Organization**—the structure of the writing.
- **Purpose**—the reason for writing, which supports the type of writing and the audience.
- **Elaboration**—the words the writer uses to convey the message.
- **Development**—the advancement of a story through vivid details and interesting plot.
- **Conventions**—the correctness of the grammar, spelling, mechanics, and usage.
- **Presentation**—the appearance of the writing.

The Writing Workshop

Since writing is an involved process that students accomplish at varying speeds, it is usually a good idea to set aside a block of time for them to work on their writing. One time-tested model that has worked well in classrooms is the Writing Workshop. In this model during a set period of time, students work individually and collaboratively (with classmates and/or with the teacher) on different writing activities. One of these activities is for students to collaborate in reviewing each other's manuscripts. One effective technique used in many workshops as a way for students to comment on aspects of each other's writing is to use the language of the traits when they comment.

Some tasks are started and finished during a workshop, while others are ongoing. A writing workshop can serve many writing-related functions:

- Students can work on a class writing assignment (ongoing or quickly accomplished).
- Students can engage in independent writing, jotting down or consulting ideas in their writing log or journal, starting or working on pieces of their own devising.

12 • Writing Handbook

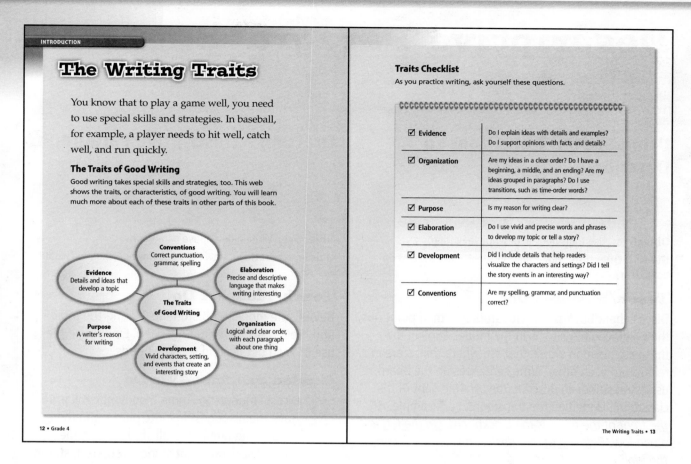

The Writing Traits

You know that to play a game well, you need to use special skills and strategies. In baseball, for example, a player needs to hit well, catch well, and run quickly.

The Traits of Good Writing

Good writing takes special skills and strategies, too. This web shows the traits, or characteristics, of good writing. You will learn much more about each of these traits in other parts of this book.

Conventions Correct punctuation, grammar, spelling

Evidence Details and ideas that develop a topic

Elaboration Precise and descriptive language that makes writing interesting

The Traits of Good Writing

Purpose A writer's reason for writing

Organization Logical and clear order, with each paragraph about one thing

Development Vivid characters, setting, and events that create an interesting story

Traits Checklist

As you practice writing, ask yourself these questions.

☑ Evidence	Do I explain ideas with details and examples? Do I support opinions with facts and details?
☑ Organization	Are my ideas in a clear order? Do I have a beginning, a middle, and an ending? Are my ideas grouped in paragraphs? Do I use transitions, such as time-order words?
☑ Purpose	Is my reason for writing clear?
☑ Elaboration	Do I use vivid and precise words and phrases to develop my topic or tell a story?
☑ Development	Did I include details that help readers visualize the characters and settings? Did I tell the story events in an interesting way?
☑ Conventions	Are my spelling, grammar, and punctuation correct?

- As previously mentioned, students can engage in peer-conferencing, giving one another advice about a piece of writing or sharing writing ideas.

- Students can select pieces for inclusion in their writing portfolio, where they keep their best work.

- Teachers can conference with individual students, reviewing student writing and discussing a given student's strengths and weaknesses as well as instructional progress.

- Teachers can engage in small-group instruction with students who need extra help with practice in specific areas of writing.

Writing Workshops are often most effective when they adhere to a dependable schedule and follow a set of clearly posted guidelines (for example, keep voices down, point out the good things about someone's writing as well as comment on aspects that might be revised, listen politely, put away materials when the workshop is over). In addition, students should know what areas of the classroom they can use during the Workshop and should have free access to writing materials, including their handbooks.

You may want to refer to the Writing Workshop pages in this *Writing Handbook Teacher's Guide* and teach one or two minilessons on writing workshop behaviors and activities so that students have a solid understanding of what is expected of them.

Introduce the Traits

Share the Writing Traits overview pages with students. Discuss each trait briefly and explain to students that their handbooks contain more information on the traits, which they can use to help them as they plan, draft, revise, edit, and publish their writing. Guide students to use their tables of content or indexes to locate where additional information can be found in their handbooks.

Descriptive Paragraph

WRITING FORMS

Minilesson 1

Using Spatial Transitions to Describe

Objective: Use transitions in descriptive writing.

Guiding Question: How can transitions make my descriptions clear?

Teach/Model—I Do

Discuss handbook p. 14 with students; then point out the boldfaced transitions in the model. Explain that these are position words that tell where things are in relation to each other. Write sentences on the board, using transitions to describe the arrangement of the classroom. Underline the transitions. For example, _At the front_ of the room is the blackboard. _On the left_ is a window. _Below that_, my desk is pushed up against the wall.

Guided Practice—We Do

Arrange three or four objects at the front of the room, such as a chair, a desk, a book, and a pencil. Work with students to write sentences with transition words that describe the setup. For example, _In the front_, there is a desk. _On top of_ the desk is an open book. Help volunteers describe the placement of the other objects in logical order (such as left to right or top to bottom), using transition words. Write the sentences on the board.

Practice/Apply—You Do

COLLABORATIVE Have small groups look at a photograph or out a window. Have them use transition words in sentences to describe a few objects they see. Have them put sentences in a logical order.

INDEPENDENT Have students write two more sentences, continuing the description their group began.

Conference/Evaluate

If students have difficulty using position words, tell them to anchor their descriptions on one object. They can then use transitions to describe everything in relation to that object.

14 • Writing

Minilesson 2

Drafting a Descriptive Paragraph

Objective: Write a descriptive paragraph.

Guiding Question: How can I help my audience see what I describe?

Teach/Model—I Do

Review the model with students, noting the topic and the details the writer included. Emphasize the use of vivid details and sensory words.

Guided Practice—We Do

 Direct students to Frame 1 on handbook p. 15. Have them suggest favorite places and then choose one familiar to all students. On the board, list details that students suggest, starting with the most noticeable feature of the place. Then guide students to suggest sentences, using the position words in the frame to describe features of the place. Have students write in their books as you write on the board.

Practice/Apply—You Do

 COLLABORATIVE Have small groups plan and complete Frame 2. Have them decide on a familiar place and list its important features. They should then fill in the frame based on the spatial relationships among the features. Have groups share and discuss what they have written.

 INDEPENDENT Have students read the directions. Tell them to use their prewriting plan from Lesson 1 or to brainstorm a new plan using Graphic Organizer 15.

Conference/Evaluate

As students draft, circulate and help them choose position words that make descriptions clear. Evaluate using the rubric on p. 104.

 Digital
• eBook
• WriteSmart
• Interactive Lessons

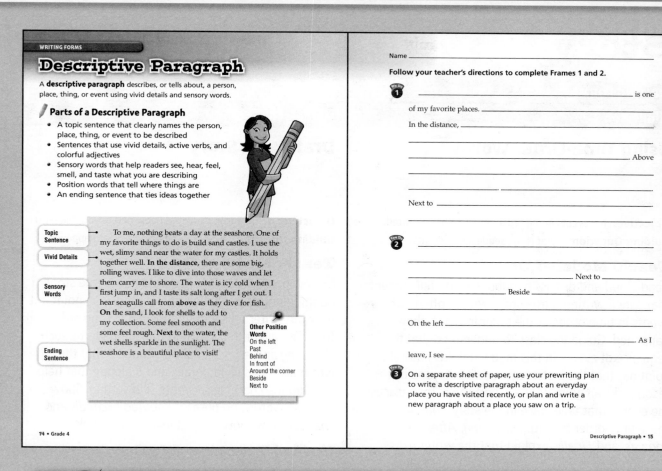

WRITING FORMS

Descriptive Paragraph

A **descriptive paragraph** describes, or tells about, a person, place, thing, or event using vivid details and sensory words.

Parts of a Descriptive Paragraph

- A topic sentence that clearly names the person, place, thing, or event to be described
- Sentences that use vivid details, active verbs, and colorful adjectives
- Sensory words that help readers see, hear, feel, smell, and taste what you are describing
- Position words that tell where things are
- An ending sentence that ties ideas together

Topic Sentence — Vivid Details — Sensory Words — Ending Sentence

To me, nothing beats a day at the seashore. One of my favorite things to do is build sand castles. I use the wet, slimy sand near the water for my castles. It holds together well. **In the distance**, there are some big, rolling waves. I like to dive into those waves and let them carry me to shore. The water is icy cold when I first jump in, and I taste its salt long after I get out. I hear seagulls call from **above** as they dive for fish. **On** the sand, I look for shells to add to my collection. Some feel smooth and some feel rough. **Next** to the water, the wet shells sparkle in the sunlight. The seashore is a beautiful place to visit!

Other Position Words
On the left
Past
Behind
In front of
Around the corner
Beside
Next to

14 • Grade 4

Name ____________________

Follow your teacher's directions to complete Frames 1 and 2.

1. ____________________ is one of my favorite places. ____________________ In the distance, ____________________ ____________________ ____________________ Above ____________________ ____________________ Next to ____________________ ____________________

2. ____________________ ____________________ Next to ____________________ Beside ____________________ ____________________ On the left ____________________ ____________________ As I leave, I see ____________________

3. On a separate sheet of paper, use your prewriting plan to write a descriptive paragraph about an everyday place you have visited recently, or plan and write a new paragraph about a place you saw on a trip.

Descriptive Paragraph • 15

Corrective Feedback

IF . . . students are unable to clearly describe the setting of their chosen place,

THEN . . . have them draw a picture of the place. This may help them visualize where objects are located in relation to one another. They can choose position words to describe where objects appear on their drawings.

Focus Trait: Elaboration

Remind students that using concrete, or exact, words makes writing more meaningful and helps create a picture in the reader's mind. On the board, write:

My friend and I went to see a show. When we got there, we smelled yummy food, so we got a bunch of stuff.

Point out that the sentence only gives a vague description of people, places, and things.

Work with students to rewrite the sentence using concrete words. Example:

My friend Leah and I biked to the movie theater. When we walked into the lobby, we smelled buttery popcorn, so we bought a bag of popcorn to share.

Grade 4 • **15**

Writing Handbook Minilessons

Story

WRITING FORMS

Minilesson 3

Using Time-Order Words

Objective: Tell events in the order in which they occurred.
Guiding Question: What is the sequence of events?

Teach/Model—I Do

Read aloud and discuss handbook p. 16. Tell students that, when writing a true story, writers often put events in time order, or the order in which they happened. Guide the class to understand that the sequence of events in this model unfolds naturally. Point out that the first event is that everyone but Jason picks an animal for a report topic. Then discuss the events that take place in the story. Point out these time-order transitions: *During, After, as soon as*, and *Finally*. Explain that the writer uses transitions to make the sequence of events clear to the reader.

Guided Practice—We Do

On the board, write these sentences: (1) *Jen looked on the floor under the seats.* (2) *Jen gave Pam her earring.* (3) *Pam lost one of her earrings on the bus.* Work with students to rewrite these events in the correct order (3, 1, 2). Then guide students to add transitional words or phrases that will make the time order more clear.

Practice/Apply—You Do

COLLABORATIVE Write these sentences on the board: *(1) The squirrel made a nest. (2) The squirrel collected leaves and twigs. (3) The squirrel slept in the nest.* Have groups rewrite these events in order (2, 1, 3), adding appropriate transitions.

INDEPENDENT Have students write three related events that happened to them, using time order and transitions.

Conference/Evaluate

Have students share their sequence of events with you to make sure they wrote them in the correct order.

16 • Writing

Minilesson 4

Drafting a Story

Objective: Write a true story that happened to you, the writer.
Guiding Question: How do I tell readers what happened?

Teach/Model—I Do

Review handbook p. 16. Read aloud the true story, pointing out its beginning and ending. Also point out how the writer tells what happened in time order, from first event to last, using transition words such as *during* and *after*. Explain to students that the writer also uses vivid details and dialogue that help develop the characters, events, and setting. Show how the words and phrases *shouted excitedly* and *snapped* show how characters feel and think.

Guided Practice—We Do

 Direct students to the frame on handbook p. 17. Tell students that, together, you will write a true story about helping a friend solve a problem. Work with students to brainstorm real experiences. Ask *Whom did you help? What problem did this person face? How did you help this person?* Then, together, complete the frame, using time order and transitions. Have students write in their books as you write on the board.

Practice/Apply—You Do

 COLLABORATIVE Have groups plan and complete Activity 2. Remind them to use dialogue and descriptive details as well as time order and transitions. Have groups share their writing.

 INDEPENDENT Have students read and follow the directions. Tell them to use their prewriting plan from Lesson 2 or to brainstorm a new plan using Graphic Organizer 4.

Conference/Evaluate

As students draft, have them evaluate their work using the rubric on p. 104.

 Digital
• eBook
• WriteSmart
• Interactive Lessons

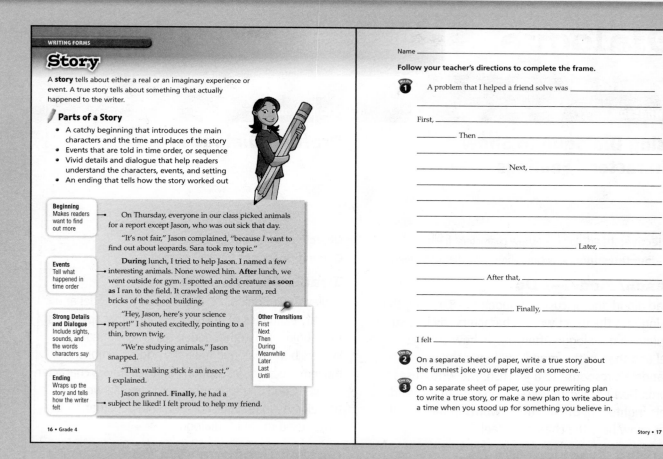

The student worktext pages show:

WRITING FORMS

Story

A **story** tells about either a real or an imaginary experience or event. A true story tells about something that actually happened to the writer.

Parts of a Story

- A catchy beginning that introduces the main characters and the time and place of the story
- Events that are told in time order, or sequence
- Vivid details and dialogue that help readers understand the characters, events, and setting
- An ending that tells how the story worked out

Beginning
Makes readers want to find out more

On Thursday, everyone in our class picked animals for a report except Jason, who was out sick that day.

"It's not fair," Jason complained, "because *I* want to find out about leopards. Sara took my topic."

Events
Tell what happened in time order

During lunch, I tried to help Jason. I named a few interesting animals. None wowed him. **After** lunch, we went outside for gym. I spotted an odd creature **as soon as** I ran to the field. It crawled along the warm, red bricks of the school building.

Strong Details and Dialogue
Include sights, sounds, and the words characters say

"Hey, Jason, here's your science report!" I shouted excitedly, pointing to a thin, brown twig.

"We're studying animals," Jason snapped.

"That walking stick *is* an insect," I explained.

Other Transitions
First
Next
Then
During
Meanwhile
Later
Last
Until

Ending
Wraps up the story and tells how the writer felt

Jason grinned. **Finally**, he had a subject he liked! I felt proud to help my friend.

16 • Grade 4

Name _____

Follow your teacher's directions to complete the frame.

1 A problem that I helped a friend solve was _____

_____

First, _____

_____ Then _____

_____

_____ Next, _____

_____

_____

_____ Later, _____

_____ After that, _____

_____ Finally, _____

I felt _____

2 On a separate sheet of paper, write a true story about the funniest joke you ever played on someone.

3 On a separate sheet of paper, use your prewriting plan to write a true story, or make a new plan to write about a time when you stood up for something you believe in.

Story • 17

 ## Corrective Feedback

IF . . . students are having a hard time coming up with vivid details,

THEN . . . have them visualize what they are trying to describe and use their five senses to capture how people, places, or things look, feel, taste, sound, or smell. For example, the words *frowned*, *slammed the locker*, and *stomped noisily* use words related to the senses of sight and sound to help show that a character felt angry.

Focus Trait: Elaboration

Tell students that an interesting true story includes words that describe and elaborate on the plot. Explain that good writers choose strong words to describe the different parts of a story: the characters, events, and setting. These words will help readers understand what happened.

Refer students to a true story they have read in a magazine or newspaper, in their textbooks, or in another book. Ask them to identify examples of strong words that help readers understand the characters, events, or setting.

Then write these sentences the board:

Tim ate a sandwich. He felt satisfied.

Have students rewrite the two sentences using stronger, more descriptive words. For example:

Tim ate a gooey, grilled-cheese sandwich.

He didn't leave a single crumb on his plate.

Grade 4 • **17**

Writing Handbook Minilessons

Dialogue

Minilesson 5

Using Dialogue to Show Characters' Feelings

Objective: Use dialogue to show characters' feelings.

Guiding Question: How can I show how characters feel?

Teach/Model—I Do

Read aloud and discuss handbook p. 18, noting that dialogue is the exact words characters say in a story. Explain that dialogue often shows how characters feel and that, in this model, dialogue shows Grandma's response to a jellyfish. The writer uses the words *Don't move* and *hissed* to show that Grandma feels frightened. Discuss other words in the model that show how the characters feel.

Guided Practice—We Do

Tell students to imagine that one friend is giving another a birthday present. Work with students to create a dialogue between the two characters that shows how pleased one friend is to receive the gift and how happy the other friend is that it is appreciated. Write suggestions on the board and help students sharpen the dialogue to better reflect the two characters' feelings.

Practice/Apply—You Do

COLLABORATIVE Have small groups work together to write dialogue for the following situation. One friend invites another to come play, but the other friend has to do chores for her mother. Groups should share their work with other groups, making constructive suggestions for improvements.

INDEPENDENT Have students write two or three lines of dialogue between two characters that show one of the characters feels worried.

Conference/Evaluate

Have students think about whether their dialogue conveys a character's feelings.

18 • Writing

Minilesson 6

Drafting Dialogue

Objective: Write dialogue.

Guiding Question: How do I write dialogue?

Teach/Model—I Do

Review handbook p. 18. Read aloud the model and identify examples of dialogue. Explain that speaker's tags (boldfaced in the model) tell *who* is speaking. Writers bring dialogue to life by adding actions, movements, and descriptions that tell *how* a character speaks. Good dialogue uses words people would actually say in real life. Point out the punctuation the writer used to set off dialogue.

Guided Practice—We Do

 Direct students to the frame on handbook p. 19. Tell students that, together, you will write dialogue. With students, brainstorm a conversation between two characters and then complete the frame. Help students use words that sound natural and show what a character is like. Have students write in their books as you write on the board.

Practice/Apply—You Do

 COLLABORATIVE Have groups plan and complete Activity 2. Remind them to use proper punctuation. Have groups share what they have written.

 INDEPENDENT Have students read the directions. Tell them to use their prewriting plan from Lesson 3 or to make a new plan. Have them use Graphic Organizer 1 with column headings *Thoughts, Actions, Words*.

Conference/Evaluate

As students draft, have them evaluate their work using the rubric on p. 104.

 Digital
• eBook
• WriteSmart
• Interactive Lessons

Dialogue

In a story, **dialogue** is the words characters say. Dialogue helps the reader imagine what the characters are like and how they act.

Parts of a Dialogue

- Words that sound like real speech
- Words that fit a character's age and personality
- Actions and movements to show how a characters feel and act
- Correct punctuation to help readers understand who is speaking and how something is being said

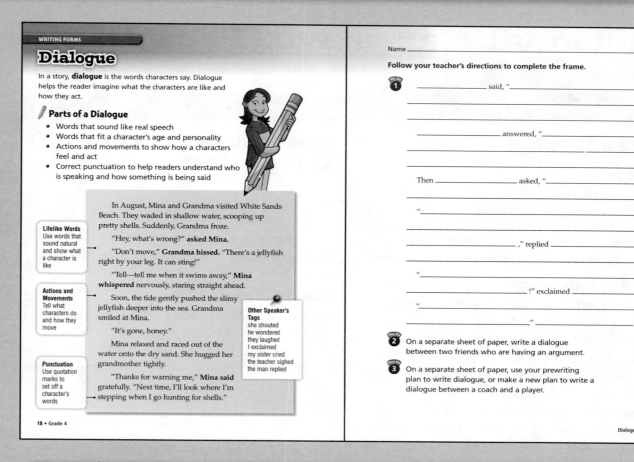

Lifelike Words
Use words that sound natural and show what a character is like

Actions and Movements
Tell what characters do and how they move

Punctuation
Use quotation marks to set off a character's words

In August, Mina and Grandma visited White Sands Beach. They waded in shallow water, scooping up pretty shells. Suddenly, Grandma froze.

"Hey, what's wrong?" **asked Mina.**

"Don't move," **Grandma hissed.** "There's a jellyfish right by your leg. It can sting!"

"Tell—tell me when it swims away," **Mina whispered** nervously, staring straight ahead.

Soon, the tide gently pushed the slimy jellyfish deeper into the sea. Grandma smiled at Mina.

"It's gone, honey."

Mina relaxed and raced out of the water onto the dry sand. She hugged her grandmother tightly.

"Thanks for warning me," **Mina said** gratefully. "Next time, I'll look where I'm stepping when I go hunting for shells."

Other Speaker's Tags
she shouted
he wondered
they laughed
I exclaimed
my sister cried
the teacher sighed
the man replied

18 • Grade 4

Name _____

Follow your teacher's directions to complete the frame.

1 _____ said, "_____
_____
_____
_____"

_____ answered, "_____
_____
_____"

Then _____ asked, "_____
_____?"

"_____
_____," replied _____

"_____
_____!" exclaimed _____

"_____
_____," _____ said.

2 On a separate sheet of paper, write a dialogue between two friends who are having an argument.

3 On a separate sheet of paper, use your prewriting plan to write dialogue, or make a new plan to write a dialogue between a coach and a player.

Dialogue • 19

Corrective Feedback

IF . . . students are having a hard time making their dialogue sound natural,

THEN . . . have pairs role play the characters and say the dialogue aloud. Direct students to make changes to help the dialogue reflect the characters' ages and personalities as well as to make the words sound more true to life.

Focus Trait: Elaboration

Tell students that elaboration is the writer's choice of words he or she uses to convey a message. The writer's words can show characters' feelings and personalities.

Explain that natural-sounding dialogue is often informal and lifelike. For example, it might include slang or sentence fragments.

Refer students to examples of dialogue in their textbook or in another book. Have them analyze the way the writer shows how characters feel.

Then write the following sentences on the board. Have students turn them into dialogue, using an appropriate voice for each character:

Carl asked his teacher for a pencil. Mr. Rich handed him a sharp pencil and told him to be careful.

For example:

"Could I borrow a pencil?" Carl asked politely.

"Watch out! It's got a sharp point," warned Mr. Rich.

Grade 4 • **19**

Fictional Narrative: Prewriting

WRITING FORMS

Minilesson 7

Using a Story Map

Objective: Use a story map to plan a fictional narrative.

Guiding Question: How can I plan my fictional narrative?

Teach/Model—I Do

Read aloud and discuss handbook p. 20. Explain that the writer first put down ideas for the characters, setting, and plot and then used the story map to sketch out the parts of a story. Point out the bold-faced headings **Setting** and **Characters** in the story map. Ask *Who are the characters? What is the setting?* Discuss the story details listed under each heading. Then point out the boldfaced heading **Plot**. Ask *What happens in the beginning of the story? the middle? the ending? What is the climax?* Guide students to understand that a story map is a kind of outline that they can use to plan and organize fictional narratives.

Guided Practice—We Do

On the board, write these story elements: (1) *John loses his backpack at school.* (2) *Pine Valley School* (3) *Mr. Rizzi helps John look for his backpack.* (4) *Mr. Rizzi and John* (5) *John thanks Mr. Rizzi.* (6) *Mr. Rizzi finds John's backpack behind the closed stage curtains.* Work with students to put the Setting, Characters, Beginning, Middle, Climax, and Ending into a story map.

Practice/Apply—You Do

COLLABORATIVE Have groups choose a story they have recently read. Then have them put the parts of the story into a story map.

INDEPENDENT Have students choose another story and put the elements into a story map.

Conference/Evaluate

Have students examine their lists to make sure they can use each of these elements in a story map.

20 • Writing

Minilesson 8

Developing the Characters, Setting, and Plot

Objective: Develop story characters, setting, and plot.

Guiding Question: How can I bring the characters, setting, and plot to life?

Teach/Model—I Do

Review handbook p. 20. Point to the story map and discuss how the writer has used details to flesh out the characters, setting, and plot. Ask students to identify specific details that the writer lists, such as the color of the kitten. Explain that details help the reader picture the characters and setting and understand events that take place in the fictional narrative.

Guided Practice—We Do

 Direct students to handbook p. 21. Tell students that, together, you will complete a story map about someone who begs her mother for permission to do something, such as babysit. Work with students to brainstorm characters, setting, and plot events. Then, together, complete the map with students' suggestions. Help students fill in each section of the story map with vivid details. Have students write in their books as you write on the board.

Practice/Apply—You Do

 COLLABORATIVE Have groups plan and complete Activity 2. Have them create a story map and then share what they have written.

 INDEPENDENT Have students read and follow the directions. Tell them to use their prewriting plan from Lesson 4 or another plan they create using Graphic Organizer 10.

Conference/Evaluate

As students draft, have them evaluate their work using the rubric on p. 104.

 Digital • eBook • WriteSmart • Interactive Lessons

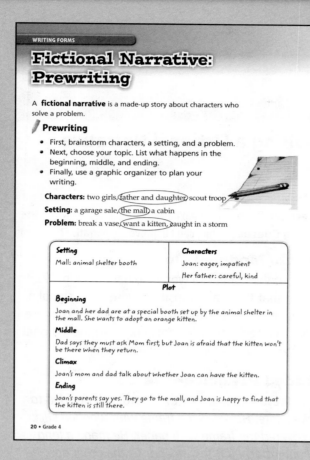

Fictional Narrative: Prewriting

A **fictional narrative** is a made-up story about characters who solve a problem.

Prewriting

- First, brainstorm characters, a setting, and a problem.
- Next, choose your topic. List what happens in the beginning, middle, and ending.
- Finally, use a graphic organizer to plan your writing.

Characters: two girls, father and daughter, scout troop

Setting: a garage sale, the mall, a cabin

Problem: break a vase, want a kitten, caught in a storm

Setting	Characters
Mall: animal shelter booth	Joan: eager, impatient
	Her father: careful, kind

Plot
Beginning
Joan and her dad are at a special booth set up by the animal shelter in the mall. She wants to adopt an orange kitten.
Middle
Dad says they must ask Mom first, but Joan is afraid that the kitten won't be there when they return.
Climax
Joan's mom and dad talk about whether Joan can have the kitten.
Ending
Joan's parents say yes. They go to the mall, and Joan is happy to find that the kitten is still there.

20 • Grade 4

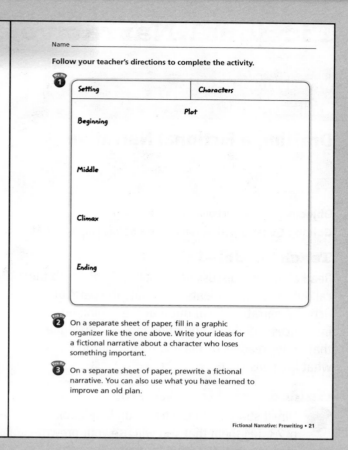

Name _____

Follow your teacher's directions to complete the activity.

1

Setting	Characters

Plot
Beginning
Middle
Climax
Ending

2 On a separate sheet of paper, fill in a graphic organizer like the one above. Write your ideas for a fictional narrative about a character who loses something important.

3 On a separate sheet of paper, prewrite a fictional narrative. You can also use what you have learned to improve an old plan.

Fictional Narrative: Prewriting • 21

Corrective Feedback

IF . . . students find it difficult to develop details for the characters, setting, or plot,

THEN . . . have them visualize what they are trying to describe. Tell them that details from these mental pictures can be used in their story maps and that they can help bring these story elements to life. For example, the setting might be *a musty historical museum crammed with antique furniture, rusty tools, and old-fashioned clothing.*

Focus Trait: Development

To help students think of ways to develop their fictional narratives, guide them to think of and list settings that interest them. For example:

A spooky, haunted old castle

The beach on a rainy day

A soccer field

Have students choose the setting that most interests them. Have them imagine what characters would be in this setting and what problems the characters would encounter there. Have students write their ideas into a story map.

Grade 4 • 21

Writing Handbook Minilessons

Fictional Narrative

| Minilesson 9 | Minilesson 10 |

Minilesson 9

Drafting a Fictional Narrative

Objective: Draft a fictional narrative.

Guiding Question: How can I write a fictional narrative?

Teach/Model—I Do

Read aloud and discuss handbook p. 22. Refer to the callouts and ask students to identify the parts of a fictional narrative. Point out that the beginning introduces a problem and often includes dialogue that draws readers in, making them want to find out what happens next.

Guided Practice—We Do

 Direct students to the frame on handbook p. 23. Tell them that you will use your prewriting plan from Lesson 4 to draft a fictional narrative. Together, review your plans for a story about a persistent child who begs her mother for permission to do something, such as babysit. Guide students to add more details about events that might take place. Then complete the frame together. Have students write in their books as you write on the board.

Practice/Apply—You Do

 COLLABORATIVE Have groups complete Activity 2 using their prewriting plans from Minilesson 8. Remind them to build up to an exciting point that will be the climax.

 INDEPENDENT Have students read and follow the directions for Activity 3. Tell them to use their prewriting plan from Minilesson 8 or to brainstorm a new plan using Graphic Organizer 10.

Conference/Evaluate

As students draft, have them evaluate their work using the rubric on p. 104.

Minilesson 10

Revising a Fictional Narrative

Objective: Revise a fictional narrative.

Guiding Question: How can I improve my narrative?

Teach/Model—I Do

Point out the boldfaced words on handbook p. 22. Explain that these are transition words that signal a change in time. Note that transition words like these establish a sequence of events and keep the fictional narrative moving along in a logical way.

Guided Practice—We Do

Write these sentences on the board: *Jeff decided to make a kite. He created a frame with wooden sticks. He covered the frame with paper. He made a long tail and attached it to one end. To the other end, he attached a flying line so that he could fly the kite. He went to a windy field.* Work with students to add transitions that will help readers follow the sequence of events *(first, then, next)*.

Practice/Apply—You Do

COLLABORATIVE Ask students to work in groups to circle the transitions in their drafts from Minilesson 9. Then have them suggest places to add other transitions.

INDEPENDENT Have students use suggestions from their groups to revise their drafts from Minilesson 9. Encourage them to add variety by using transitional phrases as well.

Conference/Evaluate

As students revise, help them determine whether their narratives move smoothly from one part to the next. Evaluate their work using the rubric on p. 104.

 Digital
- eBook
- WriteSmart
- Interactive Lessons

22 • Writing

Fictional Narrative

A **fictional narrative** tells about made-up characters who solve a problem.

Parts of a Fictional Narrative

- A beginning that introduces characters and a problem
- Descriptions that include active and colorful words
- A middle that shows how characters deal with the problem
- A climax that tells the most exciting part of the story
- An ending that tells how characters solve the problem

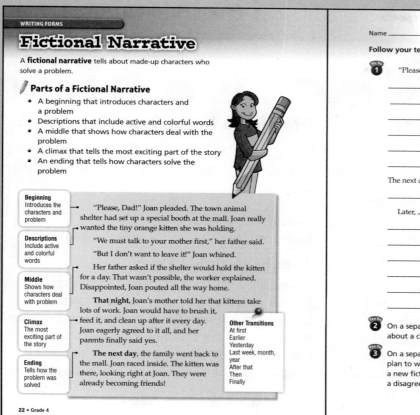

Beginning
Introduces the characters and problem

Descriptions
Include active and colorful words

Middle
Shows how characters deal with problem

Climax
The most exciting part of the story

Ending
Tells how the problem was solved

"Please, Dad!" Joan pleaded. The town animal shelter had set up a special booth at the mall. Joan really wanted the tiny orange kitten she was holding.

"We must talk to your mother first," her father said.

"But I don't want to leave it!" Joan whined.

Her father asked if the shelter would hold the kitten for a day. That wasn't possible, the worker explained. Disappointed, Joan pouted all the way home.

That night, Joan's mother told her that kittens take lots of work. Joan would have to brush it, feed it, and clean up after it every day. Joan eagerly agreed to it all, and her parents finally said yes.

The next day, the family went back to the mall. Joan raced inside. The kitten was there, looking right at Joan. They were already becoming friends!

Other Transitions
At first
Earlier
Yesterday
Last week, month, year
After that
Then
Finally

22 • Grade 4

Name _____

Follow your teacher's directions to complete the frame.

1 "Please, Mom!" _____

_____

_____

_____

_____ That night, _____

The next day, _____

Later, _____

_____ Then _____

_____ After that, _____

2 On a separate sheet of paper, write a fictional narrative about a character who loses something important.

3 On a separate sheet of paper, use your prewriting plan to write a fictional narrative, or plan and write a new fictional narrative about a character who has a disagreement with his or her best friend.

Fictional Narrative: Drafting/Revising • 23

 Corrective Feedback

IF . . . students have difficulty using transitions to establish the sequence of events,

THEN . . . have them review their completed story maps to identify places where the time or setting changes. Tell them to add appropriate words and phrases at these points of transition.

 Focus Trait: Organization

Remind students that fictional narratives are organized with a clear beginning, middle, and ending. Explain that the setting, characters, and problem are introduced in the beginning.

On the board, write this beginning to a fictional narrative:

"Oww, my leg," Claire moaned. After skidding on a patch of gravel, she had fallen and couldn't get up. Unfortunately, the bike path was deserted, and her sister Julia was far ahead.

Have students identify the setting (*a deserted bike path*), characters (*Claire and Julia*), and problem (*Claire had a bike accident and can't get up*).

Explain that the middle of a good fictional narrative often includes hints or clues about what the ending will be. Point out that these clues help readers make sense of the events so that the ending is logical.

Remind students that the ending should tell how the problem was resolved.

Grade 4 • **23**

News Report

WRITING FORMS

Minilesson 11

Writing a Headline and Lead Sentence

Objective: Write a headline and lead sentence.

Guiding Question: How do I get my audience's attention?

Teach/Model—I Do

Read aloud the definition, Parts of a News Report, and 5Ws + H list on handbook p. 24. Explain that a news report is written for a general audience, meaning that anyone could read it. Read the model aloud. Point out that the report presents only facts and has a headline to grab the reader's attention. It also has a lead sentence that provides important information about the topic right away.

Guided Practice—We Do

Work with students to come up with a list of recent special school events, such as a concert or fundraiser. List the events on the board. Guide students to choose one event and write a headline about it to grab the reader's attention, such as *Fourth-Graders Make Beautiful Music*. Then, together, write a lead sentence with a few important facts about the event, such as *The students in Mrs. Lopez's fourth-grade class played in a concert on May 14.*

Practice/Apply—You Do

COLLABORATIVE Have small groups work together to choose another event from the list and write a headline. Then have them write a lead sentence with a few important facts to go with the headline.

INDEPENDENT Have students work on their own to choose another event from the board and write a headline. Then have them write a lead sentence with a few important facts to go with that headline.

Conference/Evaluate

Circulate and offer help as needed. If students struggle to write a headline, have them think about what the most exciting part of the event was. They can describe that part in the headline.

24 • Writing

Minilesson 12

Drafting a News Report

Objective: Write a news report.

Guiding Question: How do I write a news report?

Teach/Model—I Do

Review the definition and list on handbook p. 24. Remind students that, in addition to a catchy headline, news reports need a lead sentence or paragraph that gives all the important information about the event. Tell students that many news reports also contain quotations from a participant or an onlooker.

Guided Practice—We Do

 Direct students to the frame on handbook p. 25. Read the headline and lead sentence. Work with students to come up with possible facts for the news report, such as *Students started a recycling program.* Then guide students to suggest a quotation to support the facts, such as *One student said, "It is really exciting to win this award."* Use students' suggestions to complete the report. Have students write in their books as you write on the board.

Practice/Apply—You Do

 COLLABORATIVE Have small groups work together to complete Activity 2. Remind them to write a catchy headline and to include all the important information. Have groups share their work.

 INDEPENDENT Have students read and follow the directions for Activity 3.

Conference/Evaluate

As students draft, remind them to include only facts in their news reports. Have students evaluate using the rubric on p. 104.

Digital • eBook
• WriteSmart
• Interactive Lessons

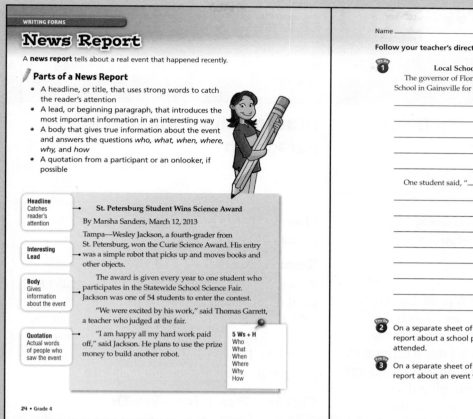

WRITING FORMS

News Report

A **news report** tells about a real event that happened recently.

Parts of a News Report

- A headline, or title, that uses strong words to catch the reader's attention
- A lead, or beginning paragraph, that introduces the most important information in an interesting way
- A body that gives true information about the event and answers the questions *who, what, when, where, why,* and *how*
- A quotation from a participant or an onlooker, if possible

Headline
Catches reader's attention

Interesting Lead

Body
Gives information about the event

Quotation
Actual words of people who saw the event

St. Petersburg Student Wins Science Award

By Marsha Sanders, March 12, 2013

Tampa—Wesley Jackson, a fourth-grader from St. Petersburg, won the Curie Science Award. His entry was a simple robot that picks up and moves books and other objects.

The award is given every year to one student who participates in the Statewide School Science Fair. Jackson was one of 54 students to enter the contest.

"We were excited by his work," said Thomas Garrett, a teacher who judged at the fair.

"I am happy all my hard work paid off," said Jackson. He plans to use the prize money to build another robot.

5 Ws + H
Who
What
When
Where
Why
How

24 • Grade 4

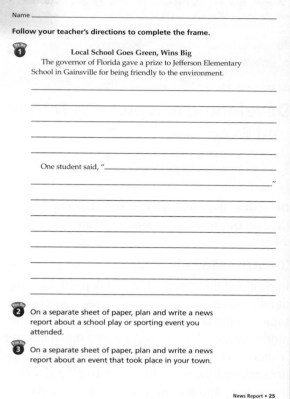

Name _____

Follow your teacher's directions to complete the frame.

1
Local School Goes Green, Wins Big
The governor of Florida gave a prize to Jefferson Elementary School in Gainsville for being friendly to the environment.

_____
_____
_____
_____

One student said, "_____
_____
_____"
_____
_____
_____
_____
_____

2 On a separate sheet of paper, plan and write a news report about a school play or sporting event you attended.

3 On a separate sheet of paper, plan and write a news report about an event that took place in your town.

News Report • 25

Corrective Feedback

IF . . . students have trouble writing a lead,

THEN . . . have them think about the questions *Who? What? When? Where? Why? How?* Remind students that their news reports should answer all of these questions. For example, for a basketball report, *Who* is the basketball team. *What* is the game they won. *Where* is the town the game took place. *Why* might be that the team had a talented player. *How* might be that the team worked hard and held extra practices.

Focus Trait: Evidence

An interview is an important writing type in which to get evidence for a news report. Tell students that whenever possible, they should interview people who observed or participated in the event that the report discusses. Advise students to write a list of questions in advance and to bring paper and a pen or pencil to record what the person says. Write the following questions on the board:

When and where did the event take place? Who else was there? What did you see, hear, and smell? How did you feel?

Have students practice interviewing each other about a recent school event, using the questions above as a guide. Encourage students to ask follow-up questions.

Grade 4 • 25

Writing Handbook Minilessons

Informational Paragraph

Minilesson 13

Developing a Topic with Details and Examples

Objective: Use details and examples to develop a topic.

Guiding Question: What details will I use to inform my readers?

Teach/Model—I Do

Read aloud and discuss handbook p. 26. Explain that details and examples help the writer explain the topic. On the board, write this sentence from the model: *Later, ancient Greeks rolled metal hoops with a short stick.* Point out that these details help readers understand how children in Greece played with hoops long ago and what the hoops looked like. Discuss other details and examples that the writer uses in this informational paragraph to help readers understand this topic.

Guided Practice—We Do

On the board, write a sports topic that your students are familiar with, such as *baseball.* Work with students to list details and examples that develop the topic. Guide them to think about how many players are on a team, how and where the sport is played, what equipment is needed, and so on.

Practice/Apply—You Do

COLLABORATIVE Write other sports topics on the board, such as *soccer, basketball, football,* or *skateboarding.* Have groups choose one topic and then list details and examples they would use to develop it.

INDEPENDENT Have students choose another informational topic and then list related details and examples on their own.

Conference/Evaluate

Have students share their lists with you to make sure they chose relevant details and examples to develop their topics.

26 • Writing

Minilesson 14

Drafting an Informational Paragraph

Objective: Write a paragraph to inform readers.

Guiding Question: How will I explain my subject?

Teach/Model—I Do

Review handbook p. 26. Read aloud the model and point out the main idea in the first sentence: *Playing with hoops is a very old custom.* Remind students that the writer uses supporting details to develop the main idea. Finally, point out the conclusion of the paragraph, which restates the main idea.

Guided Practice—We Do

 Direct students to the frame on handbook p. 27. Tell students that together you will write an informational paragraph about your school. Work with students to draft a topic sentence, such as *Our school is trying to be "greener."* Then, together, complete the frame with facts, examples, and other details. Help students write a conclusion that sums up the main idea. Have students write in their books as you write on the board.

Practice/Apply—You Do

 COLLABORATIVE Have groups plan and complete Activity 2. Tell them they can write about where this food comes from, what it looks like, and so on. Have groups share what they have written.

 INDEPENDENT Have students read and follow the directions. Tell them to use their prewriting plan from Lesson 7 or brainstorm a new plan using Graphic Organizer 15.

Conference/Evaluate

As students draft, have them evaluate their work using the rubric on p. 104.

Digital
- eBook
- WriteSmart
- Interactive Lessons

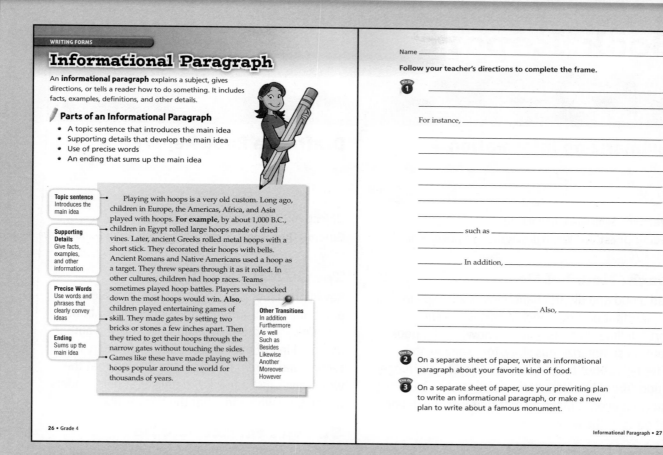

WRITING FORMS

Informational Paragraph

An **informational paragraph** explains a subject, gives directions, or tells a reader how to do something. It includes facts, examples, definitions, and other details.

Parts of an Informational Paragraph

- A topic sentence that introduces the main idea
- Supporting details that develop the main idea
- Use of precise words
- An ending that sums up the main idea

Topic sentence
Introduces the main idea

Supporting Details
Give facts, examples, and other information

Precise Words
Use words and phrases that clearly convey ideas

Ending
Sums up the main idea

Playing with hoops is a very old custom. Long ago, children in Europe, the Americas, Africa, and Asia played with hoops. **For example**, by about 1,000 B.C., children in Egypt rolled large hoops made of dried vines. Later, ancient Greeks rolled metal hoops with a short stick. They decorated their hoops with bells. Ancient Romans and Native Americans used a hoop as a target. They threw spears through it as it rolled. In other cultures, children had hoop races. Teams sometimes played hoop battles. Players who knocked down the most hoops would win. **Also**, children played entertaining games of skill. They made gates by setting two bricks or stones a few inches apart. Then they tried to get their hoops through the narrow gates without touching the sides. Games like these have made playing with hoops popular around the world for thousands of years.

Other Transitions
In addition
Furthermore
As well
Such as
Besides
Likewise
Another
Moreover
However

26 • Grade 4

Name _____

Follow your teacher's directions to complete the frame.

1 _____
_____

For instance, _____
_____
_____
_____
_____

_____ such as _____
_____

_____ In addition, _____
_____
_____

_____ Also, _____
_____
_____

2 On a separate sheet of paper, write an informational paragraph about your favorite kind of food.

3 On a separate sheet of paper, use your prewriting plan to write an informational paragraph, or make a new plan to write about a famous monument.

Informational Paragraph • 27

✔ Corrective Feedback

IF . . . students are having a hard time finding supporting details,

THEN . . . have them refer to an encyclopedia or other reference books or interview someone who knows about the topic. Encourage them to look for statistics, quotations, and other interesting facts.

✏ Focus Trait: Elaboration

Tell students that an informational paragraph includes words that help to elaborate on details the writer wants to convey. Explain that good writers elaborate on their ideas by choosing exact words to describe people, places, things, or events. Point out that precise words in the model, such as *vines* and *two bricks or stones*, clearly convey what the writer wants to say.

Now refer students to an informational paragraph in their science or social studies textbook. Ask them to

volunteer examples of precise words that help them better understand the topic.

Then write these sentences on the board:

Some frogs make loud sounds with their body parts.

Spring peepers *make loud* peeping *sounds with their* vocal sacs.

Guide students to understand that precise words in the second sentence help readers understand the topic.

Grade 4 • **27**

Writing Handbook Minilessons

Book Report

Minilesson 15

Summarizing Information

Objective: Summarize information.

Guiding Question: Which details should I include in a summary?

Teach/Model—I Do

Read aloud and discuss handbook p. 28. Explain that an important part of a book report is the *summary*, a short retelling that lets readers know what a book is about. To summarize this story, for example, the writer tells about the characters *(Lily, Charlie, judge)*, setting *(Brooklyn, New York; a tiny studio)*, and important events. Make a chart that lists the important parts of the book.

Guided Practice—We Do

On the board, write a three-column chart with these headings: *Characters, Setting, Events.* Work with students to complete the chart. First, choose a story that the class has recently read together. Then guide students to list the main characters, setting, and most important events in the story.

Practice/Apply—You Do

COLLABORATIVE Write several other story titles on the board. Have groups choose a story they remember well and then make a chart that includes the main characters, the setting, and the most important events.

INDEPENDENT Have students choose another story from the board and make a chart that lists the important parts of it.

Conference/Evaluate

Have students review their summary charts to make sure they included the most important story elements.

Minilesson 16

Drafting a Book Report

Objective: Write a book report.

Guiding Question: How do I tell readers about a book I have read?

Teach/Model—I Do

Review handbook p. 28. Read the model aloud and point out the information the writer gives about *Charlie's Paintbrush*, including the title, the author, and the kind of book. Point out the summary in the second and third paragraphs, explaining that the writer gives just a few key details that help readers understand who and what the book is about.

Guided Practice—We Do

 Direct students to the frame on handbook p. 29. Tell students that, together, you will write a book report. Have students choose a book they have read. Then, together, complete the frame, beginning with this sentence: _____ is a _____ story by _____. Help students summarize important story elements. Have students write in their books as you write on the board.

Practice/Apply—You Do

 COLLABORATIVE For Activity 2, have groups use their charts from Minilesson 15 to draft a book report. Have groups share what they have written.

 INDEPENDENT Have students read and follow the directions. Tell them to use their prewriting plan from Lesson 8 or to brainstorm a new plan using Graphic Organizer 10.

Conference/Evaluate

As students draft, have them evaluate their work using the rubric on p. 104.

 Digital
• eBook
• WriteSmart
• Interactive Lessons

28 • Writing

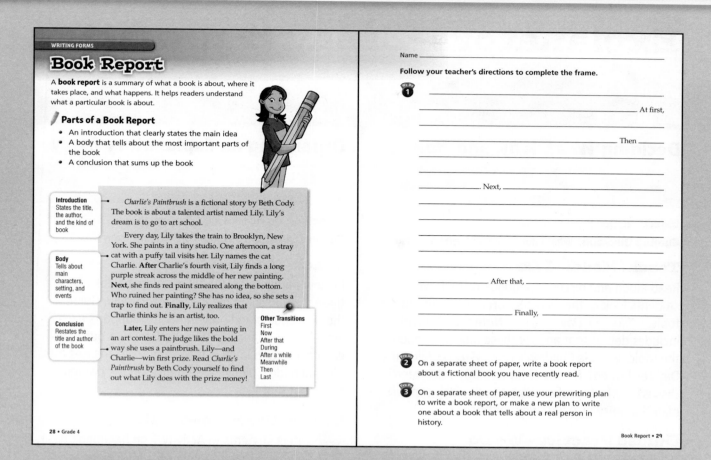

WRITING FORMS

Book Report

A **book report** is a summary of what a book is about, where it takes place, and what happens. It helps readers understand what a particular book is about.

Parts of a Book Report

- An introduction that clearly states the main idea
- A body that tells about the most important parts of the book
- A conclusion that sums up the book

Introduction
States the title, the author, and the kind of book

Body
Tells about main characters, setting, and events

Conclusion
Restates the title and author of the book

Charlie's Paintbrush is a fictional story by Beth Cody. The book is about a talented artist named Lily. Lily's dream is to go to art school.

Every day, Lily takes the train to Brooklyn, New York. She paints in a tiny studio. One afternoon, a stray cat with a puffy tail visits her. Lily names the cat Charlie. **After** Charlie's fourth visit, Lily finds a long purple streak across the middle of her new painting. **Next,** she finds red paint smeared along the bottom. Who ruined her painting? She has no idea, so she sets a trap to find out. **Finally,** Lily realizes that Charlie thinks he is an artist, too.

Later, Lily enters her new painting in an art contest. The judge likes the bold way she uses a paintbrush. Lily—and Charlie—win first prize. Read *Charlie's Paintbrush* by Beth Cody yourself to find out what Lily does with the prize money!

Other Transitions
First
Now
After that
During
After a while
Meanwhile
Then
Last

28 • Grade 4

Name _____

Follow your teacher's directions to complete the frame.

1 _____
_____ At first,
_____
_____ Then _____
_____
_____ Next, _____
_____
_____
_____
_____ After that, _____
_____
_____ Finally, _____
_____

2 On a separate sheet of paper, write a book report about a fictional book you have recently read.

3 On a separate sheet of paper, use your prewriting plan to write a book report, or make a new plan to write one about a book that tells about a real person in history.

Book Report • 29

 Corrective Feedback

IF . . . students are having a hard time summarizing the book,

THEN . . . have them create a three-column chart to list *all* of the characters, settings, and events in the book. Have them draw a line through any story elements that are *not* essential to a reader's understanding of the book.

 Focus Trait: Organization

Tell students that a book report has a particular organization. It consists of three or more paragraphs, and each paragraph has a different purpose.

- A book report begins with an *introduction* that states the main idea.

- The *body* is one or more paragraphs that summarize the most important elements of the book.

- The *conclusion* sums up the book and restates the title and author.

Refer students to the model. Have them identify the three different parts of the book report about *Charlie's Paintbrush*, reading each part aloud.

Grade 4 • 29

Writing Handbook Minilessons

Explanatory Essay: Prewriting

Minilesson 17

Deciding *What*, *Why*, and *How*

Objective: Decide which facts and details to use.

Guiding Question: What information do I need to include?

Teach/Model—I Do

Read aloud and discuss handbook p. 30. Have students look at the idea-support map. Point out the topic: *Children's Day in Japan*. Note that the writer includes details that answer these questions about the topic: *What* is Children's Day? *Why* is Children's Day celebrated? *How* is Children's Day celebrated? Discuss the facts and examples in the idea-support map that answer *what*, *why*, and *how*.

Guided Practice—We Do

On the board, write the topic *International Space Station*. Help students formulate questions about this topic. For example, they might ask *What* is the International Space Station? *Why* was it created? *How* does it gather information about space? Explain that asking *what*, *why*, and *how* helps writers decide which kinds of information belong in their explanatory essays.

Practice/Apply—You Do

COLLABORATIVE Have groups choose a topic for an explanatory essay and list facts and details about the topic that tell *what*, *why*, and *how*. Have them circle the information they would use in an essay.

INDEPENDENT Have students choose another explanatory topic and make a list of three facts or details they would include in an essay.

Conference/Evaluate

Have students share their lists with you to check that they have made appropriate decisions.

Minilesson 18

Organizing an Explanatory Essay

Objective: Determine a logical organization.

Guiding Question: How do I organize my essay?

Teach/Model—I Do

Review handbook p. 30. Have students look at the three main ideas in the idea-support map. Guide them to understand how the writer supports each main idea with facts and examples. Point out that each paragraph in an explanatory essay focuses on one main idea; all of the sentences in the paragraph tell about that idea.

Guided Practice—We Do

 Direct students to Activity 1 on handbook p. 31. Tell them that, together, you will create an idea-support map. Work with students to brainstorm a familiar holiday from another culture and write this topic at the top of the map. For example, you might write *The Day of the Dead in Mexico*. Then, together, complete the frame with main ideas and supporting facts and details. Have students write in their books as you write on the board.

Practice/Apply—You Do

 COLLABORATIVE Have groups plan and complete Activity 2 in which they create an idea-support map about their topic and then share what they have written.

 INDEPENDENT Have students read and follow the directions. Tell them to use their prewriting plan from Lesson 9 or to brainstorm a new plan using Graphic Organizer 7.

Conference/Evaluate

As students draft, have them evaluate their work using the rubric on p. 104.

 Digital
• eBook
• WriteSmart
• Interactive Lessons

30 • Writing

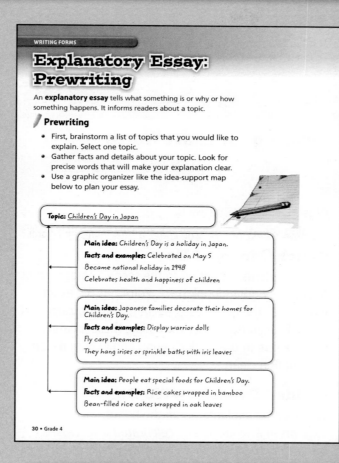

Explanatory Essay: Prewriting

An **explanatory essay** tells what something is or why or how something happens. It informs readers about a topic.

Prewriting

- First, brainstorm a list of topics that you would like to explain. Select one topic.
- Gather facts and details about your topic. Look for precise words that will make your explanation clear.
- Use a graphic organizer like the idea-support map below to plan your essay.

Topic: Children's Day in Japan

Main idea: Children's Day is a holiday in Japan.
Facts and examples: Celebrated on May 5
Became national holiday in 1948
Celebrates health and happiness of children

Main idea: Japanese families decorate their homes for Children's Day.
Facts and examples: Display warrior dolls
Fly carp streamers
They hang irises or sprinkle baths with iris leaves

Main idea: People eat special foods for Children's Day.
Facts and examples: Rice cakes wrapped in bamboo
Bean-filled rice cakes wrapped in oak leaves

30 • Grade 4

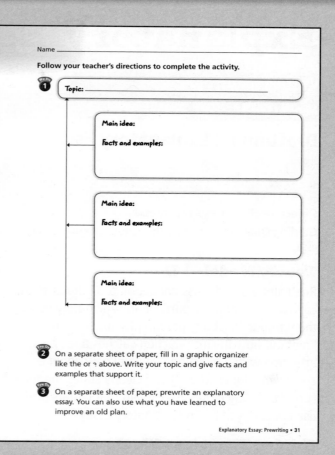

Name _____

Follow your teacher's directions to complete the activity.

1 Topic: _____

Main idea:

Facts and examples:

Main idea:

Facts and examples:

Main idea:

Facts and examples:

2 On a separate sheet of paper, fill in a graphic organizer like the one above. Write your topic and give facts and examples that support it.

3 On a separate sheet of paper, prewrite an explanatory essay. You can also use what you have learned to improve an old plan.

Explanatory Essay: Prewriting • 31

Corrective Feedback

IF . . . students find it difficult to organize their explanatory essays,

THEN . . . have them try several different patterns to figure out which one works best. They might want to use their notes to make several idea-support maps before they begin to write. Remind them to group related facts and details together.

Focus Trait: Organization

Tell students that, in a good explanatory essay, a writer uses a pattern of organization that helps readers understand the topic. Remind students that an idea-support map can be especially helpful when writers need to organize information in a logical way.

Write these different patterns of organization on the board:

Tell what happened in sequence (time order)

Tell why something happened (cause/effect)

Tell about the parts that make up a whole (analysis)

Tell how things are alike or different (compare/contrast)

Discuss each pattern of organization. Then have students identify which pattern of organization the idea-support map on p. 30 uses *(tell about the parts that make up a whole).*

Grade 4 • 31

Writing Handbook Minilessons

Explanatory Essay

Minilesson 19

Drafting an Explanatory Essay

Objective: Plan an explanatory essay.

Guiding Question: What are the parts of an explanatory essay?

Teach/Model—I Do

Read aloud and discuss handbook p. 32. Refer to the callout boxes and the parts of an explanatory essay: the introduction, body paragraphs, and conclusion. Point out how the introduction catches a reader's attention with a question (*Do you know about a special day for children?*) and clearly states the topic, (*Children's Day in Japan*). Explain that writers often use questions to begin explanatory essays.

Guided Practice—We Do

 Direct students to the frame on handbook p. 33. Have them use their plans from Minilesson 18 about a holiday. Ask students to supply facts and examples to explain this topic. Together, complete the frame, including all the parts of an explanatory essay. Have students write in their books as you write on the board.

Practice/Apply—You Do

 COLLABORATIVE Have groups plan and complete Activity 2. They may use their prewriting plans from Minilesson 18. Encourage them to think of facts and examples that will help readers understand this holiday.

 INDEPENDENT Have students read and follow directions for Activity 3. Tell them to use their prewriting plan from Minilesson 18 or make another plan using Graphic Organizer 7.

Conference/Evaluate

As students draft, have them evaluate their work using the rubric on p. 104.

Minilesson 20

Revising for Exact Words

Objective: Use precise words.

Guiding Question: How can I improve my explanatory essay?

Teach/Model—I Do

Direct students' attention to the second paragraph of the model on handbook p. 32. Point out the exact words that the writer uses, such as *warrior*, *carp*, and *irises*. Explain that exact words like these create a vivid picture in the reader's mind and help make an explanation clear.

Guided Practice—We Do

Write a brief explanation on the board, such as *Pilgrims in Massachusetts celebrated a successful harvest in 1621. For three days, they feasted on deer, corn, clams, oysters, and roast duck. Today, most people enjoy delicious things on Thanksgiving.* Work with students to identify exact words that help readers understand the explanation. *(Pilgrims, Massachusetts, deer,* and so on) Ask: *How could we change the last sentence so that it has exact words?* (Sample answer: *Today, many Americans enjoy delicious turkey, cranberry sauce, and pumpkin pie on Thanksgiving.)*

Practice/Apply—You Do

COLLABORATIVE Have groups look over their drafts from Minilesson 19 to suggest places where they could substitute more exact words.

INDEPENDENT Have students revise their drafts from Minilesson 19. If they have used enough exact words, encourage them to look for places where they can replace a word they have used too often.

Conference/Evaluate

Have students review their revised drafts to make sure the drafts include exact words.

 Digital
- eBook
- WriteSmart
- Interactive Lessons

32 • Writing

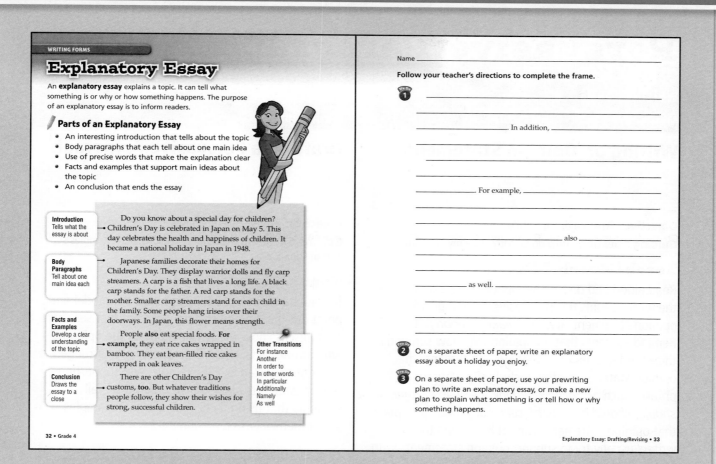

Corrective Feedback

IF . . . students have trouble organizing their explanatory essays,

THEN . . . have them review each paragraph and cross out any sentences that do not tell something about the main idea of that paragraph.

Focus Trait: Elaboration

Tell students that, in a good explanatory essay, a writer elaborates by using precise, vivid words so that readers understand the explanation. Point out that exact words in the model, such as *rice cakes* and *bamboo*, provide the reader with important details about how people in Japan celebrate Children's Day.

Write this sentence on the board:

Flowers and candy are traditional Valentine's Day gifts.

Ask *Which words are most precise?* Elicit the words *traditional*, *Valentine's Day*, and *gifts*. Ask *Which words are not precise?* Elicit the words *flowers* and *candy*.

Have students suggest exact words that could replace *flowers* and *candy*. Help students understand that writers could make the sentence clearer by replacing vague words with more specific ones, such as *roses* and *chocolates*.

Grade 4 • **33**

Writing Handbook Minilessons

Persuasive Paragraph

Minilesson 21

Writing an Opinion Statement

Objective: Write an opinion statement.

Guiding Question: How do I clearly state my opinion?

Teach/Model—I Do

Read aloud and discuss handbook p. 34. Explain that the writer begins this persuasive paragraph with an opinion statement: *A rabbit makes a good pet.* Remind students that an opinion tells how someone thinks or feels about something. Tell students that opinion statements often include signal words or phrases such as *I believe, I think, I feel, in my opinion, should, should not, might, seem,* or *probably.* Explain that opinion statements cannot be proven true, but writers usually try to support opinion statements with facts and reasons.

Guided Practice—We Do

On the board, write these sentences:

(1) *Vegetables provide vitamins, minerals, and fiber.*

(2) *Kids should eat more vegetables.*

Work with students to identify the second sentence as an opinion statement. Help them understand that the word *should* signals an opinion.

Practice/Apply—You Do

COLLABORATIVE Write this sentence on the board: *Recycling is a way to reduce waste.* Have groups turn this sentence into a clear opinion statement by adding signal words or phrases.

INDEPENDENT Have students write an opinion statement about their favorite food.

Conference/Evaluate

Have students evaluate their statements to make sure they clearly state an opinion that can be supported with facts and reasons.

Minilesson 22

Drafting a Persuasive Paragraph

Objective: Write a paragraph to persuade readers.

Guiding Question: What facts, reasons, and examples support my opinion?

Teach/Model—I Do

Review handbook p. 34. Read aloud the model and point out the opinion statement in the first sentence. Then discuss how the writer supports the opinion with strong facts, reasons, and examples arranged in order of importance. For example, one supporting reason is *rabbits make only a little noise.* Tell students that using facts, reasons, and examples strengthens a writer's argument.

Guided Practice—We Do

 Direct students to the frame on handbook p. 35. Tell students that, together, you will write a persuasive paragraph about another animal that makes a good pet. Work with students to write an opinion statement. Then, together, complete the frame with facts, reasons, and examples that support the opinion. Have students write in their books as you write on the board.

Practice/Apply—You Do

 COLLABORATIVE Have groups plan and complete Activity 2. Have students look at local newspapers and websites for ideas. Have groups share what they have written.

 INDEPENDENT Have students read and follow the directions. Tell them to use their prewriting plan from Lesson 11 or brainstorm a new plan. Have them use Graphic Organizer 15.

Conference/Evaluate

As students draft, have them evaluate their work using the rubric on p. 104.

 Digital • eBook • WriteSmart • Interactive Lessons

34 • Writing

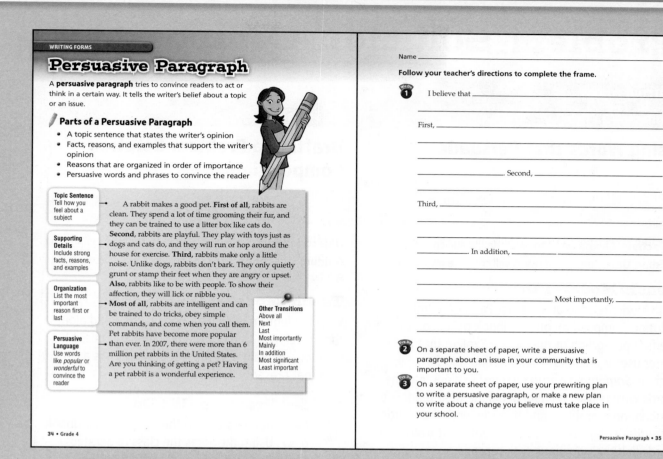

Corrective Feedback

IF . . . students are having a hard time thinking of facts, reasons, and examples to support their opinions,

THEN . . . have them find additional information about this topic. They can consult websites, current magazines and newspapers, and reference books in the school library.

Focus Trait: Evidence

Tell students that, in a good persuasive paragraph, a writer uses evidence such as specific details to share ideas that support an opinion. Point out this sentence in the model:

They spend a lot of time grooming their fur, and they can be trained to use a litter box like a cat does.

Explain that these details help readers understand why rabbits are clean. They also help support the writer's opinion that rabbits make good pets.

Write this sentence on the board:

Saturday is the most enjoyable day of the week.

Have students list details and evidence and reasons that support the statement.

Grade 4 • **35**

Problem-Solution Composition

Minilesson 23

Using Words that Persuade

Objective: Choose words to persuade the audience.

Guiding Question: What words will convince my readers?

Teach/Model—I Do

With students, read and discuss Parts of a Problem-Solution Composition on handbook p. 36. Point to the first paragraph of the model. Explain that the writer uses words that sound strong and forceful, such as *Something has to change!* Explain that the words writers use can help persuade their readers to understand a problem and to agree with the solution the writer suggests. Remind students that transition words link their opinions with reasons.

Guided Practice—We Do

Work with students to plan a problem-solution composition about crowded bus routes to school. Help students identify words or phrases that describe the problem. Then help them identify solutions (such as more buses) using persuasive words to help convince their readers. Write their suggestions on chart paper for use with Minilesson 24.

Practice/Apply—You Do

COLLABORATIVE Tell students to plan a problem-solution composition about a problem with your school's library, music room, or gym. Have pairs list words to convince their audience that the problem is important and their solution is good. Have groups save their notes.

INDEPENDENT Tell students to plan a problem-solution composition about a problem in their community. Have students write convincing words or phrases describing the problem and the solution.

Conference/Evaluate

If students are having trouble, suggest that they describe the problem aloud to partners.

36 • Writing

Minilesson 24

Drafting a Problem-Solution Composition

Objective: Write a convincing problem-solution composition.

Guiding Question: How can I convince my audience that my solution is best?

Teach/Model—I Do

With students, review handbook p. 36. Read aloud the model, pointing out the problem and possible solutions. Explain that the last paragraph is a conclusion that presents the best solution.

Guided Practice—We Do

 Have students turn to the frame on handbook p. 37. Using the ideas the class generated about bus routes in Minilesson 23, work together to put the problem and solutions into sentences. Guide students to pick the best solution to put in the concluding sentence. Have them write in their books as you write on the board.

Practice/Apply—You Do

 COLLABORATIVE Have small groups plan and complete Activity 2. They can use their notes from Minilesson 23 or choose a new problem and identify at least one solution. Have groups share and discuss their writing.

 INDEPENDENT Have students read the directions. Tell them to use their prewriting plan from Lesson 12 or brainstorm a new plan using Graphic Organizer 7.

Conference/Evaluate

Circulate and help students choose reasonable solutions. Evaluate using the rubric on p. 104.

Digital ▸ • eBook
• WriteSmart
• Interactive Lessons

Problem-Solution Composition

A **problem-solution composition** presents a problem and tells ways to solve it.

Parts of a Problem-Solution Composition
- An introduction that presents the problem
- A body that offers possible reasons and examples
- Language to persuade your audience
- A conclusion that tells the best solution

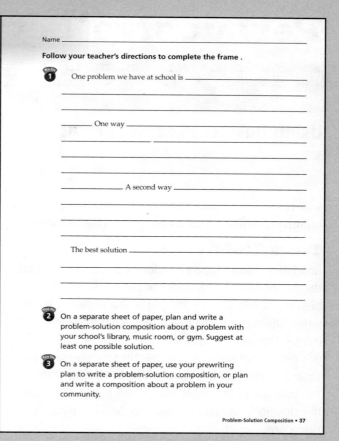

Introduction
Presents the problem

We students do not have time to eat lunch, even though we get a whole hour. It should be enough time, but it never is! The lunch lines are so long that they often take thirty minutes to get through! Then we have to gulp down our food and race back to class. Something has to change!

Solutions
Suggest ideas for fixing the problem

One way to improve things might be to stagger lunch. First, one class would go. Then, fifteen minutes later, the next class would follow, and so on. The lines would be shorter, and we

Reasons and Examples
Tell how the solutions work

would spend more time eating and less time waiting. **A second** way would be to hire another cashier and add another line. With two checkout lines, we could sit down to eat a lot faster.

Other Transitions
Next
Because
As a result
Finally
In addition
For instance
In order to

Conclusion
Names the best solution and gives reasons why it is best

Clearly, **the best solution** would be to stagger lunch. No more workers would be needed, and there would not be a need to buy another cash register. The school would just stagger the schedule. That way, we would make the most of our lunch time!

36 • Grade 4

Name _____

Follow your teacher's directions to complete the frame .

1 One problem we have at school is _____

_____

_____ One way _____

_____

_____ A second way _____

_____

The best solution _____

_____

2 On a separate sheet of paper, plan and write a problem-solution composition about a problem with your school's library, music room, or gym. Suggest at least one possible solution.

3 On a separate sheet of paper, use your prewriting plan to write a problem-solution composition, or plan and write a composition about a problem in your community.

Problem-Solution Composition • 37

✓ Corrective Feedback

IF . . . students are unable to come up with at least two reasonable solutions to their problem,

THEN . . . have them brainstorm ideas with partners or small groups. They can use other ideas that come up to prompt their own thinking. Students should record their preferred solutions in a web or other graphic organizer and provide reasons and facts or examples to support each solution.

Focus Trait: Evidence

Tell students that a strong problem-solution composition contains evidence that explains how the solution could be helpful. Good writers add details and other forms of evidence that help readers clearly understand why the solution will work.

Write *A student leader will help the school.* Explain that adding details could tell what kind of leader is needed and explain how he or she will help the school.

Write *Electing a student body president will help the school run smoothly because he or she can help the teachers and principal plan events, such as dances and book fairs.* Have students find vague ideas in their compositions and add evidence that will help show how the problem is solved.

Grade 4 • **37**

Writing Handbook Minilessons

Persuasive Letter

Minilesson 25

Using Business Letter Format

Objective: Use the correct format for a business letter.

Guiding Question: What are the parts of a business letter?

Teach/Model—I Do

Read aloud and discuss handbook p. 38. Explain that the writer, Matt Lucci, uses the correct format for a business letter. Discuss the parts of a business letter while having students examine each part in the model: the sender's address and the date; the receiver's name and address; the greeting that begins with *Dear* and ends with a comma; the body that states the purpose of the letter along with facts and details; the closing followed by a comma; and the writer's signature.

Guided Practice—We Do

On the board, write these parts of a business letter: (1) *Marie Amis* (2) *Dear Miss Evans,* (3) *Sincerely,* (4) *6 Main Street, Lauderhill, FL 33311* (5) *March 11, 2012.* (6) *Lauderhill should have a dog park. People need a place to take their dogs. I hope you will turn the old hospital grounds into a park. Then our dogs will be able to run and play off the leash.*

Work with students to put these parts in the correct format for a business letter.

Practice/Apply—You Do

COLLABORATIVE Direct groups to write a short business letter. Have them identify and label each of the six parts of the letter.

INDEPENDENT Have students write a business letter on their own, using correct format.

Conference/Evaluate

Have students share their business letters with you to make sure they have used the proper format.

38 • Writing

Minilesson 26

Drafting a Persuasive Letter

Objective: Write a letter to persuade readers.

Guiding Question: What facts, reasons, and examples support the main points of my letter?

Teach/Model—I Do

Review handbook p. 38. Read aloud the model and point out how the writer supports his opinion that the skate park needs to be repaired. He backs up his opinion with strong facts, reasons, and examples. For example, Matt says *storms caused large cracks in the concrete bowl.* Explain that using specific details strengthens a writer's argument.

Guided Practice—We Do

 Direct students to the frame on handbook p. 39. Tell students that together you will write a persuasive letter to the principal about an issue at school. For example, you might write about why your cafeteria should improve its menu. Work with students to complete the frame with facts, reasons, and examples that support the opinion. Have students write in their books as you write on the board.

Practice/Apply—You Do

 COLLABORATIVE Have groups plan and complete Activity 2. To get them started, provide them with examples of letters to the editor from local newspapers. Have groups share what they have written.

 INDEPENDENT Have students read and follow the directions. Tell them to use their prewriting plan from Lesson 13 or to brainstorm a new plan using Graphic Organizer 15.

Conference/Evaluate

As students draft, have them evaluate their work using the rubric on p. 104.

 Digital • eBook • WriteSmart • Interactive Lessons

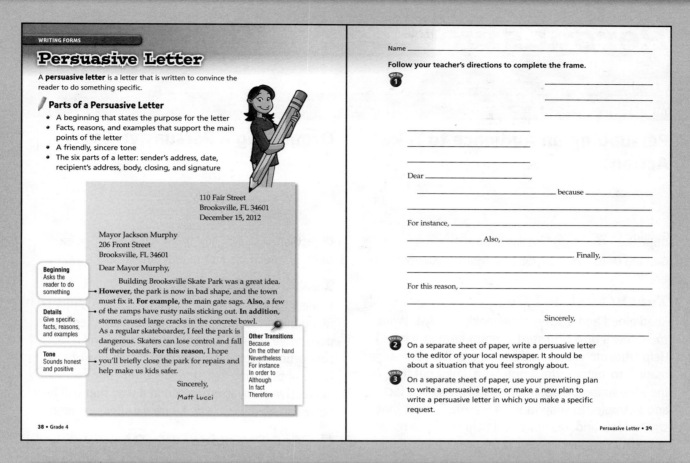

Corrective Feedback

IF . . . students are having a hard time thinking of facts, reasons, and examples to support the main points of the letter,

THEN . . . have them use websites, current magazines and newspapers, and other resources in the school library to find information about this topic.

Focus Trait: Purpose

Tell students that in a good persuasive letter, a writer sets a sincere tone that the reader can trust. The writer does this by keeping the purpose for writing in mind, and choosing the right words. Explain that some words can elicit a strong positive or negative emotional reaction.

In the model, for example, Matt says *I hope you'll briefly close the park for repairs and help make us kids safer*. Point out how specific words like *I hope* and *us kids* make the writer's voice sound friendly and sincere.

Write these sentences on the board:

You'd better send money right now to Save Our Pets.

Please consider giving today to Save Our Pets.

Guide students to understand that the first sentence uses a threatening tone and harsh language. In contrast, the second sentence is written in a polite, friendly way.

Grade 4 • **39**

Writing Handbook Minilessons

Persuasive Essay: Prewriting

Minilesson 27

Persuading an Audience to Take Action

Objective: Use strong facts and examples.

Guiding Question: How can I convince my audience to do something?

Teach/Model—I Do

Read aloud and discuss handbook p. 40. Ask *What is the writer's goal?* (To start a worm farm at school.) Help students understand how the writer persuades readers to support the worm farm. Point out that, in the idea-support map, the writer gives strong facts and examples to support each reason. Explain that strong facts and examples will help convince readers to take action.

Guided Practice—We Do

On the board, write a two-column chart with these headings: *Facts* and *Examples*. Direct students to the idea-support map and help them identify facts *(Two pounds of worms can eat a whole pound of fruits and vegetables and other waste)* and examples *(There would be less garbage for the school to send to the landfill).* Tell students that these strong facts and examples support each reason.

Practice/Apply—You Do

COLLABORATIVE Have groups choose a topic that they feel strongly about. Then have them list facts and examples that support their opinion.

INDEPENDENT Have students choose another topic they feel strongly about and list facts and examples that would persuade an audience to take action.

Conference/Evaluate

Have students look over their lists of facts and examples to make sure they are persuasive.

Minilesson 28

Organizing a Persuasive Essay

Objective: Determine how to organize a persuasive essay.

Guiding Question: How should I arrange my essay?

Teach/Model—I Do

Review handbook p. 40. Explain to students that filling out an idea-support map can help them draft persuasive essays. Point out the reason and supporting facts and examples in each box of the idea-support map. Tell students that a good persuasive essay is organized in a way that will best persuade readers to agree with a writer's opinion.

Guided Practice—We Do

 Direct students to Activity 1 on handbook p. 41. Work with students to choose a topic, such as something the school could do to improve the environment. Then, together, complete the frame with reasons, facts, and examples that support the opinion. Have students write in their books as you write on the board.

Practice/Apply—You Do

 COLLABORATIVE Have groups plan and complete Activity 2. Have them choose an opinion about something your town or community should do and create an idea-support map together. Then have groups share what they have written.

 INDEPENDENT Have students read and follow the directions. Tell them to use their prewriting plan from Lesson 14 or to brainstorm a new plan using Graphic Organizer 7.

Conference/Evaluate

As students draft, have them evaluate their work using the rubric on p. 104.

 • eBook
• WriteSmart
• Interactive Lessons

40 • Writing

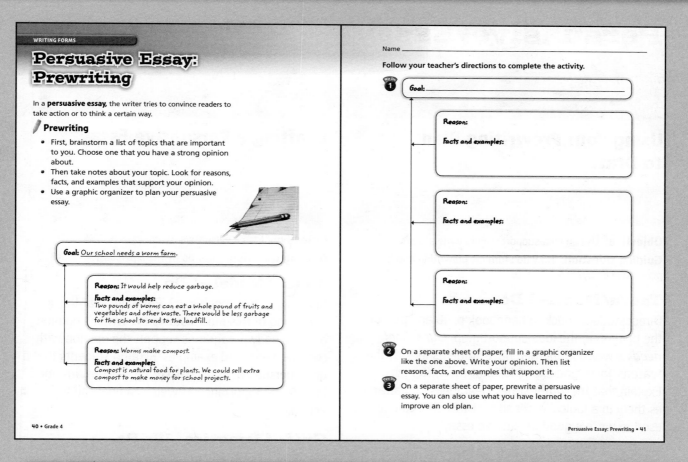

Persuasive Essay: Prewriting

In a **persuasive essay**, the writer tries to convince readers to take action or to think a certain way.

Prewriting

- First, brainstorm a list of topics that are important to you. Choose one that you have a strong opinion about.
- Then take notes about your topic. Look for reasons, facts, and examples that support your opinion.
- Use a graphic organizer to plan your persuasive essay.

Goal: Our school needs a worm farm.

Reason: It would help reduce garbage.
Facts and examples:
Two pounds of worms can eat a whole pound of fruits and vegetables and other waste. There would be less garbage for the school to send to the landfill.

Reason: Worms make compost.
Facts and examples:
Compost is natural food for plants. We could sell extra compost to make money for school projects.

40 • Grade 4

Name _____

Follow your teacher's directions to complete the activity.

1 Goal: _____

Reason:

Facts and examples:

Reason:

Facts and examples:

Reason:

Facts and examples:

2 On a separate sheet of paper, fill in a graphic organizer like the one above. Write your opinion. Then list reasons, facts, and examples that support it.

3 On a separate sheet of paper, prewrite a persuasive essay. You can also use what you have learned to improve an old plan.

Persuasive Essay: Prewriting • 41

✓ Corrective Feedback

IF . . . students find it hard to think of facts and examples that will persuade readers,

THEN . . . have them look for additional information related to their topics. Suggest that they consult magazines, newspapers, reference books, and news websites for ideas.

Focus Trait: Organization

Tell students that writers organize ideas in a way that persuades readers to agree with the writer's opinion. Explain that the most important reason should come last, right before the call to action, so that the reader feels convinced to take that action.

On the board, write the following topic: *Our school should grow a garden.*

Then write these reasons to support it.

(1) A school garden brings together students and adults in the community.

(2) School gardens encourage healthy eating.

(3) School gardens are attractive.

Help students organize the reasons from least to most important. (3, 1, 2)

Grade 4 • **41**

Writing Handbook Minilessons

Persuasive Essay

Minilesson 29

Using Your Prewriting Plan to Draft

Objective: Use an idea-support map to write a draft.

Guiding Question: How do I turn my prewriting into a persuasive essay?

Teach/Model—I Do

Direct students back to handbook p. 40 and point out the opinion in the idea-support map: *Our school needs a worm farm.* Then have students look at the reasons, facts, and examples that the writer lists. Explain that the writer states clear ideas and arranges them in a logical order so that this plan can be used to write a good persuasive essay.

Guided Practice—We Do

Work with students to turn information in the first box of the idea-support map on handbook p. 41 into a paragraph. Ask questions, such as *What is the main idea?* and *What are the supporting sentences?* Write students' suggestions on the board, work with them to choose the best ones, and then guide them to suggest transitions to connect their sentences.

Practice/Apply—You Do

COLLABORATIVE Have groups write a paragraph based on information in the second box of the idea-support map on handbook p. 41.

INDEPENDENT Have students revise their own idea-support maps. Remind them to state ideas clearly and arrange them logically, removing unnecessary ideas and moving ones that are out of order.

Conference/Evaluate

Have students share their prewriting plans to check that they are complete and accurate.

Minilesson 30

Drafting a Persuasive Essay

Objective: Plan a persuasive essay.

Guiding Question: How do I write a persuasive essay?

Teach/Model—I Do

Read aloud handbook p. 42. Point out that the beginning of this model states the writer's opinion and the body paragraphs support the opinion with reasons, facts, and examples. Remind students that a good persuasive essay has strong reasons arranged in order of importance as well as a final call to action.

Guided Practice—We Do

 Direct students to the frame on handbook p. 43. Tell them that, together, you will write a persuasive essay about how your school can help reduce energy costs by turning off lights when not in use, replacing regular light bulbs, and so on. Then, together, complete the frame using your prewriting plans from Minilessons 28 and 29 as a guide. Have students write in their books as you write on the board.

Practice/Apply—You Do

 COLLABORATIVE Have groups plan and complete Activity 2. They can use their prewriting plans from Minilesson 28 as a guide.

 INDEPENDENT Have students read and follow the directions for Activity 3. Tell them to use their prewriting plan from Lesson 15 or to make a new plan using Graphic Organizer 7.

Conference/Evaluate

As students draft, have them evaluate their work using the rubric on p. 104.

 Digital
• eBook
• WriteSmart
• Interactive Lessons

42 • Writing

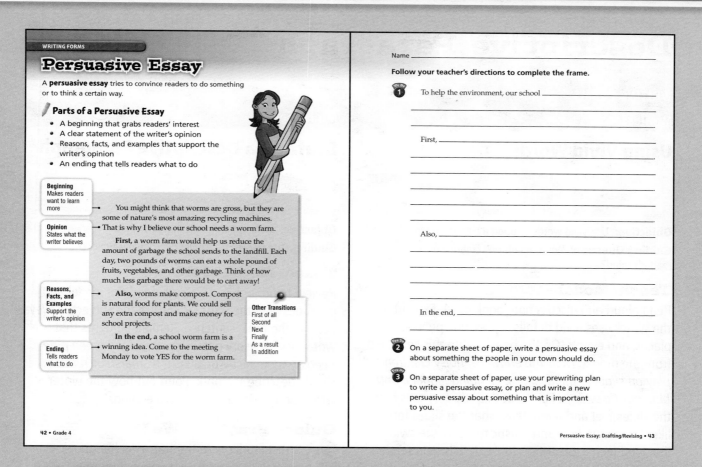

Persuasive Essay

A **persuasive essay** tries to convince readers to do something or to think a certain way.

Parts of a Persuasive Essay

- A beginning that grabs readers' interest
- A clear statement of the writer's opinion
- Reasons, facts, and examples that support the writer's opinion
- An ending that tells readers what to do

Beginning
Makes readers want to learn more

Opinion
States what the writer believes

Reasons, Facts, and Examples
Support the writer's opinion

Ending
Tells readers what to do

You might think that worms are gross, but they are some of nature's most amazing recycling machines. That is why I believe our school needs a worm farm.

First, a worm farm would help us reduce the amount of garbage the school sends to the landfill. Each day, two pounds of worms can eat a whole pound of fruits, vegetables, and other garbage. Think of how much less garbage there would be to cart away!

Also, worms make compost. Compost is natural food for plants. We could sell any extra compost and make money for school projects.

In the end, a school worm farm is a winning idea. Come to the meeting Monday to vote YES for the worm farm.

Other Transitions
First of all
Second
Next
Finally
As a result
In addition

42 • Grade 4

Name _____

Follow your teacher's directions to complete the frame.

1 To help the environment, our school _____
_____
_____

First, _____
_____
_____
_____
_____
_____

Also, _____
_____
_____
_____
_____

In the end, _____
_____

2 On a separate sheet of paper, write a persuasive essay about something the people in your town should do.

3 On a separate sheet of paper, use your prewriting plan to write a persuasive essay, or plan and write a new persuasive essay about something that is important to you.

Persuasive Essay: Drafting/Revising • 43

Corrective Feedback

IF . . . students have difficulty using their idea-support maps to draft persuasive essays,

THEN . . . have them go back to their idea-support maps and look at their reasons and the facts and examples they used to back them up. Suggest that students review their research notes or do further research to find additional persuasive reasons, facts, and examples. Then have them revise their idea-support maps.

Focus Trait: Evidence

Tell students that good writers include evidence in a persuasive essay so that readers can more easily make sense of the writer's argument. Point out that in the model the writer's argument is built on sound reasons that are backed up with persuasive facts and examples. Explain that reasons, facts, and examples must make sense to readers or they won't be persuaded.

On the board, write the following opinion: *Our town should plant more trees to help the environment.*

Then write these reasons on the board:

Trees are fun to play in.

Trees produce oxygen.

Trees are nice to look at.

Have students choose the reason that best supports this opinion. *(Trees produce oxygen.)* Then help students suggest facts and examples that will support this reason.

Grade 4 • **43**

Writing Handbook Minilessons

Descriptive Paragraph

Minilesson 31

Using Vivid Words

Objective: Use vivid words to bring a subject to life.

Guiding Question: What details will create a picture in a reader's mind?

Teach/Model—I Do

Read aloud and discuss handbook p. 44. Explain that the writer uses vivid details to describe people, places, and events. On the board, write this sentence from the model: *Near the entrance, noisy children play on slippery metal slides, climbing ladders, and blue plastic swings.* Point out that *slippery* tells how the slides feel and *metal* tells what the slides look like. The words *blue* and *plastic* tell how the swings look and feel. Explain that these details help readers picture the park in their minds.

Guided Practice—We Do

On the board, create a five-column chart with these headings: *Sight, Touch, Sound, Smell, Taste.* Work with students to find details in the model paragraph that appeal to one or more of these senses. Then write these details in the appropriate columns of the chart. Guide students to discuss how these details bring Bailey Park to life.

Practice/Apply—You Do

COLLABORATIVE Have groups choose three objects in the school. Then direct them to make charts with the headings *Look, Feel, Sound, Smell, Taste.* Have groups fill in the chart with vivid details that describe this object.

INDEPENDENT Have students make a list of vivid details to describe the school lunchroom.

Conference/Evaluate

Have students review their lists to make sure they have come up with clear, strong details.

Minilesson 32

Drafting a Descriptive Paragraph

Objective: Write a paragraph that describes.

Guiding Question: How will I describe my subject?

Teach/Model—I Do

Review handbook p. 44. Read aloud the model and point out how the writer identifies the subject, *Bailey Park*, in the topic sentence. Remind students that the writer uses sensory details such as *long green pine needles* and exact words such as *marsh* or *reeds* to clearly describe the park. Point out how the writer wraps up the description in the ending.

Guided Practice—We Do

 Direct students to the frame on handbook p. 45. Tell students that you will write a descriptive paragraph about a familiar place. Work with students to brainstorm a topic, such as your classroom or a favorite store. Then, together, complete the frame with vivid details and exact words. Have students write in their books as you write on the board.

Practice/Apply—You Do

 COLLABORATIVE Have groups plan and complete Activity 2. Encourage them to write about a well-known celebrity or community leader. Have groups share what they have written.

 INDEPENDENT Have students read and follow the directions. Tell them to use their prewriting plan from Lesson 16 or to brainstorm a new plan using Graphic Organizer 15.

Conference/Evaluate

As students draft, have them evaluate their work using the rubric on p. 104.

 Digital
• eBook
• WriteSmart
• Interactive Lessons

44 • Writing

Descriptive Paragraph

A **descriptive paragraph** describes, or tells about, a person, place, thing, or event. A descriptive paragraph helps create a picture in the reader's mind.

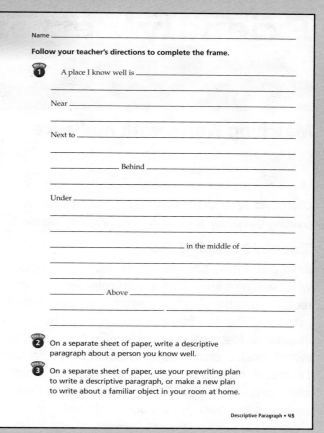

Parts of a Descriptive Paragraph

- A topic sentence that tells the subject of the paragraph
- Vivid details that clearly describe a person, place, thing, or event
- Strong words that help readers picture what is being described
- An ending that wraps up the description

Topic Sentence
Tells what the paragraph is about

Sensory Details
Tell how the subject looks, feels, sounds, smells, or tastes

Exact Words
Include specific nouns, verbs, and adjectives

Ending
Sums up the paragraph

Bailey Park is a great place to visit! A snack bar **next to** the parking lot sells yummy ice cream, cold drinks, popcorn, and other food. **Near** the entrance, noisy children play on slippery metal slides, climbing ladders, and blue plastic swings. Older kids race around the grassy soccer fields **behind** the swings. They also use the lighted basketball and tennis courts. There is a small picnic area **in the middle** of the park. You can eat your lunch **under** towering pine trees. Long green pine needles on the ground **by** the picnic tables feel as soft as a rug. Dad and I like to take the hiking trail **around** the marsh. It's a winding dirt path, which is marked with bright yellow triangles so you don't get lost. Sometimes, I hear frogs croaking in the reeds. Dad looks for interesting birds with his field glasses. Bailey Park has something for people of all ages.

Other Transitions
Above
Across
Below
Beside
Inside
Outside
At the bottom
Beyond

Name _____

Follow your teacher's directions to complete the frame.

1 A place I know well is _____

_____

Near _____

_____

Next to _____

_____

_____ Behind _____

Under _____

_____

_____ in the middle of _____

_____

_____ Above _____

_____

_____

2 On a separate sheet of paper, write a descriptive paragraph about a person you know well.

3 On a separate sheet of paper, use your prewriting plan to write a descriptive paragraph, or make a new plan to write about a familiar object in your room at home.

✓ Corrective Feedback

IF . . . students are having a hard time coming up with vivid details and exact words to describe their subject,

THEN . . . have them close their eyes and visualize the subject. Tell them to jot down words that describe what they might see, feel, hear, smell, or taste.

Focus Trait: Elaboration

Explain that in a descriptive paragraph, good writers include vivid details that can help the reader picture what is being described. In the model, for example, the writer says *Long green pine needles on the ground by the picnic tables feel as soft as a rug.* Point out that these kinds of details help convey what Bailey Park is like.

Write these sentences on the board:

Joe's Deli is dirty and crowded.

Joe's Deli is crammed with sagging wooden shelves packed with dusty cans.

Guide students to understand that the first sentence describes what Joe's Deli is like, but adding vivid details to the second sentence really makes it come alive. Ask *Which details in the second sentence help the reader picture the deli?* Elicit the words *crammed, wooden, sagging, packed,* and *dusty.*

Grade 4 • **45**

Writing Handbook Minilessons

Friendly Letter

WRITING FORMS

Minilesson 33

Matching Words with Audience

Objective: Select specific words and phrases for audience.

Guiding Question: How will my words affect my audience?

Teach/Model—I Do

Read and discuss handbook p. 46. Tell students that, when writing a letter, they should consider the recipient and the effect their words will have on that person. A letter to a friend or relative might be informal or friendly. A letter to a newspaper might be more formal. Explain that sentences in the model like *I was so excited* and *I'd love to see you* are informal and express the writer's feelings. Also note that these sentences will make Jenny's aunt feel good.

Guided Practice—We Do

On the board, write *You haven't been at school.* Work with students to make this sentence to a sick friend more personal. Explain that they can use informal words since the letter is to a friend and that they should think of things to say that would make the friend feel better, such as *I can't wait until you're back!* Write students' suggestions on the board.

Practice/Apply—You Do

COLLABORATIVE Have students imagine that they are writing a letter to an adult relative who has won a tennis tournament. On the board, write *I heard about the game.* Have groups write some words and phrases that would convey their excitement and make the relative feel good.

INDEPENDENT Have students imagine that they are writing a letter to a classmate who has lost her favorite bracelet. On the board, write *It's too bad about your bracelet.* Have students rewrite the sentence to show their sympathy for the classmate.

Conference/Evaluate

Encourage students to list precise words to describe how they feel and what happened.

46 • Writing

Minilesson 34

Drafting a Friendly Letter

Objective: Compose a friendly letter.

Guiding Question: How do I express my feelings and ideas in a friendly letter?

Teach/Model—I Do

With students, review handbook p. 46. Review the parts of the letter, including the address, date, greeting, closing, and signature. Draw students' attention to the commas used in the model. Remind them that the body of a friendly letter should have an informal, friendly voice. Go over the Closings box.

Guided Practice—We Do

 Direct students to the frame on handbook p. 47. Read the first line aloud. Have students suggest a recipient for the letter. Then help them plan details for the body of the letter. Guide students to suggest sentences to complete the frame. Have them write in their books as you write on the board.

Practice/Apply—You Do

 COLLABORATIVE Have small groups complete Activity 2. Tell them to choose a recipient, to decide on an event, to name it in the letter's opening sentence, and to include interesting details about it. Remind students to choose words with the recipient in mind.

 INDEPENDENT Have students read the directions. Tell them to use their prewriting plan from Lesson 17 or to brainstorm a new plan. Tell them to use correct letter form.

Conference/Evaluate

As students draft, circulate and help them choose words appropriate for their audiences. Evaluate using the rubric on p. 104.

 Digital
- eBook
- WriteSmart
- Interactive Lessons

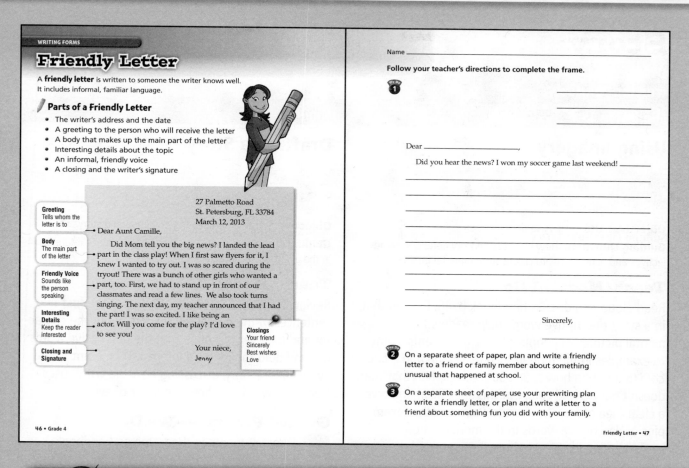

Friendly Letter

A **friendly letter** is written to someone the writer knows well. It includes informal, familiar language.

Parts of a Friendly Letter

- The writer's address and the date
- A greeting to the person who will receive the letter
- A body that makes up the main part of the letter
- Interesting details about the topic
- An informal, friendly voice
- A closing and the writer's signature

Greeting
Tells whom the letter is to

Body
The main part of the letter

Friendly Voice
Sounds like the person speaking

Interesting Details
Keep the reader interested

Closing and Signature

27 Palmetto Road
St. Petersburg, FL 33784
March 12, 2013

Dear Aunt Camille,

Did Mom tell you the big news? I landed the lead part in the class play! When I first saw flyers for it, I knew I wanted to try out. I was so scared during the tryout! There was a bunch of other girls who wanted a part, too. First, we had to stand up in front of our classmates and read a few lines. We also took turns singing. The next day, my teacher announced that I had the part! I was so excited. I like being an actor. Will you come for the play? I'd love to see you!

Your niece,
Jenny

Closings
Your friend
Sincerely
Best wishes
Love

46 • Grade 4

Name _____

Follow your teacher's directions to complete the frame.

1

_____
_____
_____

Dear _____,

Did you hear the news? I won my soccer game last weekend! _____

_____
_____
_____
_____
_____
_____
_____
_____

Sincerely,

_____

2 On a separate sheet of paper, plan and write a friendly letter to a friend or family member about something unusual that happened at school.

3 On a separate sheet of paper, use your prewriting plan to write a friendly letter, or plan and write a letter to a friend about something fun you did with your family.

Friendly Letter • 47

✓ Corrective Feedback

IF . . . students have difficulty choosing words to suit their audience,

THEN . . . have them consult a thesaurus and a dictionary to improve word choice. Tell them to make sure they check the definitions of unfamiliar synonyms before they use them in their writing.

✏ Focus Trait: Purpose

Explain to students that when their writing purpose is to write a friendly letter, they can use informal language. The language will sound like the words they would say aloud. Tell students to take a few minutes to think about expressions they use when talking with friends.

If necessary, prompt students by asking *How do you greet your friends? What do you say when you are excited?* Have volunteers share expressions and then record them on the board. Tell students that, when they write their letters, they should recall their purpose and use familiar expressions to capture their own personalities on the page.

Grade 4 • **47**

Writing Handbook Minilessons

Story

Minilesson 35

Using Imagery

Objective: Use imagery to describe.

Guiding Question: How can I use sensory details, vivid adjectives and active verbs to create strong mental images?

Teach/Model—I Do

Read aloud and discuss handbook p. 48. Explain that, in a story, descriptive words help readers form mental pictures of people, places, and events. Point to examples in the model, such as *like he had a bad cold* to describe how Juan sounded. Explain that Juan doesn't have a bad cold, but this specific image gives a clear idea of how he sounds. Point to other examples of descriptive words in the model or in classroom books. Discuss how these make the writing clear and interesting.

Guided Practice—We Do

On the board, write *The train conductor shouted.* Guide students to think about how they might make the sentence more descriptive, such as *The train conductor boomed like an elephant.*

Practice/Apply—You Do

COLLABORATIVE Write the following sentences on the board: *The bus stopped. The doors opened.* Have groups work together to add or change words or phrases to make the sentence more descriptive.

INDEPENDENT Have students choose two sentences from the model and use descriptive words to make them even more vivid.

Conference/Evaluate

Have students evaluate their sentences to make sure they have used descriptive words to make their stories come to life.

Minilesson 36

Drafting a Story

Objective: Write an interesting and engaging story.

Guiding Question: How can I keep my audience interested in the events and characters in my story?

Teach/Model—I Do

Review handbook p. 48. Point out that the first two sentences of the model tell readers about the character and the event. Explain that the descriptive words get and hold the reader's interest. Then point to the events in the story, discussing how the writer uses transition words to show the order of events.

Guided Practice—We Do

 Direct students to the frame on handbook p. 49. Say that, together, you will write a story about a boy who wants to win a spelling bee. Guide students to write a first line, such as *Even though he knew his words well, Michael was really nervous about the spelling bee.* Together, complete the frame by adding imagery and writing the steps the boy took to win. Have students write in their books as you write on the board.

Practice/Apply—You Do

 COLLABORATIVE Have pairs of students plan and complete Activity 2. Tell them to use descriptive words and sequence words. Have groups share what they have written.

 INDEPENDENT Have students read and follow the directions. Tell them to use their prewriting plan from Lesson 18 or to brainstorm a new plan using Graphic Organizer 10.

Conference/Evaluate

As students draft, have them evaluate their work using the rubric on p. 104.

 Digital
- eBook
- WriteSmart
- Interactive Lessons

48 • Writing

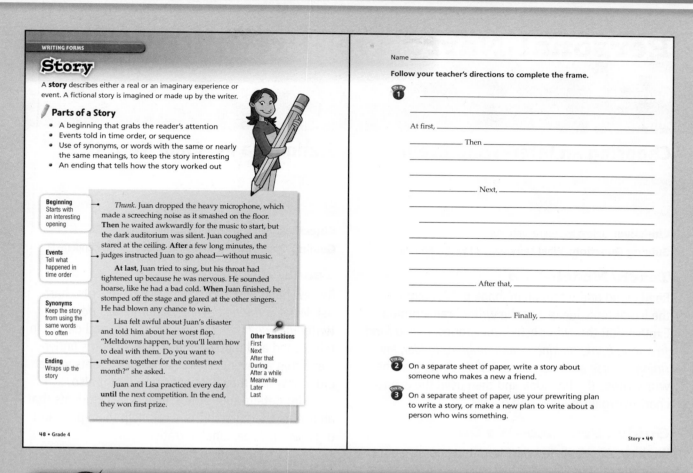

WRITING FORMS

Story

A **story** describes either a real or an imaginary experience or event. A fictional story is imagined or made up by the writer.

Parts of a Story

- A beginning that grabs the reader's attention
- Events told in time order, or sequence
- Use of synonyms, or words with the same or nearly the same meanings, to keep the story interesting
- An ending that tells how the story worked out

Beginning Starts with an interesting opening

Events Tell what happened in time order

Synonyms Keep the story from using the same words too often

Ending Wraps up the story

Thunk. Juan dropped the heavy microphone, which made a screeching noise as it smashed on the floor. **Then** he waited awkwardly for the music to start, but the dark auditorium was silent. Juan coughed and stared at the ceiling. **After** a few long minutes, the judges instructed Juan to go ahead—without music.

At last, Juan tried to sing, but his throat had tightened up because he was nervous. He sounded hoarse, like he had a bad cold. **When** Juan finished, he stomped off the stage and glared at the other singers. He had blown any chance to win.

Lisa felt awful about Juan's disaster and told him about her worst flop. "Meltdowns happen, but you'll learn how to deal with them. Do you want to rehearse together for the contest next month?" she asked.

Juan and Lisa practiced every day **until** the next competition. In the end, they won first prize.

Other Transitions
First
Next
After that
During
After a while
Meanwhile
Later
Last

Name ______

Follow your teacher's directions to complete the frame.

1 ______

At first, ______ Then ______

______ Next, ______

______ After that, ______

______ Finally, ______

2 On a separate sheet of paper, write a story about someone who makes a new a friend.

3 On a separate sheet of paper, use your prewriting plan to write a story, or make a new plan to write about a person who wins something.

Corrective Feedback

IF . . . students are having difficulty coming up with descriptive words and phrases,

THEN . . . have them form pictures in their minds of how a character acts or talks or how an event unfolds. Ask questions such as *What does the audience look like or do when the boy wins the spelling bee? Clap politely? Jump up and cheer loudly?* Once they have an image in their minds, have students describe it as they have pictured it.

Focus Trait: Elaboration

Tell students that, when writing a story, one way to elaborate and find just the right word or phrase is to look in a thesaurus. Explain that a thesaurus is a book that lists words and gives synonyms, or words that are similar in meaning, for each word. Point out that thesauruses list words in alphabetical order, like dictionaries. In addition, word processing programs often include a thesaurus.

Model using a thesaurus to find a synonym for a less descriptive word, such as *look*. On the board, write some of the words you find, such as *gaze, stare, glare,* and *peek*. Discuss how one of these words might be a more descriptive choice than *look*, and how it might help to elaborate to add meaning and clarity. Give another word, such as *walk*, and have students practice looking up words and their synonyms.

Writing Handbook Minilessons

Personal Narrative: Prewriting

Minilesson 37

Choosing an Interesting Event

Objective: Select an interesting true story.

Guiding Question: What story should I write about?

Teach/Model—I Do

Read aloud and discuss handbook p. 50. Point out the list of topic ideas that the writer brainstormed. Explain that the writer listed true stories: *giving food to a food bank, making a hummingbird feeder*, and *riding a horse at Windy Farm*. Tell students that the writer chose the first idea and then used the events chart to organize ideas and details.

Guided Practice—We Do

Work with students to brainstorm true stories about experiences your class has had, such as taking a field trip or listening to a guest speaker. Help students list suggestions on the board. Guide them to decide which experience would make the most interesting personal narrative. Have a volunteer put a star beside it.

Practice/Apply—You Do

COLLABORATIVE Have groups brainstorm a list of topics for true stories that happened to them. Have them select the topic that would be most interesting and that would have plenty of events and details to write about.

INDEPENDENT Have individuals brainstorm a list of topics for true stories and pick one that they would most like to write about. Remind students that they should be able to explain and justify their choices.

Conference/Evaluate

Remind students to consider whether their story has enough events and details to write about.

Minilesson 38

Planning a Personal Narrative

Objective: Plan a personal narrative.

Guiding Question: How will I tell about what happened?

Teach/Model—I Do

Review handbook p. 50. Point out the events chart. Ask *What is the first event? What details does the writer include?* Then discuss the events and details in the second and third sections. Help students understand that an events chart can outline events in the order in which they happened and that it also provides details about these events. Tell students that an events chart like this one can help them plan and organize their personal narratives.

Guided Practice—We Do

 Direct students to Activity 1 on handbook p. 51. Say that, together, you will create an events chart for the starred class story from Minilesson 37. Then, together, complete the chart with events and details that tell about this story. Have students write in their books as you write on the board.

Practice/Apply—You Do

 COLLABORATIVE Have groups plan and complete Activity 2. Tell them to work together to create an events chart and then share their work with other groups.

INDEPENDENT Have students read and follow the directions. Tell them to use their prewriting plan from Lesson 19 or brainstorm a new plan using either Graphic Organizer 4 or an events chart.

Conference/Evaluate

As students draft, have them evaluate their work using the rubric on p. 104.

 Digital • eBook • WriteSmart • Interactive Lessons

50 • Writing

Personal Narrative: Prewriting

A **personal narrative** tells about something that happened to the writer and describes how the writer feels about the events.

Prewriting for Personal Narrative

- Brainstorm a list of true stories that happened to you.
- Pick one story that made a strong impression on you.
- Use a graphic organizer to plan your writing.

Topic Ideas

Giving food to a food bank

Making a hummingbird feeder

Riding a horse at Windy Farm

Event: My class wanted to give food to a food bank.

Details: My uncle is a chef. He offered to give us cooking lessons at his restaurant.

Event: Class met at my uncle's restaurant.

Details: We unpacked our cooking tools. My uncle showed us how to make different dishes. My group made pumpkin pie.

Event: We took the food to the food bank.

Details: Ms. Chao, the head of the food bank, thanked us. She said it would be the best Thanksgiving food a lot of people had. Everyone clapped for us. I felt great.

---

50 • Grade 4

Name _____

Follow your teacher's directions to complete the activity.

1

> Event:
> Details:
>
> Event:
> Details:
>
> Event:
> Details:

2 On a separate sheet of paper, fill in a graphic organizer like the one above. Write your ideas for a personal narrative about something you did to help others.

3 On a separate sheet of paper, prewrite a personal narrative. You can also use what you have learned to improve an old plan.

Personal Narrative: Prewriting • 51

✓ Corrective Feedback

IF . . . students have difficulty thinking of details to include in their events charts,

THEN . . . have them ask themselves questions such as *Who? Where? What?* Explain that the answers to such questions help writers think of details that belong in their personal narratives.

Focus Trait: Organization

Tell students that writers organize their personal narratives in ways that help readers better understand the story. For example, writers often use time order to tell what happened since time order helps readers follow the story in the same order in which the events happened.

Explain that an events chart can help writers arrange the events and details of a personal narrative.

Write these sentences on the board:

(1) She showed us rough sketches for her new book.

(2) A children's book artist visited our class.

(3) We asked her questions about her sketches.

Have students explain how they would use an events chart to organize these events in time order (2, 1, 3). Elicit details they might add to the chart.

Grade 4 • **51**

Writing Handbook Minilessons

Personal Narrative

Minilesson 39

Keeping Readers Interested

Objective: Use details that will bring a narrative to life.

Guiding Question: How will I keep my readers interested?

Teach/Model—I Do

Read aloud and discuss handbook p. 52. Explain that the beginning of the model grabs the reader's interest with a question. Point out that the writer makes the story more interesting by including details about the experience and how people felt about it. Illustrate this by pointing out the descriptive details in the second paragraph: *My group made pumpkin pie.* Also, point out the dialogue at the end, which brings Ms. Chao and her feelings to life.

Guided Practice—We Do

Work with students to add interesting details to your events charts from Activity 1 on handbook p. 51. Ask *Which details will help readers picture what happened? Which details will help readers understand our feelings about what happened?* Have students write their ideas in their events charts as you write on the board.

Practice/Apply—You Do

COLLABORATIVE Have groups discuss their events charts from Activity 2 on handbook p. 51. Tell them to add descriptive details to their events charts. Remind them to include details about the experience and how people felt about it.

INDEPENDENT Have students brainstorm details and feelings about their events charts from Activity 3 on handbook p. 51. Have them add descriptive details to their events charts.

Conference/Evaluate

Have students share their revised charts with you to make sure they added appropriate details. Remind them that they can also add dialogue to bring feelings and experiences to life.

52 • Writing

Minilesson 40

Drafting a Personal Narrative

Objective: Write a personal narrative.

Guiding Question: What will I tell readers about my experience?

Teach/Model—I Do

Review handbook p. 52. Refer to the callouts and have students identify the parts of a personal narrative: the *beginning, the events and details of the body paragraphs,* and the *ending.*

Guided Practice—We Do

 Direct students to the frame on handbook p. 53. Tell students that you will work together to write about a class experience. Have students complete the first sentence. Then, together, complete the frame with interesting events and details. Use your prewriting plan from handbook p. 51 as a guide. Have students write in their books as you write on the board.

Practice/Apply—You Do

 COLLABORATIVE Have groups plan and complete Activity 2. Encourage them to write about a class activity, such as a musical performance. Have groups share their work.

 INDEPENDENT Have students read and follow the directions. Tell them to use their prewriting plan from handbook p. 51 or to brainstorm a new plan using either Graphic Organizer 4 or an events chart.

Conference/Evaluate

Have students review their drafts to be sure they have told events in time order and included the kind of details that will keep readers interested.

 Digital
• eBook
• WriteSmart
• Interactive Lessons

Personal Narrative

A **personal narrative** is a true story about something that happened to the writer. It tells how the writer feels about the events.

Parts of a Personal Narrative
- A beginning that grabs readers' interest
- Events that really happened to the writer, told in time order
- Interesting details about the events
- The writer's feelings about what happened

Beginning
Makes readers want to find out more

Events
Tell what happened in time order

Interesting Details
Include sights, sounds, and feelings

Ending
Tells how the writer felt

Have you ever wanted to be a chef? Everyone in my class got to be one this year. We wanted to donate food to a food bank. My uncle is a chef, and he offered to give us cooking lessons at his restaurant.

To start, the class met at the restaurant and unpacked our tools. **Then** my uncle showed us how to make different dishes. My group made pumpkin pie. It was hard work, but it was worth it!

Finally, we packed up the food and took it to the food bank. The head of the food bank, Ms. Chao, was waiting for us.

"This will be the best Thanksgiving food a lot of people have ever had! Thank you!" she said. **At the end,** everyone clapped for us, and I felt great.

Other Transitions
First
Second
During
After a while
Meanwhile
Later
Last

52 • Grade 4

Name _____

Follow your teacher's directions to complete the frame.

1   I had an amazing time when our class went _____

_____

To start, _____

_____

_____ Then _____

_____

_____

_____

_____

_____ Later, _____

_____

_____

_____ Last, _____

_____

2   On a separate sheet of paper, write a personal narrative about one of the best things you ever did with your class.

3   On a separate sheet of paper, use your prewriting plan to write a personal narrative, or plan and write a new personal narrative about something you or your class did that helped other people.

Personal Narrative: Drafting/Revising • 53

Corrective Feedback

IF . . . students have difficulty organizing and drafting their personal narratives,

THEN . . . have them tell a classmate what happened so that, together, they can review events and come up with more details. Also remind students to use appropriate transitions to make the order of events clear.

Focus Trait: Development

Tell students that writers usually get and develop their ideas during the prewriting phase of a writing project. However, writers can still develop or add ideas while they are drafting or revising a piece of writing.

Direct students to the model on page 52 and tell them to imagine that they are revising this personal narrative. Ask *Wouldn't it be good to show how some of the other students enjoyed this experience? And wouldn't it be good to discuss some of the other dishes the students made?*

Point out that these are ideas that could be added during either the drafting or revising phases. Then work with students to list possible details that might develop these ideas, such as:

My friend Alma thought it was the best Thanksgiving she had ever had, too.

We also made turkey, cranberry sauce, and mashed potatoes.

Grade 4 • 53

Writing Handbook Minilessons

Summary

Minilesson 41

Using Your Own Words

Objective: Use your own words to summarize.

Guiding Question: How do I retell a story in my own words?

Teach/Model—I Do

With students, read and discuss Parts of a Story Summary and the model on handbook p. 54. Explain that, in a summary, writers use their own words to tell about the most important events in a story. Point out the part of the model that says *On the day of the test, there is a horrible storm.* Then read the description from the text *It was one of those storms where the rain came down in washtubs, but the stage was scheduled to go.* Point out how the summary gives just the essential information about what happened.

Guided Practice—We Do

Choose a reading selection the whole class has read. Then work together to identify the main events in the text. Write the events on the board. Have volunteers summarize the selection in their own words.

Practice/Apply—You Do

COLLABORATIVE Choose a passage from a story, such as "The World According to Humphrey," and write it on the board: *They talked and talked and Dad got out some cards and they played a game called Crazy Eights and another one called Pig where they put their fingers on their noses and laughed like hyenas.* Have groups work together to summarize the passage.

INDEPENDENT Have students choose another passage from the same story and summarize it in their own words.

Conference/Evaluate

Circulate and help students determine which details are important and which are not needed.

Minilesson 42

Drafting a Summary

Objective: Write a summary of the main events in a story.

Guiding Question: How can I describe what a story is about in a few sentences?

Teach/Model—I Do

Have students review handbook p. 54. Read the model aloud, pointing out the topic sentence, the story problem, the main events, and the boldfaced transitions. Go over the list in the Other Transitions box.

Guided Practice—We Do

 Help students choose a reading selection to summarize. Guide them to name the story problem and the important events. Write phrases they suggest on the board. Then work with students to put those events into sentences to complete the frame. Have students write in their books as you write on the board.

Practice/Apply—You Do

 COLLABORATIVE Have small groups plan and complete Activity 2. Have them choose a story, list the story's problem and important events, and then fill in the frame. Remind them to use transitions to organize and link ideas. Groups can then share their writing.

 INDEPENDENT Have students read the directions. Tell them to use their prewriting plan from Lesson 21 or to brainstorm a new plan using Graphic Organizer 4.

Conference/Evaluate

As students draft, circulate and help them determine which details are important and which are not needed in a summary. Evaluate using the rubric on p. 104.

 Digital • eBook • WriteSmart • Interactive Lessons

54 • Writing

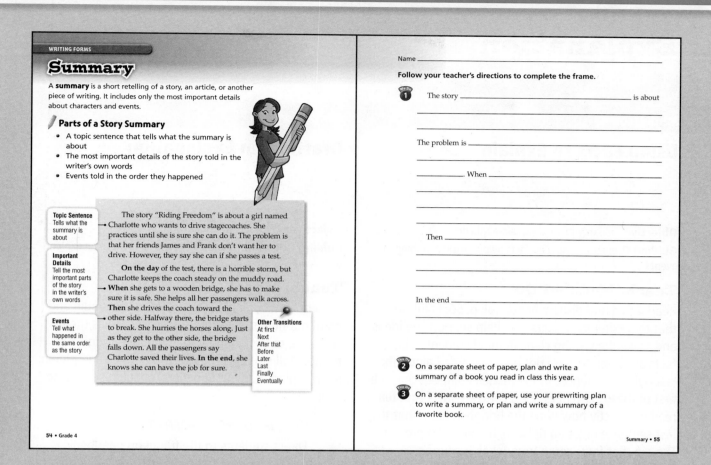

Summary

A **summary** is a short retelling of a story, an article, or another piece of writing. It includes only the most important details about characters and events.

Parts of a Story Summary

- A topic sentence that tells what the summary is about
- The most important details of the story told in the writer's own words
- Events told in the order they happened

Topic Sentence Tells what the summary is about

Important Details Tell the most important parts of the story in the writer's own words

Events Tell what happened in the same order as the story

The story "Riding Freedom" is about a girl named Charlotte who wants to drive stagecoaches. She practices until she is sure she can do it. The problem is that her friends James and Frank don't want her to drive. However, they say she can if she passes a test.

On the day of the test, there is a horrible storm, but Charlotte keeps the coach steady on the muddy road. **When** she gets to a wooden bridge, she has to make sure it is safe. She helps all her passengers walk across. **Then** she drives the coach toward the other side. Halfway there, the bridge starts to break. She hurries the horses along. Just as they get to the other side, the bridge falls down. All the passengers say Charlotte saved their lives. **In the end**, she knows she can have the job for sure.

Other Transitions
At first
Next
After that
Before
Later
Last
Finally
Eventually

54 • Grade 4

Name

Follow your teacher's directions to complete the frame.

1 The story _____ is about

_____

_____

The problem is _____

_____

_____ When _____

_____

Then _____

_____

_____

In the end _____

_____

_____

2 On a separate sheet of paper, plan and write a summary of a book you read in class this year.

3 On a separate sheet of paper, use your prewriting plan to write a summary, or plan and write a summary of a favorite book.

Summary • 55

Corrective Feedback

IF . . . students have trouble deciding what is important to include in their summary,

THEN . . . have them ask themselves the *five Ws and an H: who? what? when? where? why? how?* Their summary should briefly answer all of these questions.

Focus Trait: Evidence

Remind students that a summary does not have to include every detail from a story. Removing unimportant details will make a summary clearer and easier to understand. Write the following on the board:

The television was broken. Andrew liked to watch shows about gadgets. Andrew and his sister went outside. They played a game with their neighbors.

Ask students to identify which detail in the paragraph is less important than the others. (*Andrew liked to watch shows about gadgets.*) Have students suggest ways to rewrite the paragraph to include only important details.

Grade 4 • **55**

Writing Handbook Minilessons

Explanation

Minilesson 43

Using Facts to Explain

Objective: Identify facts to explain nonfiction text.

Guiding Question: How do facts help to explain a thing or event?

Teach/Model—I Do

Read aloud and discuss handbook p. 56. Point out that the writer gave facts that help support the ideas and make the writing clear. Remind students that facts are true; they are not opinions. Read aloud the last pair of sentences in the model. Point out that the first of these sentences gives concrete facts that tell readers exactly how wide the bridge is. Note that the last sentence gives an opinion; it cannot be proven. Explain that facts come from reliable sources— books, encyclopedias, and websites—and that writers should verify, or check, facts they use.

Guided Practice—We Do

Work with students to think of facts that might be added to make the model even more interesting *(its height, people who explored the area)*. Then work with students to write, on the board, other explanatory text topics, such as *How was the Lincoln Memorial built?* Work with students to write several facts about the topic you would like to know, such as *Who built it? What material was used?*

Practice/Apply—You Do

COLLABORATIVE Tell groups to use the topic *Bronx Zoo* for generating facts. Have them write a list of details they would need to learn to explain their topic.

INDEPENDENT Have students choose another topic and list facts they would need to find out in order to explain the topic.

Conference/Evaluate

Have students evaluate their lists to make sure they refer to facts they would need to look up.

56 • Writing

Minilesson 44

Drafting an Explanation

Objective: Use facts to explain a thing or event.

Guiding Question: How can I use facts to make an explanation clearer?

Teach/Model—I Do

Review handbook p. 56. Read aloud the model and point out how the writer uses facts, such as the first sentence, to explain how the Rainbow Bridge was formed. Tell students that they may voice an opinion in an explanation but in general should use facts to support it.

Guided Practice—We Do

 Direct students to the frame on handbook p. 57. Mention that, together, you will write an explanation about how the Washington Monument was built. Model how to look up facts on reputable websites. Then work with students to write an introduction and add facts such as *The Washington Monument reaches more than 555 feet in height.* Together complete the frame. Have students write in their books as you write on the board.

Practice/Apply—You Do

 COLLABORATIVE Have groups plan and complete Activity 2. Tell them to use websites, books, and encyclopedias to find facts. Have groups share what they have written.

 INDEPENDENT Have students read and follow the directions. Tell them to use their prewriting plan from Lesson 22 or brainstorm a new plan using Graphic Organizer 3.

Conference/Evaluate

As students draft, have them evaluate their work using the rubric on p. 104.

 Digital
• eBook
• WriteSmart
• Interactive Lessons

Explanation

An **explanation** is writing that explains, or tells why or how something happens. The purpose of an explanation is to give readers information about a topic.

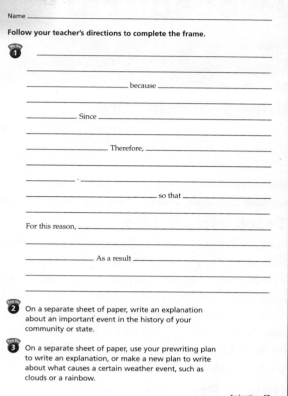

Parts of an Explanation

- A beginning that introduces the topic
- Information that is organized in a way that makes sense
- Facts and examples that support the topic
- An ending that sums up the main points

Beginning Tells what the explanation is about	Rainbow Bridge in southern Utah was formed millions of years ago. Rain and melted snow ran down Navajo Mountain. **When** the water flowed off the mountain, it created Bridge Creek. As the creek flowed toward the Colorado River, it passed through a canyon.
Organization Presents information in a way that makes sense	For centuries, the creek washed over layers of rock in the canyon. The rushing water slowly wore away the rock **so that** it created thin rock walls. Eventually, the water broke through the thin walls and made a hole. **As a result**, a colorful stone bridge was
Facts and Examples Include details that help develop the explanation	carved out of the rock. The bottom of the bridge is reddish brown. The top is pink with dark red streaks. These rich colors come from iron and other minerals. Today, Rainbow Bridge arches high above Bridge Creek. It stretches more than 200 feet from
Ending Draws the explanation to a close	one side to the other. Rainbow Bridge is one of the world's natural wonders!

Other Transitions
Because
Thus
Therefore
Consequently
In order to
Since
Accordingly
For this reason

56 • Grade 4

Name _____

Follow your teacher's directions to complete the frame.

1 _____
_____
_____ because _____
_____
_____ Since _____
_____
_____ Therefore, _____
_____
_____ . _____
_____ so that _____
_____
For this reason, _____
_____
_____ As a result _____
_____
_____

2 On a separate sheet of paper, write an explanation about an important event in the history of your community or state.

3 On a separate sheet of paper, use your prewriting plan to write an explanation, or make a new plan to write about what causes a certain weather event, such as clouds or a rainbow.

Explanation • 57

Corrective Feedback

IF . . . students are having a hard time coming up with facts,

THEN . . . remind them that a fact is something that can be proven. For example, *The Washington Monument is 555 feet and 5 1/8 inches tall* can be proven because the monument can be measured. Have students write down a few facts and opinions, exchange papers with partners, and discuss which items are facts and which are opinions.

Focus Trait: Elaboration

Tell students that, when they write an explanation, they can make it more interesting by elaborating and using details. Write the following sentences on the board: *The Amazon River is long. It is the second longest river in the world.* Help volunteers connect the sentences to make the details clearer. *(The Amazon River is the second longest river in the world.)* Explain that there are other ways to use elaboration to make sentences clearer, such as breaking up sentences that are too long, beginning sentences in different ways, and varying the lengths of the sentences. Using the model, have students identify specific examples of elaboration that are clear and show the meaning the writer intends. Then have students revise their own explanations to make their sentences clear.

Grade 4 • **57**

Procedural Composition

WRITING FORMS

Minilesson 45

Using Sequential Order

Objective: Use sequential order for sets of instructions.

Guiding Question: How can I best show the order of steps?

Teach/Model—I Do

Point to the model on handbook p. 58. Tell students that, when they write instructions for a Procedural Composition, they need to plan and organize their ideas in sequential, or time, order. Point out the steps shown in the model, and explain that they are in exactly the same order in which the process should be done. Emphasize this by making a flow chart that shows the steps in order.

Guided Practice—We Do

On the board, write a set of instructions out of order. For example: *Rinse your mouth. Move the toothbrush up and down to clean your teeth. Put toothpaste on your toothbrush.* Draw a flow chart on the board and help students place the steps in sequential order.

Practice/Apply—You Do

COLLABORATIVE On the board, write another set of instructions, such as *Dry your hands on a towel. Turn on warm water. Rub your hands together under the water for at least twenty seconds.* Have groups use flowcharts to organize the steps in sequential order.

INDEPENDENT Write a third set of instructions on the board, such as *Press the two slices of bread together. Spread peanut butter on one slice of bread. Spread jelly on another slice of bread.* Have students work on their own to make a flow chart that puts the steps in sequential order.

Conference/Evaluate

With students, clarify how steps build upon one another as the process is carried out. Use questions, such as *Should you press the two slices of bread together before or after you put peanut butter on one slice?*

58 • Writing

Minilesson 46

Drafting a Procedural Composition

Objective: Compose clear and sequential instructions.

Guiding Question: How can I explain how to do something?

Teach/Model—I Do

Discuss the model, pointing out the topic sentence, the steps in the process, and the boldfaced transitions on handbook p. 58. Go over the list in the Other Transitions box. Then suggest a familiar process, such as preparing cereal for breakfast. List the steps involved and number them.

Guided Practice—We Do

 1 Point out the topic sentence in the frame on handbook p. 59. Ask students to name steps they might take to prepare for an important test. Choose four of those suggestions and help students identify the order in which they should be completed. Together, write sentences to complete the frame. Have students write in their books as you write on the board.

Practice/Apply—You Do

 2 **COLLABORATIVE** Have groups plan and complete Activity 2. Have them decide on a simple process to describe and then list the steps involved. Have groups share and discuss their writing.

 3 **INDEPENDENT** Have students read the directions. Tell them to use their prewriting plan from Lesson 23 or to brainstorm a new plan using Graphic Organizer 4.

Conference/Evaluate

Circulate and help students choose transitions that organize ideas sequentially. Evaluate using the rubric on p. 104.

 Digital
- eBook
- WriteSmart
- Interactive Lessons

Procedural Composition

A **procedural composition** tells how to do something. It presents step-by-step directions for how to complete a process.

Parts of a Procedural Composition

- A topic sentence that tells what readers will learn
- Steps in the process that are arranged in sequential order
- Transitions that make the order clear
- A conclusion, or ending, that tells the outcome of the process

Topic Sentence
Names the process

Steps
Tells what to do in sequence

Transitions
Make the order clear

Conclusion
Tells what results from following the steps

You can show the beauty of fall by drying colorful leaves for art projects. **First,** find leaves on the ground. Maple leaves are very pretty and great to use. **Before** you bring the leaves inside, shake off any water or bugs. **Next,** press the leaves between two paper towels to get rid of any water. **After that,** put each leaf between two sheets of paper. **Then** put your leaf-and-paper sandwich inside a thick, heavy book. Close the book and stack another big book on top. **After about two weeks,** your leaves should **finally** be dry. Your dried leaves can make colorful bookmarks. You can also paste leaves onto colored paper to make art to decorate your walls. You can even string them together to make yourself a beautiful chain of leaves to wear around your neck or wrist!

Other Transitions
Meanwhile
Later
Last
Second
Third

Name _____

Follow your teacher's directions to complete the frame.

1 Preparing for a big test takes time, energy, and concentration.

First, _____

_____ Next, _____

_____

_____

_____

Then _____

_____

_____

_____

_____ After that, _____

_____

_____

_____

Finally, _____

2 On a separate sheet of paper, plan and write a procedural composition about how to make your favorite craft project or healthy snack.

3 On a separate sheet of paper, use your prewriting plan to write a procedural composition, or plan and write a new procedural composition for something you do every day.

Corrective Feedback

IF . . . students have difficulty including all the necessary steps in their instructions,

THEN . . . have them draw separate, simple cartoons of the steps they can visualize in the process. Have them arrange the cartoons in order and then ask a partner to "narrate" the process. Any missing steps should become obvious.

Focus Trait: Organization

Tell students that they can do two things that can help organize information in sequential order. First, they can write the descriptions of steps in order in their instructions. Then they can use transition words to make the order and connections clear. On the board, write:

Buy soil, seeds, and trays. Fill trays with soil. Plant seeds one inch apart. Water seeds daily. Watch them sprout.

Review the boldfaced transition words in the model and the Other Transitions on handbook p. 58. Then have students suggest transitions to add to the paragraph on the board. Remind them that their transitions should make the paragraph clearer and flow more smoothly. Possible answer:

Before you begin, buy soil, seeds, and trays. First, fill trays with soil. Next, plant seeds one inch apart. Then, water seeds daily. Finally, watch them sprout.

Grade 4 • **59**

Research Report: Prewriting

WRITING FORMS

Minilesson 47

Seeking an Answer to a Question

Objective: Use the Internet to find answers to questions.

Guiding Question: What words can I use to find an answer to questions on the Internet?

Teach/Model—I Do

Read aloud and discuss handbook p. 60. Explain that writers often use the Internet to find information for reports. Point to section II and explain that it answers the question, *What are some threats to bald eagles?* Discuss how to use a shortened form of this question as key words for a search engine. Note that key words need not always be in the form of a question but that they should always be as brief and specific as possible. Write *bald eagle threats* on the board and discuss why this phrase would be useful for finding information.

Guided Practice—We Do

On the board, write a research question, such as *How far away is the moon from Earth?* Write student suggestions for key words for an Internet search for the answers to this question. Work with students to practice leaving out unimportant words and emphasizing important ones (for example, *distance Earth moon*).

Practice/Apply—You Do

COLLABORATIVE Write several other research questions, such as *What are the different kinds of squirrels?* or *What important things did President Abraham Lincoln do?* Have groups choose one question and write key words for an Internet search.

INDEPENDENT Have students choose another question and write key words on their own.

Conference/Evaluate

Have students evaluate their key words to determine if they will answer the question.

60 • Writing

Minilesson 48

Using an Outline to Organize

Objective: Make an organized outline with main topics.

Guiding Question: What main topics belong in my outline?

Teach/Model—I Do

Review handbook p. 60. Explain that in an outline, main topics follow Roman numerals and details follow capital or lower-case letters. Point out the organization of the outline, showing how the first main idea includes general facts about the bald eagle and the second includes threats to bald eagles. Tell students that an outline should organize information in a logical manner like this.

Guided Practice—We Do

 Direct students to Activity 1 on handbook p. 61. Tell them that, together, you will write an outline about grizzly bears. Work with students to find information on the Internet. On the board, write main ideas such as *physical description*. Help students discuss which main ideas and details to include as well as ways to organize the outline. Guide them to complete the frame. Have students write in their books as you write on the board.

Practice/Apply—You Do

 COLLABORATIVE Have groups plan and complete Activity 2. Have groups share what they have written.

 INDEPENDENT Have students read and follow the directions. Tell them to use their prewriting plan from Lesson 24 or brainstorm a new plan using an outline.

Conference/Evaluate

As students draft, have them evaluate their work using the rubric on p. 104.

 Digital
- eBook
- WriteSmart
- Interactive Lessons

Research Report: Prewriting

A **research report** uses facts and details from outside sources to inform readers about a topic.

✏ Prewriting

- First, choose a topic for your research report.
- Then do research about your topic. Jot down notes on index cards.
- Using your notes, make an outline to organize your report. Each main topic in your outline will be a paragraph in your report.

Outline

I. **Bald eagle**
   A. Called "America's bird"
   B. Seen on pictures, coins, flags

II. **Threats to bald eagles**
   A. Hurt by use of pesticide called DDT
   B. Disappeared in some parts of U.S.
   C. EPA - only 412 pairs in U.S. in 1950

III. **How bald eagles were saved**
   A. Listed as endangered in 1967
   B. Government banned DDT
   C. About 115,000 eagles in U.S. by 1990s
   D. Taken off endangered list in 2007

Name _____

Follow your teacher's directions to complete the activity.

1

Outline

I. _____
   A. _____
   B. _____
   C. _____

II. _____
   A. _____
   B. _____
   C. _____

III. _____
   A. _____
   B. _____
   C. _____

 2 On a separate sheet of paper, create an outline like the one above. Then outline the main ideas and supporting facts and details that you will use in a report about an endangered animal.

 3 On a separate sheet of paper, prewrite an outline for a research report. You can also use what you have learned to improve an old outline.

✔ Corrective Feedback

IF . . . students are having a hard time coming up with key words for research,

THEN . . . have them work with the indexes of various informational texts. Explain that the terms found in an index often include key words that can help readers find information on the Internet. For example, in a book about the cardinal, possible index terms might be *habitat* or *life cycle*. Have students choose a few key words from an index and then study the page or pages on which they find information about those key words. Then have them practice using these key words for an Internet search.

✏ Focus Trait: Organization

Tell students that outlining is a good way to organize ideas. However, some students may find that once they begin outlining, their topics are too broad and their outline is too long. Explain that when this happens, writers can narrow their topic focus by asking questions such as *What kind?* For example, if a student's topic is *Owls*, one way to narrow the topic is to focus on one kind of owl, such as the barn owl.

Model narrowing the number of ideas in a report by narrowing the topic. Write *Flags* on the board and ask students to name kinds of flags, such as their state flag or the American flag. Point out that now that the topic has been narrowed, it is easier to research and write about it. Write several other broad topics on the board, such as *Flowers*, *State Symbols*, and *Dogs*, and have students come up with narrower topics by asking *What kind?*

Grade 4 • **61**

Writing Handbook Minilessons

Research Report

Minilesson 49

Avoiding Plagiarism

Objective: Write in your own words to avoid plagiarism.

Guiding Question: How can I use information from other sources and rewrite it in my own words?

Teach/Model—I Do

Read aloud and discuss handbook p. 62. Explain that the facts the writer used came from research sources and that the writer paraphrased them, or rewrote them in his or her own words. Tell students that *plagiarism* is copying someone else's writing word for word and that it should never be done. Find a passage from a book and then model how to paraphrase it, reading the passage aloud, closing the book, and then rewriting what you read in your own words.

Guided Practice—We Do

Write a sentence on the board from a book or website, such as *Visitors look in wonder at the one-mile deep, 277-mile long Grand Canyon.* Read the passage aloud several times and then erase it. Work with students to rewrite the sentence in their own words. For example: *The Grand Canyon is one mile deep and 277 miles long. It is a thrilling sight.*

Practice/Apply—You Do

COLLABORATIVE Have students find a passage from an informational text and read it several times. As they read, tell them to note key ideas and details and paraphrase them. Then have students close the book and rewrite the passage in their own words

INDEPENDENT Have students choose another passage and rewrite it in their own words.

Conference/Evaluate

Have students compare their rewrites with the original sources to make sure they didn't plagiarize.

Minilesson 50

Drafting a Research Report

Objective: Draft a research report with an introduction, facts to support main ideas, and a conclusion.

Guiding Question: What ideas do I want to include in my draft?

Teach/Model—I Do

Review handbook p. 62. Explain that this is the writer's final version; before writing this, the writer first did research and wrote an outline and then wrote a first draft. Point out that first drafts help writers get down ideas that they can revise later.

Guided Practice—We Do

 Direct students to the frame on handbook p. 63. With students review the research and outline you did together in Minilesson 48. Work with them to write a first draft based on the notes and outline. Write suggestions for one of the main ideas on the board, such as *description: Grizzly bears can weigh up to 790 pounds or more.* Together, complete the frame. Have students write in their books as you write on the board.

Practice/Apply—You Do

 COLLABORATIVE Have groups complete Activity 2. Remind them that they will revise and proofread later. Have groups share their work.

 INDEPENDENT Have students read and follow the directions. Tell them to use their prewriting plan from Lesson 25 or brainstorm a new plan using an outline.

Conference/Evaluate

As students draft, have them evaluate their work using the rubric or on p. 104.

Digital • eBook • WriteSmart • Interactive Lessons

62 • Writing

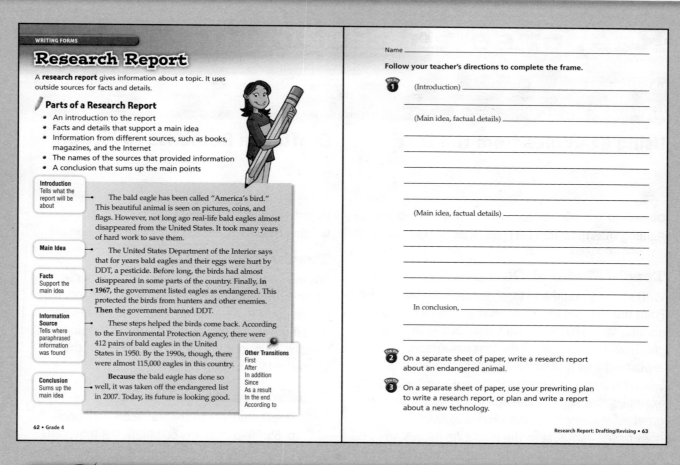

Research Report

A **research report** gives information about a topic. It uses outside sources for facts and details.

Parts of a Research Report

- An introduction to the report
- Facts and details that support a main idea
- Information from different sources, such as books, magazines, and the Internet
- The names of the sources that provided information
- A conclusion that sums up the main points

Introduction
Tells what the report will be about

The bald eagle has been called "America's bird." This beautiful animal is seen on pictures, coins, and flags. However, not long ago real-life bald eagles almost disappeared from the United States. It took many years of hard work to save them.

Main Idea

The United States Department of the Interior says that for years bald eagles and their eggs were hurt by DDT, a pesticide. Before long, the birds had almost disappeared in some parts of the country. Finally, **in 1967**, the government listed eagles as endangered. This protected the birds from hunters and other enemies. **Then** the government banned DDT.

Facts
Support the main idea

Information Source
Tells where paraphrased information was found

These steps helped the birds come back. According to the Environmental Protection Agency, there were 412 pairs of bald eagles in the United States in 1950. By the 1990s, though, there were almost 115,000 eagles in this country.

Other Transitions
First
After
In addition
Since
As a result
In the end
According to

Conclusion
Sums up the main idea

Because the bald eagle has done so well, it was taken off the endangered list in 2007. Today, its future is looking good.

62 • Grade 4

Name _____

Follow your teacher's directions to complete the frame.

1 (Introduction) _____

(Main idea, factual details) _____

(Main idea, factual details) _____

In conclusion, _____

2 On a separate sheet of paper, write a research report about an endangered animal.

3 On a separate sheet of paper, use your prewriting plan to write a research report, or plan and write a report about a new technology.

Research Report: Drafting/Revising • 63

✓ Corrective Feedback

IF . . . students are having a hard time rewriting information in their own words,

THEN . . . have them use a thesaurus to find synonyms for words in the original passage. Explain that they can find synonyms for words in the original text and use these words when they paraphrase. Emphasize that it takes more than simply replacing words with synonyms to avoid plagiarism, however; have them practice using different sentence structures or even breaking up a long sentence or combining several short ones.

Focus Trait: Elaboration

Tell students that when they write a research report, it is important to elaborate on your ideas by using descriptive words that create a mental picture for the reader. Nouns and adjectives should be specific, not general, and there should be strong, specific action verbs as well. On the board, write *Grizzlies have blond to black fur with white or gray ends.* Ask students to point to "dull" or "overly general" words. Then ask students to offer suggestions for improving them. For example, the opening words could be replaced with the more vivid words. Likewise, the rest of the sentence can be made both more vivid and more precise (for example: *Grizzlies range in color from golden blond to dark black, with fur that usually glistens with white or gray tips.*)

Grade 4 • **63**

Response to Fiction

WRITING FORMS

Minilesson 51

Using Examples from the Text

Objective: Use examples from a text to support a response.

Guiding Question: How can I support my opinion about a text with examples?

Teach/Model—I Do

With students, read and then discuss handbook p. 64. Point out that the model gives the writer's opinion about a story character and supports it with examples from the story. Read the first paragraph, explaining that it states the reader's opinion that Stormy is a great character. Point out reasons and examples that support the opinion (reasons: *he's a great adventurer, he's courageous*; examples: *he goes to sea, farms, sees the world; he battles an octopus*). Explain that words such as *for instance* and *in addition* help link the opinion and reasons.

Guided Practice—We Do

Help students choose a story they all have read and guide them to give opinions about a character in it. Then help students identify examples that support their opinions.

Practice/Apply—You Do

COLLABORATIVE Guide students to look back at another story they read together. Have small groups write a sentence stating their opinion of a character. Then ask groups to write at least one example from the story that supports the opinion.

INDEPENDENT Have students write a sentence stating their opinion of another character from the same story. Have them find one or two examples in the story to support their opinion.

Conference/Evaluate

Encourage students having trouble writing an opinion to use judgment words, such as *think, feel, believe, best,* or *worst*. Point out that these words are used to state opinions and personal feelings about a topic.

64 • Writing

Minilesson 52

Drafting a Response to Fiction

Objective: Write a response to fiction.

Guiding Question: How can I best support my opinion?

Teach/Model—I Do

Review handbook p. 64. Point out the writer's opinion in the model and the reasons and examples that support it. Remind students that the boldfaced transitions in the model link the writer's opinion to reasons. Point out the descriptive words in the Character Words box.

Guided Practice—We Do

 Direct students to the frame on handbook p. 65. Help students complete the topic sentence, using a character from another story they have read. Work with students to identify reasons why the character is interesting. Have them suggest sentences to complete the frame giving examples that support their opinions. Have students write in their books as you write on the board.

Practice/Apply—You Do

 COLLABORATIVE Have small groups plan and complete Activity 2. Tell them to complete the topic sentence with their group's opinion and then finish the paragraph together. Have groups share and discuss their work.

 INDEPENDENT Have students read the directions. Ask them to use their prewriting plan from Lesson 26 or use Graphic Organizer 7 to brainstorm a new plan.

Conference/Evaluate

As students draft, circulate and help them choose examples that support their opinions. Evaluate using the rubric on p. 104.

Digital
• eBook
• WriteSmart
• Interactive Lessons

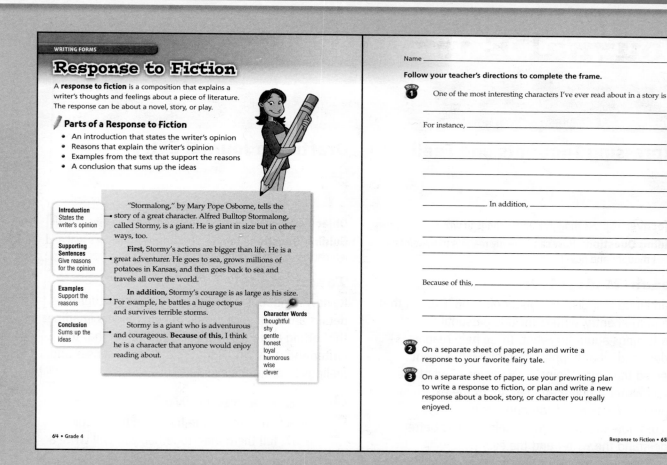

WRITING FORMS

Response to Fiction

A **response to fiction** is a composition that explains a writer's thoughts and feelings about a piece of literature. The response can be about a novel, story, or play.

Parts of a Response to Fiction

- An introduction that states the writer's opinion
- Reasons that explain the writer's opinion
- Examples from the text that support the reasons
- A conclusion that sums up the ideas

Introduction
States the writer's opinion

"Stormalong," by Mary Pope Osborne, tells the story of a great character. Alfred Bulltop Stormalong, called Stormy, is a giant. He is giant in size but in other ways, too.

Supporting Sentences
Give reasons for the opinion

First, Stormy's actions are bigger than life. He is a great adventurer. He goes to sea, grows millions of potatoes in Kansas, and then goes back to sea and travels all over the world.

Examples
Support the reasons

In addition, Stormy's courage is as large as his size. For example, he battles a huge octopus and survives terrible storms.

Conclusion
Sums up the ideas

Stormy is a giant who is adventurous and courageous. **Because of this,** I think he is a character that anyone would enjoy reading about.

Character Words
thoughtful
shy
gentle
honest
loyal
humorous
wise
clever

64 • Grade 4

Name _____

Follow your teacher's directions to complete the frame.

1 One of the most interesting characters I've ever read about in a story is
_____

For instance, _____
_____
_____
_____
_____

_____ In addition, _____
_____
_____
_____

Because of this, _____
_____
_____

2 On a separate sheet of paper, plan and write a response to your favorite fairy tale.

3 On a separate sheet of paper, use your prewriting plan to write a response to fiction, or plan and write a new response about a book, story, or character you really enjoyed.

Response to Fiction • 65

✓ Corrective Feedback

IF . . . students are unable to come up with at least one example to support their opinion,

THEN . . . have them ask themselves, *Why do I like/dislike this book/story/character?* The answer to the question should lead them to an example in the work that supports their opinion.

✏ Focus Trait: Elaboration

Remind students that using specific words will help readers understand their opinions about a piece of fiction. It will also help readers understand their opinions about a piece of fiction. Write this statement on the board:

I *like* Maniac Magee *because the main character is great.* Elicit from students how the opinion can be strengthened by using a more specific word.

Example: *I liked Maniac Magee because the main character is unique and gets into all sorts of trouble.*

Have partners revise the words they can make more specific.

Grade 4 • **65**

Journal Entry

Minilesson 53

Expressing Thoughts and Feelings

Objective: Express thoughts and feelings in writing.

Guiding Question: How can I get my readers to understand what I thought and how I felt?

Teach/Model—I Do

Read aloud and discuss handbook p. 66. Explain that, in a journal entry, writers include personal thoughts and feelings about an event. These help readers understand what happened and how the event affected the writer. Point to examples of what the model writer thought and felt about the experience. (Example: *I was a little bit nervous because…*) Discuss how these sentences help readers better understand the writer and the event.

Guided Practice—We Do

On the board, write a few scenes that will evoke feelings in children, such as *taking a big test* or *winning a game or contest.* Tell students to place themselves in one of these scenes. Help them come up with words that describe their feelings, such as *My heart pounded.* Write their descriptions on the board.

Practice/Apply—You Do

COLLABORATIVE Have small groups choose an event you listed or another event they have experienced. Have them work together to create a few sentences they might include in a journal entry about it. Tell them to include their thoughts and feelings about the event.

INDEPENDENT Have students choose an event on their own and express their thoughts and feelings about it.

Conference/Evaluate

Encourage students to ask themselves, *Did I use words and phrases that help readers understand how I felt and what I thought?*

Minilesson 54

Drafting a Journal Entry

Objective: Write a journal entry that is clear and thoughtful.

Guiding Question: How can I clearly describe the event and let readers understand how it made me feel?

Teach/Model—I Do

Review handbook p. 66, noting how the writer uses details and sequence words to help readers imagine the setting and follow the action. Explain that the writer also uses words that relate to the senses and feelings to bring the events to life.

Guided Practice—We Do

 Direct students to the frame on handbook p. 67. Tell them that, together, you will write a journal entry about the first day of school. Work with students to "set the scene" in the first paragraph (*It was the first day of school.*). Use sensory details to show what was happening and what feelings came about. Plan and write the sequence of events together, ending with a description of how the writer felt about the event. Have students write in their books as you write on the board.

Practice/Apply—You Do

 COLLABORATIVE Have groups plan and complete Activity 2. Tell them to set the scene clearly and to use words that express their thoughts and feelings. Have groups share what they have written.

 INDEPENDENT Have students read and follow the directions. Tell them to use their prewriting plan from Lesson 27 or brainstorm a new plan using Graphic Organizer 10.

Conference/Evaluate

As students draft, have them evaluate their work using the rubric on p. 104.

 Digital ▸ • eBook
• WriteSmart
• Interactive Lessons

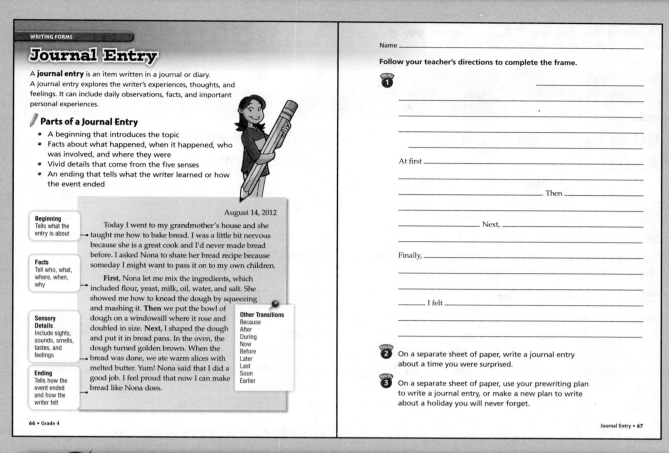

WRITING FORMS

Journal Entry

A **journal entry** is an item written in a journal or diary. A journal entry explores the writer's experiences, thoughts, and feelings. It can include daily observations, facts, and important personal experiences.

Parts of a Journal Entry

- A beginning that introduces the topic
- Facts about what happened, when it happened, who was involved, and where they were
- Vivid details that come from the five senses
- An ending that tells what the writer learned or how the event ended

Beginning Tells what the entry is about

Facts Tell who, what, where, when, why

Sensory Details Include sights, sounds, smells, tastes, and feelings

Ending Tells how the event ended and how the writer felt

August 14, 2012

Today I went to my grandmother's house and she taught me how to bake bread. I was a little bit nervous because she is a great cook and I'd never made bread before. I asked Nona to share her bread recipe because someday I might want to pass it on to my own children.

First, Nona let me mix the ingredients, which included flour, yeast, milk, oil, water, and salt. She showed me how to knead the dough by squeezing and mashing it. **Then** we put the bowl of dough on a windowsill where it rose and doubled in size. **Next**, I shaped the dough and put it in bread pans. In the oven, the dough turned golden brown. When the bread was done, we ate warm slices with melted butter. Yum! Nona said that I did a good job. I feel proud that now I can make bread like Nona does.

Other Transitions
Because
After
During
Now
Before
Later
Last
Soon
Earlier

66 • Grade 4

Name _____

Follow your teacher's directions to complete the frame.

At first _____

_____ Then _____

_____ Next, _____

Finally, _____

_____ I felt _____

② On a separate sheet of paper, write a journal entry about a time you were surprised.

③ On a separate sheet of paper, use your prewriting plan to write a journal entry, or make a new plan to write about a holiday you will never forget.

Journal Entry • 67

Corrective Feedback

IF . . . students are having a hard time expressing their thoughts and feelings,

THEN . . . have them imagine they are telling a trusted friend about the experience and that this person asks them questions about how they felt or thought about the events. For example, *What exactly were you thinking when you met your new teacher? How were you feeling?* Encourage students to use sensory words to help readers understand their thoughts and feelings. For example, *My palms were sweaty and my heart was racing as I opened the classroom door.*

Focus Trait: Elaboration

Tell students that they can elaborate to make their journals more interesting by using precise words and clear details.

Model elaborating by writing sentences on the board and modifying them so that the writer's personality shows through:

I was scared when the nurse held up the needle.

When the nurse held up the needle, I swallowed hard. It seemed like it was a foot long! My arm would never be the same!

Work with students to compare the two passages, pointing to words and phrases that let the writer's personality show through.

Write the following sentence on the board. Then work with students to elaborate by rewriting or adding to it: *I was so happy when we won the game.*

Grade 4 • 67

Public Service Announcement

WRITING FORMS

Minilesson 55

Using Language to Affect Audience

Objective: Use language that appeals to feelings.

Guiding Question: How can I make my writing more persuasive by using language that targets emotions?

Teach/Model—I Do

Read aloud and discuss handbook p. 68. Explain that a public service announcement uses words that stir up readers' feelings and cause readers to act a certain way. Point out the "Be smart!" in the first paragraph. Explain that this sentence is persuasive because it makes readers feel a certain way: if they don't agree with the writer and take action, they aren't "smart." On the board, write *Keep your friends safe!* Discuss how this sentence appeals to readers' emotions and stirs them to action.

Guided Practice—We Do

On the board, write an idea for a public service announcement, such as *Don't litter!* Work with students to write a sentence that appeals to readers' emotions and persuades them to take action. You may want to give students a frame such as *When you litter,* _____.

Practice/Apply—You Do

COLLABORATIVE Write several other ideas for public service announcements, such as *recycle to reduce waste* and *buckle your seat belts.* Have groups choose one idea and write several sentences that appeal to readers' emotions and stir them to take action.

INDEPENDENT Have students choose another idea and write a few sentences about it on their own.

Conference/Evaluate

Have students evaluate their sentences to make sure they stir readers to action.

68 • Writing

Minilesson 56

Drafting a Public Service Announcement

Objective: Write a persuasive public service announcement.

Guiding Question: How can I write and organize my public service announcement so that it persuades readers?

Teach/Model—I Do

Review handbook p. 68. Point out the first and last paragraphs, discussing how the writer uses words that appeal to readers' emotions. Discuss the organization, noting how the writer explains the subject, then gives facts to support the subject, and finally ends with a call to action.

Guided Practice—We Do

 Direct students to handbook p. 69. Say that, together, you will write a public service announcement about crossing the street safely. On the board write, *60,000 pedestrians were killed by cars in 2009.* Work with students to use this sentence to write an introduction. Then fill in the frame with supporting details and steps readers can take to safely cross the street. End with a call to action. Have students write in their books as you write on the board.

Practice/Apply—You Do

 COLLABORATIVE Have groups plan and complete Activity 2. Have groups share what they have written.

 INDEPENDENT Have students read and follow the directions. Tell them to use their prewriting plan from Lesson 28 or brainstorm a new plan using Graphic Organizer 7.

Conference/Evaluate

As students draft, have them evaluate their work using the rubric on p. 104.

Digital • eBook • WriteSmart • Interactive Lessons

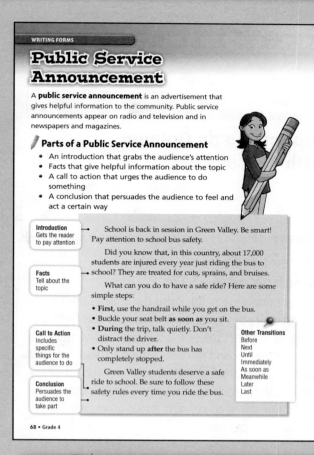

Public Service Announcement

A **public service announcement** is an advertisement that gives helpful information to the community. Public service announcements appear on radio and television and in newspapers and magazines.

 Parts of a Public Service Announcement

- An introduction that grabs the audience's attention
- Facts that give helpful information about the topic
- A call to action that urges the audience to do something
- A conclusion that persuades the audience to feel and act a certain way

Introduction Gets the reader to pay attention	School is back in session in Green Valley. Be smart! Pay attention to school bus safety.
Facts Tell about the topic	Did you know that, in this country, about 17,000 students are injured every year just riding the bus to school? They are treated for cuts, sprains, and bruises.
Call to Action Includes specific things for the audience to do	What can you do to have a safe ride? Here are some simple steps: • **First,** use the handrail while you get on the bus. • Buckle your seat belt **as soon as** you sit. • **During** the trip, talk quietly. Don't distract the driver. • Only stand up **after** the bus has completely stopped.
Conclusion Persuades the audience to take part	Green Valley students deserve a safe ride to school. Be sure to follow these safety rules every time you ride the bus.

Other Transitions
Before
Next
Until
Immediately
As soon as
Meanwhile
Later
Last

68 • Grade 4

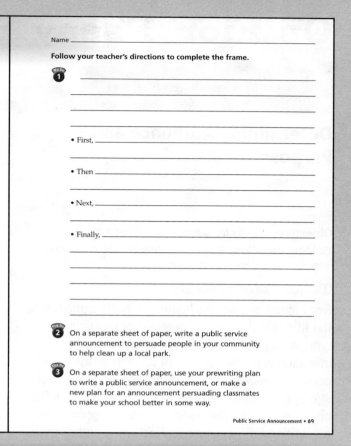

Name _____

Follow your teacher's directions to complete the frame.

1 _____
_____
_____
_____
_____

• First, _____

• Then _____

• Next, _____

• Finally, _____
_____
_____
_____
_____

2 On a separate sheet of paper, write a public service announcement to persuade people in your community to help clean up a local park.

3 On a separate sheet of paper, use your prewriting plan to write a public service announcement, or make a new plan for an announcement persuading classmates to make your school better in some way.

Public Service Announcement • 69

✓ Corrective Feedback

IF . . . students are having difficulty coming up with persuasive words that appeal to readers' emotions,

THEN . . . explain that advertisements often use similar ways to stir up readers' emotions by appealing to such basic needs as safety, health, and love. For example, a public service announcement about exercising every day might include *Stay healthy and live longer by exercising every day.* Point out that this appeals to readers' need to be healthy. Have students think of ways they can stir up their readers' feelings about another basic need.

✏ Focus Trait: Organization

Tell students that they can use a computer to get a sense of how to organize their public service announcements. One way to do this is to read other public service announcements. Students can find public service announcements of a charity, such as the American Red Cross, by doing an Internet search of key words, such as *public service announcement Red Cross.* Explain that they can also find public service announcements posted in various places in their community, such as grocery stores and recreation centers.

Have students read one such announcement and discuss its various parts: (1) an introduction that grabs readers' attention, (2) details that support the opinion presented, (3) and a call to action at the end. Discuss how this organization helps to make the announcement more effective. Have students also identify words and phrases in the announcement that appeal to readers' emotions. Work with students to make an outline showing the organization of the announcement.

Grade 4 • **69**

Writing Handbook Minilessons

Opinion Essay: Prewriting

Minilesson 57

Determining Audience and Purpose

Objective: Identify the purpose and audience for writing.

Guiding Question: How can I determine who my writing is intended for and why I am writing it?

Teach/Model—I Do

Read aloud and discuss handbook p. 70. Explain that the title tells the writer's *purpose*, or reason for writing: to persuade the audience what the best invention was. The purpose of opinion essays is to persuade readers to agree with an opinion you feel strongly about. Before you prewrite, you must decide on a purpose and the audience—or the people you are writing for—because it affects how and what you write: an opinion paper about not littering, for example, might be different for an audience of children as opposed to adults. The audience in the model is *classmates and teacher* because it is a classroom assignment.

Guided Practice—We Do

On the board, write an opinion, such as *Dogs make better pets than cats.* Work with students to identify the purpose. The audience should be people who would be interested in your opinion. Ask students to identify audiences, such as classmates or cat owners, and to explain how they might change what and how they write for each.

Practice/Apply—You Do

COLLABORATIVE Write several other opinions for opinion essays, such as *our classroom needs a pet.* Have groups choose one opinion and write a purpose and audience.

INDEPENDENT Have students choose another opinion and write a purpose and audience.

Conference/Evaluate

Have students evaluate their purpose and audience to make sure they fit together.

70 • Writing

Minilesson 58

Supporting an Opinion with Reasons

Objective: Support an opinion with reasons, facts, and details.

Guiding Question: How can I support my opinions?

Teach/Model—I Do

Review handbook p. 70. Point out that in the idea-support map, the writer gives reasons and facts and details to support them. Explain that the writer supports the second reason by writing *Surf Internet.* She also gives other details for each reason. Tell students that, in an opinion essay, giving more than one fact or detail to support a reason makes the writing more persuasive.

Guided Practice—We Do

 Direct students to Activity 1 on handbook p. 71. Tell students that together you will complete an idea-support map on how planting a school garden could be educational, or teach them things. Work with students to decide on the purpose and audience for the essay. Then, together, complete the map with reasons, facts, and details. Have students write in their books as you write on the board.

Practice/Apply—You Do

 COLLABORATIVE Have groups plan and complete Activity 2. Have them share what they have written.

 INDEPENDENT Have students read and follow the directions. Tell them to use their prewriting plan from Lesson 29 or brainstorm a new plan using Graphic Organizer 7.

Conference/Evaluate

As students draft, have them evaluate their work using the rubric on p. 104.

 Digital
- eBook
- WriteSmart
- Interactive Lessons

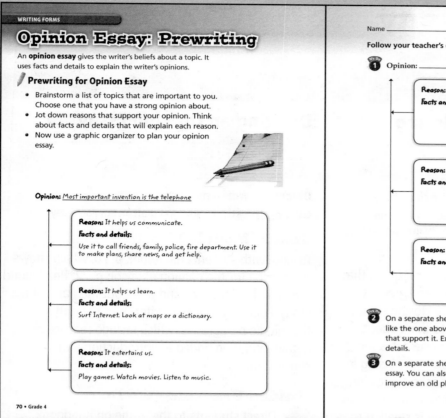

Opinion Essay: Prewriting

An **opinion essay** gives the writer's beliefs about a topic. It uses facts and details to explain the writer's opinions.

Prewriting for Opinion Essay

- Brainstorm a list of topics that are important to you. Choose one that you have a strong opinion about.
- Jot down reasons that support your opinion. Think about facts and details that will explain each reason.
- Now use a graphic organizer to plan your opinion essay.

Opinion: _Most important invention is the telephone_

> **Reason:** It helps us communicate.
> **Facts and details:**
> Use it to call friends, family, police, fire department. Use it to make plans, share news, and get help.

> **Reason:** It helps us learn.
> **Facts and details:**
> Surf Internet. Look at maps or a dictionary.

> **Reason:** It entertains us.
> **Facts and details:**
> Play games. Watch movies. Listen to music.

70 • Grade 4

Name _____

Follow your teacher's directions to complete the activity.

1 Opinion: _____

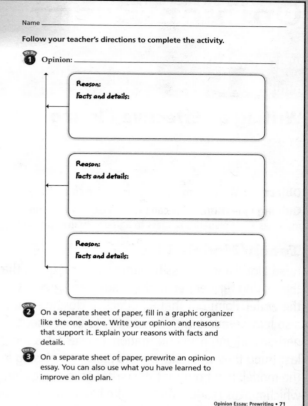

> **Reason:**
> **Facts and details:**

> **Reason:**
> **Facts and details:**

> **Reason:**
> **Facts and details:**

2 On a separate sheet of paper, fill in a graphic organizer like the one above. Write your opinion and reasons that support it. Explain your reasons with facts and details.

3 On a separate sheet of paper, prewrite an opinion essay. You can also use what you have learned to improve an old plan.

Opinion Essay: Prewriting • 71

✔ Corrective Feedback

IF . . . students are having a hard time coming up with a purpose and audience,

THEN . . . have them think about something they feel strongly about, such as adopting a classroom pet. Have them ask themselves, *What is something that I care about? What things would I like to see change? What is something that I think is the best or worst, like a movie or book?* Once students have decided on a purpose, have them determine an audience by asking themselves *Who would be interested in reading my opinion? My classmates? My neighbors? My relatives?*

✎ Focus Trait: Purpose

Tell students that when their purpose for writing is to write an opinion essay, they can get ideas for their own essays by reading other opinion essays. Explain that one kind of an opinion essay is an editorial, which often appears in newspapers in the Opinion/ Editorial section. Students can go to a newspaper's website and check this section to think about the writer's purpose and the audience the writer is writing for. They can also study the reasons and facts used to support the opinion to think about how to support their own reasons.

Model finding an editorial on a website for a newspaper geared towards children, or print out an editorial to share with students. Have students read the editorial and decide what the purpose for writing is and what details the writer includes to support her opinion. Discuss who they think the writer's audience is and why.

Grade 4 • **71**

Opinion Essay

WRITING FORMS

Minilesson 59

Writing an Effective Closing

Objective: Write a strong, clear, persuasive closing.

Guiding Question: How can I write a closing that sums up my ideas and persuades readers to agree with my opinion?

Teach/Model—I Do

Read aloud and discuss handbook p. 72. Explain that the closing further persuades readers to agree with the writer. Point out that an effective closing should also leave readers with something to think about, perhaps adding new information, because it is the last thing they will read. Reread aloud the closing in the model. Point out that the writer asks a question, which makes readers think. In the last two sentences, he explains that even though a phone is small, it is extremely important.

Guided Practice—We Do

On the board, write *The phone is the most important invention.* Work with students to think of another closing that sums up the opinion and/or leaves the audience with something to think about. Print out a short article about the phone today and have students use facts from it. For example, *There are almost 300 million cell phones in our country today. That's almost one phone for every American!*

Practice/Apply—You Do

COLLABORATIVE Have groups come up with other closings for the telephone essay, either using the facts you provided or restating the opinion in other ways. Remind students to leave readers with something to think about.

INDEPENDENT Have students write another closing on their own.

Conference/Evaluate

Have students evaluate their closing to make sure it restates the opinion and is memorable.

Minilesson 60

Drafting an Opinion Essay

Objective: Write a strong opinion essay.

Guiding Question: How do I draft an opinion essay?

Teach/Model—I Do

Review with students handbook p. 70, which shows the outline for the opinion essay on p. 72. Read aloud the model on page 72 and point out the parts of the essay. Point out that the writer used the outline for the middle paragraphs, which include reasons and details, and then added an introduction and conclusion.

Guided Practice—We Do

 Direct students to the frame on handbook p. 73. Then refer to the graphic organizer they filled out on p. 71 about why planting a garden is educational. Tell students that together you will draft an opinion essay about this topic. Work with students to study the outline and decide what to put in the frame. Then, together, complete the frame, adding a beginning and an ending. Help students suggest strong endings. Have students write in their books as you write on the board.

Practice/Apply—You Do

 COLLABORATIVE Have groups plan and complete Activity 2. Tell them to write a strong ending. Have groups share what they have written.

 INDEPENDENT Have students read and follow the directions. Tell them to use their prewriting plan from Lesson 30 or brainstorm a new plan using Graphic Organizer 7.

Conference/Evaluate

As students draft, have them evaluate their work using the rubric on p. 104.

 Digital • eBook • WriteSmart • Interactive Lessons

Opinion Essay

An **opinion essay** expresses the writer's beliefs about a topic. An opinion is a statement that cannot be proved true.

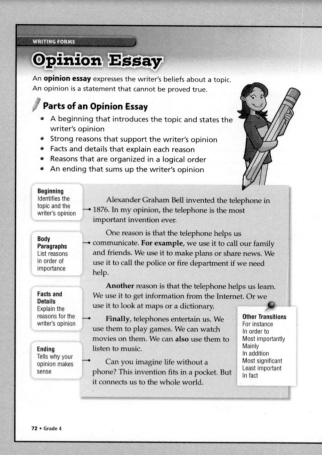

Parts of an Opinion Essay

- A beginning that introduces the topic and states the writer's opinion
- Strong reasons that support the writer's opinion
- Facts and details that explain each reason
- Reasons that are organized in a logical order
- An ending that sums up the writer's opinion

Beginning
Identifies the topic and the writer's opinion

→ Alexander Graham Bell invented the telephone in 1876. In my opinion, the telephone is the most important invention ever.

Body Paragraphs
List reasons in order of importance

→ One reason is that the telephone helps us communicate. **For example,** we use it to call our family and friends. We use it to make plans or share news. We use it to call the police or fire department if we need help.

Facts and Details
Explain the reasons for the writer's opinion

→ **Another** reason is that the telephone helps us learn. We use it to get information from the Internet. Or we use it to look at maps or a dictionary.

Finally, telephones entertain us. We use them to play games. We can watch movies on them. We can **also** use them to listen to music.

Other Transitions
For instance
In order to
Most importantly
Mainly
In addition
Most significant
Least important
In fact

Ending
Tells why your opinion makes sense

→ Can you imagine life without a phone? This invention fits in a pocket. But it connects us to the whole world.

72 • Grade 4

Name _____

Follow your teacher's directions to complete the frame.

 I believe that _____

_____

_____

One reason is that _____

_____

_____

Second, _____

_____

_____

Finally, _____

_____

_____ For example, _____

In conclusion, _____

_____

_____

 On a separate sheet of paper, write an opinion essay about another invention that you think is important. Be sure to support your opinion with strong reasons.

On a separate sheet of paper, use your prewriting plan to write an opinion essay, or make a new plan to write about a custom or tradition you feel strongly about.

Opinion Essay: Drafting/Revising • 73

✓ Corrective Evidence

IF . . . students are having a hard time coming up with an effective closing,

THEN . . . have them reread the model and decide how the writer's conclusion makes them think about what life would be like without the telephone. Tell them to ask themselves questions such as, *How would my life be different without _____? How can I expand on this idea to create an effective closing?* In addition, have them reread the information you printed out to find facts they might include in the closing to leave the reader with something to think about.

Focus Trait: Elaboration

Tell students that writers of opinion essays try to hold readers' attention by making their reasons and evidence interesting as well as convincing. Point out that one way to make writing sound more interesting is to replace everyday words and phrases with language that is more descriptive and precise. On the board, write *The telephone is used for a lot of things. The telephone lets us talk to people.* Guide students to suggest ways to replace common, everyday words and phrases such as "a lot of things" and "lets us talk to people" with more descriptive or precise language. For example, *The telephone is used for a wide variety of purposes. The telephone allows us to communicate with anyone at a moment's notice.* Discuss with students why these sentences are more interesting to read than the previous ones.

Grade 4 • **73**

Writing Handbook Minilessons

Prewriting

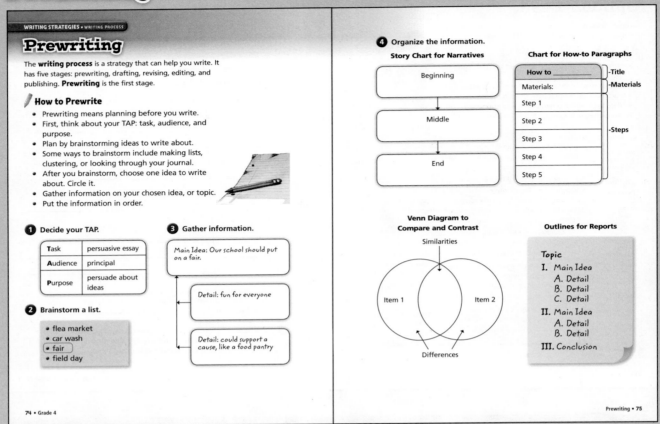

Prewriting

WRITING STRATEGIES • WRITING PROCESS

Prewriting

The **writing process** is a strategy that can help you write. It has five stages: prewriting, drafting, revising, editing, and publishing. **Prewriting** is the first stage.

How to Prewrite
- Prewriting means planning before you write.
- First, think about your TAP: task, audience, and purpose.
- Plan by brainstorming ideas to write about.
- Some ways to brainstorm include making lists, clustering, or looking through your journal.
- After you brainstorm, choose one idea to write about. Circle it.
- Gather information on your chosen idea, or topic.
- Put the information in order.

1 Decide your TAP.

Task	persuasive essay
Audience	principal
Purpose	persuade about ideas

2 Brainstorm a list.
- flea market
- car wash
- fair
- field day

3 Gather information.

Main Idea: Our school should put on a fair.

Detail: fun for everyone

Detail: could support a cause, like a food pantry

4 Organize the information.

Story Chart for Narratives: Beginning → Middle → End

Chart for How-to Paragraphs: How to ____ -Title, Materials: -Materials, Step 1, Step 2, Step 3, Step 4, Step 5 -Steps

Venn Diagram to Compare and Contrast: Similarities, Item 1, Item 2, Differences

Outlines for Reports:
Topic
I. Main Idea
   A. Detail
   B. Detail
   C. Detail
II. Main Idea
   A. Detail
   B. Detail
III. Conclusion

74 • Grade 4

Prewriting • 75

WRITING STRATEGY

Minilesson 61

Introducing Prewriting

Objective: Understand how to use the prewriting handbook pages.

Guiding Question: How do I use these pages to help me come up with ideas for my writing?

Teach/Model

Have students read p. 74. Explain that the steps on this page show how a student begins a persuasive essay by determining the TAP, brainstorming a list of ideas, choosing one idea, and gathering information.

Practice/Apply

Have students discuss making lists, clustering, using a journal, and other ways that they can brainstorm ideas.

74 • Writing

Minilesson 62

Organizing Information

Objective: Understand how to use a graphic organizer to put information in order.

Guiding Question: How can I use a graphic organizer to arrange information?

Teach/Model

Explain to students that they can fill in a graphic organizer to arrange information. Point out how the writer listed the main idea and added details in the idea-support map on p. 74.

Practice/Apply

Have students look at the graphic organizers on p. 75. Discuss how they can use each graphic organizer to arrange information for different purposes.

Drafting

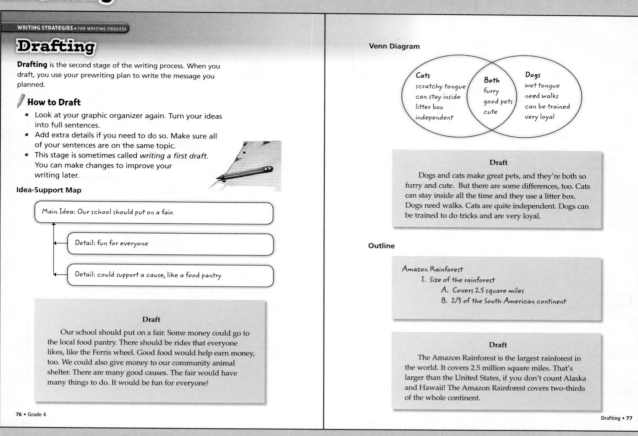

Drafting

Drafting is the second stage of the writing process. When you draft, you use your prewriting plan to write the message you planned.

How to Draft

- Look at your graphic organizer again. Turn your ideas into full sentences.
- Add extra details if you need to do so. Make sure all of your sentences are on the same topic.
- This stage is sometimes called *writing a first draft.* You can make changes to improve your writing later.

Idea-Support Map

Main Idea: Our school should put on a fair.

Detail: fun for everyone

Detail: could support a cause, like a food pantry

Draft

Our school should put on a fair. Some money could go to the local food pantry. There should be rides that everyone likes, like the Ferris wheel. Good food would help earn money, too. We could also give money to our community animal shelter. There are many good causes. The fair would have many things to do. It would be fun for everyone!

76 • Grade 4

Venn Diagram

Cats
scratchy tongue
can stay inside
litter box
independent

Both
furry
good pets
cute

Dogs
wet tongue
need walks
can be trained
very loyal

Draft

Dogs and cats make great pets, and they're both so furry and cute. But there are some differences, too. Cats can stay inside all the time and they use a litter box. Dogs need walks. Cats are quite independent. Dogs can be trained to do tricks and are very loyal.

Outline

Amazon Rainforest
   I. Size of the rainforest
      A. Covers 2.5 square miles
      B. 2/3 of the South American continent

Draft

The Amazon Rainforest is the largest rainforest in the world. It covers 2.5 million square miles. That's larger than the United States, if you don't count Alaska and Hawaii! The Amazon Rainforest covers two-thirds of the whole continent.

Drafting • 77

WRITING STRATEGY

Minilesson 63

Introducing Drafting

Objective: Understand how to use the drafting handbook pages.

Guiding Question: How do I use these pages to help me start writing?

Teach/Model

Have students read p. 76. Explain that the example on this page shows how a student used the prewriting graphic organizer to write the first draft of a persuasive essay.

Practice/Apply

Have students read the examples on p. 77. Discuss how the examples show two more ways students can use their graphic organizers to write their drafts.

Minilesson 64

Going from Organizer to Draft

Objective: Understand how to use a graphic organizer to draft.

Guiding Question: How can I use my prewriting plan draft?

Teach/Model

Explain to students that one way to start a rough draft is to review the information in their graphic organizer and then write a topic sentence. Then they can follow that first sentence with details. Point out how the writer did this for the Venn diagram. Remind them that they can revise later.

Practice/Apply

Have students discuss how the student used the information in the outline to write a topic sentence and then begin drafting details as support.

Writing • 75

Writing Handbook Minilessons

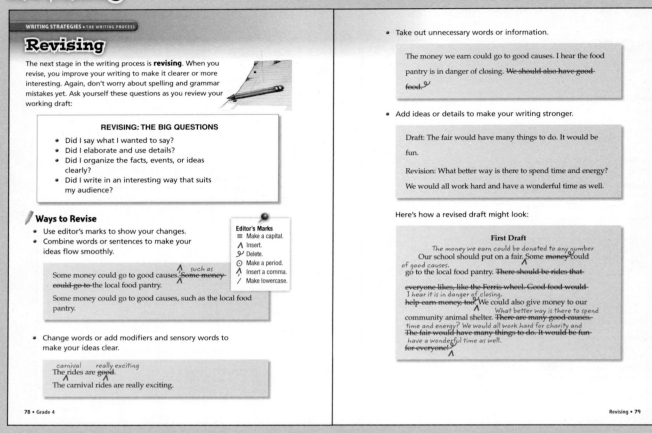

Revising

Revising

The next stage in the writing process is **revising**. When you revise, you improve your writing to make it clearer or more interesting. Again, don't worry about spelling and grammar mistakes yet. Ask yourself these questions as you review your working draft:

REVISING: THE BIG QUESTIONS
- Did I say what I wanted to say?
- Did I elaborate and use details?
- Did I organize the facts, events, or ideas clearly?
- Did I write in an interesting way that suits my audience?

Ways to Revise
- Use editor's marks to show your changes.
- Combine words or sentences to make your ideas flow smoothly.

Editor's Marks
- ≡ Make a capital.
- ∧ Insert.
- ℘ Delete.
- ⊙ Make a period.
- ∧ Insert a comma.
- / Make lowercase.

Some money could go to good causes. Some money could go to the local food pantry.

Some money could go to good causes, such as the local food pantry.

- Change words or add modifiers and sensory words to make your ideas clear.

The rides are good.

The carnival rides are really exciting.

78 • Grade 4

- Take out unnecessary words or information.

The money we earn could go to good causes. I hear the food pantry is in danger of closing. We should also have good food.

- Add ideas or details to make your writing stronger.

Draft: The fair would have many things to do. It would be fun.

Revision: What better way is there to spend time and energy? We would all work hard and have a wonderful time as well.

Here's how a revised draft might look:

First Draft

The money we earn could be donated to any number
Our school should put on a fair. Some money could
of good causes.
go to the local food pantry. There should be rides that
everyone likes, like the Ferris wheel. Good food would
I hear it is in danger of closing.
help earn money, too. We could also give money to our
What better way is there to spend
community animal shelter. There are many good causes.
time and energy? We would all work hard for charity and
The fair would have many things to do. It would be fun
have a wonderful time as well.
for everyone!

Revising • 79

WRITING STRATEGY

Minilesson 65

Introducing Revising

Objective: Understand how to use the revising handbook pages.

Guiding Question: How do I use these pages to help me revise my writing?

Teach/Model

Have students read p. 78. Explain that the examples on this page show how a student revised parts of a persuasive essay by combining two sentences, adding a modifier, and changing the word *good*.

Practice/Apply

Have students read the examples on p. 79. Discuss how these examples show two more ways students can revise to improve their drafts.

76 • Writing

Minilesson 66

Using Editor's Marks

Objective: Understand how to use editor's marks to revise a draft.

Guiding Question: How can I use editor's marks to show changes I want to make?

Teach/Model

Explain to students that they can use editor's marks to show changes as they revise a draft. Have them review the chart on p. 78. Then point out two editor's marks that a student uses in the revised first draft.

Practice/Apply

Have students discuss what the student has added, taken out, changed, or combined to revise the persuasive essay draft.

Editing and Publishing

WRITING STRATEGIES • WRITING PROCESS

Editing

Editing, or proofreading for errors, is the fourth stage of the writing process.

✏ Editing

- Check for mistakes in punctuation, capitalization, spelling, and grammar. You can use a dictionary and a grammar book to help.
- Make sure your paragraphs are indented.
- Use editing marks to show corrections on your paper.
- Use the spelling and grammar checker if you are working on a computer. Be sure to double-check your work for errors the checker won't catch.

Editor's Marks
≡ Make a capital.
∧ Insert.
𝒚 Delete.
⊙ Make a period.
⋏ Insert a comma.
/ Make lowercase.

Revised Draft

Dear Principal Martinez,

The key to a great ~~far~~ is good food and ~~exsiting~~ rides. *fair* *exciting*

That's what makes people come out and spend money⊙

Our school could rent a Ferris wheel⋏ a giant slide, and maybe

some other rides, too. ≡we could pay back the rental fees from

the money ~~erned~~ at the fair. Food would be easy. Students and *earned*

parents could work together to make ~~delishus~~ food to sell. As *delicious*

you can see, I don't think rides or food for the fair would be a

problem.

Sincerely,
Amanda

Publishing

The last stage of the writing process is **publishing**. Before you publish, you can go back to any stage to fix or improve your writing.

- Decide how you want to publish. You might publish by sharing a written piece, giving an oral report, or giving a multimedia presentation.
- Type or write a clean copy of your piece.
- When you give a presentation, write note cards with the main ideas to guide your oral reporting or multimedia presentation.
- If you use multimedia, use a computer to choose pictures, charts, audio, or video to go with your writing.

Why We Should Have a School Fair
by Amanda Fleming

I believe our school should put on a fair. The money we earn could be donated to any number of good causes. Some could go to the local food pantry. We could also give money to our community animal shelter. I hear they're in danger of closing. What better way is there to spend our time and energy? We would be learning a lot about planning, budgets, and cooperating as a school. Just think, we would all be working hard for charity while having a wonderful time!

WRITING STRATEGY

Minilesson 67

Introducing Editing

Objective: Understand how to use the editing and publishing handbook pages.

Guiding Question: How do I use these pages to check my writing for mistakes?

Teach/Model

Have students read p. 80. Explain that the example on this page shows how Amanda checked for mistakes and then used editor's marks to show corrections in her revised draft.

Practice/Apply

Have students discuss the mistakes in punctuation, capitalization, spelling, and grammar that Amanda caught in her revised draft.

Minilesson 68

Introducing Publishing

Objective: Understand how to use the editing and publishing handbook pages.

Guiding Question: How do I publish my writing?

Teach/Model

Have students read p. 81. Point out that Amanda's persuasive essay is now polished and ready to be published. Explain that there are several ways to publish a piece of writing.

Practice/Apply

Have students discuss how Amanda might decide to publish her edited persuasive essay.

Writing Handbook Minilessons

Evidence

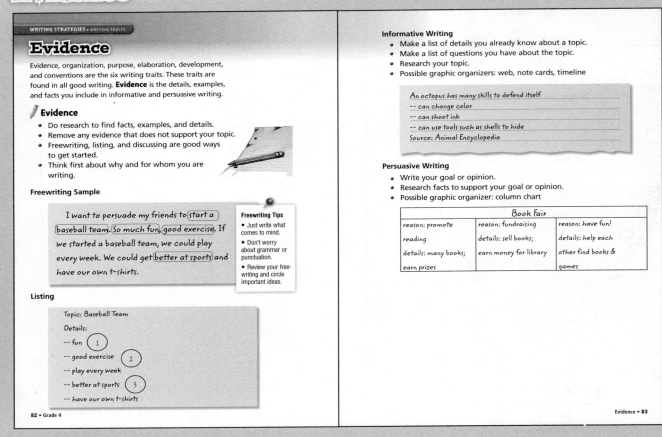

Evidence

Evidence, organization, purpose, elaboration, development, and conventions are the six writing traits. These traits are found in all good writing. **Evidence** is the details, examples, and facts you include in informative and persuasive writing.

Evidence
- Do research to find facts, examples, and details.
- Remove any evidence that does not support your topic.
- Freewriting, listing, and discussing are good ways to get started.
- Think first about why and for whom you are writing.

Freewriting Sample

I want to persuade my friends to start a baseball team. So much fun, good exercise. If we started a baseball team, we could play every week. We could get better at sports and have our own t-shirts.

Freewriting Tips
- Just write what comes to mind.
- Don't worry about grammar or punctuation.
- Review your freewriting and circle important ideas.

Listing

Topic: Baseball Team
Details:
-- fun (1)
-- good exercise (2)
-- play every week
-- better at sports (3)
-- have our own t-shirts

82 • Grade 4

Informative Writing
- Make a list of details you already know about a topic.
- Make a list of questions you have about the topic.
- Research your topic.
- Possible graphic organizers: web, note cards, timeline

An octopus has many skills to defend itself
-- can change color
-- can shoot ink
-- can use tools such as shells to hide
Source: Animal Encyclopedia

Persuasive Writing
- Write your goal or opinion.
- Research facts to support your goal or opinion.
- Possible graphic organizer: column chart

Book Fair		
reason: promote reading	reason: fundraising	reason: have fun!
details: many books; earn prizes	details: sell books; earn money for library	details: help each other find books & games

Evidence • 83

WRITING STRATEGY

Minilesson 69

Introducing Evidence

Objective: Understand how to locate evidence to support a topic.

Guiding Question: How do I think of facts, details, and examples to support my topic?

Teach/Model

Have students read p. 82. Explain that the examples on this page show how a student used freewriting and listing to collect evidence about starting a baseball team. Point out the freewriting tips in the box and discuss them.

Practice/Apply

Have students use freewriting or listing to think of topics and evidence for a piece of writing about a hobby they enjoy, like playing soccer.

78 • Writing

Minilesson 70

Finding Topics for Different Kinds of Writing

Objective: Find topics for different forms of writing.

Guiding Question: What topics should I think about for informative or persuasive writing?

Teach/Model

Have students read p. 83. For each form of writing, discuss which graphic organizers they might want to use and what topics they will think about or find evidence for.

Practice/Apply

Have students think about topics and evidence for a piece of informative or persuasive writing.

Organization

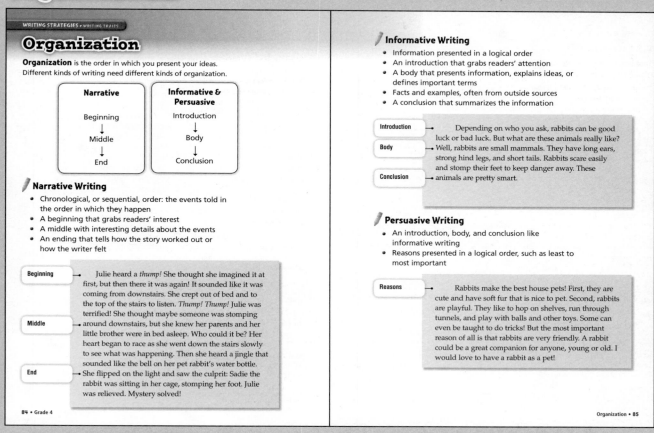

Minilesson 71

Organizing Narrative Writing

Objective: Understand how to organize narrative writing.

Guiding Question: How do I present my ideas in narrative writing?

Teach/Model

Have students read p. 84. Emphasize that different forms of writing have different kinds of organization. Point out that the example of narrative writing on this page tells about events in the order in which they happen.

Practice/Apply

Have students discuss what happens in the beginning, middle, and ending in the example.

Minilesson 72

Organizing Informative and Persuasive Writing

Objective: Understand how to organize informative and persuasive writing.

Guiding Question: How do I present my ideas in informative and persuasive writing?

Teach/Model

Have students read p. 85. Point out that both examples include an introduction, a body, and a conclusion.

Practice/Apply

Guide students to fill in a Venn diagram about the similarities and differences between the organization of the two examples.

Writing • **79**

Writing Handbook Minilessons

Purpose and Elaboration

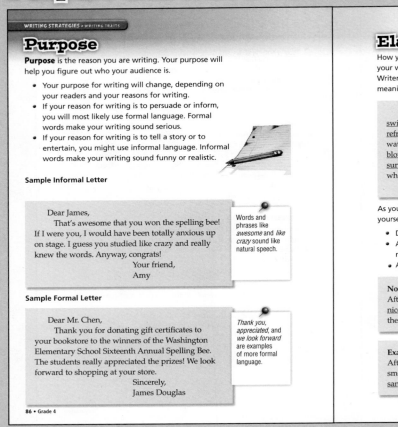

WRITING STRATEGIES • WRITING TRAITS

Purpose

Purpose is the reason you are writing. Your purpose will help you figure out who your audience is.

- Your purpose for writing will change, depending on your readers and your reasons for writing.
- If your reason for writing is to persuade or inform, you will most likely use formal language. Formal words make your writing sound serious.
- If your reason for writing is to tell a story or to entertain, you might use informal language. Informal words make your writing sound funny or realistic.

Sample Informal Letter

Dear James,
    That's awesome that you won the spelling bee! If I were you, I would have been totally anxious up on stage. I guess you studied like crazy and really knew the words. Anyway, congrats!
                        Your friend,
                        Amy

Words and phrases like awesome *and* like crazy *sound like natural speech.*

Sample Formal Letter

Dear Mr. Chen,
    Thank you for donating gift certificates to your bookstore to the winners of the Washington Elementary School Sixteenth Annual Spelling Bee. The students really appreciated the prizes! We look forward to shopping at your store.
                        Sincerely,
                        James Douglas

Thank you, appreciated, and we look forward are examples of more formal language.

86 • Grade 4

Elaboration

How you choose to elaborate on the ideas and details in your writing helps create a picture in your reader's mind. Writers use **exact words** to make their writing more meaningful and interesting.

During the summer, I <u>swim</u> every morning. It's so <u>refreshing</u> to <u>dive</u> into the water on a <u>hot</u>, <u>sticky</u> day. I <u>blow bubbles</u> under the <u>surface</u> and <u>jump</u> up only when I need more air.

On Sundays we go, <u>Grandma</u> and I, To pick <u>wild berries</u> And <u>bake</u> one big pie. I wash the fruit, She <u>molds</u> the <u>crust</u>. Once it's all done, She says, "Try it. You must!"

As you revise, look for unclear or boring words. Ask yourself these questions:

- Do my **verbs** show exactly what is happening?
- Are the people, places, and things easy for my readers to see? Do the **nouns** create a clear picture?
- Are there **other words** I can add or change?

Not Exact:
After school Jeff and I <u>went</u> to the <u>store</u>. The smell of <u>nice</u> bread filled the air. We <u>got a bunch of stuff</u> for the picnic.

Exact:
After school Jeff and I <u>biked</u> to the <u>delicatessen</u>. The smell of <u>fresh</u> bread filled the air. We <u>bought tuna sandwiches</u> for the picnic.

Try replacing dull or unclear words with new vocabulary words.

Purpose/Elaboration • 87

WRITING STRATEGY

Minilesson 73

Understanding Purpose

Objective: Understand that the purpose for writing will determine when to use formal or informal language.

Guiding Question: How do I decide whether to use formal or informal language in my writing?

Teach/Model

Have students read p. 86. Explain that Amy and James use different styles of language in the examples. Discuss the purpose each writer has for writing. Point out that Amy uses informal language in the first letter, but James uses formal language in the second letter.

Practice/Apply

Have students identify the writers' purposes in each letter and why informal or formal language was used.

80 • Writing

Minilesson 74

Understanding Elaboration

Objective: Understand how to elaborate using exact words.

Guiding Question: How can I make my writing clear and interesting?

Teach/Model

Have students read p. 87. Explain that exact words help create a picture in a reader's mind. Point out the underlined nouns, verbs, and adjectives in the two examples on this page.

Practice/Apply

Have students discuss how the writer replaced the underlined words in the first passage at the bottom of the page with more specific words. Challenge students to think of other exact words the writer may have used.

Development

WRITING STRATEGIES • WRITING TRAITS

Development

Good writers **develop** narratives with interesting details and clear descriptions.

- Describe characters and settings using interesting words and descriptions.
- Develop events and experiences that describe conflicts and how they are resolved in the story.
- Write different kinds of sentences that begin in different ways.

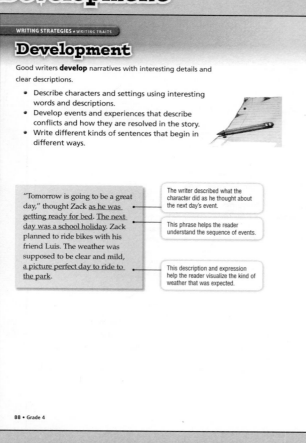

"Tomorrow is going to be a great day," thought Zack <u>as he was getting ready for bed. The next day was a school holiday.</u> Zack planned to ride bikes with his friend Luis. The weather was supposed to be clear and mild, <u>a picture perfect day to ride to the park.</u>

> The writer described what the character did as he thought about the next day's event.

> This phrase helps the reader understand the sequence of events.

> This description and expression help the reader visualize the kind of weather that was expected.

Use a variety of sentence beginnings.

Too Many Sentences Beginning the Same Way

Hailey looked at her art project. She picked up her paintbrush. She added one more stroke of red. She put the brush down. She thought, "Now I am ready for the art show."

Varied Beginnings

Hailey looked at her art project. <u>Then</u> she picked up a paintbrush and added one more stroke of red. <u>After setting her brush down,</u> she thought, "Now I am ready for the art show."

Use different sentence lengths.

Too Many Sentences of the Same Length

Baseball is a popular sport around the world. Many towns and schools in other countries have started baseball programs. Children are now able to play on organized teams. Girls and boys can both join Little League teams here in the US. They can easily play on the same teams.

Varied Lengths

Baseball is a popular sport around the world. Since many towns and schools in other countries have started baseball programs, children are now able to play on organized teams. Both girls and boys can play together on organized Little League teams in the US.

Use different kinds of sentences.

Similar Sentences

Snails are slimy creatures. They carry their houses on their backs. They live in many kinds of places. Some of these are on the land, in the ocean, or in freshwater lakes.

Varied Sentences

What is a slimy creature that carries its house on its back? It's a snail! Snails live in many kinds of places. Some of these are on the land, in the ocean, or in freshwater lakes.

WRITING STRATEGY

Minilesson 75

Understanding Development

Objective: Understand how to develop good narratives.

Guiding Question: How do I make narratives interesting and easy to understand?

Teach/Model

Have students read the top of p. 88. Explain that good writers do more than just list a sequence of events when they write a story. Instead they add details and descriptions that help readers understand why the characters act as they do.

Practice/Apply

Have students read the model on p. 88. Discuss how the underlined text gives readers information about the story and helps to make the story more interesting to read.

Minilesson 76

Using Sentence Variety

Objective: Understand how to develop sentences that vary.

Guiding Question: How can I vary my sentences to make my writing more interesting?

Teach/Model

Have students read p. 89. Explain that the three pairs of examples show different ways to vary sentences. Point out how writers can use different sentence beginnings, a mix of short and long sentences, and different kinds of sentences to make readers want to continue reading.

Practice/Apply

Have students develop three related sentences about a topic. Remind them to develop sentences that are varied and that include interesting words and details.

Writing • **81**

Writing Handbook Minilessons

Conventions

WRITING STRATEGIES ▪ WRITING TRAITS

Conventions

Conventions are rules about grammar, spelling, punctuation, and capitalization. One way to make sure you are following the rules when you write or edit is to have an editing checklist.

Sample Editing Checklist

> **Punctuation**
> ___ Did I use correct end punctuation in my sentences?
> ___ Did I use commas correctly in compound sentences?
> ___ Did I use quotation marks correctly?
> **Capitalization**
> ___ Did I start every sentence with a capital letter?
> ___ Did I capitalize proper nouns?
> **Spelling**
> ___ Did I spell all of my words correctly?
> **Grammar**
> ___ Did my sentences have correct subject-verb agreement?
> ___ Did I avoid run-on sentences and fragments?

Common Errors

Fragments and Run-Ons
A sentence should have a **subject** and a **verb**. It starts with a capital letter and ends with a period.

Wrong Way	Right Way
The sheep in the field.	The sheep in the field are ready to be sheared.
Can shear them to gather the wool.	The farmers can shear them to gather the wool.
Wool made from sheep was one of the first textiles people around the world make clothing from wool.	Wool made from sheep was one of the first textiles. People around the world make clothing from wool.

Compound and Complex Sentences
A **compound sentence** combines two sentences. The clauses are separated by a comma and a coordinating conjunction. A **complex sentence** has an independent and a dependent clause and does not need a comma.

Wrong Way	Right Way
The barn is only half-painted but it already looks great!	The barn is only half-painted, but it already looks great!
The cows are fed, after they are milked.	The cows are fed after they are milked.

Subject-Verb Agreement
Make sure the subject and verb of your sentence agree.

Wrong Way	Right Way
Joan plant tree in the schoolyard.	Joan plants a tree in the schoolyard.
José and Marisol paints a mural near the playground.	José and Marisol paint a mural near the playground.
The students wants to make recess better.	The students want to make recess better.

Possessives
Use an apostrophe to show that a noun is possessive.

Wrong Way	Right Way
That is Barrys football.	That is Barry's football.
Alexs mother brings sandwiches and juice to our game's.	Alex's mother brings sandwiches and juice to our games.
All the boy's new jerseys are red.	All the boys' new jerseys are red.

WRITING STRATEGY

Minilesson 77

Using an Editing Checklist

Objective: Follow rules about grammar, spelling, punctuation, and capitalization.

Guiding Question: How do I use an editing checklist to improve my writing?

Teach/Model

Have students read p. 90. Explain that the checklist shows the kinds of errors that a writer looks for when writing or editing a draft.

Practice/Apply

Using the editing checklist, have students review drafts of their own writing to make sure they have followed these rules.

Minilesson 78

Understanding Common Errors

Objective: Understand common mistakes in writing.

Guiding Question: What mistakes should I look for when I edit my writing?

Teach/Model

Have students read the examples of common errors in the charts on pp. 90–91. Discuss grammar and punctuation mistakes that are illustrated in each chart.

Practice/Apply

Have students check their own writing to make sure they have written sentences with a subject and a verb, used correct subject-verb agreement, and correctly punctuated compound or complex sentences and possessives.

82 • Writing

Writing Workshop

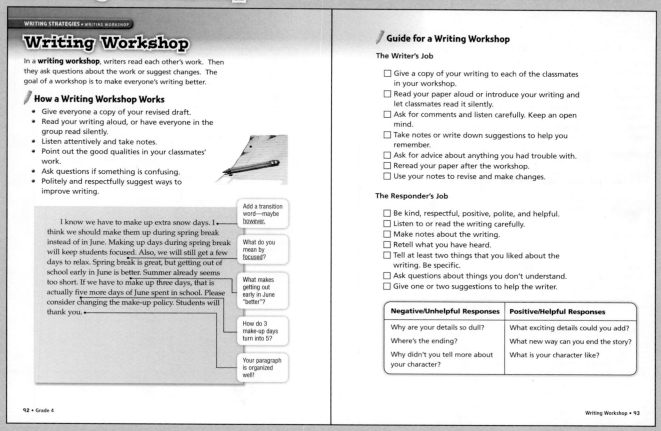

WRITING STRATEGIES • WRITING WORKSHOP

Writing Workshop

In a **writing workshop**, writers read each other's work. Then they ask questions about the work or suggest changes. The goal of a workshop is to make everyone's writing better.

How a Writing Workshop Works

- Give everyone a copy of your revised draft.
- Read your writing aloud, or have everyone in the group read silently.
- Listen attentively and take notes.
- Point out the good qualities in your classmates' work.
- Ask questions if something is confusing.
- Politely and respectfully suggest ways to improve writing.

> I know we have to make up extra snow days. I think we should make them up during spring break instead of in June. Making up days during spring break will keep students focused. Also, we will still get a few days to relax. Spring break is great, but getting out of school early in June is better. Summer already seems too short. If we have to make up three days, that is actually five more days of June spent in school. Please consider changing the make-up policy. Students will thank you.

Add a transition word—maybe however.

What do you mean by focused?

What makes getting out early in June "better"?

How do 3 make-up days turn into 5?

Your paragraph is organized well!

92 • Grade 4

Guide for a Writing Workshop

The Writer's Job

☐ Give a copy of your writing to each of the classmates in your workshop.
☐ Read your paper aloud or introduce your writing and let classmates read it silently.
☐ Ask for comments and listen carefully. Keep an open mind.
☐ Take notes or write down suggestions to help you remember.
☐ Ask for advice about anything you had trouble with.
☐ Reread your paper after the workshop.
☐ Use your notes to revise and make changes.

The Responder's Job

☐ Be kind, respectful, positive, polite, and helpful.
☐ Listen to or read the writing carefully.
☐ Make notes about the writing.
☐ Retell what you have heard.
☐ Tell at least two things that you liked about the writing. Be specific.
☐ Ask questions about things you don't understand.
☐ Give one or two suggestions to help the writer.

Negative/Unhelpful Responses	Positive/Helpful Responses
Why are your details so dull?	What exciting details could you add?
Where's the ending?	What new way can you end the story?
Why didn't you tell more about your character?	What is your character like?

Writing Workshop • 93

WRITING STRATEGY

Minilesson 79

Understanding the Writing Workshop

Objective: Understand how a writing workshop works.

Guiding Question: How can a writing workshop help improve my writing?

Teach/Model

Have students read p. 92. Review the bulleted steps. Explain that the example shows how a student points out strengths and weaknesses in a classmate's writing.

Practice/Apply

Have students discuss the comments made by the workshop reader in the example on this page. Ask if they agree or disagree with the comments and why.

Minilesson 80

Using a Workshop Checklist

Objective: Use a checklist as a guide for a writing workshop.

Guiding Question: In a writing workshop, what is the writer's job? What is the responder's job?

Teach/Model

Have students read p. 93. Explain that these checklists will guide them in a writing workshop. Point out that the first list guides the writer, while the second list guides student readers who respond to a piece of writing.

Practice/Apply

Have students hold a writing workshop using the two checklists and the chart on this page to offer helpful responses.

Writing • 83

Writing Handbook Minilessons

Using the Internet

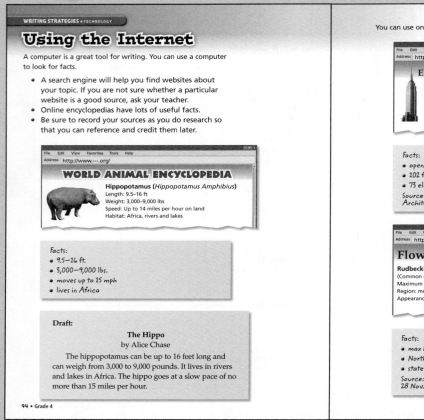

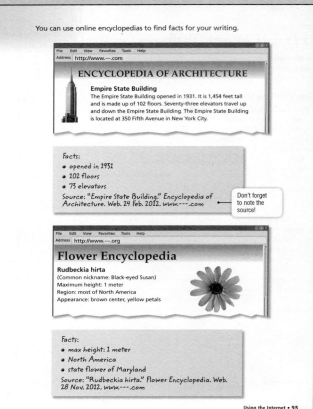

WRITING STRATEGY

Minilesson 81

Using the Internet for Writing

Objective: Understand how to use the Internet to find facts.

Guiding Question: How do I use the Internet for my writing?

Teach/Model

Have students read p. 94. Explain that they can use the Internet to find websites or online encyclopedias to learn about a topic. Point out that the example on this page shows how Alice used an online encyclopedia to draft an informational paragraph about hippos.

Practice/Apply

Ask students which search engines, websites, and online encyclopedias they have used to look for facts. List examples on the board. Guide them to understand which examples are reliable sources of information.

84 • Writing

Minilesson 82

Using Online Encyclopedias

Objective: Understand how to use an online encyclopedia.

Guiding Question: How can I use an online encyclopedia to find facts?

Teach/Model

Explain to students that one way to find facts for their writing is by using an online encyclopedia. Have them read the examples on p. 95. Point out how a student found facts using the Encyclopedia of Architecture and the Flower Encyclopedia.

Practice/Apply

Have students use an online encyclopedia to find three facts about a planet, an inventor, or an animal in the rainforest. Remind them to record their sources.

Writing for the Web

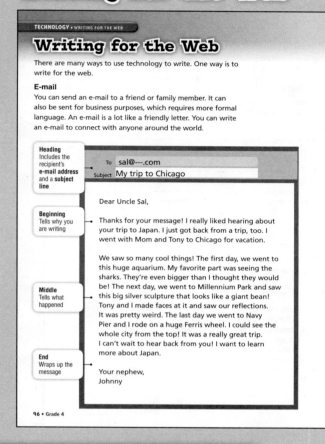

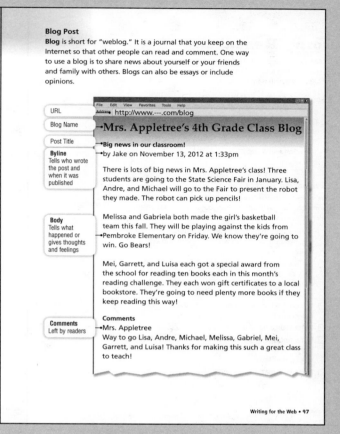

WRITING STRATEGY

Minilesson 83

Writing an E-mail

Objective: Understand how to write an e-mail.

Guiding Question: How do I write an e-mail to friends or family members?

Teach/Model

Have students read p. 96. Explain that the example on this page shows Johnny's e-mail to his Uncle Sal. Referring to the call-outs, discuss the format of an e-mail.

Practice/Apply

Have students use a computer to write an e-mail to a friend or family member. Remind them that an e-mail is similar to a friendly letter.

Minilesson 84

Writing a Blog Post

Objective: Understand how to write a blog post.

Guiding Question: What are the key parts of a blog post?

Teach/Model

Have students read p. 97. Explain that the example on this page shows how a blog post is set up and what elements it includes. Point out the call-outs, and discuss each one. Have students tell who wrote the blog post and what the post is about.

Practice/Apply

Help students use a computer to create a blog post about their own class. Remind them to include a blog name, a post title, a byline, and a body that tells what happened or shares their thoughts and feelings.

Writing • 85

Writing Handbook Minilessons

Doing Research

WRITING STRATEGIES

Doing Research

The best way to support your points in your informative or persuasive writing is to use facts and details. The best way to find facts and details is to do research.

Sources of Information

- Books
- Encyclopedias
- Magazines and Newspapers
- The Internet
- Television and Videos
- Interviews

Remember to record your sources so that you can cite them later.

Evaluating Sources

Some sources are better than others or have more reliable information. How can you tell which sources are good? When looking at a new source, ask yourself these questions:

☐ Is the source published by an institution, organization, or person who knows the subject well?

☐ If it is a website, is it trustworthy? (Sites with .edu, .org, or .gov are usually educational, nonprofit, or government websites and can have good information.)

☐ Is there background information in the author's biography or author's website?

☐ Is the source up to date?

☐ Is the purpose or point of view of the source stated? If there is more than one side to the issue, are both sides presented?

☐ Is the information complete?

98 • Grade 4

Finding Information

One way to find information is to search in your library's electronic card catalog or use an Internet search engine. In order to find good sources of information, you need to search using good keywords.

A **keyword** is a word or phrase about a subject. A good keyword to start with might be the topic of your research.

Tips:

- Narrow your topic down to a specific keyword. If you pick something too broad, your search will get hundreds of results.
- Don't pick anything too specific or you won't find enough results to get enough information.

Less Effective Keywords	Effective Keywords
cars	the first car
old cars	Model T
inventors	Henry Ford
Grandma's red 1957 Chevy	1957 Chevys

Parts of a Nonfiction Book

- A **table of contents** shows how the book is organized and lists names and page numbers of chapters
- A **glossary** gives definitions of special words used in the book
- A **bibliography** lists sources the author used when writing the book
- An **index** is an alphabetical list of topics covered in the book

Doing Research • 99

WRITING STRATEGY

Minilesson 85

Finding Reliable Sources

Objective: Determine which sources of information are reliable.

Guiding Question: How can I tell whether a source is good?

Teach/Model

Have students read p. 98. Explain that it is important for them to choose a reliable source of information when they are looking for facts and details for their informative or persuasive writing. Point out that the checklist on this page will help them decide whether their sources are good.

Practice/Apply

Refer students to the bulleted list on this page. Have them discuss which sources they have used to find facts and details and how they can evaluate each one.

86 • Writing

Minilesson 86

Finding Good Sources of Information

Objective: Understand how to find good sources.

Guiding Question: How do I find good sources of information?

Teach/Model

Have students read p. 99. Explain that choosing effective keywords is one way to find good sources of information. Point out the tips for choosing a keyword. Then discuss how to use the parts of a nonfiction book to find specific facts and details.

Practice/Apply

Have students list several possible keywords for an Internet search on a favorite athlete or other public figure. Help them to narrow their keywords.

Notetaking

RESEARCH • NOTETAKING

Notetaking

You will find a great deal of information when you research. One way to keep track of it and stay organized is to take notes.

Note Cards

You can take notes on your research in two ways.

1. You can write a main idea or a research question at the top of the card. Then write details or the answer to your research question below. At the bottom, include your source.

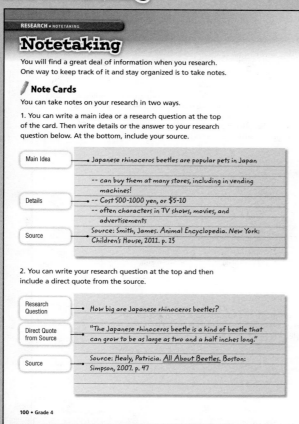

Main Idea → Japanese rhinoceros beetles are popular pets in Japan

Details →
-- can buy them at many stores, including in vending machines!
-- Cost 500-1000 yen, or $5-10
-- often characters in TV shows, movies, and advertisements

Source → Source: Smith, James. *Animal Encyclopedia*. New York: Children's House, 2011. p. 13

2. You can write your research question at the top and then include a direct quote from the source.

Research Question → How big are Japanese rhinoceros beetles?

Direct Quote from Source → "The Japanese rhinoceros beetle is a kind of beetle that can grow to be as large as two and a half inches long."

Source → Source: Healy, Patricia. *All About Beetles*. Boston: Simpson, 2007. p. 47

100 • Grade 4

Writing to Learn

Think-Aloud on Paper

- As you read, write notes about what you are reading.
- Write notes on what you understand about the topic.
- You might write notes on what images you picture as you read, what you predict will happen in a story, or how what you read is like something you have experienced.

Learning Logs

- A learning log is a place for you to comment on, ask questions about, or make connections to your reading.
- In the "Note-Taking" column, write the exact words you read.
- In the "Note-Making" column, write your reactions to or questions about what you read.

Learning Log: "Starting a Garden"	
Note-Taking	Note-Making
"Plant seeds in the spring." "Choose good plants for your garden." "You should see sprouts about ten days after you plant your seeds."	What day is the best day to plant seeds? I want to plant cucumbers and tomatoes. Cucumbers are tasty. Is there anything I can do to make my plants grow faster?

Notetaking • 101

WRITING STRATEGY

Minilesson 87

Taking Notes

Objective: Understand how to take notes.

Guiding Question: How do I take notes when I research information?

Teach/Model

Have students read p. 100. Explain that the examples on this page show two different ways that students used note cards to keep track of information about Japanese rhinoceros beetles.

Practice/Apply

Have students research a different insect, such as a firefly, a praying mantis, or a leafcutter ant. Have them take notes using each method for making note cards.

Minilesson 88

Using a Learning Log

Objective: Understand how to use a learning log.

Guiding Question: How can I use a learning log while I read?

Teach/Model

Have students read p. 101. Explain that one way to take notes while reading is to use a learning log. Point out how a student did this for the topic *starting a garden*.

Practice/Apply

Have individuals practice writing in a learning log as they read a short sample text. Have small groups compare the exact words they quoted in the first column and the reactions they recorded in the second column.

Writing • 87

Writing Handbook Minilessons

Writing to a Prompt

WRITING STRATEGIES • TEST PREP

Writing to a Prompt

A **prompt** is a writing assignment. Sometimes teachers give timed writing assignments for class exercises or tests.

Writing to a Prompt

- Read the prompt carefully.
- Note whether it asks you to give information, express thoughts and feelings, or persuade someone.
- Look for clues that tell what to include. For non-fiction, you might see *fact, opinion, examples, reasons.* For stories, *conflict, characters, plot.*
- Plan your writing, and then write. Restate key words from the prompt in your topic sentence.
- Some prompts have time limits. Plan how to best use your time.

Prompt: Think of a place you would like to visit. Write a paragraph explaining where you want to go and why you want to go there.

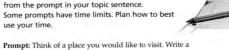

I would like to visit the Grand Canyon. My aunt Carol went to visit it last year and brought back many photos. The cliffs and rocks looked beautiful. Aunt Carol said that the Grand Canyon is even bigger in person than it looks in the photos! It does not look like any place I have ever been to before. I want to see it with my own eyes someday.

102 • Grade 4

Written Prompts

A **written prompt** is a statement or question that asks you to complete a writing task. Here is an example of a written prompt that asks for a personal narrative:

> Almost everyone has had an interesting experience visiting a new place. Think about your own experience in a new place. It may have happened during a visit to another state, to a museum, or to some other place. Now tell or recount a story to your reader about what happened when you visited that place.

Here are some other examples of written prompts:

Narrative Writing	Persuasive Writing
These prompts ask you to "tell a story."	These prompts ask you to "convince" or "persuade."
Informative Writing	**Response to Literature**
These prompts may ask you to "tell or explain why."	These prompts ask you to answer questions about a piece you read.

Picture Prompts

A **picture prompt** is a statement or question about a picture. It asks you to tell something about the picture. Here is an example of a picture prompt that asks for a description.

Picture yourself in this scene. Write a composition for your teacher in which you tell what you see.

Writing to a Prompt • 103

WRITING STRATEGY

Minilesson 89

Writing to a Prompt

Objective: Understand how to write to a prompt.

Guiding Question: How do I write to a prompt?

Teach/Model

Have students read p. 102. Explain that the example on this page shows how a student wrote to a prompt, using a graphic organizer to plan a personal narrative paragraph. Point out how the student restated key words from the prompt in the topic sentence of the paragraph.

Practice/Apply

Have students use the prompt on this page to write a personal narrative paragraph. Remind them to follow the bulleted list of steps for writing to a prompt.

88 • Writing

Minilesson 90

Understanding Different Kinds of Prompts

Objective: Understand different kinds of prompts.

Guiding Question: How do I write to different kinds of prompts?

Teach/Model

Have students read p. 103. Explain that this shows two kinds of prompts: one that is written and one that is a picture. Point out the examples of a written prompt for a personal narrative and the picture prompt for a description. Then discuss the other examples of written prompts in the chart.

Practice/Apply

Have students use the picture prompt on this page to write a short description.

Checklists and Rubrics

Checklists and Rubrics

A **rubric** is a chart that helps you when you write and revise.
Score 6 tells you what to aim for in your writing.

	• Focus • Support	• Organization
Score 6	My writing is focused and supported by facts or details.	My writing has a clear introduction and conclusion. Ideas are clearly organized.
Score 5	My writing is mostly focused and supported by facts or details.	My writing has an introduction and a conclusion. Ideas are mostly organized.
Score 4	My writing is mostly focused and supported by some facts or details.	My writing has an introduction and a conclusion. Most ideas are organized.
Score 3	Some of my writing is focused and supported by some facts or details.	My writing has an introduction or a conclusion, but might be missing one. Some ideas are organized.
Score 2	My writing is not focused and is supported by few facts or details.	My writing might not have an introduction or a conclusion. Few ideas are organized.
Score 1	My writing is not focused or supported by facts or details.	My writing is missing an introduction and a conclusion. Few or no ideas are organized.

104 • Grade 4

• Elaboration • Purpose	• Conventions • Development • Evidence
Purpose is strong. Writing grabs readers' interest. Word choices strongly support the purpose and audience.	Writing has no errors in spelling, grammar, capitalization, or punctuation. It includes description, details, and/or reasons.
Purpose is clear. Writing holds readers' interest. Most word choices support the purpose and audience.	Writing has few errors in spelling, grammar, capitalization, or punctuation. It includes descriptions, details, and/or reasons.
Purpose is clear, but could be stronger in the beginning or end. Overall writing holds readers' interest. Word choices good.	Writing has some errors in spelling, grammar, capitalization, or punctuation. It includes some description, details, and/or reasons.
Purpose is clear at the beginning or end. Some of the writing interests readers. Few word choices support the purpose and audience.	Writing has some errors in spelling, grammar, capitalization, or punctuation. It includes a few examples of description, details, and/or reasons.
Purpose is mostly unclear. Writing does not include desciption and does not hold readers' interest. Weak word choices.	Writing has many errors in spelling, grammar, capitalization, or punctuation. Little variety of sentences. Some sentences are incomplete.
Purpose is unclear. Writing is not interesting to read.	Writing has many errors in spelling, grammar, capitalization, or punctuation.

Checklists and Rubrics • 105

WRITING STRATEGY

Minilesson 91

Introducing Rubrics

Objective: Understand what a rubric is and how it is organized.

Guiding Question: What is a rubric, and how is it organized?

Teach/Model

Have students read pp. 104–105. Explain that the rubric on these pages is a chart with four headings across the top and a scoring guide from 6 to 1 down the left side. Tell students that they can use a rubric to determine how well a piece of writing fulfills each listed trait or characteristic.

Practice/Apply

Discuss each of the four headings at the top of the rubric. Have students review the writing traits on handbook pp. 82–90.

Minilesson 92

Using a Rubric to Improve Writing

Objective: Use a rubric to improve a piece of writing.

Guiding Question: How can I use a rubric to improve my writing?

Teach/Model

Model how to use the rubric to assign a score to a writing sample. Explain that students can use a rubric as a guide when revising and editing their writing. A rubric gives them feedback about what improvements need to be made. Remind them that the checklists in the Writing Forms section of the handbook can also help guide the revision process.

Practice/Apply

Have students use the rubric to evaluate a sample of their own writing.

Writing • 89

Writing Handbook Minilessons

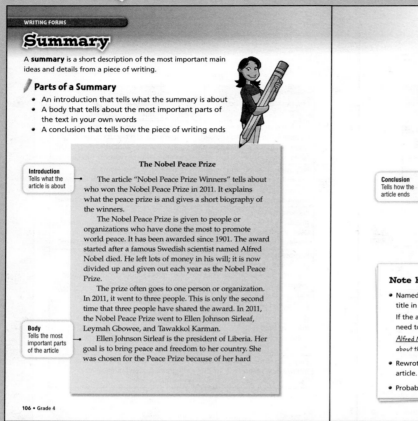

WRITING FORMS

Summary

A **summary** is a short description of the most important main ideas and details from a piece of writing.

Parts of a Summary
- An introduction that tells what the summary is about
- A body that tells about the most important parts of the text in your own words
- A conclusion that tells how the piece of writing ends

The Nobel Peace Prize

Introduction Tells what the article is about →

The article "Nobel Peace Prize Winners" tells about who won the Nobel Peace Prize in 2011. It explains what the peace prize is and gives a short biography of the winners.

The Nobel Peace Prize is given to people or organizations who have done the most to promote world peace. It has been awarded since 1901. The award started after a famous Swedish scientist named Alfred Nobel died. He left lots of money in his will; it is now divided up and given out each year as the Nobel Peace Prize.

The prize often goes to one person or organization. In 2011, it went to three people. This is only the second time that three people have shared the award. In 2011, the Nobel Peace Prize went to Ellen Johnson Sirleaf, Leymah Gbowee, and Tawakkol Karman.

Body Tells the most important parts of the article →

Ellen Johnson Sirleaf is the president of Liberia. Her goal is to bring peace and freedom to her country. She was chosen for the Peace Prize because of her hard

work for women's rights. She hopes that girls around the world will see her as a role model.

Leymah Gbowee is also from Liberia and is a peace activist. She led a group in Liberia to fight for women to get the right to vote in elections. She also helped to end a civil war in her country. Gbowee got the Peace Prize for helping women to have more freedom and for keeping women safe.

The third winner, Tawakkol Karman, also won the prize for her work with women. She is the first Arab woman ever to win the Nobel Peace Prize. Her goal is to bring freedom and self-esteem to people in her country.

Conclusion Tells how the article ends →

These three women received their awards at a ceremony in Oslo, Norway. The Peace Prize ceremony is held in Oslo every year.

Note how the author of this piece:
- Named the article in the first paragraph, putting the article's title in quotation marks.

  If the author of this piece had been summarizing a book, she would need to italicize or underline the title.

  Alfred Nobel: A Biography, is a book by Kenne Fant. It tells interesting facts about the Swedish scientist who created the famous Nobel Peace Prize.
- Rewrote the article using her own words instead of copying from the article.
- Probably made the summary much shorter than the article.

106 • Grade 4

Summary • 107

WRITING MODELS AND FORMS

Minilesson 93

Understanding the Summary

Objective: Understand the summary.

Guiding Question: How can I use these pages to help me write a good summary?

Teach/Model

Have students read the definition and bulleted points. Explain that the example on these pages is a summary of an article, "Nobel Peace Prize Winners." Then have students read to the end of p. 107.

Practice/Apply

Have students identify the introduction, body, and conclusion of the summary. Discuss what the author tells about the article "Nobel Peace Prize Winners" in each part of her summary.

90 • Writing

Minilesson 94

Recognizing Important Details

Objective: Recognize important main ideas and details.

Guiding Question: Which main ideas and details will I include in my summary?

Teach/Model

Explain to students that a summary includes only the main ideas and details that are necessary for readers to understand the original piece of writing. Discuss the main ideas and details the author used in her summary of "Nobel Peace Prize Winners."

Practice/Apply

Have students write a summary of a short nonfiction article they have read. Remind them to include only the most important main ideas and details.

Cause-and-Effect Essay

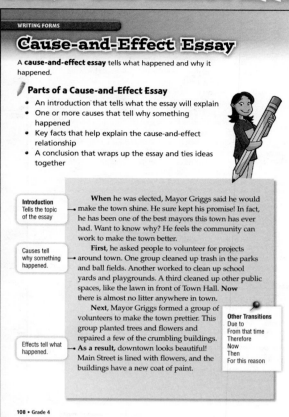

WRITING FORMS

Cause-and-Effect Essay

A **cause-and-effect essay** tells what happened and why it happened.

Parts of a Cause-and-Effect Essay

- An introduction that tells what the essay will explain
- One or more causes that tell why something happened
- Key facts that help explain the cause-and-effect relationship
- A conclusion that wraps up the essay and ties ideas together

Introduction
Tells the topic of the essay

When he was elected, Mayor Griggs said he would make the town shine. He sure kept his promise! In fact, he has been one of the best mayors this town has ever had. Want to know why? He feels the community can work to make the town better.

Causes tell why something happened.

First, he asked people to volunteer for projects around town. One group cleaned up trash in the parks and ball fields. Another worked to clean up school yards and playgrounds. A third cleaned up other public spaces, like the lawn in front of Town Hall. **Now** there is almost no litter anywhere in town.

Next, Mayor Griggs formed a group of volunteers to make the town prettier. This group planted trees and flowers and repaired a few of the crumbling buildings.

Effects tell what happened.

As a result, downtown looks beautiful! Main Street is lined with flowers, and the buildings have a new coat of paint.

Other Transitions
Due to
From that time
Therefore
Now
Then
For this reason

Body
Has key facts that help explain cause-and-effect relationships

The mayor **also** started a program to persuade people to bring their old books to the public library. The library got so many books, they did not have space to put them all! **In addition,** he asked people to give food to the homeless shelter **so that** everyone who lives in our town can get enough to eat.

Then Mayor Griggs decided to do something about crime. He hired more police officers and encouraged neighbors to form neighborhood watch groups. **Because** he did, there has been much less crime, especially in the downtown area.

Conclusion
Ties ideas together

All in all, life is better in our town because of Mayor Griggs. Not only has life in town improved, but people are working together. **Because** of the mayor's work, there is a stronger sense of community. **More than that,** downtown looks beautiful. People who live in our town feel safe. This has become a wonderful place to live **since** Mayor Griggs was elected.

Note how the author of this piece:

- Introduced the topic of the essay.
  Other ways she could have introduced the essay include telling how the mayor made the town more beautiful or safer.
  The town has never been more beautiful than it has been since Mayor Griggs took office.
- Showed cause-and-effect relationships in paragraph 5:
  He hired more police officers and encouraged neighbors to form neighborhood watch groups. **Because he did,** *there has been much less crime, especially in the downtown area.*

108 • Grade 4

Cause-and-Effect Essay • 109

WRITING MODELS AND FORMS

Minilesson 95

Understanding Cause and Effect

Objective: Understand the cause-and-effect essay.

Guiding Question: How can I use these pages to help me write a good cause-and-effect essay?

Teach/Model

Have students read the definition and bulleted points. Explain that the example on these pages is a cause-and-effect essay about how Mayor Griggs improved his town. Point out a few examples of how Mayor Griggs's acts changed the town and explain that these are causes and effects.

Practice/Apply

Have students identify cause-and-effect relationships in the essay. On the board, list causes and effects in a T-map.

Minilesson 96

Using Cause-and-Effect Transitions

Objective: Use cause-and-effect transition words.

Guiding Question: How will I use transition words in my essay to signal cause-and-effect relationships?

Teach/Model

Explain to students that the author of this essay used cause-and-effect transition words to connect ideas clearly. Point out *as a result* in the third paragraph. Discuss the cause-and-effect relationship that this transition signals to the reader.

Practice/Apply

Have students find the words *so that* and *because* in this essay. Have them discuss the cause-and-effect relationships that these transitions signal.

Writing • **91**

Writing Handbook Minilessons | **349**

Writing Handbook Minilessons

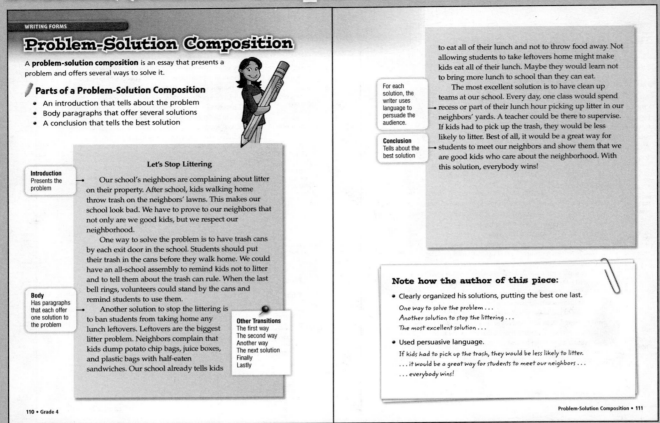

WRITING MODELS AND FORMS

Minilesson 97

Understanding Problem and Solution

Objective: Understand the problem/solution composition.

Guiding Question: How do I use these pages to help me write a good problem/solution composition?

Teach/Model

Ask students to read the definition and bulleted points. Tell them that the example on these pages presents solutions to the problem of students' littering near the school. Then have students read to the end of p. 111.

Practice/Apply

Have students identify the three solutions that the author presented in this essay.

92 • Writing

Minilesson 98

Using Order of Importance

Objective: Organize solutions in order of importance.

Guiding Question: How will I organize my solutions in a problem/solution composition?

Teach/Model

Point out how the author organized the solutions in this essay. Explain that he put the best solution last. Elicit that the author did this to make a strong argument that will convince his audience.

Practice/Apply

Have students brainstorm three solutions to a problem in your school, such as bullying or switching to healthy snacks. Have students list their solutions in order of importance, with the best solution last.

Compare-and-Contrast Essay

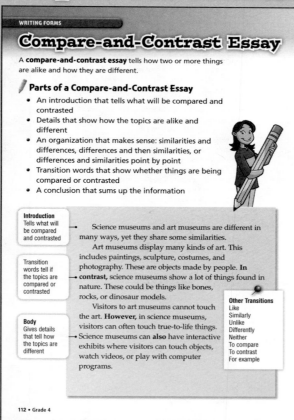

WRITING FORMS

Compare-and-Contrast Essay

A **compare-and-contrast essay** tells how two or more things are alike and how they are different.

Parts of a Compare-and-Contrast Essay

- An introduction that tells what will be compared and contrasted
- Details that show how the topics are alike and different
- An organization that makes sense: similarities and differences, differences and then similarities, or differences and similarities point by point
- Transition words that show whether things are being compared or contrasted
- A conclusion that sums up the information

Introduction
Tells what will be compared and contrasted

Transition words tell if the topics are compared or contrasted

Body
Gives details that tell how the topics are different

Science museums and art museums are different in many ways, yet they share some similarities.

Art museums display many kinds of art. This includes paintings, sculpture, costumes, and photography. These are objects made by people. **In contrast,** science museums show a lot of things found in nature. These could be things like bones, rocks, or dinosaur models.

Visitors to art museums cannot touch the art. **However,** in science museums, visitors can often touch true-to-life things. Science museums can **also** have interactive exhibits where visitors can touch objects, watch videos, or play with computer programs.

Other Transitions
Like
Similarly
Unlike
Differently
Neither
To compare
To contrast
For example

112 • Grade 4

Body
Gives details that tell how the topics are similar

The art museum in our town is often very quiet. People walk through it slowly and examine the art silently. **By contrast,** the science museum is sometimes very loud. There are more kids who visit it each day. They talk as they play with the exhibits.

On the other hand, both museums have displays that show how people lived long ago. For example, the art museum shows Native American art, including costumes, tools, and jewelry. You can see some of these same kinds of things at the science museum in the rooms about how people used to live. Also, **both** museums can be great places to visit on a rainy day. Art and science museums are filled with things to explore. **Both** museums encourage you to learn in an exciting way. They are great places to visit on a school field trip or with your family.

Conclusion
Sums up the information

Art museums and science museums are equally great places to visit. No matter which one you visit, you are sure to have an interesting experience!

Note how the author of this piece:

- Organized the essay with differences first and then similarities. Other ways he could have organized the essay include giving similarities first and then differences, or giving similarities and differences on the same topic within the same paragraph.
- Used transition words, such as:

  alike, different, in contrast, however, both

Compare-and-Contrast Essay • 113

WRITING MODELS AND FORMS

Minilesson 99

Understanding the Compare-and-Contrast Essay

Objective: Understand the compare-and-contrast essay.

Guiding Question: How can I use these pages to help me write a good compare-and-contrast essay?

Teach/Model

Have students read the definition and bulleted points. Explain that the essay on these pages compares and contrasts science museums and art museums. Then have students read to the end of p. 113.

Practice/Apply

Have students create a Venn diagram. Direct them to fill in the diagram with details from the essay that tell how science and art museums are alike and different.

Minilesson 100

Using Transitions to Signal Comparisons and Contrasts

Objective: Use transitions to signal comparisons and contrasts.

Guiding Question: How do I use transition words to make my compare-and-contrast essay clear?

Teach/Model

Point out boldfaced words in this essay, such as *in contrast, however, also,* and *both.* Explain to students that the author used transition words to signal comparisons and contrasts.

Practice/Apply

Have students discuss how transition words help them understand the topic and the organization of the essay.

Writing • 93

Writing Handbook Minilessons

How-to Essay

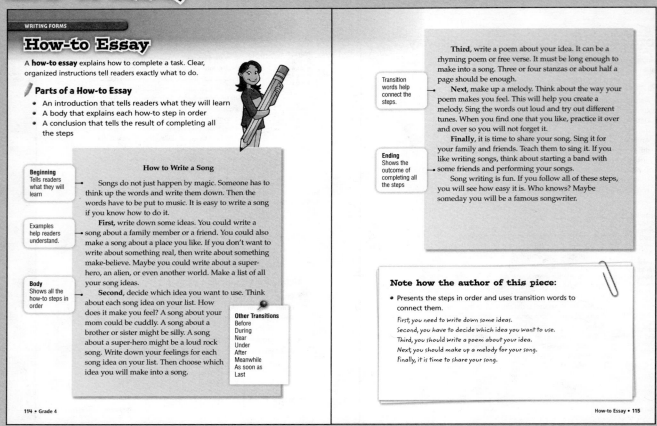

WRITING MODELS AND FORMS

Minilesson 101

Understanding the How-to Essay

Objective: Understand how to use the information presented about the how-to essay.

Guiding Question: How can I use these pages to help me write a good how-to essay?

Teach/Model

Have students read the definition and bulleted points. Add that a how-to essay should mention any materials required to complete the task. Have the students read to the end of p. 115. Point out that the boldfaced transition words show how the steps connect in order.

Practice/Apply

Have students locate and tell how the introduction and conclusion do what the bulleted points say they will do.

94 • Writing

Minilesson 102

Using Sequential Order

Objective: Put steps in order.

Guiding Question: How do I connect my steps in a how-to essay without numbering them?

Teach/Model

Explain to students that the writer linked ideas in this essay with sequence words such as *first, second,* and *finally,* which replace numbered steps in a how-to essay.

Practice/Apply

Have students locate the boldface transition words and discuss other sequence words that might be used in place of them. (Examples: *after this* or *then* for *next; last* instead of *finally.*)

Explanation

WRITING FORMS

Explanation

An **explanation** is writing that explains something or tells how or why something happens. When you write an explanation, you provide readers with information about a specific topic.

Parts of an Explanation

- An introduction that gets readers interested in the topic
- A body that uses logical order to present facts and examples explaining the topic
- A conclusion that sums up the explanation in a meaningful way

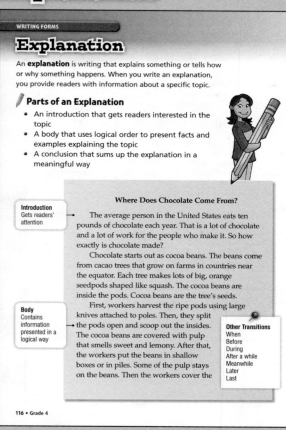

Where Does Chocolate Come From?

Introduction
Gets readers' attention

The average person in the United States eats ten pounds of chocolate each year. That is a lot of chocolate and a lot of work for the people who make it. So how exactly is chocolate made?

Chocolate starts out as cocoa beans. The beans come from cacao trees that grow on farms in countries near the equator. Each tree makes lots of big, orange seedpods shaped like squash. The cocoa beans are inside the pods. Cocoa beans are the tree's seeds.

Body
Contains information presented in a logical way

First, workers harvest the ripe pods using large knives attached to poles. Then, they split the pods open and scoop out the insides. The cocoa beans are covered with pulp that smells sweet and lemony. After that, the workers put the beans in shallow boxes or in piles. Some of the pulp stays on the beans. Then the workers cover the

Other Transitions
When
Before
During
After a while
Meanwhile
Later
Last

116 • Grade 4

beans with big banana leaves. After about a week in the sun, the pulp breaks down and the beans begin to taste like chocolate. Next, the workers put the beans on bamboo mats to dry. The beans are dried for several days. During this drying process, the beans lose most of their moisture and about half their weight. The dried beans are hard. They have a deep brown center, and they smell like chocolate. Now the workers load the cocoa beans into sacks. They put the sacks onto trucks, boats, and planes and send them to chocolate factories all around the world.

Finally, chocolate makers in the factories roast the beans and grind them up. The ground cocoa beans turn into a thick chocolate liquid. The liquid is made into solid unsweetened chocolate, cocoa butter, or cocoa powder. Other ingredients can be added to sweeten and flavor the chocolate.

Conclusion
Wraps up the topic in a meaningful way

It takes a lot of work to make cocoa beans into chocolate. But once you have chocolate, you can use it to make other things. Most of them are sweet, like cakes, candy, ice cream, and cookies. Unsweetened chocolate can also be mixed with spicy ingredients like onions, garlic, and chili peppers to make a special sauce for Mexican meals. However you use it, chocolate is one of the most delicious foods you will ever eat.

Explanation • 117

WRITING MODELS AND FORMS

Minilesson 103

Understanding the Explanation

Objective: Understand the explanation.

Guiding Question: How can I use these pages to help me write a good explanation?

Teach/Model

Have students read the definition and bulleted points. Point out that the example on these pages explains where chocolate comes from. Then have students read to the end of p. 117.

Practice/Apply

Write this question on the board: *Where does chocolate come from?* Have students give an answer based on their reading of this explanation.

Minilesson 104

Using Precise Words and Phrases

Objective: Use precise words and phrases.

Guiding Question: What precise words and phrases can I use to make my explanation clear?

Teach/Model

Point out examples of precise words and phrases in the fourth paragraph: *roast, ground cocoa beans, thick chocolate liquid.* Mention that the author used precise language to make this explanation clear.

Practice/Apply

On the board, write *Chocolate comes in different ways.* Have students rewrite the sentence with precise words and phrases. (Example: *Chocolate comes in different forms such as bars, chips, and chunks.)*

Writing • 95

Writing Handbook Minilessons

Science Observation Report

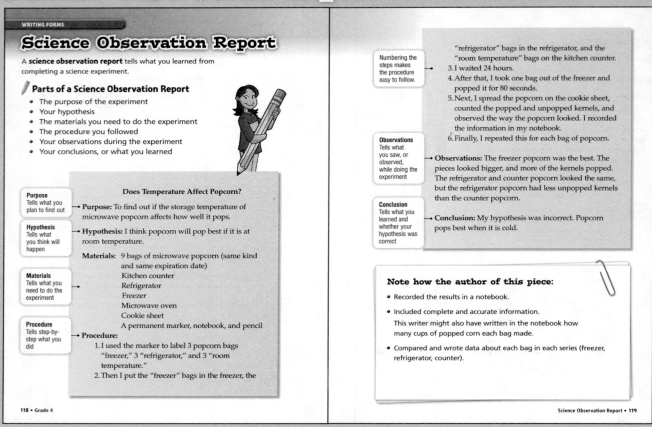

Science Observation Report

A **science observation report** tells what you learned from completing a science experiment.

Parts of a Science Observation Report
- The purpose of the experiment
- Your hypothesis
- The materials you need to do the experiment
- The procedure you followed
- Your observations during the experiment
- Your conclusions, or what you learned

Purpose
Tells what you plan to find out

Hypothesis
Tells what you think will happen

Materials
Tells what you need to do the experiment

Procedure
Tells step-by-step what you did

Does Temperature Affect Popcorn?

- **Purpose:** To find out if the storage temperature of microwave popcorn affects how well it pops.
- **Hypothesis:** I think popcorn will pop best if it is at room temperature.

Materials: 9 bags of microwave popcorn (same kind and same expiration date)
Kitchen counter
Refrigerator
Freezer
Microwave oven
Cookie sheet
A permanent marker, notebook, and pencil

- **Procedure:**
  1. I used the marker to label 3 popcorn bags "freezer," 3 "refrigerator," and 3 "room temperature."
  2. Then I put the "freezer" bags in the freezer, the

118 • Grade 4

Numbering the steps makes the procedure easy to follow.

"refrigerator" bags in the refrigerator, and the "room temperature" bags on the kitchen counter.
3. I waited 24 hours.
4. After that, I took one bag out of the freezer and popped it for 80 seconds.
5. Next, I spread the popcorn on the cookie sheet, counted the popped and unpopped kernels, and observed the way the popcorn looked. I recorded the information in my notebook.
6. Finally, I repeated this for each bag of popcorn.

Observations
Tells what you saw, or observed, while doing the experiment

- **Observations:** The freezer popcorn was the best. The pieces looked bigger, and more of the kernels popped. The refrigerator and counter popcorn looked the same, but the refrigerator popcorn had less unpopped kernels than the counter popcorn.

Conclusion
Tells what you learned and whether your hypothesis was correct

- **Conclusion:** My hypothesis was incorrect. Popcorn pops best when it is cold.

Note how the author of this piece:
- Recorded the results in a notebook.
- Included complete and accurate information. This writer might also have written in the notebook how many cups of popped corn each bag made.
- Compared and wrote data about each bag in each series (freezer, refrigerator, counter).

Science Observation Report • 119

WRITING MODELS AND FORMS

Minilesson 105

Understanding the Science Observation Report

Objective: Understand the science observation report.

Guiding Question: How can I use these pages to help me write a good science observation report?

Teach/Model

Tell students to read the definition and bulleted points. Explain that the example on these pages is a science observation report about a microwave popcorn experiment. Have students read to the end of p. 119.

Practice/Apply

Have students discuss the purpose, hypothesis, and conclusion of this microwave popcorn experiment.

96 • Writing

Minilesson 106

Using Time-Order Words

Objective: Use time-order words to explain a procedure.

Guiding Question: How can I use time-order words to make my science observation report clear?

Teach/Model

Explain to students that the author used time-order words to explain the step-by-step procedure in this report. Point out that time-order words such as *Then* and *After that* help make the order of the steps clear.

Practice/Apply

Have students identify other time-order words in this report. (Examples: *Next, Finally*) Have them discuss how using time-order words and numbering the steps makes the procedure easy to follow.

Research Report

WRITING FORMS

Research Report

A **research report** uses facts and details from outside sources to inform readers about a topic.

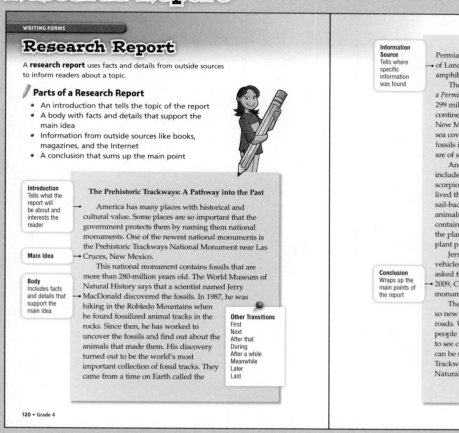

Parts of a Research Report

- An introduction that tells the topic of the report
- A body with facts and details that support the main idea
- Information from outside sources like books, magazines, and the Internet
- A conclusion that sums up the main point

Introduction
Tells what the report will be about and interests the reader

Main Idea

Body
Includes facts and details that support the main idea

The Prehistoric Trackways: A Pathway into the Past

America has many places with historical and cultural value. Some places are so important that the government protects them by naming them national monuments. One of the newest national monuments is the Prehistoric Trackways National Monument near Las Cruces, New Mexico.

This national monument contains fossils that are more than 280-million years old. The World Museum of Natural History says that a scientist named Jerry MacDonald discovered the fossils. In 1987, he was hiking in the Robledo Mountains when he found fossilized animal tracks in the rocks. Since then, he has worked to uncover the fossils and find out about the animals that made them. His discovery turned out to be the world's most important collection of fossil tracks. They came from a time on Earth called the

Other Transitions
First
Next
After that
During
After a while
Meanwhile
Later
Last

120 • Grade 4

Information Source
Tells where specific information was found

Permian Period. According to the New Mexico Bureau of Land Management, the monument contains fossils of amphibians, reptiles, insects, plants, and petrified wood.

There is a book about the monument called *Traces of a Permian Seacoast*. It says the Permian Period was 251 to 299 million years ago. Back then, all the Earth's continents were one big supercontinent called Pangea. New Mexico was near the equator. A shallow tropical sea covered its southern part. That is why some of the fossils in the Prehistoric Trackways National Monument are of sea animals like brachiopods.

Ancient animals that lived along the seacoast included different kinds of fish, insects, spiders, and scorpions. Amphibians, like snakes and salamanders, lived there, too. So did big predators like the ferocious sail-backed dimetrodon. Fossils from all of these animals can be found in the new monument. It also contains fossils of logs, trees, and other plants. Some of the plants were like those we see today. The Walchia plant probably looked like a modern Norfolk Pine tree.

Jerry MacDonald worried that hikers and all-terrain vehicles might destroy these valuable fossils. So, he asked the United States Government to protect them. In 2009, Congress agreed to make this area a national monument.

Conclusion
Wraps up the main points of the report

The Prehistoric Trackways National Monument is so new that there are no signs, hiking paths, or smooth roads. Work is underway for that to change. For now, people can hike, ride horses, or drive off-road vehicles to see certain parts of the monument. More of the fossils can be seen at the Jerry MacDonald Paleozoic Trackways collection in the New Mexico Museum of Natural History and Science.

Research Report • 121

WRITING MODELS AND FORMS

Minilesson 107

Understanding the Research Report

Objective: Understand the research report.

Guiding Question: How can I use these pages to help me write a good research report?

Teach/Model

Ask students to read the definition and bulleted points. Explain that the example on these pages is a report about Prehistoric Trackways National Monument. Add that research reports give information in the author's own words and often include a works-cited page at the end. Then have students read to the end of p. 121.

Practice/Apply

Have students identify the main idea of this research report and three facts and details that support it.

Minilesson 108

Identifying Sources of Information

Objective: Identify outside sources of information.

Guiding Question: How do I tell where I found information for my report?

Teach/Model

Explain to students that one way to identify a source of information is by citing it in the report itself. Discuss how the author did this in the second paragraph. Point out the sentence that begins *According to the New Mexico Bureau of Land Management.*

Practice/Apply

Have students find two other information sources the author cites in this report. *(World Museum of Natural History, Traces of a Permian Seacoast)*

Writing • **97**

Writing Handbook Minilessons

Graphs, Diagrams, and Charts

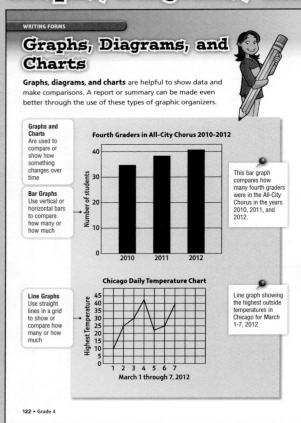

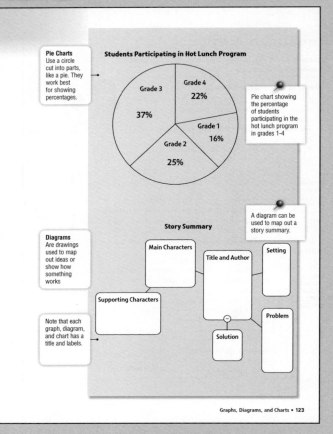

WRITING MODELS AND FORMS

Minilesson 109

Understanding Graphs, Diagrams, and Charts

Objective: Understand graphs, diagrams, and charts.

Guiding Question: How do I use graphs, diagrams, or charts to make my report or summary better?

Teach/Model

Have students read the definition on p. 122. Then discuss each of the examples given on these pages.

Practice/Apply

Have students use the first three graphic organizers to answer these questions: *In which year were the most fourth graders in All-City Chorus? Which March day was warmest in Chicago? Which grade has 37 percent of its students in the hot lunch program?*

98 • Writing

Minilesson 110

Using Titles and Labels

Objective: Use titles and labels on graphic organizers.

Guiding Question: What titles and labels can I use to make my graphs, diagrams, and charts clear?

Teach/Model

Explain to students that using titles and labels on graphic organizers helps the reader interpret the information that is shown. Point out that the bar graph, line graph, pie chart, and story summary on these pages all have clear titles and labels.

Practice/Apply

Have students create a bar graph, a line graph, or a pie chart to represent data about their classroom or school. Remind them to use a clear title and labels.

Character Description

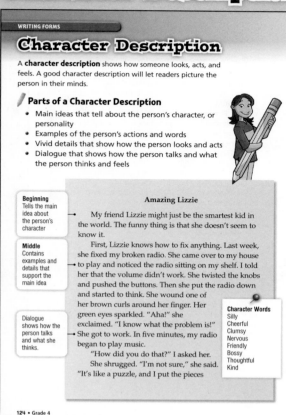

Character Description

A **character description** shows how someone looks, acts, and feels. A good character description will let readers picture the person in their minds.

Parts of a Character Description

- Main ideas that tell about the person's character, or personality
- Examples of the person's actions and words
- Vivid details that show how the person looks and acts
- Dialogue that shows how the person talks and what the person thinks and feels

Beginning
Tells the main idea about the person's character

Middle
Contains examples and details that support the main idea

Dialogue
shows how the person talks and what she thinks.

Amazing Lizzie

My friend Lizzie might just be the smartest kid in the world. The funny thing is that she doesn't seem to know it.

First, Lizzie knows how to fix anything. Last week, she fixed my broken radio. She came over to my house to play and noticed the radio sitting on my shelf. I told her that the volume didn't work. She twisted the knobs and pushed the buttons. Then she put the radio down and started to think. She wound one of her brown curls around her finger. Her green eyes sparkled. "Aha!" she exclaimed. "I know what the problem is!" She got to work. In five minutes, my radio began to play music.

"How did you do that?" I asked her.

She shrugged. "I'm not sure," she said. "It's like a puzzle, and I put the pieces

Character Words
Silly
Cheerful
Clumsy
Nervous
Friendly
Bossy
Thoughtful
Kind

124 • Grade 4

together." This was the same answer I got when Lizzie fixed our computer printer, TV, and toaster.

Second, Lizzie knows something about everything. She can tell you how clouds are formed or how many different kinds of birds are found in Canada. Do you want to know how bridges are built? Just ask Lizzie. Sometimes she'll give a short answer, like she did with the radio. Other times, she gets excited and won't stop talking. One time I asked her how jelly beans are made. For the next twenty minutes, she told me all about jelly bean factories. Some people might think that this would be annoying. But Lizzie makes learning fun. She might even crack a good joke. "Hey, why did the jelly bean go to school?" she asked me. "Because he wanted to be a smartie!" Then she bent over and laughed her head off.

Lizzie never brags about being smart. She says that everyone knows something that other people don't. I guess she's right. But to me, Lizzie sure seems like a smartie in a world of jelly beans.

Vivid descriptions show how the person acts and feels.

Ending Reviews the main idea of the character description

Note how the authors of this piece:

- Described the person's appearance by mentioning her hair and eye color.

 Other ways to describe how a person looks include telling about her age, clothing, or unique physical features.

 No one believes that Lizzie is only nine because she is so tall.
 Lizzie always wears shorts and sneakers.
 Lizzie has freckles across her nose and a dimple on her right cheek.

Character Description • 125

Minilesson 111

Understanding the Character Description

Objective: Understand character description.

Guiding Question: How do I use these pages to help me write a good character description?

Teach/Model

Ask students to read the definition and the bulleted points. Explain that the example on these pages describes a character named Lizzie. Point out that the author described how Lizzie looks, acts, and feels. Then have students read to the end of p. 125.

Practice/Apply

Have students write a short scene describing something else Lizzie might do based on the details provided in the character description. Encourage them to draw a picture of her.

Minilesson 112

Using Vivid Details

Objective: Use vivid details to bring a character to life.

Guiding Question: What details will I use to describe how a character looks, acts, and feels?

Teach/Model

Explain that the author used vivid details to describe Lizzie. Point out these details: *She wound one of her brown curls around her finger* and *she bent over and laughed her head off.* Tell students that these details help the reader picture what Lizzie looks like and how she acts.

Practice/Apply

Have students write sentences describing a real person or an imaginary character. Ask them to add at least three vivid details.

Writing • 99

Writing Handbook Minilessons

Personal Narrative

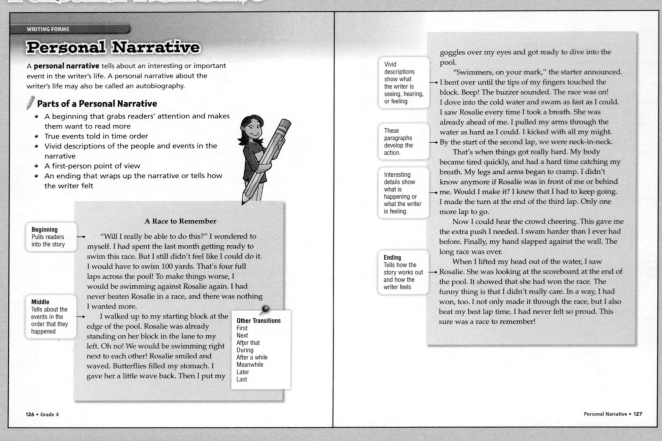

WRITING MODELS AND FORMS

Minilesson 113

Understanding the Personal Narrative

Objective: Understand the personal narrative.

Guiding Question: How can I use these pages to help me write a good personal narrative?

Teach/Model

Have students read the definition and bulleted points. Explain that the example on these pages is a personal narrative about a swimming race. Point out that the author used the first-person point of view: *I, me, my, myself.* Then ask students to read to the end of p. 127.

Practice/Apply

Have students list the interesting details and vivid descriptions in this personal narrative that help bring people and events to life.

100 • Writing

Minilesson 114

Using Time Order

Objective: Tell events in the order in which they happened.

Guiding Question: How do I tell what happened in my personal narrative?

Teach/Model

Explain to students that a personal narrative tells what happened in time order. Point out that the author arranged events in the swimming race in the order in which they happened, linking them with transitions such as *Then* and *By the start of the second lap.*

Practice/Apply

Have students write about an important event in their own lives using time order to narrate the sequence of events.

Biography

WRITING FORMS

Biography

A **biography** is a true story that tells about the main events in a person's life. It explains why the person is special or interesting, or how he or she made a difference.

Parts of a Biography

- A beginning that introduces the person to readers
- A middle with interesting facts and details about the person
- Events told in time order, or sequence
- An ending that wraps up the biography or gives a final thought

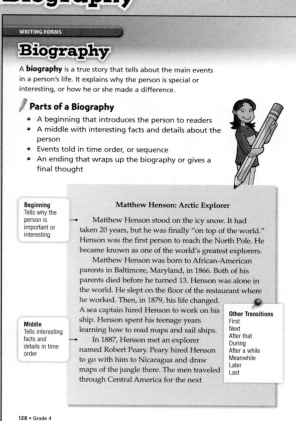

Matthew Henson: Arctic Explorer

Beginning
Tells why the person is important or interesting

Matthew Henson stood on the icy snow. It had taken 20 years, but he was finally "on top of the world." Henson was the first person to reach the North Pole. He became known as one of the world's greatest explorers.

Matthew Henson was born to African-American parents in Baltimore, Maryland, in 1866. Both of his parents died before he turned 13. Henson was alone in the world. He slept on the floor of the restaurant where he worked. Then, in 1879, his life changed. A sea captain hired Henson to work on his ship. Henson spent his teenage years learning how to read maps and sail ships.

Middle
Tells interesting facts and details in time order

In 1887, Henson met an explorer named Robert Peary. Peary hired Henson to go with him to Nicaragua and draw maps of the jungle there. The men traveled through Central America for the next

Other Transitions
First
Next
After that
During
After a while
Meanwhile
Later
Last

128 • Grade 4

two years. When the trip ended, Peary decided to go after his real dream. He wanted to be the first person in the world to reach the North Pole. He asked Henson to go with him.

Between 1891 and 1908, Peary and Henson tried to reach the North Pole four times. Each time, they started from base camps in Greenland or Canada. Then they traveled north. The trips were very dangerous. The weather was extremely cold and windy. The men also had trouble finding food. Henson became stronger, though. He made friends with the Eskimo and learned a lot from them. He learned how to break trails, hunt for food, and make clothing from animal fur. Henson even learned how to build sleds and run a dog team. These skills helped the men survive.

Keep readers interested with stories about what the person experienced.

In April 1909, Peary and Henson tried one last time to reach the North Pole. The men didn't have a lot of supplies and could make only one trip. Henson ran the lead sled and moved quickly. In five days, Henson traveled over 200 miles. He reached the North Pole shortly before Peary did. Henson became the first person to reach what is known as the top of the world.

Unfortunately, Henson didn't have a lot of time to celebrate. People didn't believe that he and Peary really reached the North Pole. They had to prove that they were telling the truth. Then, Peary took all the credit. He said that he was the first one to reach the North Pole.

Ending
Wraps up the biography and gives a final thought

Finally, in 1937, people learned the truth. Henson received many awards after that, including the Congressional Medal of Honor. He even had schools and a ship named after him. Matthew Henson died in 1955. He is still remembered as one of the world's greatest explorers.

Biography • 129

WRITING MODELS AND FORMS

Minilesson 115

Understanding the Biography

Objective: Understand the biography.

Guiding Question: How can I use these pages to help me write a good biography?

Teach/Model

Tell students to read the definition and the bulleted points on p. 128. Explain that the example on these pages is a biography of the African-American explorer Matthew Henson. Then have students read to the end of p. 129.

Practice/Apply

Have students discuss why Matthew Henson is important or how he made a difference based on their reading of facts and details in this biography.

Minilesson 116

Including Facts

Objective: Use facts to tell about a person's life.

Guiding Question: How do I include facts in my biography?

Teach/Model

Remind students that a biography includes details about a person's life. Explain that the author told about the main events in Matthew Henson's life, beginning with his birth and ending with his death. Point out that the author included facts like dates to describe when these happened. Point out the dates in the model.

Practice/Apply

Using dates and details in this biography, have students make a timeline of Matthew Henson's life.

Writing • **101**

Writing Handbook Minilessons

Fictional Narrative

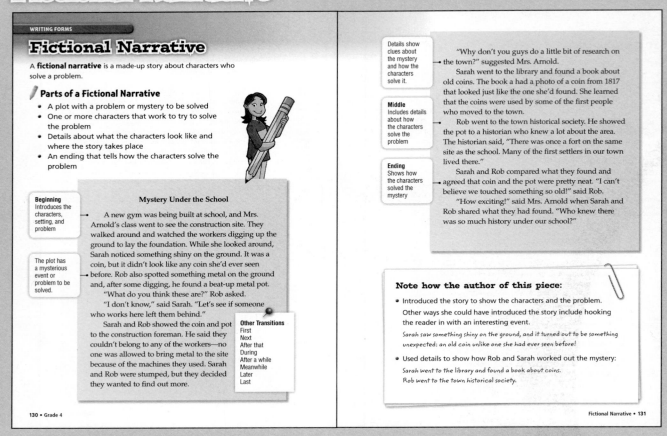

Minilesson 117

Understanding the Fictional Narrative

Objective: Understand the fictional narrative.

Guiding Question: How can I use these pages to help me write a good fictional narrative?

Teach/Model

Tell students to read the definition and bulleted points. Add that a fictional narrative includes dialogue. Have students read to the end of p. 131.

Practice/Apply

Have students list the details and dialogue that help them understand the characters and setting in this fictional narrative. Discuss how each detail contributes to the story.

102 • Writing

Minilesson 118

Understanding Plot

Objective: Understand the plot of a fictional narrative.

Guiding Question: What elements do I include in the plot of my fictional narrative?

Teach/Model

Explain to students that the plot of a fictional narrative is the sequence of story events. It includes a problem the characters solve and a solution. Point out that the problem in "Mystery Under the School" is introduced in the beginning and solved in the middle and ending.

Practice/Apply

Have students list the sequence of story events in "Mystery Under the School." Make sure that they can identify the problem and how Rob and Sarah solve it.

Play

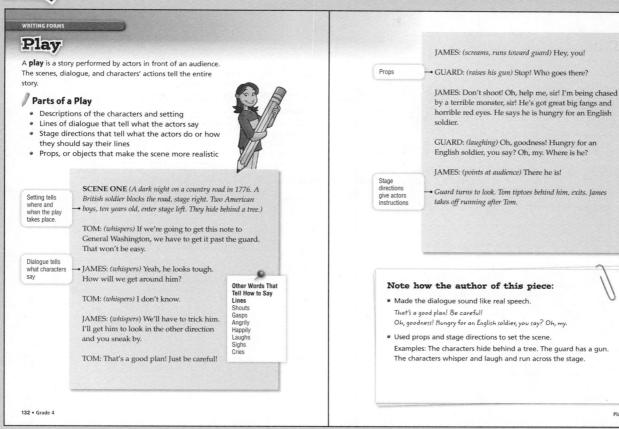

WRITING FORMS

Play

A **play** is a story performed by actors in front of an audience. The scenes, dialogue, and characters' actions tell the entire story.

Parts of a Play

- Descriptions of the characters and setting
- Lines of dialogue that tell what the actors say
- Stage directions that tell what the actors do or how they should say their lines
- Props, or objects that make the scene more realistic

Setting tells where and when the play takes place.

SCENE ONE (*A dark night on a country road in 1776. A British soldier blocks the road, stage right. Two American boys, ten years old, enter stage left. They hide behind a tree.*)

TOM: (*whispers*) If we're going to get this note to General Washington, we have to get it past the guard. That won't be easy.

Dialogue tells what characters say

JAMES: (*whispers*) Yeah, he looks tough. How will we get around him?

TOM: (*whispers*) I don't know.

Other Words That Tell How to Say Lines
Shouts
Gasps
Angrily
Happily
Laughs
Sighs
Cries

JAMES: (*whispers*) We'll have to trick him. I'll get him to look in the other direction and you sneak by.

TOM: That's a good plan! Just be careful!

132 • Grade 4

JAMES: (*screams, runs toward guard*) Hey, you!

Props

GUARD: (*raises his gun*) Stop! Who goes there?

JAMES: Don't shoot! Oh, help me, sir! I'm being chased by a terrible monster, sir! He's got great big fangs and horrible red eyes. He says he is hungry for an English soldier.

GUARD: (*laughing*) Oh, goodness! Hungry for an English soldier, you say? Oh, my. Where is he?

JAMES: (*points at audience*) There he is!

Stage directions give actors instructions

Guard turns to look. Tom tiptoes behind him, exits. James takes off running after Tom.

Note how the author of this piece:

- Made the dialogue sound like real speech.
  That's a good plan! Be careful!
  Oh, goodness! Hungry for an English soldier, you say? Oh, my.
- Used props and stage directions to set the scene.
  Examples: The characters hide behind a tree. The guard has a gun. The characters whisper and laugh and run across the stage.

Play • 133

WRITING MODELS AND FORMS

Minilesson 119

Understanding the Play

Objective: Understand the elements of a play.

Guiding Question: How can I use these pages to help me write a good play?

Teach/Model

Have students read the definition and bulleted points. Add that some plays are divided into acts and scenes. Explain that this scene from a play is set during the American Revolution in the 18th century. Then have students read to the end of p. 133.

Practice/Apply

Have students discuss how the setting, stage directions, and props help set this scene.

Minilesson 120

Using Dialogue

Objective: Use dialogue in a play.

Guiding Question: How do I use dialogue in a play?

Teach/Model

Explain to students that this play scene consists of lines of dialogue that are spoken by three actors who play Tom, James, and a British soldier. Point out that the characters' names are written in capital letters and the stage directions are written in italics.

Practice/Apply

Have three volunteers perform the play, reading lines of dialogue. Remind them to use the stage directions as a guide for how they should speak their lines. Next, ask students to write dialogue for the following scene in the play.

Writing • 103

Writing Handbook Minilessons

Tall Tale/Myth

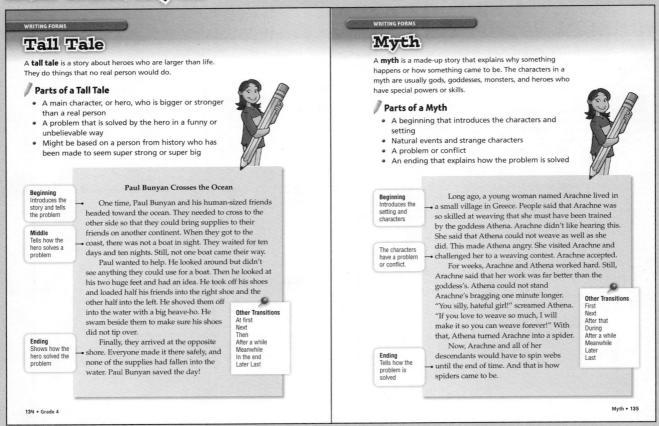

WRITING MODELS AND FORMS

Minilesson 121

Understanding the Tall Tale

Objective: Understand the tall tale.

Guiding Question: How can I use this page to help me write a tall tale?

Teach/Model

Ask students to read the definition and the bulleted points on p. 134. Explain that the tall tale on this page, "Paul Bunyan Crosses the Ocean," is about a hero who solves a problem in an unbelievable way. Then have students read to the end of the page.

Practice/Apply

Have students discuss the characteristics that make Paul Bunyan a hero. Encourage them to recall stories about other heroes they have read about in tall tales and write their own brief tall tale.

Minilesson 122

Understanding the Myth

Objective: Understand the myth.

Guiding Question: How can I use this page to help me write a myth?

Teach/Model

Have students read the definition and bulleted points on p. 135. Explain that the example on this page is a retelling of a Greek myth about a weaver named Arachne and the goddess Athena. Ask students to read to the end of the page.

Practice/Apply

Have students discuss the setting, the characters, and the conflict in this myth. Ask *According to this myth, how did spiders come to be?* Have students share other myths they have heard.

Opinion Essay

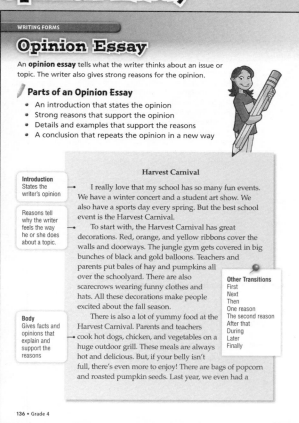

Opinion Essay

An **opinion essay** tells what the writer thinks about an issue or topic. The writer also gives strong reasons for the opinion.

Parts of an Opinion Essay

- An introduction that states the opinion
- Strong reasons that support the opinion
- Details and examples that support the reasons
- A conclusion that repeats the opinion in a new way

Introduction
States the writer's opinion

Reasons tell why the writer feels the way he or she does about a topic.

Body
Gives facts and opinions that explain and support the reasons

Harvest Carnival

I really love that my school has so many fun events. We have a winter concert and a student art show. We also have a sports day every spring. But the best school event is the Harvest Carnival.

To start with, the Harvest Carnival has great decorations. Red, orange, and yellow ribbons cover the walls and doorways. The jungle gym gets covered in big bunches of black and gold balloons. Teachers and parents put bales of hay and pumpkins all over the schoolyard. There are also scarecrows wearing funny clothes and hats. All these decorations make people excited about the fall season.

There is also a lot of yummy food at the Harvest Carnival. Parents and teachers cook hot dogs, chicken, and vegetables on a huge outdoor grill. These meals are always hot and delicious. But, if your belly isn't full, there's even more to enjoy! There are bags of popcorn and roasted pumpkin seeds. Last year, we even had a

Other Transitions
First
Next
Then
One reason
The second reason
After that
During
Later
Finally

Strong descriptions convince readers to agree with the opinion.

big table with bowls of fruit, pies, and other treats. Of course, caramel apples are my favorite food to eat at the Harvest Carnival. Some of them are plain with only caramel. Others are covered in chocolate chips or peanuts.

Last, the Harvest Carnival has a lot of really fun games. In one game, you try to throw a ping-pong ball into a goldfish bowl. If you do it, you get to bring the goldfish home. In another game, you can win a prize by running with an egg in a spoon without dropping it. There is even a cake walk and a pie-eating contest. I spend all afternoon playing the games at the Harvest Carnival, and I still don't want to leave at the end of the day.

Conclusion
Repeats the focus statement in a new way

My school has a lot of great events throughout the year. But nothing beats the Harvest Carnival. After all, where else can you see beautiful decorations, eat yummy food, and play exciting games?

Note how the author of this piece:

- Gave a reason in the topic sentence of each paragraph.

  To start with, the Harvest Carnival has great decorations.
  There is also a lot of yummy food at the Harvest Carnival.
  Last, the Harvest Carnival has a lot of really fun games.

- Used strong language and descriptions to convince readers that her reasons make sense.

  Red, orange, and yellow ribbons cover the walls and doorways.
  All these decorations **make people excited** about the fall season.
  These meals are always **hot** and **delicious.**

136 • Grade 4

Opinion Essay • 137

Minilesson 123

Understanding the Opinion Essay

Objective: Understand the opinion essay.

Guiding Question: How can I use these pages to help me write a good opinion essay?

Teach/Model

Tell students to read the definition and the bulleted points that follow it. Explain that the opinion essay on these pages tells what the author thinks about the school's yearly Harvest Carnival. Then have students read to the end of p. 137.

Practice/Apply

Have students look at the introduction and the conclusion of the essay. Have them write the author's opinion statement in their own words.

Minilesson 124

Supporting Opinions with Strong Reasons

Objective: Use strong reasons to support an opinion.

Guiding Question: What reasons will I use to support my opinion in an opinion essay?

Teach/Model

Explain to students that the author's opinion about the Harvest Carnival is supported with strong reasons. Point out transition words, such as *To start with* and *Last,* that link the opinion and reasons that support it.

Practice/Apply

Have students list three reasons from the essay that support the author's opinion. Then have them find details and examples that support each reason.

Writing • 105

Writing Handbook Minilessons

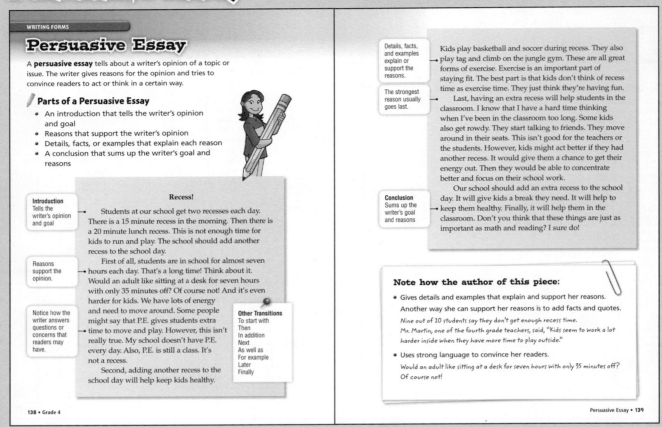

WRITING MODELS AND FORMS

Minilesson 125

Understanding the Persuasive Essay

Objective: Understand the persuasive essay.

Guiding Question: How can I use these pages to help me write a good persuasive essay?

Teach/Model

Ask students to read the definition and bulleted points. Explain that the persuasive essay on these pages tells about the author's opinion of recess at her school. Then have students read to the end of p. 139.

Practice/Apply

Have students look at the introduction and the conclusion of the essay. Ask them to explain the author's opinion about recess at her school and her goal.

106 • Writing

Minilesson 126

Using Persuasive Language

Objective: Use strong language to convince an audience.

Guiding Question: What words and phrases can I use in my persuasive essay to convince my readers?

Teach/Model

Tell students that a persuasive essay uses strong, convincing words. Point out examples of persuasive language in this essay, such as *That's a long time!* and *I sure do!* Explain that the author used persuasive language to convince readers to accept her viewpoint.

Practice/Apply

Have students find other examples of strong words and phrases that the author used in this essay to convince her readers.

Response to Literature: Play

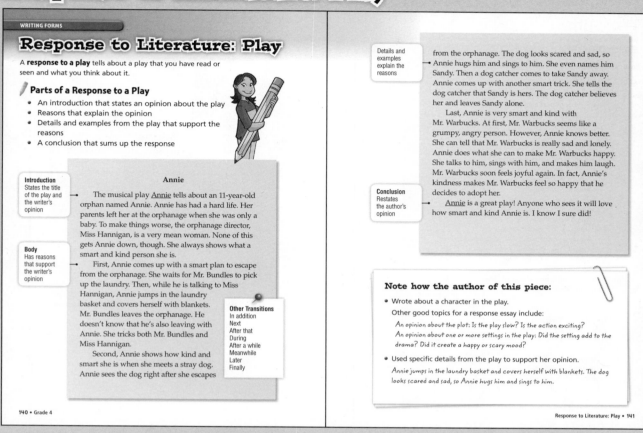

WRITING FORMS

Response to Literature: Play

A **response to a play** tells about a play that you have read or seen and what you think about it.

Parts of a Response to a Play
- An introduction that states an opinion about the play
- Reasons that explain the opinion
- Details and examples from the play that support the reasons
- A conclusion that sums up the response

Introduction
States the title of the play and the writer's opinion

Body
Has reasons that support the writer's opinion

Annie

The musical play Annie tells about an 11-year-old orphan named Annie. Annie has had a hard life. Her parents left her at the orphanage when she was only a baby. To make things worse, the orphanage director, Miss Hannigan, is a very mean woman. None of this gets Annie down, though. She always shows what a smart and kind person she is.

First, Annie comes up with a smart plan to escape from the orphanage. She waits for Mr. Bundles to pick up the laundry. Then, while he is talking to Miss Hannigan, Annie jumps in the laundry basket and covers herself with blankets. Mr. Bundles leaves the orphanage. He doesn't know that he's also leaving with Annie. She tricks both Mr. Bundles and Miss Hannigan.

Second, Annie shows how kind and smart she is when she meets a stray dog. Annie sees the dog right after she escapes

Other Transitions
In addition
Next
After that
During
After a while
Meanwhile
Later
Finally

140 • Grade 4

Details and examples explain the reasons

from the orphanage. The dog looks scared and sad, so Annie hugs him and sings to him. She even names him Sandy. Then a dog catcher comes to take Sandy away. Annie comes up with another smart trick. She tells the dog catcher that Sandy is hers. The dog catcher believes her and leaves Sandy alone.

Last, Annie is very smart and kind with Mr. Warbucks. At first, Mr. Warbucks seems like a grumpy, angry person. However, Annie knows better. She can tell that Mr. Warbucks is really sad and lonely. Annie does what she can to make Mr. Warbucks happy. She talks to him, sings with him, and makes him laugh. Mr. Warbucks soon feels joyful again. In fact, Annie's kindness makes Mr. Warbucks feel so happy that he decides to adopt her.

Conclusion
Restates the author's opinion

Annie is a great play! Anyone who sees it will love how smart and kind Annie is. I know I sure did!

Note how the author of this piece:
- Wrote about a character in the play.
  Other good topics for a response essay include:
  An opinion about the plot: Is the play slow? Is the action exciting?
  An opinion about one or more settings in the play: Did the setting add to the drama? Did it create a happy or scary mood?
- Used specific details from the play to support her opinion.
  Annie jumps in the laundry basket and covers herself with blankets. The dog looks scared and sad, so Annie hugs him and sings to him.

Response to Literature: Play • 141

WRITING MODELS AND FORMS

Minilesson 127

Understanding the Response to a Play

Objective: Understand a response essay about a play.

Guiding Question: How can I use these pages to help me write a good response to a play?

Teach/Model

Ask students to read the definition and the bulleted points that follow it. Explain that the response to a play on these pages tells how the author felt about the musical play *Annie*. Then instruct students to read to the end of p. 141.

Practice/Apply

Have students write an opinion about a play that they have read or seen. Challenge them to list reasons that explain their opinions.

Minilesson 128

Using Specific Details and Examples

Objective: Use strong details and examples as support.

Guiding Question: What details and examples should I use to explain the reasons in my response essay?

Teach/Model

Tell students that the author used strong details and examples from *Annie* to explain her opinion about the play. For example, the detail *She tricks both Mr. Bundles and Miss Hannigan* in the second paragraph supports the reason that Annie is smart.

Practice/Apply

Have students find other details and examples from the play that the author uses to explain the reasons for her opinion.

Writing • **107**

Writing Handbook Minilessons

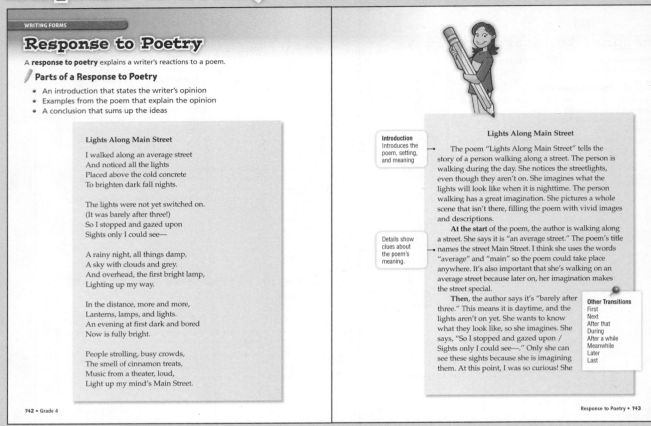

Response to Poetry

WRITING FORMS

Response to Poetry

A **response to poetry** explains a writer's reactions to a poem.

Parts of a Response to Poetry

- An introduction that states the writer's opinion
- Examples from the poem that explain the opinion
- A conclusion that sums up the ideas

Lights Along Main Street

I walked along an average street
And noticed all the lights
Placed above the cold concrete
To brighten dark fall nights.

The lights were not yet switched on.
(It was barely after three!)
So I stopped and gazed upon
Sights only I could see—

A rainy night, all things damp,
A sky with clouds and grey.
And overhead, the first bright lamp,
Lighting up my way.

In the distance, more and more,
Lanterns, lamps, and lights.
An evening at first dark and bored
Now is fully bright.

People strolling, busy crowds,
The smell of cinnamon treats,
Music from a theater, loud,
Light up my mind's Main Street.

142 • Grade 4

Lights Along Main Street

Introduction Introduces the poem, setting, and meaning

The poem "Lights Along Main Street" tells the story of a person walking along a street. The person is walking during the day. She notices the streetlights, even though they aren't on. She imagines what the lights will look like when it is nighttime. The person walking has a great imagination. She pictures a whole scene that isn't there, filling the poem with vivid images and descriptions.

Details show clues about the poem's meaning.

At the start of the poem, the author is walking along a street. She says it is "an average street." The poem's title names the street Main Street. I think she uses the words "average" and "main" so the poem could take place anywhere. It's also important that she's walking on an average street because later on, her imagination makes the street special.

Then, the author says it's "barely after three." This means it is daytime, and the lights aren't on yet. She wants to know what they look like, so she imagines. She says, "So I stopped and gazed upon / Sights only I could see—." Only she can see these sights because she is imagining them. At this point, I was so curious! She

Other Transitions
First
Next
After that
During
After a while
Meanwhile
Later
Last

Response to Poetry • 143

WRITING MODELS AND FORMS

Minilesson 129

Understanding the Response to Poetry

Objective: Understand a response to poetry.

Guiding Question: How can I use these pages to help me write a good response to poetry?

Teach/Model

Ask students to read the definition, bulleted points, and poem on p. 142. Explain that the composition starting on p. 143 is a response to "Lights Along Main Street." Then have students read to the end of p. 145.

Practice/Apply

After reading the composition, ask students to identify how the author feels about "Lights Along Main Street." Have them find reasons that explain this opinion.

108 • Writing

Minilesson 130

Quoting Poetry Correctly

Objective: Quote two or more lines of poetry correctly.

Guiding Question: How do I quote two or more lines of poetry in my response to poetry composition?

Teach/Model

Point out the pair of quoted lines from "Lights Along Main Street" in the third paragraph of this composition. Explain that the author put quotation marks around the lines and used a slash (/) with a space before and after it to show where one line ends and the next begins.

Practice/Apply

Have students quote two consecutive lines from "Lights Along Main Street" or another poem to complete this sentence: *My two favorite lines are _____.*

Response to Poetry

could have imagined anything. She could have imagined a busy street with people walking and having fun. Instead, she imagines something very dark.

Indeed, she sees, "A rainy night, all things damp / A sky with clouds and grey." The author pictures a dark evening with rain. "All things damp" means that it has been raining for a long time. When it rains for a while, everything gets a little wet. **Further**, the author sees "clouds and grey." This sounds like the kind of night when you don't even want to go outside because it is so wet and rainy.

Next, the author sees "the first bright lamp." Here, I picture this dark scene where everything is sad and quiet. Then, out of the dim street scene, a light! The lamp is so bright that it stands out against the darkness. She says it is "lighting up my way." Now, she can see in front of her. Instead of seeing just the grey sky, the author can see the street. At first, she just sees more and more light. This means the street looks brighter.

Finally, in the light, everything looks happy. She sees people walking and gathering in a store. She also smells cinnamon and hears music. These lines are so important because these are the first people, smells, and sounds in the poem. Before, when it was dark outside, the poem was dark and empty. Now, when the lights are on, the poem is filled with people and things to smell and hear.

> **Body**
> Digs in further to find meaning in the poem

> **More details** help to discuss the poem's meaning.

The last line is: "Light up my mind's Main Street." I like that the author says it is her mind's street, and not just any street. This is not "an average street" or even "Main Street" anymore. This shows that the author now loves the street. It is no longer dark and dreary outside. Now it is bright and full of music. All of this is in her imagination, so I think she is really happy.

When I finished reading the poem, I looked back at the title: "Lights Along Main Street." I noticed that the focus of the title isn't darkness or rain. The focus is on light. The author never gets to see the lights turn on. However, she imagines what it would look like. Her imagination is so bright and full. I believe this is what the poem is about—finding excitement and happiness in dark places.

> **Conclusion**
> Sums up the main idea of the poem

Note how the author of this piece:

- Ends the response by going back to the beginning (the title). The author also could have ended the piece by talking about something general in the poem:
  I notice that the ideas of light and dark come up again and again in the poem.

- Shows what the poem did not say, but could have:
  She could have imagined a busy street with people walking and having fun.

144 • Grade 4

Response to Poetry • 145

WRITING MODELS AND FORMS

Minilesson 131

Analyzing Sensory Details

Objective: Analyze sensory details in a response to poetry.

Guiding Question: How do I analyze a poem's sensory details in my composition?

Teach/Model

Have students reread the last stanza of "Lights Along Main Street" (p. 142). Point out the writer's discussion of details from this stanza in the sixth and seventh paragraphs (pp. 144–145). Explain that the writer analyzed sensory details to find the poem's meaning.

Practice/Apply

Have students make a chart with the headings *Sight, Sound, Smell, Touch.* Have them list details in "Lights Along Main Street" that appeal to these senses.

Minilesson 132

Analyzing Figurative Language

Objective: Analyze figurative language in a poetry response.

Guiding Question: How do I analyze a poem's figurative language for my composition?

Teach/Model

Ask students to reread the last stanza of "Lights Along Main Street" (p. 142). Point out the writer's discussion of the stanza's last line in the seventh paragraph (p. 145) of the composition. Explain that the writer analyzed "my mind's Main Street" to find the poem's meaning.

Practice/Apply

Have students identify the type of figurative language "my mind's Main Street" is and determine whether they agree with the writer's analysis of it.

Writing • **109**

Writing Handbook Minilessons

Author Response

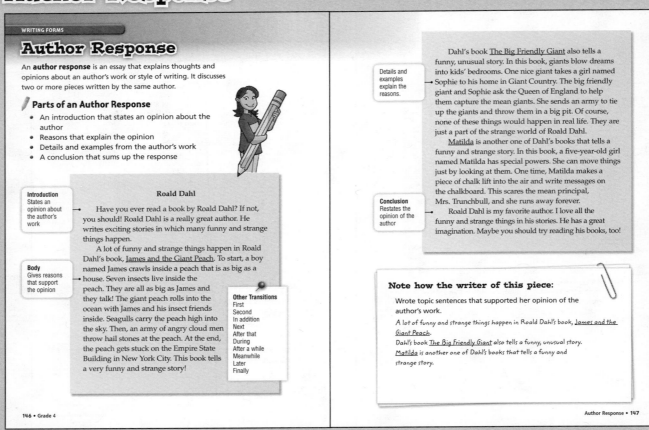

WRITING FORMS

Author Response

An **author response** is an essay that explains thoughts and opinions about an author's work or style of writing. It discusses two or more pieces written by the same author.

Parts of an Author Response
- An introduction that states an opinion about the author
- Reasons that explain the opinion
- Details and examples from the author's work
- A conclusion that sums up the response

Introduction
States an opinion about the author's work

Body
Gives reasons that support the opinion

Roald Dahl

Have you ever read a book by Roald Dahl? If not, you should! Roald Dahl is a really great author. He writes exciting stories in which many funny and strange things happen.

A lot of funny and strange things happen in Roald Dahl's book, James and the Giant Peach. To start, a boy named James crawls inside a peach that is as big as a house. Seven insects live inside the peach. They are all as big as James and they talk! The giant peach rolls into the ocean with James and his insect friends inside. Seagulls carry the peach high into the sky. Then, an army of angry cloud men throw hail stones at the peach. At the end, the peach gets stuck on the Empire State Building in New York City. This book tells a very funny and strange story!

Other Transitions
First
Second
In addition
Next
After that
During
After a while
Meanwhile
Later
Finally

146 • Grade 4

Details and examples explain the reasons.

Dahl's book The Big Friendly Giant also tells a funny, unusual story. In this book, giants blow dreams into kids' bedrooms. One nice giant takes a girl named Sophie to his home in Giant Country. The big friendly giant and Sophie ask the Queen of England to help them capture the mean giants. She sends an army to tie up the giants and throw them in a big pit. Of course, none of these things would happen in real life. They are just a part of the strange world of Roald Dahl.

Matilda is another one of Dahl's books that tells a funny and strange story. In this book, a five-year-old girl named Matilda has special powers. She can move things just by looking at them. One time, Matilda makes a piece of chalk lift into the air and write messages on the chalkboard. This scares the mean principal, Mrs. Trunchbull, and she runs away forever.

Conclusion
Restates the opinion of the author

Roald Dahl is my favorite author. I love all the funny and strange things in his stories. He has a great imagination. Maybe you should try reading his books, too!

Note how the writer of this piece:

Wrote topic sentences that supported her opinion of the author's work.

A lot of funny and strange things happen in Roald Dahl's book, James and the Giant Peach.

Dahl's book The Big Friendly Giant also tells a funny, unusual story.

Matilda is another one of Dahl's books that tells a funny and strange story.

Author Response • 147

WRITING MODELS AND FORMS

Minilesson 133

Understanding the Author Response

Objective: Understand the author response essay.

Guiding Question: How can I use these pages to help me write a good author response?

Teach/Model

Ask students to read the definition and bulleted points. Tell them that the author response on these pages discusses three books by Roald Dahl. Then have students read to the end of p. 147.

Practice/Apply

Ask students to identify the opinion in this essay. Then have them find reasons that explain the opinion and details and examples that explain the reasons.

110 • Writing

Minilesson 134

Writing Book Titles Correctly

Objective: Write book titles correctly.

Guiding Question: How do I write the titles of books in an author response essay?

Teach/Model

Call attention to the three books by Roald Dahl that are discussed in this author response essay. Tell students that book titles are underlined. Explain that the first, last, and important words are capitalized.

Practice/Apply

Have students think of an author they would like to write a response essay about. Have them list two books by this author, writing the titles correctly.

Book Review/Report

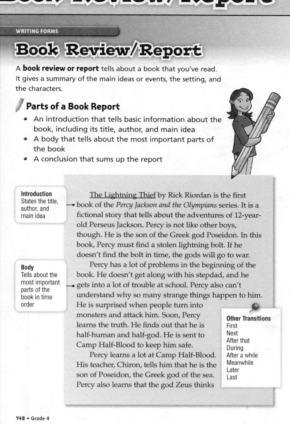

WRITING FORMS

Book Review/Report

A **book review or report** tells about a book that you've read. It gives a summary of the main ideas or events, the setting, and the characters.

Parts of a Book Report

- An introduction that tells basic information about the book, including its title, author, and main idea
- A body that tells about the most important parts of the book
- A conclusion that sums up the report

Introduction
States the title, author, and main idea

The Lightning Thief by Rick Riordan is the first book of the *Percy Jackson and the Olympians* series. It is a fictional story that tells about the adventures of 12-year-old Perseus Jackson. Percy is not like other boys, though. He is the son of the Greek god Poseidon. In this book, Percy must find a stolen lightning bolt. If he doesn't find the bolt in time, the gods will go to war.

Body
Tells about the most important parts of the book in time order

Percy has a lot of problems in the beginning of the book. He doesn't get along with his stepdad, and he gets into a lot of trouble at school. Percy also can't understand why so many strange things happen to him. He is surprised when people turn into monsters and attack him. Soon, Percy learns the truth. He finds out that he is half-human and half-god. He is sent to Camp Half-Blood to keep him safe.

Percy learns a lot at Camp Half-Blood. His teacher, Chiron, tells him that he is the son of Poseidon, the Greek god of the sea. Percy also learns that the god Zeus thinks

Other Transitions
First
Next
After that
During
After a while
Meanwhile
Later
Last

148 • Grade 4

These paragraphs give more information about the main characters and events.

that Poseidon stole his lightning bolt. If the bolt is not returned in 14 days, Zeus will go to war against Poseidon. Percy is given a quest. He must go to the Underworld, find the bolt, and return it to Zeus on Mount Olympus before the 14 days have passed. Percy takes two friends on the quest to help him. He takes Grover, a satyr, and Annabeth, the daughter of Athena.

Percy, Grover, and Annabeth must travel from New York to Los Angeles to get to the Underworld. The trip is hard. The friends battle monsters along the way. Ares, the god of war, plays a lot of tricks on them. Luckily, Percy has a special shield that keeps him safe.

Things don't get any easier for Percy when he finally gets to the Underworld. Hades, the god of the Underworld, says he doesn't have the bolt. Hades also says that his helm of darkness is missing. He accuses Percy of stealing both. To prove it, Hades says that the lightning bolt is in Percy's back pack. And it is! Percy, Grover, and Annabeth escape the Underworld and go back to New York.

At the end of the book, Percy goes to Mount Olympus on the 600th floor of the Empire State Building. He gives the lightning bolt to Zeus. He also meets his dad for the first time. Percy then tells the gods that he thinks the god Kronos caused all of the trouble. Kronos ruled before Zeus did. Now he wants to bring down the Greek gods. Percy leaves Mount Olympus at the end of the meeting. Everyone kneels and calls him a hero. Finally, Percy goes home to be with his mother.

Conclusion
Restates the title and author, and gives an opinion of the book

The Lightning Thief by Rick Riordan is an exciting, action-packed book. But, it's only the beginning of Percy Jackson's story. I can't wait to read the rest of the books in the series to find out what happens next!

Book Review/Report • 149

WRITING MODELS AND FORMS

Minilesson 135

Understanding the Book Review

Objective: Understand the book review or report.

Guiding Question: How can I use these pages to help me write a good book review or report?

Teach/Model

Tell students to read the definition and bulleted points. Explain that the book report on these pages tells about *The Lightning Thief* by Rick Riordan. Then ask them to read to the end of p. 149.

Practice/Apply

Have students find the opinion in the conclusion of this book report. Ask *Does this book report make you want to read* The Lightning Thief?

Minilesson 136

Giving a Summary of a Book

Objective: Understand how to give a summary of a book.

Guiding Question: How do I give a summary of a book for my book report?

Teach/Model

Have students review Summary on pp. 106–107. Then explain that this book report briefly describes the main events, the setting, and the characters in *The Lightning Thief*. Point out that the summary tells only the most important parts of the book, using time order.

Practice/Apply

Using information in this book report, have students create a story map that identifies the main events, the setting, and the characters in *The Lightning Thief*.

Writing • **111**

Personal Narrative

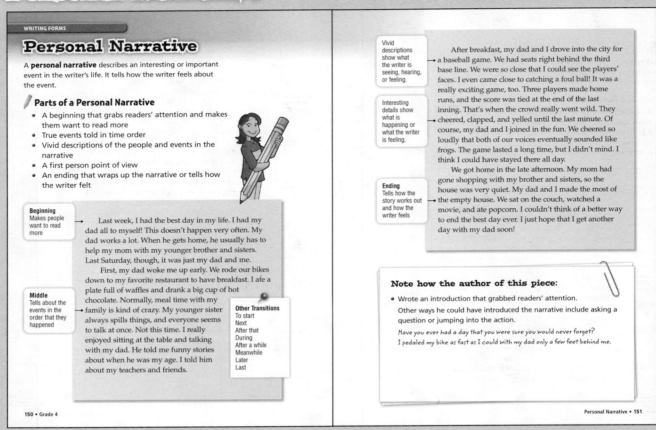

WRITING MODELS AND FORMS

Minilesson 137

Understanding the Personal Narrative

Objective: Understand the personal narrative.

Guiding Question: How can I use these pages to help me write a good personal narrative?

Teach/Model

Instruct students to read the definition and the bulleted points that follow it. Explain that the example on these pages is a personal narrative about a very enjoyable day the writer experienced. Then have students read to the end of p. 151.

Practice/Apply

Have students make a list of the vivid descriptions in this personal narrative that help them understand the people and events.

112 • Writing

Minilesson 138

Using First-Person Point of View

Objective: Use first-person point of view in a personal narrative.

Guiding Question: From what point of view will I write my personal narrative?

Teach/Model

Explain to students that most personal narratives are written from the first-person point of view, or when the narrator who tells the story also takes part in the action. Point out the pronouns *I, my,* and *me* in the first paragraph of the personal narrative.

Practice/Apply

Have students write a paragraph about an enjoyable day they experienced. Remind them to use the first-person point of view.

Labels and Captions

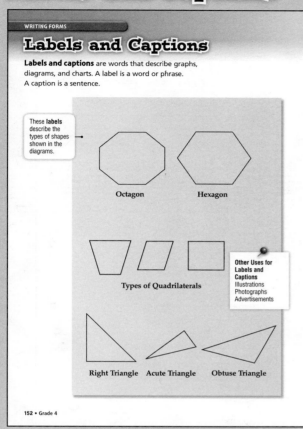

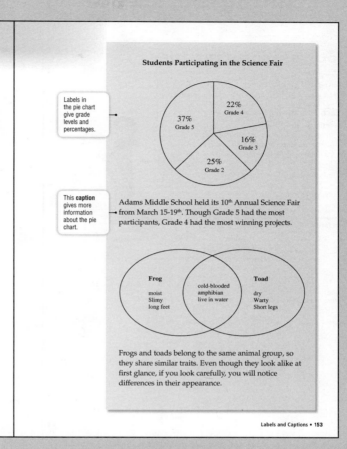

Minilesson 139

Understanding Labels

Objective: Understand the use of labels.

Guiding Question: How can I use these pages to help me write good labels for graphs, diagrams, and charts?

Teach/Model

Instruct students to read the definition on p. 152. Then explain that the labels on these pages help describe different kinds of graphs, diagrams, and charts. Tell students to closely examine labels on the graphic organizers on pp. 152–153.

Practice/Apply

Have students find examples of labels for graphic organizers in textbooks, magazines, or newspapers. Ask them to discuss what makes a good label.

Minilesson 140

Understanding Captions

Objective: Understand the use of captions.

Guiding Question: How can I use these pages to help me write good captions for graphs, diagrams, and charts?

Teach/Model

Tell students to read the two captions on p. 153. Point out that captions are written in sentences. Explain that captions are brief yet should be clear and accurate.

Practice/Apply

Provide students with a graph, diagram, or chart that does not have a caption but could include one to explain its ideas. Have them write a one- or two-sentence caption that gives information about the graphic organizer.

Writing • 113

Writing Handbook Minilessons

Notetaking Strategies

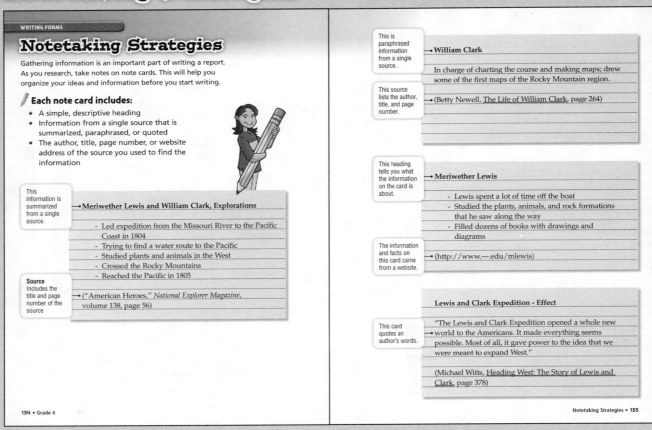

WRITING FORMS

Notetaking Strategies

Gathering information is an important part of writing a report. As you research, take notes on note cards. This will help you organize your ideas and information before you start writing.

Each note card includes:
- A simple, descriptive heading
- Information from a single source that is summarized, paraphrased, or quoted
- The author, title, page number, or website address of the source you used to find the information

This information is summarized from a single source.

→ **Meriwether Lewis and William Clark, Explorations**

- Led expedition from the Missouri River to the Pacific Coast in 1804
- Trying to find a water route to the Pacific
- Studied plants and animals in the West
- Crossed the Rocky Mountains
- Reached the Pacific in 1805

Source Includes the title and page number of the source

→ ("American Heroes," *National Explorer Magazine*, volume 138, page 56)

154 • Grade 4

This is paraphrased information from a single source.

→ **William Clark**

In charge of charting the course and making maps; drew some of the first maps of the Rocky Mountain region.

This source lists the author, title, and page number.

→ (Betty Newell, The Life of William Clark, page 264)

This heading tells you what the information on the card is about.

→ **Meriwether Lewis**

- Lewis spent a lot of time off the boat
- Studied the plants, animals, and rock formations that he saw along the way
- Filled dozens of books with drawings and diagrams

The information and facts on this card came from a website.

→ (http://www.---.edu/mlewis)

Lewis and Clark Expedition - Effect

This card quotes an author's words.

→ "The Lewis and Clark Expedition opened a whole new world to the Americans. It made everything seems possible. Most of all, it gave power to the idea that we were meant to expand West."

(Michael Witts, Heading West: The Story of Lewis and Clark, page 378)

Notetaking Strategies • 155

WRITING MODELS AND FORMS

Minilesson 141

Using Note Cards

Objective: Understand how to take notes using note cards.

Guiding Question: How do I use these pages to help me make note cards for my report?

Teach/Model

Tell students to read the introduction and the bulleted points. Explain that the sample note cards on these pages show different ways to take notes about the explorers Meriwether Lewis and William Clark. Ask students to read to the end of p. 155.

Practice/Apply

Have students examine the sources that are listed on each note card. Have them discuss how information from magazines, books, and websites is cited.

114 • Writing

Minilesson 142

Summarizing, Paraphrasing, and Quoting

Objective: Summarize, paraphrase, or quote information.

Guiding Question: How do I summarize, paraphrase, or quote information on my note cards?

Teach/Model

Point out that the first and third note cards summarize information, the second card restates information using different words, and the last card quotes an author.

Practice/Apply

Have students take notes on another explorer, such as Henry Hudson or Ponce de Leon. Ask them to make a series of note cards that summarize, paraphrase, and quote information from different sources.

Journal

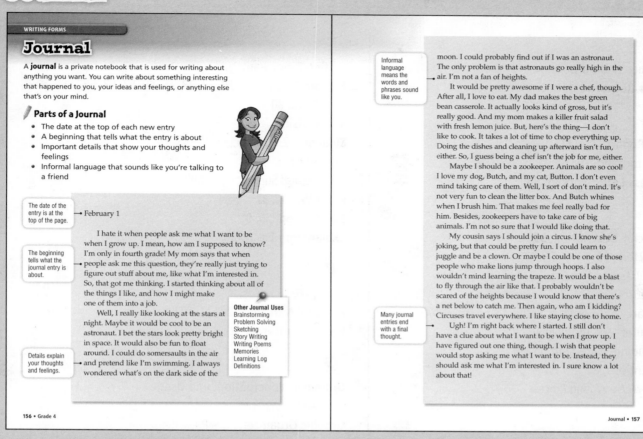

WRITING FORMS

Journal

A **journal** is a private notebook that is used for writing about anything you want. You can write about something interesting that happened to you, your ideas and feelings, or anything else that's on your mind.

Parts of a Journal

- The date at the top of each new entry
- A beginning that tells what the entry is about
- Important details that show your thoughts and feelings
- Informal language that sounds like you're talking to a friend

The date of the entry is at the top of the page.

→ February 1

The beginning tells what the journal entry is about.

I hate it when people ask me what I want to be when I grow up. I mean, how am I supposed to know? I'm only in fourth grade! My mom says that when people ask me this question, they're really just trying to figure out stuff about me, like what I'm interested in. So, that got me thinking. I started thinking about all of the things I like, and how I might make one of them into a job.

Details explain your thoughts and feelings.

Well, I really like looking at the stars at night. Maybe it would be cool to be an astronaut. I bet the stars look pretty bright in space. It would also be fun to float around. I could do somersaults in the air and pretend like I'm swimming. I always wondered what's on the dark side of the

Other Journal Uses
Brainstorming
Problem Solving
Sketching
Story Writing
Writing Poems
Memories
Learning Log
Definitions

156 • Grade 4

Informal language means the words and phrases sound like you.

moon. I could probably find out if I was an astronaut. The only problem is that astronauts go really high in the air. I'm not a fan of heights.

It would be pretty awesome if I were a chef, though. After all, I love to eat. My dad makes the best green bean casserole. It actually looks kind of gross, but it's really good. And my mom makes a killer fruit salad with fresh lemon juice. But, here's the thing—I don't like to cook. It takes a lot of time to chop everything up. Doing the dishes and cleaning up afterward isn't fun, either. So, I guess being a chef isn't the job for me, either.

Maybe I should be a zookeeper. Animals are so cool! I love my dog, Butch, and my cat, Button. I don't even mind taking care of them. Well, I sort of don't mind. It's not very fun to clean the litter box. And Butch whines when I brush him. That makes me feel really bad for him. Besides, zookeepers have to take care of big animals. I'm not so sure that I would like doing that.

My cousin says I should join a circus. I know she's joking, but that could be pretty fun. I could learn to juggle and be a clown. Or maybe I could be one of those people who make lions jump through hoops. I also wouldn't mind learning the trapeze. It would be a blast to fly through the air like that. I probably wouldn't be scared of the heights because I would know that there's a net below to catch me. Then again, who am I kidding? Circuses travel everywhere. I like staying close to home.

Many journal entries end with a final thought.

Ugh! I'm right back where I started. I still don't have a clue about what I want to be when I grow up. I have figured out one thing, though. I wish that people would stop asking me what I want to be. Instead, they should ask me what I'm interested in. I sure know a lot about that!

Journal • 157

Minilesson 143

Understanding the Journal

Objective: Understand the journal.

Guiding Question: How can I use these pages to help write entries in a journal?

Teach/Model

Ask students to read the definition and bulleted points. Explain that the journal entry on these pages tells the writer's ideas and feelings about his or her interests. Then have students read to the end of p. 157.

Practice/Apply

Have students discuss the Other Journal Uses box on p. 156. Ask them to write a journal entry that fits one or more of these purposes.

Minilesson 144

Using Informal Language

Objective: Use informal language in a journal.

Guiding Question: What natural-sounding words and phrases should I use in my journal entries?

Teach/Model

Explain to students that this journal entry uses words and phrases that seem as if the writer is talking to a friend. For example, point out *awesome, gross,* and *here's the thing* in the third paragraph of the entry.

Practice/Apply

Have students find additional examples of informal language that the writer used in this journal entry. Have them discuss how these words and phrases reflect the writer's personality.

Writing • 115

Writing Handbook Minilessons

Index

Writing Handbook Minilessons

Read Aloud Passages

Table of Contents

Read Aloud Passages

LESSON 1
Sideline Support

Players and fans were keeping cool with soft drinks and ice cream on the hottest day of July and the first day of the Little League tournament. Brett, an outfielder, was watching the game from the bench. *Crack!* Fans erupted in a chorus of cheers.

"Cheers for someone other than me," came a small voice from beside Brett. Brett was surprised to see that the speaker was Omar, one of the younger boys on the team. The few times Omar had spoken at all, his words usually **consisted** of *yes, no, coach,* or some combination of the three.

"Excuse me?" said Brett, still not **positive** the words had come from Omar.

"I've had it." Frustration was obvious from the **peculiar** strain in Omar's voice. "Just being here now puts me in a bad **mood**. I show up to every practice. I do whatever Coach asks. And where am I during the games? On the bench! Why is that? Does Coach think the other players try harder or have more **talent** than I have? Are they simply more **advanced** than I am?"

"Don't be silly!" laughed Brett. "I played less than you during my first year, and I didn't even know how to hold a bat **properly**! And you know what? I had a blast. It's just a matter of looking at the situation differently. My Dad would call it an *attitude tune-up.*"

"*Attitude tune-up?*" responded a surprised Omar. "How can I look at the season for anything but what it is—a disaster!"

"How can you even **mention** such a word?" asked Brett in an astonished tone. "We're out in the fresh air, spending time with our friends. It's a great day!"

"Practice hard, keep a positive attitude, and your playing time will come," added Brett, trying to **comfort** his teammate. "Whether Coach **intends** to put you in today or not, enjoy this day at the ballpark!"

Another wave of cheers hit the stands as a second run was scored. A small smile appeared on Omar's face as he looked at his new friend. Then, without waiting a moment longer, he jumped up to support his team.

LESSON 2
The Troublemaker Who Healed a Nation

A man whose middle name means "troublemaker" sounds like an unlikely candidate for a Nobel Peace Prize. But Nelson Rolihlahla Mandela won that honor for his struggle to bring peace and harmony to the troubled nation of South Africa.

Born in 1918, Mandela grew up at a time when an all-white government ruled his country, even though most of its citizens were black. This government forced a policy of **segregation** on Mandela's people. This meant blacks weren't allowed equal rights based on their race and were forced to live separately from whites.

During his boyhood in the country, Mandela had few **encounters** with unfair treatment. He was more influenced by the values of his tribe, the Xhosa. The Xhosa's belief in dignity and self-respect gave him confidence. And, being the son of a village chief, young Mandela was expected to think of the needs of others.

Mandela would often **recall** one childhood event that taught him a valuable lesson about respect. One day, Mandela and his friends were trying to ride a donkey that **preferred** to be left alone. When Mandela took his turn, the donkey thrust him into a thorn bush. The sting of the thorns only went skin deep, but his friends' laughter cut the proud boy to the bone. At that moment, Mandela realized that disrespectful treatment was the cruelest punishment of all.

As a law student in Johannesburg, Mandela suffered far worse insults. Mandela's mistreatment by unfair whites fueled his **dream** of ending segregation. During his long fight against **injustice**, Mandela was often on the run from police. In 1964, he was **captured**. The government sentenced him to life on Robben Island, a bleak prison camp.

Mandela was Robben Island's most famous prisoner. Many world leaders expressed concern about his safety. Prison officials offered Mandela **numerous** privileges, but he refused special treatment. He insisted that **nourishing** food and warm blankets were every prisoner's right.

At first, Mandela fought his guards and made fun of them. However, the many books he read in prison fostered deeper understanding of others. Eventually, he realized his jailers were victims of an unfair system. The guards were uneducated. Ignorance and fear of change were the true enemies of justice.

When he was released from prison in 1990, Mandela worked with the white government to ensure fair and dignified treatment for all races. Mandela became South Africa's first President elected in a democracy, and today he remains a leading **example** of a fighter who won his battle by seeking peace.

LESSON 3
Bridging the Gap

Try to imagine a world without computers. Can you? Computers make it possible to send text messages, do research, keep in touch with family and friends, and stay tuned to world events. In the United States, most people have access to a computer at school, at home, or at a library. However, many children in the world do not have **access** to computers or the Internet. As a result, they don't have a chance to develop the skills that could help them get a good job later in life. Equally important, they can't learn about and become connected to the worldwide community.

The Kasiisi (kuh-seé-see) Primary School is in rural western Uganda, East Africa. The school is a four-hour drive from the capital city of Kampala. Rough roads and rugged terrain make travel to the **remote** community of Kasiisi a challenge. At times, the roads to this **isolated** area are **impassable**. Families work hard but have little money. For most families, a computer would be impossible to **obtain**. Thanks to an organization called One Laptop Per Child, or OLPC, computers have come to Kasiisi. In 2009, OLPC donated 100 laptops to Kasiisi Primary School and to two other schools nearby.

Since 2006, OLPC has given more than two million laptops to schools around the world. OLPC laptops are built to last. They are small, lightweight, and rugged. The sturdy green frame and rubber-coated keyboard can handle **extremes** such as scorching temperatures that other laptops can't. Each laptop comes fully loaded with software kids can use for e-mail, research, games, and Internet access.

Other groups are also trying to bridge the gap between people who have computers and people who don't. A group called Hole-in-the-Wall has set up learning stations at school playgrounds in India. The main feature of each center is a computer that kids can use whenever they are at recess. Students use the computers to work on school projects, explore the Internet, and take **virtual** tours of faraway places.

Computers are important tools for learning and for life. Exploring the Internet can inspire children to become **avid** explorers of the world. It can get them excited about learning and encourage them to **devour** new information. Photo and document-sharing programs allow people to **preserve** and save memories, customs, and stories. Hopefully, someday all people on earth—no matter where they are— will have these opportunities.

LESSON 4
Bookmobile Rescue

Jessica had just come out of her building early Saturday morning when she saw Alex running toward her.

"Help!" called Alex.

"What is it?" asked Jessica with an **innocent** look. She **speculated** that Alex was in trouble. He had the guilty look of a crime **suspect**—probably because some **scheme** he was cooking up had gone wrong.

"I have a BIG problem!" replied Alex. "The local branch of the library is closed for repairs!"

"So?" asked Jessica, glad the problem wasn't worse.

"We have a report due on Monday, and I need to do some research!" Alex responded. "I don't have a computer at home anymore, remember?"

How could Jessica forget? There had been **burglaries** in the area recently. The thieves had stolen several computers. **Regretfully**, she recalled that Alex's was one of them.

"May I use your computer?" asked Alex.

"Sorry, you can't. Mom just took our computer to be repaired, "said Jessica. "But maybe she can **assist** us."

Jessica and Alex ran up to Jessica's apartment.

"Mom," said Jessica. "Alex has to do research for a report due on Monday. Neither of us has a computer to use at home. Alex says that the local branch of the library is closed. Will you do us a **favor** and take us to the main library, please?"

"Why don't you just wait for the bookmobile? While the local branch is closed, the bookmobile is stopping all over the neighborhood. It should get to our block anytime now."

"The bookmobile!" said Alex and Jessica. "Perfect!"

Alex and Jessica went outside and talked about Alex's report while they waited. His report was on the Johnson Space Center in Houston, Texas. Jessica thought the topic was boring, but Alex loved anything about space.

Before long, the City Bookmobile rolled down the street and parked at the end of the block. Alex and Jessica took off down the street.

"I just need to find some information on how astronauts train for space flights," Alex explained to the librarian.

"I have a few books on the space program," said the librarian. "But you'll find more information online. Use one of our computers to explore the Space Center's website."

"Awesome!" said Alex. He sat down and started to click through the website. Jessica helped take notes.

"It says here that **prior** to 1971, astronauts returning from the moon were checked to make sure they hadn't brought space germs back to Earth!"

"Weird!" said Jessica. "Space germs sound freaky. I **misjudged** this topic. There's some interesting stuff here."

"And we wouldn't have found it if your Mom hadn't remembered the bookmobile," said Alex. "This place is great. And we didn't even have to leave our block!"

LESSON 5

Mighty Joe Magarac

In western Pennsylvania, on the banks of three mighty rivers, lies the steel town of Pittsburgh. Pittsburgh was once the steel capital of the world. It was home to mighty steel mills and the mighty steelworkers who made the steel that built this great nation.

Of all the mighty steelworkers in Pittsburgh, the mightiest and most **memorable** was Joe Magarac.

Sometime in the 1930s, or so the steelworkers say, young Joe sprouted up full grown from the iron ore in the Pennsylvania hills. He was literally made of steel. A giant of a man, he towered over other steelworkers like a colossal steel crane.

Young Joe reported for work at the Pittsburgh steel mills. He worked longer and harder than any other steelworker ever had or ever could. In fact, they say Joe made steel 24 hours a day, 365 days a year.

Joe could bend giant steel beams with his bare hands. He could dip his hands into pots of molten steel, scoop up the boiling metal, and pour it into molds! The sight **horrified** other steelworkers. They were afraid for Joe. But how can you hurt a man of steel?

You might think a giant steel man would be an **outcast**, not liked by the folks around him. But Joe was a hero to the steelworkers. One time, a huge pot of melted steel broke loose from the giant chains high above a mill floor. Before anyone could yell "Watch out!" Joe caught the immense melting pot just before it landed on fifty workers below!

In the 1940s, there was a **shortage** of ships. The country needed many new ones—fast. So Joe Magarac got busy. He worked double, then triple, speed. In just one week, Joe made enough steel to build a whole new **seafaring** fleet.

Joe bundled up all the steel with a giant chain and carried it to the shipyards of the eastern seaboard. Then he helped with the shipbuilding. In fact, he built a whole battleship by himself—in one night!

But all the work near the **tidal** waters wasn't good for poor Joe. Sadly, the salt water from the **foaming** Atlantic Ocean rusted his joints. Soon Joe was in terrible **condition**. His mighty steel body had **betrayed** him.

Back in Pittsburgh, the steelworkers heard that Joe had a **yearning** to return home. So they built a special railroad car just to carry Joe home. It was as long as a football field, with a vast, flat bed for Joe. It took ten steam engines to pull it. When Joe saw it, he almost cried with joy. (Of course, he had to stop before he rusted his eyes shut!)

Joe lay down on that railroad car and rode home to Pittsburgh in style. The steelworkers greeted him with cheers. They needed Joe's help in the mills. But by this time, Joe's working days were over. After fixing his tired joints, Joe disappeared back into the hills he came from. And no one heard of or saw him again.

LESSON 6

The Tunguska Event

More than 100 years ago, in a remote region of Earth, an **extraordinary** event happened. It is known as the Tunguska Event because it took place near the Tunguska River in Siberia. Siberia, part of Russia, is a cold, snowy region near the North Pole where few people live. The region is known for deep forests, freezing winters, and herds of wild reindeer.

The Tunguska Event happened early in the morning of June 30, 1908. People who saw it said that suddenly, high above the forest, the northern sky lit up as if it were on fire. The air grew hot, and ferocious winds roared down from the sky. There was a huge explosion high up in the air, so powerful that the ground below shook violently. People heard deafening bangs.

As the fiery light in the sky began to **fade**, people stared in **awe** at the wreckage on the ground. Something **indescribable** had just happened. Over an area of 800 square miles, millions of trees had been flattened. They lay on their sides like piles of toothpicks. Everything was destroyed—but why? The cause of the destruction was a mystery.

The effects of the blast were felt for thousands of miles. People reported a **luminous** glow in the sky that lasted for hours.

Many years went by before scientists were able to enter the blast zone to find out what happened. The harsh conditions of the Siberian wilderness prevented them from reaching the site. Finally, in 1927, a group of **daring** scientists succeeded.

Leonid Kulik, an expert in meteorites, led the team. Meteorites are rocks from space that enter the Earth's atmosphere. Team members asked locals to share their memories of that morning in 1908. Many people had been so **alarmed** by the explosion that they refused to say anything. Others, though, were willing to **convey** their experience.

The scientists listened to eyewitness descriptions. They studied the damage. They noticed the way the trees had fallen. They concluded that a huge meteorite, measuring about 120 feet across and weighing 220 million pounds, had entered Earth's atmosphere. As the rock hurled toward Earth, it heated the air around it to super-hot temperatures. The rock **reacted** to the heat and burst into pieces. The force of the explosion knocked down trees and shook the ground below for thousands of miles.

Scientists have been **conferring** for decades about the Tunguska Event. Most agree with Kulik's conclusion that it was caused by a meteorite. Scientists think that a meteorite of that size enters Earth's atmosphere about every 300 years. Who knows when or where the next one will arrive?

LESSON 7
Steven Spielberg: A Filmmaker's Journey

It's not always easy to figure out what you want to do for a living, especially when you're growing up. You **focus** on one career idea and then switch to another and another. But some people discover their dream job early. Seeds are planted in their youth that guide them like bread crumbs along a particular path. That's what happened to Steven Spielberg. From a young age, he set his sights on filmmaking. Once he found his **target** career, it was full speed ahead!

Steven was born in Cincinnati, Ohio, in 1946. Since his family moved a lot, Steven was often lonely, and he used his imagination to keep himself company. His father was a big fan of science fiction. Steven found the genre **entertaining**, too. He became especially fascinated with extraterrestrial life. He created an imaginary alien character that became his constant companion.

At the age of twelve, Steven began to show an interest in filmmaking. Eventually, he earned a merit badge in Boy Scouts for filmmaking. He also made his first amateur film that year, called *The Last Gun*.

After high school, Steven made a film called *Amblin'*. It was this film that helped him land a job at Universal Studios in California. Soon the filmmaker was Hollywood bound!

In Hollywood, Steven's first big success came in 1975 with his movie *Jaws*. It is about a giant, people-eating shark that terrorized a small fishing village. Steven used intense close-up **angles** and shocking **jolts** of action. Audiences found the film **thrilling** to watch. Many people were scared right out of their seats! The poster used to **advertise** the movie attracted a lot of people to the theater. *Jaws* made 260 million dollars in ticket

sales and won two Academy Awards for music and editing. But the young Hollywood filmmaker was just getting started.

Steven wanted to make a movie that would **promote** a sense of wonder about aliens. He had many sci-fi-**generated** ideas, such as traveling through time and meeting aliens from outer space. Steven worked with an author, Melissa Mathison, who had written a novel about a kind alien who befriended some curious children on the planet Earth. From this book, the movie, *E.T.: The Extra-Terrestrial*, was born. *E.T.* broke sales records around the world, and many movie **critics** consider it one of the best science fiction movies ever made.

Today Steven Spielberg's movies have grossed nearly 8 billion dollars. He is the most successful filmmaker of all time. Looks like the once-lonely boy from Ohio has had quite a fantastic journey himself!

LESSON 8
Jazzy Jasmine

On a bright Saturday morning, Jasmine marched into Herbert's Music **Studio** to pick up her new saxophone. She had been playing the school's saxophone for a month. Now, she would have a shiny instrument of her own. Jasmine just knew she would look **glorious** playing it—like Jack "the Saxman" Monroe, who played in the high school band. When he blew through the curved, golden bell of his saxophone, everyone stopped to watch. Even picnickers, enjoying an outdoor **feast** of hot dogs, chips, and soda would pause when the Saxman played.

As Mr. Herbert pulled the saxophone from its sleek black case, Jasmine saw rays of sunlight **streak** across the metal to make the instrument shine like real gold. She **yanked** her mom's hand. "Isn't it beautiful?"

Her mother nodded. "Can I make a **schedule** of payments by the month?" she asked Mr. Herbert.

"Of course!" he said.

When Jasmine got home, she invited her best friend, Saji, over. As Saji sat on the sofa, Jasmine blew into the saxophone with all her strength. Her fingers raced up and down the pearl-like keys. She rocked back and forth on her heels and twisted her hips. A wild blast of sounds blared from the horn.

Jasmine held her head up high. "Well, how do I look?" Saji's eyebrows moved together, like they did when she was **concerned** about a test.

"Is there something stuck inside?" Saji asked.

Jasmine wasn't going to let her good mood be **ruined**. She stuck out her chin. "This is just how Jack 'the Saxman' plays. I've watched him."

"Have you *listened* to him?" Saji asked.

"Well, yeah, sort of." Jasmine plopped on the sofa.

"When he plays you can tell he really feels the music," Saji said. "That's why he moves around."

After Saji went home, Jasmine moped around the house. Her shiny saxophone lay by a **model** train in the upstairs bedroom she shared with her sister, Annie. She knew she could *act* like the Saxman, but could she ever *sound* like him?

Jasmine sat down at the kitchen table. Annie's coloring book lay open. The page was **smeared** with orange—Annie's favorite color. "I would have chosen pink," Jasmine mused. "And I would have colored inside the lines, too." Annie hadn't learned how to yet. Suddenly, a smile spread across Jasmine's face. Wasn't playing saxophone a lot like that? Like practicing until you could stay inside the lines, while still being able to use your own special colors?

As Jasmine raced up the stairs to her room and to her saxophone, she shouted, "Look out, Saxman! Here comes Jazzy Jasmine!"

LESSON 9
Is Sasquatch Out There?

Have you heard the legend of Sasquatch? Picture a hairy, human-like creature between 6 and 15 feet tall with large feet. Sasquatch may or may not exist in the real world, but it definitely exists in legend. Legends are stories about amazing events people believe happened in the not-so-distant past. They can be scary, funny, or unusual and might be repeated to warn, thrill, or amuse us. Legends are even reported in newspapers and **reference** materials.

Legends may begin with something that has actually happened, but, over time, tellers **borrow** or change details. For example, they may change a story's setting and say the event happened in a **local** place. It is not any one person's **fault**. Have you ever played the game "Telephone"? One person whispers to a friend, who whispers what was heard to the next person, who whispers to the next, and so on. The last person reports what was heard, and it is never exactly what the first person said. Legends are repeated by many people over time, and in the process they are changed, just like the message in a game of "Telephone."

There have been debates for many years about whether or not Sasquatch really exists. Even though no one has found fossils or bones of such a creature, some scientists, including Jane Goodall, have claimed they believe Sasquatch may be real. Many people have created false pictures of Sasquatch as a joke.

They don't **apologize** for sharing false evidence. In fact, some brag about it.

Some people have **insisted** that Sasquatch is real. In 1957, Albert Ostman described such an incident. In 1924, he claimed he was mining for gold when Sasquatch kidnapped him. He was picked up in his sleeping bag, carried 25 miles, and set down among Sasquatch's family. They didn't hurt him. Ostman never yelled, **fainted** from fear, or cried. On the sixth day, he simply fed Sasquatch a lot of chewing tobacco, and when old Sas got sick, Ostman escaped.

In 1967, Roger Patterson and Bob Gimlin claimed to have captured Sasquatch on film in a piece of footage that might be **proof** of Sasquatch's existence, but it's very blurry. Is it **genuine**, or is it fake? No one knows for sure.

Most people laugh at the idea of an enormous hairy creature with big feet that trudges through **slimy** mud, sleeps in the wild, and is scared of humans. But the legend, at least, is alive and well.

LESSON 10
Mexican Dove

Most people **towered** over Frida Kahlo. People called her "the dove" because she seemed so fragile and small. Yet she used her **stubborn** interest in art to shout her story to the world.

Frida was born near Mexico City, Mexico, which is far south of the **border** between the United States and Mexico. When she was a child, the Mexican people were fighting a war to gain their freedom from Spain, so Frida would have heard gunshots while she was growing up. Frida's gentle family likely would have been kind to any soldiers who might have come near their home. If Frida were to see one **hauling** himself over the wall behind her home into her yard, then asking **permission** to stay for dinner, Frida and her mother would probably have fed him.

Frida had many troubles as she grew up. As a young child, she had polio, a horrible disease that caused her to have a weak leg. When she was a bit older, she was in a bus accident that broke her leg and her back. Frida never fully recovered and was in great pain for the rest of her life. She had surgery thirty-five times so that doctors could try to fix her leg.

Frida must have felt **discouraged** because of all the hardships she had to endure, but she never gave up. Instead of allowing her feelings to be trapped inside, she used her pain and hardship to make her paintings spectacular. Often Frida had to paint while lying in a hospital bed, but she used that time to make amazing art. Some of her paintings were

mournful, such as the self-portrait where she is shown seated in a gray suit against a brown and tan background. Scissors in hand, her long, curling locks of hair lie at her feet.

However, Kahlo almost always used vibrant colors and symbols that the native Mexicans used in their ancient art. Frida told the world about her feelings and thoughts through these paintings. From her art, the world learned about Frida and also about Mexico and its people.

Frida **toured** other countries to show people her paintings. In fact, the Louvre, a famous museum in Paris, France, organized a **debut** of her art. Museum visitors were very impressed, and the Louvre bought one of Frida's paintings. It was the first time the museum had ever bought a painting from a Mexican artist.

Frida was a strong person whose life touches people even today. Her paintings allowed her to **triumph** over hardships. They also inspire us. When we view one of her paintings, we know we can overcome many problems, because Frida did.

LESSON 11
The Big Storm

My soccer coach canceled our evening practice last Tuesday because a big storm was expected to hit our area. Sure enough, by six o'clock, the autumn leaves were **whirling** in our yard. Soon the trees were rocking back and forth. The rain began with big lazy drops, but it quickly became a drumming downpour that **rapidly** filled the gutters with water. We were warm in our house, but the thermometer on our kitchen window showed that the outside temperature had dropped sharply. I pressed my nose against the window and watched my breath **condense** in a little patch of fog against the glass.

My father wasn't having as much fun. He was worrying about a section of roof that he had been meaning to fix all summer. When water began to drip from our kitchen ceiling, he groaned and placed a pot beneath the **source** of the leak. To cheer him up, I pointed out the window to our duck lawn ornament. Its wooden wings were **rotating** so fast in the wind that we both burst out laughing.

"Thanks for showing me that, Son," said Dad. "I needed a good laugh right about now."

As the light faded, I listened to the wind **rage** in wild gusts. I heard loud snaps and cracks as branches broke and fell in the woods behind our house. It's exciting but a little scary to **experience** such a powerful storm. When the lights flickered and went out, we lit the emergency candles that we keep in case of a power outage. Bathed in candlelight, our house looked like an **ancient** castle. My dad said it was impossible to

predict when we would regain electricity. Luckily, he had replaced the batteries in our flashlights. He had also made sure our battery-operated radio was working.

We tuned in to the weather report. A crackly voice reported that nearby weather stations had **registered** the highest wind speeds in more than ten years! Some roads had been closed due to flooding, but the storm hadn't caused any major damage.

By the time I curled up in bed, the roof had stopped leaking and the wind had died down. I fell asleep bathed in moonlight shining through my window.

LESSON 12
Safe from Harm

Jia sat in the living room. Holding her hamster Rosy always made her feel better, and she needed it, listening to her parents talking.

"It's just so dry," said her dad.

"I know; one large rainstorm and we'll be in trouble," her mother replied.

Jia knew what they were talking about. It was all over the news. Northern California was in the middle of a drought. There had been almost no rain for two years. Where Jia's family lived, the drought meant real danger. Their house had been **constructed** on the side of a steep hill. A heavy rain could turn the dry earth into slippery mud. The mud could slide down the hill at great speed, **crushing** everything in its path.

The next week, Jia and her parents made several trips into town to Grandmother's **tenement**. They took with them any **possessions** that they could not replace if something happened to their house. Jia took the letters she had saved from her pen pals. On the last trip, Jia decided to leave Rosy with her grandmother, too.

"Are you sure?" her mother asked.

She was. She couldn't imagine something happening to her favorite pet.

The family's preparations had been a good idea. Just two weeks later, the weather forecast predicted heavy rain. The police told everyone to leave the area. Then, the rains fell in mad rushes of water. Jia watched it from the safety of her grandmother's window. Jia watched the rain fall every day, for five long days.

"I don't like the rain anymore," Jia complained.

"Why not?" her mother asked. "We need rain after all the dry years."

"I just can't stand the way the house **trembles** from the storm," Jia shuddered. "It feels like the whole world could fall apart."

When the rain finally stopped, Jia begged her parents to let her go with them to check on their house. It was not a pleasant drive. Each mile revealed more **wreckage**. As they crossed a river, Jia could see **debris** floating in high water. When they got to her neighborhood, she saw her friend Sara's house. Nothing but **rubble** remained. A huge **slab** of mud had completely pushed the house off its foundation. Jia felt awful for her friend, but she was relieved that no one had been in the house when it slid.

When they turned the corner, Jia was overjoyed to see her home practically untouched. The huge **timbers** of the old house had stood the test. As happy as she was, Jia couldn't help thinking about Sara, who had lost everything. Suddenly Jia turned to her parents.

"We need to go back to Grandma's," she announced. "I think Sara is going to need Rosy."

LESSON 13

On My Way to Meet the Khan: Excerpts from Marco Polo's Adventures

Imagine traveling from Venice, Italy, to China as a seventeen-year-old. It would be a very long trip from which you would not return for many years. Marco Polo began that journey in 1271. When he returned, the people of Europe loved the stories he told about his travels. His stories gave people in Europe a clear **vision** of the difficult journey and of China so far away.

Here are retellings of a few of his stories:

After leaving the kingdom of Kirman, you ride over a plain full of birds, with many fruit trees and herds of cattle. After this abundance, you must cross a mountain where it is so cold by Venetian **standards** that you must **huddle** under all of your clothes.

In the city of Ormus, the wind blows hot during the summer. People must leave the city and build homes over the river. Everyone must be **alert** to the wind's approach. The wind can suffocate a person, so people stand up to their chins in the river's water.

On the way to Sapurgan you pass over a plain, a great mountain, and a desert. On the fourth day of travel, there is a river of fresh water where, in **weariness**, one can stop and rest.

In the province of Vokhan, a great range of mountains with **fractured** rocks rises. High in the mountains lies a lake from which flows a river. Here is a rich plain full of wild game. **Graceful** sheep with great horns run smoothly in the wind. The mountains around this plain are so high that no birds fly near the summits, and fires do not warm one. It takes forty days to travel through these rugged mountains.

The desert of Lop is vast. Before making the month-long crossing of the desert, people must prepare well. It is not a place to be **stranded** without enough food or water.

Near the city of Changanor, the Khan has a palace he likes to visit because there are many streams and bodies of water near there. The swans, cranes, pheasants, and other birds make quite a **display**. The Khan has **concluded** that people should grow grain there just for the birds.

Most Europeans at the time would never see the plants, animals, and fascinating places Polo described, but his stories piqued their interest in and fascination with a land far away.

LESSON 14

Wicked Wind

Imagine you are lying in your bed late at night when you hear something strange that gives you goose bumps. The noise starts as a distant hum that gets louder and louder until it sounds like a train is about to crash through your door. Now you can hear sirens wailing outside. Your mother opens the door and yells, "Tornado! Come quick!"

Tornado Forces

Tornadoes are violent, spinning winds that usually form from huge thunderstorms called supercells. These storms contain the strongest winds on earth. Some of them have 300-mile-per-hour winds that can pick up a car and **transport** it across an entire state. Large tornadoes can destroy buildings and whole towns. This kind of destruction can change the **social** structures of communities. People can become separated from family members and neighbors just when they need them most.

The damage these monsters leave behind can create **obstacles** that make life very difficult for survivors. Roads are often blocked, and then people can't get to safety. Some lose their jobs because the buildings they worked in are gone. Medical help, food, water, and shelter are often **scarce** after a storm passes. The great need for these resources can lead to angry **exchanges**, or arguments, between survivors and those they need to help them.

Preparing for a Tornado

Even though a tornado is a horrible, scary event, if you live in an area where tornadoes occur frequently, you can take steps to prepare for one and to survive. A prepared person **transfers** needed items to a safe place long before tornado season starts. First, you should find a solid **chamber**, such as a basement room, to run to when a tornado approaches. If you don't have a basement, choose a room in the middle of your home, away from windows. The surrounding rooms **reinforce** the middle room, making it safer.

Set aside space in your tornado room for **storage**. Store at least three days' worth of food and water in your room, such as **excess** canned goods and other food that won't spoil. In addition to food, store medical supplies, a flashlight, and a battery-operated radio.

Even though your chances of ever being hit by a tornado are small, it is smart to be ready just in case. If you are prepared, you will know exactly what to do when the wicked wind comes late at night or any other time.

LESSON 15
Forests are Forever

At first glance, a forest may seem like it is made up of a lot of trees and nothing more. A closer inspection, however, shows that a forest is much more than just trees.

Forests are home to many living things. Indeed, forests are one of the main **habitats** on Earth. That is because many **species** of animals and plants live and thrive there. Many of the **organisms** that live in forests are visible, of course, but others are tiny and cannot be seen by the naked eye. Bacteria, for example, leave no **traces** that are visible unless you are using a microscope or other magnification.

Deep in the woods, away from the bright sunlight and the sound of traffic on the highway, the forest seems **vast**. If you are planning to go exploring, it's a good idea to travel in a group!

The actions of humans can **directly affect** the organisms that live in the forest, and not always in negative ways. There are, in fact, a **variety** of good things people can do.

These include everything from taking care to remove your trash and recycling it to using products that do not pollute the atmosphere.

Products that pollute the atmosphere cause weak spots in the ozone layer. The ozone is a part of Earth's upper atmosphere that shields the planet from harmful rays from the sun. Many people believe that the ozone layer must be saved so that the **radiation** is blocked. That's why so many pollutants have been **banned**—pollutants eat away at the ozone layer and leave our planet vulnerable.

LESSON 16
Getting the Story

In 1887, a young reporter for a New York City newspaper received a daring first assignment: go undercover and expose the conditions at a well-known mental institution. "Could I pass a week in the insane ward at Blackwell's Island?" the reporter later wrote. "I said I could and I would. And I did."

The reporter's name was Nellie Bly. At a time when there were few women journalists, Bly was determined to prove herself **worthy** of the job. Going into a mental hospital must have set her stomach **churning** nervously, but it wasn't the first challenging **situation** she'd plunged into, and it wouldn't be the last.

Bly was born Elizabeth Cochran in a small town in Pennsylvania. She landed her first newspaper job—and took her pen name—at the *Pittsburgh Dispatch*. When that paper's popular columnist declared that a woman who worked for a living was a "monstrosity," Bly **swelled** with indignation. Women didn't **deserve** such an insult! She fired off a letter to the paper. Impressed, the editors hired her. For her first story, Bly interviewed working women, then described their lives and **defended** their abilities, in an article called "The Girl Puzzle." Nellie Bly cared about people's lives and had a knack for getting them to talk to her. She wasn't **satisfied** when the *Dispatch* assigned her to write about fashion and flowers, so she packed her bags and left her editors a note: "I'm off for New York. Look out for me. Bly."

The editors didn't have to look out for long. Nellie Bly's name soon began to appear in the *New York World*, the paper that sent her undercover to the mental institution. Because of what she wrote about the cruel treatment there, horrified officials began to make changes. For another story, she got herself arrested, then wrote about the harsh treatment of prisoners. She exposed a health clinic that used unqualified doctors.

Nellie Bly was a pioneer in investigative reporting. Readers **relied** on her to dig for the facts and get "the story behind the story." She developed a strong **reputation** for her work. But another kind of story made her an international celebrity. Her newspaper wanted to send a reporter around the world to try to beat the record of a character in the novel, *Around the World In 80 Days*. Naturally, Bly wanted the assignment. When she threatened to go to another newspaper if they sent a man instead, her paper gave in. Refusing to be **escorted** by a chaperone, Bly circled the world by steamship, train, handcart, and burro— sending stories back to her eager readers. She arrived home in 72 days, 6 hours, and 11 minutes, breaking the fictional record. Nellie Bly said she could do it, and she did.

LESSON 17
Let Me Be Brave

Many people witnessed Liinah Bukenya win the 50-meter backstroke in the 2003 Special Olympics in Dublin, but they did not see all of the difficulties she had to overcome just to be there.

Even though Liinah was born with a mental disability, she always wanted to swim. Her coach started her with armband floats, but as she gained **confidence**, Liinah was able to **graduate** to swimming without help. At first, she could barely make it across the pool. The more she practiced, the better she got. Soon Liinah sped through the water like a fish.

Then, just two months before the Special Olympics, tragedy strikes. Liinah's father suddenly dies. Knowing that she **performs** better with her parents in attendance, she is faced with a problem. If she **confesses** this to her coach, he may cut her from the team. If she doesn't tell anyone, she will have to face her fears alone. Liinah decides to swallow her sadness and keep practicing.

Before she knows it, the day of the biggest race of her life is upon her. Liinah's stomach is jumpy as she waits for the race to start. Her eager eyes scan the large crowd. It is her first trip away from her home in Uganda, and she feels completely alone. Even though her family can't attend, two Irish social workers helping **foster** children in Uganda have met Liinah in her country. Liinah looks into the crowd and catches their smiling faces. She smiles back, takes a deep breath, and **patiently** waits for the start of the race.

Suddenly, the buzzer sounds, and Liinah springs into action. Using every muscle, she glides swiftly through the water. She is in the lead, but she knows other racers are close behind and working to catch her. Liinah's muscles scream for

her to slow down, but she will **disobey** the urge until she reaches the edge of the pool. Suddenly, the crowd cheers, and Liinah knows she has won!

Later, in a grand **ceremony**, Queen Sylvia Nagginda of Uganda presents Liinah with a shiny gold medal to **reward** her hard work. The medal is a sparkling **symbol** of Liinah's great effort. She smiles as the queen gives her a big hug.

LESSON 18
Theseus and the Minotaur

There is a story that long ago, a mean-spirited king ruled the Greek island of Crete. His name was King Minos. One of the king's mean-spirited hobbies was using his navy to attack the city of Athens. Minos attacked the city often, and loudly **boasted** that no one could stop him.

The people of Athens grew tired of the attacks, so they made a deal with King Minos. Every nine years, the Athenians sent seven boys and seven girls to the island of Crete. These young people were devoured by the Minotaur, a horrible monster that lived there. In exchange, King Minos **ceased** his attacks on Athens.

The Minotaur had the head of a bull and the body of a man. It lived in a giant maze called a labyrinth. The maze was so complicated that anyone who entered it became hopelessly lost. Escape from the Minotaur was impossible.

Years passed, and soon it was time to for the Athenians to send a group of young people to their terrible fate. There was much weeping and sorrow as the **unfortunate** children were selected. However, one young man bravely volunteered to go. He was Prince Theseus, son of the Athenian king.

Theseus boldly **declared** that he would kill the Minotaur and put an end to the Athenians' sacrifice. Theseus's father begged him not to go, but the prince refused to listen. He was both **resourceful** and brave. He knew that somehow he would succeed. No amount of pleading could **coerce** him to change his mind.

When the ship carrying the doomed Athenians arrived in Crete, King Minos's beautiful daughter Princess Ariadne noticed the handsome prince at once. She fell in love with him. She wrote Theseus a note. In it, she offered to help him kill the Minotaur and escape from the labyrinth.

Ariadne had **devised** a clever plan. Before Theseus and the other youths entered the cave, she gave him a ball of string and a sword. She told him to tie one end of the string to the labyrinth's front gate and unravel it as he searched for the Minotaur.

Theseus told the others to wait by the gate. Then he did as Ariadne had instructed. He found the monster deep in the maze. The Minotaur **glared** at Theseus and wondered how he had managed to **acquire** a sword. Theseus wasted no time. He raised the sword above his head and killed the Minotaur with a single blow. Then he followed the path of the string back to the gate. Theseus **beamed** with pride as he led the others to freedom.

LESSON 19
The Father of India

Imagine living in a place where those in charge were from another country. Even though your ancestors had lived on the land for thousands of years, another government took over and decided who could own land, how much tax your family had to pay on simple things like salt, whether you could go to school, and what you could do when you grew up. India, a land of both **drought** and heavy rains, had been ruled by the British for a hundred years. But one day, one man would **dedicate** his life to persuading the British to give India its freedom.

Many Indians wanted to be free of the British, but they didn't agree with one another on how to win their freedom. In the midst of all the disagreements, Mohandas K. Gandhi, a small, frail-looking man, got everyone's attention. Though he adopted simple clothes and a modest lifestyle, Gandhi was an engaging speaker. In his work to **overcome** unfair British laws, Gandhi gave many persuasive speeches in the British Empire. Heads of government in London's **capitol** building took notice. In his speeches, Gandhi stated that only by acting together in protest, could Indians free themselves. Gandhi won over many Indians and became a leader of a new **association** called the Congress party.

Gandhi reasoned that the best way to resist unfair rules was to protest without **violence**. Peaceful action was persuasive action, even when British police were hitting, yelling, or arresting protesters. When Indians used nonviolence in **conflicts** with British police, there was a lot of **publicity** that embarrassed the British. This caused people around the world to support India's struggles.

One of the most famous things Gandhi did was to lead people on a march that protested unfair salt laws. The British believed all of the salt belonged to them and they could tax Indians whatever they wanted for it. Gandhi, and thousands of people who marched with him, walked for twenty-three days to the city of Dandi. Perhaps the **brilliant** sea, sparkling in the sun, offered the weary protesters hope. Turning toward the **horizon**, Gandhi reached down to pick up a lump of salt. This

action sent a message to the British that the people of India would no longer obey their unfair salt laws.

It took many years of practicing non-violence before Gandhi and his supporters could persuade the British to give India its independence. Then, in 1947, Gandhi and his supporters saw the birth of a free India. Indians honored him by calling him the "father of the nation."

LESSON 20
Race Against Death

In 1925, the only doctor in the small city of Nome, Alaska, sent a desperate telegram through the U.S. Army Signal **Corps**: *"An epidemic of diphtheria is almost inevitable here…. I am in urgent need of one million units of diphtheria antitoxin…."* No one needed an **interpreter** to understand the danger. Diphtheria was a deadly, fast-spreading disease. Several children had already died, and the clock was ticking. If the doctor didn't get the antitoxin, or medicine, thousands of people in Nome and in surrounding villages would die.

But it was January and Nome was ice-bound. A blizzard was brewing, and the only pilot who could safely fly in dangerous weather was away on a trip. Only one form of transportation was left: the dogsled. In 1925, mushers, the drivers of dogsleds, and their sled dogs were the ones who brought mail and **supplies** to Nome and other remote parts of Alaska. Most of the mushers were Native Athabascans and Inuits, and they were the best in the **territory**. But the nearest medicine was almost 700 miles away, and it would take a musher twenty-five days to get it to Nome.

Then, someone **proposed** an idea: What about a relay? If each musher took a different leg of the journey and handed off the medicine to the next musher, could they make it? Believing it was their **duty** to try, a team of twenty mushers quickly organized a race against death.

The race began in the town of Nenana, where the first musher took the medicine and sped along the frozen Tanana River to the Yukon. Every village along the way offered its best team and driver. When the doctor in Nome reported more cases of diphtheria, a reporter who lived there said, "All hope is in the dogs and their heroic drivers."

With no one but their dogs to **accompany** them, the mushers drove on. The **route** took them over mountains, through forests, and across the shifting ice of Norton Sound. When the blizzard hit, finding a **landmark** in the thick, swirling snow was almost impossible. One driver's team got tangled up with a reindeer. Another's hands were so **clumsy** with frostbite that he could barely pass the medicine to the next driver. Several dogs died. But the mushers pushed on. And at 5:30 in the morning on February 2, the last musher and his dogs arrived in the waiting city of Nome.

Together, the dedicated teams covered the distance in less than six days, delivering life-saving medicine to an ice-bound city and winning the race against death.

LESSON 21

Fun and Games on the Range

It's another boring night at home. The TV is **blaring**; the telephone shrieks. The **combination** of noises jangles your nerves. You're wearing stereo headphones to muffle your ears. Suddenly, your mother's voice cuts through the **racket**. "It's 9:30! I **suggest** you turn off the lights and get to bed, so you'll wake up ready for school tomorrow."

Now picture the same basic scene in a different setting. The year is 1850. Your bedroom is a corner of a one-room cabin on a vast prairie. Your grass-stuffed mattress rests on a shelf. Otherwise, you'd be sharing the floor with mice or the occasional rattlesnake.

The soundtrack has changed, too. Chirping crickets and the lonesome cries of owls, coyotes, and other **nocturnal** animals have replaced the hubbub of modern appliances. There aren't even any electric lights to switch off!

What would you be doing at 9:30 at night? Chances are, you'd already be fast asleep. Early bedtimes were a must on America's frontier. It took a lot of **effort** to get through a day that started before sunrise. In those days, children were expected to get up **promptly** to help their parents. Chores included feeding farm animals, collecting firewood, and hanging beef jerky outside to dry. Afterwards, children often trudged miles to school. Arrival at their one-room schoolhouse didn't mean a chance to rest, however! Students swept the floors and carried in drinking water and firewood while teachers got ready to **introduce** their lessons.

Did pioneers ever relax? Sure. Families considered a few hours of reading by candlelight a treat. If the weekly mail had arrived, parents enjoyed letters or months-old newspapers, magazines, or catalogs from back East. Children did homework.

Didn't pioneers get to have any fun? They thought they had plenty! Pioneers loved a party. In those days, however, most parties involved hard work! Such gatherings were called "bees." Bees gave distant neighbors a chance to visit and to get big jobs done faster. After sewing quilts, shucking corn, peeling apples, or building a barn, people chatted over homemade pie, cider, and donuts. Sometimes a fiddler or a harmonica player,

or even someone who could beat time with a washboard and spoons, provided music for dancing.

Marbles, checkers, and jumping rope were popular games. Children also practiced strange **feats**, such as running alongside a barrel hoop they rolled with a stick.

Are you starting to **appreciate** those boring nights at your house?

LESSON 22

Jane's Big Ideas

Jane Addams was a tiny woman with big ideas. She had those ideas during a time when women were not expected to have them. Jane Addams was so **intelligent** and so persuasive that many of her ideas became laws. Jane Addams was one tough cookie.

Addams was born in 1860 in Cedarville, Illinois. She lived comfortably with her family in a big house. At the time, she was expected to grow up, marry a nice man, and take care of a big house and her own children. But Addams wanted something different. She wanted to go to college. This was unheard of during her time.

Addams would not listen. She went away to college, becoming one of the first women in America to attend a university. In college, Addams had heated discussions with her classmates and professors. Her ideas grew bigger. She wondered: Why were women **denied** the right to vote?

Many people did not **approve** of her ideas. Women at the **polls**? No. A woman's place was in the home. But Addams kept pushing. She wrote a pamphlet entitled *Why Women Should Vote*. It was a persuasive list of arguments that helped people become **informed** on the issues. In it, she confirmed that women were great at tending a home and raising children. Wouldn't they also be great, then, at taking care of things in the community? Why shouldn't they become involved in **politics**?

Addams wrote about her ideas. Some people listened. Addams also spoke about her ideas in public. Many thought her rousing speeches were **disorderly** and unladylike, but Addams wasn't concerned. She continued making speeches. She became Vice President of the National American Woman Suffrage Association. This group tried to persuade the **legislature** to consider women's rights in lawmaking. Jane Addams lived to see the Nineteenth **Amendment** passed, which gave women the right to vote.

Jane Addams worked for more than women's rights, though. In Chicago, she set up a center called Hull House, which helped people who had moved to the growing city from all over the world. Addams recognized the need for good schooling for everyone. She once said, "America's future will be determined by the home and the school. The child becomes largely what he is taught; hence we must watch what we teach, and how we live." Addams also worked for world peace. During World War I, she traveled all over the world, speaking about peace between nations.

In the final years of her life, people showed their appreciation of Addams's dedication. She became one of the **candidates** for the Nobel Peace Prize. In 1931, Jane Addams was the first American woman to receive this honor.

LESSON 23
Deserts on the Move?

Creeping Sands

Madinah is a young woman from Sudan, a country on the **continent** of Africa. Growing up, she listened to her older relatives talk about what her home used to be like. It was full of greenery, they told her, with grasses and plants covering the land. But now there are sand dunes everywhere. Sand has drifted across the roads and even crept inside the houses.

Are deserts really on the move? In some places, they are. But even in countries thousands of miles from a desert, there's more desert-like land than ever before. Places once filled with dense forests are now covered with sand dunes. Areas like the one where Madinah lives—where people built houses, grew crops, and raised animals—now look as if they've never been civilized. Sandstorms turn major cities dark in the middle of the day.

As the land changes, people's lives change, too. Some don't have enough food or water. Many leave their homes in search of opportunities to work. In some countries, people have gone to war over any natural resources that remain.

Damage Control

Deserts have always grown and shrunk over time, but they're not **independent**—they need help to move. Lately, they've had a lot of help—from humans. If you destroy forests to make room for building or farming, nothing stops the soil from blowing away or the sand from blowing in. Plants can't take root in the dry, **shallow** dirt that's left. If you keep planting crops without giving the land a rest, soon the land won't be healthy enough for crops to grow. With few plants to help keep **moisture** close to the earth, rainwater will quickly **evaporate**. For example, in Beijing, China, sandstorms from a desert called the Gobi can turn the city dark at noon and could one day blow across the ocean to other countries.

Just as humans helped cause the problem, they're helping to solve it. China is building a new Great Wall. It's a Great Green Wall, and it's made of trees to keep the sand from blowing. In many places, people are giving up their **customs** of slashing and burning forests to clear the land for farms. They're protecting the soil from wind by covering it with layers of straw. They're growing crops on one half of their land and letting the other half rest. People are also planting trees. Maybe one day, Madinah's home will be green once again.

LESSON 24
New Friends in the Newsroom

Anna was so **exhausted** that she immediately slumped down in her seat. The bus took an hour each way because the city was so big. Plus, she had just started a new school and she felt like an **intruder** there. Everyone already had a **bond** with a friend, so she was on her own as the new kid.

When Anna's mom got a job in the city, they had moved away from the rolling farmland that Anna had known all her life—miles and miles away. There were so many things Anna missed about the country, such as the **enclosure** where Mr. Reyes kept his animals. Once his llama had even **charged** at her and spit on her shoe! The thing she missed the most, though, was her friend Maya. Her mom called her "Anna's best compadre." They had been **inseparable** friends since they were preschoolers.

Anna really wanted to make friends at her new school, so last week she signed up for the school newspaper.

Tomorrow was the first meeting, and she was nervous.

The next day, Anna walked into the newsroom just in time to hear Mr. Fletcher, the **chief** editor, call out, "Sit down, everyone. I picked a **companion** for each of you to work with, and that's why you're in assigned seats. Our next issue is due Friday, and each team is going to write an article."

Anna looked at her teammate and said, "Hi, I'm Anna."

"I'm Sarah; nice to meet you. Are you new here? I haven't seen you before."

"Yeah, I started at school a month ago. I moved here from the country," Anna said shyly.

"That's so cool!" Sarah exclaimed. "I've never even left the city. Hey, we should write an article about how people have **suffered** when they move from the home they know to an unknown place! If we write it together we can get it done by the end of the week!"

Anna and Sarah met every day that week to work on their piece. On Friday, they turned it in to Mr. Fletcher, and he loved it! He said he might even put it on the front page!

As they were walking away, Sarah said, "Hey Anna, want to come home with me after school? Anya and Carrie are coming, too."

"Absolutely!" Anna smiled widely.

When Anna got back home, her mom called out, "How did it go?"

Anna called back, "I had fun! We're going swimming at the city pool on Sunday. It kind of made me miss Maya, though. Can I call her?"

Her mom smiled with **affection** and said, "Sure."

LESSON 25

The Future of Flight

Our world is shrinking fast, but don't panic! Our world is not really shrinking, but because air travel has made it easy to move from place to place, it sometimes feels that way. In past **centuries**, people traveled using horses, steam trains, and ships. It was very difficult and expensive to travel, and very few people did it. Today, a trip that used to take months takes only a matter of hours. The **progress** we have made in the field of flight gives many more people access to other cultures and opportunities.

While few people would **dispute** the idea that air travel is fast and safe, environmentalists are concerned that all this air travel could hurt our planet. Like all forms of **mechanical** transportation, airplanes produce carbon dioxide. They also leave clouds in the sky called vapor trails. The carbon dioxide and vapor trails can make the earth warmer. Scientists call carbon dioxide a greenhouse gas, because it makes the earth warmer—like a greenhouse in a garden.

Scientists have **calculated** that airplanes are a **superior** form of transportation for long trips. There is less **waste** of time when passengers reach their destinations more quickly. Also, airplanes produce fewer greenhouse gases than cars, trains, or buses; and newer, more efficient planes are coming soon.

An airplane **inspector** might not see a big difference on the outside of a newly designed plane compared to an older plane. But the new airplanes are made of a strong material that is completely different from materials in older airplanes. Designers use this new material anywhere they can. It is stronger than metal, yet much lighter. In fact, the **average** plane made with this material will be almost 40% lighter than planes used to be. This means the new planes will burn much less fuel. Designers call the new material a composite.

The future of aviation is full of promise because of new technology. You will be able to see more places all around the world, and it will cost less to do it. Someday airplanes will even fly into space. This will make it possible to travel to the other side of the earth in about an hour. One day, you might **insert** a key in the ignition of your own private plane. You'll leave New York in the morning, have lunch in Sydney, Australia, and be back in New York for dinner!

Resources

Table of Contents

Linguistic Transfer Support

In the charts that follow, the mark • identifies areas in which primary language speakers may have some difficulty pronouncing and perceiving spoken English. The sound may not exist in the primary language, may exist but be pronounced somewhat differently, or may be confused with another sound. Sound production and perception issues affect phonics instruction.

CONSONANTS

Sound	Spanish	Vietnamese	Hmong	Cantonese	Haitian Creole	Korean	Khmer
/b/ as in bat			•	•		•	
/k/ as in cat and kite			•				
/d/ as in dog				•		•	
/f/ as in fan						•	
/g/ as in goat			•	•		•	•
/h/ as in hen					•		
/j/ as in jacket	•	•	•	•		•	
/l/ as in lemon						•	
/m/ as in money							
/n/ as in nail							
/p/ as in pig			•				
/r/ as in rabbit	•		•	•	•	•	
/s/ as in sun			•				
/t/ as in teen		•	•				
/v/ as in video	•			•		•	•
/w/ as in wagon	•		•				•
/y/ as in yo-yo							
/z/ as in zebra	•		•	•		•	•
/kw/ as in queen			•				
/ks/ as in X-ray			•	•			

SHORT VOWELS

Sound	Spanish	Vietnamese	Hmong	Cantonese	Haitian Creole	Korean	Khmer
short a as in hat	•	•		•		•	
short e as in set	•		•	•	•	•	
short i as in sit	•	•	•	•	•	•	
short o as in hot	•		•			•	
short u as in cup	•		•	•	•	•	

LONG VOWELS

Sound	Spanish	Vietnamese	Hmong	Cantonese	Haitian Creole	Korean	Khmer
long *a* as in d<u>a</u>te			•	•			
long *e* as in b<u>e</u>				•		•	
long *i* as in <u>i</u>ce				•			
long *o* as in r<u>oa</u>d			•	•			
long *u* as in tr<u>ue</u>				•		•	

VOWEL PATTERNS

Sound	Spanish	Vietnamese	Hmong	Cantonese	Haitian Creole	Korean	Khmer
oo as in b<u>oo</u>k	•	•	•		•	•	•
aw as in s<u>aw</u>	•					•	

DIPHTHONGS

Sound	Spanish	Vietnamese	Hmong	Cantonese	Haitian Creole	Korean	Khmer
oy as in b<u>oy</u>		•					
ow as in h<u>ow</u>	•						

R-CONTROLLED VOWELS

Sound	Spanish	Vietnamese	Hmong	Cantonese	Haitian Creole	Korean	Khmer
ir as in b<u>ir</u>d	•	•	•	•	•	•	•
ar as in h<u>ar</u>d	•	•	•	•	•	•	•
or as in f<u>or</u>m	•	•	•	•	•	•	•
air as in h<u>air</u>	•	•	•	•	•	•	•
ear as in h<u>ear</u>	•	•	•	•	•	•	•

CONSONANT DIGRAPHS

Sound	Spanish	Vietnamese	Hmong	Cantonese	Haitian Creole	Korean	Khmer
sh as in <u>sh</u>oe	•*	•		•			•
ch as in <u>ch</u>ain		•	•				
th as in <u>th</u>ink	•	•	•	•	•	•	•
ng as in si<u>ng</u>	•		•		•		

CONSONANT BLENDS

Sound	Spanish	Vietnamese	Hmong	Cantonese	Haitian Creole	Korean	Khmer
bl, *tr*, *dr*, etc. (start of words) as in <u>bl</u>ack, <u>tr</u>ee, <u>dr</u>ess		•	•	•		•	
ld, *nt*, *rt*, etc. (end of words) as in co<u>ld</u>, te<u>nt</u>, sta<u>rt</u>		•	•	•	•	•	•

* Spanish speakers from Mexico or Central America who also speak Nahuatl or a Mayan language will be familiar with this sound, written as an *x* in words like *mixteca* (pronounced *mishteca*).

Sound–Symbol Transfer Support

The following charts identify sound–symbol transfer issues for four languages that use the Roman alphabet. (The remaining three do not.) The mark • identifies symbols which do not represent the corresponding sound in the writing system of the primary language.

CONSONANTS

Sound	Spanish	Vietnamese	Hmong	Haitian Creole
b as in <u>b</u>at			•	
c as in <u>c</u>at		•	•	•
as in <u>c</u>ent		•	•	
d as in <u>d</u>og				
f as in <u>f</u>ish				
g as in <u>g</u>oat			•	
as in <u>g</u>iant	•		•	
h as in <u>h</u>en	•			
j as in <u>j</u>acket	•	•	•	
k as in <u>k</u>ite			•	
l as in <u>l</u>emon				
m as in <u>m</u>oon				
n as in <u>n</u>ice				
p as in <u>p</u>ig				
qu as in <u>qu</u>een	•		•	•
r as in <u>r</u>abbit	•		•	
s as in <u>s</u>un			•	
t as in <u>t</u>een			•	
v as in <u>v</u>ideo	•			
w as in <u>w</u>agon		•	•	
x as in <u>X</u>-ray		•	•	•
y as in <u>y</u>o-<u>y</u>o	•			
z as in <u>z</u>ebra	•	•	•	

CONSONANT DIGRAPHS

Sound	Spanish	Vietnamese	Hmong	Haitian Creole
sh as in <u>sh</u>oe	•			
ch as in <u>ch</u>air				•
th as in <u>th</u>ink	•			•
as in <u>th</u>at				

VOWELS AND VOWEL PATTERNS

Sound	Spanish	Vietnamese	Hmong	Haitian Creole
a as in b<u>a</u>t	•		•	
aCe as in d<u>a</u>te	•	•		
ai as in r<u>ai</u>n	•	•	•	•
ay as in d<u>ay</u>	•		•	•
au as in <u>au</u>thor	•	•	•	•
aw as in s<u>aw</u>	•	•	•	•
e as in b<u>e</u>t	•		•	•
ee as in s<u>ee</u>d	•	•	•	•
ea as in t<u>ea</u>	•	•	•	•
ew as in f<u>ew</u>	•	•	•	•
i as in s<u>i</u>t	•		•	•
iCe as in p<u>i</u>pe	•	•	•	•
o as in h<u>o</u>t	•		•	•
o as in r<u>o</u>de	•	•	•	•
oo as in m<u>oo</u>n	•	•	•	•
oo as in b<u>oo</u>k	•		•	•
oa as in b<u>oa</u>t	•	•	•	•
ow as in r<u>ow</u>	•	•	•	•
ow as in h<u>ow</u>	•	•	•	•
ou as in s<u>ou</u>nd	•	•	•	•
oi as in b<u>oi</u>l			•	•
oy as in b<u>oy</u>		•	•	•
u as in c<u>u</u>p	•	•	•	•
uCe as in J<u>u</u>ne	•	•		
ui as in s<u>ui</u>t	•	•	•	•
ue as in bl<u>ue</u>	•	•	•	•
y as in tr<u>y</u>	•	•	•	•
ar as in st<u>ar</u>			•	•
er as in f<u>er</u>n	•		•	•
ir as in b<u>ir</u>d	•		•	•
or as in t<u>or</u>n	•		•	
ur as in b<u>ur</u>n	•		•	

English–Spanish Vocabulary Transfer Support

English and Spanish share some basic linguistic characteristics. Both languages use word parts like prefixes and suffixes, and both have verbs that change in form. The example words below are not intended to be cognates, but words that illustrate the similar meanings of the word parts. Note that Haitian Creole, Cantonese, Hmong, and Vietnamese do not use word parts to construct new words in the same way that English does.

PREFIXES

English Word Part or Parts	English Example Words	Spanish Word Part or Parts	Spanish Example Words	Word Part Purpose
un-, non-, in-, dis-	unhappy nonstop incorrect dislike	*in-, des-/dis-* *no* plus the verb *sin* plus the noun or verb	infeliz, incorrecto desconocido disparejo no gustar sin parar	Means "not"
re-	redo	*re-*	rehacer	Means "again"
pre-	preteen	*pre-*	preescolar	Means "before"

SUFFIXES

English Word Part or Parts	English Example Words	Spanish Word Part or Parts	Spanish Example Words	Word Part Purpose
-ful	powerful	*-oso/a*	poderoso/a	Means "with"; turns a noun into an adjective
-able	readable likeable	*-ible* *-able*	legible agradable	Turns a verb into an adjective
-less	fearless careless	*sin* plus the noun prefix *des-*	sin miedo descuidado	Means "without"; turns a noun into an adjective
-ness	happiness	*-idad*	felicidad	Turns an adjective into a noun
-ion/-tion, -ment	reaction payment amazement	*-ción/-sión* verb stem + *-o*	reacción conclusión pago asombro	Turns a verb into a noun
-ly	quickly	*-mente*	rápidamente	Turns an adjective into an adverb

Qualitative Spelling Inventory (QSI)

You may use this inventory and the **Qualitative Spelling Inventory Checklist** (pages 398–399) to gather information about where students fall within a specific developmental level. In this QSI, the words are presented in increasing difficulty. As the spelling assessment proceeds, you will see what features students are learning by the quality of their spelling and the number of words and features they spell correctly. With the words in ascending difficulty, consider stopping the assessment when students make enough errors to determine a phase of spelling. To avoid frustration level testing, small groups can continue this or another list the next day.

The inventory and the checklist will help you identify what students have learned, what they are still "using but confusing" and thus need to learn, and what is beyond their present level. The inventory can be given at the beginning and end of the year and one or two times in between to monitor progress.

Students who score between 40% and 90% on the **Qualitative Spelling Inventory** can begin instruction on grade level. Consider alternate lists for students who score below 40% and above 90%.

Grade 1	Grade 2	Grade 3	Grade 4	Grade 5	Grade 6
1. net	1. class	1. paint	1. shown	1. scowl	1. pledge
2. pig	2. went	2. find	2. thirst	2. beneath	2. advantage
3. job	3. chop	3. comb	3. lodge	3. pounce	3. changeable
4. bell	4. when	4. knife	4. curve	4. brighten	4. inspire
5. trap	5. milk	5. scratch	5. suit	5. disgrace	5. conference
6. chin	6. shell	6. crawl	6. bounce	6. poison	6. relying
7. with	7. sock	7. throat	7. middle	7. destroy	7. amusement
8. drum	8. such	8. voice	8. clue	8. weary	8. conclusion
9. track	9. sleep	9. nurse	9. traced	9. sailors	9. carriage
10. bump	10. boat	10. weigh	10. hurry	10. whistle	10. advertisement
11. smoke	11. size	11. waving	11. noisier	11. chatting	11. description
12. pool	12. plain	12. letter	12. striped	12. legal	12. appearance
13. slide	13. tight	13. useful	13. collar	13. human	13. cooperation
14. shade	14. knife	14. tripping	14. medal	14. abilities	14. democratic
15. brave	15. start	15. early	15. skipping	15. decided	15. responsible
16. white	16. fought	16. dollar	16. palace	16. settlement	16. invisible
17. pink	17. story	17. mouthful	17. civil	17. surround	17. official
18. father	18. clapped	18. starry	18. wrinkle	18. treasure	18. commission
19. batted	19. saving	19. slammed	19. fossil	19. service	19. civilize
20. hugging	20. funny	20. thousand	20. disappear	20. confession	20. inherited
	21. patches	21. circle	21. damage	21. frequency	21. accidental
	22. pinned	22. laughter	22. capture	22. commotion	22. spacious
	23. village	23. carried	23. parading	23. evidence	23. sensibility
	24. pleasure	24. happiest	24. trouble	24. predict	24. composition
	25. question		25. imagine	25. community	25. accomplish
			26. favorite	26. president	26. opposition
				27. responsible	
				28. sensibility	
				29. symphonies	
				30. permission	

Qualitative Spelling Inventory Checklist

This checklist can assist you in identifying a phase of spelling development for each student and whether the student is in the early, middle, or late part of that phase.

When a feature is regularly spelled correctly, check "Yes." If the feature is spelled incorrectly or is omitted, check "No." The last feature that you check as "Often" corresponds to the student's phase of development.

Student's Name _____

Letter Name–Alphabetic Phase

EARLY

- Are beginning and ending consonants included?   Yes _____   No _____   Often _____
- Is there a vowel in each word?   Yes _____   No _____   Often _____

MIDDLE

- Are consonant digraphs and blends correct? (**sh**ade/**tr**ack)   Yes _____   No _____   Often _____

LATE

- Are short vowels spelled correctly? (h**i**d, ch**o**p, s**u**ch)   Yes _____   No _____   Often _____
- Are *m* and *n* included in front of other consonants? (bu**m**p, pi**n**k)   Yes _____   No _____   Often _____

Within Word Pattern Phase

EARLY

- Are long vowel spellings in single-syllable words "used but confused"? (SLIED for *slide*, MAIK for *make*)   Yes _____   No _____   Often _____
- Is there a vowel in each word?   Yes _____   No _____   Often _____

MIDDLE

- Are most long vowels in single-syllable words spelled correctly but some long vowel spellings still "used but confused"? (MANE for *main*)   Yes _____   No _____   Often _____

LATE

- Are *r*- and *l*-controlled vowels in single-syllable words spelled correctly? (st**ar**t/mi**lk**)   Yes _____   No _____   Often _____

Syllables and Affixes Phase

EARLY

- Are inflectional endings added correctly to base words with short vowel patterns? (hug**ging**, pin**ned**)   Yes _____ No _____ Often _____

MIDDLE

- Are inflectional endings added correctly to base words with long vowel patterns? (wa**ving**, stri**ped**)   Yes _____ No _____ Often _____

LATE

- Are unaccented final syllables spelled correctly? (cat**tle**, accur**ate**)   Yes _____ No _____ Often _____

- Are less frequent prefixes and suffixes spelled correctly? (**con**fession, **pro**duction, cap**ture**, coll**ar**)   Yes _____ No _____ Often _____

Derivational Relations Phase

EARLY

- Are multisyllabic words spelled correctly? (expansion, community)   Yes _____ No _____ Often _____

MIDDLE

- Are unaccented vowels in derived words spelled correctly? (prohibition, opp**o**sition)   Yes _____ No _____ Often _____

LATE

- Are words from derived forms spelled correctly? (comp**e**tition, confid**ent**)   Yes _____ No _____ Often _____

- Are absorbed prefixes spelled correctly? (**ir**relevant, **ac**complish)   Yes _____ No _____ Often _____

Adapted from Words Their Way *by Donald Bear, Marcia Invernizzi, Shane Templeton, & Francine Johnston (Englewood Cliff, NJ: Prentice-Hall 2004).*

▶ Comprehensive List of Spelling/Phonics Lessons and Words, Grades K–6

The effectiveness of word study instruction begins with its word list. The lessons and words on pages 400–410 are organized by the phases of spelling development to guide your selection of lessons for students, based on assessment results. Lessons that are not in your grade-level version of this Guide can be accessed online at **www.thinkcentral.com**.

Emergent Phase

LATE

Letters *Aa–Jj*
Grade K, Lesson 1

The Letters in Your Name
Grade K, Lesson 2

Letters *Aa–Tt*
Grade K, Lesson 3

The Alphabet
Grade K, Lesson 4

Beginning Sounds in Words
Grade K, Lesson 5

Beginning Sounds in Words
Grade K, Lesson 6

Beginning Sounds /m/*m*, /s/*s*
Grade K, Lesson 7

Beginning Sounds /m/*m*, /s/*s*, /t/*t*
Grade K, Lesson 8

Beginning Sounds /t/*t*, /k/*c*, /p/*p*
Grade K, Lesson 9

Beginning Sounds /n/*n*, /m/*m*
Grade K, Lesson 14

Beginning Sounds /p/*p*, /f/*f*
Grade K, Lesson 16

Beginning Sounds /d/*d*, /r/*r*, /g/*g*
Grade K, Lesson 21

Letter Name– Alphabetic Phase

EARLY

Ending Sounds in Words
Grade K, Lesson 10

Ending Sounds /s/*s*, /p/*p*, /t/*t*
Grade K, Lesson 11

Ending Sounds /g/*g*, /b/*b*
Grade K, Lesson 18

Short *a* /ă/
Grade K, Lesson 12

Words with -*an*, -*ap*, -*at*
Grade K, Lesson 13

Short *a* Words and High-Frequency Words
Grade K, Lesson 15

Short *i* /ĭ/
Grade K, Lesson 17

Words with Short *a* and Short *i*
Grade K, Lesson 19

Words with -*ig*, -*in*, -*it*
Grade K, Lesson 20

Short *o* /ŏ/
Grade K, Lesson 22

MIDDLE

Words for One and More than One (-*s*)
Grade K, Lesson 23

Words with -*at*, -*it*, -*ot*
Grade K, Lesson 24

Words with Short *o* and Short *e*
Grade K, Lesson 25

Words with -*et* and -*en*
Grade K, Lesson 26

Short *u* /ŭ/
Grade K, Lesson 27

Words with Short *e* and Short *u*
Grade K, Lesson 28

Words with -*ap*, -*up*, -*op*
Grade K, Lesson 29

Words with Short Vowels
Grade K, Lesson 30

Words with Short *a*
Grade 1, Lesson 1
1. am
2. at
3. sat
4. man
5. dad
6. mat

Words with Short *i*
Grade 1, Lesson 2
1. if
2. is
3. him
4. rip
5. fit
6. pin

Words with Short *o*
Grade 1, Lesson 3
1. log
2. dot
3. top
4. hot
5. lot
6. ox

Words with Short *e*
Grade 1, Lesson 4
1. yet
2. web
3. pen
4. wet
5. leg
6. hen

Words with Short *u*
Grade 1, Lesson 5
1. up
2. bug
3. mud
4. nut
5. hug
6. tub

Words with Short *a*
Grade 1, Lesson 6
1. an
2. bad
3. can
4. had
5. cat
6. ran

Words with Short *i*
Grade 1, Lesson 7
1. in
2. will
3. did
4. sit
5. six
6. big

Words with Short *o*
Grade 1, Lesson 8
1. on
2. got
3. fox
4. pop
5. not
6. hop

Words with Short *e*
Grade 1, Lesson 9
1. yes
2. let
3. red
4. ten
5. bed
6. get

Words with Short *u*
Grade 1, Lesson 10
1. us
2. sun
3. but
4. fun
5. bus
6. run

Words with *th*
Grade 1, Lesson 11
1. that
2. then
3. this
4. them
5. with
6. bath

Words with *ch*
Grade 1, Lesson 12
1. chin
2. chop
3. much
4. chip
5. rich
6. chick

Words with *sh*, *wh*
Grade 1, Lesson 13
1. ship
2. shop
3. which
4. when
5. whip
6. fish

Short Vowels *a*, *i*
Grade 2, Lesson 1
1. sad
2. dig
3. jam
4. glad
5. list
6. win
7. flat
8. if
9. fix
10. rip
11. kit
12. mask

Short Vowels *o*, *u*, *e*
Grade 2, Lesson 2
1. wet
2. job
3. hug
4. rest
5. spot
6. mud
7. left
8. help
9. plum

10. nut
11. net
12. hot

LATE

Consonant Blends with *r, l, s*
Grade 2, Lesson 5
1. spin
2. clap
3. grade
4. swim
5. place
6. last
7. test
8. skin
9. drag
10. glide
11. just
12. stage

Common Final Blends *nd, ng, nk, nt, xt, mp*
Grade 2, Lesson 6
1. next
2. end
3. camp
4. sank
5. sing
6. drink
7. hunt
8. stand
9. long
10. stamp
11. pond
12. bring

Words with *ar*
Grade 1, Lesson 21
1. far
2. arm
3. yard
4. art
5. jar
6. bar
7. barn
8. bark
9. card
10. yarn

Double Consonants and *ck*
Grade 2, Lesson 7
1. rock
2. black
3. trick
4. kick
5. full
6. dress
7. neck
8. add
9. spell
10. stuck
11. class
12. doll

Words with *th, sh, wh, ch*
Grade 2, Lesson 8
1. dish
2. than
3. chest
4. such
5. thin
6. push
7. shine
8. chase
9. white
10. while
11. these
12. flash

Short Vowels
Grade 3, Lesson 1
1. crop
2. plan
3. thing
4. smell
5. shut
6. sticky
7. spent
8. lunch
9. pumpkin
10. clock
11. gift
12. class
13. skip
14. swing

Within Word Pattern Phase

EARLY

Words with Long *a*
Grade 1, Lesson 14
1. came
2. make
3. brave
4. late
5. gave
6. shape

Words with Long *i*
Grade 1, Lesson 15
1. time
2. like
3. kite
4. bike
5. white
6. drive

Long Vowels *a, i*
Grade 2, Lesson 3
1. cake
2. mine
3. plate
4. size
5. ate
6. grape
7. prize
8. wipe
9. race

10. line
11. pile
12. rake

Words with Long *o*
Grade 1, Lesson 16
1. so
2. go
3. home
4. hole
5. no
6. rope
7. joke
8. bone
9. stove
10. poke

Words with Long *e*
Grade 1, Lesson 17
1. me
2. be
3. read
4. feet
5. tree
6. keep
7. eat
8. mean
9. sea
10. these

Words with Long *a*
Grade 1, Lesson 18
1. play
2. grain
3. sail
4. mail
5. may
6. rain
7. way
8. day
9. stay
10. pain

Words with Long *o*
Grade 1, Lesson 19
1. show
2. row
3. grow
4. low
5. blow
6. snow
7. boat
8. coat
9. road
10. toad

Words with *er, ir, ur*
Grade 1, Lesson 22
1. her
2. fern
3. girl
4. sir
5. stir
6. bird
7. fur
8. hurt
9. turn
10. third

Words with *oo* (/o͞o/)
Grade 1, Lesson 23
1. look
2. book
3. good
4. hook
5. brook
6. took
7. foot
8. shook
9. wood
10. hood

Words with *oo, ou, ew*
Grade 1, Lesson 24
1. soon
2. new
3. noon
4. zoo
5. boot
6. too
7. moon
8. blew
9. soup
10. you

Words with Long *i*
Grade 1, Lesson 28
1. my
2. try
3. sky
4. fly
5. by
6. dry
7. pie
8. cried
9. night
10. light

Long Vowels *o, u*
Grade 2, Lesson 4
1. doze
2. nose
3. use
4. rose
5. pole
6. close
7. cute
8. woke
9. mule
10. rode
11. role
12. tune

Contractions
Grade 2, Lesson 10
1. I'm
2. don't
3. isn't
4. can't
5. we'll
6. it's
7. I've
8. didn't
9. you're
10. that's
11. wasn't
12. you've

Words with *ai, ay*
Grade 2, Lesson 12
1. pay
2. wait
3. paint
4. train
5. pail
6. clay
7. tray
8. plain
9. stain
10. hay
11. gray
12. away

Words with *ee, ea*
Grade 2, Lesson 13
1. free
2. teach
3. teeth
4. please
5. beach
6. wheel
7. team
8. speak
9. sneeze
10. sheep
11. meaning
12. weave

Long *o* (*o, oa, ow*)
Grade 2, Lesson 14
1. own
2. most
3. soap
4. float
5. both
6. know
7. loan
8. goat
9. flow
10. loaf
11. throw
12. coach

Long *i* (*i, igh, y*)
Grade 2, Lesson 17
1. night
2. kind
3. spy
4. child
5. light
6. find
7. right
8. high
9. wild
10. July
11. fry
12. sigh

MIDDLE

Words with *ar*
Grade 2, Lesson 19
1. car
2. dark
3. arm
4. star
5. park
6. yard

7. party
8. hard
9. farm
10. start
11. part
12. spark

Words with *or, ore*
Grade 2, Lesson 20
1. horn
2. story
3. fork
4. score
5. store
6. corn
7. morning
8. shore
9. short
10. born
11. tore
12. forget

Words with *er*
Grade 2, Lesson 21
1. father
2. over
3. under
4. herd
5. water
6. verb
7. paper
8. cracker
9. offer
10. cover
11. germ
12. master

Homophones
Grade 2, Lesson 22
1. meet
2. meat
3. week
4. weak
5. mane
6. main
7. tail
8. tale
9. be
10. bee
11. too
12. two

Words with *oo (ew, oo, ou)*
Grade 2, Lesson 26
1. root
2. crew
3. spoon
4. few
5. bloom
6. grew
7. room
8. you
9. stew
10. boost
11. scoop
12. flew

Words with *oo (book)*
Grade 2, Lesson 27
1. took
2. books
3. foot
4. hoof
5. cook
6. nook
7. hood
8. wood
9. stood
10. shook
11. crook
12. cookbook

Words with *ai, ay, igh, y*
Grade 2, Lesson 29
1. aim
2. snail
3. bay
4. braid
5. ray
6. always
7. gain
8. sly
9. chain
10. shy
11. bright
12. fright

Words with *oa, ow, ee, ea*
Grade 2, Lesson 30
1. seated
2. keeps
3. speed
4. seen
5. means
6. clean
7. groan
8. roast
9. bowls
10. crow
11. owe
12. grown

V-C-e Spellings
Grade 3, Lesson 2
1. spoke
2. mile
3. save
4. excuse
5. cone
6. invite
7. cube
8. price
9. erase
10. ripe
11. broke
12. flame
13. life
14. rule

More Long *a* and Long *e* Spellings
Grade 3, Lesson 3
1. lay
2. real

3. trail
4. sweet
5. today
6. dream
7. seem
8. tea
9. treat
10. afraid
11. leave
12. bait
13. screen
14. speed

More Long *o* Spellings
Grade 3, Lesson 4
1. load
2. open
3. told
4. yellow
5. soak
6. shadow
7. foam
8. follow
9. glow
10. sold
11. window
12. coach
13. almost
14. throat

Spelling Long *i*
Grade 3, Lesson 5
1. slight
2. mild
3. sight
4. pie
5. mind
6. tie
7. pilot
8. might
9. lie
10. tight
11. blind
12. fight
13. die
14. midnight

Vowel + /r/ Sounds in *air* and *fear*
Grade 3, Lesson 16
1. air
2. wear
3. chair
4. stairs
5. bare
6. bear
7. hair
8. care
9. pear
10. pair
11. share
12. near
13. ear
14. beard

Words with *aw, al, o*
Grade 2, Lesson 25
1. tall
2. saw
3. dog
4. draw
5. call
6. fall
7. soft
8. paw
9. ball
10. yawn
11. log
12. small

More Short and Long Vowels
Grade 3, Lesson 6
1. math
2. toast
3. easy
4. socks
5. Friday
6. stuff
7. paid
8. cheese
9. June
10. elbow
11. program
12. shiny
13. piles
14. sticky

Words with *ou, ow*
Grade 1, Lesson 25
1. how
2. now
3. cow
4. owl
5. ouch
6. house
7. found
8. out
9. gown
10. town

Words with *ow, ou*
Grade 2, Lesson 28
1. cow
2. house
3. town
4. shout
5. down
6. mouse
7. found
8. loud
9. brown
10. ground
11. pound
12. flower

LATE

Three-Letter Clusters
Grade 3, Lesson 7
1. three
2. scrap
3. street

4. spring
5. thrill
6. scream
7. strange
8. throw
9. string
10. scrape
11. spray
12. threw
13. strong
14. scratch

Unexpected Consonant Spellings
Grade 3, Lesson 8
1. itch
2. wreck
3. knee
4. patch
5. wrap
6. knot
7. watch
8. knife
9. stretch
10. write
11. knew
12. knock
13. match
14. wrong

Vowel Sound in *town*
Grade 3, Lesson 9
1. clown
2. round
3. bow
4. cloud
5. power
6. crown
7. thousand
8. crowd
9. sound
10. count
11. powder
12. blouse
13. frown
14. pound

Vowel Sound in *talk*
Grade 3, Lesson 10
1. talk
2. cross
3. awful
4. law
5. cloth
6. cost
7. crawl
8. chalk
9. also
10. raw
11. salt
12. wall
13. lawn
14. always

Vowel Sound in *joy*
Grade 3, Lesson 11
1. joy
2. point

Comprehensive Word List

3. voice
4. join
5. oil
6. coin
7. noise
8. spoil
9. toy
10. joint
11. boy
12. soil
13. choice
14. boil

Homophones
Grade 3, Lesson 12
1. hole
2. whole
3. its
4. it's
5. hear
6. here
7. won
8. one
9. our
10. hour
11. their
12. there
13. fur
14. fir

Contractions
Grade 3, Lesson 13
1. I'd
2. he's
3. haven't
4. doesn't
5. let's
6. there's
7. wouldn't
8. what's
9. she's
10. aren't
11. hasn't
12. couldn't
13. he'd
14. they're

Vowel + /r/ Sounds
Grade 3, Lesson 14
1. horse
2. mark
3. storm
4. market
5. acorn
6. artist
7. March
8. north
9. barking
10. stork
11. thorn
12. forest
13. chore
14. restore

Vowel + /r/ Sound in nurse
Grade 3, Lesson 15
1. nurse
2. work
3. shirt

4. hurt
5. first
6. word
7. serve
8. curly
9. dirt
10. third
11. worry
12. turn
13. stir
14. firm

Words with /j/ and /s/
Grade 3, Lesson 17
1. age
2. space
3. change
4. jawbone
5. jacket
6. giant
7. pencil
8. circle
9. once
10. large
11. dance
12. jeans
13. bounce
14. huge

Spelling the /k/ and /kw/ Sounds
Grade 3, Lesson 18
1. shark
2. check
3. queen
4. circus
5. flake
6. crack
7. second
8. squeeze
9. quart
10. squeak
11. quick
12. coldest
13. Africa
14. Mexico

Vowel Sounds in *spoon* and *wood*
Grade 3, Lesson 19
1. mood
2. wooden
3. drew
4. smooth
5. blue
6. balloon
7. true
8. crooked
9. chew
10. tooth
11. hooves
12. cool
13. food
14. pooch

ough* and *augh
Grade 3, Lesson 28
1. taught
2. thought

3. rough
4. laugh
5. bought
6. cough
7. ought
8. caught
9. fought
10. daughter
11. tough
12. through
13. enough
14. brought

Short *o* and Long *o*
Grade 4, Lesson 4
1. block
2. shown
3. oatmeal
4. wrote
5. fellow
6. scold
7. coast
8. odd
9. locate
10. slope
11. throat
12. host
13. online
14. shock
15. solve
16. known
17. remote
18. stock
19. boast
20. globe

Homophones
Grade 4, Lesson 5
1. wait
2. weight
3. heard
4. herd
5. days
6. daze
7. heel
8. heal
9. peak
10. peek
11. sent
12. cent
13. scent
14. feet
15. feat
16. vain
17. vane
18. vein
19. miner
20. minor

Short *a* and Long *a*
Grade 4, Lesson 1
1. blade
2. gray
3. past
4. afraid
5. magic
6. delay
7. amaze
8. drain
9. maybe

10. break
11. sale
12. hang
13. stain
14. glass
15. raft
16. jail
17. crayon
18. fact
19. stale
20. steak

Short *e* and Long *e*
Grade 4, Lesson 2
1. west
2. steep
3. member
4. gleam
5. fresh
6. freedom
7. speed
8. steam
9. beast
10. believe
11. speck
12. kept
13. cheap
14. pretend
15. greed
16. shelf
17. least
18. eager
19. reason
20. chief

Short *i* and Long *i*
Grade 4, Lesson 3
1. skill
2. crime
3. grind
4. tonight
5. brick
6. flight
7. live
8. chill
9. delight
10. build
11. ditch
12. decide
13. witness
14. wind
15. district
16. inch
17. sigh
18. fright
19. remind
20. split

Vowel Sounds /ŭ/, /yo͞o/, and /o͞o/
Grade 4, Lesson 6
1. bunch
2. fruit
3. argue
4. crumb
5. crew
6. tune
7. juice
8. refuse
9. truth

10. young
11. clue
12. trunk
13. amuse
14. suit
15. rude
16. trust
17. dew
18. stuck
19. rescue
20. brush

Vowel Sounds /o͞o/ and /o͝o/
Grade 4, Lesson 7
1. bloom
2. cookbook
3. tool
4. shampoo
5. put
6. wool
7. stool
8. proof
9. prove
10. group
11. brook
12. foolish
13. bush
14. crooked
15. booth
16. raccoon
17. hook
18. groom
19. roof
20. soup

Vowel Sounds /ou/ and /ô/
Grade 4, Lesson 8
1. aloud
2. bald
3. hawk
4. south
5. faucet
6. proud
7. claw
8. tower
9. stalk
10. couple
11. howl
12. false
13. dawn
14. allow
15. drown
16. pause
17. fault
18. cause
19. amount
20. cloudier

Vowel + /r/ Sounds
Grade 4, Lesson 9
1. spark
2. prepare
3. cheer
4. tear
5. scarf
6. scare
7. repair
8. earring

9. scarce
10. weird
11. sharp
12. rear
13. spare
14. gear
15. hairy
16. compare
17. alarm
18. harsh
19. upstairs
20. square

More Vowel + /r/ Sounds
Grade 4, Lesson 10
1. learn
2. dirty
3. worn
4. sore
5. thirst
6. burn
7. record
8. cure
9. board
10. course
11. worth
12. early
13. return
14. pure
15. world
16. search
17. worse
18. thirteen
19. sport
20. current

Syllables and Affixes Phase

EARLY

Compound Words
Grade 1, Lesson 20
1. bedtime
2. sunset
3. bathtub
4. sailboat
5. flagpole
6. backpack
7. playpen
8. raincoat
9. inside
10. himself

Base Words with -ed, -ing
Grade 1, Lesson 26
1. mix
2. mixed
3. hop
4. hopped
5. hope
6. hoping
7. run
8. running
9. use
10. used

Base Words with -er, -est
Grade 1, Lesson 27
1. hard
2. harder
3. hardest
4. fast
5. faster
6. fastest
7. slow
8. slower
9. slowest
10. sooner

Words with Suffixes -ly, -y, -ful
Grade 1, Lesson 29
1. sad
2. sadly
3. slow
4. slowly
5. dust
6. dusty
7. trick
8. tricky
9. help
10. helpful

Compound Words
Grade 2, Lesson 15
1. cannot
2. pancake
3. maybe
4. baseball
5. playground
6. someone
7. myself
8. classroom
9. sunshine
10. outside
11. upon
12. nothing

Base Words with Endings -ed, -ing
Grade 2, Lesson 9
1. liked
2. using
3. riding
4. chased
5. spilled
6. making
7. closed
8. hoping
9. baked
10. hiding
11. standing
12. asked

Base Words with Endings -ed, -ing
Grade 2, Lesson 16
1. running
2. clapped
3. stopped
4. hopping
5. batted
6. selling
7. pinned
8. cutting
9. sitting
10. rubbed
11. missed
12. grabbed

Base Words with Endings -s, -es
Grade 2, Lesson 11
1. hens
2. eggs
3. ducks
4. bikes
5. boxes
6. wishes
7. dresses
8. names
9. bells
10. stamps
11. dishes
12. grapes

Suffixes -ly, -ful
Grade 2, Lesson 23
1. helpful
2. sadly
3. hopeful
4. thankful
5. slowly
6. wishful
7. kindly
8. useful
9. safely
10. painful
11. mouthful
12. weakly

Long e Spelled y
Grade 2, Lesson 18
1. happy
2. pretty
3. baby
4. very
5. puppy
6. funny
7. carry
8. lucky
9. only
10. sunny
11. penny
12. city

Prefixes re-, un-
Grade 2, Lesson 24
1. unhappy
2. retell
3. untangle
4. unkind
5. repaint
6. refill
7. unlike
8. remake
9. unpack
10. reread
11. unlock
12. replay

Compound Words
Grade 3, Lesson 20
1. birthday
2. anyone
3. sometimes
4. everything
5. homework
6. afternoon
7. airplane
8. grandmother
9. something
10. without
11. himself
12. faraway
13. sunburned
14. daylight

Words with -ed and -ing
Grade 3, Lesson 21
1. coming
2. swimming
3. dropping
4. tapping
5. taping
6. invited
7. saving
8. stared
9. planned
10. changing
11. joking
12. loved
13. gripped
14. tasted

Changing Final y to i
Grade 3, Lesson 22
1. cities
2. cried
3. puppies
4. hurried
5. stories
6. flies
7. parties
8. tried
9. pennies
10. fried
11. carried
12. babies
13. spied
14. ponies

The Suffixes -ful, -ly, and -er
Grade 3, Lesson 23
1. singer
2. loudly
3. joyful
4. teacher
5. fighter
6. closely
7. powerful
8. farmer
9. quickly
10. careful
11. friendly
12. speaker
13. wonderful
14. truly

The Prefixes re- and un-
Grade 3, Lesson 24
1. unfold
2. rejoin
3. untie
4. reheat
5. unfair
6. unclear
7. repaid
8. rewrite
9. unhurt
10. recheck
11. unlucky
12. unwrap
13. reuse
14. unsure

The Suffixes -less and -ness
Grade 3, Lesson 25
1. painless
2. sickness
3. sadness
4. helpless
5. thankless
6. kindness
7. hopeless
8. darkness
9. fearless
10. thickness
11. careless
12. goodness
13. spotless
14. softness

Compound Words
Grade 4, Lesson 11
1. somebody
2. fireplace
3. nearby
4. toothbrush
5. homesick
6. make-believe
7. anything
8. all right
9. goodbye
10. forehead
11. classmate
12. flashlight
13. haircut
14. twenty-two
15. driveway
16. alarm clock
17. baby-sit
18. airport
19. forever
20. mailbox

Words with -ed or -ing
Grade 4, Lesson 12
1. rising
2. traced
3. stripped
4. slammed
5. dancing
6. striped
7. winning

8. snapping
9. bragging
10. handled
11. dripped
12. begged
13. dared
14. skipped
15. hitting
16. spotted
17. raced
18. dimmed
19. spinning
20. escaped

More Words with -ed or -ing
Grade 4, Lesson 13
1. wiped
2. covered
3. mapped
4. pleasing
5. slipped
6. putting
7. traveled
8. seeking
9. visiting
10. mixed
11. shipped
12. phoning
13. offered
14. smelling
15. hiking
16. checking
17. fainted
18. landed
19. becoming
20. wandering

Final Long e
Grade 4, Lesson 14
1. turkey
2. lonely
3. colony
4. steady
5. hungry
6. valley
7. hockey
8. starry
9. melody
10. movie
11. duty
12. drowsy
13. chimney
14. plenty
15. daily
16. alley
17. fifty
18. empty
19. injury
20. prairie

Changing Final y to i
Grade 4, Lesson 15
1. tiniest
2. hobbies
3. copied
4. countries
5. pitied
6. easier

7. laziest
8. families
9. spied
10. happiest
11. ladies
12. friendlier
13. studied
14. busier
15. breezier
16. prettiest
17. noisier
18. healthier
19. butterflies
20. funniest

Words with /k/, /ng/, and /kw/
Grade 4, Lesson 16
1. risky
2. track
3. topic
4. blank
5. question
6. pocket
7. monkey
8. junk
9. equal
10. ache
11. public
12. attack
13. struck
14. earthquake
15. picnic
16. banker
17. electric
18. blanket
19. mistake
20. stomach

Prefixes re-, un-, dis-
Grade 4, Lesson 18
1. unused
2. refresh
3. dislike
4. replace
5. unpaid
6. redo
7. disorder
8. unplanned
9. distrust
10. rewind
11. untrue
12. unload
13. recall
14. displease
15. uneven
16. rebuild
17. restart
18. uncover
19. untidy
20. discolor

Suffixes -ful, -less, -ness, -ment
Grade 4, Lesson 19
1. colorful
2. weakness
3. movement
4. endless

5. truthful
6. illness
7. cheerful
8. useless
9. beautiful
10. restless
11. clumsiness
12. pavement
13. peaceful
14. fondness
15. neatness
16. speechless
17. statement
18. wasteful
19. penniless
20. treatment

Words with -ed or -ing
Grade 5, Lesson 16
1. scrubbed
2. listening
3. stunned
4. knitting
5. carpeting
6. wandered
7. gathering
8. beginning
9. skimmed
10. chatting
11. shrugged
12. bothering
13. whipped
14. quizzed
15. suffering
16. scanned
17. ordered
18. totaled
19. answered
20. upsetting

More Words with -ed or -ing
Grade 5, Lesson 17
1. tiring
2. borrowed
3. freezing
4. delivered
5. whispered
6. losing
7. decided
8. amazing
9. performing
10. resulting
11. related
12. attending
13. damaged
14. remarked
15. practicing
16. supported
17. united
18. expected
19. amusing
20. repeated

Changing Final y to i
Grade 5, Lesson 18
1. duties
2. earlier

3. loveliest
4. denied
5. ferries
6. sunnier
7. terrified
8. abilities
9. dirtier
10. scariest
11. trophies
12. cozier
13. enemies
14. iciest
15. greediest
16. drowsier
17. victories
18. horrified
19. memories
20. strategies

Suffixes: -ful, -ly, -ness, -less, -ment
Grade 5, Lesson 19
1. lately
2. settlement
3. watchful
4. countless
5. steadily
6. closeness
7. calmly
8. government
9. agreement
10. cloudiness
11. delightful
12. noisily
13. tardiness
14. forgetful
15. forgiveness
16. harmless
17. enjoyment
18. appointment
19. effortless
20. plentiful

Prefixes: in-, un-, dis-, mis-
Grade 5, Lesson 24
1. mislead
2. dismiss
3. insincere
4. unable
5. indirect
6. mistreat
7. disaster
8. dishonest
9. insecure
10. unknown
11. incomplete
12. unequal
13. unstable
14. misspell
15. disagree
16. informal
17. discover
18. unwise
19. mislaid
20. disgrace

MIDDLE

Words with Syllable Pattern CV
Grade 1, Lesson 30
1. even
2. open
3. begin
4. baby
5. tiger
6. music
7. paper
8. zero
9. table
10. below

VCCV Syllabication
Grade 3, Lesson 26
1. person
2. helmet
3. until
4. carpet
5. Monday
6. enjoy
7. forget
8. problem
9. Sunday
10. garden
11. order
12. mistake
13. umpire
14. herself

Words with Double Consonants
Grade 3, Lesson 27
1. jelly
2. bottom
3. pillow
4. happen
5. butter
6. lesson
7. cherry
8. sudden
9. arrow
10. dollar
11. hello
12. rabbit
13. letter
14. button

Words Ending with -er or -le
Grade 3, Lesson 29
1. apple
2. river
3. little
4. October
5. ladder
6. summer
7. purple
8. later
9. November
10. giggle
11. uncle
12. winter
13. center
14. double

Comprehensive Word List   **405**

Words that Begin with a- or be-
Grade 3, Lesson 30
1. below
2. about
3. belong
4. around
5. again
6. alone
7. because
8. above
9. between
10. alive
11. behind
12. begin
13. along
14. before

Words with VCV Pattern
Grade 4, Lesson 21
1. event
2. humor
3. rapid
4. music
5. relief
6. planet
7. detail
8. unite
9. frozen
10. figure
11. siren
12. polite
13. hotel
14. protest
15. punish
16. defend
17. relay
18. habit
19. student
20. moment

VCCV and VCV Patterns
Grade 4, Lesson 22
1. dentist
2. final
3. finish
4. narrow
5. shelter
6. ahead
7. corner
8. hollow
9. divide
10. famous
11. recent
12. silver
13. capture
14. cabin
15. dinner
16. minus
17. minute
18. value
19. reward
20. broken

Words with VCCV Pattern
Grade 4, Lesson 23
1. poster
2. secret
3. whether
4. author
5. rocket
6. bushel
7. agree
8. bucket
9. ticket
10. declare
11. chicken
12. clothing
13. apron
14. whiskers
15. degree
16. gather
17. achieve
18. rather
19. bracket
20. machine

Words with VCCCV Pattern
Grade 4, Lesson 24
1. hundred
2. supply
3. single
4. middle
5. explain
6. surprise
7. pilgrim
8. sandwich
9. instead
10. complete
11. monster
12. settle
13. address
14. farther
15. sample
16. although
17. turtle
18. athlete
19. orchard
20. kingdom

Words with VV Pattern
Grade 4, Lesson 25
1. idea
2. lion
3. usual
4. radio
5. liar
6. poem
7. India
8. piano
9. January
10. quiet
11. poet
12. science
13. diary
14. violin
15. period
16. February
17. cereal
18. video
19. meteor
20. rodeo

Final Schwa + /r/ Sound
Grade 4, Lesson 26
1. enter
2. banner
3. sugar
4. shower
5. motor
6. collar
7. labor
8. finger
9. mirror
10. beggar
11. favor
12. bother
13. fever
14. doctor
15. temper
16. actor
17. polar
18. sweater
19. traitor
20. whenever

Final Schwa + /l/ Sound
Grade 4, Lesson 27
1. title
2. towel
3. battle
4. pedal
5. metal
6. simple
7. eagle
8. special
9. total
10. trouble
11. nickel
12. gentle
13. barrel
14. model
15. tangle
16. ankle
17. marvel
18. juggle
19. squirrel
20. riddle

More Vowel + /r/ Sounds
Grade 5, Lesson 7
1. earth
2. peer
3. twirl
4. burnt
5. smear
6. further
7. appear
8. worthwhile
9. nerve
10. pier
11. squirm
12. weary
13. alert
14. murmur
15. thirsty

Short Vowels
Grade 6, Lesson 1
1. batch
2. reject
3. vanish
4. sloppy
5. rhythm
6. blunder
7. strict
8. meadow
9. recover
10. cleanse
11. text
12. mystery
13. expand
14. bluff
15. promptly
16. initials
17. statue
18. polish
19. somehow
20. dreadful

Short Vowels
Grade 5, Lesson 1
1. breath
2. wobble
3. blister
4. crush
5. direct
6. promise
7. grasp
8. numb
9. hymn
10. shovel
11. gravity
12. frantic
13. swift
14. feather
15. comic
16. bundle
17. solid
18. weather
19. energy
20. stingy

Long a and Long e
Grade 5, Lesson 2
1. awake
2. feast
3. stray
4. greet
5. praise
6. disease
7. repeat
8. display
9. braces
10. thief
11. ashamed
12. sleeve
13. waist
14. beneath
15. sheepish
16. reverse
17. worship
18. career
19. research
20. volunteer

Long i and Long o
Grade 5, Lesson 3
1. sign
2. groan
3. reply
4. thrown
5. strike
6. mighty
7. stroll
8. compose
9. dough
10. height
11. excite
12. apply
13. slight
14. define
15. odor
16. spider
17. control
18. silent
19. brighten
20. approach

Vowel Sounds: /o͞o/, /yo͞o/
Grade 5, Lesson 4
1. glue
2. flute
3. youth
4. accuse
5. bruise
6. stew
7. choose
8. loose
9. lose
10. view
11. confuse
12. cruise
13. jewel
14. execute
15. route
16. cartoon
17. avenue
18. include
19. assume
20. souvenir

VCCV Pattern
Grade 5, Lesson 11
1. bargain
2. journey
3. pattern
4. arrive
5. object
6. suppose
7. shoulder
8. permit
9. sorrow
10. tunnel
11. subject
12. custom
13. suggest
14. perhaps

16. release
17. remain
18. sway
19. training
20. niece

15. lawyer
16. timber
17. common
18. publish
19. burden
20. scissors

VCV Pattern
Grade 5, Lesson 12
1. human
2. exact
3. award
4. behave
5. credit
6. basic
7. vivid
8. evil
9. modern
10. nation
11. robot
12. panic
13. select
14. cousin
15. item
16. police
17. prefer
18. menu
19. novel
20. deserve

VCCCV Pattern
Grade 5, Lesson 13
1. conflict
2. orphan
3. instant
4. complex
5. simply
6. burglar
7. laundry
8. laughter
9. employ
10. anchor
11. merchant
12. improve
13. arctic
14. mischief
15. childhood
16. purchase
17. dolphin
18. partner
19. complain
20. tremble

VV Pattern
Grade 5, Lesson 14
1. actual
2. cruel
3. patriot
4. diet
5. museum
6. casual
7. ruin
8. pioneer
9. trial
10. visual
11. realize
12. create
13. riot
14. genuine

15. area
16. annual
17. audio
18. dial
19. theater
20. influence

Vowel Sounds: /ou/, /ô/, /oi/
Grade 5, Lesson 5
1. ounce
2. sprawl
3. launch
4. loyal
5. avoid
6. basketball
7. moist
8. haunt
9. scowl
10. naughty
11. destroy
12. saucer
13. pounce
14. poison
15. August
16. auction
17. royal
18. coward
19. awkward
20. encounter

Vowel + /r/ Sounds
Grade 5, Lesson 6
1. glory
2. aware
3. carton
4. adore
5. aboard
6. dairy
7. ordeal
8. pardon
9. warn
10. vary
11. barely
12. torch
13. barge
14. soar
15. beware
16. absorb
17. armor
18. stairway
19. perform
20. former

Words with VCCV Pattern
Grade 4, Lesson 20
1. million
2. collect
3. lumber
4. pepper
5. plastic
6. borrow
7. support
8. thirty
9. perfect
10. attend
11. canyon
12. traffic

13. fortune
14. danger
15. soccer
16. engine
17. picture
18. survive
19. seldom
20. effort

LATE

Words with Final /j/ and /s/
Grade 4, Lesson 17
1. glance
2. judge
3. damage
4. package
5. twice
6. stage
7. carriage
8. since
9. practice
10. marriage
11. baggage
12. office
13. message
14. bridge
15. chance
16. notice
17. ridge
18. manage
19. palace
20. bandage

Words with Silent Consonants
Grade 4, Lesson 29
1. half
2. comb
3. mortgage
4. honor
5. fasten
6. kneel
7. wreath
8. calm
9. answer
10. handsome
11. wrinkle
12. listen
13. fetch
14. yolk
15. climb
16. honest
17. knuckle
18. plumber
19. limb
20. folktale

Unusual Spellings
Grade 4, Lesson 30
1. meant
2. routine
3. style
4. flood
5. month
6. pleasant
7. guess
8. women

9. either
10. against
11. disguise
12. sweat
13. magazine
14. guard
15. receive
16. wonder
17. league
18. type
19. ceiling
20. money

Three-Syllable Words
Grade 4, Lesson 28
1. library
2. another
3. hospital
4. example
5. deliver
6. history
7. however
8. several
9. vacation
10. important
11. victory
12. imagine
13. camera
14. potato
15. remember
16. together
17. memory
18. favorite
19. continue
20. president

Homophones
Grade 5, Lesson 8
1. steel
2. steal
3. aloud
4. allowed
5. ring
6. wring
7. lesson
8. lessen
9. who's
10. whose
11. manor
12. manner
13. pedal
14. peddle
15. berry
16. bury
17. hanger
18. hangar
19. overdo
20. overdue

Compound Words
Grade 5, Lesson 9
1. wildlife
2. uproar
3. home run
4. headache
5. top-secret
6. teammate
7. wheelchair

8. light bulb
9. well-known
10. throughout
11. life preserver
12. barefoot
13. part-time
14. warehouse
15. overboard
16. post office
17. outspoken
18. up-to-date
19. awestruck
20. newscast

Final Schwa + /r/ Sound
Grade 5, Lesson 10
1. cellar
2. flavor
3. cougar
4. chapter
5. mayor
6. anger
7. senator
8. passenger
9. major
10. popular
11. tractor
12. thunder
13. pillar
14. border
15. calendar
16. quarter
17. lunar
18. proper
19. elevator
20. bitter

Final Schwa + /l/ Sound
Grade 5, Lesson 15
1. formal
2. whistle
3. label
4. puzzle
5. legal
6. angle
7. normal
8. needle
9. angel
10. pupil
11. struggle
12. level
13. local
14. bicycle
15. channel
16. global
17. stumble
18. quarrel
19. article
20. fossil

Final /n/ or /ən/, /chər/, /zhər/
Grade 5, Lesson 21
1. nature
2. certain
3. future
4. villain

5. mountain
6. mixture
7. pleasure
8. captain
9. departure
10. surgeon
11. texture
12. curtain
13. creature
14. treasure
15. gesture
16. fountain
17. furniture
18. measure
19. feature
20. adventure

Unstressed Syllables
Grade 5, Lesson 23
1. entry
2. limit
3. talent
4. disturb
5. entire
6. wisdom
7. dozen
8. impress
9. respond
10. fortress
11. neglect
12. patrol
13. kitchen
14. forbid
15. pirate
16. spinach
17. adopt
18. frighten
19. surround
20. challenge

Words from Other Languages
Grade 5, Lesson 20
1. salsa
2. mattress
3. tycoon
4. burrito
5. bandana
6. tomato
7. poncho
8. dungarees
9. lasso
10. patio
11. siesta
12. cargo
13. vanilla
14. tsunami
15. iguana
16. plaza
17. caravan
18. hammock
19. pajamas
20. gallant

Plurals
Grade 6, Lesson 19
1. echoes
2. halves
3. solos

4. leaves
5. heroes
6. cliffs
7. scarves
8. potatoes
9. pianos
10. volcanoes
11. sheriffs
12. calves
13. tomatoes
14. cellos
15. wolves
16. ratios
17. stereos
18. yourselves
19. studios
20. bookshelves

Long Vowels
Grade 6, Lesson 2
1. scene
2. bracelet
3. mute
4. strive
5. faithful
6. devote
7. rhyme
8. succeed
9. coax
10. rely
11. conceal
12. forgave
13. lonesome
14. delete
15. confine
16. exceed
17. terrain
18. reproach
19. abuse
20. defeat

**Vowel Sounds:
/ou/, /o͞o/, /ô/, /oi/**
Grade 6, Lesson 3
1. mound
2. gloomy
3. caution
4. annoy
5. dawdle
6. counter
7. haughty
8. rejoice
9. devour
10. thoughtful
11. flawless
12. maroon
13. droop
14. doubt
15. bamboo
16. hoist
17. oyster
18. exhausted
19. scoundrel
20. boundary

Vowel + /r/ Sounds
Grade 6, Lesson 4
1. source
2. flirt
3. hurdle

4. parka
5. frontier
6. forward
7. radar
8. earnest
9. afford
10. urban
11. discard
12. smirk
13. rehearse
14. mourn
15. surface
16. parcel
17. yearn
18. fierce
19. starch
20. formula

Words with *ie* or *ei*
Grade 6, Lesson 6
1. brief
2. field
3. reign
4. review
5. fiery
6. receipt
7. relieve
8. conceited
9. neither
10. foreign
11. grief
12. veil
13. freight
14. belief
15. deceive
16. yield
17. beige
18. perceive
19. seize
20. leisure

Derivational Relations Phase

EARLY

Final /ĭj/, /ĭv/, /ĭs/
Grade 5, Lesson 22
1. storage
2. olive
3. service
4. relative
5. cabbage
6. courage
7. native
8. passage
9. voyage
10. knowledge
11. image
12. creative
13. average
14. justice
15. detective
16. postage
17. cowardice
18. adjective

19. village
20. language

Suffix: *-ion*
Grade 5, Lesson 25
1. elect
2. election
3. tense
4. tension
5. react
6. reaction
7. confess
8. confession
9. decorate
10. decoration
11. contribute
12. contribution
13. express
14. expression
15. imitate
16. imitation
17. connect
18. connection
19. admire
20. admiration

Word Parts: *com-, con-, pre-, pro-*
Grade 5, Lesson 26
1. produce
2. company
3. protect
4. preview
5. contain
6. combat
7. prejudge
8. commotion
9. contest
10. prefix
11. progress
12. computer
13. confide
14. convince
15. prospect
16. confirm
17. preflight
18. provide
19. propose
20. promotion

Homophones
Grade 6, Lesson 5
1. waist
2. waste
3. patience
4. patients
5. rite
6. right
7. write
8. muscle
9. mussel
10. principal
11. principle
12. summary
13. summery
14. sight
15. cite
16. site
17. stationary
18. stationery

19. coward
20. cowered

Final /ər/
Grade 6, Lesson 7
1. fiber
2. similar
3. regular
4. barrier
5. superior
6. grammar
7. rumor
8. character
9. director
10. acre
11. consider
12. junior
13. senior
14. solar
15. scholar
16. razor
17. surrender
18. particular
19. familiar
20. laser

Final /ən/, /əl/, and /ər/
Grade 6, Lesson 8
1. triangle
2. mental
3. error
4. panel
5. litter
6. pollen
7. gallon
8. cancel
9. abandon
10. rival
11. soldier
12. recycle
13. salmon
14. counsel
15. rural
16. vehicle
17. citizen
18. monitor
19. physical
20. oxygen

Words with *-ed* or *-ing*
Grade 6, Lesson 9
1. happening
2. limited
3. forgetting
4. equaled
5. fitting
6. reasoning
7. labored
8. permitting
9. scrapped
10. tutoring
11. admitted
12. honored
13. skidding
14. pardoned
15. modeling
16. preferred
17. scarred

18. favored
19. glistening
20. shuddered

Endings and Suffixes
Grade 6, Lesson 10
1. reserved
2. unlikely
3. purposeful
4. adorable
5. amazement
6. gentleness
7. sparkling
8. homeless
9. excitement
10. mileage
11. graceful
12. sincerely
13. advanced
14. usable
15. amusement
16. entirely
17. wireless
18. excluding
19. scarcely
20. changeable

Final /īz/, /īv/, and /īj/
Grade 6, Lesson 15
1. revise
2. advantage
3. memorize
4. active
5. organize
6. criticize
7. shortage
8. advertise
9. attractive
10. college
11. explosive
12. exercise
13. encourage
14. summarize
15. wreckage
16. recognize
17. positive
18. percentage
19. sensitive
20. heritage

Suffixes: -ion or -ation
Grade 6, Lesson 11
1. correct
2. correction
3. explore
4. exploration
5. admire
6. admiration
7. subtract
8. subtraction
9. examine
10. examination
11. separate
12. separation
13. alter
14. alteration
15. preserve

16. preservation
17. reflect
18. reflection
19. substitute
20. substitution

Spelling /sh/
Grade 6, Lesson 18
1. section
2. shallow
3. direction
4. musician
5. rash
6. position
7. astonish
8. pressure
9. attention
10. crucial
11. impression
12. official
13. emotion
14. bashful
15. delicious
16. establish
17. ancient
18. situation
19. suspicion
20. permission

Prefixes: dis-, ex-, inter-
Grade 6, Lesson 20
1. disobey
2. explosion
3. dislike
4. interview
5. disapprove
6. interoffice
7. Internet
8. disallow
9. disappear
10. international
11. disrespect
12. exchange
13. exclaim
14. dissolve
15. disconnect
16. interact
17. distaste
18. export
19. disappoint
20. interstate

Prefixes: pre-, pro-
Grade 6, Lesson 21
1. prediction
2. project
3. prevent
4. prepaid
5. prevail
6. proclaim
7. prehistoric
8. prejudge
9. preapprove
10. pregame
11. precaution
12. preorder
13. prescreen
14. preshow
15. pretreat

16. prolong
17. process
18. protrude
19. provision
20. production

More Words with -ion
Grade 6, Lesson 13
1. circulate
2. circulation
3. conclude
4. conclusion
5. instruct
6. instruction
7. possess
8. possession
9. introduce
10. introduction
11. except
12. exception
13. discuss
14. discussion
15. collide
16. collision
17. oppose
18. opposition
19. estimate
20. estimation

Suffixes: -ent, -ant, -able, -ible, -ism, -ist
Grade 5, Lesson 27
1. vacant
2. insistent
3. reversible
4. patriotism
5. finalist
6. honorable
7. contestant
8. observant
9. urgent
10. pessimist
11. comfortable
12. absorbent
13. optimism
14. journalism
15. novelist
16. terrible
17. frequent
18. laughable
19. radiant
20. collectible

Greek Word Parts
Grade 5, Lesson 28
1. telephone
2. autograph
3. microscope
4. photograph
5. televise
6. biology
7. microphone
8. paragraph
9. symphony
10. telegraph
11. megaphone
12. microwave
13. photocopy
14. biography

15. saxophone
16. telescope
17. calligraphy
18. xylophone
19. homophone
20. homograph

Latin Word Roots
Grade 5, Lesson 29
1. inspect
2. export
3. erupt
4. predict
5. respect
6. bankrupt
7. dictate
8. porter
9. report
10. spectacle
11. deport
12. interrupt
13. dictator
14. import
15. disrupt
16. portable
17. transport
18. spectator
19. verdict
20. dictionary

More Words from Other Languages
Grade 5, Lesson 30
1. ballet
2. echo
3. bouquet
4. cassette
5. coupon
6. safari
7. portrait
8. barrette
9. depot
10. courtesy
11. petite
12. denim
13. brunette
14. buffet
15. garage
16. khaki
17. crochet
18. chorus
19. essay
20. alphabet

MIDDLE

Prefixes: in-, im-, ir-, il-
Grade 6, Lesson 12
1. illegal
2. indent
3. imperfect
4. irregular
5. insecure
6. illogical
7. inappropriate
8. impatient
9. individual
10. inability
11. impolite

12. illegible
13. irresistible
14. immobile
15. impartial
16. inaudible
17. improper
18. ineffective
19. immovable
20. irrational

Word Parts: com-, con-
Grade 6, Lesson 14
1. contrast
2. contact
3. compound
4. concentrate
5. combine
6. comment
7. conference
8. compete
9. community
10. convert
11. conversation
12. commute
13. constitution
14. conduct
15. consumer
16. continent
17. composition
18. communicate
19. compliment
20. condition

Suffixes: -ent, -ant
Grade 6, Lesson 16
1. confident
2. confidence
3. fragrant
4. fragrance
5. excellent
6. excellence
7. decent
8. decency
9. truant
10. truancy
11. brilliant
12. brilliance
13. resident
14. residence
15. evident
16. evidence
17. occupant
18. occupancy
19. reluctant
20. reluctance

Suffixes: -able/-ible, -ate
Grade 6, Lesson 17
1. visible
2. enjoyable
3. celebrate
4. incredible
5. horrible
6. desperate
7. cooperate
8. valuable
9. appreciate
10. considerate

11. audible
12. delicate
13. washable
14. graduate
15. capable
16. miserable
17. sensible
18. fortunate
19. noticeable
20. responsible

Words with Silent Letters
Grade 6, Lesson 22
1. aisle
2. align
3. island
4. crumbs
5. gnaw
6. design
7. knotty
8. bustle
9. shepherd
10. soften
11. sword
12. thistle
13. knock
14. wrestle
15. column
16. autumn
17. knowledge
18. debt
19. numb
20. raspberry

Suffixes: *-ic, -ure, -ous*
Grade 6, Lesson 23
1. fantastic
2. culture
3. curious
4. nervous
5. posture
6. jealous
7. scientific

8. generous
9. signature
10. dangerous
11. tragic
12. gigantic
13. sculpture
14. precious
15. lecture
16. serious
17. specific
18. fracture
19. romantic
20. ambitious

Prefixes: *de-, trans-*
Grade 6, Lesson 24
1. transform
2. deject
3. destruct
4. detour
5. transmit
6. default
7. describe
8. defend
9. transplant
10. descend
11. derail
12. defrost
13. transcript
14. deploy
15. dethrone
16. deodorize
17. transatlantic
18. decompose
19. decrease
20. transaction

Word Parts
Grade 6, Lesson 25
1. existence
2. refreshment
3. convention
4. intermission
5. uneventful
6. perfectly

7. completion
8. improvement
9. information
10. attendance
11. reversible
12. invention
13. development
14. respectful
15. unhappiness
16. preparation
17. irrigate
18. disagreement
19. unbelievable
20. concentration

Words from Other Languages
Grade 6, Lesson 26
1. opera
2. vague
3. antique
4. drama
5. tornado
6. debut
7. stampede
8. gourmet
9. unique
10. academy
11. sonnet
12. brochure
13. cocoon
14. fatigue
15. mosquito
16. diploma
17. fiesta
18. debris
19. cafeteria
20. quartet

Greek Word Parts
Grade 6, Lesson 27
1. geography
2. democracy
3. microbiology
4. technology

5. thermos
6. automatic
7. mythology
8. democratic
9. thermometer
10. chronology
11. automobile
12. aristocrat
13. thermal
14. geology
15. aristocracy
16. geometry
17. anthology
18. apology
19. thermostat
20. psychology

Latin Word Roots
Grade 6, Lesson 28
1. prescribe
2. contract
3. manufacture
4. progression
5. vocal
6. manual
7. audience
8. eject
9. impose
10. management
11. Congress
12. expose
13. inject
14. audition
15. manuscript
16. vocabulary
17. objection
18. manicure
19. proposal
20. extract

Greek and Latin Word Parts
Grade 6, Lesson 29
1. pedal
2. peddler

3. pedestrian
4. pedestal
5. centipede
6. dental
7. dentist
8. dentures
9. vocalize
10. vocalist
11. vocation
12. memoir
13. memorial
14. tripod
15. podium
16. memorable
17. manager
18. manifest
19. mortal
20. mortified

Words Often Confused
Grade 6, Lesson 30
1. desert
2. dessert
3. hardy
4. hearty
5. moral
6. morale
7. laying
8. lying
9. personal
10. personnel
11. formally
12. formerly
13. healthy
14. healthful
15. precede
16. proceed
17. conscious
18. conscience
19. immigrate
20. emigrate

Teacher's Notes

Leveled Readers Database

Guided Reading Level	Title	Grade Pack	DRA Level	Lexile Level	Genre	Word Count
M	Linney Twins Get Cooking, The	4 ●	28	610	Science Fiction	968
M	Magic of Teamwork, The	4 ●	28	530	Fantasy	873
M	Painting the Ocean	4 ●	28	400	Realistic Fiction	885
M	Recipe for Learning	4 ●	28	620	Realistic Fiction	879
N	Animal Doctors	4 ●	30	710	Narrative Nonfiction	801
N	Animals Helping People	4VR	34	940	Informational Text	1,016
N	Check Out the Library	4VR	30	820	Informational Text	839
N	Elizabeth's Stormy Ride	4 ●	34	310	Historical Fiction	815
N	King Midas and the Golden Touch	4 ●	30	550	Myth	759
N	Nina Wows KWOW	4 ●	30	NP	Play	791
N	Sailing to Safety	4 ●	34	560	Historical Fiction	1,005
N	Squash in the Schoolyard	4VR	34	700	Informational Text	620
N	Zeebo Encounter, The	4 ●	30	NP	Play	884
O	Amazing Birds of Antarctica	4 ●	34	650	Narrative Nonfiction	619
O	Ants of All Kinds	4VR	38	890	Informational Text	898
O	Community Teamwork	4VR	38	910	Informational Text	1,101
O	Friends on a Field Trip	4 ◆	38	NP	Play	1,266
O	Isadora Duncan	4 ●	38	780	Biography	915
O	John Wesley Powell	4 ●	38	830	Biography	888
O	Keeping Safe in an Earthquake	4VR	38	780	Informational Text	949
O	Kids Can Save the Planet	4 ●	34	690	Informational Text	703
O	Plants of the Redwood Forest	4 ●	38	730	Informational Text	913
O	Princess and the Manatee, The	4 ■	38	710	Fantasy	1,655
O	Really, Really Cold!	4VR	38	690	Informational Text	781
O	Reptiles As Pets	4VR	38	800	Informational Text	1,109

- Go to www.thinkcentral.com for the complete *Journeys* Online Leveled Readers Database.
- Search by grade, genre, title, or level.

Author's Purpose	Cause and Effect	Compare and Contrast	Conclusions	Fact and Opinion	Main Ideas and Details	Sequence of Events	Story Structure	Text and Graphic Features	Theme	Understanding Characters
●	●	●	●			●	●			●
●	●	●	●			●	●		●	
	●	●	●			●	●		●	●
●			●			●	●		●	●
●		●	●	●	●		●	●		
●	●	●	●	●	●	●				
●				●	●					
●	●		●			●	●		●	●
	●		●			●	●		●	●
		●	●			●	●		●	●
●		●	●			●	●			●
●	●			●						
			●			●	●		●	●
●	●	●	●	●	●			●		
●			●	●	●					
●	●					●				
●		●	●			●	●		●	●
●	●	●	●	●	●	●		●		
●	●	●	●	●	●	●		●		
●	●				●			●		
●	●		●	●				●		
●		●	●		●			●		
●	●		●			●	●		●	●
●	●	●	●		●			●		
●		●	●	●	●			●		

Leveled Readers Database

Guided Reading Level	Title	Grade Pack	DRA Level	Lexile Level	Genre	Word Count
O	Seal Who Wanted to Live, The	4 ●	38	520	Fantasy	846
O	Sharing a Dream	4 ●	38	830	Biography	913
P	Amazing Balina, The	4 ◆	38	660	Tall Tale	1,379
P	Artists in Training	4VR	38	790	Informational Text	813
P	Behind the Scenes	4VR	38	930	Informational Text	894
P	Dangerous Waves	4VR	38	670	Informational Text	915
P	Father's Garden, A	4 ◆	38	600	Realistic Fiction	1,129
P	First Woman Doctor, The	4 ●	38	650	Biography	880
P	Flying into History	4 ●	38	790	Narrative Nonfiction	846
P	Forever Green	4VR	38	930	Informational Text	846
P	Friendly Field Trip, A	4 ▲	38	NP	Play	1,278
P	Golden Age of Sail, The	4VR	38	720	Informational Text	870
P	Lives of Social Insects, The	4 ●	38	910	Informational Text	886
P	Mississippi Marvis Barnes	4 ●	38	360	Tall Tale	874
P	Now Showing in Your Living Room	4 ●	38	800	Informational Text	885
P	Parker's Problem	4 ●	38	430	Realistic Fiction	850
P	Planes, Trains, and Snowmobiles	4VR	38	900	Informational Text	692
P	Remarkable Robots	4VR	38	950	Informational Text	994
P	Songs for the People	4 ●	38	810	Biography	732
P	Volcanoes	4 ●	38	660	Informational Text	704
Q	Balina	4 ▲	40	600	Tall Tale	1,325
Q	Beltons' Imagination, The	4 ▲	40	780	Fantasy	1,506
Q	Dad's Garden	4 ▲	40	630	Realistic Fiction	1,104
Q	Lewis and Clark's Packing List	4VR	40	810	Informational Text	936
Q	Mystery on Maple Street, The	4 ▲	40	490	Realistic Fiction	1,153

ONLINE LEVELED READERS DATABASE

- Go to www.thinkcentral.com for the complete *Journeys* Online Leveled Readers Database.
- Search by grade, genre, title, or level.

Author's Purpose	Cause and Effect	Compare and Contrast	Conclusions	Fact and Opinion	Main Ideas and Details	Sequence of Events	Story Structure	Text and Graphic Features	Theme	Understanding Characters
●	●		●			●	●		●	●
●	●		●		●	●		●		
●			●			●	●		●	●
●		●	●		●					
●	●		●		●			●		
●	●		●		●	●				
	●		●				●		●	●
●	●	●	●	●	●			●		
●	●	●	●	●	●			●		
		●	●		●					
●		●	●				●		●	●
	●	●			●					
●	●				●					
●			●			●	●		●	●
●	●	●	●	●	●			●		
			●			●	●		●	●
●	●	●	●	●	●			●		
●			●		●			●		
●	●		●	●	●	●				
●	●	●	●	●	●			●		
●			●			●	●		●	●
●	●	●	●			●			●	
●	●		●				●			●
●		●	●	●	●			●		
	●		●			●	●		●	●

Leveled Readers Database

Guided Reading Level	Title	Grade Pack	DRA Level	Lexile Level	Genre	Word Count
Q	Separate Worlds	4VR	40	730	Informational Text	858
Q	Stagecoach Travel	4VR	40	680	Informational Text	916
Q	Summer with Uncle Vince	4 ◆	40	610	Fantasy	1,497
Q	Tornadoes	4VR	40	980	Informational Text	872
Q	What Happened on Maple Street?	4 ◆	40	370	Realistic Fiction	1,252
R	Big, Dangerous Wave, The	4 ◆	40	700	Informational Text	1,212
R	Golden Age of Radio, The	4VR	40	950	Informational Text	1,031
R	Habitat for Humanity	4 ▲	40	860	Informational Text	1,146
R	Helping with Houses	4 ◆	40	770	Informational Text	1,121
R	Icy Adventure, An	4 ▲	40	980	Narrative Nonfiction	1,066
R	Laura Ingalls Wilder	4 ◆	40	640	Biography	1,478
R	New Name for Lois, A	4 ◆	40	480	Historical Fiction	1,383
R	People's President, The	4 ◆	40	790	Biography	1,254
R	President for the People, A	4 ◆	40	610	Biography	1,193
R	Romare Bearden	4VR	40	890	Informational Text	1,005
R	Rural Veterinarian, A	4 ▲	40	890	Narrative Nonfiction	1,390
R	Sisters Play Soccer	4 ◆	40	430	Realistic Fiction	1,426
R	Soccer Sisters	4 ▲	40	580	Realistic Fiction	1,541
R	Story of Perseus, The	4 ◆	40	540	Myth	1,263
R	Taking Care of Animals	4 ◆	40	690	Narrative Nonfiction	1,343
R	Truth About Rodents, The	4VR	40	940	Informational Text	912
R	Visit to Antarctica, A	4 ◆	40	770	Narrative Nonfiction	1,035
R	Whisper	4 ■	40	620	Tall Tale	1,866
R	Writer from the Prairie	4 ▲	40	830	Biography	1,434
S	A.L.L. to the Rescue	4 ■	40	NP	Play	1,452

- Go to www.thinkcentral.com for the complete *Journeys* Online Leveled Readers Database.
- Search by grade, genre, title, or level.

Author's Purpose	Cause and Effect	Compare and Contrast	Conclusions	Fact and Opinion	Main Ideas and Details	Sequence of Events	Story Structure	Text and Graphic Features	Theme	Understanding Characters
●	●	●	●	●	●			●		
●					●					
●	●	●	●			●	●		●	
●	●	●	●	●	●			●		
	●		●			●	●		●	●
●	●		●	●	●	●		●		
●		●	●	●	●	●		●		
●	●		●	●	●	●		●		
●	●		●	●	●	●		●		
●			●	●	●			●		
●	●	●	●	●	●	●		●		
●	●	●	●			●	●		●	●
●	●		●	●	●	●		●		
●	●		●	●	●			●		
●		●	●	●	●	●		●		
●		●	●	●			●	●		
	●		●			●	●		●	●
	●	●	●			●	●		●	●
	●		●			●	●		●	●
●		●	●	●	●		●	●		
●	●	●		●	●	●				
●			●					●		
●	●	●	●			●	●		●	●
●	●	●	●	●	●	●		●		
●	●		●			●	●		●	●

Leveled Readers Database

Guided Reading Level	Title	Grade Pack	DRA Level	Lexile Level	Genre	Word Count
S	Amazing Game, The	4 ◆	40	NP	Play	1,285
S	Animals of the Redwood Forest	4 ◆	40	710	Informational Text	1,484
S	Arthropods Everywhere!	4 ◆	40	730	Informational Text	1,304
S	Arthropods Rule!	4 ▲	40	860	Informational Text	1,337
S	Champion of Change, A	4 ▲	40	1010	Biography	1,341
S	Champions on Ice	4 ■	40	840	Narrative Nonfiction	1,880
S	Come to Nicodemus	4 ■	40	940	Historical Fiction	1,866
S	Dangerous Trip, A	4 ◆	40	640	Historical Fiction	1,359
S	Dex Is a Hero	4 ◆	40	610	Science Fiction	1,492
S	Dragon's View, A	4 ■	40	670	Fantasy	2,317
S	Gentle Redwood Giants	4 ■	40	1160	Informational Text	1,776
S	Gift for Grandpa, A	4 ◆	40	500	Realistic Fiction	1,440
S	Gramp's Favorite Gift	4 ▲	40	810	Realistic Fiction	1,481
S	Helen Keller's Lifelong Friend	4 ▲	40	810	Narrative Nonfiction	1,377
S	Helen Keller's Special Friend	4 ◆	40	560	Narrative Nonfiction	1,472
S	Hero Weighs In, A	4 ▲	40	880	Science Fiction	1,488
S	Jackson Pollock in Action	4 ▲	40	1000	Biography	1,263
S	Life Among the Redwoods	4 ▲	40	970	Informational Text	1,410
S	Life of Jackson Pollock, The	4 ◆	40	770	Biography	1,155
S	Little Hare and the Thundering Earth	4 ▲	40	850	Historical Fiction	1,426
S	Long Ago in Greece	4VR	40	770	Informational Text	692
S	Mill Girls	4VR	40	910	Informational Text	884
S	Perilous Passage	4 ▲	40	800	Historical Fiction	1,273
S	Shirley Chisholm	4 ◆	40	730	Biography	1,396
S	Stuck at Camp	4 ■	40	840	Realistic Fiction	2,198

ONLINE LEVELED READERS DATABASE

- Go to www.thinkcentral.com for the complete *Journeys* Online Leveled Readers Database.
- Search by grade, genre, title, or level.

Author's Purpose	Cause and Effect	Compare and Contrast	Conclusions	Fact and Opinion	Main Ideas and Details	Sequence of Events	Story Structure	Text and Graphic Features	Theme	Understanding Characters
	●		●			●	●		●	●
●		●	●	●	●			●		
●	●	●	●		●			●		
●	●	●	●		●			●		
●	●	●	●	●	●	●		●		
●	●	●	●	●	●	●		●		
	●	●	●			●	●		●	●
●	●		●			●	●		●	●
●	●	●	●			●	●			●
●	●	●	●			●	●		●	●
●		●	●	●	●			●		
●	●		●			●	●		●	●
●	●		●			●	●		●	●
●	●	●	●	●	●	●		●		
●	●	●	●	●	●	●		●		
●	●	●	●			●	●			●
●	●	●	●			●		●		
●		●	●		●			●		
●	●	●	●	●	●	●		●		
	●	●	●			●	●		●	●
		●			●			●		
●			●		●					
●	●		●			●	●		●	●
●	●	●	●	●	●	●		●		
●	●		●			●	●		●	●

Leveled Readers Database

Guided Reading Level	Title	Grade Pack	DRA Level	Lexile Level	Genre	Word Count
S	Think Before You Speak	4 ■	40	580	Realistic Fiction	1,910
S	Thurgood Marshall	4 ◆	40	630	Biography	1,264
S	Tough Times	4VR	40	830	Informational Text	971
S	Trading Talents	4 ■	40	650	Realistic Fiction	1,952
S	Tsunami	4 ▲	40	780	Informational Text	1,239
S	Voice for Equality, A	4 ▲	40	890	Biography	1,263
T	Adventure of Perseus, The	4 ▲	44	660	Myth	1,261
T	Helping Wild Animals	4 ■	44	1030	Narrative Nonfiction	2,126
T	Love Those Bugs!	4 ■	44	970	Informational Text	1,798
T	Magic of Movies, The	4 ▲	44	800	Informational Text	1,304
T	Making Movies	4 ◆	44	590	Informational Text	1,297
T	Math Today and Tomorrow	4 ■	44	770	Science Fiction	2,035
T	Nature Destroys, Nature Renews	4 ■	44	1020	Informational Text	994
T	Time Tag	4 ▲	44	NP	Play	1,196
T	Two Against the Mississippi	4 ■	44	900	Historical Fiction	2,187
T	Volunteer!	4 ■	44	920	Informational Text	1,387
U	Be Afraid	4 ■	50	NP	Play	1,431
U	Chief Washakie	4 ■	44	1090	Biography	2,073
U	Leader for All, A	4 ■	44	880	Biography	1,500
U	Story of Dorothea Lange, The	4 ■	50	880	Biography	1,954
U	Writer Who Changed America, The	4 ■	44	1000	Biography	1,976
V	Critics in Hollywood	4 ■	50	1080	Informational Text	1,839
V	Heroes of the Antarctic	4 ■	50	900	Narrative Nonfiction	1,900
V	Story of Icarus, The	4 ■	50	760	Myth	1,640
W	Luciano Pavarotti	4 ■	60	980	Biography	1,704

- Go to www.thinkcentral.com for the complete *Journeys* Online Leveled Readers Database.
- Search by grade, genre, title, or level.

Author's Purpose	Cause and Effect	Compare and Contrast	Conclusions	Fact and Opinion	Main Ideas and Details	Sequence of Events	Story Structure	Text and Graphic Features	Theme	Understanding Characters
	●	●	●			●	●		●	●
●	●	●	●		●	●		●		
●	●	●	●	●	●	●				
		●	●				●		●	●
●	●	●	●		●	●				
●	●	●	●		●	●		●		
	●	●	●			●	●		●	●
●		●	●	●	●		●	●		
●	●	●	●					●		
●	●	●	●	●	●	●		●		
●	●	●	●	●	●	●		●		
	●	●	●				●			●
●	●	●	●	●	●			●		●
●	●	●	●			●	●		●	●
●		●	●	●	●					
			●			●	●		●	●
●	●	●	●	●	●	●		●		
●	●		●		●	●		●		
	●	●	●		●	●				
●	●		●	●	●	●		●		
●	●	●	●	●	●	●		●		
	●		●			●	●		●	●
●	●	●	●	●	●	●		●		

Literature Discussion

For small-group literature discussion, use the suggested trade book titles on the pages that follow, or select age-appropriate texts from your library or classroom collection.

Engage students in discussions to build understanding of the text, deepen comprehension, and foster their confidence in talking about what they read. Encourage students to share their ideas about the text and also to build upon one another's ideas.

 Classic

 Science

 Social Studies

 Music

 Math

 Art

Suggested Trade Book Titles

BIOGRAPHY

Bertrand, Diane Gonzales. *Ricardo's Race/La carrera de Ricardo.* A bilingual biography of Ricardo Romo, a talented runner as a youth who later earned a Ph.D. in history and became a college president. Piñata, 2007 (32p).

Burleigh, Robert. *Paul Cézanne: A Painter's Journey.* Rejecting the opinions of others, the young Cézanne followed his own vision, becoming one of the world's greatest artists. Abrams, 2006 (31p).

Dunn, Joe. *Abraham Lincoln.* This biography of the president who saw the United States through its most divisive period is told in a graphic-novel format. Abdo & Daughters, 2007 (32p).

FitzGerald, Dawn. *Vinnie and Abraham.* Abraham Lincoln sat for Vinnie Ream, an eighteen-year-old sculptor, as she prepared to create a life-size statue that now stands in the U.S. Capitol. Charlesbridge, 2000 (48p).

Guzmán, Lila and Rick. *Ellen Ochoa: First Latina Astronaut.* In 1993, aboard the space shuttle *Discovery,* Ochoa became the first Latina astronaut. **Available in Spanish as** *Ellen Ochoa: La primera astronauta latina.* Enslow, 2006 (32p).

Guzmán, Lila and Rick. *Frida Kahlo: Painting Her Life.* This biography tells about the Mexican painter who is best known for her self-portraits. **Available in Spanish as** *Frida Kahlo: Pintó su vida.* Enslow, 2006 (32p).

Martin, Jacqueline Briggs. *Snowflake Bentley.* Wilson A. Bentley, fascinated with snow, devoted his life to photographing snowflakes. Houghton, 1998 (32p).

Miller, Barbara Kiely. *George Washington Carver.* This famous African American scientist was a dedicated professor, taught farmers how to keep their fields productive, and invented hundreds of uses for various crops. **Also available in Spanish.** Weekly Reader, 2007 (24p).

Parker, Robert Andrew. *Piano Starts Here.* This is the story of jazz virtuoso Art Tatum's enthusiasm for music as a young boy. Schwartz & Wade, 2008 (40p).

Ray, Deborah Kogan. *Down the Colorado.* John Wesley Powell became the first person to scientifically explore the Colorado River and the Grand Canyon. Farrar, 2007 (48p).

Streissguth, Tom. *Wilma Rudolph.* Stricken by polio as a child and told she would never walk again, Wilma Rudolph won multiple Olympic medals in track. Lerner, 2007 (120p).

Taylor, Gaylia. *George Crum and the Saratoga Chip.* Chef George Crum's efforts to please his customers result in the invention of the potato chip. Lee & Low, 2006 (32p).

Wyckoff, Edwin Brit. *Heart Man.* Although he worked as a janitor, Vivien Thomas was an African American medical technician who directed the first 100 open-heart surgeries. Enslow, 2008 (32p).

Yoo, Paula. *Sixteen Years in Sixteen Seconds: The Sammy Lee Story.* A Korean American boy realizes his dream to become an Olympic diving champion. Lee & Low, 2005 (32p).

Zalben, Jane Breskin. *Paths to Peace.* From Gandhi to Princess Diana and beyond, the author profiles people who have devoted their lives to helping others. Dutton, 2006 (48p).

FANTASY

Birney, Betty G. *Friendship According to Humphrey.* Humphrey, the hamster of Room 26, isn't sure what to make of the new class pet. Puffin, 2006 (150p).

Dahl, Roald. *Charlie and the Chocolate Factory.* Although there are five lucky winners of a tour through Willy Wonka's chocolate factory, Charlie is most special of all. **Available in Spanish as** *Charlie y la fábrica de chocolate.* Puffin, 2007 (176p).

Einhorn, Edward. *A Very Improbable Story.* On the morning of a big soccer match, Ethan wakes up with a cat on his head that won't move until he wins a game of probability. Charlesbridge, 2008 (32p).

Helgerson, Joseph. *Horns and Wrinkles.* Claire and her cousin Duke discover that trolls in the nearby Mississippi River are causing havoc in the community. Houghton, 2008 (240p).

Lechner, John. *Sticky Burr: Adventures in Burrwood Forest.* The adventures of Sticky and his friends are supplemented with information about forest life. Candlewick, 2008 (56p).

Selden, George. *The Cricket in Times Square.* First published in 1960, the story follows Chester Cricket as he leaves his Connecticut home and becomes "the most famous musician in New York City." **Available in Spanish as** *Un grillo en Times Square.* Yearling, 1999 (176p).

Van Allsburg, Chris. *Jumanji.* When Judy and Peter discover a mysterious board game in the park, a fantastic adventure begins—one that won't end until someone wins the game. **Also available in Spanish.** Houghton, 1981 (31p).

Vernon, Ursula. *Nurk.* Nurk the shrew lives a quiet life until he receives a letter asking for help and gets involved in finding a kidnapped dragonfly prince. Harcourt, 2008 (144p).

HISTORICAL FICTION

Armstrong, Jennifer. *Magnus at the Fire.* Magnus the horse and his team are retired from pulling a steam pumper when their firehouse gets its first fire engine, but Magnus won't be put out to pasture that easily. Simon & Schuster, 2005 (32p).

Borden, Louise. *The Greatest Skating Race.* Piet, a Dutch boy, takes on a dangerous mission: to escort two younger children to the safety of their aunt's house in Belgium during World War II. McElderry, 2004 (48p).

Casanova, Mary. *The Klipfish Code.* Marit and her brother are sent to live with their grandfather when the Nazis invade Norway, but Marit finds a way to help the resistance movement. Houghton, 2007 (240p).

Celenza, Anna Harwell. *Gershwin's Rhapsody in Blue.* A New York newspaper is advertising the upcoming debut of George Gershwin's new jazz concerto, but George hasn't composed it yet! Charlesbridge, 2006 (32p).

Kinsey-Warnock, Natalie. *Nora's Ark.* When torrential rain floods a Vermont river valley, Nora's grandparents welcome a host of neighbors into their unfinished house on a hill. HarperCollins, 2005 (32p).

Tingle, Tim. *Crossing Bok Chitto.* In pre-Civil War Mississippi, Martha, a Choctaw girl, begins a life-saving friendship with African American slaves across the river. Cinco Puntos, 2008 (40p).

INFORMATIONAL TEXT

Buckley, Annie and James Buckley, Jr. *Inside Photography.* The work of three active photographers—in fashion, news, and animal photography—is covered, highlighting attributes unique to each style. Child's World, 2007 (32p).

Claybourne, Anna. *Deep Oceans.* Covering methods of travel to the deep ocean and the life forms found there, this book speculates about how ocean exploration will change in the future. Heinemann, 2008 (48p).

Davies, Nicola. *Oceans and Seas.* The wonders of the sea, from its animals and plants to its tides and waves, are explained. Kingfisher, 2007 (48p).

Gaff, Jackie. *I Wonder Why Pine Trees Have Needles and Other Questions About Forests.* In a question-and-answer format, a broad scope of information about forests is covered. Kingfisher, 2007 (32p).

Graham, Ian. *The Best Book of Speed Machines.* Throughout history, people have designed vehicles to move ever faster. Kingfisher, 2008 (32p).

Harrison, David L. *Cave Detectives.* When a Missouri road crew uncovered a cave in 2001, scientists discovered evidence of several prehistoric species. Chronicle, 2007 (48p).

Hirschi, Ron. *Lions, Tigers, and Bears: Why Are Big Predators So Rare?* Large animals such as grizzly bears and killer whales are fierce predators, but environmental changes threaten their existence. Boyds Mills, 2007 (40p).

Hiscock, Bruce. *Ookpik: The Travels of a Snowy Owl.* Born in the Arctic, a young snowy owl must find a region with a more plentiful food supply. Boyds Mills, 2008 (30p).

Hodgkins, Fran. *The Whale Scientists.* Scientists are trying to learn why whales strand themselves on beaches when death is the usual result. Houghton, 2007 (64p).

Hoena, B. A. *Shackleton and the Lost Antarctic Expedition.* This graphic novel is an account of Ernest Shackleton and his crew, who in 1907 escaped disaster on an attempt to reach the South Pole. Capstone, 2006 (32p).

Howard, Amanda. *Robbery File: The Museum Heist.* Thieves who stole two paintings from Amsterdam's Van Gogh Museum in 2002 left behind clues, which scientists studied using forensic techniques to solve the crime. Bearport, 2008 (32p).

Jenkins, Steve. *Living Color.* The wide range of color in the animal world serves many purposes, from evading predators to attracting a mate. Houghton, 2007 (32p).

Kurlansky, Mark. *The Cod's Tale.* This is the story of how the humble codfish helped shape the history of the world. Putnam, 2001 (48p).

Literature Discussion

Lewin, Ted. *Tooth and Claw: Animal Adventures in the Wild.* The author relates some of his wildest animal encounters. HarperCollins, 2003 (112p).

Marx, Trish. *Steel Drumming at the Apollo.* A boys' steel drum band from Schenectady, New York, takes its talents to the Apollo Theater in New York City. Lee & Low, 2007 (56p).

Price, Sean. *Smokestacks and Spinning Jennys.* Beginning in the 1760s, the rapid replacement of manual work with machines initiated the Industrial Revolution. Raintree, 2007 (32p).

Quigley, Mary. *Mesa Verde.* Scientists have made surprising discoveries in their excavation of Mesa Verde. Heinemann, 2005 (48p).

Raczka, Bob. *Here's Looking at Me.* Since 1484, artists' self-portraits have revealed many clues about how they think of themselves. Millbrook, 2006 (32p).

Reynolds, Jan. *Frozen Land.* The Inuit continue to pass down their traditions, even as outside influences change their culture. Lee & Low, 2007 (32p).

Schulman, Janet. *Pale Male: Citizen Hawk of New York City.* A red-tailed hawk and his mate rear twenty-three chicks over a nine-year period on a Fifth Avenue apartment building, winning both enemies and champions in the process. Knopf, 2008 (40p).

Sitarski, Anita. *Cold Light: Creatures, Discoveries, and Inventions That Glow.* For hundreds of years people have been intrigued by animals and things that glow—something every firefly chaser can relate to. Boyds Mills, 2007 (48p).

Spilsbury, Richard. *Cartoons and Animation.* Animation has changed a great deal since its earliest years; an overview of contemporary techniques and career possibilities is presented. Heinemann, 2008 (56p).

Wechsler, Doug. *Frog Heaven: Ecology of a Vernal Pool.* Over the course of one year, a vernal pool in Delaware supports a rich variety of animal and plant life. Boyds Mills, 2006 (48p).

Whipple, Heather. *Hillary and Norgay.* Since Edmund Hillary and Tenzing Norgay first reached the top of the highest mountain in the world in 1953, mountain climbing has never been the same. Crabtree, 2007 (32p).

Wilkes, Angela. *The Best Book of Ballet.* All aspects of ballet are explained, from basic dance positions to acting in a performance. Kingfisher, 2007 (32p).

MYSTERY

Dowd, Siobhan. *The London Eye Mystery.* When Ted and Katrina's visiting cousin, Salim, boards a London tourist ride but doesn't disembark, the two must race against time to find out what happened. Fickling, 2008 (336p).

Konigsburg, E. L. *From the Mixed-Up Files of Mrs. Basil E. Frankweiler.* Claudia and her brother Jamie camp out in the Metropolitan Museum of Art, where they are caught up in a mystery involving a statue. Aladdin, 2007 (176p).

Nilsen, Anna. *The Great Art Scandal.* Readers must use clues to match 32 of the world's greatest artists to the paintings they created. **Available in Spanish as El gran escándalo en el arte.** Kingfisher, 2003 (48p).

Pinkwater, Daniel. *The Artsy Smartsy Club.* Nick, Loretta Fischetti, Bruno Ugg, and Henrietta (Nick's 6-foot-tall, 266-pound chicken) discover the sidewalk art of Lucy Casserole. HarperCollins, 2005 (165p).

Simon, Seymour. *Einstein Anderson, Science Detective: The Gigantic Ants and Other Cases.* Science whiz Einstein Anderson solves a variety of mysteries, including a snake that chases people and a machine that can stop hurricanes. Morrow, 1998 (165p).

POETRY

Brown, Calef. *Flamingos on the Roof.* Twenty-nine humorous, irresistible nonsense poems play with language. Houghton, 2006 (64p).

Carroll, Lewis. *Jabberwocky.* Carroll's classic poem is interpreted anew through the illustrations of Christopher Myers. Hyperion, 2007 (32p).

Florian, Douglas. *Comets, Stars, the Moon, and Mars.* Poems explore the universe in both its vastness and its intimate detail. Harcourt, 2007 (56p).

Grimes, Nikki. *Oh, Brother!* Twenty poems tell the story of two boys who adjust to becoming brothers when their parents marry. Amistad, 2007 (32p).

Lewis, J. Patrick. *Please Bury Me in the Library.* An array of poems in various forms celebrate libraries, books, and the joy of reading. Harcourt, 2005 (32p).

Mora, Pat. *Yum! ¡Mmmm! ¡Qué Rico!* The haiku in this collection celebrate foods that originated in the Americas. Lee & Low, 2007 (32p).

Shields, Carol. *Almost Late to School and More School Poems.* These school poems take many forms including a concrete poem, poems for two voices, and a jump rope rhyme. Puffin, 2005 (48p).

Sidman, Joyce. *Song of the Water Boatman and Other Pond Poems.* Each of these lyrical poems about pond life is accompanied by a brief paragraph elaborating on that poem's subject. Houghton, 2005 (32p).

REALISTIC FICTION

Blume, Judy. *Tales of a Fourth-Grade Nothing.* Peter finds that it's not easy being the older brother of a mischievous two-year-old. Puffin, 2007 (128p).

Blume, Lesley M. M. *Cornelia and the Audacious Escapades of the Somerset Sisters.* Cornelia is beguiled by her new elderly neighbor, Virginia Somerset, through Virginia's captivating stories of her life. Yearling, 2008 (192p).

Cheng, Andrea. *Shanghai Messenger.* A Chinese American girl is invited to spend the summer in China with relatives she has never met. Lee & Low, 2005 (40p).

Danziger, Paula. *Amber Brown Goes Fourth.* Amber must start fourth grade as she copes with her parents' divorce and the fact that her best friend moved away. **Available in Spanish as** *Ámbar en su cuarto y sin su amigo.* Puffin, 2007 (112p).

DeGross, Monalisa. *Donavan's Double Trouble.* Donavan's struggles in fourth grade include his math class and his beloved Uncle Vic, who has returned from overseas combat in a wheelchair. Amistad, 2007 (192p).

Frazee, Marla. *A Couple of Boys Have the Best Week Ever.* James and Eamon spend a week at Nature Camp, but exploring nature isn't nearly as interesting as doing indoor activities. Harcourt, 2008 (40p).

Greene, Stephanie. *Sophie Hartley, on Strike.* Sophie learns that going on strike to protest her housekeeping chores only creates more problems. Clarion, 2006 (160p).

Hannigan, Katherine. *Ida B.* Fun-loving, home-schooled Ida B must face public school and other changes when her mother becomes seriously ill. **Available in Spanish as** *Ida B: . . . y sus planes para potenciar el diversión, evitar desastres y (posiblemente) salvar al mundo.* HarperCollins, 2006 (256p).

Kyi, Tanya Lloyd. *Jared Lester, Fifth-Grade Jester.* Jared knows his fantasy of becoming a court jester is far-fetched, until he learns that the Queen will be passing through town. Annick, 2006 (74p).

Lin, Grace. *The Year of the Dog.* Pacy hopes to "find herself" as the Chinese Year of the Dog begins. Little, Brown, 2007 (160p).

Lombard, Jenny. *Drita, My Homegirl.* Maxine, a popular fourth-grader, befriends Drita, the new girl from Kosovo. Puffin, 2006 (144p).

Mills, Claudia. *Being Teddy Roosevelt.* Inspired by the perseverance of Teddy Roosevelt, whom he is studying for a school project, Riley is determined to find a way to acquire a saxophone. Farrar, 2007 (96p).

Paterson, Nancy Ruth. *The Winner's Walk.* Case warms quickly to a dog that follows him home one day, but when he learns that it was trained to help a girl with disabilities, he must decide what to do. Farrar, 2006 (128p).

Ransom, Candice. *Seeing Sky-Blue Pink.* Maddie isn't sure whether she can trust her new stepfather or whether she'll like living in the country. Carolrhoda, 2007 (122p).

Smith, Charles R., Jr. *Winning Words: Sport Stories and Photographs.* Quotations and stories about overcoming fears and trying one's hardest are presented. Candlewick, 2008 (80p).

Tate, Lindsey. *Kate Larkin, the Bone Expert.* Recovering from an injury gives curious Kate an opportunity to learn about the science of broken bones. Holt, 2008 (64p).

Urban, Linda. *A Crooked Kind of Perfect.* Zoe dreams of playing the piano, but her parents buy her an organ instead, and soon she's practicing for the Perform-O-Rama organ competition. Harcourt, 2007 (214p).

TRADITIONAL TALE

Babbitt, Natalie. *Jack Plank Tells Tales.* In a boarding house run by Nina's mother, the residents try to help find a new job for Jack Plank, a pirate who doesn't plunder well and has recently been sacked. Michael di Capua, 2007 (144p).

Giovanni, Nikki. *The Grasshopper's Song.* In this twist on an Aesop fable, Jimmy Grasshopper sues the Ants for failing to appreciate his artistic endeavors. Candlewick, 2008 (56p).

Johnson, Paul Brett. *Fearless Jack.* In this Appalachian folktale, Jack wins fame and fortune after killing ten yellow jackets with one whack. Margaret K. McElderry, 2001 (32p).

Kellogg, Steven. *Sally Ann Thunder Ann Whirlwind Crockett.* Sally Ann, wife of Davy Crockett, fears nothing—and proves it when braggart Mike Fink tries to scare her. William Morrow, 1995 (48p).

Mosel, Arlene. *Tikki Tikki Tembo.* This Chinese folktale tells the story of a boy whose long name gets in the way of his rescue from a well. Henry Holt, 1968 (32p).

Nolen, Jerdine. *Hewitt Anderson's Great Big Life.* Tiny Hewitt, the son of giants, finds a way to ease his parents' worries about his small size. Simon & Schuster, 2005 (40p).

Professional Bibliography

Abbott, M. (2001). Effects of traditional versus extended word-study spelling instruction on students' orthographic knowledge. *Reading Online, 5(3).*

Barrentine, Shelley. "Engaging with reading through interactive read-alouds." *The Reading Teacher, 50(1):* 36–43.

Baumann, J. F., Edwards, E. C., Font, G., Tereshinski, C. A., Kame'enui, E. J., & Olejnik, S. (2003). Teaching morphemic and contextual analysis to fifth-grade students. *Reading Research Quarterly, 37(2),* 150–176.

Bear, D. R., Invernizzi, M., Templeton, S., & Johnston, F. (2012). *Words their way: Word study for phonics, vocabulary, and spelling instruction* (5th Ed.). Upper Saddle River, NJ: Pearson/Prentice-Hall.

Beck, I., McKeown, M. G., & Kucan, L. (2008). *Creating robust vocabulary.* New York: Guilford.

Berninger, V. W., Abbott, R. D., Nagy, W., & Carlisle, J. (2009). Growth in phonological, orthographic, and morphological awareness in grades 1 to 6. *Journal of Psycholinguistic Research. 39(2),* 141–163.

Berninger, V. W., Vaughan, K., & Abbott, R. D. (2000). Language-based spelling instruction: Teaching children to make multiple connections between spoken and written words. *Learning Disability Quarterly, 23,* 117–135.

Biemiller, A. (2005). Size and sequence in vocabulary development: Implications for choosing words for primary grade vocabulary instruction. In E. H. Hiebert & M. L. Kamil (Eds.), *Teaching and learning vocabulary: Bringing research to practice* (pp. 223–242). Mahwah, NJ: Lawrence Erlbaum Associates.

Bowers, P. N., & Kirby, J. R. (2010). Effects of morphological instruction on vocabulary acquisition. *Reading and Writing: An Interdisciplinary Journal. 23(5),* 515–537.

Brooks, A., Begay, K., Curtin, G., Byrd, K., & Graham, S. (2000). Language-based spelling instruction: Teaching children to make multiple connections between spoken and written words. *Learning Disability Quarterly, 2,* 117–135.

Carlisle, J. F. (2010). Effects of instruction in morphological awareness on literacy achievement: An integrative review. *Reading Research Quarterly, 45(4),* 464–487.

Clay, Marie M. *Becoming Literate: The Construction of Inner Control.* Heinemann, 1991.

Clay, Marie M. *Change Over Time in Children's Literacy Development.* Heinemann, 2001.

Conrad, N. J. (2008). From reading to spelling and spelling to reading: Transfer goes both ways. *Journal of Educational Psychology, 100(4),* 869–878.

Dale, E., & O'Rourke, J. (1981). *Living word vocabulary.* Chicago: World Book/Childcraft International.

Ehri, L. C. (2005). Learning to read words: Theory, findings, and issues. *Scientific Studies of Reading, 9(2),* 167–188.

Fountas, Irene. C. and G. S. Pinnell. *Guided Reading: Good First Teaching for All Children.* Heinemann, 1996.

Fountas, Irene C. and G. S. Pinnell. *Guiding Readers and Writers: Teaching Comprehension, Genre, and Content Literacy.* Heinemann, 2001.

Fountas, Irene C. and G. S. Pinnell. *Leveled Books, K–8: Matching Texts to Readers for Effective Teaching.* Heinemann, 2005.

Fountas, Irene C. and G. S. Pinnell. *Teaching for Comprehending and Fluency: Thinking, Talking, and Writing About Reading, K–8.* Heinemann, 2006.

Henderson, E. H., & Templeton, S. (1986). The development of spelling abilities through alphabet, pattern, and meaning. *Elementary School Journal, 86,* 305–316.

Hiebert, E. H. (2005). In pursuit of an effective, efficient vocabulary curriculum for elementary students. In E. H. Hiebert & M. L. Kamil (Eds.), *Teaching and learning vocabulary: Bringing research to practice* (pp. 243–263). Mahwah, NJ: Lawrence Erlbaum Associates.

Holdaway, Don. *The Foundations of Literacy.* Ashton Scholastic, 1979 (also Heinemann).

Invernizzi, M., & Hayes, L. (2004). Developmental-spelling research: A systematic imperative. *Reading Research Quarterly, 39,* 2–15.

Juel, C, & Minden-Cupp, C. (2000). Learning to read words: linguistic units and instructional strategies. *Reading Research Quarterly, 35,* 458–492.

Kieffer, M. J., & Lesaux, N. K. (2007). Breaking down words to build meaning: Morphology, vocabulary, and reading comprehension in the urban classroom. *Reading Teacher, 61(2),* 134–144.

Morris, D., Bloodgood, J. W., Lomax, R. G., & Perney, J. (2003). Developmental steps in learning to read: A longitudinal study in kindergarten and first grade. *Reading Research Quarterly, 38,* 302–328.

Morris, D., Nelson, L., & Perney, J. (1986). Exploring the concept of "spelling instructional level" through the analysis of error-types. *Elementary School Journal, 87,* 181–200.

Nunes, T., & Bryant, P. (2006). *Improving literacy by teaching morphemes.* London: Routledge.

Ouellette, G. P., & Sénéchal, M. (2008). A window into early literacy: Exploring the cognitive and linguistic underpinnings of invented spelling. *Scientific studies of reading, 12(2),* 195–219.

Pikulski, J., & Templeton, S. (2010). *Comprehensive vocabulary instruction for reading and school success* (Professional Paper). Boston: Houghton Mifflin Harcourt.

Pinnell, Gay Su and Irene C. Fountas. *The Continuum of Literacy Learning, Grades K–8: Behaviors and Understandings to Notice, Teach, and Support.* Heinemann, 2007.

Santoro, L. E., Chard, D. J., Howard, L., & Baker, S. K. (2008). Making the most of classroom read-alouds to promote comprehension and vocabulary. *The Reading Teacher, 61,* 396–408.

Templeton, S. (2003). Teaching of spelling. In J. Guthrie (Senior Ed.), *Encyclopedia of Education* (2nd Ed.) (pp. 2302–2305). New York: Macmillan.

Templeton, S. (2011). Teaching spelling in the English/language arts classroom. In D. Lapp & D. Fisher (Eds.), *The handbook of research on teaching the English language arts* (3rd ed.) (pp. 247–251). IRA/NCTE: Erlbaum/Taylor Francis.

Templeton, S. (2012). The vocabulary-spelling connection and generative instruction: Orthographic development and morphological knowledge at the intermediate grades and beyond. In J. F. Baumann & E. J. Kame'enui (Eds.), *Vocabulary instruction: Research to Practice* (2nd ed.) New York: Guilford Press.

Templeton, S., & Bear, D. R. (Eds.). (1992). *Development of orthographic knowledge and the foundations of literacy: A memorial festschrift for Edmund H. Henderson.* Hillsdale, NJ: Lawrence Erlbaum Associates.

Templeton, S., & Bear, D. R. (2006). *Spelling and Vocabulary.* Boston: Houghton Mifflin.

Templeton, S., & Bear, D. R. (2011). Phonemic awareness, word recognition, and spelling. In T. Rasinski (Ed.), *Developing reading instruction that works.* Bloomington, IN: Solution Tree Press.

Templeton, S., Bear, D. R., Invernizzi, M., & Johnston, F. (2010). *Vocabulary their way: Word study with middle and secondary students.* Boston: Allyn & Bacon.

Templeton, S., Bear, D. R., & Madura, S. (2007). Assessing students' spelling knowledge: Relationships to reading and writing. In J. R. Paratore & R. L. McCormack (Eds.), *Classroom literacy assessment: Making sense of what students know and do.* New York: Guilford Press.

Templeton, S., & Gehsmann, K. (in press). *Teaching reading and writing, K-8: The developmental approach.* Boston: Pearson/Allyn & Bacon.

Templeton, S., & Morris, D. (1999). Questions teachers ask about spelling. *Reading Research Quarterly, 34,* 102–112.

Templeton, S., & Morris, D. (2000). Spelling. In M. Kamil, P. Mosenthal, P. D. Pearson, & R. Barr (Eds.), *Handbook of reading research: Vol. 3* (pp. 525–543). Mahwah, NJ: Lawrence Erlbaum Associates.

White, T. G. (2005). Effects of systematic and strategic analogy-based phonics on Grade 2 students' word reading and reading comprehension. *Reading Research Quarterly, 40*(2), 234–255.

Zeno, S. M., Ivens, S. H., Millard, R. T., & Duvvuri, R. (1996). *The educator's word frequency guide.* New York: Touchstone Applied Science Associates

CONTENTS

K–8 Scope and Sequence for McGraw-Hill Mathematics

Glencoe *

NUMERATION AND NUMBER THEORY	K	1	2	3	4	5	6	6	7	8
Count	■	■	■	■						
Skip-count		■	■	■	■					
Ordinal numbers	■	■	■	■						
Place value										
whole numbers		■	■	■	■	■	■	■	■	■
decimals				■	■	■	■	■	■	■
Compare and order										
whole numbers	■	■	■	■	■	■	■	■	■	■
decimals				■	■	■	■	■	■	■
fractions and mixed numbers			■	■	■	■	■	■	■	■
integers							■	■	■	■
rationals									■	■
irrationals										■
Round										
whole numbers			■	■	■	■	■	■	■	■
decimals					■	■	■	■	■	■
fractions and mixed numbers					■	■	■	■	■	■
Exponents						■	■	■	■	■
Scientific notation							■	■	■	■
Square roots									■	■
Factors and multiples				■	■	■	■	■	■	■
Common factors/greatest common factor (GCF)					■	■	■	■	■	■
Common multiples/least common multiple (LCM)					■	■	■	■	■	■
Divisibility rules					■	■	■	■	■	■
Even and odd numbers		■	■	■	■					
Prime and composite numbers					■	■	■	■	■	■
Prime factorization						■	■	■	■	■
Relative primes									■	■

GRADE 4
NUMERATION AND NUMBER THEORY
Count, 40-41, 74, 141, 150-151
Skip-count, 128-129, 150-151
Ordinal numbers, 82-83
Place value
  whole numbers
    expanded form, 8-10, 16, 23, 25-26, 32, 69, 173
    to hundreds, 4-7, 32-33
    to thousands, 4-11, 32-33
    to millions, 24-27, 32-33
    abacus, 51, 465
  decimals
    tenths and hundredths, 450-458, 476-477
Compare and order
  whole numbers, 12-13, 32-33, 42-43, 74-75
  decimals, 456-458, 476-477
  fractions and mixed numbers, 382-383, 402-403
Round
  whole numbers, 20-23, 32-33
  decimals, 464-465, 476-477
  fractions and mixed numbers, 382-385, 402-403
Factors and multiples, 128-129, 131-136, 170-173, 184, 206-208, 211, 302-303, 380-381
Common factors/greatest common factor (GCF), 152-153
Common multiples/least common multiple (LCM), 426-427
Divisibility rules, 156-157, 297
Even and odd numbers, 73
Prime and composite numbers, 285

* *Mathematics: Applications and Connections Courses 1–3* ©1998

Glencoe *

WHOLE NUMBER COMPUTATION	K	1	2	3	4	5	6	6	7	8
Addition										
Meaning of addition	■	■	■	■	■					
Properties		■	■	■	■	■	■		■	
Basic facts	■	■	■	■	■					
Fact families		■	■	■	■					
Missing addends		■	■	■	■	■		■	■	
Add 2-digit numbers		■	■	■	■	■	■	■	■	
Add 3-digit numbers			■	■	■	■	■	■	■	
Add greater numbers			■	■	■	■	■	■	■	
Add money amounts		■	■	■	■	■	■	■	■	
Mental math strategies		■	■	■	■	■	■	■	■	
Estimate sums		■	■	■	■	■	■	■	■	
Write/solve number sentences		■	■	■	■	■	■	■	■	
Solve equations				■	■	■	■	■	■	
Subtraction										
Meaning of subtraction		■	■	■	■	■				
Properties		■	■	■	■	■				
Basic facts		■	■	■	■					
Fact families		■	■	■	■					
Subtract 2-digit numbers		■	■	■	■	■	■	■	■	
Subtract 3-digit numbers			■	■	■	■	■	■	■	
Subtract greater numbers				■	■	■	■	■	■	
Subtract money amounts		■	■	■	■	■	■	■	■	
Mental math strategies		■	■	■	■	■	■	■	■	
Estimate differences		■	■	■	■	■	■	■	■	
Write/solve number sentences		■	■	■	■	■	■	■	■	
Solve equations					■	■	■	■	■	

Chart continued on page T3

GRADE 4
WHOLE NUMBER COMPUTATION
Addition
Meaning of addition, 44-49
Properties
  order, zero, grouping, 52-53, 74-75
Basic facts, 44-45
Fact families, 58-59
Missing addends, 58-59
Add 2-digit numbers, 48-54, 74-75
Add 3-digit numbers, 48-54, 74-75
Add greater numbers, 12-13, 42-43, 74-75
Add money amounts, 39-47, 50-53, 55-57, 59, 75, 83
Mental math strategies, 44-47, 54
Estimate sums, 46-50, 55, 74, 77, 181, 193, 217, 385, 410-412,
    434-437, 464-465
  front-end, 55
  round, 46-50, 53, 54, 77
Write/solve number sentences, 472-473

Subtraction
Meaning of subtraction, 58-61
Properties
  zero, 68-69
Basic facts, 58-59
Fact families, 58-59
Subtract 2-digit numbers, 56-67, 74-75
  across zeros, 68-69
Subtract 3-digit numbers, 56-67, 74-75
  across zeros, 68-69
Subtract greater numbers, 62-65, 74-75
Subtract money amounts, 39, 58-69, 72, 75
Mental math strategies, 58-61, 74-75
Estimate differences, 60-65, 68-69, 74-75, 77, 434-437, 464-465
Write/solve number sentences, 472-473

* *Mathematics: Applications and Connections   Courses 1–3   ©1998*

Chart continued from page T2

Glencoe *

WHOLE NUMBER COMPUTATION	K	1	2	3	4	5	6		6	7	8
Multiplication											
Meaning of multiplication		●	●	●	●	●					
Properties			●	●	●	●	●		●	●	●
Basic facts			●	●	●	●					
Fact families				●	●	●					
Missing factors				●	●	●	●				
Multiply three factors				●	●	●					
Multiply powers of 10					●	●	●		●	●	●
Multiply by 1-digit multiplier				●	●	●	●		●		
Multiply by 2-digit multiplier					●	●	●		●	●	●
Multiply money amounts					●	●	●			●	●
Mental math strategies					●	●	●		●	●	●
Estimate products					●	●	●		●	●	●
Write/solve number sentences			●	●	●	●	●		●	●	●
Solve equations						●	●		●	●	●
Division											
Meaning of division		●	●	●	●	●					
Properties				●	●	●	●				
Basic facts				●	●	●					
Fact families					●	●					
Divide powers of 10					●	●	●		●	●	●
Divide by 1-digit divisor				●	●	●	●		●		
Divide by 2-digit divisor					●	●	●		●	●	●
Zeros in quotient					●	●	●		●	●	●
Divide money amounts					●	●	●			●	●
Mental math strategies					●	●	●		●	●	●
Estimate quotients					●	●	●		●	●	●
Write/solve number sentences			●	●	●	●	●		●	●	●
Solve equations						●	●		●	●	●

GRADE 4
WHOLE NUMBER COMPUTATION

Multiplication
Meaning of multiplication, 124-127
Properties
    order, zero, one, grouping , 128-130, 132-133, 137,
        140-141, 143, 162-163
Basic facts, 128-137, 144-145, 152-153, 162-163
Fact families, 154-155, 162-163
Missing factors, 151, 153
Multiply three factors, 140-142, 162-163
Multiply powers of 10, 206-207
Multiply by 1-digit multiplier, 128-135, 143, 162-163, 170-202
    with greater numbers, 226-227, 232-233
Multiply by 2-digit multiplier, 178-181, 184, 188, 198, 204-236,
    259
Multiply money amounts, 192-193, 198-199, 224-225
Mental math strategies, 128-137, 170-173, 178, 182, 184, 188,
    192, 198, 206-209, 217, 227
Estimate products, 172-173, 178-180, 184, 188, 190, 193, 198,
    208-209, 216-218, 224-225, 227
Write/solve number sentences, 125-126, 130, 133, 141-142, 147

Division
Meaning of division, 146-149
    divisibility rules for 2, 5 and 10, 154-157, 297
Properties
    zero, identity, 146-148, 154-155
Basic facts, 146-153
Fact families, 154-155, 162-163
Divide powers of 10, 278-279, 302-303
Divide by 1-digit divisor, 282-289, 296, 312-313
    with greater numbers, 292-293, 296, 304-305, 312-313
Divide by 2-digit divisor, 302-313, 381
Zeros in quotient, 154-155, 290-291, 296, 312-313
Divide money amounts, 286-293
Mental math strategies, 278-281, 288, 296, 297, 302-303, 306,
    312-313
Estimate quotients, 280-281, 286, 290, 296, 312-313
Write/solve number sentences, 147, 150-151, 153-155, 283-284,
    306

Glencoe *

FRACTIONS AND MIXED NUMBERS	K	1	2	3	4	5	6		6	7	8
Concepts											
Meaning of fractions	■	■	■	■	■	■	■		■	■	■
Equivalent fractions				■	■	■	■		■	■	■
Simplest form				■	■	■	■		■	■	■
Least common denominator (LCD)						■	■		■	■	■
Compare and order			■	■	■	■	■		■	■	■
Round					■	■	■		■	■	■
Mixed numbers					■	■	■		■	■	■
relate improper fractions					■	■	■		■	■	■
Find fraction of a number						■	■		■	■	■
Reciprocals							■		■	■	■
Computation											
Add fractions											
like denominators					■	■	■		■	■	■
unlike denominators						■	■		■	■	■
Add mixed numbers					■	■	■		■	■	■
Estimate sums					■	■	■		■	■	■
Subtract fractions											
like denominators					■	■	■		■	■	■
unlike denominators						■	■		■	■	■
Subtract mixed numbers					■	■	■		■	■	■
Estimate differences					■	■	■		■	■	■
Multiply fractions						■	■		■	■	■
Multiply mixed numbers							■		■	■	■
Estimate products						■	■		■	■	■
Divide fractions						■	■		■	■	■
Divide mixed numbers							■		■	■	■
Estimate quotients						■	■		■	■	■
Relate fractions and decimals					■	■	■		■	■	■
Relate fractions and percents						■	■		■	■	■
Write and solve number sentences					■	■	■		■	■	■
Solve equations							■		■	■	■

GRADE 4
FRACTIONS AND MIXED NUMBERS
Concepts

Meaning of fractions, 368-373
  parts of a set, 372-373, 386, 402-403
  parts of a whole, 368-369, 386, 402-403
Equivalent fractions, 376-379, 382-383, 386, 402-403, 405, 426-429, 442-443
Simplest form, 380-381, 384-386, 402-403, 410-411, 414-418, 420-421, 442-443
Least common denominator (LCD), 426-427
Compare and order, 382-383, 402-403
Round, 384-385, 402-403
Mixed numbers, 384-386, 402-403, 434-437, 442-443
  relate improper fractions, 384-385

Computation

Add fractions
  like denominators, 410-415, 442-443
  unlike denominators, 428-431, 442-443
Add mixed numbers, 434-437, 442-443
Estimate sums, 434-437, 442-443
Subtract fractions
  like denominators, 416-421, 442-443
  unlike denominators, 428-431, 442-443
Subtract mixed numbers, 434-437, 442-443
Estimate differences, 434-437, 442-443
Relate fractions and decimals, 450-455, 458, 476-477
Write and solve number sentences, 414, 417, 420, 429, 442

* *Mathematics: Applications and Connections Courses 1–3 ©1998*

Glencoe *

DECIMALS	K	1	2	3	4	5	6	6	7	8
Concepts										
Place value				■	■	■	■	■	■	■
Equivalent decimals					■	■	■	■	■	■
Compare and order					■	■	■	■	■	■
Round					■	■	■	■	■	■
Relate decimals and fractions				■	■	■	■	■	■	■
Relate decimals, fractions, and percents						■	■	■	■	■
Terminating and repeating decimals							■	■	■	■
Scientific notation									■	■
Computation										
Add decimals					■	■	■	■	■	■
Subtract decimals					■	■	■	■	■	■
Estimate sums and differences					■	■	■	■	■	■
Multiply by whole number						■	■	■	■	■
Multiply by decimal						■	■	■	■	■
Estimate products						■	■	■	■	■
Divide by whole number						■	■	■	■	■
Divide by decimal							■	■	■	■
Zeros in quotient and dividend						■	■	■	■	■
Estimate quotients						■	■	■	■	■
Mental math strategies					■	■	■	■	■	■
Write/solve number sentences				■	■	■	■	■	■	■
Solve equations					■	■	■	■	■	■

GRADE 4
DECIMALS

Concepts

Place value
  tenths and hundredths, 450-455, 458, 476-477
Compare and order, 450-458, 476-477
Round, 464-465
Relate decimals and fractions, 450-455, 458

Computation

Add decimals, 466-469, 476-477
Subtract decimals, 466-467, 470-471, 476-477
Estimate sums and differences, 464-465, 476-477
Mental math strategies, 466-471
Write/solve number sentences, 465, 468-469
Solve equations, 466-471

Glencoe *

GEOMETRY	K	1	2	3	4	5	6	6	7	8
Patterns	■	■	■	■	■	■	■			
Points, lines, line segments, rays, angles		■	■	■	■	■	■	■	■	■
Classify angles			■	■	■	■	■	■	■	■
Measure and estimate angles				■	■	■	■	■	■	■
Identify 3-dimensional shapes	■	■	■	■	■	■	■	■	■	■
Identify 2-dimensional shapes	■	■	■	■	■	■	■	■	■	■
Classify polygons			■	■	■	■	■	■	■	■
Classify triangles				■	■	■	■	■	■	■
Classify quadrilaterals				■	■	■	■	■	■	■
Similarity					■	■	■	■	■	■
Congruence		■	■	■	■	■	■	■	■	■
Symmetry		■	■	■	■	■	■	■	■	■
Circles					■	■	■	■	■	■
Use geometric formulas					■	■	■	■	■	■
Constructions						■	■	■	■	■
Tessellations				■	■	■	■		■	■
Transformations					■	■	■	■	■	■
Coordinate geometry			■	■	■	■	■	■	■	■
Spatial reasoning	■	■	■	■	■	■	■	■	■	■
Relationships in a right triangle								■	■	■
Pythagorean theorem								■	■	■
Tangent, sine, cosine, ratios										■

GRADE 4
GEOMETRY

Patterns, 197, 320-321, 324, 363, 441
Points, lines, line segments, rays, angles, 328-329, 332, 336, 358-359
Classify angles, 332-336, 354, 358-359
Identify 3-dimensional shapes, 320-323, 358-359
Identify 2-dimensional shapes, 324-327, 358-359
Classify polygons, 324-327, 338-339, 354, 358-359, 373, 413
Classify triangles, 23, 320-322, 324-327, 335, 354, 358-359
Classify quadrilaterals, 324-327, 330, 358-359
Similarity, 340-343
Congruence, 340-342, 358-359
Symmetry, 344-345, 358-359
Circles, 327, 358-359, 441
Tessellations, 338-339
Transformations, 346-347, 358-359
Coordinate geometry, 458-459
Spatial reasoning, 15, 23, 67, 89, 109, 137, 139, 173, 183, 197,
  223, 227, 233, 251, 259, 269, 295, 323, 327, 331, 335, 357, 370,
  385, 393, 415, 440

* *Mathematics: Applications and Connections Courses 1–3* ©1998

Glencoe *

MEASUREMENT, TIME, MONEY	K	1	2	3	4	5	6	6	7	8
Measurement										
Estimate and measure length										
nonstandard units		■	■	■	■		■	■		
metric/customary units		■	■	■	■	■	■	■	■	■
Estimate and measure capacity										
nonstandard units	■	■	■	■	■					
metric/customary units		■	■	■	■	■	■	■	■	■
Estimate and measure mass/weight										
nonstandard units	■	■	■	■	■					
metric/customary units		■	■	■	■	■	■	■	■	■
Convert units				■	■	■	■	■	■	■
Compute with denominate numbers				■	■	■	■	■	■	■
Temperature	■	■	■	■	■	■	■	■	■	■
Perimeter			■	■	■	■	■	■	■	■
Circumference		■				■	■	■	■	■
Area		■	■	■	■	■	■	■	■	■
Surface area						■	■	■	■	■
Volume				■	■	■	■	■	■	■
Relate surface area and volume							■	■	■	■
Angle measure					■	■	■	■	■	■
Precision					■	■	■	■	■	■
Indirect measurement							■	■	■	■
Measurement sense	■	■	■	■	■	■	■	■	■	■
Time										
Read a calendar	■	■	■	■	■					
Estimate and tell time	■	■	■	■	■	■	■	■		
Find elapsed time			■	■	■	■	■	■		
Convert units		■	■	■	■	■	■	■	■	■
Money										
Find values of coins and bills	■	■	■	■				■		
Make change		■		■	■	■	■	■		
Compare and order	■	■	■	■	■	■	■	■		
Round			■	■	■	■	■	■	■	■
Estimate and compute with money amounts		■	■	■	■	■	■	■	■	■

GRADE 4
MEASUREMENT, TIME, MONEY

Measurement

Estimate and measure length
  nonstandard units, 259
  metric/customary units, 242-245, 252, 270-271, 291
Estimate and measure capacity
  nonstandard units, 256-259, 262-264
  metric/customary units, 256-259, 262-264, 270-271
Estimate and measure mass/weight
  nonstandard units, 256-259, 262-264
  metric/customary units, 256-259, 262-264, 270-271, 291
Convert units, 244-245, 247, 270-271, 307
Temperature, 255-256, 270-271
  Celsius, 255-256, 270-271
  Fahrenheit, 255-256, 270-271
Perimeter, 250-252, 270-271
Circumference, 343
Area, 348-351, 358-359, 371
Volume, 352-353, 358-359
Precision, 242-243, 246-248
Measurement sense, 242-243, 246-248, 253

Time

Read a calendar, 85-87, 114-115
Estimate and tell time, 82-89, 96, 114-115
Find elapsed time, 84-89, 96, 114-115
Convert units, 82-83

Money

Find values of coins and bills, 40-43, 74-75
Make change, 39-41, 43, 54, 74-75, 155
Compare and order, 39, 42-43, 70, 74-75
Round, 42-43
Estimate and compute with money amounts
  add/subtract, 39-47, 50, 52-53, 55-57, 59, 74-75, 83
  multiply, 192-193, 196, 198-199, 224-225, 232-233
  divide, 153, 155, 160, 279-281, 285, 295-296, 302-303, 306, 381

Glencoe *

PROBLEM SOLVING	K	1	2	3	4	5	6	6	7	8
Use the problem-solving process	■	■	■	■	■	■	■	■	■	■
Use/find a pattern	■	■	■	■	■	■	■	■	■	■
Use/make a table		■	■	■	■	■	■	■	■	■
Use/draw a picture/diagram	■	■	■	■	■	■	■	■	■	■
Use logical reasoning	■	■	■	■	■	■	■	■	■	■
Interpret data	■	■	■	■	■	■	■	■	■	■
Guess, test, and revise	■	■	■	■	■	■	■	■	■	■
Use/make a model	■	■	■	■	■	■	■	■	■	■
Make an organized list	■	■	■	■	■	■	■	■	■	■
Use estimation		■	■	■	■	■	■	■	■	■
Choose a strategy	■	■	■	■	■	■	■	■	■	■
Write a number sentence	■	■	■	■	■	■	■	■	■	■
Check for reasonable answers	■	■	■	■	■	■	■	■	■	■
Choose the operation	■	■	■	■	■	■	■	■	■	■
Act it out	■	■	■	■				■	■	■
Choose the method	■	■	■	■	■	■	■	■	■	■
Work backward	■	■	■	■	■	■	■	■	■	■
Solve multistep problems			■	■	■	■	■	■	■	■
Identify extra information			■	■	■	■	■	■	■	■
Solve a similar/simpler problem				■	■	■	■	■	■	■
Identify missing information			■	■	■	■	■	■	■	■
Use alternate solution methods					■	■	■		■	■
Interpret the quotient and remainder					■	■	■			
Conduct an experiment				■	■	■	■	■	■	■
Use a fraction vs. use a decimal					■	■	■	■	■	■
Write an equation						■	■	■	■	■
Use a formula						■	■	■	■	■
Eliminate possibilities							■	■	■	■
Use the Pythagorean theorem									■	■
Factor polynomials										■
Classify information	■	■	■	■	■	■	■	■	■	■

Glencoe *

MATHEMATICAL REASONING	K	1	2	3	4	5	6	6	7	8
Decision making		■	■	■	■	■	■	■	■	■
Critical thinking	■	■	■	■	■	■	■	■	■	■

GRADE 4
PROBLEM SOLVING
Use the problem-solving process, 14-15, 28-31, 66-67, 70-73, 88-89, 110-113, 182-183, 194-197, 222-223, 228-231, 294-295, 308-311, 330-331, 354-357, 394-395, 398-401, 432-433, 472-475
Use/find a pattern, 138-139
Use/make a table, 14-15
Use/draw a picture/diagram, 354-357, 432-433
Use logical reasoning, 2, 3, 7, 27, 30, 51, 133, 141, 173, 207, 230, 260-261, 293, 310, 327, 335, 345, 373, 400, 440, 443, 471, 475
Interpret data, 28-31, 110-113, 194-197
Guess, test, and revise, 294-295
Use/make a model, 48, 376-377, 450-453
Make an organized list, 330-331
Use estimation, 228-231
Choose a strategy, 222-223
Write a number sentence, 472-475
Check for reasonable answers, 266-269
Choose the operation, 66-67, 158-161, 438-441
Choose the method, 222-223
Work backward, 88-89
Solve multistep problems, 182-183, 398-401
Identify extra information, 70-73
Solve a similar/simpler problem, 462-463
Identify missing information, 70-71
Use alternate solution methods, 222-223
Interpret the quotient and remainder, 308-311
Conduct an experiment, 394-395

GRADE 4
MATHEMATICAL REASONING
Decision making, 13, 19, 23, 53, 55, 57, 67, 69, 87, 99, 103, 109, 141, 145, 153, 173, 187, 191, 193, 213, 221, 223, 245, 255, 266, 279, 297, 299, 331, 339, 351, 359, 389, 393, 395, 401, 425, 431, 437, 440, 453, 461
Critical thinking, 3, 5, 9, 12, 14, 25, 33, 41, 42, 44, 46, 49, 52, 56, 60, 63, 66, 75, 85, 88, 91, 95, 101, 104, 107, 115, 125, 129, 132, 135, 138, 140, 147, 150, 152, 154, 157, 163, 170, 172, 175, 179, 182, 189, 192, 199, 206, 208, 211, 215, 222, 224, 226, 233, 243, 244, 247, 250, 257, 260, 263, 271, 278, 280, 283, 287, 290, 292, 294, 301, 302, 305, 313, 321, 329, 330, 333, 344, 347, 349, 353, 359, 369, 372, 375, 377, 380, 382, 384, 391, 397, 403, 411, 414, 417, 420, 427, 429, 432, 435, 443, 451, 454, 456, 462, 464, 467, 468, 470, 477

* *Mathematics: Applications and Connections Courses 1–3 ©1998*

Glencoe *

ESTIMATION	K	1	2	3	4	5	6		6	7	8
Strategies											
Rounding			●	●	●	●	●		●	●	●
Front-end					●	●	●		●	●	●
Compatible numbers				●	●	●	●		●	●	●
Clustering						●	●			●	●
Patterns	●	●	●	●	●	●	●		●	●	●
Choose the computation method				●	●	●	●		●	●	●
Capture-recapture							●				
Use fractions, decimals, and percent interchangeably							●		●	●	●
Numbers/Operations											
Whole numbers	●	●	●	●	●	●	●				
sums and differences		●	●	●	●	●	●		●	●	●
products and quotients			●	●	●	●	●		●	●	●
Money			●	●	●	●	●				
sums and differences			●	●	●	●	●		●	●	●
products and quotients				●	●	●	●		●	●	●
Decimals					●	●	●				
sums and differences					●	●	●		●	●	●
products and quotients						●	●		●	●	●
Fractions/mixed numbers					●	●	●				
sums and differences					●	●	●		●	●	●
products and quotients						●	●		●	●	●
Percent							●		●	●	●
Estimate square roots										●	●
Measurement											
Length, capacity, mass/weight	●	●	●	●	●	●	●		●	●	●
Time		●	●	●	●	●	●				
Temperature			●	●	●	●	●				
Perimeter, area, volume			●	●	●	●	●		●	●	●
Angle measure					●	●	●		●	●	●
Problem Solving											
Check for reasonableness		●	●	●	●	●	●		●	●	●
Estimation vs. exact answers				●	●	●	●		●	●	●
Over- and under-estimating						●	●		●	●	●

GRADE 4
ESTIMATION

Strategies
Rounding, 172-173, 178-180, 184, 188, 190, 196, 208-209, 384-385, 464-465
Front-end, 55, 61, 209
Compatible numbers, 280-281, 304-305

Numbers/Operations
Whole numbers
  sums and differences, 46-50, 55, 60-64, 68-69, 74, 77, 181, 193, 217, 384-385, 410-412, 434-437, 464-465
  products and quotients, 172-173, 178-180, 184, 188, 190, 196, 204-205, 280-281, 286, 290, 296
Money
  sums and differences, 46-47, 49-50, 52-53, 63-64, 69
  products and quotients, 172-173, 181, 185, 189-190, 192-193
Decimals
  sums and differences, 464-465, 476-477
Fractions/mixed numbers
  sums and differences, 437

Measurement
Length, capacity, mass/weight, 242-243, 248, 252-253, 257-258, 264
Time, 83, 86
Temperature, 255-256
Perimeter, area, volume, 351

Problem Solving
Check for reasonableness, 49, 52, 62-63, 68, 178-179, 188-189, 192, 210, 215, 224, 258, 264, 266-267, 271
Estimation vs. exact answers, 228-231

Glencoe *

TECHNOLOGY	K	1	2	3	4	5	6		6	7	8
Calculator											
Patterns	●	●	●	●	●	●	●		●	●	●
Computation	●	●	●	●	●	●	●		●	●	●
Choose a calculation method		●	●	●	●	●	●		●	●	●
Order of operations				●	●	●	●		●	●	●
Fractions and decimals					●	●	●		●	●	●
Special keys				●	●	●	●		●	●	●
Computer											
Spreadsheets			●	●	●	●	●		●	●	●
Patterns	●	●	●	●	●	●	●		●	●	●
Simulations				●	●	●	●		●	●	●
Functions			●	●	●	●	●		●	●	●
Graphs	●	●	●	●	●	●	●		●	●	●

GRADE 4
TECHNOLOGY

Calculator
Patterns
  palindromes, 357
Computation
  addition/subtraction, 7, 9, 10, 13, 15, 23, 27, 33, 45, 47, 51, 53, 61, 68, 69, 75, 83, 385, 437, 465
  multiplication, 125, 127, 131, 133, 137, 139, 141, 151, 161, 163, 170-171, 173, 181-182, 189, 191-193, 199, 206, 209, 213, 223-227
Choose a calculation method, 151, 219, 292, 457
Fractions and decimals, 386
Special keys, 292-293, 428-429

Computer
Spreadsheets, 73, 119, 161, 219, 231, 311, 475
Patterns, 363
Simulations, 401
Functions, 219, 458
Graphs, 37, 113, 203, 275, 401, 407, 441

* *Mathematics: Applications and Connections Courses 1–3 ©1998*

Glencoe *

MENTAL MATH	K	1	2	3	4	5	6		6	7	8
Basic Addition/Subtraction Fact Strategies											
Use patterns		■	■	■	■	■					
Count on		■	■	■	■	■					
Count back		■	■	■	■	■					
Use doubles		■	■	■	■						
Use doubles plus 1		■	■	■	■						
Make 10		■	■	■	■						
Skip count		■	■	■	■	■					
Add/subtract 9		■	■	■	■						
Use related facts		■	■	■	■	■					
Use fact families		■	■	■	■	■					
Use properties		■	■	■	■	■					
Basic Multiplication/Division Fact Strategies											
Use patterns			■	■	■	■					
Break apart numbers				■	■	■					
Use square numbers				■	■	■					
Use related facts			■	■	■	■					
Use fact families			■	■	■	■					
Use properties			■	■	■	■					
Computation Strategies											
Use patterns			■	■	■	■	■		■		
Count on/count back			■	■	■	■	■		■		
Add/subtract multiples of powers of 10			■	■	■	■	■		■		
Multiply/divide multiples of powers of 10				■	■	■	■		■		
Multiply/divide by multiples of powers of 10					■	■	■		■		
Use properties			■	■	■	■	■		■		
Work left to right				■	■	■	■				
Break apart numbers				■	■	■	■				
Use compensation				■	■	■			■		
Use divisibility rules					■	■	■		■		
Use equivalence among fractions, decimals, percents						■	■		■		
Compatible numbers					■	■	■		■		

GRADE 4
MENTAL MATH
Basic Addition/Subtraction Fact Strategies
Use patterns, 44-45, 58-59, 74-75
Count on, 40-41, 74-75
Count back, 141, 150-151, 162-163
Use doubles, 53
Use doubles plus 1, 46-47
Make 10, 46-47
Skip count, 128-129, 150-151
Add/subtract 9, 46-47
Use related facts, 58-59
Use fact families, 58-59
Use properties, 52-53, 74-75

Basic Multiplication/Division Fact Strategies
Use patterns, 105, 125, 129, 135, 138-139, 143, 154, 157, 161, 170-171, 206-207
Break apart numbers, 134, 211
Use square numbers, 143
Use related facts, 147, 150, 154-155
Use fact families, 154-155
Use properties, 128-130, 132, 137, 140, 143

Computation Strategies
Use patterns, 44-45, 58-59, 74-75, 105, 125, 129, 135, 138-139, 143, 154-155, 157, 161, 170-171, 206-207, 278-279, 296, 302-303
Count on/count back, 40-41, 74-75, 150-151, 162-163
Add/subtract multiples of powers of 10, 46-47, 58-59
Multiply/divide multiples of powers of 10, 170-171, 206-208, 211, 302-303, 312-313
Multiply/divide by multiples of powers of 10, 208-209, 278-279, 302-303
Use properties, 52-53, 128-130, 132, 137, 140, 143, 302-303, 312-313
Work left to right, 46-47, 58-59
Break apart numbers, 134, 211
Use compensation, 46-47, 58-59
Use divisibility rules, 156-157, 297

Glencoe *

PATTERNS, RELATIONSHIPS, FUNCTIONS	K	1	2	3	4	5	6		6	7	8
Patterns											
Number patterns											
repeating patterns		■	■	■	■	■	■		■		
growing patterns			■	■	■	■	■		■		
computation patterns			■	■	■	■	■		■		
skip-counting patterns		■	■	■	■						
place-value patterns		■	■	■	■	■	■		■		
even and odd number patterns			■	■	■	■	■				
use a calculator/computer		■	■	■	■	■	■				
Number sequences					■	■	■		■		
Fibonacci sequence							■		■		
Pascal's triangle							■		■		
Geometric/spatial patterns		■	■	■	■	■	■		■		
Statistical patterns				■	■	■	■		■		

GRADE 4
PATTERNS, RELATIONSHIPS, FUNCTIONS
Patterns
Number patterns
  repeating patterns, 125, 154, 161, 170, 206-207
  growing patterns, 93, 129, 131, 138, 170, 173, 206-207, 245, 302
  computation patterns, 59, 89, 93, 105, 125, 157, 161, 170, 173, 181-182, 196, 206, 278-279, 296, 302
  skip-counting patterns, 128, 151
  place-value patterns, 8-9
  even and odd number patterns, 73
  use a calculator/computer, 151, 363
Geometric/spatial patterns, 197, 320-321, 324, 363, 441
  transformations, 346-347
  tessellations, 338-339
Statistical patterns, 94-95, 98-103

Chart continued on page T10

* *Mathematics: Applications and Connections Courses 1–3* ©1998

Chart continued from page T9

SCOPE AND SEQUENCE

Glencoe *

PATTERNS, RELATIONSHIPS, FUNCTIONS	K	1	2	3	4	5	6	6	7	8
Relationships										
Sorting and classifying	▪									
Number relationships										
inequalities			▪	▪	▪	▪	▪	▪	▪	▪
factors, multiples				▪	▪	▪	▪	▪	▪	▪
divisibility rules					▪	▪	▪	▪	▪	▪
Geometric relationships										
shapes	▪	▪	▪	▪	▪	▪	▪	▪	▪	▪
perimeter, area, volume				▪	▪	▪	▪	▪	▪	▪
circumference, surface area						▪	▪	▪	▪	▪
graphing ordered pairs			▪	▪	▪	▪	▪	▪	▪	▪
Functions										
Meaning	▪	▪	▪	▪	▪	▪	▪	▪	▪	▪
Function tables								▪	▪	▪
Geometric functions								▪	▪	▪
Linear functions									▪	▪

Glencoe *

RATIO, PROPORTION, PERCENT	K	1	2	3	4	5	6	6	7	8
Ratio										
Meaning						▪	▪	▪	▪	▪
Equal ratios						▪	▪	▪	▪	▪
Rate							▪	▪	▪	▪
Tangent, sine, & cosine ratios										▪
The Golden Ratio										▪
Proportion										
Meaning						▪	▪	▪	▪	▪
Solve proportions							▪	▪	▪	▪
Scale drawings							▪	▪	▪	▪
Similar figures							▪	▪	▪	▪
Scale up or down							▪	▪	▪	▪
Indirect measurement									▪	▪
Dilations										▪
Tangent, sine, cosine ratio										▪
Percent										
Meaning						▪	▪	▪	▪	▪
Relate fractions and percents						▪	▪	▪	▪	▪
Relate decimals and percents						▪	▪	▪	▪	▪
Percents greater than 100% and less than 1%							▪	▪	▪	▪
Percent of a number							▪	▪	▪	▪
Percent one number is of another							▪	▪	▪	▪
Find number when percent of it is known							▪	▪	▪	▪
Estimate percents							▪	▪	▪	▪
Mental math							▪	▪		▪
Percent applications										
circle graphs							▪	▪	▪	▪
simple/compound interest							▪	▪	▪	▪
discount/sale price						▪	▪	▪	▪	▪
sales tax							▪	▪	▪	▪
percent of change							▪	▪	▪	▪
Dilations										▪

GRADE 4
PATTERNS, RELATIONSHIPS, FUNCTIONS
Relationships
Number relationships
  inequalities, 4-5, 12-13, 16, 25-26, 32-33, 42-43, 47, 50, 64, 74, 90, 149, 155, 157, 172-173, 180, 185, 188-190, 198, 207, 209, 218, 226-227, 292-293, 296, 304-305, 456-458
  factors, multiples, 128-129, 131-136, 170-171, 184, 206-208, 211, 302-303, 380-381
  divisibility rules, 297
Geometric relationships
  shapes, 320-322, 324-327, 340-342, 346-347, 352-353
  perimeter, area, volume, 250-251, 348-353
  graphing ordered pairs, 104-105

Functions
Meaning, 459
Function tables, 22, 232, 459

---

* *Mathematics: Applications and Connections Courses 1–3 ©1998*

Glencoe *

ALGEBRA	K	1	2	3	4	5	6	6	7	8
Expressions, Equations, Inequalities										
Patterns, relationships, functions		■	■	■	■	■	■	■	■	■
Inverse operations		■	■	■	■	■	■	■	■	■
Properties					■	■	■	■	■	■
Use order of operations					■	■	■	■	■	■
Write/solve number sentences	■	■	■	■	■	■	■	■	■	■
Evaluate algebraic expressions					■	■	■	■	■	■
Inequalities		■	■	■	■	■	■	■	■	■
Solve 1-step equations										
with integer solutions						■	■		■	■
with two variables									■	■
Solve 2-step equations							■		■	■
Use formulas						■	■		■	■
Positive/Negative Numbers										
Integers										
meaning of							■	■	■	■
absolute value							■	■	■	■
properties							■	■	■	■
compare and order							■	■	■	■
add and subtract							■	■	■	■
multiply and divide								■	■	■
graph integers on the number line								■	■	■
Rational numbers										
identify and simplify rational numbers									■	■
rational numbers as decimals									■	■
compare and order rational numbers									■	■
solve equations with rational number solutions									■	■
scientific notation								■	■	■
properties									■	■
Real numbers										
identify and classify real numbers									■	■
Negative exponents									■	■
Square roots									■	■
Irrational numbers									■	■
Density property										■
Coordinate Graphing										
Locate points on a number line		■	■	■	■	■	■	■	■	■
Graph coordinates in first quadrant		■	■	■	■	■	■	■	■	■
Graph coordinates in four quadrants							■	■	■	■
Graph functions							■	■	■	■
Graph equations							■		■	■
Transformations on a coordinate plane								■	■	■
Quadratic functions										■
To solve systems of equations										■
Slope									■	■
Polynomials										
Represent and simplify polynomials										■
Add, subtract and multiply polynomials										■
Factor polynomials										■
Multiply binomials										■

GRADE 4
ALGEBRA
Expressions, Equations, Inequalities
Patterns, relationships, functions, *See* Patterns, Relationships, Functions
Inverse operations, 151, 153
Properties, 52-53, 74-75, 128-130, 132, 137, 140, 143
Write/solve number sentences, 125-126, 130, 133, 141-142, 147, 150-151, 154-155, 278, 472-473
Evaluate algebraic expressions, 227
Inequalities
  use >, < symbols, 13, 16, 32, 43, 75, 149, 180, 207, 209, 218, 245, 248, 252, 383, 422, 456-458, 476

Coordinate Graphing
Locate points on a number line, 12-13, 22, 456
Graph coordinates in first quadrant, 458-459

Glencoe *

STATISTICS AND GRAPHING	K	1	2	3	4	5	6	6	7	8
Gather and Collect Data										
Collect data	●	●	●	●	●	●	●	●	●	●
Conduct a survey		●	●	●	●	●	●	●	●	●
Tally		●	●	●	●	●	●	●	●	●
Conduct an experiment or simulation			●	●	●	●	●	●	●	●
Use sampling					●	●	●	●	●	●
Organize and Represent Data										
Sort and order data	●	●	●	●	●	●	●	●	●	●
Make a list	●	●	●	●	●	●	●	●	●	●
Make a table/graph/schedule	●	●	●	●	●	●	●	●	●	●
Frequency tables			●	●	●	●	●	●	●	●
Venn diagrams	●	●	●	●	●	●	●	●	●	●
Tree diagrams			●	●	●	●	●	●	●	●
Concrete graphs	●	●	●	●	●			●		
Pictographs	●	●	●	●	●	●	●	●	●	●
Line plots		●	●	●	●	●	●	●	●	●
Bar graphs	●	●	●	●	●	●	●	●	●	●
Double bar graphs				●	●	●	●	●	●	●
Line graphs				●	●	●	●	●	●	●
Double line graphs					●	●	●	●	●	●
Circle graphs					●	●	●	●	●	●
Stem-and-leaf plots					●	●	●	●	●	●
Histograms						●	●	●	●	●
Box-and-whisker plots							●	●	●	●
Scatter plots							●	●	●	●
Computer generated displays	●	●	●	●	●	●	●	●	●	●
Use a database/spreadsheet					●	●	●	●	●	●
Analyze Data and Draw Conclusions										
Read and interpret data	●	●	●	●	●	●	●	●	●	●
Make predictions and generalizations	●	●	●	●	●	●	●	●	●	●
Identify and describe trends			●	●	●	●	●	●	●	●
Find mode, range, mean and median				●	●	●	●	●	●	●
Quartiles							●	●	●	●
Misleading statistics						●	●	●	●	●

GRADE 4
STATISTICS AND GRAPHING

Gather and Collect Data
Collect data, 18-19, 28-29, 35, 56-57, 83, 90-103, 110-112, 114-115, 117, 133, 139, 141, 153, 181, 194-195, 202-203, 216, 220-221, 254-255, 274-275, 383, 406-407, 419, 441
Conduct a survey, 7, 90, 95, 103, 141, 181, 203, 281
Tally, 2, 7, 29, 94-95, 102, 180, 301, 394
Conduct an experiment or simulation, 394-397

Organize and Represent Data
Sort and order data, 35, 56-57, 94-95, 98-101, 114, 254-255, 406
Make a list, 330-331
Make a table/graph/schedule, 14-15, 28-29, 37, 84-85, 94-95, 97, 100-103, 106-111, 113, 194-195, 203, 275, 316-317, 354-355, 383, 401, 407, 419, 441, 458-459
Frequency tables, 94-95, 97
Venn diagrams, 31, 354-355
Tree diagrams, 82
Concrete graphs, 94-95
Pictographs, 83, 94-95, 112, 117, 139, 153, 181, 209, 419
Line plots, 28-29, 87-91, 100-102
Bar graphs, 37, 80, 100-103, 109, 115-117, 183, 191, 202-203, 216, 249, 285
Line graphs, 106-109, 112, 115, 119, 231, 275
Circle graphs, 383, 419, 441
Stem-and-leaf plots, 103
Computer generated displays, 37, 73, 113, 119, 161, 203, 219, 231, 275, 311, 401, 407, 441, 475
Use a database/spreadsheet, 73, 119, 161, 219, 231, 311, 475

Analyze Data and Draw Conclusions
Read and interpret data, 28-29, 83, 90-91, 93, 96-103, 110-112, 115, 117, 133, 139, 153, 194-195, 202-203, 216, 220-221, 274-275, 406-407, 419, 441
Make predictions and generalizations, 3, 19, 57, 70, 73, 99, 124, 145, 187, 221, 231, 255, 299, 308, 311, 339, 389, 396-397, 401, 425, 432-433, 461
Identify and describe trends, 106-107
Find mode, range, mean and median, 90-93, 96, 99, 114, 117, 133

Glencoe *

PROBABILITY	K	1	2	3	4	5	6	6	7	8
Meaning		●	●	●	●	●	●	●	●	●
Conduct an experiment/simulation			●	●	●	●	●	●	●	●
Simple events			●	●	●	●	●	●	●	●
Independent events				●	●	●	●	●	●	●
Dependent events					●	●	●	●	●	●
Theoretical/experimental probability					●	●	●	●	●	●
Record outcomes				●	●	●	●	●	●	●
Predict outcomes	●	●	●	●	●	●	●	●	●	●
Tree diagrams				●	●	●	●	●	●	●
Sample space					●	●	●	●	●	●
Combinations	●	●	●	●	●	●	●		●	●
Counting principle					●	●	●	●	●	●
Permutations						●	●	●	●	●
Use area models						●	●	●	●	●

GRADE 4
PROBABILITY

Meaning, 390-391
Conduct an experiment/simulation, 396-397
Simple events, 390-393
Independent events, 390-393
Theoretical/experimental probability, 396-397
Record outcomes, 396-397
Predict outcomes, 3, 19, 57, 70, 73, 99, 124, 145, 187, 221, 231, 255, 299, 308, 311, 339, 389, 396-397, 401, 425, 432-433, 461
Tree diagrams, 182-183
Combinations, 182-183

* *Mathematics: Applications and Connections   Courses 1–3   ©1998*

Perspectives on Meeting Individual Needs

Learning Styles

Students have many different styles of learning mathematics. Three of the most common learning styles are based on different modalities. A kinesthetic learning style entails learning from hands-on and whole-body activities; a visual learning style relies on observations, drawing, and reading; and an auditory or oral learning style uses listening and discussing. Some children are very flexible in their learning styles; that is, they can switch among learning styles, depending on the nature of the problem. Other children may be less flexible; for example, they may simply learn better by modeling problems (kinesthetic) and not understand how a sketch (visual) can help to solve a problem. To accommodate children's different learning styles, you should be flexible in how you present problems to children and in allowing children to explain or show how they figured out a problem's answer.

Howard Gardner, in his book *Multiple Intelligences: The Theory in Practice,* lists the seven types of intelligence that every student brings to the learning process:

- Logical-mathematical intelligence is shown in a sensitivity to and ability to understand logical or mathematical patterns, and in the ability to handle long or complex forms of reasoning;

- Linguistic intelligence manifests itself in sensitivity to the nuances of language;

- Musical intelligence is the ability to appreciate and to reproduce rhythmic sounds and pitch;

- Spatial intelligence involves the perception of the visual and spatial world;

- Kinesthetic intelligence is the control of one's own body movements and the skillful handling of objects;

- Interpersonal intelligence is the capacity to recognize and respond to the moods, temperaments, motivations, and needs of other people;

- Intrapersonal intelligence involves the ability to understand and respond to one's own needs, desires, strengths, and weaknesses.

Everyone has aspects of all seven intelligences, but individuals will vary in how strongly each intelligence has been developed and in how flexibly they can access and apply the different intelligences in the context of particular types of problems.

As you plan each lesson, it may help you to consider how well different students will perform. Choose two or three students in your class and ask yourself how the lesson you are preparing for tomorrow will work for them. Does one student prefer to model and another to listen closely? If so, how will you accommodate these different styles? Will this lesson work well in a small group, or will it need to be individually paced? Are there places where the students you are thinking about might have difficulty understanding? What contingency plans are available? How might the lesson proceed if a student gave an answer that could turn into a teachable moment? Think about different children for each lesson. This exercise will help you to focus on students' individual learning styles.

Students Acquiring English

Never underestimate what students acquiring English can do. For example, do not automatically assume that they cannot solve word problems; try them and see. And don't isolate a student acquiring English when using small groups: include at least one bilingual student who speaks that child's native language (who can work with and translate for the student acquiring English) and English-speaking students (who can model how to use English when working on mathematics).

- If a problem seems a little difficult, try to simplify the English. Use active voice, present tense, short sentences.

- If a student has trouble providing a solution, encourage the use of the native language.

- If someone else in the class speaks the native language, ask that child to translate for the rest of the class. Ask the second child if the first child's solution seems reasonable.

- When speaking to the class, be sure to enunciate carefully. (This does not mean to speak louder since, when you speak louder, your face may become contorted, and students acquiring English may think you are angry.)

- Avoid asking rhetorical questions, since students may take them literally.

- Be strategic in the questions that you ask students. The easiest questions to understand are those that call for simple yes-or-no answers.

- When asking a series of yes-or-no questions, be sure to vary the pattern so that the correct answers are not either all yes or all no. After yes-or-no questions, students should also be exposed to some multiple-choice questions.

- Finally, students can understand questions that ask who, what, when, where, how, and why. If a student does not understand a particular kind of question, try to simplify it by using one at an easier level.

Gifted and Talented

Gifted and talented students often come up with interesting angles and insights into the mathematical nature of the problems they solve. To help gifted students develop their reasoning skills, try to pose problems that challenge at all levels of understanding and achievement, and that encourage a diversity of approaches to solution.

- Note each child's particular talents and try to connect those talents to specific curricular areas as well as to real-life applications.

- Find local or national contests that involve literary and artistic creativity, and encourage students to exercise their abilities by submitting entries.

- Seek out local businesses that might welcome student-created banners or displays in their windows.

- Encourage preparation of a class magazine or newspaper, and engage interested students forming the editorial and production staff.

- Suggest the formation of a book club or circulating library, with students sharing and reviewing their favorite books and stories.

- Introduce interested students to the stock market, then encourage them to choose stocks and track their progress over a period of time.

- Moderate panel discussions of historical figures, with students researching and then "becoming" real personages whose lives or ideas they find interesting or inspirational.

The most important objective of tailoring instruction to gifted and talented students is to support and encourage their talents in any way possible. Specific strategies should be adjusted on a regular basis to reflect the students' changing needs and interests.

Inclusion

Children of various abilities will do their best work in an atmosphere in which they feel valued and in which they are made aware that you expect them to think and learn on an equal footing with their classmates. For some children, showing that you value them and have high expectations of them may mean starting each day by listening to their cares and concerns. You can also help them increase their participation by warning them in advance that you will be calling on them and by giving them extra response time. You may initially accept children's one-word answers and then, as the year progresses, encourage students to use phrases, full sentences, and eventually, more fully elaborated explanations. Be sure to communicate to the entire class that everyone is expected to work hard, to value all their classmates as individuals with varying strengths and abilities, and to help one another.

There are many different kinds of special needs students, so it is important to understand the specific nature of each child's needs and to customize your teaching approach accordingly.

- All children, but especially those with special needs, require consistent and well-understood classroom routines.
- Presenting all information both aurally and visually will benefit students with special needs.
- Everyone should know how roles and responsibilities are distributed when doing small-group work.
- Group roles and responsibilities should be posted, and children should be referred to them as the need arises.
- All students should know what criteria are used for assessing whether mathematics work needs to be redone, is acceptable, or excels.

Gender Fair Classrooms

It is important to be aware of messages that girls receive, in school and out of school, about their mathematical abilities and whether mathematics will be important to them as they grow older. Girls often receive the message that they will not need mathematics when they grow up, or that it is okay not to make an effort in mathematics. If such messages come from well-meaning family members, you may need to discuss with the student's family how such messages can discourage their children and hurt their performance in school.

In the classroom, boys sometimes monopolize the teacher's attention by calling out answers or by behaving in inappropriate ways. Also, questions that emphasize critical thinking are sometimes directed at boys more than at girls. You should evaluate your management routines early in the year to be sure that girls are given at least as many meaningful opportunities to participate in class discussions as boys.

Cooperating to Teach

Most elementary schools employ teachers who specialize in teaching students acquiring English, students with special needs, and gifted students. By working together with these teachers, you should be able to provide your students with a more coherent mathematics program. For instance, you might share lesson plans with specialty teachers and ask them for suggestions on how to adapt lessons for specific students in your class. You might also ask specialist teachers to preteach some mathematics concepts so that their students are prepared when they encounter the ideas in your class. Specialists might also help you to better assess your students' understanding of the mathematics that you are teaching. In all cases, the important thing to focus on is: What are my students comprehending? How can I be sure that every one of them has a meaningful and fair chance at learning this material?

Six Perspectives on Cooperative Learning

1 A Way to Teach Academic Content

Learning collaboratively in small groups is an effective instructional method for learning math. In Grade Four, motivation to learn comes in part from the building of classroom community. Providing students with opportunities to talk about and act upon mathematical ideas is combined with practicing cooperative skills such as listening, and checking for agreement or understanding.

2 An Approach to Learning

Cooperative approaches build on basic research about how the brain learns: by developing concepts through relevant discussion, by testing ideas against those of others, and through gaining support and help from others. Activities are built into Grade Four where students think on their own, communicate ideas with a variety of partners, help each other, and learn cooperative skills such as restating, coming to agreement, and reflecting.

3 A Community of Learners

A learning community may include teachers collaborating with teachers to improve instruction, or administrators, teachers, students, and parents collaborating to foster relevant and consistent student learning. In Grade Four, this can be students collaborating with parents to learn math used in the home, or bringing parents to school to participate in family math events.

4 Diversity as an Asset

Cooperative groups capitalize on the heterogeneity of the modern classroom by bringing together students with different learning strategies and strengths. Fourth Graders are encouraged to value diversity in the group as providing unique perspectives. Students bring their personal experiences and interests to bear on math topics.

5 A Foundation for Success

Most businesses and industries rely heavily on teamwork. Through learning with partners and consulting and comparing with other pairs, Grade Four students begin to build the kinds of work relationships and cooperative skills that will serve them later in almost any field of endeavor.

6 Cooperation Is Content That Is Learned in Stages

The goals for students at this grade level fall into five stages. To help you achieve these goals, the following strategies have been built into the program:

1. Developing cooperation in community-building activities that also teach mathematical content
   - Concentric Circles Strategy: sharing ideas or answers quickly in two circles with several different partners
   - People Graphs Strategy: lining up by shared characteristics, making observations, discussing

2. Teaching collaboration through work with several partners
   - Partners Check Strategy: checking each other's thinking, problem-solving methods, or strategies
   - Partners Brainstorm Strategy: generating ideas by combining and expanding individual lists

3. Beginning to develop teamwork by having two pairs (two sets of partners) meet
   - Pairs Compare Strategy: working individually; comparing with a partner; joining another pair to compare strategies, methods, or answers
   - Pairs Experiment Strategy: partners working on an experiment; joining another pair to share and discuss results; producing a joint report

4. Developing teamwork in groups of three, four, or more
   - Triads Practice: working side by side in a group of three, discussing and sharing methods and outcomes.
   - Group Discussion with Round Robin Strategy: learning equal participation by taking turns clockwise; responding verbally in a group of three or four
   - Group Product Strategy: working together in a group; organizing the task; coming to agreement; completing a product; presenting it to the class
   - Huddle Strategy: counting off to number group members; conferring on the answer to a question posed by the teacher; being ready to represent the group when number is called

5. Learning complex teamwork with division of labor or belonging to more than one group
   - Jigsaw Strategy: learning one segment of the group assignment; teaching it to teammates; integrating the parts to form a whole problem, solution, or product
   - Jigsaw Strategy with Expert Groups: learning one segment of the group assignment by working with an "expert group" which also plans how to teach it; teaching it to teammates; integrating the parts to form a whole problem, solution, or product

Chapter 1   Lesson 2   p. 5

Ex. 14: Possible answer: a. Increase the tens digit by 1 to get 775; b. decrease the hundreds digit by 1 to get 665; c. 1,100 is 1 thousand 1 hundred, so increase the thousands digit by 1 and the hundreds digit by 1 to get 1,865.

Chapter 1   Lesson 8   p. 28

Ex. 3: Statements may vary. Possible answer: The same number of students, six students, had first names with 4 letters and 6 letters, which was more than for any other number of letters.

Ex. 4: Answers may vary. Possible answer: The statement would no longer be true because there would be seven students with 5 letters in their first names, and this would be more than for any other number of letters.

Ex. 5: Answers may vary. Possible answer: The line plot; it is easier to see how the data varies, the most common data, and the least common data.

Ex. 6: Answers may vary. Possible answer: the results of the survey show that nobody's name was longer than 13 letters, so having more letters is extremely unusual; predictions may vary; check students' reasoning.

Chapter 1   Performance Assessment   p. 35

Question 2: Possible answer: a table with heads "Country" and "Number of Immigrants" to organize the data; order, from greatest to least: Mexico—126,561, China—65,578, Philippines—63,457, Great Britain—18,783, Jamaica—17,241.

Question 3: Possible answer: About 130,000 immigrants came from Mexico that year, which was about 60,000 more than the next largest group, and about 2,000 fewer immigrants came from the Philippines than from China.

Chapter 1   Math-Science-Technology Connection   p. 37

Ex. 1: African Elephant, Black Rhinoceros, Hawaiian Monk Seal, Mauritus Parakeet, Nene, Orangutan, Wooly Spider Monkey; Arabian Oryx, Florida Cougar, Indian Tiger, Japanese Crane, Polar Bear, Red Wolf, Siberian Tiger; compare the numbers in the third and fourth columns.

Ex. 2: African Elephant, Orangutan, Polar Bear, Black Rhinoceros, Indian Tiger, Hawaiian Monk Seal, Arabian Oryx, Nene, Wooly Spider Monkey, Japanese Crane, Siberian Tiger, Red Wolf, Florida Cougar, Mauritus Parakeet; Hawaiian Monk Seal, Arabian Oryx, Nene, Wooly Spider Monkey, Japanese Crane, Siberian Tiger, Red Wolf, Florida Cougar, Mauritus Parakeet.

Chapter 2   What Do You Know?   p. 39

Ex. 2: Answers may vary. Possible answer: 1 five-dollar bill, 2 dimes, 7 pennies; 5 one-dollar bills, 1 quarter, 2 pennies; 5 one-dollar bills, 5 nickels, 2 pennies.

Chapter 2   Lesson 4   p. 46

Ex. 7: Rounding up: estimated sum is greater than exact sum—$26 + 37 = 63$, $30 + 40 = 70, 70 > 63$; rounding down: estimated sum is less than exact sum—$23 + 34 = 57, 20 + 30 = 50, 50 < 57$; rounding one up and one down: estimated sum may be either less than or greater than exact sum—$24 + 47 = 71$, $20 + 50 = 70, 70 < 71; 55 + 23 = 78, 60 + 20 = 80, 80 > 78$.

Chapter 2   Lesson 12   p. 91

Ex. 1: Needed information—price of milk; not needed—price of Late Riser and items not in Hearty Meal

Ex. 2: Needed information—price of Late Riser and items in the special; not needed—cost of Hearty Meal and items not in Late Riser; possible answer: no; the cost of the items separately would be 20¢ less than the cost of the special.

Ex. 3: Needed information—price of eggs Benedict; not needed—price of all items except juice

Chapter 3   Lesson 4   p. 91

Ex. 3: Answers may vary. Possible answer: 1. the mode, the response that occurs most often, is 2 books—more students read 2 books than any other number; 2. the range shows the difference between the greatest and least number of books read; 3. the median, the number in the middle if you arranged the responses in order, is 3—so at least half the responses are 3 books or greater.

Chapter 3   Lesson 5   p. 94

Question 1: Each stick figure stands for 8 votes, to show the number of votes for country music; to show 20 votes for R&B, use $2\frac{1}{2}$ figures.

Chapter 3   Lesson 6   p. 100

Question 1: Possible answer: Counted the number of Xs in the line plot for each animal, found that number on the scale of the bar graph, then drew the bar to that height.

Question 2: Possible answer: Both make it easy to compare the data; the bar graph makes it easier to read exact numbers because the data can be read from the scale.

Chapter 3   Lesson 6   p. 103

Ex. 4:
Union School District
Number Of Students In Fourth Grade

Stem	Leaves
1	8
2	0 5 5 8
3	2 2 6 6

2 | 5 stands for 25 students.

Chapter 3   Lesson 7   p. 104

Question 1: Start at zero, go right 3 blocks, then go up 8 blocks to get to Marcella's home.

Question 2: No; (8, 3) would mean go right 8 blocks and then go up 3 blocks to get to Roberto's home.

Question 3: Possible answer: The order tells by a rule how to find the location—the first number tells how far to go right and the second number how far to go up.

Chapter 3   Lesson 8   p.106

Question 1: Answers may vary. Possible answer: For each month in the table, found the number of students on the scale of the line graph, placed a point above the month at that height, then connected the points.

Chapter 3   Lesson 8   p. 107

Question 2: Possible answer: The number of new subscribers decreases, as between months 4 and 5; the number of new subscribers stays the same, as between months 2 and 3.

Chapter 4   Lesson 10   p. 154

Ex. 1: $2 \times 8 = 16, 8 \times 2 = 16, 16 \div 2 = 8, 16 \div 8 = 2$

Ex. 2: $4 \times 5 = 20, 5 \times 4 = 20, 20 \div 4 = 5, 20 \div 5 = 4$

Ex. 3: $6 \times 1 = 6, 1 \times 6 = 6, 6 \div 1 = 6, 6 \div 6 = 1$

Ex. 4: $9 \times 4 = 36, 4 \times 9 = 36, 36 \div 4 = 9, 36 \div 9 = 4$

Ex. 5: $8 \times 8 = 64, 64 \div 8 = 8$

Chapter 4 Lesson 10 p. 155

Ex. 1: 3 x 6 = 18, 6 x 3 = 18, 18 ÷ 6 = 3, 18 ÷ 3 = 6

Ex. 2: 4 x 7 = 28, 7 x 4 = 28, 28 ÷ 7 = 4, 28 ÷ 4 = 7

Ex. 3: 5 x 5 = 25, 25 ÷ 5 = 5

Ex. 4: 8 x 9 = 72, 9 x 8 = 72, 72 ÷ 8 = 9, 72 ÷ 9 = 8

Ex. 5: 9 x 5 = 45, 5 x 9 = 45, 45 ÷ 5 = 9, 45 ÷ 9 = 5

Ex. 6: 7 x 2 = 14, 2 x 7 = 14, 14 ÷ 2 = 7, 14 ÷ 7 = 2

Ex. 7: 9 x 7 = 63, 7 x 9 = 63, 63 ÷ 7 = 9, 63 ÷ 9 = 7

Ex. 8: 1 x 8 = 8, 8 x 1 = 8, 8 ÷ 8 = 1, 8 ÷ 1 = 8

Ex. 9: 4 x 8 = 32, 8 x 4 = 32, 32 ÷ 8 = 4, 32 ÷ 4 = 8

Ex. 10: 7 x 7 = 49, 49 ÷ 7 = 7

Ex. 11: 7 x 8 = 56, 8 x 7 = 56, 56 ÷ 8 = 7, 56 ÷ 7 = 8

Ex. 12: 9 x 9 = 81, 81 ÷ 9 = 9

Chapter 5 Lesson 2 p. 173

Ex. 20: Answers may vary. Possible answer: They can buy 3 bicycles at most, so they should buy 2 deluxe and 1 foldable bicycle; if they buy 2 deluxe and 1 foldable bicycle, they will get 2 bicycles that are of better quality.

Chapter 5 Developing Math Sense p. 185

Ex. 1: 3 x $1,000 = $3,000; no; since $1,397 > $1,000, the exact cost is greater than $3,000.

Ex. 2: 8 x $40 = $320; yes; since $42 > $40, the exact amount is greater than $320.

Ex. 3: 6 x 50 = 300; no; since 48 < 50, the exact number of clowns is less than 300.

Ex. 4: 30 x $9 = $270; yes; since 34 > 30, her exact earnings are greater than $270.

Ex. 5: 50 x $7 = $350; no; since 47 < 50, the exact amount is less than $350.

Ex. 6: 5 x 20 = 100; yes; since 24 > 20, the exact number of bears is greater than 100.

Ex. 7: 9 x 20 = 180; no; since 15 < 20, the exact number of cups is less than 180.

Ex. 8: 4 x 10 = 40; yes; since 12 > 10, his exact number of hours is greater than 40.

Chapter 5 Lesson 8 p. 194

Ex. 5: Answers may vary. Possible answer: Offer a discount to senior citizens on Tuesdays because the fewest number of people attend on that day, and there are fewer adults than children so the discount should help to increase these numbers.

Chapter 6 Lesson 4 p. 215

Ex. 10: To find 50 x 45, multiply the product 5 x 45 by 10, or attach a zero to the product 5 x 45; this works because 50 = 5 tens, or 5 x 10, so 50 x 45 = 5 x 10 x 45 = 5 x 45 x 10 = 225 x 10 = 2,250.

Chapter 6 Lesson 8 p. 230

Ex. 4: Students' problems could involve finding the amount recycled in a year given a daily amount. Accept any reasonable explanation of choice of method.

Chapter 7 Developing Number Sense p. 253

Ex. 3: Answers may vary. Lengths over 10 cm (1 dm) would be easier with the width of the hand, and those over 1 m, with the length of a stride.

Chapter 7 Lesson 5 p. 259

Ex. 25: Students may estimate using inches, centimeters, or millimeters. Students may suggest using their hand span to estimate the length of their desk, chalkboard, and other items.

Chapter 9 Lesson 11 p. 354

Ex. 4:

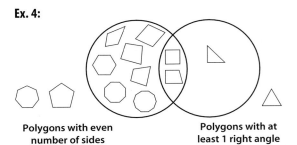

Polygons with even number of sides Polygons with at least 1 right angle

Chapter 10 Lesson 8 p. 390

Question 1: Possible results: Spinner 1—players had almost the same number of points, Spinner 2—blue had the most points, Spinner 3—yellow had the most points and the red had no points, Spinner 4—red had the most points.

Chapter 10 Lesson 9 p. 392

Ex. 5: Answers may vary. Possible answer: a. Agree—there are two possible outcomes, head or tail, and there are two favorable outcomes, head or tail, so the probability of getting a head or tail is 2/2, or 1; b. agree—7 does not appear on the number cube, so there is no favorable outcome out of the six possible outcomes, 1, 2, 3, 4, 5, and 6, so the probability is 0/6, or 0.

Chapter 10 Lesson 12 p. 400

Ex. 2: Answers may vary. Students should realize that they need to conduct an experiment to solve.

Chapter 12 Lesson 5 p. 465

Question 1: Start from the decimal point (four beads on the fourth wire). Look at the next wire up—6 beads pushed to the left for 6 ones. Look at the next wire up—3 beads pushed to the left for 3 tens. Look at the first wire below the decimal-point wire—no beads pushed to the left for 0 tenths. Look at the next wire down—5 beads pushed to the left for 5 hundredths.

Ex. 1: Start from the decimal point (four beads on the fourth wire). Look at the next wire up—8 beads pushed to the left for 8 ones. Look at the first wire below the decimal-point wire—1 bead pushed to the left for 1 tenth. Look at the next wire down—4 beads pushed to the left for 4 hundredths.

Ex. 2: Start from the decimal point (four beads on the fourth wire). Look at the next wire up—5 beads pushed to the left for 5 ones. Look at the first wire below the decimal-point wire—3 beads pushed to the left for 3 tenths. Look at the next wire down—7 beads pushed to the left for 7 hundredths.

Ex. 3: Start from the decimal point (four beads on the fourth wire). Look at the next wire up—1 bead pushed to the left for 1 one. Look at the next wire up—2 beads pushed to the left for 2 tens. Look at the first wire below the decimal-point wire— no beads pushed to the left for 0 tenths. Look at the next wire down—3 beads pushed to the left for 3 hundredths.

Ex. 4: Start from the decimal point (four beads on the fourth wire). Look at the next wire up—8 beads pushed to the left for 8 ones. Look at the next wire up—5 beads pushed to the left for 5 tens. Look at the first wire below the decimal-point wire—7 beads pushed to the left for 7 tenths. Look at the next wire down—5 beads pushed to the left for 5 hundredths.

Books for the Teacher

Apelman, Maja, and Julie King. *Exploring Everyday Math: Ideas for Students, Teachers, and Parents.* Portsmouth, NH: Heinemann, 1993.

Artzt, Alice F., and Claire M. Newman. *How to Use Cooperative Learning in the Mathematics Class.* Reston, VA: National Council of Teachers of Mathematics, 1990.

Barnett, Carrie, et al. *Mathematics Teaching Cases: Fractions, Decimals, Ratios, & Percents—Hard to Teach and Hard to Learn?* Portsmouth, NH: Heinemann, 1994.

Beaumont, Vern, et al. *How to Teach Perimeter, Area, and Volume.* Reston, VA: National Council of Teachers of Mathematics, 1986.

Billstein, R., et al. *A Problem Solving Approach to Mathematics for Elementary School Teachers.* Menlo Park, CA: Benjamin Cummings, 1987.

Borasi, Raffaella. *Learning Mathematics Through Inquiry.* Portsmouth, NH: Heinemann, 1992.

Bresser, Rusty. *Math and Literature (Grades 4–6).* Portsmouth, NH: Heinemann, 1996.

Brown, Ruth, ed. *Math Across Cultures.* San Francisco, CA: Exploratorium, 1995.

Burns, Marilyn. *About Teaching Mathematics: A K–8 Resource.* Portsmouth, NH: Heinemann, 1992.

Cooney, Thomas J., ed. *Teaching and Learning Mathematics in the 1990s.* (1990 Yearbook) Reston, VA: National Council of Teachers of Mathematics, 1990.

Copeland, Richard W. *How Children Learn Mathematics: Teaching Implications of Piaget's Research.* New York: Macmillan, 1984.

Corwin, Rebecca B. *Talking Mathematics: Supporting Children's Voices.* Portsmouth, NH: Heinemann, 1995.

Cruikshank, Douglas, and Linda J. Sheffield. *Mathematics for Elementary Children: A Foundation for the Future.* Columbus, OH: Merrill, 1988.

Cuevas, Gilbert, and Mark Driscoll, eds. *Reaching All Students with Mathematics.* Reston, VA: National Council of Teachers of Mathematics, 1993.

Del Grande, John, et al. *Geometry and Spatial Sense: Addenda Series, Grades K–6.* Reston, VA: National Council of Teachers of Mathematics, 1993.

Farrell, Margaret A., ed. *Imaginative Ideas for the Teacher of Mathematics.* Reston, VA: National Council of Teachers of Mathematics, 1988.

Feinberg, Miriam M. *Solving Word Problems in the Primary Grades: Addition and Subtraction.* Reston, VA: National Council of Teachers of Mathematics, 1988.

Frank, Marjorie. *The Kids' Stuff: Book of Math for the Middle Grades.* Nashville, TN: Incentive Pub., 1988.

Holmes, Emma E. *Children Learning Mathematics: A Cognitive Approach to Teaching.* Englewood Cliffs, NJ: Prentice-Hall, 1985.

House, Peggy A., ed. *Connecting Mathematics Across the Curriculum. (1995 Yearbook)* Reston, VA: National Council of Teachers of Mathematics, 1995.

Hughes, Martin. *Children and Number: Difficulties in Learning Mathematics.* New York: Basil Blackwell, 1986.

Kennedy, Leonard M., and Steve Tipps. *Guiding Children's Learning of Mathematics.* Belmont, CA: Wadsworth, 1988.

Lilburn, Pat, and Pam Rawson. *Let's Talk Math: Encouraging Children to Explore Ideas.* Portsmouth, NH: Heinemann, 1994.

Lindquist, Mary, et al. *Making Sense of Data: Addenda Series, Grades K–6.* Reston, VA: National Council of Teachers of Mathematics, 1992.

Marks, John L., and A. A. Hiatt. *Teaching Elementary School Mathematics for Understanding.* New York: McGraw-Hill, 1985.

Mokros, Jan. *Beyond Facts & Flashcards: Exploring Math with Your Kids.* Portsmouth, NH: Heinemann, 1996.

Musser, Gary L., and William F. Burger. *Mathematics for Elementary Teachers: A Contemporary Approach,* 2nd ed. New York: Macmillan, 1991.

Neyland, Jim, ed. Mathematics *Education: A Handbook for Teachers, Volume 1.* Reston, VA: National Council of Teachers of Mathematics, 1994.

Rowan, Thomas, and Barbara Bourne. *Thinking Like Mathematicians: Putting the K–4 NCTM Standards into Practice.* Portsmouth, NH: Heinemann, 1994

Sprung, Barbara, et al. *What Will Happen If... : Young Children and the Scientific Method.* New York: Education Equity Concepts, Inc., 1985.

Stevenson, Frederick W. *Exploratory Problems in Mathematics.* Reston, VA: National Council of Teachers of Mathematics, 1992.

Thiessen, Diane, and Margaret Matthias, eds. *The Wonderful World of Mathematics: A Critically Annotated List of Children's Books in Mathematics.* Reston, VA: National Council of Teachers of Mathematics, 1992.

Trafton, Paul R., ed. *New Dictionaries for Elementary School Mathematics: 1989 Yearbook.* Reston, VA: National Council of Teachers of Mathematics, 1989.

Webb, Norman L., ed. *Assessment in the Mathematics Classroom. (1993 Yearbook)* Reston, VA: National Council of Teachers of Mathematics, 1993.

Zaslavsky, Claudia. *Multicultural Math: Hands-On Math Activities from Around the World.* New York: Scholastic Inc., 1994.

_____ . *The Multicultural Math Classroom: Bringing in the World.* Portsmouth, NH: Heinemann, 1995.

Recommended Periodicals

Cooperative Learning. Santa Cruz, CA: International Association for the Study of Cooperation in Education (IASCE).

Teaching Children Mathematics. Reston, VA: National Council of Teachers of Mathematics.

Technology & Learning. Dayton, OH: Peter Li, Inc.

Books for the Student

Daniel, Becky. *Math Thinkercises.* Carthage, IL: Good Apple, 1988.

Dunn, Patricia. *Math Trivial Pursuit—Intermediate Level.* Carthage, IL: Good Apple, 1989.

Embry, Lynn, and Betty Bobo. *Math America.* Carthage, IL: Good Apple, 1987.

Laycock, Mary, et al. *Geoblocks and Geojackets: Metric Version.* Hayward, CA: Activity Resources, 1988.

Wells, David. *Can You Solve These? Mathematical Problems to Test Your Thinking Powers.* New York: Parkwest, 1985.

INDEX

ACKNOWLEDGMENTS

COVER PHOTOGRAPHY Jade Albert for MMSD; t.m. John Eastcott and Yva Monatiuk/Animals/Animals; 1. MMSD.

PHOTOGRAPHY CREDITS All photographs are by the Macmillan/McGraw-Hill School Division (MMSD) and Scott Harvey for MMSD except as noted below.

Chapter 1 7: Johan Elbers/Sygma; b. Perkins/Beckett, Summer 1989, American Museum of Natural History; • 8: Hiro Komine; • 8: b. Dave Mager for MMSD; • 12: Yoichiro Miyazaki/FPG International; Tom Sanders/The Stock Market; • 13: Reuters/Corbis-Bettmann; • 18: t. AP/Wide World Photos; • 19: P & F Communications for MMSD; • 20: Pierre Perrin/Sygma; • 27: Nick Dolding/Tony Stone Images; • 30: t.r. Peter J. Bryant/Tony Stone Images; m.r. Jeff Greenberg/Photo Researchers, Inc.; m.l. Tim Davis/Photo Researchers, Inc.; b. Patrick Forestier/Sygma; • 36: t. Daniel J. Cox/Natural Exposures; m. Charles V. Angelo/Photo Researchers, Inc.; • 36-37: Tim Davis/Photo Researchers, Inc.; b.l. Michael Durham/Ellis Nature Photos; • 37: b. A.H. Rider/Photo Researchers, Inc.; t. Daniel J. Cox/Liaison International; **Chapter 2** 38: b. Henley & Savage/The Stock Market; • 38–39: Wes Thompson/The Stock Market; • 44: Eising/StockFood America; • 48: Corbis-Bettmann; • 49: Corbis-Bettmann; • 62: Dept. of the Treasury Bureau of Engraving; • 68: Jose Carrillo/Stock Boston; • 69: Graham Lawrence/Picture Perfect; • 72: Sepp Seitz/Woodfin Camp & Assoc.; • 78: t.m. Lee E. Battaglia/Photo Researchers; • 78: b.l. Ancient Art and Architecture Collection; • 79: t.l. Herbert W. Booth III/Liaison International; m. Ken Cavanagh/Photo Researchers; b.r. Lee F. Snyder/Photo Researchers; r.m. Russell D. Curtis/Photo Researchers; **Chapter 3** 80: m.i. Myrleen Cate/Tony Stone Images; • 80–81: Henry Horenstein/Viesti Associates; • 80-81: Mark Stephenson/Westlight; • 82: Lawrence Migdale; • 87: b. Michele Burgess/The Stock Market; • 89: Jason Bleibtreu/Sygma; • 93: Peter Fisher/The Stock Market; • 100: Photographer Photos Co./Gamma-Liaison; • 101: b.l. Tom McHugh/Photo Researchers; b.m. Tim Flach/Tony Stone Images; • 106: t. Susanah Druck; • 109: North Wind Picture Archive; • 112: t.l. George A. Dillon/Stock Boston, Inc.; t.r. Monkmeyer/Collins; • 113: Lawrence Migdale.• 119: Ned Matura/Liaison International; **Chapter 4** 122: Stephen Frisch/Stock Boston; • 129: t.r. Daemmrich/The Image Works; • 132: t. Bob Daemmrich/Stock Boston, Inc.; m. Bob Daemmrich/Stock Boston, Inc.; • 134: t. Dave Tillotson/The Houston Chronicle; • 137: t. Archive Photos; b. Bridgeman/Art Resource, Inc.; • 144: b. Ed Bock/Stock Market; t.r. Jerry Koontz/The Picture Cube, Inc.; • 145: Laura Dwight; • 146: Daemmrich/Stock Boston; • 153: Eric Neurath/Stock Boston; • 158: LeDuc/Monkmeyer; • 160: t.m.r. Bob Krist/Stock Market; • 160: b.r. Sonlight Images for MMSD; • 161: John Terence Turner/FPG International; • 166: t.r. Tom McHugh/Photo Researchers; m.l., b.r. Don Mason/The Stock Market; • 167: t.l. Tom Brakefield/The Stock Market; m.r. Dan Gair/The Picture Cube, Inc.; t.m. J. Giannotti/The Picture Cube, Inc.; b.m. ZEFA-Cutouts/The Stock Market; b.l. Kennan Ward/The Stock Market; **Chapter 5** 167F: Lena Williams, "A Silk Blouse on the Assembly Line? (Yes, the Boss's)," The New York Times, 5 February 1995, sec. F; • 168: b. Oz Charles; • 168–169: PhotoDisc; • 170: Erik S. Lesser/Silver Image; • 171: UPI/Corbis-Bettmann; • 172: Mike Powell/Allsport USA; • 181: Picture Network International, Ltd. • 188: Superstock, Inc.; • 189: William Taufic/The Stock Market; • 191: Roger Wood/(c) Corbis; • 192: Dennis Cox/ChinaStock; • 193: Steven Ferry; • 194: t. Dennis MacDonald/PhotoEdit; • 195: from Marketing; • 196: l. Chris Sorensen/The Stock Market; b.r. James Kozyra/Liaison International; • 197: t.r. Superstock, Inc.; • 202: l. Calvin Larsen/Photo Researchers; • 202: r. Liane Enkens/Stock Boston, Inc.; **Chapter 6** 204: b. Seth Resnick/Liaison International; • 204–205: John Matchett/Picture Perfect; • 206: D. Young-Wolff/PhotoEdit; • 213: John M. Roberts/Stock Market; • 214: Gary Braasch/Woodfin Camp & Assoc.; • 220: t. Nick Vedros, Vedros & Assoc./Tony Stone Images; b. Tony Freeman/Photo Edit; • 220: t.l. C.T. Tracy/FPG International; • 223: David Lissy/FPG International; • 226: t.r. courtesy Jeff Mantus; • 229: m.r. courtesy Megan McAtee; • 230: t.l. Eunice Harris/The Picture Cube; 231: b.r. Ellen B. Senisi/ Photosynthesis; **Chapter 7** 240-241: Roger Steene/Ellis Nature Photography; • 240: i. Pedro Coll/The Stock Market; • 242: t.r. Courtesy of Kim Harrison; • 244: m. Peter Skinner/Photo Researchers; b. Fred McConnaughey/Photo Researchers; • 247: t. Jeremy Stafford-Deitsch/Ellis Nature Photography; Tom McHugh/Steinhart Aquarium/Photo Researchers; • 256: t. David Lissy/Folio; • 257: t.m.l. PhotoDisc • Brent Petersen/The Stock Market; • 261: Lawrence Migdale/Stock Boston, Inc.; • 262: Bill Barley/Photri; • 263: b.l. David Young-Wolfe/PhotoEdit; • 263: b.r. Superstock, Inc.; • 265: b. Bob Gibbons/Photo Researchers; • 265: Mark Richards/PhotoEdit; • 268: b.l. Jon Feinaersh/The Stock Market; m.l. Tony Freeman/PhotoEdit; t.r. David McGlynn/FPG International; t.l. Tom McHugh/Steinhart Aquarium/Photo Researchers; r.m.b. Michael Gadomski/Photo Researchers; b.r. Tony Freeman/PhotoEdit; • 274: Stephen Dalton/Photo Researchers; **Chapter 8** 276: m. J. Mil Stein/The Image Works; • 278: t. Dowling/Gamma Liaison; • 280: t. Gary Wolinski/Stock Boston, Inc.; • 281: t. Joseff Neltu/Stock Boston, Inc.; • 290: t.r. Toyohiko Yamada/FPG International; • 293: b.r. Erich Lessing/Art Resource, Inc.; • 297: t. Chuck Pefley/Stock Boston, Inc.; • 298: b.r. PhotoDisc vol. 1; b.l. PhotoDisc vol. 24; t.l. PhotoDisc vol. 1; t.r. Stephanie Myers; • 300: t. Focus On Sports; • 310: m.l. Bob Randall for MMSD; b.r. Coco McCoy/Rainbow; t.r. Bob Raskid/Monkmeyer; m. Superstock, Inc.; m. Phyllis Picordi/Stock Boston, Inc.; • 316: b.l. Photo Researchers; • 316: t.r. Michael Holford; • 317: b.l. Coco McCoy/Rainbow; **Chapter 9** 318: Art Wolfe/Tony Stone Images; • 320: t.r. Superstock, Inc.; • 323: t.r. Will & Deni McIntyre/Photo Researchers; • 326: Sinclair Stammers/Photo Researchers; t.r. Stephen Johnson/Tony Stone Images; 328: Joseph Stella/Art Resource, Inc.; 329: m. Tom & Pat Leeson/Photo Researchers; l. Hans Lutz/Okapia/Photo Researchers; • 332: t.m. Tom & Pat Leeson/Photo Researchers; l. Jim Levin for MMSD.• 334: m. Photri/The Stock Market; r. Rockefeller Center Photo; r. David Young-Wolfe/Photo Researchers; • 336: t.l. NASA; • 338: Prepaid to Cordon Art Museum B.V.; b. Robert Frerck/Tony Stone International; r. NYU/Peter Freed; Cordon Art Museum B.V.; • 340: r. Denver Art Museum Collection; • 344: Jim Harrison/Stock Boston, Inc.; • 345: m.l. Jim Corwin/Stock Boston, Inc.; m.r. Alfred Pasieka/Science Photo Library/Photo Researchers; l. Raymond Barnes/Tony Stone Images; • 346: Joel Gordon; • 351: Wolfgang Hoyt; • 355: b.l. Michal Heron/The Stock Market; • 361: Grenoble Musee/Art Resource, Inc.; • 362: b.r. European Photo/FPG International; t.l. Scala/Art Resource, Inc.; b.l. Archivo Cameraphoto Venezia/Art Resource, Inc.; t.r. Eric Corle/Stock Boston, Inc.; • 363: Coco McCoy/Rainbow; **Chapter 10** 373: Allen/Liaison International; • 379: b. William S. Nawrocki/Nawrocki Stock Photo, Inc.; • 380: t.r. Universtiy Museum Archives/University of PA; • 382: t.l. Mario Ruiz/The Stock Market; • 384: t.r. Brian Smith; • 400: b.l. Monkmeyer/Leduc; b.l. The Stock Market; **Chapter 11** 408: m.i. inset Bill Aron/Photo Edit, bkgnd. Aaron Rezny/The Stock Market; • 415: b.r. Richard Pranitzke/Photo Researchers; • 420: t.r. Collins/Monkmeyer; • 423: Giraudon/Art Resource; • 428: t.l. Courtesy Andre Pierre Lincy; • 438: b.r. David Ball/The Picture Cube; t.r. Don Mason/The Stock Market; • 439: b.l. Constance Hansen/The Stock Market; b.l. Al Assid/The Stock Market; b.l. Esbin Anderson/The Image Works; • 440: b.r. Gabe Palmer/The Stock Market; b.r. Andy Levin/Photo Researchers; b.l. Elena Roonaid/PhotoEdit; m.r. Jose Paiaez/Stock Market; • 446: b.l. D. Young-Wolff/PhotoEdit; • 447: r., t.l. Photo Disc vol. 8; **Chapter 12** 448: m. Cynthia Johnson/Gamma Liaison; • 454: t.r. Thayer Syme/FPG International; • 456: Kevin Schafer/Tony Stone Images; • 462: Fredrik D. Bodin/Stock Boston, Inc.; • 464: t. Michelle Michaels; • 468: t.l. Tom & Dee Ann McCarthy/The Stock Market; • 470: m. Roger Ressmeyer/Corbis; t.r. NASA/Photo Researchers; • 474: b.r. Michael Newman/PhotoEdit; • 480: m.r., m.l. Bettmann/Corbis; • 481: Frank Rossotto/The Stock Market.

ILLUSTRATION CREDITS Bernard Adnet: 249, 250 • Ken Bowser: 205, 208, 219, 220, 224, 409, 414, 424, 433, 449, 452, 462, 479 • Hal Brooks: 2, 12, 17, 20, 25, 28 • Tom Cardamone: 7, 87, 137, 191, 202, 213, 265, 293, 297, 327, 343, 379, 415, 465 • Susan Johnston Carlson: 277, 278, 280, 285, 291, 292, 294, 297, 300, 302, 308 • Anthony Cericola: 252, 258, 264, 268, 319, 322, 336, 351 • Eldon Doty: 473 • Brian Dugan: 18, 98, 217, 270, 388, 389, 406, 407 • Annie Gusman: 26, 35, 150,160, 161, 166 • Henry Hill: 243–247, 267, 269, 271, 274, 275 • WB Johnston: 254, 266, 267, 334, 348, 368–370, 398 • Stanford Kay: 90, 96, 118, 349, 450, 453, 459, 473-475 • Deborah Haley Melmon: 40, 47 • Marion Nixon: 220, 230, 231, 393 • Lori Osieki: 70, 71 • Michael Racz: 20, 21 • Margaret Robinson: 202 • Douglas Schneider: 354 • Stephen Schudlich: 52, 53, 55, 58, 72, 76 • Remy Simard: 84–86, 93, 94, 108, 112, 113, 117, 124, 136, 138, 165 • Matt Straub: 152, 248, 259, 273, 280, 291, 295, 302, 308, 309. 315. 380, 395 • Beata Szpura: 14, 15 • Gary Torrisi: 324-326 • Joe VanDerBos: 3. 33. 39, 42. 43. 63, 77, 214, 215, 233 • Nina Wallace: 104, 105, 114, 125, 126, 129, 130, 132, 151, 153, 156, 162, 164, 186, 187, 196, 201 • Susan Williams: 183, 196, 201, 372, 373, 375, 405 • Rose Zgodzinski: 209, 223, 233, 367, 379, 383

All photographs are by the McGraw-Hill School Division (MMSD), Ken Karp for MMSD, David Mager for MMSD, Scott Harvey for MMSD, Bonnie West for MMSD, Monica Stevenson for MMSD, and Doug David for MMSD.

All props and illustrations are by the McGraw-Hill School Division (MMSD), Jeff Hernandez for MMSD, Raymond Hernandez for MMSD, Carmen Pujols for MMSD, Marina Brolin for MMSD, William Touchet for MMSD, Daniel DelValle for MMSD, and Deirdre Kennedy for MMSD.

DIRECTIONS: To convert a raw score into percentage scores, find the column that indicates the total number of items. Then find the row that matches the number of items that the student answered correctly. The intersection of the two rows gives the percent correct.

TOTAL NUMBER OF ITEMS

Number Correct	70	69	68	67	66	65	64	63	62	61	60	59	58	57	56	55	54	53	52	51	50	49	48	47	46	45	44	43	42	41	40	39	38	37	36	35	34	33	32	31	30	29	28	27	26	25	24	23	22	21	20	19	18	17	16	15	14	13	12	11	10
1	1	1	1	1	2	2	2	2	2	2	2	2	2	2	2	2	2	2	2	2	2	2	2	2	2	2	2	2	2	2	3	3	3	3	3	3	3	3	3	3	3	3	4	4	4	4	4	4	5	5	5	5	6	6	6	7	7	8	8	9	10
2	3	3	3	3	3	3	3	3	3	3	3	3	3	4	4	4	4	4	4	4	4	4	4	4	4	4	5	5	5	5	5	5	5	5	6	6	6	6	6	6	7	7	7	7	8	8	8	9	9	10	10	11	11	12	13	13	14	15	17	18	20
3	4	4	4	4	5	5	5	5	5	5	5	5	5	5	5	5	6	6	6	6	6	6	6	6	7	7	7	7	7	7	8	8	8	8	8	9	9	9	9	10	10	10	11	11	12	12	13	13	14	14	15	16	17	18	19	20	21	23	25	27	30
4	6	6	6	6	6	6	6	6	6	7	7	7	7	7	7	7	7	8	8	8	8	8	8	9	9	9	9	9	10	10	10	10	11	11	11	11	12	12	13	13	13	14	14	15	15	16	17	17	18	19	20	21	22	24	25	27	29	31	33	36	40
5	7	7	7	7	8	8	8	8	8	8	8	8	9	9	9	9	9	9	10	10	10	10	10	11	11	11	11	12	12	12	13	13	13	14	14	14	15	15	16	16	17	17	18	19	19	20	21	22	23	24	25	26	28	29	31	33	36	38	42	45	50
6	9	9	9	9	9	9	9	10	10	10	10	10	10	11	11	11	11	11	12	12	12	12	13	13	13	13	14	14	14	15	15	15	16	16	17	17	18	18	19	19	20	21	21	22	23	24	25	26	27	29	30	32	33	35	38	40	43	46	50	55	60
7	10	10	10	10	11	11	11	11	11	11	12	12	12	12	13	13	13	13	13	14	14	14	15	15	15	16	16	16	17	17	18	18	18	19	19	20	21	21	22	23	23	24	25	26	27	28	29	30	32	33	35	37	39	41	44	47	50	54	58	64	70
8	11	12	12	12	12	12	13	13	13	13	13	14	14	14	14	15	15	15	15	16	16	16	17	17	17	18	18	19	19	20	20	21	21	22	22	23	24	24	25	26	27	28	29	30	31	32	33	35	36	38	40	42	44	47	50	53	57	62	67	73	80
9	13	13	13	13	14	14	14	14	15	15	15	15	16	16	16	16	17	17	17	18	18	18	19	19	20	20	20	21	21	22	23	23	24	24	25	26	26	27	28	29	30	31	32	33	35	36	38	39	41	43	45	47	50	53	56	60	64	69	75	82	90
10	14	14	15	15	15	15	16	16	16	16	17	17	17	18	18	18	19	19	19	20	20	20	21	21	22	22	23	23	24	24	25	26	26	27	28	29	29	30	31	32	33	34	36	37	38	40	42	43	45	48	50	53	56	59	63	67	71	77	83	91	100
11	16	16	16	16	17	17	17	17	18	18	18	19	19	19	20	20	20	21	21	22	22	22	23	23	24	24	25	26	26	27	28	28	29	30	31	31	32	33	34	35	37	38	39	41	42	44	46	48	50	52	55	58	61	65	69	73	79	85	92	100	
12	17	17	18	18	18	18	19	19	19	20	20	20	21	21	21	22	22	23	23	24	24	24	25	26	26	27	27	28	29	29	30	31	32	32	33	34	35	36	38	39	40	41	43	44	46	48	50	52	55	57	60	63	67	71	75	80	86	92	100		
13	19	19	19	19	20	20	20	21	21	21	22	22	22	23	23	24	24	25	25	25	26	27	27	28	28	29	30	30	31	32	33	33	34	35	36	37	38	39	41	42	43	45	46	48	50	52	54	57	59	62	65	68	72	76	81	87	93	100			
14	20	20	21	21	21	22	22	22	23	23	23	24	24	25	25	25	26	26	27	27	28	29	29	30	30	31	32	33	33	34	35	36	37	38	39	40	41	42	44	45	47	48	50	52	54	56	58	61	64	67	70	74	78	82	88	93	100				
15	21	22	22	22	23	23	23	24	24	25	25	25	26	26	27	27	28	28	29	29	30	31	31	32	33	33	34	35	36	37	38	38	39	41	42	43	44	45	47	48	50	52	54	56	58	60	63	65	68	71	75	79	83	88	94	100					
16	23	23	24	24	24	25	25	25	26	26	27	27	28	28	29	29	30	30	31	31	32	33	33	34	35	36	36	37	38	39	40	41	42	43	44	46	47	48	50	52	53	55	57	59	62	64	67	70	73	76	80	84	89	94	100						
17	24	25	25	25	26	26	27	27	27	28	28	29	29	30	30	31	31	32	33	33	34	35	35	36	37	38	39	40	40	41	43	44	45	46	47	49	50	52	53	55	57	59	61	63	65	68	71	74	77	81	85	89	94	100							
18	26	26	26	27	27	28	28	29	29	30	30	31	31	32	32	33	33	34	35	35	36	37	38	38	39	40	41	42	43	44	45	46	47	49	50	51	53	55	56	58	60	62	64	67	69	72	75	78	82	86	90	95	100								
19	27	28	28	28	29	29	30	30	31	31	32	32	33	33	34	35	35	36	37	37	38	39	40	40	41	42	43	44	45	46	48	49	50	51	53	54	56	58	59	61	63	66	68	70	73	76	79	83	86	90	95	100									
20	29	29	29	30	30	31	31	32	32	33	33	34	34	35	36	36	37	38	38	39	40	41	42	43	43	44	45	47	48	49	50	51	53	54	56	57	59	61	63	65	67	69	71	74	77	80	83	87	91	95	100										
21	30	30	31	31	32	32	33	33	34	34	35	36	36	37	38	38	39	40	40	41	42	43	44	45	46	47	48	49	50	51	53	54	55	57	58	60	62	64	66	68	70	72	75	78	81	84	88	91	95	100											
22	31	32	32	33	33	34	34	35	35	36	37	37	38	39	39	40	41	42	42	43	44	45	46	47	48	49	50	51	52	54	55	56	58	59	61	63	65	67	69	71	73	76	79	81	85	88	92	96	100												
23	33	33	34	34	35	35	36	37	37	38	38	39	40	40	41	42	43	43	44	45	46	47	48	49	50	51	52	53	55	56	58	59	61	62	64	66	68	70	72	74	77	79	82	85	88	92	96	100													
24	34	35	35	36	36	37	38	38	39	39	40	41	41	42	43	44	44	45	46	47	48	49	50	51	52	53	55	56	57	59	60	62	63	65	67	69	71	73	75	77	80	83	86	89	92	96	100														

SCORING CHART

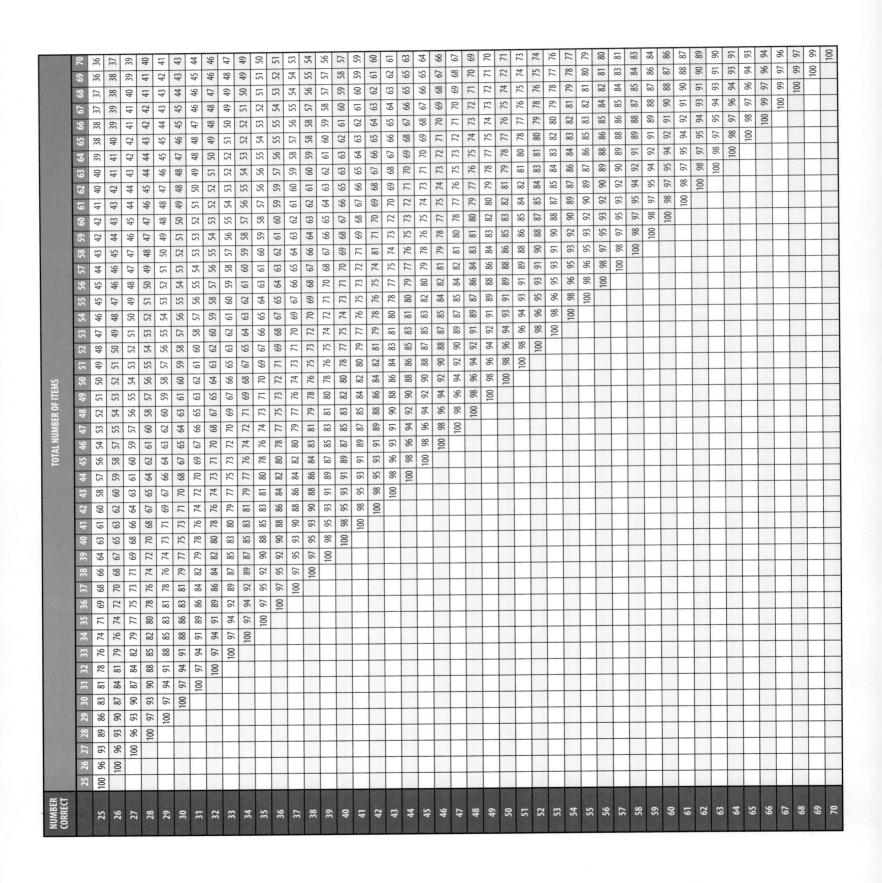

Teacher's Notes